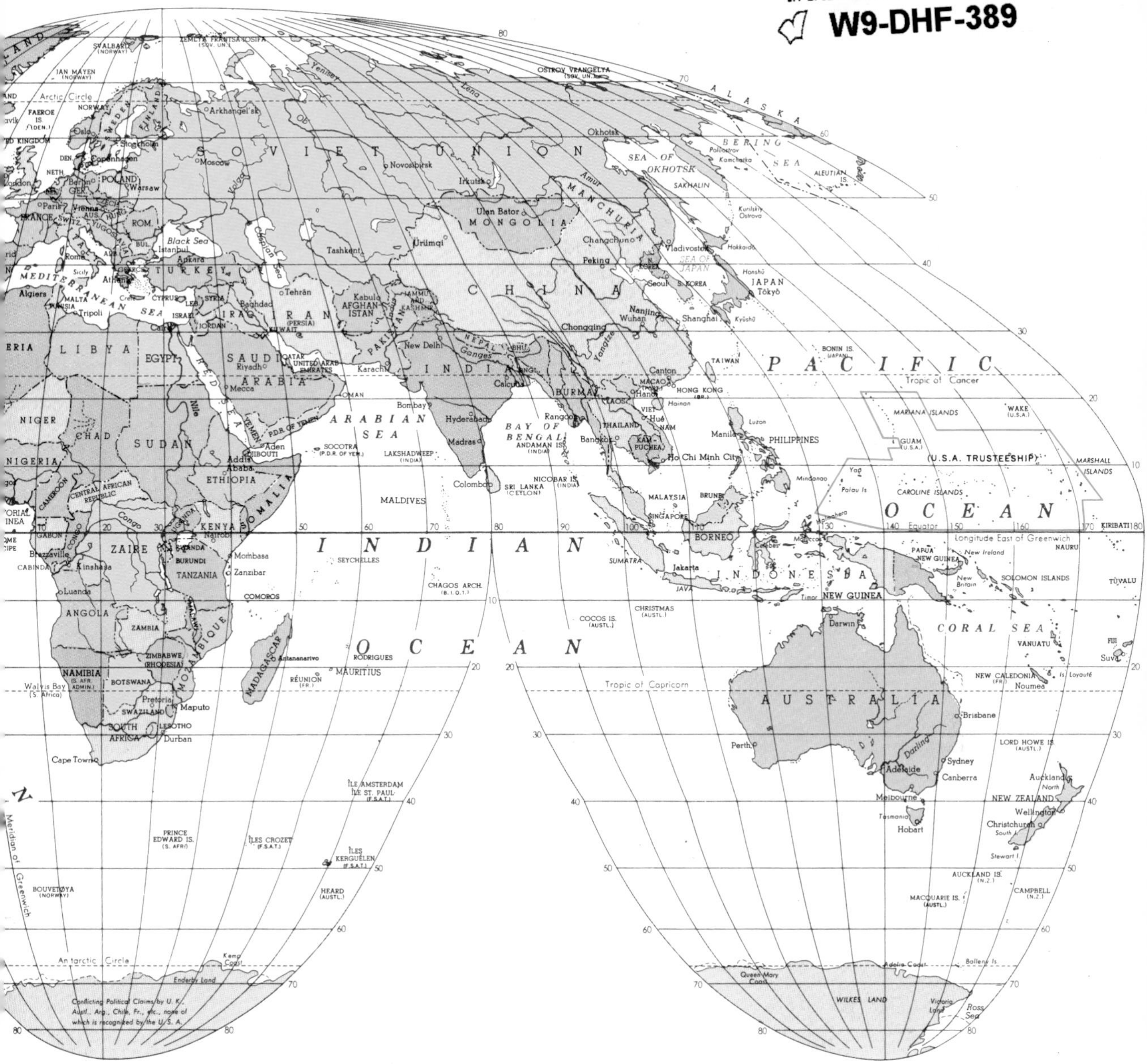

Goode's Homolosine Equal Area Projection

INTERNATIONAL BUSINESS
Theory and Managerial Applications

The Irwin Series in Management and The Behavioral Sciences

L. L. Cummings and E. Kirby Warren Consulting Editors

INTERNATIONAL BUSINESS
Theory and Managerial Applications

Robert Grosse

Duane Kujawa

Both of the
University of Miami

1988

IRWIN

Homewood, Illinois 60430

Acquisitions editor: William R. Bayer
Developmental editor: Ann M. Granacki
Project editor: Gladys True
Production manager: Carma W. Fazio
Artist: Rolin Graphics, Inc.
Cover photo: Michel Tcherevkoff
End paper map: From Goode's World Atlas © Copyright 1987 by Rand McNally & Company, R.L. 87-S-153
Compositor: Better Graphics, Inc.
Typeface: 10/12 Garamond Light (ITC)
Printer: R. R. Donnelley & Sons Company

ISBN 0-256-03281-5

Library of Congress Catalog Card No. 87-82182

Printed in the United States of America

1 2 3 4 5 6 7 8 9 0 DO 5 4 3 2 1 0 9 8

To Alan, Amanda, David, Laura, and Matthew

PREFACE

International business is the field of study that focuses on business activities that cross national boundaries. It includes exports and imports—the subject of traditional international trade discussions—as well as foreign direct investment, international banking, international transfer of technology, global business strategy, and many more topics. Our concern in this book is to present a panorama of the most important activities in international business and to offer a framework for thinking about them from the perspective of the company manager.

There are many important challenges and problems that face firms that do business outside of their home countries. How do you handle foreign exchange? How can exchange risk be managed? What are some ways of dealing with foreign governments and of operating effectively in diverse legal environments? Is it possible to avoid some of the business problems that may arise due to cultural differences among people from different countries? What strategies exist for coping with the competition of rival firms from different countries? All of these questions and others are treated in this book. Conclusive answers are not always possible, but logical methods for dealing with the questions are developed and analyzed.

Many of the concerns of decisionmakers in international business have to do with environmental factors such as government policies and economic conditions in different countries. Such issues as the oil crises of the 1970s and the international debt crisis of the 1980s have forced companies in all industries to come to grips with higher inflation and interest rates and greater risks of currency inconvertibility in virtually all less-developed countries. The evolution of multinational firms has meant that older MNEs from the United States and Western Europe are encountering new and tougher competition from younger rival firms in Japan, Korea, Brazil, and even within their own countries. These conditions really go to the core of business at the end of the 20th century. Whether a firm is international or not, its competitors may come from different countries, its suppliers likewise may be foreign or domestic, and the environment in which it operates may depend on activities of foreign governments and firms.

It is in this context that the present book has been written. Although its focus is international, the decisionmaking methods and considerations presented in the book generally apply to domestic firms as well. From another perspective, it is our hope that the content of this book will be developed further in the traditional courses in finance, marketing, and management. There can be little doubt that business around the world has become open to foreign competitors, foreign markets, and foreign supply sources; so any manager should understand the implications of these phenomena for the firm.

This text was designed for the survey course in international business. It is a comprehensive text, designed to be used in a one-semester course, with the selection of chapters left to the instructor's discretion. It should also prove useful as a reference source both in subsequent courses and in business experience.

The text is distinctive from others in the field because of its unifying theme of "competitive advantanges," which gives continuity to what are all too often studied as free-standing topics. Also, throughout the text, real-life business situations are cited to clarify the material being discussed and to make it more exciting and interesting. The cases presented in the text give further opportunity for understanding the material in its practical aspects and applications.

ACKNOWLEDGMENTS

We would like to thank the many people who contributed their time, talents, and efforts toward the completion of this book. Most importantly, John Hixon, Steve Bracken, and Mike Hornstein, MBA students at the University of Miami, all worked diligently and carefully to gather information and check the facts that appear in these pages. In addition, our secretary, Bunny Russian, very capably helped to coordinate the project and keep track of our communications with the publisher and business people who gave inputs into the book.

There are more than 100 business people who provided information and interpretations about their firms' international business activities that are incorporated in the book. Those with whom we worked most closely are the several senior executives in multinational firms and international banks who are also members of our International Business & Banking Institute's Board of Advisers: Bernie Hamilton, Gene Rostov, Donn Davis, Bill Young, Gonzalo Valdes-Fauli, George Reeves, George Williams, Antonia Shusta, John Polychron, Yves Bobillier, Juan Yanes, Archie Monroe, Nigel Simpson, Ralph Llop, Burt Landy, John Rednall, and Carlton de Souza. In addition, we would like to thank Steve Vogel, Jim Widmer, Gus Franco, David Friedsom, Jerry Brock, John Hume, and Ernesto Garuolis. Others assisted in various important ways that we truly appreciate.

Our intellectual debts are to many scholars, but we would like to mention specifically Jack Behrman, whose views and encouragement stimulated this project. Others have also substantially influenced us in our own professional development, and their influences are reflected in this book. These scholars include: Vern Terpstra, Bob Hawkins, Ingo Walter, Gunter Dufey, Steve Robock, Alan Rugman, Dave Ricks, Jeff Arpan, Bill Ogram, Jim Goodnow, Hans Schollhammer, John Daniels, Jose de la Torre, Larry Franko, Raj Aggarwal, Bal Bhatt, Steve Kobrin, Ivan Vernon, Don Pattilo, Riad Ajami,

Rosalie Tung, Dick Moxon, Mike Czinkota, Subhash Jain, Arvind Phatak, Phil Grub, Russ Root, Laurent Jacque, John Dunning, Irene Lange, Moises Naim, Jean-Francois Hennart, Ian Giddy, Gerard Watzke, Bob Vichas, John Weber, George Tesar, Jim Sood, Ken Simmonds, Bill Renforth, David Rutenberg, Alex Murray, John Ryans, and Attila Yaprak.

Our colleagues who read all or some of the manuscript and offered very valuable comments include: Ravi Sarathy, Northeastern University; Bruce Johnson, Gustavus Adolphus College; John Garland, University of Kansas; John Thanopoulos, University of Akron; Warren J. Bilkey, University of Wisconsin; Richard Moxon, University of Washington; Dan Brenenstuhl, Arizona State University; Stephen W. Miller, St. Louis University; and J. J. Boddewyn, Baruch College. We enjoyed working with them on this project.

While this book reflects valuable inputs and influences from all of these people, we want to note that we alone take responsibility for its contents. In closing, we invite you—professor or student—to share your thoughts on this book with us. A good text is one that *lives* and that reflects the needs and interests of both professors and students as both they and the field evolve over time. We think this is a good text and would value your comments to make it even better.

Robert Grosse
Duane Kujawa

Miami, Florida

CONTENTS

INTERNATIONAL BUSINESS
Theory and Managerial Applications

PART 1

INTRODUCTION

1

ISSUES AND CONCEPTS

In some ways, international business is an extension of domestic business; in other ways, it is not. The purpose of this chapter is to introduce you to the "real world" of international business by discussing actual companies and what they are actually doing internationally. The effects of international activities on different business functions—as illustrated by these same case examples—are then introduced. The discussion covers the effects of these activities on product definition, marketing research and marketing management, financing, personnel issues, accounting practices, and taxation. A key conclusion to this point is that different firms behave quite differently. But then we must ask what factors in the environment give rise to these behavioral differences and why firms operate differently in the international arena. Implicit in what has been said thus far is the fact that the major focus of this chapter, and of this book, is on multinational corporations. The chapter also discusses importing and exporting and the activities of governments that relate to them, and it summarizes the general organization of the book. The main goals of the chapter are to:

1. Illustrate important differences between international business and domestic business.
2. Identify the entities involved in international business.
3. Illustrate how important business functions vary firm by firm internationally and raise the question of why this occurs.
4. Present the organization of this book.

Introduction

What is "international business"? To some people, it means "big business." These people see international business as dominated by giant corporations whose economic power is so great that it may even compromise the political autonomy of nation-states. Other people equate international business with "international trade," thinking only in terms of exports and imports. Some of these people may work for firms that sell products to overseas markets; others may work for firms that are battling foreign-made products right here in their home market. For such people, international business can mean either big opportunities or big problems.

Figure 1-1 presents several alternative characterizations of international business, which, as illustrated, can encompass individuals, companies, banks, and governments, and can include trade in goods and services (exports and imports), ownership of foreign plants and companies (direct investment), technology transfers, loans, and so on. But aren't all of these "definitions" of international business really talking about manifestations of international business activity? There's really more to international business—especially for students in schools of business administration. Let's look at a few cases to illustrate what international business is all about.

International Business Highlights—Ampex, Citicorp, Dow, and Honda[1]

Ampex

Ampex Corporation develops, manufactures, and markets audio-video, magnetic tape, and data-memory products worldwide to the broadcast industry. It is headquartered in California and has several plants in the United States—as well as wholly owned manufacturing subsidiaries in England, Belgium, Hong Kong, Mexico, Australia, and Taiwan. Ampex shares ownership with local partners at joint-venture subsidiaries in Japan, Brazil, and Mexico. Its annual sales are above $500 million. About 40 percent of its sales and nearly 50 percent of its employees are outside the United States. At the top, Ampex is organized into four main product divisions with profit/loss responsibility. Foreign plant managements, like domestic plant managements, operate within their respective divisions, but with varying degrees of international integration. For example, plants in Europe and Australia manufacture and assemble Ampex products that are sold in those foreign markets. In contrast, plants in Taiwan and Mexico assemble components and products for subsequent processing and sale in the United States. An international division, separate from the product divisions, handles U.S. exports—which are about one third of U.S. production.

The ability to generate new products has been the key to the success of

Figure 1-1 **Examples of International Business Activities**

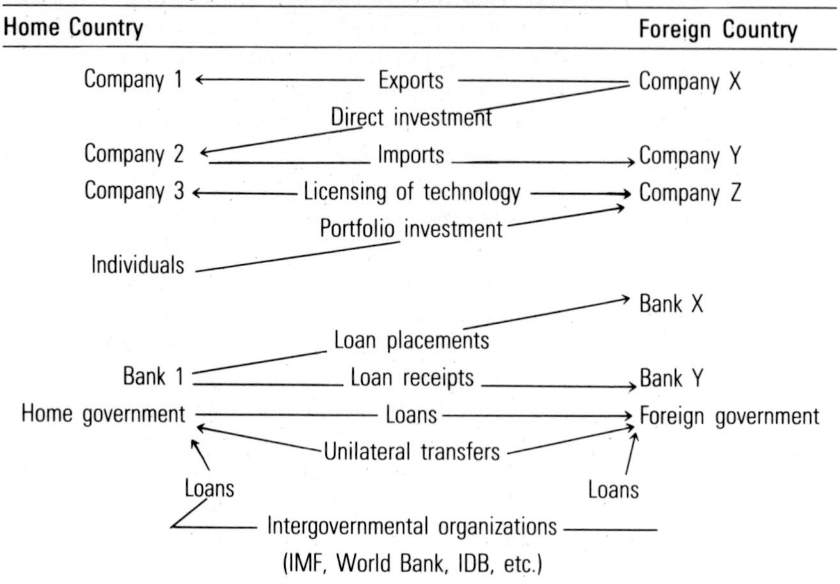

Ampex over the years. Ampex is a high-tech company that typically plows back about 7 percent of its revenues into research and development (R&D). It is also a company whose products "grow old" quickly because of the interplay between rapidly changing technologies and competitive marketplaces. Ampex conducts almost all of its R&D in the United States and views other industrialized countries as important for marketing opportunities. The company sometimes licenses foreign firms to manufacture products using proprietary technology. Several Japanese companies, for example, have been licensed to manufacture videotape recorders using Ampex product technology.

Citicorp

One of the world's largest financial services institutions, Citicorp operates in 42 states in the United States and in 92 countries other than the United States. It has a customer relationship with one out of every five U.S. households, and its assets totaled $173.6 billion at the end of 1985. Citicorp is headquartered in New York City, but nearly half of its 81,000 employees and two thirds of its offices were located overseas in 1985. Slightly over half (54 percent) of its net income was generated overseas that year. Citicorp, which calls itself a "global financial services business," is organized at the top into three major business units focusing on commercial banking, consumer banking, and investment banking. It is diversified by customer base, geographic presence, and product line. As might be expected, there is considerable coordination among the different customer and product-oriented operating units both within each country or region and among countries and regions.

The financial services industry is becoming increasingly competitive, and Citicorp's competitive strategy is based on innovation, customer orientation, and management decentralization. Citicorp notes, for example, that a key support element cutting across all three of its major business units is its advanced information processing and transmission capabilities. Citicorp worldwide operates 160 data centers working through 20,000 terminals—7,000 of which are located in its customers' facilities. In the past few years the company has spent over $500 million in developing and implementing electronic information-handling technologies, and it contends that it is now the world leader in electronic banking for commercial applications. It also contends that these technologies give it special capabilities for generating new products in an industry where old-line, mature products are no longer very profitable. Cases in point here include the establishment of "Citifunds," an Asian-based cash management account marketed to non-U.S. customers with high net worth and the revitalization of its Diners Club and other travel and entertainment-related businesses by enabling more efficient, lower-cost operations. In addition, Citicorp sells its funds transfer service to some 7,000 financial institutions located around the world.

Dow

A globally integrated producer of chemical, health care, and other consumer and industrial products, Dow Chemical Company is headquartered in Michigan and has numerous facilities in the United States, Canada, Europe, the Orient, and Latin America. Dow's foreign operations range from wholly owned subsidiaries, such as those in Canada, The Netherlands, Italy, Greece, Germany, Mexico, Argentina, and Colombia, to joint ventures, such as those in the United Kingdom, Spain, The Netherlands, France, Italy, Germany, Argentina, Ecuador, Colombia, Chile, Mexico, Japan, India, Australia, New Zealand, and Malaysia. In 1985, Dow's sales revenues totaled over $11.5 billion. About 55 percent of Dow's sales are outside the United States—as are about 40 percent of its 53,000 employees.

Dow's top-level organizational operating structure is geographically defined into six regions: The U.S.A., Canada, Europe, Latin America, Brazil, and the Pacific. The president of Dow Chemical Europe, for example, has operations responsibility for the entire European region. Management and technical personnel at various organizational levels within the regional divisions coordinate with their counterparts in other divisions on major investment, production allocation, and similar decisions. About one quarter of Dow Chemical U.S.A.'s production is exported to customers in the other five regions.

Dow's mainstream production is in chemical intermediates, and over the years the company has been especially successful in developing families of products around a common product core—as with styrene plastic. Dow is deliberately expanding its presence in specialty chemicals, pharmaceuticals, and other health and consumer products that are less capital intensive and less sensitive to cyclical declines than are chemical intermediates. The company's basic R&D is done in the United States, but applications research, which focuses on adapting products to meet the capabilities and needs of local users, is conducted in the United States and the foreign divisions. The overseas subsidiaries, whether wholly or partially owned by Dow, produce under licensing agreements with the parent company.

Honda

Honda Motor Company, Ltd. manufactures and sells motorcycles, automobiles, and power products (e.g., portable generators, outboard motors, and lawn mowers). It is headquartered in Tokyo and operates several factories in Japan, as well as wholly owned subsidiaries in Belgium, Brazil, Italy, Thailand, and the United States. Honda performs additional overseas production at minority-held subsidiaries and 50-50 joint ventures in Indonesia, Iran, Nigeria, Peru, Taiwan, Thailand, and the Philippines. Honda's worldwide sales are about 3,000 billion yen per year (about US$21 billion using an exchange rate of approximately 152 yen per dollar, the rate in January 1987). About 70 percent of the company's revenues come from overseas markets. Direct exports from Japan represent approximately one fifth of total Japanese production. (Data on domestic and overseas employment are not routinely made available by the company.)

Honda eschews formal organization structures. Functionally, however, the parent maintains direct responsibility for the manufacture and sale of all products in Japan. Honda Research & Development Company, Ltd. (a Japan-based subsidiary) provides product R&D and product designs and Honda Engineering Company, Ltd. (also a Japan-based subsidiary) performs process-related R&D and manufactures production tooling and equipment for Honda plants worldwide. The situation of the U.S. subsidiary illustrates organizational relationships internationally. The president of Honda of America is also a managing director and member of the board of directors of the parent company. Operational coordination is achieved via varied contacts involving managerial and technical personnel at the parent and subsidiary in the product divisions and specialty areas (e.g., Honda Engineering for use of production technology and equipment).

Honda Motor's growth has traditionally been production driven. It has had to develop markets as outlets for its continuously expanding, low-cost production capabilities. Large markets, which include domestic and foreign segments, enable Honda to take advantage of its large-scale production facilities for certain parts and components, such as motorcycle engines, and to put such low-cost production to its competitive advantage. This was the situation, for example, when Honda first established motorcycle production at its U.S. plant in Ohio (1979). Engines were imported from Japan until sales in the U.S. market became large enough to justify producing engines in Ohio (1984).

Production R&D, conducted at Honda Engineering in Japan, is heavily oriented toward robotics and automated production equipment that have general applicability in Honda plants worldwide. Product R&D, as related, for example, to motorcycle models, is less monolithic. It uses market-generated information from both foreign and domestic operations and technical design expertise housed at Honda Research & Development Company in Japan. Honda licenses companies in 27 foreign countries to produce and sell Honda products.

The Conduct of International Business

Ampex, Citicorp, Dow, and Honda have a lot in common. They export something of value from their home countries and also produce abroad. They implement overseas activities via wholly owned foreign subsidiaries, joint ventures, and licensing arrangements that display obvious dependence on the parent company. They generally center their R&D at home. But Ampex, Citicorp, Dow, and Honda differ in important ways too. Ampex produces abroad to export back to the U.S. market in some cases. Its R&D is centered in the home market, while Dow, Citicorp, and Honda conduct product application and consumer research in foreign markets. The four companies exhibit very different organization structures at the top: the divisionalizing of Ampex is on a product basis; that of Citicorp and Dow, on a hybrid product, customer, and/or geographic basis; and that of Honda, on a functional basis. What are the implications of these observations for managers? Let's explore them.

Product Impact

Product variations are required to accommodate different technical considerations, such as the electrical characteristics of broadcast equipment, different use conditions, such as the chemicals used in agricultural applications, and different consumer preferences, such as the infatuation of Americans with powerful, heavy-duty motorcycles (compared, for example, to the smaller, scooter-type motorcycles preferred in some European countries). Product design for different markets also incorporates cost considerations related to scale economies in production, the use of standardized components on a global basis, and the production skills available in the work force at the foreign plant.

For some of the same reasons, the use of certain kinds of production processes, machinery, and equipment may vary between domestic and foreign operations. These are *process* variations. The level of production at a domestic plant may vary with demand conditions in a foreign country or with interruptions of production (caused by a strike, for example) at a foreign plant.

Honda, as the world's leading motorcycle manufacturer for over two decades, is maintaining its commitment to expanding the worldwide market for motorcycles through a steady stream of new products and technologies. . . . Thus, in Japan alone, 27 new models were introduced last year, including several scooter models, and a technological breakthrough, the CX500 Turbo, the world's first mass-produced turbocharged motorcycle.

Source: Honda Motor Company, Ltd., 1982 *Annual Report.*

Marketing Impact

Marketing is similarly complicated. Marketing research must now be coordinated among the different countries served—not only to determine product needs but also to arrive at product sales estimates used in setting production and inventory levels and purchasing and staffing needs. Pricing and promotional strategies must be determined for geographically segmented markets with different competitive characteristics. Successful marketing also requires understanding country-specific distribution systems, packaging preferences and standards, and so on.

Continuous development of new products and services is the essence of the competitive advantage for Dow Chemical.

Emphasis will be appropriately balanced between new product development and pure research. The budgeting of research expenses and capital will be integrated with global product strategies. Increased attention will be placed on coordinating global research and technology management so that new developments can be moved worldwide more efficiently and more quickly.

Source: Dow Chemical Company, 1985 *Annual Report.*

Financial Impact

Finance is concerned with handling cash flows and funding needs in both domestic and foreign operations, in home country and foreign country currencies. Dow Chemical, for example, uses a capital budgeting procedure to evaluate a plant investment proposal in Germany characterized by cash flows denominated in both deutsche marks and U.S. dollars. Moving funds internationally is also a major concern. Ampex needs Mexican pesos to pay the wages of its workers at its assembly plant just south of the Mexican-U.S. border. Dow wants to bring home its profits from its Dutch subsidiary; Honda, the licensing fees from its Costa Rican licensee. The currency denomination of assets and of debt funds is also important. What happens, for instance, to Citicorp's loans denominated in Argentinean pesos if pesos cannot be converted to dollars—or to the U.S. dollar value of Dow's Canadian dollar debt should the relative value of the Canadian dollar climb? Can Citicorp and Dow somehow protect themselves against the risk involved here?

The tests of the past few years extended to the fundamental financial management of the Company. Managing a global enterprise during uncertain economic times requires a top-notch financial function. . . . In 1983, the efforts of our Treasury Department resulted in a gain of more than $65 million on foreign exchange.
Source: Dow Chemical Company, 1983 *Annual Report.*

Personnel Impact

Personnel concerns are also different when a company is dealing with foreign operations. Honda uses Japanese nationals in managerial and technical positions at its U.S. subsidiary; Ampex uses Americans at its British subsidiary. How are these parent company expatriates in turn managed? What career paths do they tread? Do they mix well with local nationals? Another concern is the management of workers at the foreign plant. The industrial relations environment must be analyzed on several issues—for example, the wage determination process, the implementation of technological change, the propensity for industrial conflict, and the composition, magnitude, and determination of nonwage compensation.

Accounting Impact

Financial accounting systems must be developed to reflect operations consolidated on a global basis. Dow Chemical presents a dollar-denominated, consolidated financial report on its worldwide activities—even though its foreign subsidiaries deal in and report their own operations in their own currencies. How is this accomplished? How can managerial accounting systems be designed to convey meaningful information to parent company management when operations cross a variety of national environments?

The consolidated financial statements include the accounts of Citicorp and its wholly owned subsidiary, Citibank, N.A., and their majority-owned subsidiaries, after the elimination of all material intercompany transactions.

Affiliates which are 20 percent to 50 percent owned are carried under the equity method of accounting and the pro rata share of their income (loss) is included in other revenue. Income from investments in less than 20 percent-owned companies is recognized when dividends are received.
Source: Citicorp, 1985 *Annual Report.*

Throughout this annual report, Japanese yen amounts for the fiscal year ended February 28, 1986 have been translated into United States dollars solely for convenience at the rate of Y180.55 = U.S.$1, the noon buying rate on February 28, 1986 in New York City for cable transfers in yen as certified for customs purposes by the Federal Reserve Bank of New York.
Source: Honda Motor Company, Ltd., 1985 *Annual Report.*

Tax Impact

Ampex, Citicorp, Dow, and Honda operate internationally within various national tax jurisdictions. Most governments, the United States and Japan included, like to collect taxes. Operating entities, such as parent companies and subsidiaries, generate profits (or losses) and are taxed. Profits can be moved around, however, between parent and subsidiaries depending, for example, on what the latter pay for imported components, management fees, and royalties. Nonetheless, the U.S. Internal Revenue Service reserves the right to determine these charges (for tax purposes) for firms operating in the United States and, for example, felt that Honda of America owed $12 million more in its 1982 taxes than it actually paid.[2]

As a U.S. corporation, all of Citicorp's foreign pretax earnings are subject to domestic taxation currently if earned by a foreign branch, or when earnings are effectively repatriated, if earned by a foreign subsidiary or affiliate. . . . In addition, certain of Citicorp's domestic income is subject to foreign income tax where the payor of such income is domiciled overseas.
Source: Citicorp, 1983 *Annual Report.*

Certainly, more could be said about the differences between operating just domestically as compared to operating internationally. In fact, that is what this whole book is all about. Table 1-1 presents the differences noted above in summary form. Later in the book, each of these traditional functional areas of management, as put into practice in the international business setting, is discussed in substantial detail.

Subsequent Levels of Analysis

From a management perspective, the differences between operating domestically and operating internationally are substantial. Noting these differences constitutes a first level of analysis. But what gives rise to these differences? This *second level* of analysis involves understanding and appreciating the environmental and institutional peculiarities that uniquely affect international business and that influence or determine the nature of the management functions. Included in this level of analysis are the pressures resulting in

Table 1-1 **How the Management Functions Differ in International Business**

Management Topics	Selected Highlights of International Business Dimensions of Operations
Product	Adaptive to differences in technical requirements, use conditions, scale economies, consumer preferences, available production skills, and available materials.
Process	Adaptive, as noted above—with emphasis on scale economies and available production skills and materials.
Marketing	Marketing research—decentralized, market specific, yet coordinated across different countries to identify commonalities. Distribution, packaging, promotion, etc. usually market specific. Pricing set via competitive conditions in geographically segmented markets.
Finance	Concerned with cash flows and funding needs in both domestic and foreign currencies, capital budgeting for foreign operations and currency denomination of debt. Focus is on the financial and business risks associated with such activities and on the methods available for reducing or offsetting these risks.
Personnel	Selecting, motivating, and rewarding personnel on foreign assignments. Justification for using expatriate personnel. Managing industrial relations internationally.
Accounting	Accounting for foreign transactions and consolidating financial statements at the multinational level. Developing and implementing informative managerial accounting systems internationally. Minimizing taxes on a global corporate basis.

international trade and investment, the operations of foreign exchange markets, and the politically determined presence of trade and investment barriers and incentives. Cultural barriers are also relevant. These and other related topics are discussed in considerable detail in the chapters that follow.

As discussed above, the management functions are different because of international operations and the roots of these differences are found in environmental differences. A *third level* of analysis is needed, however, to explain why there are differences in how companies operate internationally. Look at how Ampex, Citicorp, Dow, and Honda differ. Why do these differences exist? This third level of analysis focuses on how each company operates within a specific competitive and technological setting and within its own corporate culture and on how this may either expand or constrain its options. Ampex, for example, produces offshore for consumption in the United States because of labor cost differences; Dow does not. Honda assembles and markets heavy-duty motorcycles in the United States, as does its main domestic competitor, Harley-Davidson. It imports lighter-weight vehicles that cater to other market segments where there is no domestic competition. Why? Ampex is not especially concerned with product modifications to meet the needs of foreign customers; Dow is to some extent. Citicorp has identified global customers with global needs. Honda is very market sensitive in its product planning. Why? All four companies view international operations as important to their success strategies, and yet their strategies vary considerably. Why? The following text also deals with these questions and provides the student with a solid perspective on the rationales for differing managerial decisions that result in differing approaches to operating internationally.

Topics aside from the Multinational Corporation

Thus far, the discussion has focused totally on the multinational corporation. But international business involves a much more diverse set of actors than just multinational corporations.

Governments

As implied from the above, governments are also certainly relevant. They usually implement their policies via specific agencies, and these policies and agencies are certainly proper subjects for this text. In addition, governments often own companies that compete with private sector firms—so these companies will be discussed. International institutions, typically constituted via government action, help define the environment within which international business functions. The International Monetary Fund, the World Bank, and the International Labor Office are examples of such institutions.

Culture

As noted briefly above, culture is also an important variable in international business where firms operate cross-culturally. People are products of specific cultural settings, and international business is conducted through people. Culture affects values, communications, institutions, and so on. Most often it is seen as being national or subnational in character. But there is also the "corporate culture"—people in firms are groups too, and they often share common values, interests, hierarchies, and the like. International business deals with home country and host country cultures within a corporate culture. Finding commonalities among these three cultural groups often facilitates successful operations. The topic of culture is addressed specifically in Chapter 11. The influences of culture, however, will be manifested in various other chapters—especially those dealing with international business operations in the functional areas.

Exporting/Importing

The four companies presented above are all pretty big companies. International business, however, is also relevant for small and medium-sized firms. Today, many of these firms are involved in exporting and in the foreign

"Home" to most of the countries of the world, the United Nations has a tremendous impact on international business via, for example, its Center on Transnational Corporations and Conference on Trade and Development (UNCTAD)

Wide World Photos

sourcing of materials or parts. The example of RECO International, B.V., a Dutch-owned food and beverage processor and distributor, comes to mind. This $12 million (sales) firm operates four factories in Europe and has recently begun exporting processed bananas from an Ecuadoran plant to the United States. The Ecuadoran plant, built with World Bank funds and utilizing automated processing equipment provided by an Australian firm, is government owned. Like the Ecuadoran government, many other governments, including that of the United States, do much to promote exports—providing tax breaks, special foreign marketing assistance, and so forth. These activities are usually fairly well publicized. Some governments also have special policies that are meant to encourage imports. These often take the form of special tariff reductions on goods imported from selected countries. A case in point here is the duty-free import into the United States of many manufactured goods under the Generalized System of Preferences (GSP) and the Caribbean Basin Initiative (CBI). Export/import management is the subject of Chapter 18. Government activities pertaining to international trade are also discussed in this chapter—and in other chapters as appropriate.

Why Study International Business?

The answer to this question should be fairly obvious by now. People should study international business because —

1. Almost all of the large enterprises in the United States, Western Europe, and Japan are multinational in character.
2. Many small and medium-sized firms are also involved internationally. This may take the form of export or import operations, support activities directly related to international trade (e.g., freight forwarders, customs brokers), professional services pertaining to international trade or multinational operations (e.g., accounting/auditing, banking, legal counsel), and so on. Some of these firms may also be involved in overseas plant investment or licensing arrangements with foreign firms.
3. Competitive environments are typically industry specific, and industries today are very often competitive internationally. Overseas investment, incidentally, is not a requirement for international competitiveness. International trade, or the potential for such, can also link markets. A popular case in point here would be the U.S. steel industry, which has contracted considerably in the face of expanding imports.
4. Public policy issues often relate to international trade, investment, and finance. Today, any country's economic policies must consider the foreign sector. These policies are directly concerned with structuring business-to-government and business-to-business relationships in ways consistent with national interests. Many domestic public issues and policies also have important spillover effects for international business. For example, the British manufacturer of Austin-Healey sports cars abandoned exporting to the United States when it felt that it was in no position to meet U.S. auto safety requirements while remaining competitive. What have air quality standards done to the competitiveness of domestic versus imported steel in the U.S. market? The number of examples here is endless!

Specific data and information on the scope and magnitude of international trade and investment and on the form and extent of multinational corporate activity are presented in the next three chapters. Public policy issues are analyzed in several of the chapters that follow.

Clearly, international business is important to managers. *The Wall Street Journal, Business Week, Forbes,* and other business periodicals typically include articles and commentary on global business activities and on the changing global environment affecting business. Academe also recognizes the importance of international business. To ensure that people study international business, the U.S. business school accrediting agency, the American Assembly of Collegiate Schools of Business (AACSB), now requires that all bachelor's- and master's-level degree programs include a "worldwide business component." From the student's personal perspective, however, the study of international business should also be important. Many business school graduates are or will be employed by firms engaged in international business. Even more business school graduates are or will be employed by firms in industries characterized by, or at least influenced by, international trade or investment. All business school graduates, as business practitioners, will be influenced by public policies pertinent to national interests and the

From Le Havre to Singapore to Sydney, international trade means moving the goods—from packaging and insuring, to shipping and getting paid.

Milton & Joan Mann/Cameramann International

dynamics of a world economy. Business practitioners have a responsibility to operate in a manner consistent with these policies and to work constructively to influence them. "Good citizenship," when viewed in this perspective, means good business too!

Comments on the Content and Organization of Materials Presented in This Book

Introduction

As is evident from all of the preceding, the multinational enterprise (MNE) is the key figure in international business—especially for students of business administration. The MNE is also the key figure in this text. The focus is not exclusive, however. Other forms of international business and other issue areas are also discussed. The next chapter presents the operational concepts that affect decision making in the MNE. That chapter and this one constitute the introductory materials.

Manager in the World Economy

The next part, "Manager in the World Economy," provides a thorough discussion of the environments and the institutional and theoretical frameworks within which international business is conducted. The topics covered in this part include international trade and foreign direct investment patterns and theories, with added commentary on their relevance to business decisions; the international financial markets and how firms dealing in these markets operate; and the more important business-government issues, such as trade and investment barriers (e.g., tariffs, quotas, exchange restrictions), the partial elimination of these barriers via economic integration, and the methods used by governments in evaluating the potential advantages and disadvantages of investments by foreign firms in manufacturing and other types of operations.

Managing the MNE

Part 3, "Managing the MNE," deals with the challenges and opportunities of multinational operations and with the means by which MNEs develop and sustain a competitive presence. The first chapter focuses on culture. The other nine chapters cover the traditional, and not so traditional, management decision-making areas of organization structure and business strategy, marketing, accounting and taxation, finance and control, industrial relations, personnel, export/import management, and technology transfer.

Doing Business in . . .

Part 4 consists of three chapters focusing on selected, fairly distinctive environments within which international business functions. These are the developed countries, the less developed countries (LDCs), and the communist countries.

A Look to the Future

The final two chapters take a look at the future. The commentary is structured around analyses of several industries and around political developments affecting the MNE.

Conclusions

International business is presented in this chapter as being the domain of multinational enterprises and smaller firms that engage in export/import activities or provide related support functions and of political activities that directly and indirectly influence international trade and finance. International business is implemented via management functions that have to account for different and compelling environmental circumstances—and that are unique unto themselves in some instances, such as those concerned with foreign exchange markets and host country assessments of the desirability of foreign direct investment.

Ampex, Citicorp, Dow Chemical, and Honda were cited as examples of international businesses that operated in ways common to all and in ways unique to each. Different aspects of each company's situation were highlighted and subsequently categorized by management function. This procedure resulted in fairly distinctive descriptions of differences in management functions consistent with the international (versus purely domestic) content of the operational environment.

The idea of "level of analysis" was introduced. Three levels were identified: identification of the differences between operating domestically and internationally, discussion of the environmental circumstances giving rise to these differences, and analysis of the rationales for making management decisions in international business in light of these differences.

The importance of studying international business was discussed. Business today is international! Almost invariably, firms and industries are internationally involved. Business school graduates may find themselves working for an MNE or dealing with management problems occasioned by competition from foreign companies in their industries. Public policy issues, including those often identified with ostensibly domestic problems, strongly influence international business activities.

The general outline of the text was presented. Its five parts were identified: "Introduction" (including the concept of the MNE), "Manager in the World Economy" (analyzing the more significant environmental influences), "Managing the MNE" (focusing on the management functions), "Doing Business in . . ." (covering developed countries, LDCs, and communist countries), and "A Look to the Future" (examining industry and political trends). The authors believe that this five-dimensional format covers all of the essential topics necessary for a substantial introduction to international business. For many students, the topics covered in this text will constitute their only academic experience with international business. Other students will use this text as an introduction to courses in international management, marketing, finance, etc. The text has been designed to serve the needs of both groups.

Questions

1. What is "international business"?
2. What activities of a firm characterize it as being in international business?
3. How important is international business to Ampex? Citicorp? Dow? Honda? Is the domestic competitiveness of these firms in any way affected by their international business success?
4. How might the four firms be different or similar in international business—especially in these areas: product design, marketing, finance, industrial relations, personnel, and accounting and taxation?

5. Why study international business?
6. What are the differences among the three levels of analysis? Is there a logical progression through the levels?
7. Judging from the general knowledge you have, how important is international business to the following firms: IBM, Exxon, Sears, Coca-Cola, Holiday Inns, and General Motors? How do their international business activities differ?
8. How would you differentiate between international business and international trade?
9. Can you identify a current public policy issue that is related to international business? How is that issue important to you as a consumer or citizen? How would it be important to you if you were a business manager? What do you think the government should do in this case? Why?
10. Why do you think a small or new firm would get involved in international business? Would your answer differ if the firm were in, say, Belgium rather than the United States?

References

The Wall Street Journal. Keep current on daily issues related to international business and the activities of MNEs. Read the International Section, especially.

Business Week. Feature articles often refer to international issues or analyze the corporate strategy of an MNE.

Economist. Especially strong on environmental analysis, economic or political, and on non-U.S. MNEs.

Fortune. In-depth analysis and presentation of the Fortune 500 and other companies.

Annual reports. Select a company. Study its annual reports for the past five years. Note how "international" fits into its business strategy. Identify the relationships between its domestic business and its international business.

Endnotes

1. The case information presented here is based on company interviews conducted by the authors or annual reports published by the companies.
2. Honda Motor Company, Ltd., 1982 *Annual Report,* pp. 20-21.

2

THE MULTINATIONAL ENTERPRISE AND COMPETITIVE ADVANTAGES

This chapter introduces the multinational enterprise as the key actor in international business. An even broader definition of firms that do international business, namely international contractors, shows that this book applies to both small and large firms. The chapter presents a conceptual framework that is used throughout the rest of the book, namely the theory of competitive advantage. The main goals of the chapter are to:

1. Describe the multinational enterprise (**MNE**) and show how both large and small firms can be MNEs.
2. Explain the theory of competitive advantage and show how competitive advantages can be used by firms to benefit from doing international business.
3. Explain the concept of internalization, which can help managers and students alike to understand why MNEs act as they do.
4. Provide examples of the use of competitive advantages in international business, such as the Caterpillar case, that shed more light on the concepts and on their applications in actual business situations.

Introduction

This chapter focuses on the **multinational enterprise (MNE),** the single most important actor in international business. Clearly, the national governments that set the "rules of the game" in business are important; and other, nonmultinational firms that participate in international business are also important. But the MNE dominates by virtue of the size and scope of its international transactions, the frequency of those transactions, and other measures of international business, including the visibility of its activities in the public eye.

Consider the forms of international business discussed in Chapter 1, which are categorized in Table 2-1 (intergovernmental transactions have been ignored here). Multinational firms carry out the vast majority of business in every category. Recognize that, while MNEs do carry out the bulk of the *value* of transactions in international business, they do not necessarily undertake the largest *number* of transactions. Many small firms are involved, particularly in exports and imports.

Basically, through their internal transactions among affiliates and their external transactions with unrelated clients, multinational firms do the following: they export and import; they move funds internally through loans, payments for technology, overhead, and so on, and they borrow from and lend to unrelated parties; they exchange ownership of assets across national

Table 2-1 **Some Estimates of MNE Participation in International Business** (in billions of current U.S. dollars)

	World	United States
Exports (1985)	1,782.9	213.1
Foreign direct investment (1985)*		232.7 stock 19.7 flow
Licensing:		
Of affiliates (1985)	n.a.	4.1
Of unrelated firms		
Other contractual dealings:		
With affiliates (1985)	n.a.	2.5
With unrelated firms		
International commercial bank lending (1985)	506,337	355,945

* Foreign direct investment *must* be done by MNEs, by definition.

Sources: *International Financial Statistics,* 1986 yearbook; *Survey of Current Business,* August 1986; Federal Financial Institutions Examination Council, "Country Exposure Lending Survey" (December 1985); and Bank for International Settlements, "Semi-annual International Banking Statistics" (June 1986).

borders; and they pass uncountable amounts of information internationally among their affiliates and with unrelated parties. These activities are the essence of international business. Figure 2-1 presents another look at international business, picturing the MNE as the central actor.

As illustrated in Figure 2-1, the MNE is a central organizing institution for international transactions involving money, goods, and information. The MNE not only seeks to earn profits for its owners; it also generates income for suppliers in more than one country, provides outputs for customers in more than one country, provides additional competition for firms in each country, involves banks in financing these activities in each country, and operates under the rules set by governments in each of the jurisdictions involved. Rather than having separate firms or individuals carry out these various activities, the MNE groups them all together under one management structure.

This chapter explains what a multinational enterprise is, what kinds of activities it undertakes, and why it undertakes them. The central idea is to get the reader to think about the kinds of problems and decisions that face an MNE manager. In the next section, we define the MNE, according to several criteria. Then the section "Examples of MNEs" lists a number of large, relatively visible MNEs and discusses some of their attributes. By using the

Figure 2-1 **The Multinational Enterprise in International Business**

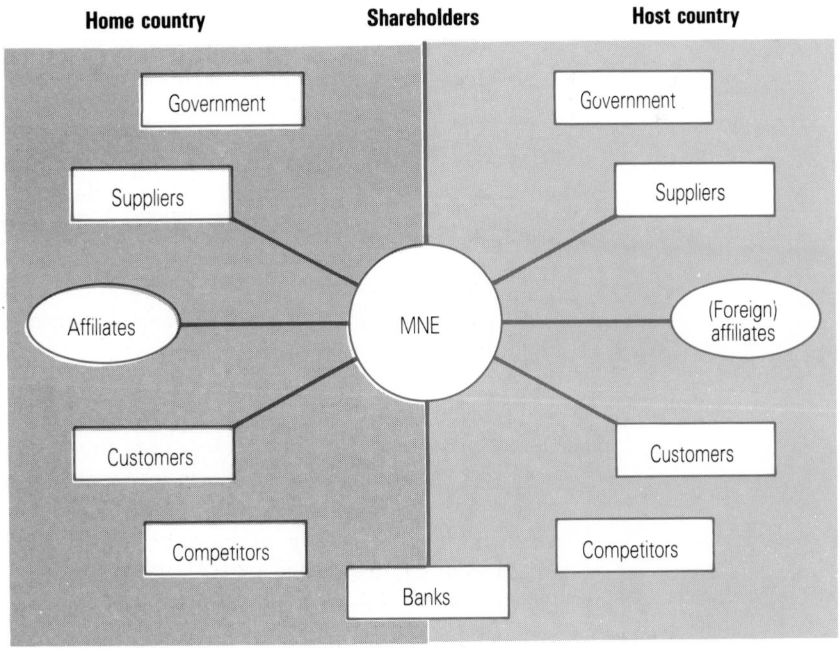

theory of competitive advantage, described in the section that follows, a manager can decide what information to gather and how to use that information to make careful decisions about MNE activities ranging from capital budgeting to dealing with governments. Competitive advantage is utilized throughout the text as a general framework for thinking about the issues facing the MNE manager and for defining the basic rationale of the key decisions that MNE managers make.

Characteristics of the Multinational Enterprise

No single definition of the MNE has received wide acceptance at this time. Some analysts view large, dominant firms that do at least some international business (such as those appearing in the Fortune 500) as the relevant ones. Others include only firms that have owners from more than one country. Even the label is arguable—the United Nations calls the firms "transnational corporations," and the AFL-CIO calls them "multinational companies." While no definition can be completely objective, Vernon and Wells have offered a view that covers the concept fairly well. Their view is that multinational enterprises are companies

> *made up of a cluster of affiliated firms [that], although in different countries, nevertheless share distinguishing characteristics as follows:*
> 1. *They are linked by ties of common ownership.*
> 2. *They draw on a common pool of resources, such as money and credit, information systems, trade names and patents.*
> 3. *They respond to some common strategy.*[1]

In this view, the MNE may be privately or governmentally owned; it may be very large or relatively small; its ownership may be held by investors from any number of countries; and it may engage in any number of forms of international business—as long as it possesses owned affiliates in more than two countries. This may be called a *functional* definition of the MNE, since it focuses on the functioning of the firm and not on its ownership structure or other characteristics. The one necessary function of an MNE is foreign direct investment, through which the firm obtains or creates affiliates in at least three countries.

Typically, the firms discussed in this book not only have affiliates in three or more countries but also possess the other characteristics of multinational ownership and large size, as shown in the next section. The key point of our definition is that firms need *not* possess these latter characteristics in order to use the strategies and organization structures discussed in later chapters. The ability to utilize more than one country as the firm's market or production site (and to face the concomitant opportunities and constraints) is the distinguishing feature of the MNE. From this arise the competitive advantages peculiar to multinational firms.

The International Contractor

The central focus of international business is on the multinational enterprise, or more accurately on the **international contractor** (INC). The MNE has been defined as a firm with subsidiaries, branches, or other controlled affiliates in three or more countries. The INC is a more broadly defined firm, with business activities in at least two countries. The minimum number of countries involved in *inter*national business is two; hence the international contractor is a firm that carries out such business. This definition encompasses firms ranging from small exporters all the way to EXXON and IBM, with affiliates in dozens of countries; all of them are really firms of interest to this book.

Due to the increasing limitations that many countries impose on ownership of local firms by foreigners, firms that carry out substantial international business are finding more and more nonownership forms of activity to undertake (e.g., licensing, franchising, turnkey ventures, and other more complex contracting arrangements, in addition to simple exporting). Also, small firms often discover that international business can be carried out through nonownership forms that do not require the large amounts of resources that operation of subsidiaries does. Thus, the MNE is an international contractor that utilizes ownership of foreign-controlled firms. The INC is a firm, large or small, that participates in business in at least two countries, through owned affiliates or other contractual forms. (This issue is discussed in more detail in Chapter 25.)

International contracting has become quite common in raw materials industries and in public utilities (such as telephone and electric power companies). Firms such as Exxon, Texaco, ITT, and GTE find themselves in the late 1980s (especially in less developed countries) with fewer foreign investments in oil wells or telephone operating companies and more technical consulting agreements with host country firms that monopolize these industries. International banking has traditionally relied on correspondent relationships among banking firms in different countries to provide international services. Even in manufacturing, contracting out to provide managerial or technical services has become very common for large as well as small firms in international business.

In sum, our interest is in the international activities of firms, hence in the international contractor. Because the largest and most successful firms in most industries of the world have two or more foreign affiliates, much of our analysis will look specifically at multinational enterprises.

Examples of MNEs

The list of multinational enterprises according to our definition would number in the thousands. Instead of trying to create such a list, we consider a small number of very successful MNEs and a few of their competitive characteristics. Our purpose is to discover not only which companies are multinational but also to see what enables them to operate successfully at the international level. Table 2-2 lists 36 large U.S.-based multinationals that a study by Peters and Waterman (1982) regarded as having been highly successful from 1961 to 1980.

Table 2-2 **Characteristics of Top-Performing, U.S.-Based MNEs**

Company	Technology Intensity (R&D/sales)	Annual Sales ($ millions)	Number of Foreign Countries with Affiliates	Capital per Worker (assets per employee)
Electronics				
Amdahl	17.7	462	12	127.9
Data General	10.5	804	25	47.6
Digital Equipment	9.0	4,019	23	59.9
Emerson Electric	2.6	3,472	23	n.a.
Hewlett-Packard	10.0	4,266	29	51.3
IBM	6.0	34,364	46	89.2
Intel	14.5	900	n.a.	36.2
National Semiconductor	9.9	1,152	12	31.2
Raychem	9.3	561	13	46.6
Schlumberger	5.4	6,284	n.a.	79.4
Texas Instruments	5.5	4,327	16	32.9
Wang Laboratories	7.5	1,322	18	72.6
Eastman Kodak	6.6	10,815	28	77.8
Cosmetics and Health Care Products				
Avon	1.8	3,001	31	58.0
Johnson & Johnson	6.3	5,761	53	52.8
Bristol-Myers	4.5	3,600	54	78.9
Chesebrough-Pond's	1.0	1,623	39	40.6
Revlon	4.9	2,351	33	99.7
Procter & Gamble	2.4	12,301	23	116.4
Chemicals				
Dow Chemical	4.3	10,618	43	208.6
DuPont	2.6	33,331	36	166.7
Merck	10.5	3,063	35	148.6

Notice that the vast majority of these firms spend much more on research and development (R&D), and thus are more technology intensive, than the U.S. industry average of 2.1 percent of sales spent on R&D. Also, most of them possess affiliates in far more than the three countries needed to be considered a multinational enterprise. Notice, finally, that the group is spread over a wide variety of industries, despite their similarity of above-average commitments to technology and international diversification.

A similar listing of non-U.S. MNEs cannot be as detailed, because far less information is available on those firms. By ranking firms according to size

Table 2-2 (*concluded*)

Company	Technology Intensity (R&D/sales)	Annual Sales ($ millions)	Number of Foreign Countries with Affiliates	Capital per Worker (assets per employee)
Electrical Appliances				
Maytag	n.a.	441	1	114.3
Industrial Machinery				
Caterpillar	3.6	6,469	12	134.3
Dana	1.7	2,423	7	59.1
3M	5.3	6,600	23	63.1
Clothing				
Levi Strauss	n.a.	2,572	5	360.0
Oil				
Amoco	0.5	29,900	27	420.2
Project Management				
Boeing	7.6	9,035	2	79.3
Fluor	n.a.	7,336	7	121.0
Services (e.g., hotels, retail sales, restaurants)				
Delta Air Lines	n.a.	3,607	0	86.8
Disney Productions	n.a.	1,089	2	97.8
K mart	n.a.	16,999	1	27.5
Marriott	n.a.	2,541	n.a.	18.8
McDonald's	n.a.	2,715	30	29.3
Wal-Mart	n.a.	3,124	0	n.a.

Sources: Thomas J. Peters and Robert H. Waterman *In Search of Excellence* (New York: Harper & Row, 1982), Standard & Poor's, *Business Week,* and Moody's. All of these firms passed Peters and Waterman's tests for "excellent" performance during 1961–80.

(defined as annual sales converted into U.S. dollars), however, a listing can be created. Table 2-3 presents a group of the largest non-U.S. MNEs, which appear in the *Fortune* list of the 500 largest non-U.S. industrial companies. These companies are classified by profitability (defined as gross profits divided by total assets), size, country of parent company, industry, and capital intensity (defined as total assets divided by total employees).

Despite the proliferation of countries represented, the industrial concentration of these large, non-U.S. firms is striking: over half are in the petroleum and automotive industries. Most of the firms are in European countries, but Japan has more entries (eight companies) in the list than any other single country.

What can account for the uneven distribution of MNEs across countries

Table 2-3 **Characteristics of the Largest Non-U.S. Multinationals**

Name	Profits/ Assets	Annual Sales ($ billions)	Industry	Country	Assets per Employee
1. Royal Dutch Shell	0.071	84.865	Petroleum	Netherlands/UK	463.56
2. British Petroleum	0.037	50.662	Petroleum	UK	302.51
3. ENI	−0.002	25.798	Petroleum, chemicals	Italy	183.26
4. Toyota	0.081	24.111	Motor vehicles	Japan	25.79
5. IRI	n.a.	23.354	Petroleum	Italy	n.a.
6. Unilever	0.057	21.599	Food, soaps, cosmetics	UK/Netherlands	35.16
7. Elf-Aquitaine	0.044	20.662	Petroleum	France	221.66
8. Matsushita Electrical Industrial	0.059	19.993	Electrical appliances	Japan	127.37
9. Pemex	0.0002	19.405	Petroleum	Mexico	213.39
10. Hitachi	0.034	18.486	Electronics	Japan	127.01
11. Cie. Française des Petroles	0.014	18.159	Petroleum	France	244.8
12. Philips	0.023	17.835	Electronics	Netherlands	44.47
13. Nissan	0.021	17.513	Motor vehicles	Japan	135.24
14. Petrobras	0.046	17.087	Petroleum	Brazil	235.83
15. Siemens	0.025	16.638	Electronics	Germany	48.17
16. Volkswagenwerk	0.008	16.035	Motor vehicles	Germany	43.79
17. Daimler-Benz	0.044	15.274	Motor vehicles	Germany	45.39
18. Bayer	0.035	15.108	Chemicals	Germany	57.32
19. Kuwait Petroleum	0.057	16.691	Petroleum	Kuwait	1,140.16
20. Nippon Steel	0.008	14.785	Metal manufacturing	Japan	666.54
21. Hoechst	0.042	14.555	Chemicals	Germany	50.20

and industries? Certainly, no single factor is the key. The next section presents a viewpoint that offers both an understanding of some of the important factors involved and ways for managers to utilize these factors in operating their own companies.

The Theory of Competitive Advantage

Defining Competitive Advantages

Studies of MNEs during the 1960s and 1970s have shown that these firms typically compete in domestic and foreign markets on the basis of **competitive advantages** that are based on company-specific characteristics. That

Table 2-3 (*concluded*)

Name	Profits/ Assets	Annual Sales ($ billions)	Industry	Country	Assets per Employee
22. BASF	0.041	14.184	Chemicals	Germany	66.31
23. Mitsubishi Heavy Industries	0.006	17.781	Motor vehicles, industrial equipment	Japan	189.56
24. Petróleos de Venezuela	0.13	13.598	Petroleum	Venezuela	392.83
25. Fiat	0.024	13.547	Motor vehicles	Italy	65.55
26. BAT Industries	0.097	13.461	Tobacco	UK	54.76
27. Imperial Chemical Industries	0.076	13.426	Chemicals	UK	89.39
28. Nestlé	0.067	13.242	Food, beverages	Switzerland	68.21
29. General Motors of Canada	0.233	12.584	Motor vehicles	Canada	64.39
30. Renault	−0.134	12.227	Motor vehicles	France	50.19
31. Nippon Steel	0.0002	11.995	Metal manufacturing, steel	Japan	234.27
32. Thyssen	0.009	11.776	Metal manufacturing, steel	Germany	47.81
33. Esso Petroleum	0.18	5.271	Petroleum	UK	864.47
34. Canadian Pacific	0.02	11.300	Metal manufacturing, steel, mining	Canada	118.51
35. Toshiba	0.021	11.288	Electrical appliances	Japan	112.46
36. Volvo	0.029	10.518	Motor vehicles	Sweden	93.52

Source: "The International 500 Ranked by Sales," *Fortune,* August 19, 1985.

is, an MNE usually possesses some **proprietary asset**—a new production process, a superior sales location, facilities that realize economies of scale in production or distribution, and so on (or a combination of such assets)—that allows it to achieve lower costs or higher revenues than its competitors.[2]

For example, Pfizer Corporation has discovered that it can successfully transfer product differentiation strategies developed in one country to other countries in which it does business in pharmaceuticals; the company has managed its internal resources to obtain economies of scale in advertising and physical distribution for its differentiated products. Westinghouse Electric Corporation has demonstrated an ability to negotiate contracts to provide major power-generating facilities with governments in less developed countries and Eastern Europe; it now possesses a competitive advantage in government contracting and a protected business position in several national markets. Mobil Oil, Caterpillar Tractor, and several other firms have developed internal "codes of conduct" that they publicize widely and use to convince governments and social pressure groups that the company is acting in the interest of the country involved; this is a kind of competitive advantage in social goodwill, since it is expected to result in more favorable treatment of the company by each government or social pressure group. Hewlett-Packard, IBM, and many Japanese companies have corporate philosophies that are passed on to employees and substantially followed by the companies' executives—leading to superior internal labor and personnel relations than in many other firms. L. M. Ericcson, the Swedish telecommunications manufacturer, has developed small electronic switching systems that suit many customers that need less-extensive, less-costly telephone systems than those produced and sold by its major rivals in international business—Ericcson has developed a market niche advantage. Each of these examples of competitive advantages gives the company the ability to outcompete its rivals in a particular business situation.

Many of these proprietary characteristics are not limited to multinational firms; in fact, most of them pertain to successful domestic firms as well. Table 2-4 lists a number of commonly cited attributes that create competitive advantages for multinational firms. Advantages that exist for both domestic and multinational firms are discussed in this section; specifically multinational advantages are discussed in the following section.

Historically, 20th-century MNEs began primarily in extractive industries, ranging from oil to bananas to copper.[3] These multinationals competed on the basis of their access to supplies of natural resources and to substantial markets. By the advent of World War II, many of these advantages had been partially or completely competed away, and thus the firms were vulnerable to competition from other firms and to greater regulation by governments.

Most of the post-World War II analyses of MNEs (e.g., Vernon 1966 and Kindleberger 1969) focused on **proprietary technology** as the basis for the competitive strength of such firms. Indeed, many of the most successful U.S.-based MNEs in the 1950s and 60s produced high-tech products in such industries as pharmaceuticals (e.g., Pfizer, Johnson & Johnson, and Merck), data processing (e.g., IBM, Burroughs, Honeywell), telecommunications (e.g., ITT, GTE), chemicals (e.g., Dow, Du Pont, Monsanto), and electronic instruments (e.g., Eastman Kodak, Texas Instruments). The competitive advantage came from some technology created or purchased by the firm that the firm was able to utilize in production to generate better or less-expensive products than were produced by its competitors. For example, Du Pont created distinctive products such as nylon, rayon, and more recently Kevlar; IBM was a leader in moving data processing from electromechanical computations to electronic processing; and Eastman Kodak created a higher-quality paper for photographs than its rivals.

Early analyses also focused on the marketing advantages possessed by MNEs (e.g., Vernon 1966 and Caves 1971). Particularly important in this case is the firm's ability to differentiate its product from others. By establishing a **brand or trade name,** the firm may be able to attract additional buyers due to name recognition and trust. Examples of industries in which firms possess

Table 2-4 **Competitive Advantages of Multinational Enterprises**

Advantage	Description
General Competitive Advantages	
Proprietary technology	Product, process, or management technology held by a firm that others can obtain only through R&D or contracting with the possessor
Goodwill based on brand or trade name	Reputation for quality, service, etc., developed through experience
Scale economies in production	Large-scale production facilities that lower unit costs of production
Scale economies in purchasing	Lower costs of inputs through purchasing large quantities
Scale economies in financing	Access to funds at a lower cost for larger firms
Scale economies in distribution	Shipments of large quantities of products/inputs to necessary locations, lowering unit shipping costs
Scale economies in advertising	Sales in several markets, allowing somewhat standardized advertising across markets
Government protection	Free or preferential access to a market limited by government fiat
Human resource management	Skill at fostering teamwork among employees and optimizing productivity
Multinational Competitive Advantages	
Multinational marketing capability	Knowledge of and access to markets in several countries
Multinational sourcing capability	Reliable access to raw materials, intermediate goods, etc., in several countries that reduces single-source costs
Multinational diversification	Operations in several countries so that country risk and business risk are reduced
Managerial experience in several countries	Skill for managing multicountry operations gained through experience in different countries (learning curve gains)

this type of advantage include electrical appliances (e.g., General Electric, Maytag, Sunbeam), health care products (e.g., Bristol-Myers, Colgate-Palmolive, Procter & Gamble), foods (e.g., Coca-Cola, Kraft, RJR-Nabisco), and pharmaceuticals. In this case, the advantage arises from the firm's developing a reputation for high-quality products, good service after the product has been purchased, and/or good value relative to competitors' products. These characteristics become identified with the brand or trade name, enabling the firm to sell more output or charge higher prices than competitors.

More recent analysts have looked at multinational firms as holders of a variety of such competitive assets, no one of which is necessary by itself. A

Kodak office tower in Rochester, New York.

Courtesy Eastman Kodak Company

fairly extensive list of those advantages appears in Table 2-4. Let us consider the rest of the advantages listed.

Scale economies in production exist when a firm is able to operate a production facility that attains lower costs per unit at large levels of output than the costs achieved by competitors in production facilities that have lower output capacities. That is, as the scale (volume) of production is increased by increasing the size of the production facility, unit costs can be decreased at higher levels of output. (This does *not* mean that companies producing more of a product necessarily have lower costs; such a result may also occur when some producers are producing at quantities below their minimum-cost level of output). Scale economies in production are important in many industries, especially those that are heavily capital intensive, such as the automotive, airframe manufacturing, industrial chemical, and oil industries. General Motors, for example, is able to achieve substantially lower production costs for its cars than American Motors or Chrysler, each of which produces in smaller facilities and at lower volumes of output.

Scale economies in purchasing can be attained by firms that are able to buy inputs in large quantities and thus reduce their unit costs. This competitive advantage is usually available to larger firms, which are able to purchase larger quantities than their rivals. It also tends to arise for firms with more standardized production, as the selection of inputs becomes more predictable and larger stocks become justifiable. By contracting to buy literally millions of pounds of beef on a regular basis, such companies as Burger King and McDonald's reduce their hamburger cost far below that of local, single-location restaurants.

Scale economies in financing exist for firms that are able to borrow large sums of funds, and thus can obtain "quantity discounts." IBM, because of its very large size (and also because of its extremely good creditworthiness), can borrow at interest rates similar to those paid by the largest commercial banks for their own funds. A small computer manufacturer or component maker will pay far higher rates. By borrowing in the eurocurrency markets (which are restricted to fairly large-scale transactions, as discussed in Chapter 6), IBM or another large firm may find even lower rates than those available to smaller firms.

Scale economies in distribution arise when the firm is able to contract for shipping to several destinations and for large quantities of products to serve its several markets. The per unit cost of distributing products often falls when the selling firm can contract for multiple shipments and high volumes. (The firm may even purchase its own distribution system, if the cost of so doing is less than the cost of contracting with outside distributors.)

Scale economies in advertising may be attainable when the firm sells products in several countries and it can standardize the promotion across countries. In industrial countries, adjusting for language differences, such standardization can often be carried out, and advertising costs can thus be reduced. On the contrary, when products are introduced into very different countries (e.g., less developed nations), the promotion and even the product often need to be adapted to local conditions, and these scale economies cannot be realized. Exxon has used its "Put a tiger in your tank" promotional campaign successfully around the world; in the late 1980s, Beatrice Foods placed the company logo on its products of all sorts around the world (as opposed to previous promotion that downplayed the Beatrice connection).

Government protection is another source of competitive advantage. These advantages are often ignored, since they are based, not on the firm's activities in the market, but rather on the legal framework and negotiations with regulators. Nonetheless, managers should be aware that in every country temporary or permanent protection from competition may be obtained from the government. Whether it be operation of the telephone company (which AT&T monopolized until 1984 in most of the United States) or establishment of an import-replacing plant to produce pharmaceuticals, the firm may obtain exclusive rights or other protection from the host government. Such protection precludes other firms from competing, or makes their entry and operations far less profitable than the protected firm's activities. Also, dealing with the government as its supplier of products or services can generate a protected environment for the firm, since governments tend to deal with reliable suppliers without switching frequently. Literally thousands of firms in the United States earn all or most of their income from selling to the U.S. government. Such relationships tend to be fairly stable; and they are common in other countries as well.

Human resource management has proven to be a very important advantage for Japanese firms competing with U.S.-based MNEs in the 1970s and 1980s. When the firm's managers are able to create a working environment that stimulates employees' productivity, this enables the firm to lower its unit costs and improve the quality of the product. Countless stories have been told (e.g., William Ouchi's Theory Z) about Japanese firms' greater success at managing "people resources" than their U.S. rivals. Of course, many successful U.S. firms similarly have achieved superior human resource management as well (cf. the list of firms in Table 2.2).

Multinational Competitive Advantages

All of the advantages already discussed can be used at the international level as well as domestically. Scale economies in purchasing, production, distribution, or financing may be even greater for a firm that is able to spread its sales over several countries rather than just one. A technological lead can be exploited in many countries without necessarily reducing its value. Similarly, the other domestic competitive advantages can be extended to include foreign business. This section examines four competitive advantages that are primarily limited to MNEs, though some of them can be attained by domestic firms that contract with foreign firms.

Perhaps the most important is **multinational marketing** capability, which enables the firm to sell its products in many national markets simultaneously. Compared to competitors that operate in only one national market, the MNE gains a key advantage in being able to sell its excess production in other markets, due to its sales affiliates in those markets. The affiliates function as gatherers of information about market demands, regulatory conditions, and other business intelligence that could benefit the firm, and this enables the firm to quickly take advantage of markets for selling its output. The wider the firm's net of affiliates, the greater is its possibility of maximizing its revenues. From another perspective, shortfalls in demand in one country can be remedied by sending excess output to other countries where the firm encounters an excess demand beyond the ability of the local affiliate to supply.

Another fundamental multinational competitive advantage is **multinational sourcing** of production, which enables the firm to minimize production costs by using facilities in low-cost countries. This advantage enables the

MNE to reduce its costs relative to local competitors in any one country. Very frequently in the 1980s, firms have set up offshore production facilities in Asian countries (such as Singapore, South Korea, and Taiwan) or Mexico, where labor costs are low, to assemble machinery, clothing, or other products for sale in the United States or Europe. (In some cases, the MNE could realize this advantage through contracting with a local Korean or Mexican firm to do the assembly rather than through investing in local production.)

A third multinational advantage is the risk-reducing benefit of **international diversification.** Many MNEs use facilities in several countries to produce the same products for several markets. That way, if a strike, war, or just a machine breakdown occurs in any one country, markets can be served from the other production sites. Major chemical companies produce the basic petrochemicals, such as ethanol, polyethylene, and butyl rubber, in a "portfolio" of countries, so their supply is assured in the event of a nationalization, a work stoppage, or the like in any one country. Similarly, they try to establish multiple sources of raw materials, such as oil and metals, and even of other inputs, such as labor, in order to avoid dependence on one supplier country. Thus, by operating multiple sourcing and marketing affiliates, the MNE gains this important risk-reducing capability.

Finally, managerial experience in several countries gives the firm the advantage of know-how in dealing with business situations in different countries. This advantage generally helps the MNE possessing experienced managers relative to other MNEs without such people. Host country firms in each nation may possess managers with even more experience in that particular environment; hence, these firms possess a competitive advantage relative to all MNEs. Skill in managing a multi-country operation is itself a scarce factor of production; and firms with managers who possess such skill will presumably obtain better results than firms without them.

Managers of MNEs and potential competitors seek to obtain and benefit from these competitive advantages. While firms can generally either create such advantages from their own activities or buy them from other firms or individuals, we will consider throughout the book many specific ways in which firms can obtain proprietary assets and benefit from them.

Sources of Competitive Advantages

A basic framework of competitive strategy, used fairly widely by business analysts, views companies as organizations that carry out a set of economic activities. Let us define the economic activity of the firm as essentially production, subdivided into obtaining necessary inputs, actually producing goods or services, distributing to points of sale, and marketing them to customers. Figure 2-2 presents a sketch of the basic aspects of production in which competitive advantages may arise.

At purchasing, the first stage, inputs are assembled for production of the product or service. Then, either in that location or after transferring the inputs elsewhere, basic production is carried out. If additional assembly is needed, it may be done in the same location or at one or more assembly or finishing facilities. Finally, the product or service is marketed to customers in the same location and/or other locations.

Notice that at each step of the production process the firm must choose combinations of inputs—manpower, physical capital, financial capital, and information—that will generate the output; it must decide how to organize them, and it must decide how to deal with the risks involved. Managers should do this to minimize the cost of completing the economic activity. So, for example, if it is less expensive to buy components than to produce them internally, the firm should contract out for the components. Similarly, if the firm chooses to bear the risk of losses, rather than contract with an outside insurance provider to cover that possibility, it is providing "self-insurance." In all, the firm can be viewed as a value-maximizing organization that decides on optimal combinations of inputs at each stage of the production process to generate its output and thus profit. Two key points here are (1) that the firm must attempt to evaluate the impact on profits, not only of its own activities, but also of the activities of its rivals and of other outside actors (e.g., governments); and (2) that the firm must consider the functioning of its own internal market, including the "people problems" of labor/personnel relations that must be solved to achieve optimal outputs. From this scheme, we can derive the main competitive advantages that have been noted elsewhere (e.g., Porter, 1980, 1985, and Grosse, 1984) and we can see many additional areas in which advantages may arise.

Obtaining Competitive Advantages

The goal of competitive strategy is to obtain, utilize, and sustain competitive advantages to the optimal level. Given the advantages discussed above, and others that may be uncovered, the manager needs to see how the firm can obtain these advantages and when it is desirable to do so. Of course, in simple economic terms, it will be best to obtain each competitive advantage up to the point where the additional economic benefit gained is just equal to the additional cost of obtaining or extending that advantage. (The decision is complicated, however, by uncertainty about future conditions, difficulties in valuing the advantages, and the unclear accessibility of some of them.)

The challenge to managers is to carve out competitive positions based on these advantages; so their potential values must be measured. Perhaps the best way to begin any such evaluation is to consider the possibility of purchasing a competitive advantage from another firm, as opposed to creating it internally within the firm. This "make-versus-buy" decision can be made on the bases of expected revenues, expected costs, and expected risks, just as with the purchase of production inputs. For example, the managerial experience gained from operating in a particular country can either be produced internally through the company's business over time or purchased in the market, by hiring a manager from the outside. A distribution system can be constructed by the firm itself or purchased from another firm—as Nestlé did recently with its purchase of Carnation and as Imperial Chemicals (a British firm) did with its purchase of Atlas Chemicals (a U.S. firm with many

Figure 2-2 **Competitive Advantages in the Production Process**

Purchasing $\xrightarrow{\text{Distribution}}$ Basic production $\xrightarrow{\text{Distribution}}$ Assembly, finishing $\xrightarrow{\text{Distribution}}$ Sale to customers

The Production Process*

* Inputs used at each stage of production:

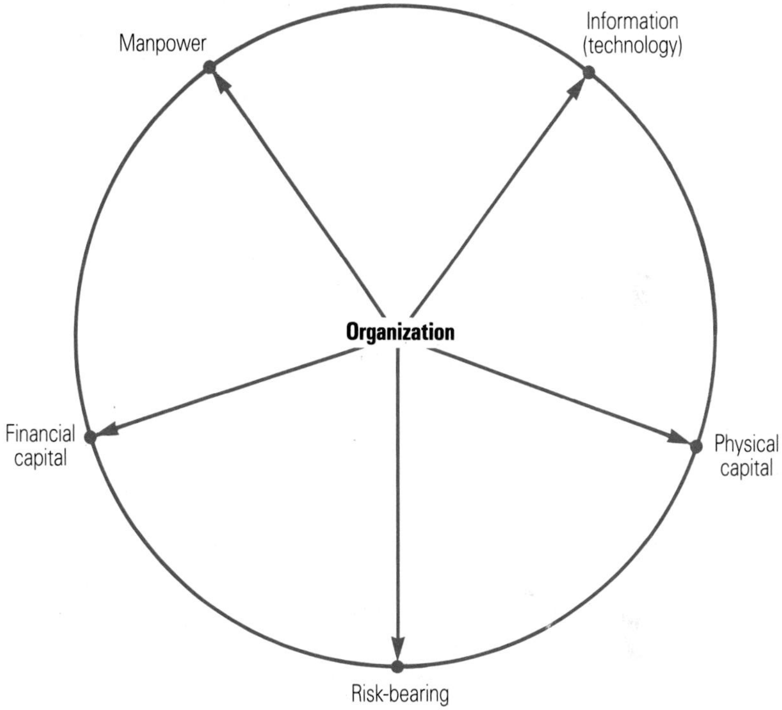

affiliates in the United States and Latin America) in the 1970s. Technology may be purchased through a licensing agreement or developed within the firm—or even obtained by buying another company, as in the 1983 purchase of Rolm (a telephone switching equipment manufacturer) by IBM. Even a brand name can be obtained without spending many years to develop goodwill in dealings with customers for a particular product; the firm seeking a brand name advantage can simply buy a branded line from another company, or even buy the whole company—an acquisition strategy followed very successfully in food products by Beatrice Foods and Heinz during the past 20 years. (Heinz, for example, bought Weight Watchers.)

In each of the above examples, the firm seeking to obtain a competitive advantage must evaluate the costs and benefits expected from that advantage not only in terms of the firm's own activities but also in terms of the responses that may be expected from its important competitors at home and abroad. The competitive gains from achieving scale economies in production may be zero if all important competitors build large-scale plants too. Thus, while the make-versus-buy view can be applied by the firm to each competitive advantage, the ultimate decision to pursue an advantage depends on the expected reaction of competitors, the firm's own activities, and the amount of time needed by competitors to duplicate the advantage.

The choice even to consider making or buying a particular competitive advantage rests on the assessment of how important that advantage is (or will become) in competition. Economies of scale in distribution, for example, may offer an advantage to firms possessing their own distribution channels, but the advantage may be so slight compared to the costs facing other firms using outside suppliers of distribution that the benefits may not warrant investment in the channels. Instead, the key competitive factor in that industry may be proprietary technology or advertising effectiveness. So rather than focus efforts on accruing as many competitive advantages as possible, the manager should assess the relative importance of each advantage in the industry (and country) and then pursue those that offer the greatest benefits—usually those that create the greatest barriers to entry to and exit from the industry. (Exit barriers are those difficulties facing firms trying to leave a business, such as the problem of selling machinery or other assets specific to that business.)

Internalization

Perhaps the most useful concept to employ in studying the strategies (and also the regulation) of MNEs is **internalization.** This term, popularized by Buckley and Casson (1976) and Rugman (1981), refers to the extension of ownership by a firm to cover new markets, new sources of materials, and new stages of the production process.[4] Internalization covers many of the same ideas as horizontal and vertical integration, as discussed in the economics literature related to industrial organization.

Briefly, horizontal integration is the expansion of a firm to carry out the same activity in a market other than the one in which it originally operated. Every time Sheraton Hotels builds a new hotel in another city, that company has integrated horizontally. On the other hand, vertical integration is the expansion of a firm into a stage of the production process other than that of its original business. A company that manufactures wood furniture can integrate vertically by expanding its activities to include lumber production or the sale of the furniture through its own stores, rather than through furniture stores belonging to others. (The firm could also do both.)

The key differences between integration and internalization are (1) that *internalization emphasizes the strategic choices* of the firm in deciding whether to buy inputs or to buy suppliers and whether to sell to other firms or to buy those firms and deal with their customers directly and (2) that internalization covers transactions outside the scope of horizontal or vertical integration, such as the purchase of labor, capital and technology.

To understand this idea better, consider a company that refines petroleum as its only business. This firm may choose to buy or build another oil refinery located in another market—this would be **horizontal integration,** that is, entry into a similar business and stage of the production process in a different location. As a second strategy, the oil refining firm may choose to buy a chain of gasoline stations, in order to extend its sales downstream to final customers. Alternatively, the firm may choose to buy into oil exploration and producing (either through acquisition or creation of a new firm), in this case integrating vertically in the upstream direction. Either of these two cases of **vertical integration** is also a form of internalization, in which additional levels of the production process are brought into the same firm. Finally, the firm may choose to hire a scientist(s) or engineer(s) involved in oil refining research, so that the firm could gain a new low-cost processing technology. By internalizing this research, the firm avoids the need to rely on an outside supplier of the R&D. In all of these examples, the firm is internalizing additional transactions; when a firm does this across national borders, it becomes multinational. Figure 2-3 illustrates this idea.

Hence, just as in the cases of most of the competitive advantages discussed previously, internalization may be either domestic or international; it does not exist solely in the province of MNEs.

Other classic examples of vertical integration include most mineral and metal industries, in which a few firms have succeeded in creating huge structures that stretch from mining or drilling all the way to sales to final consumers. Exxon, Texaco, Shell, and British Petroleum exemplify international internalization of the oil industry.[5] Kennecott and Anaconda, the copper industry; Reynolds and Kaiser, the aluminum industry; and so on. In each case, the firm owns some of the natural resource, it explores for and produces some of the metal or mineral, and it then processes and distributes the downstream products, often all the way to final consumers in many national markets.

Firms may choose to take advantage of their proprietary assets through internalization when the gains from buying or establishing the new operation outweigh the costs and risks of doing so. For example, it does not necessarily make sense for McDonald's to integrate upstream into cattle raising to service the firm's restaurants, if contracting with cattle ranchers or slaughterhouses proves satisfactory. (Typically, the benefits of internalization are lower when there are a large number of such suppliers than when there are a few, powerful suppliers.) On the other hand, it does make economic sense for a steelmaker to integrate backward into the mining and production of iron ore or for a lumber company to internalize the growing and cutting of timber. In each of these cases, the firm faces a limited number of suppliers that can virtually hold the lumber or steel company hostage for higher prices, unless the firm owns the raw materials supply itself.[6]

Figure 2-3 **Internalization in the Oil Industry**

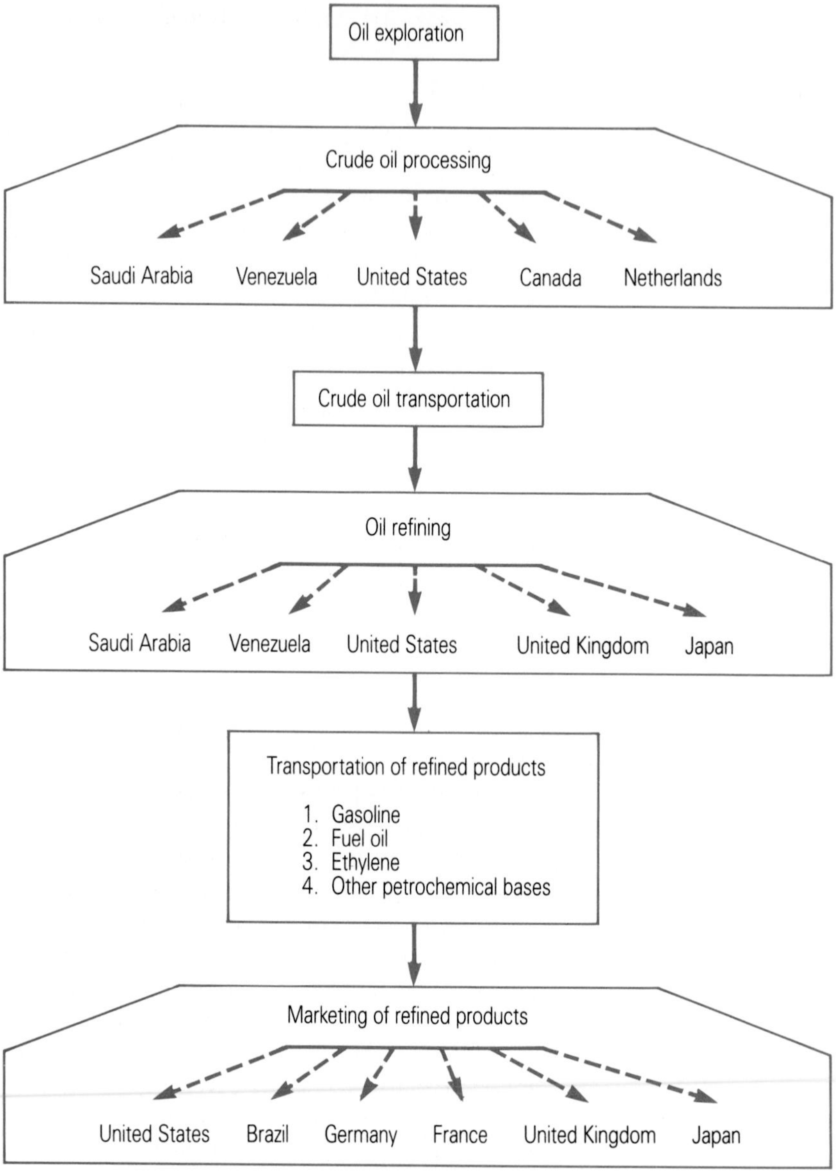

Internalization is a powerful concept that instructs the firm's decision makers on how to proceed in maximizing the gains from its proprietary assets.

Internalization applies to domestic or international business, but it is especially vital at the transnational level. In the case of horizontal international integration, the firm gains:

1. A diversified portfolio of markets, including the home country and the countries where affiliates are located.
2. Multiple sources of output, which conceivably can be shipped to any markets that require it.
3. New opportunities to achieve scale economies and to learn about new markets (learning curve effects).

In the case of vertical international integration, the firm gains:

1. New or multiple sources of raw materials, which preclude events in any one country from interrupting the full range of the firm's activities (backward integration).
2. New market outlets, which preclude any one country's economic condition from limiting the firm's sales (forward integration).
3. Experience in new markets (learning curve effects).

Internal and External Constraints (Opportunities)

According to the concept of competitive strategy developed above, competitive advantages may be gained from a variety of business activities. So far, we have looked at production and marketing, but the other areas cannot be ignored. It is useful to emphasize two of them here. First, the issue of labor and personnel relations is one that has concerned U.S.-based firms, especially in the 1970s and 1980s (for example, because of work rules, high wages, and low productivity), and that has operated as a competitive advantage for many Japanese firms. The optimal use of a firm's internal resources must include human resources, and policies need to be developed to deploy people effectively. Ouchi's (1979) "Theory Z" offers a set of techniques to accomplish this goal, as does the Peters and Waterman (1982) view. Many analysts have argued that the competitive weakness of U.S. firms in international business can be traced to a failure to develop strength in this area. While one cannot simply conclude that Japanese management style in general is "optimal" in some sense, Theory Z does focus attention on the key internal issue of human resource management. (The discussion in Chapter 20 pursues this issue of Japanese management and competitiveness.)

A second additional constraint or opportunity to keep in mind is the issue of government/business relations. In principle, any firm can follow the competitive strategy sketched above in any country it chooses. In fact, there are numerous country-specific factors (in addition to cost conditions) that make it worthwhile to discuss government relations here as well.[7] No matter how conclusive the analysis of competitive strategy, a firm may not pursue the tactic of foreign direct investment to establish a subsidiary in some country if that country does not allow foreign direct investment (FDI)! Or, in a less-extreme case, regardless of the firm's internal gains of efficiency through FDI, if the taxes, tariffs, and other regulatory costs are too biased in favor of maintaining the home country facility, then the appropriate strategy is *not* to invest. This last point, relating to national (production and regulatory) cost conditions, is analyzed in detail in Chapter 3 in the section on "comparative advantage." Let us next look at the means available to the multinational firm for participating in international business, exploiting its competitive advantages.

Taking Advantage of Competitive Advantages

The final step for the manager in creating a competitive strategy is to determine how to benefit from the firm's accumulated competitive advantages. The solution depends, of course, on the specific set of advantages obtained by the firm and on the competitive conditions in the industries and countries in which it competes. A natural resource company will generally be very limited in its ability to own mines, wells, land, or other sources of raw materials in most countries of the world today. Instead, raw materials must often be purchased through long-term contracts or in spot markets—and a key advantage may accrue to firms that have multiple suppliers. Manufacturers of mature industrial products may need to reduce costs by seeking low-cost assembly locations—perhaps in newly industrializing countries such as Mexico, Taiwan, or Malaysia. Manufacturers of military goods may need to produce some of their components and/or products in foreign countries, to comply with government restrictions in the (foreign) purchasing countries—regardless of cost conditions that favor other sites.

An array of vehicles for doing business in various national markets is sketched in Table 2-5, which also suggests several criteria for choosing among the alternative methods of exploiting competitive advantages. Notice that the "bottom line" is not a simple cash flow analysis of market-serving alternatives; rather, it is a strategic evaluation of how the method fits into the firm's full global organization and strategy. For example, a project in Japan whose net present value is lower than that of an alternative project in France may be accepted if the impact of the project in Japan is to reduce the profitability of a competitor in Japan and thus limit the competitor's ability to compete in other markets as well.[8] Similarly, a project with a lower net present value than that of some other alternative should be chosen if the more profitable project demands too much of the firm's scarce management time or if it presents too great an exposure to economic, political, or foreign exchange risk. All in all, market-serving alternatives should be chosen on the basis of their total impact on the global corporation and not just on the basis of their expected returns as independent activities.

Table 2-5 **Methods for Exploiting Competitive Advantages through Foreign Involvement**

Form of Foreign Involvement	Decision Criteria*						
	Added Income	Capital Commitment	Management Commitment	Technology Commitment	Political Risk	Flexi-bility	Impact on Rivals
Exports†	?	Low	Low	Low	Low	High	?
Contracting‡	?	Low	Possibly high	Possibly high	Low	?	?
Partially owned direct investment§	?	?	Possibly high	High	Medium	Low	?
Wholly owned direct investment ‖	?	High	High	Low	High	?	?

* Each column represents a dimension for decision making that should be considered when choosing a method to use in exploiting a competitive advantage. The rankings will differ from company to company and also across countries.
†Examples: (*a*) direct, (*b*) through a distributor, (*c*) through a trading company.
‡Examples: (*a*) licensing technology, (*b*) franchising, (*c*) management contracting.
§Examples: (*a*) joint venture with local company, (*b*) joint venture with foreign company, (*c*) joint venture with government.
‖ Examples: (*a*) assembly plant for local sales, (*b*) basic manufacturing, (*c*) raw materials extraction, (*d*) offshore assembly plant.

The multinational firm may exploit its competitive advantages through multiple vehicles in various markets—ownership of a factory or office in each country is unnecessary. Hilton Hotels earns a substantial return on its business activities in different countries, even though most of the hotels in the chain worldwide are franchised out to independent hotel owners. Similarly, pharmaceuticals manufacturers routinely contract with other firms in their industry to produce their drugs under "tolling" agreements, which are essentially licenses to manufacture ethical drugs using the proprietor firm's name. The Dow Chemical pharmaceuticals plant in Argentina formulates drugs for Eli Lilly, Brazil's Astra, and other multinational drug companies; in other countries, Dow contracts out to other firms to produce its products in the same manner. The correct strategy depends on the entire competitive position of the company in all of its markets.

Overall, the firm needs to take stock of its own competitive advantages, plus those of its competitors, and select a strategy that emphasizes its strengths and minimizes the impact of its weaknesses. The multinational firm must consider the strategies of its competitors not only in its home market but also in every relevant foreign market. And finally, managers must realize that no matter how strong the competitive advantage, other firms are likely to chip away at it, so that ultimately the advantage will be gone.[9] For a firm to be competitive in the long run, it must regularly review its competitive position in its various markets and products and then adjust its strategy to take advantage of environmental and internal changes.

A Caterpillar Tractor Company plant in Tanggu, China.

Courtesy Caterpillar, Inc.

An Example—Caterpillar Tractor Company

Consider the example of Caterpillar Tractor Company (or Cat), one of the world's largest manufacturers of diesel engines and earthmoving and construction machinery, and until recently a highly profitable firm as well. Since the dramatic decline in demand for its products, this $7 billion company has been performing far less satisfactorily, showing losses for the past two years. How could Caterpillar take advantage of the approach presented above?

First, Caterpillar needs to take stock of its competitive advantages and those of its major competitors. From the list of advantages presented in Table 2-4, Cat is generally perceived to possess a highly respected brand name, which conveys an image of quality and good service. Relative to multinational competitors such as International Harvester, Allis-Chalmers, Komatsu, and Ford, it does *not* possess any particular economies of scale in production, financing, and so on that the others lack. (However, relative to local competitors in many countries, it does possess some of these advantages.) Cat's long experience in international business may give its managers an advantage over rivals in dealing with problems in a wide variety of countries. On the issue of technology, most construction machinery is considered to be maturing or standardized in the product life cycle, so again Cat probably does not possess a major advantage over other firms in this area. Finally, some outside observers (e.g., Peters and Waterman, *In Search of Excellence*) believe that Cat maintains a significantly better internal work environment and a harmony between blue- and white-collar workers that leads to greater productivity than that of other firms. (Hout et al. argued that another Cat strength is its international distribution network, which is superior to those of its competitors.)

The main competitive disadvantages facing Cat may be the firm's large investments in inventory and in plant and equipment, which are weighing down its financial position during the current time of deep recession in its main businesses. In boom times these characteristics would probably be great advantages, but in the early 1980s smaller size would most likely have served Cat better than the excess capacity that then existed. (By mid-1983, Caterpillar had reduced its global employment almost one third, to 60,000.)

Second, Caterpillar needs to decide which competitive strengths it wants to obtain. Perhaps new technology can be developed to give the firm a lead in providing smaller or less costly equipment to the market. Perhaps greater decentralization of production to foreign locations would enable Cat to attain a protected position in some host countries that want to reduce their imports. And perhaps investment in upstream and downstream business activities, such as metalworking or the manufacture of engine accessories, would strengthen Cat's production capabilities. Each of these, and possibly other competitive advantages, should be considered for acquisition by Caterpillar.

Third, Caterpillar needs to choose how to utilize the additional competitive advantages obtained. For example, new technology could be developed internally or obtained by purchasing an outside firm. (Cat acquired Solar Turbine Corporation, a turbine engine manufacturer, in 1982.) In this manner, Cat can continue to maintain its high-quality image, competing on the basis of product durability and excellent service. Large possibilities exist for reducing production costs by moving parts of the production process offshore to low-wage countries. Following this strategy, Cat could become competitive on the basis of price in some product lines, while still utilizing product differentiation as its main strategy.

In each aspect of the new strategy development, Cat needs to judge the reactions of its rivals in order to estimate the effectiveness of its own steps. If Komatsu is able to compete with low prices and high-quality products because of the dollar's appreciation relative to the yen, then Cat may choose to compete more strongly in the Japanese market (where Caterpillar already has a joint venture with Mitsubishi). If American rivals face even greater difficulties than Caterpillar does, then perhaps some of their complementary operations could be acquired at very low prices.

This sketch (developed by the authors) of possible alternatives facing Caterpillar Tractor Company is intended simply to illustrate the use of the proposed analytic framework. Similar reasoning could be used for any large or small firm competing at the international level; the framework used here provides an approach to strategic decision making.

Conclusions

The multinational enterprise is unquestionably the central actor in international business today. Multinational firms function as major vehicles for transfer of technology and other knowledge, international financial flows, and exports/imports of goods and services. The multinational firms include huge manufacturers such as IBM and Dow Chemical—but they also include service sector companies such as Hilton Hotels, Citibank, and Merrill Lynch. In addition, many smaller firms are multinational in the sense that they possess affiliates in three or more countries. Much of the strategy designed for the large multinationals is relevant to these smaller firms as well.

The theory of the multinational enterprise is being advanced by analysts along many lines. Competitive advantage and internalization are two concepts that have been widely discussed in the recent literature. Both concepts recognize the highly imperfect competition that characterizes international (and domestic) business throughout the world. Both offer perspectives to the manager for capitalizing on the firm's relative strengths in competition with rival firms. Although this is not the only view of the MNE that has merit, it does offer a wide range of applications to decision makers.

Given the perspective outlined in this chapter, we can analyze decisions made in international business as part of the competitive strategy of the firm. In the next few chapters, we will consider some of the environmental conditions facing firms in international business. Then we will look at competitive strategies for decision makers in the various functional areas.

Questions

1. What are the important differences between a multinational enterprise and a domestic company? Why are these differences important?
2. Explain the competitive advantages of Caterpillar Tractor Company. What strategy do you think the company should follow during the current severe downturn in farm and construction equipment sales?
3. Why are the largest multinational enterprises concentrated in a few industries such as petroleum and motor vehicles? Why are the most profitable MNEs (measured in terms of, for example, profits per share) *not* concentrated in any one or two industries?
4. How can a company such as Apple Computer Corporation best take advantage of its competitive advantages in foreign markets? Discuss opportunities in both developed countries and LDCs.
5. Should a chemical company such as Dow Chemical Corporation inter-

nalize its supply of oil for making petrochemicals by entering the oil business? What other choices does Dow have to assure competitive access to the raw materials it needs for production around the world?

6. What competitive advantages are possessed by Citibank? How can it use those advantages in international banking competition?
7. Perez Trading Company is a small Los Angeles-based firm that serves as an exporter for several small U.S. manufacturing companies and as an importer for several more U.S. firms. Almost all of the firm's business is done with Latin American customers or suppliers. The only foreign activities that Perez has are sales offices in Mexico and Peru. Is this a multinational company? What do you think are Perez' competitive advantages? Do you regard its 20 years' experience in this business as a competitive advantage?
8. Why are about half of the world's largest multinational enterprises based in the United States? Does this *country* possess some advantage that its companies obtain automatically? Is that advantage changing over time?
9. What characteristics give companies such as Sheraton Hotels and Holiday Inns the ability to compete in foreign markets? Do you regard these companies as MNEs?
10. Given the nationalizations of foreign oil companies by governments in OPEC (a cartel of Oil Producing and Exporting Countries) during the past decade, do you expect that Exxon, Texaco, and other companies will no longer be multinational in the future? What are these companies doing to maintain their international operations?

References

Alchain, Armen, and Harold Demsetz. "Production, Information Costs, and Economic Organization." *American Economic Review,* December 1972.

Buckley, Peter, and Mark Casson. *The Future of the Multinational Enterprise.* London: Macmillan, 1976.

Casson, Mark. "Transactions Costs and the Theory of the Multinational Enterprise." In *New Perspectives in International Business,* ed. Alan Rugman. London: Croom Helm, 1982.

_______. *General Theories of the Multinational Enterprise: A Critical Examination.* University of Reading Discussion Papers, no. 77, January 1984.

Caves, Richard. "International Corporations: The Industrial Economics of Foreign Investment." *Economica,* February 1971.

Davidson, William, and Donald McFetridge. "International Technology Transactions and the Theory of the Firm." *Journal of Industrial Economics,* March 1984.

Dunning, John. "Trade, Location of Economic Activity, and the Multinational Enterprise: A Search for an Eclectic Approach." In *The International Allocation of Economic Activity,* ed. Bertil Ohlin. New York: Holmes & Meier, 1977.

Grosse, Robert. *The Theory of Foreign Direct Investment.* University of South Carolina Essays in International Business, December 1981.

———. *Competitive Advantages and Multinational Enterprises.* University of Miami Discussion Papers in International Business, no. 84-7, November 1984.

———. "An Imperfect Competition Theory of the MNE." *Journal of International Business Studies,* Spring 1985.

Hennart, Jean-François. *The Multinational Enterprise.* Ann Arbor: University of Michigan Press, 1982.

Horst, Thomas. "Firm and Industry Determinants of the Decision to Invest Abroad: An Empirical Study." *Review of Economics and Statistics,* 1972.

Hout, Thomas; Michael Porter; and Eileen Rudder. "How Global Companies Win Out." *Harvard Business Review,* September-October 1982.

Kindleberger, Charles. *Direct Investment Abroad.* New Haven, Conn.: Yale University Press, 1969.

Lall, Sanjaya. "Monopolistic Advantages and Foreign Involvement by U.S. Manufacturing Industry." *Oxford Economic Papers,* March 1980.

Ouchi, William. *Theory Z.* New York: Basic Books, 1979.

Peters, Thomas J., and Robert H. Waterman. *In Search of Excellence.* New York: Harper & Row, 1982.

Porter, Michael. *Competitive Strategy.* New York: Free Press, 1980.

Porter, Michael. *Competitive Advantages.* New York: Free Press, 1985.

Rugman, Alan. *Inside the Multinationals.* London: Croom Helm, 1981.

Swedenborg, B. *The Multinational Operations of Swedish Firms: An Analysis of Determinants and Effects.* Stockholm: Industrial Institute for Economic and Social Research, 1979.

Vernon, Raymond. "International Investment and International Trade in the Product Cycle." *Quarterly Journal of Economics,* 1966.

———. *Storm over the Multinationals.* Cambridge, Mass.: Harvard University Press, 1977.

Vernon, Raymond, and Louis T. Wells, Jr. *Manager in the International Economy.* Englewood Cliffs, N.J.: Prentice-Hall, 1981.

Watson, Craig. "Counter-Competition Abroad to Protect Home Markets." *Harvard Business Review,* January-February, 1982.

Williamson, Oliver. *Markets and Hierarchies: Analysis and Antitrust Implications.* New York: Free Press, 1975.

———. "The Modern Corporation: Origins, Evolution, Attributes." *Journal of Economic Literature,* December 1981.

Endnotes

1. R. Vernon and L. Wells, *Manager in the International Economy,* 4th ed. (Englewood Cliffs, N.J.: Prentice-Hall, 1981), p. 4.
2. Some competitive advantages are not *firm specific* but general to firms of some particular type. For example, MNEs based in the United States had a competitive advantage in the 1960s, when the U.S. dollar was overvalued, because they had access to cheaper financing than foreign firms. Also, firms from Switzerland have been relatively unharmed by world wars, since Switzerland has been consistently neutral in wartime. Along another dimension, many economies of scale are realized by very large firms; such economies are not limited to just one firm in an industry or country.
3. M. Wilkins, *The Emergence of Multinational Enterprise* (Cambridge, Mass.: Harvard University Press, 1970).
4. Internalization also refers to bringing an "externality" that markets fail to price from the outside into a firm. For example, governments try to force pollution control costs, previously an externality, onto polluting firms. The firm may use internalization to bring market power within its command by acquiring competitors and then raising prices to monopolized customers. Thus, internalization does not always connote improvement of economic welfare or efficiency.
5. It is interesting to note that the great vertical integration of the oil industry has been reduced by the participation of OPEC countries at the oil-producing stage; those countries are beginning to integrate downstream into processing, and eventually into the marketing of final products.
6. Conceivably, the use of long-term contracts, if they are enforced, could offer the firms the same level of assurance of supply and negate the need for ownership of the raw material (i.e., internalization of the source of supply).
7. Dunning (1977) has pioneered the idea of focusing on three of the factors discussed in this section. He calls them ownership advantages (proprietary assets), internalization advantages (as we do here), and location advantages (country-specific factors).
8. Watson (1982) discusses this idea of challenging international competitors in their home markets as a competitive strategy. He concludes that forcing your competitors to compete actively in their home markets will reduce their ability to put resources into competing in your home market.
9. Following the international product cycle for any product demonstrates the stages during which proprietary technology, strong advertising and effective distribution channels, and low-cost production are the key competitive advantages. See, for example, Vernon (1977) and Vernon and Wells (1981).

Case
Mom & Pop's Restaurants, Inc.

Introduction

Sitting at his personal computer one evening in 1987, Pop Westerfield was thinking about the growing food business that he had built up over the past 10 years and that constantly seemed to present him with new, major problems. Just last week, the Burger King restaurant chain had introduced stuffed potatoes and a new salad bar in all of its restaurants, throughout his territory of Illinois, Indiana, and southern Michigan. McDonald's was likewise expanding its menu to compete more and more with traditional restaurants such as Mom & Pop's. Pop was beginning to think that he should consider entering some new areas that were not as highly competitive for restaurant business, such as nearby Canada.

The Existing Business

The Westerfields had entered the restaurant business with a small, unassuming operation in Homewood, Illinois, in 1979. Pop, at age 33, had decided that he was unwilling to continue at his job with a large automotive parts firm in Chicago, given the unabated crisis in the industry since 1973. Even while growing up, he had had the desire to open a small business, and restaurants looked like a suitable environment for his easygoing manner and his enjoyment of good food. Every day, while commuting to work in the mid-1970s, Pop had passed an attractive family restaurant at the corner of Halsted Avenue and Third Street in Homewood. When a For Sale sign appeared in the window one day in 1978, Pop began to consider the possibility of taking over the business. In early 1979, he finally decided to jump at the opportunity. After a few weeks of fact-finding concerning the owner's asking price, suppliers, the costs of the foods needed to supply his restaurant, taxes, and so forth, Pop made an offer for the building, which was accepted.

The initial "strategy," if it can be called that, was to serve very good meals in traditional American style at reasonable prices. No advertising was undertaken, except for installing the new sign proclaiming "Mom & Pop's Restaurant" (Mrs. Westerfield had agreed to join him in this entrepreneurial venture). Even in the first few months, business picked up enough to pay the bills and generate a small operating profit for the firm. When construction of a new roadway nearby took place in 1980, Mom & Pop's found itself the beneficiary of twice as much traffic on Halsted Avenue and of twice as many customers. By the end of 1982, Mom suggested that they look into the possibility of opening up another restaurant to take advantage of their apparently successful formula of simple, home-cooked meals, medium prices, and quiet atmosphere.

After deliberating on this suggestion for a few weeks, Mom and Pop decided to pursue the expansion. Pop hired a Realtor friend to check out the availability of corner properties within 10 miles of the initial building, either to buy or rent. Then, armed with a list of four possible locations, the Westerfields chose the one that offered the least commuting problems from their home and from the existing business. The second venture followed the same path as the first, with almost immediate moderate success. By 1985, Mom and Pop had opened three more restaurants—one near their son's college in South Bend, Indiana, and the other two through an arrangement with a trusted friend who lived in Detroit (both of these restaurants were located in the suburbs of Detroit).

In early 1987, the Westerfields owned six restaurants using the Mom & Pop name, all of which were in the three locations noted above. The last one was started in late 1986, located in a new shopping center just off Interstate 94 near Skokie, Illinois. (Another start-up had failed, due to last-minute difficulties in agreeing on the rental of space in a new building in Chicago.) At this point, the firm employed 9 full-time salaried staff members and about 40 wage-earning waiters, waitresses, cooks, busboys, and other helpers. The firm's financial statements appear below.

Luckily, Pop had found a capable office manager to keep his books and watch over the daily activities of the restaurant chain. He himself, therefore, had more time to think about the future of the business and about the problems and opportunities that arose frequently. The threat of increased competition from the large, well-financed hamburger chains struck him as serious enough to look into alternative markets for long-run survival. The near failure of the second restaurant when road construction almost eliminated customers' access to the building also made him realize the desirability of diversifying into more locations. While neither of the Westerfields was willing to move far from home, they both thought that southern Canada along the border with Michigan would provide a possible starting point for expanding into that country. Pop's main concern was with choosing a method of dealing with one or several restaurants that were so distant from the existing businesses and, another nontrivial factor, so expensive to open and operate.

The Canadian Situation

At the time that Mr. Westerfield began to look seriously into a Canadian venture, that country's government had recently reversed its policy toward foreign firms. During the previous decade, Canada had required that all foreign direct investment projects obtain permission from the Foreign Investment Review Agency. This agency was charged with evaluating the impact of proposed investments on Canadian income, employment, and ownership of the Canadian economy. A number of projects were rejected during that period. After several years of serious recession in the early 1980s, Canada's government decided to switch its policy in favor of an open attitude, seeking to attract foreign direct investment and stimulate economic growth. As part of the new strategy, the agency itself had its name changed to Investment Canada. All of this meant that Mr. Westerfield discovered a very responsive Canadian government when he inquired about Canadian laws and rules pertaining to the opening of a new restaurant.

Given the liberal government policies, Mom & Pop's needed primarily to decide on a type of venture to establish and on a location for it. The range of possibilities included a new restaurant, set up in a new location; purchase of an existing restaurant; creation of a joint venture with a local partner who knew the market; franchise of the firm's name and use of proprietary food preparations; and some combination of these choices. A sketch of the costs and benefits of each choice is given below.

A *green field* (or *de novo*) *investment* would require site selection, major financing, legal assistance to comply with local laws, and employment of basically all-new staff. From his previous experiences, Pop knew that the start-up cost of the restaurant would be in the neighborhood of $150,000. The Canadian location might offer somewhat lower costs, but dealing with unknown contingencies arising from the new environment would probably leave the total cost about the same. None of the current employees was willing to move to the Windsor, Canada, area (across the river from Detroit), although the Westerfields' oldest son would be a possibility after his college graduation in another year. There appeared to be no significant limitations on importing any needed equipment or food into Canada, though this point needed to be checked in more detail once the specific location was chosen. The tax situation really confused Mr. Westerfield, but he had heard repeatedly that Canadian taxes were similar to U.S. taxes and that the U.S. government would not double-tax his Canadian earnings.

An *acquisition* of an existing Canadian restaurant would cost somewhat less than the new venture, but it still involved many of the other problems. The lower financial cost and the potential availability of existing staff were very attractive to Pop. However, the purchase of an existing facility would bring with it the problems as well as the benefits of the previous business. Given their experience with acquisitions in the past, neither of the Westerfields was overly concerned with the problems likely to be involved.

A *joint venture* was an approach that they had never tried. By finding a local partner, the Westerfields could reduce all the costs of doing business in Canada. The drawbacks of this strategy are that there is a real risk that the partner may not be a good businessperson or a reliable one and that the earnings from the venture have to be shared with the partner. Management of the joint venture could be a troubling issue, since one of the partners would have to trust the other to run it.

The least costly possibility for entering the Canadian market would be to *franchise* out the name Mom & Pop's, as well as some of the proprietary parts of the business, to a local firm. In this case, Mom & Pop's would allow the franchisee to use the restaurant name and would also help the franchisee to

MOM & POP'S RESTAURANTS, INC.
Balance Sheet, Year-End 1986
(in $U.S. 000)

Assets		*Liabilities*	
Cash	215	Notes payable	643
Marketable securities	68	Accounts payable	274
Accounts receivable	47	Taxes due	59
Inventory	180	Long-term debt	28
Fixed assets	1,302	Retained earnings	217
		Shareholders' equity	591
Total Assets	1,812	Total Liabilities	1,812

MOM & POP'S RESTAURANTS, INC.
Income Statement, 1986
(in $U.S. 000)

Sales		3,152
Cost of goods sold		
Materials	1,051	
Labor	988	
Utilities	213	
Depreciation	130	
Gross profit		770
Selling expense	249	
Overhead	296	
Interest expense	67	
Net income before tax		158
Income taxes	47	
Net income after taxes		111

set up and operate the facility. The full set of responsibilities (and sharing of revenues) would be determined in negotiations with the franchisee.

As a last possibility, the Westerfields could try some *combination* of the other strategies. For example, they could set up a joint venture and sell some of the proprietary food preparations to it on a fee basis. Or they could agree on a franchising operation but take some ownership position in that firm. The number of combinations is limited only by the imagination of the Westerfields (and, of course, to some extent by Canadian laws).

Without going into a detailed capital budgeting analysis, Pop felt that it would be best to compare the good and bad points of each alternative and choose the one that seemed best, on balance.

This case was written by Professor Robert Grosse in 1987 as a basis for class discussion.

PART 2

MANAGER IN THE WORLD ECONOMY

3

INTERNATIONAL TRADE

This chapter discusses the economics of international trade. First, patterns of international trade since World War II are described. Then a number of theories are offered to help explain why trade patterns exist and why they differ between countries and products. These theories can also be used to understand why firms export and import as part of their business activities. The main goals of the chapter are to:

1. Demonstrate patterns of trade to give an idea of which countries and which products have been most important during the past half-century.
2. Explain why these patterns exist, based mainly on the theories of comparative cost advantage and the international product cycle.
3. Point out aspects of international trade that do not fit these theories very well and note some new concepts that attempt to deal with these aspects.
4. Show criteria that company managers can use to make international business decisions involving trade—specifically to show how trade fits into the activities of the MNE.

Introduction

The way in which international trade fits within the total range of international business activities has shifted dramatically in the post-World War II period. Early in this century, exports and imports, typically between unrelated firms, comprised the vast majority of intercountry business. At present, however, intra-MNE trade dominates international trade and foreign-owned production is even larger. This chapter seeks to illuminate the role of trade in the new context.

This first section presents some measures of trade flows and sketches some of the underlying influences that have caused the flows to grow and shift as they do. Then the text focuses on the most fundamental theory of international trade, the comparative cost view. The third section explains the international product cycle, a more recent view that focuses on the demand side and the technology factor. The fourth section discusses some of the important discrepancies between the theories and actual trade patterns—issues such as the Leontief paradox and the cross-hauling of exports of the same type of product in both directions between two countries. The final section reviews the material and relates it specifically to the manager's concerns.

Let us begin with a look at some empirical evidence on trade patterns. Table 3-1 presents a number of comparisons between international trade

Table 3-1 **World Trade Data** (in billions of U.S. dollars)

	1950	1960	1970	1980	1985
World					
Exports*	57.9	115.5	284.7	1,868.3	1,784.5
Imports†	59.3	121.0	298.4	1,923.4	1,879.3
Industrial countries					
Exports	36.4	83.9	220.3	1,239.4	1,258.5
Imports	39.8	85.5	227.2	1,369.6	1,361.4
Oil-exporting LDCs					
Exports	4.2	7.2	17.1	296.5	143.8
Imports	2.3	5.3	9.6	134.3	110.7
United States					
Exports	10.3	20.6	43.2	220.8	213.1
Imports	9.6	16.4	42.7	257.0	361.6
Nonoil LDCs					
Exports	17.6	24.7	46.5	312.0	352.3
Imports	17.3	30.1	60.5	399.7	387.7

* Export values are free on board (FOB).
† Import values include cost of insurance and freight (CIF).

Source: International Monetary Fund, *International Financial Statistics* (Supplement on Trade Statistics), 1986.

flows earlier in the post-World War II period and those that have been occurring most recently. Ignoring the cost of insurance and freight, which causes the total figures for exports and imports to be slightly different, some definite trends can be seen. For instance, the industrialized countries maintained a fairly even balance in their aggregate trade flows up until the 1970s. By 1980, these countries showed an annual trade deficit (i.e., imports greater than exports) of about 10 percent with respect to the rest of the world, primarily the oil-exporting countries. The United States in particular maintained a surplus of exports over imports until the recent period, and since 1970 has incurred a substantial deficit in its trade account. Oil-exporting less developed countries (LDCs) have consistently exported much greater value than they have imported, but of course the situation since the 1973 OPEC oil embargo and price hike is much more striking—exports were 121 percent greater than imports in 1980, for example. Then, with the drastic oil price decline in 1985, oil-exporting LDCs shifted back toward the historical situation, maintaining a 29 percent trade surplus.

Table 3-2 presents another look at 20th-century international trade, this time comparing the volume of trade in various highly aggregated industrial sectors. Notice the huge shift in the composition of trade in the 1960s, toward manufactured goods, and in the 1970s toward minerals (especially oil) and away from other industries. Trade in minerals accounted for about 17 percent of the total in 1970, but for about 30 percent of the total in 1980, after the two major OPEC price hikes. Manufacturing, in comparison, fell from about 61

Table 3-2 **Development of World Exports and Production between 1960 and 1984**

	1960	1968	1970	1973	1975	1980	1984
World exports (billions of U.S. dollars, FOB)							
Total	129	240	313	575	875	1,989	1,915
Agricultural products	40	54	64	120	150	299	280
Minerals	22	41	52	96	207	569	454
Manufactures	65	141	192	348	501	1,095	1,148
Other	2	4	5	11	17	26	100
Percentages of total trade							
Total	100	100	100	100	100	100	100
Agricultural products	31	23	20	21	17	15	15
Minerals	17	17	17	17	24	29	24
Manufactures	50	59	61	61	57	55	60
Other	2	1	2	1	2	1	1

Source: General Agreement on Tariffs and Trade, *International Trade, 1984/85* (Geneva: GATT, 1985), p. 4.

percent of total exports in 1970 to about 51 percent of the total in 1980. The original relationship was approximately reestablished in 1985, due to the oil price decline.

Both of these tables point up an aspect of international trade that is usually de-emphasized in discussions of the reasons for trading and the distribution of benefits from trade: one fundamental basis for international trade is the *availability of natural resources* in each country. Any nation that possesses known and accessible deposits of oil can export it, while other nations must either import oil or utilize substitute products (such as coal or other energy sources). The fact that a small number of nations possess most of the world's known and accessible oil deposits gives them a near-monopoly position as producers; and in the 1970s they used that position to raise prices and curtail output—leading to the large jump in LDC exports and mineral exports in Tables 3-1 and 3-2. In the 1980s, however, both prices and quantities of oil sold in world markets were declining, due to the demand curtailment and substitution effects encouraged by the increases in oil prices. Chapters 8 and 24 explore some additional aspects of the oil industry and its relations to international business; here, we are mainly concerned with oil's surge to a substantial percentage of total world trade (about 16 percent in 1980). Thus, a very important basis for a country's export/import activities is resource availability.

The next section continues to look at trade from a macroeconomic perspective, focusing on cost conditions that affect trade patterns. Then we present some additional rationales for trade and empirical examples before considering how the decision maker can utilize these perspectives in operating a firm.

Theories of International Trade—Comparative Advantage

Among the various views of the underlying *reasons* for trade, the cost-based theory has been developed extensively over more than two centuries, and a number of additional views have been offered to explain much of what it ignores. Anyone trying to understand the full set of reasons for the trade that takes place today should recognize at the outset that no single theory explains it all. Trade in different products occurs for different reasons. Trade in services differs in many ways from trade in tangible products. The theories collectively deal with all types of trade, and individually or collectively they can be used to construct policy, either for government regulators or for company managers.

The **comparative cost theory** of international trade, as developed by Ricardo and refined by Heckscher, Ohlin, and Samuelson,[1] states that *a country will gain from international trade if it specializes in the production and export of products that require relatively more input of its abundant production factors and if it imports products that require relatively more input of its scarce production factors.* If we assume that prices in each country are proportional to costs and that costs are determined by the availability of production factors, then the "comparative advantage" theory leads to these results.

Before proceeding with this very powerful concept, consider the simple bases that led to the above conclusions. The first step toward today's comparative cost theory was taken by Adam Smith in *The Wealth of Nations,* published in 1776. Smith reasoned that nations would gain from free trade, as long as each partner had an **absolute** cost **advantage** in producing some product. For example, if England and France both produce machinery and wine, the production possibilities, assuming complete specialization in *either* machinery *or* wine, are:

	Machinery	Wine
England	100*	40
France	30	120

* These quantities are units of output, using all available factors of production.

This means that each country has an absolute advantage: England in the production of machinery, France in the production of wine. If there are no barriers to trade between these countries, then each can specialize in producing its advantageous product and trade with the other, thus obtaining more of both goods than before trade. (This result is explained in detail below for the case of comparative advantage.)

The second step toward today's comparative cost theory was taken by David Ricardo in *Principles of Political Economy and Taxation,* published in 1817. Ricardo showed that just as there are gains from trade under conditions of absolute advantage for each country, there are also gains from trade when one country has an absolute advantage in producing *both* products (as long as its relative superiority differs between products). His example involved England and Portugal producing cloth and wine as shown in the table below. (The quantities are the man-hours of input needed to produce the same amount of output for each product.)

	Wine	Cloth
England	120	100
Portugal	80	90

Portugal has an *absolute* advantage in producing both products, but it has a relative or **comparative advantage** in producing wine. (That is, Portugal's superiority in wine production is 120/80, or 1.5, while Portugal's superiority in cloth production is only 100/90, or 1.1.) In the absence of trade barriers and as long as prices are proportional to costs, both England and Portugal can obtain more wine and cloth if Portugal specializes in producing (and exporting) wine and England does likewise with cloth. In Ricardo's words:

> *Though she [Portugal] could make cloth with the labor of 90 men, she would import it from a country where it required the labor of 100 men to produce it, because it would be advantageous to her rather to employ her capital in the production of wine, for which she would obtain more cloth from England than she could produce by diverting a portion of her capital from the cultivation of vines to the manufacture of cloth. (Ricardo 1971, p. 154)*

Although 20th-century analysts have produced much more detailed assessments of the comparative cost theory, most of the newer work is still based fundamentally on Ricardo's insight.[2]

Comparative Cost Theory

The easiest way to demonstrate the main implications of this theory is with an example involving two countries, two products, and two factors of production. Let us assume that each country's availability of factors of production has already led to a set of domestic costs for producing each product (before trade takes place), and proceed from there.

Notice that the theory as presented so far relates to the benefits that a *country* would expect if it allowed international trade to take place. The company manager should view this information as a basis for choosing countries for production and export or countries for import sales. So, if it happens that lower costs of producing product A exist in country 1, then the manager should look at possibilities for producing that product there and for importing it into country 2, based on the theory of comparative advantage. Now let us see why this is true.

Just to emphasize that country size is not necessarily important in determining relative costs, consider the United States and Honduras as examples. Let us work with a pair of standardized products that are clearly related to each country's relative endowment of production factors (e.g., agricultural land and physical capital).

For the sake of our discussion, the United States and Honduras are assumed to possess the characteristics depicted in Table 3-3 and Figure 3-1. In this situation, the United States is a substantially larger producer of both good A *(electrical appliances,* such as toasters, blenders, and coffee pots) and good B *(bananas).* Nonetheless, the United States and Honduras may both be able to consume more of each product under free trade than if they use only their domestic capabilities for production to satisfy their own consumption.

These two exhibits demonstrate the capabilities of each country to produce bananas and appliances, assuming that all available productive re-

Table 3-3 **Production and Consumption Possibilities for the United States and Honduras** (in 000 bushels of bananas/month and 000 appliances/month)

United States		Honduras	
Appliances	Bananas	Appliances	Bananas
200	0	60	0
160	20	50	15
120*	40*	40*	30*
100	50	30	40
60	70	20	55
0	100	0	80

* Equals initial production and consumption points.

sources are utilized in these two industries. That is, if all of the people, machinery, and land in Honduras were used to produce bananas, they could produce 80,000 bushels of bananas per month. If all of these same productive resources were used to produce appliances, they could make 60,000 appliances per month. Finally, if some of the people, machinery, and land were used to produce each product, the trade-offs appear as points along the production possibilities curve (or as pairs of output possibilities in Table 3-3). Notice that the P-P curves in Figure 3-1 have been drawn as straight lines, implying that no diminishing returns occur as specialization increases. This also means that, with trade, each country will be induced to specialize completely in the production of one product. If diminishing returns did occur, then trade generally would lead to incomplete specialization in each country.[3] The actual points on the production possibilities curves where consumers in each country choose to purchase appliances and bananas are determined by their preferences, as reflected in indifference curves I_{Hon} and I_{US}.

Factors of Production

The theory of comparative advantage states that the production possibilities of each country arise from the productive capabilities of its factors of production. In our example, we can assume that banana production is more land intensive and that appliances production is more machinery intensive. Furthermore, we must assume that, in relative terms, Honduras possesses more fertile land compared to machinery and that the United States possesses more machinery relative to fertile land (or that the **relative productivities** of land and labor give each country the advantage shown). Stated in measurable terms:

Figure 3-1 **Production and Consumption Possibilities for the United States and Honduras**

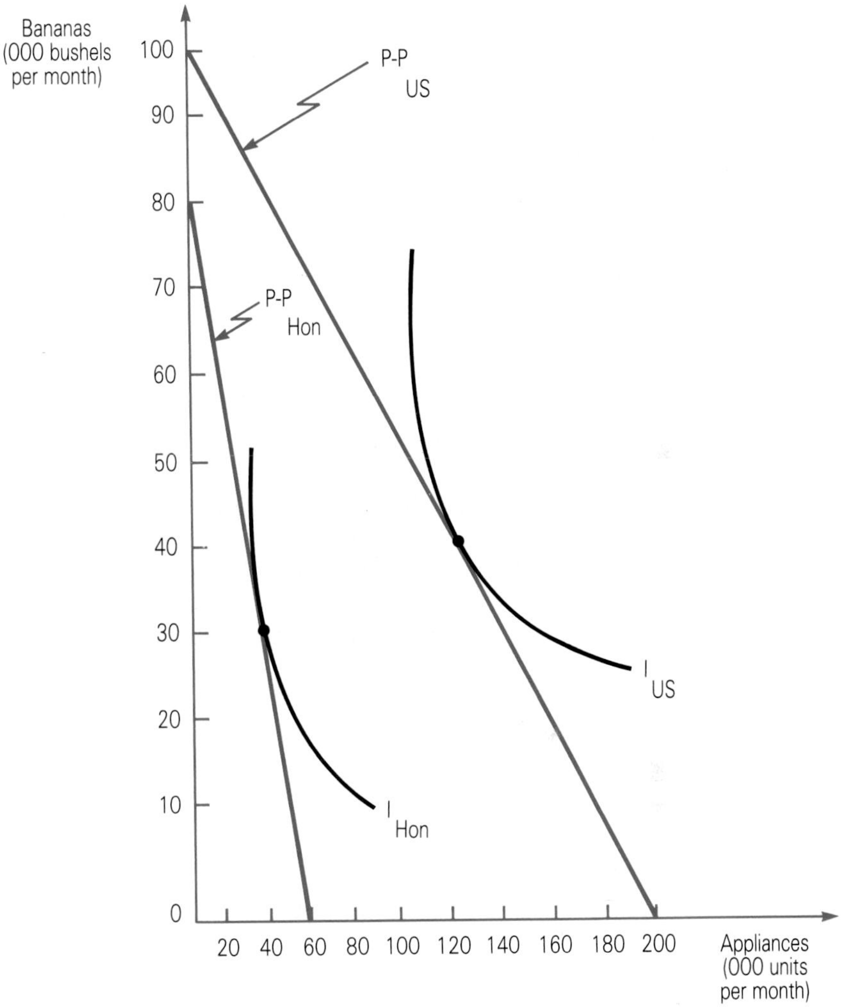

$$\frac{\text{Quantity of fertile land}_{\text{Hon}}}{\text{Quantity of available machinery}_{\text{Hon}}} > \frac{\text{Quantity of fertile land}_{\text{US}}}{\text{Quantity of available machinery}_{\text{US}}}$$

If these conditions do hold, then Table 3-1 is a reasonable representation of each country's possibilities. The United States, because of its larger endowments of all production factors, could produce more of either product than Honduras; but the United States is *relatively* more productive in appliances, and Honduras in bananas.

From our initial production/consumption points for each country, we can reason that trade will be beneficial if it leads each country to a final consumption point in which more of either or both goods is consumed, and less of neither. So the final consumption of appliances and bananas must be at least as much as each one of the entries in the table below. Remember that the choice of the initial consumption point is determined by consumers' tastes in each country, limited by the production possibilities. Gains from trade occur only if consumers in each country are able to consume on a higher indifference curve (or at least on the same curve), compared to pretrade conditions.[4]

Initial Consumption (and Production)

	A	B
United States	120	40
Honduras	40	30

Note: Appliances are measured in thousands of appliances per month; bananas are measured in thousands of bushels per month.

Now consider the relative efficiencies of each country in producing each good. If Honduras were to specialize completely in the production of bananas, the country could produce 80,000 bushels per month (that is, 80 units of 1,000 bushels/month each, and *no* appliances), compared to the U.S. capability to specialize and produce 100,000 bushels per month (i.e., 100 units). Similarly, by specializing in appliance production, Honduras could produce 60,000 appliances per month (and *no* bananas) and the United States could produce 200,000 appliances per month. Clearly, the United States possesses an *absolute* advantage in the production of both products. however, we can also see that each country has a *relative* (or comparative) advantage in the production of one product.

Assuming complete specialization in the production of *appliances,* the United States has an advantage of $^{200}/_{60} = 3.33$ over Honduras. If complete specialization in *banana* production were carried out, the United States would maintain an advantage of $^{100}/_{80} = 1.20$ over Honduras. Thus, the United States has a *comparative advantage* in producing appliances.

On the other side, Honduras would operate at a disadvantage in producing either product. However, the disadvantage in producing bananas is only $^{80}/_{100} = 0.8$, while the disadvantage in producing appliances is $^{60}/_{200} = 0.3$. Honduras possesses a comparative advantage (i.e., less disadvantage) in producing bananas. In other words, Honduras possesses factors of production (i.e., land, labor, and machinery) that are relatively more efficient in producing bananas, and the United States possesses factors of production that are relatively more efficient at producing appliances.

The doctrine of comparative advantage states that when such relative production advantages exist and are reflected in prices, then each country will be better off by specializing and trading, rather than remaining economically independent. These results are more likely to occur (1) the fewer the restrictions that are placed on trade, (2) the lower the transactions costs involved, (3) the wider the gap in production advantages, and (4) the easier it is for productive resources to be shifted into the advantageous industry in each country.

Posttrade Production Points

By considering posttrade production points, it can be seen numerically that trade may improve each country's consumption. If each country specializes where it has a comparative advantage, then posttrade production will be as in the table below. Pretrade consumption of each product by *both* countries combined was 160 units per month of appliances and 70 units per month of bananas. Now total production exceeds each of these figures—so it remains only to price the products and distribute the output—unquestionably, each country is *potentially* better off.

Posttrade Production (units/month)

	A	B
United States	200	0
Honduras	0	80

The final consumption points will depend on consumers' preferences in each country, as reflected in the indifference curves for that country. We do know, however, that the United States will export *at most* 80 units of appliances per month and will demand *at least* 40 units per month of bananas in exchange, in order to remain at least as well off as before trade. Honduras, similarly, will be willing to export *at most* 50 units per month of bananas in exchange for *at least* 40 units of appliances per month, so that consumers there will be no worse off than before trade. Any trade of 40-80 units of appliances per month for 40-50 units of bananas per month will make each country better off than it was before.[5] We can assume that the final consumption points are as shown in the table below.

Posttrade Consumption (units/month)

	A	B
United States	150	45
Honduras	50	35

Implicitly, this means that the posttrade relative prices are 45 bushels of bananas/50 appliances = 0.9 bananas/appliances, or 1.11 appliances/bananas. That is, final consumption possibilities (if graphed on Figure 3-1) have a slope of more than the pretrade U.S. trade-off and less than the Honduran one.

Next, let us consider *prices* explicitly, to show that each country is better off in financial as well as real terms. The adjustment from pre- to posttrade prices can take place through changes in domestic prices in each country or through changes in the exchange rate, or both. To focus our attention on "international prices," let us allow only the exchange rate to change, while domestic prices in each country remain constant.

Assume that the domestic price of bananas in the United States before trade was 200 appliances per 100 bushels of bananas, or 2 to 1. If an appliance cost $10, then one bushel (i.e., one unit) of bananas cost $20, according to Figure 3-1. In Honduras, the pretrade value of a bushel of bananas was three fourths of an appliance. If an appliance cost 200 lempira, then a bushel of bananas cost 150 lempira.

Once international trade is allowed, there must be some rate of exchange between lempira and dollars. Looking at the pretrade domestic prices, appliances were worth 200 lempira or $10, a ratio of 20 lempira/dollar, and bananas were worth 150 lempira or $20, a ratio of 7.5 lempira/dollar. As long as the exchange rate falls somewhere between these ratios, bilateral trade will make each country better off in financial terms. Let us assume, then, that the exchange rate becomes 15 lempira/dollar.

This exchange rate means that U.S. consumers who want to buy Honduran appliances or bananas will face dollar prices of 200 lempira/15 lempira per dollar = $13.33 per appliance and 150 lempira/15 lempira per dollar = $10 per bushel of bananas. On the other hand, Honduran consumers looking at possible purchases of U.S. appliances and bananas will see lempira prices of $10 × 15 lempira per dollar = 150 lempira per appliance and $20 × 15 lempira per dollar = 300 lempira per bushel of bananas. Clearly, U.S. consumers will benefit from importing bananas and Honduran consumers will benefit from importing appliances. Since each country is large enough to satisfy total demand for the product it exports, then complete specialization may occur in each (though not necessarily, due to various market imperfections—tariffs, factor immobility between industries, etc.).

If the exchange rate were to change to a level outside the range of 7.5-20 lempira/dollar, a disequilibrium would exist. At any exchange rate below 7.5 lempira/dollar, both countries would want to buy appliances and bananas from the United States. And at any rate above 20 lempira/dollar, both countries would want to buy both products from Honduras. For example, if the rate is 5 lempira/dollar, then Hondurans can import appliances for 50 lempira/appliance and bananas for 10 lempira/bushel and U.S. consumers have to pay $40 for imported appliances and $30/bushel for imported bananas. In this case, both countries would buy both products from the United States, until the exchange rate moved above 7.5 lempira/dollar or until U.S. prices of appliances and bananas rose enough to accomplish the same result. (Alternatively, Honduran prices could fall to generate this result. The actual adjustment will depend on which prices are more flexible—domestic prices or exchange rates—but the result will be the same.)

This relatively simple framework is intended to demonstrate the potential real and financial gains available to any pair of countries that begin bilateral trade in two commodities. These results will generally obtain for situations involving many countries and many products, as long as relative production efficiencies differ.[6] The very important problems that arise from market imperfections such as government controls and monopolistic company practices are ignored in this chapter—though they are critical factors for managerial decision making.[7] Our only purpose here has been to present one underlying economic rationale for trade.

The International Product Cycle

The **international product cycle** is a concept developed by Raymond Vernon in the mid-60s, based on the product life cycle in marketing analysis.[8] This concept is far more intuitively appealing than the comparative advantage theory as an explanation of post-World War II trade (and investment), especially regarding manufactured goods (in particular, differentiated products). The product cycle theory explicitly incorporates the multinational enterprise as an actor that undertakes international trade (and also foreign direct investment). It focuses on market expansion and technological innovation, which are relatively de-emphasized in the comparative advantage theory. Finally, it is a dynamic view, exploring the reasons why trade flows shift over time. In all, it puts the phenomenon of international trade in a context that makes business sense in a world of changing technology and multiple markets that faces any firm.

The theory of the international product cycle has two fundamental tenets. First, technology is a critical factor in product creation and development, and the existence of proprietary technology gives some firms advantages over others. Second, market size and structure are critical factors in determining trade patterns.

The cycle itself comprises three stages: the new product stage, the maturing product stage, and the standardized product stage. These stages are more or less analogous to the stages of the domestic product life cycle, though the decline and cessation of production of a product are ignored.

New Product Stage

A *new product* is created by some firm or firms and does not exist prior to this. For example, pocket calculators, automobiles, specific drugs, and nuclear power plants were each created by one or a few firms whose scientists and engineers developed each of these products. When such an invention is sold in the market, it is called an **innovation,** or a **new product.** The first step toward a new product, then, is the process of scientific research, which leads to inventions.

The conditions under which an innovation will succeed depend greatly on the type of product and the type of market. If we consider manufactured products and national markets, we would expect a lot of innovations in nations where sufficient scientists and engineers are available and where purchasers have sufficient incomes to buy the products. Vernon, in his reasoning in the mid-1960s, explained that the largest percentage of new products would be introduced in the largest single national market with the highest per capita income—the United States. That is, he believed that innovations had the best chance for success in the United States at that time because the United States then had more scientists and engineers and a higher per capita income than any other country.

Also important in the new product stage is **flexibility** in production, to suit the needs and desires of new purchasers.[9] Generally, when a new product is introduced, we would expect the demand for it to be relatively price inelastic. Purchasers who have no perfect substitutes available for the new product are likely to be more concerned (initially) with the product's useful characteristics than with its price. As the innovating firm receives feedback from purchasers about performance, reliability, and so on, it can alter the product to suit purchasers' preferences. Close contact with the market is therefore a very important factor in this stage. To achieve flexibility, then, the innovating firm will probably want to locate in or near a major potential market, where good communications are available. Once again, the United States is a very likely candidate for such a firm's location, though of course today Western European countries and Japan serve about equally well as appropriate markets for new products.

As the innovating firm discovers additional customers for sales of the new product, foreign demand may be sought, or it may arise through requests for exports. If the innovating firm is a multinational, it may face the choice between exporting and setting up production in foreign markets. Smaller firms would generally look just at exporting, or perhaps contracting with a foreign firm to produce the product abroad. Thus, the initial entry of the new product into international business will probably occur through exports, and sooner or later that step may be followed by foreign production. Figure 3-2 presents an overview of the international product cycle, assuming that initial production occurs in the United States.

Notice that as the new product stage progresses, exports provide a growing share of total sales. If sale of the new product is truly profitable, the innovating firm is likely to attract competitors both in the United States and abroad. Depending on the firm's success in retaining its proprietary ability to make the product, competition will arise sooner or later. Exports and the start-up of foreign production (in panel 2 of Figure 3-2) may be carried out either by the innovating firm or by competing firms, depending on the ability

Figure 3-2 **The International Product Cycle**

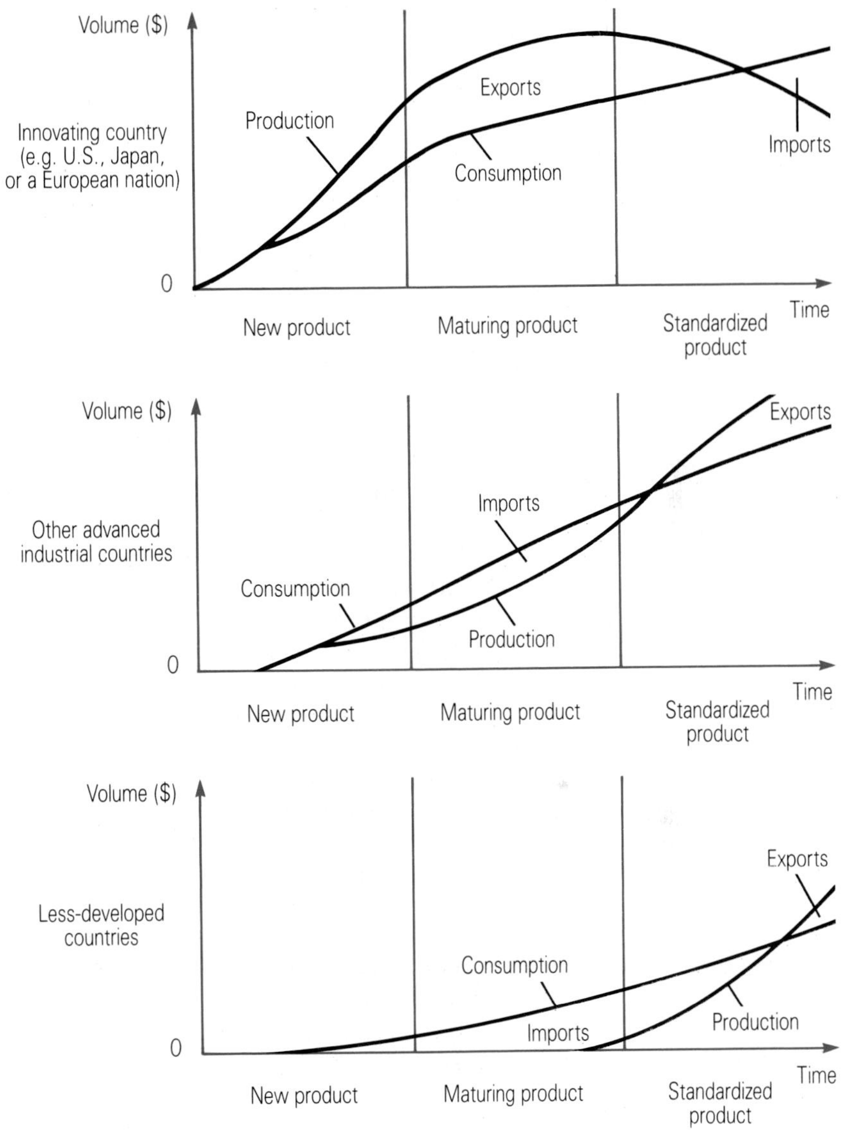

of these firms to gain information about the product and access to foreign markets.

Two distinct shifts in the nature of the new business mark the transition from the new product stage to the maturing product stage. First, the likelihood that competitors will begin making the product, in the home country or abroad, means that *price* competition is likely to become more important. The innovating firm itself may establish facilities abroad, to achieve lower-cost production as well as to serve foreign markets (especially in Europe, Canada, and Japan) with a product capable of being adapted to local market requirements. Second, the fact that competitors exist at all means that technology is diffusing, so that the original firm does not maintain its monopoly of the product.

Maturing Product Stage

Each of these shifts leads toward the **maturing product** stage, which involves global diffusion of the product through exports and also through foreign production via foreign direct investment. This second stage is characterized by more price-elastic demand for the product, more standardization of the production process, and a change in company strategy away from a focus on production (of this particular product) and toward market protection. Both local and foreign competitors typically challenge the innovating firm in its home market and abroad. In this stage, product differentiation is typical and pursuit of new markets by competing firms becomes active.

Production in the home country typically levels off in this stage, as market growth slows. Lower-cost production methods and locations are often sought as price competition increases. Toward the end of this stage, foreign production may even be exported to the home country. Notice that both competition and production tend to spread from the home country to other industrial countries first, and later to less developed countries.

Standardized Product Stage

Finally, the **standardized product** stage occurs when technology relevant to the product becomes widely available, and price becomes the main basis for competition. In this stage, production of standardized products (or components) is often shifted to low-cost locations, including less developed countries. (see Figure 3-2, bottom panel). Also typical of the standardized product stage is offshore assembly, in which parts of the product are still produced in the home country—but assembly is done in cheap-labor countries, for final sale in many countries. Strategically, firms often try to avoid pure price competition in the standardized product stage by differentiating their products.

The Pocket Calculator

The standard pocket calculator offers a clear example of a product moving through the international product cycle. This "product" is defined here to be the battery-operated, hand-held computational instrument that adds, subtracts, multiplies, and divides electronically. Scientists at Sunlock Comptometer Corporation invented the product in 1961 and began marketing it soon afterward. At about $1,000 per calculator, the instrument was not cheap. But it performed functions formerly reserved for large computers and mechanical calculators, while offering the user a simple, portable, and independent computational capability. The alternative in terms of portability and independence from electrical outlets was the slide rule, which had far less accuracy than the 6-10 digits usually available in a calculator.

Ignoring the refinements that allow pocket calculators to carry out complex calculations, store results, and even act as microcomputers, let us continue to look at the simple, four-function product. (The others can be defined as separate products, to avoid confusion.) Within eight years of the introduction of pocket calculators, several additional firms (including a number of Japanese manufacturers) had entered the market with competing products and the price had dropped to about $400 per calculator. Hewlett-Packard, Texas Instruments, Casio (a Japanese firm), and other electronics manufacturers developed similar models, which forced all manufacturers of pocket calculators to compete on price grounds, in the United States and in several foreign markets. Each of these developments indicates a move into the maturing product stage. (The new product stage lasted for perhaps four to six years.)

In the early 1970s, more firms entered the market, several began to assemble their calculators in offshore locations such as Taiwan and Singapore, and price competition became truly fierce. In 1971, Bowmar Corporation, an American firm, introduced a four-function calculator that retailed for $240. By 1975, these calculators sold routinely for $10-15 and sometimes for even less. One could argue that pocket calculators had reached the standardized product stage by 1975, with the production technology widely available, price competition (hence costs) of utmost importance, and product differentiation widely used.

Thus, the international product cycle for simple calculators was completed in less than fifteen years. The product itself remains in widespread demand, but producers now compete on the basis of price, other product characteristics, and distribution, rather than on the basis of proprietary technology and new markets.

Development of the Polaroid Land Camera

Contrast the case of the pocket calculator with that of the Polaroid Land camera. In 1947, Edwin Land, the founder and manager of Polaroid Corporation, introduced a new photographic process. He had invented an instant-developing film that allowed a photographer to snap a picture and simply wait a few minutes for chemicals on the film to develop the final snapshot. First marketed in 1948, the Polaroid Land camera enjoyed a monopoly position for several decades.

Initially, the Polaroid Land camera took only black-and-white photographs and the film processing was done inside the camera. In 1963, Polaroid introduced an improved version that processed the film outside the camera. (Each snapshot was removed from the camera immediately after the picture-taking, in a "sandwich" of developing chemicals, film negative, and print paper. Then the print was pulled away from the other materials, which were discarded.) Later, improved prints of both black-and-white and color pictures were offered. In 1972, Polaroid introduced another modification of the camera, which now gives the final print directly from the camera after each picture. (The print develops in a few seconds, with no materials to be discarded.)

If the instant-developing camera is regarded as one product, ignoring its improvements over the years, then one can conclude that the new product stage in this case lasted approximately 30 years. During that time, Polaroid had a monopoly on the market worldwide, expanding sales through both direct exports and foreign marketing and production affiliates. Today, 42 percent of the firm's sales come from foreign operations located in 22 countries.

It was only in 1976, when Kodak introduced an instant-developing camera using somewhat different technology, that competition began for this product. Then, in 1984, a patent infringement case against Kodak was won by Polaroid, which forced Kodak out of the market for instant-developing cameras. In 1987, the instant-developing camera was still in the late new product or early maturing product stage—a huge contrast with the pocket calculator's cycle. Today, Polaroid's proprietary technology continues to play a major role in competition for instant-developing cameras. Price competition has become more important, though not dominant, in Polaroid's effort to entice photographers away from single-lens reflex and Instamatic cameras. Thus, the international product cycle provides an appealing description of the sequence of events that takes place in the lives of many products—but as we see with the instant-developing camera, it does *not* explain *when* the stages will begin or end.

While the theory of the international product cycle offers us a wealth of insights into international trade and the activities of multinational firms, it leaves some important questions unanswered. This theory does not tell us how long each stage will last, though it does illuminate key competitive aspects of each stage. Nor does it tell us explicitly how or when a firm should choose between exporting and setting up a local plant abroad, though it does mention costs as an important concern. It does not explain which country's firms are most likely to produce in any given market, nor which firms will move first. Lastly, the theory is decidedly vague on the definition of a "product." Despite these limitations, as compared with other theories available today, the theory gives us substantial managerial insights into trade patterns in manufacturing.

An especially fortunate aspect of the theory of the international product cycle is its compatibility with the theory of comparative advantage. If we focus on trade that occurs primarily on the basis of comparative national cost conditions, then the standardized product stage of the international product

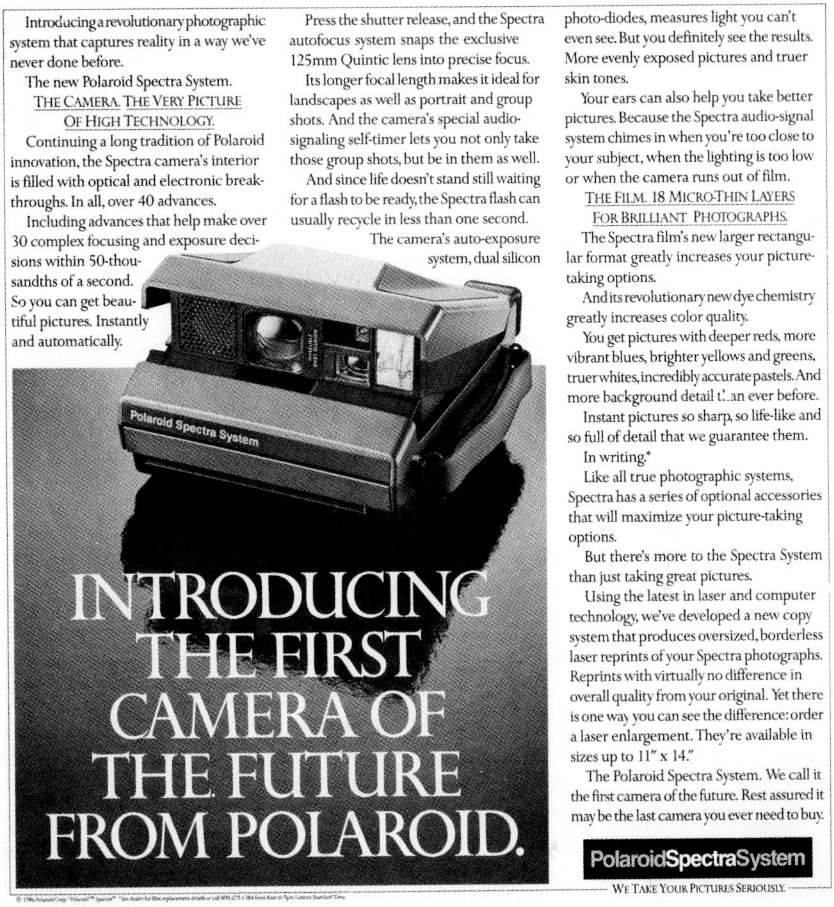

The latest version of Polaroid's instant-developing camera.

Courtesy Polaroid.

cycle outlines broad aspects of such trade and the comparative advantage view lays out a solid theoretical framework for analysis and decision making.

* * * * *

One additional theory of international trade that is based on demand-side considerations deserves comment at this point. Staffan Linder (1961) created a theory based on similarity of **demand patterns** to explain trade patterns in manufactured products. This theory was developed in the early 1960s, at about the same time that the theory of the international product cycle was attempting to move emphasis in trade theory to the demand side. Linder reasoned that a major determinant of trade patterns was the level of a country's economic development. Countries at similar levels of development would have similar demand patterns and would be likely to trade among themselves. Intuitively, this idea is sensible, and one can think of the pharmaceuticals industry, the computer industry, and many others that display large trade volumes among developed countries, and relatively little involving LDCs (with the exception of the offshore assembly done in LDCs for sale in developed countries). Linder's theory offers an underlying reason for expecting so much trade in manufactured goods among developed countries, even when many of their cost conditions are very similar.

Empirical Controversies and New Theories

The Leontief Paradox

A large part of the international economic policy of governments worldwide is based on the concept of comparative advantage. That is, national governments tend to view the gains from trade as being quite real and they try to obtain a larger share of the total gains for themselves. The United States has traditionally been the clearest and most consistent advocate and example of free-trade policy. Following the principle of comparative advantage, the United States, then, should specialize in the production and export of products in which the country has an advantage. Which ones are they?

One might expect that if we focus simply on capital-intensive versus labor-intensive goods, the United States would export the former and import the latter. Certainly, with its abundant capital resources, the United States would be expected to behave in this way. A study by (subsequent Nobel Prize-winning economist) Wassily Leontief in 1953 showed that, in fact, export goods from the United States are relatively more labor intensive and import-competing goods are relatively more capital intensive! What happened to the theory of comparative advantage? Table 3-4 shows Leontief's results and those of two other similar investigations covering different years.

A number of explanations have been given for what is now called the **Leontief paradox.** Some authors have attributed the findings to trade barriers that distort trade flows; others have looked at differences in natural resource availability across countries; still others have focused on differences in the characteristics of labor across countries.[10] Most analysts today agree that this last factor plays a large part in determining U.S. trade flows (and also foreign direct investment flows). If we measure the "quality" of labor inputs (i.e., their productivity), rather than just man-hours of work, it turns out that the United States tends to specialize in producing and exporting products that use relatively more "high-quality" labor (e.g., technology-intensive products that require more highly educated labor). Several analysts, including Keesing (1966) and Gruber, Mehta, and Vernon (1967), found empirical evidence supporting this point. This explanation is quite consistent with the international product cycle, which is based on the development of new technology and which sees the United States as the country most likely to be the source of new products.

Table 3-4 **Leontief Paradox Studies: Capital and Labor Requirements in U.S. Exports and Import-Competing Replacements**

Year for Input-Output Structure (I-O) and Trade Pattern	Factor Requirements per Million Dollars of Product	Exports	Competitive Imports	Ratio of Exports to Imports
(1) 1899 I-O and trade structure (Whitney)	Capital stock	$2,621,200	$2,589,700	
	Labor (person-years)	1,122.5	1,240.2	
	Capital/labor ratio	$2,335.1	$2,088.3	1.118
(2) 1947 I-O and trade structure (Leontief)	Capital stock	$2,550,780	$3,091,339	
	Labor (person-years)	182	170	
	Capital/labor ratio	$14,010	$18,180	0.771
(3) 1958 I-O and 1962 trade structure (Baldwin)	Capital stock	$1,876,000	$2,132,000	
	Labor (person-years)	131	119	
	Capital/labor ratio	$14,200	$18,000	0.789

(1) William G. Whitney, "The Structure of the American Economy in the Late Nineteenth Century," unpublished Ph.D. dissertation, Harvard University, 1968, calculated from table V-3.
(2) Wassily W. Leontief, "Factor Proportions and the Structure of American Trade: Further Theoretical and Empirical Analysis," *Review of Economics and Statistics* 38, no. 4 (November 1956), pp. 392, 397.
(3) Robert E. Baldwin, "Determinants of the Commodity Structure of U.S. Trade," *American Economic Review* 61, no. 1 (March 1971), table 1 on p. 134.

Source: Charles P. Kindleberger and Peter H. Lindert, *International Economics*, 6th ed. (Homewood, Ill.: Richard D. Irwin, 1978), p. 92.

Both the theory of the international product cycle and the technology-based theory have had to be reevaluated since the early 1970s, to recognize the comparable levels of development and market size in the European Community and Japan relative to the United States. Today, it is possible to argue that both of these theories provide plausible reasons for trade to begin among the industrial countries once an innovation has taken place, but neither of them is able to explain where to look for innovations.[11]

Cross-Hauling or "Intra-Industry Trade"

Each of the theories discussed above gives reasons why one should expect exports of any given product in one direction between countries; none of them explains **cross-hauling,** or two-way trade, of the same goods between two countries. Yet trade statistics are full of examples of two-way trade in apparently the same products between various trading partners. A simple reason for this unexpected phenomenon is that the statistics include many products in one aggregated category, so that what appears to be one product really turns out to be many. Indeed, much of the evidence is of exactly this type. Also, multistage production (including offshore assembly) leads to trade flows of one product both into and out of the same country where processing is done, while the actual items being moved are first inputs and then outputs of the product. However, after misclassified products have been excluded, there still turns out to be a substantial amount of cross-hauling in exactly the same products.

Lisa Blum (1984) has shown that cross-hauling occurs in U.S. international trade in many industries, possibly because (1) the market size is large enough to absorb the total combined sales; and/or (2) companies find that it is strategically useful to export products to competitors' markets, and/or (3) product differentiation may provide sufficient preferences to allow more than one supplier of the product to survive, and/or (4) large economies of scale in production limit domestic entry in an industry, into which foreign producers may export. No complete rationale has been established to explain two-way trade in the same products, but Blum's work provides clear evidence and plausible hypotheses that may lead to a new theory encompassing this phenomenon.[12]

The Direction of New Trade Theories

Most of the new trade theories to emerge in the 1970s and 1980s have used the base of industrial organization theory to explore the impact of imperfect competition (or monopolistic competition) on trade flows. By allowing for proprietary technology or economies of scale, such theories are able to better explain the trade flows among industrial countries in the past twenty years. (See, for example, Ethier 1983 and Lancaster 1980.) Clearly, these two factors are important determinants of current trade among industrial countries.

Another avenue of investigation that has been very productive is to consider trade as part of multinational business, along with foreign direct investment and other international business activities. Beginning with the general view of the international product cycle, several writers (such as Hirsch 1976 and Grosse 1985) have examined in more detail the relationships between trade and direct investment by multinational firms. First, trade can be seen as a substitute for direct investment when the MNE seeks to supply foreign markets or to obtain inputs for use in the home market. Second, trade can be seen as a complement for direct investment when the MNE seeks to fill out product lines beyond those produced locally in any affiliate. The appendix to this chapter presents a model showing such an analysis.

Conclusions

Each of the trade theories discussed can be recast in a microeconomic context, focusing on individual firms. The lesson to be learned from the comparative cost view, for example, is that when costs are very important in competition, it may be best for a firm to produce its products in low-cost countries, rather than try to serve markets from its home country alone. Certainly, this lesson has been learned by the many U.S.-based electronics firms that now manufacture in Singapore, South Korea, or Hong Kong to lower their production costs. Alternatively, a firm may find it best to import some products from low-cost suppliers, rather than try to produce them itself. In fact, many export-import firms make their entire business from finding low-cost suppliers in various countries and sales in others—profiting from the use of comparative cost advantages in each product.

The theory of the international product cycle offers the manager advice about the dynamics of many industries, as competition shifts from being based on proprietary technology, to product differentiation, to price (cost) minimizing. The high-tech firm may choose to leave the markets for its products when they enter the maturing or standardized stage, in order to concentrate its efforts on developing new products and competing on the basis of its technology. The firm with a respected brand name may choose to focus its efforts on finding low-cost production sites and establishing an international distribution network, to minimize delivery costs.

The other theories can also be used as guides for decision making. In every case, the firm needs to consider other alternatives besides exports (for example, foreign direct investment). The appendix to this chapter presents a model that relates exports, foreign direct investment, and other contractual forms for doing international business that may add useful insights for making these choices.

Looking specifically at individual countries, it appears that U.S. companies are competing successfully in export markets with products that are relatively intensive in human capital. This may be restated in terms of companies' competitive advantages: U.S. firms can succeed in export markets where the proprietary skills of these firms (such as technology and management know-how) are relatively important. Foreign firms can export to the United States products whose competitiveness depends more on other factors of production (e.g., low-wage labor, natural resources, different management skills).

Questions

1. How can the manager of an international company use the comparative advantage theory in decision making? For example, suppose that the company is Apple Computers and the manager is looking for a site to locate a new plant.
2. Explain the stages of the international product cycle. How can a manager use this theory in decision making? Use the case of the auto industry to help illustrate your answer.
3. What are the main export products/services of the United States today? Why are U.S. exporters able to compete successfully in these markets? (Figure 7-4 in Chapter 7 lists the main merchandise products, and Figure 7-3 shows several key service categories.)
4. Is the exchange rate important in the theory of comparative advantage? Why or why not?
5. Explain Leontief's paradox. Be sure to discuss several reasons why the paradox may be more apparent than real.
6. What competitive advantage do the OPEC countries possess that allows them to compete in export markets? What theory of international trade covers this example?

7. At what stage of the international product cycle are personal computers? Based on that view, what do you expect to happen in this market during the rest of the 1980s?
8. At what stage of the international product cycle is the automobile? What do you expect to happen in this market during the rest of the 1980s?
9. Given the information below, what should each *country* do? Why?

	Computers	Paper
United States	50	40
Canada	100	60

Note: Each cell represents the number of hours of labor input needed to produce one unit of output of each product.

10. How does international trade relate to foreign direct investment? (Use the appendix to this chapter for help, if you wish.)

References

Baldwin, Robert. "Determinants of the Commodity Structure of U.S. Trade," *American Economic Review,* March 1971.

Blum, Lisa. "Intra-Industry Trade and Market Structure: A Time Trend Analysis." Paper presented at the Academy of International Business annual meeting, 1984.

Buckley, Peter, and Robert D. Pearce. "Exports in the Strategy of Multinational Enterprises." *Journal of Business Research,* (1984).

Ethier, Wilfred. *Modern International Economics.* New York: W. W. Norton, 1983.

Grosse, Robert. "An Imperfect Competition Theory of the MNE," *Journal of International Business Studies,* Winter 1985.

Gruber, W. H.; Dileep Mehta; and Raymond Vernon. "The R&D Factor in International Investment of U.S. Industries," *Journal of Political Economy,* February 1967.

Haberler, Gottfried. *The Theory of International Trade.* London: William Hodge, 1950.

Hirsch, S. "An International Trade and Investment Theory of the Firm." *Oxford Economic Papers,* July 1976.

Hufbauer, Gary. *Synthetic Materials and the Theory of International Trade.* Cambridge, Mass.: Harvard Univ. Press, 1966.

Keesing, Donald. "Labor Skills and Comparative Advantage," *American Economic Review,* May 1966.

Kindleberger, Charles, and Peter Lindert. *International Economics.* 6th ed. Homewood, Ill.: Richard D. Irwin, 1978.

Krugman, Paul. "New Theories of Trade among Industrial Countries," *American Economic Review,* May 1983.

Lancaster, Kelvin. "Intra-Industry Trade under Perfect Monopolistic Competition." *Journal of International Economics,* May 1980.

Linder, Staffan. *An Essay on Trade and Transformation.* New York: John Wiley & Sons, 1961.

Ricardo, David. *Principles of Political Economy and Taxation.* Harmondsworth, Middlesex, England: Penguin Books, 1971. (Originally published in 1817.)

Vernon, Raymond. "International Investment and International Trade in the Product Cycle." *Quarterly Journal of Economics,* May 1966.

Endnotes

1. The current state of development of this theory is presented in Kindleberger and Lindert (1978).
2. Ricardo's analysis assumes constant opportunity costs in shifting production from one product to another in a given country. This point has been criticized by Haberler (1950) and others; and current economics texts use the increasing-cost approach. The present text uses Ricardo's model because it allows more clarity in the exposition. See Kindleberger and Lindert (1978), chapters 2-4, for an excellent presentation of the pure theory.
3. Normally, we would expect diminishing returns to occur as production is specialized more and more in the one product, hence using less and less efficient resources for producing it. And we would therefore expect *incomplete* specialization in each country. Our example simplifies the economics substantially; and any international trade text can be used to explore the added concerns of incomplete specialization. Graphically, the results of trade with incomplete specialization between two equal-sized countries would be:

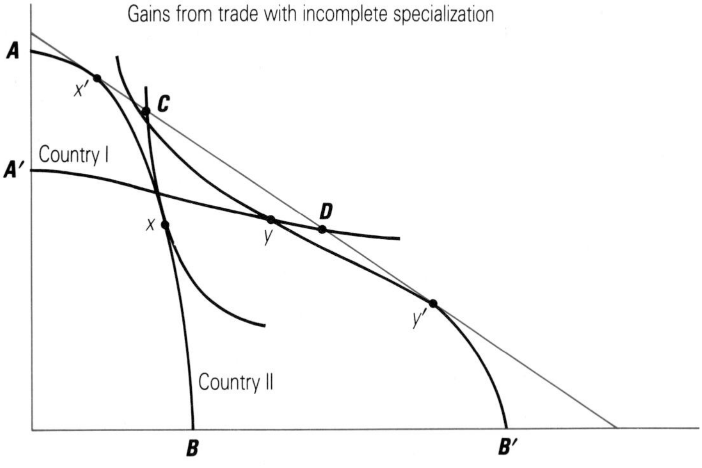

where Country 1 produces and consumes initially at *Y*, and Country 2 at *X*. With trade, each country partially specializes its production, at points *X′* and *Y′*, and each can consume both goods at some point on segment *CD*, which is above the original indifference curves.

4. In fact, consumers may choose a little less of one good and a lot more of the other, after trade, as long as they end up consuming on a higher indifference curve. To keep matters simple, we will assume that consumers choose more of both products, when available.
5. Thus, comparative advantage analysis not only tells us which country will specialize in production of what product; it also tells us what the limits will be on the real rate of exchange.
6. See Kindleberger and Lindert (1978) for a full and careful treatment of these issues.
7. Government controls are discussed in Chapter 8; monopolistic practices are treated in the appendix to this chapter as well as elsewhere in the text.
8. Vernon's theory appeared as "International Investment and International Trade in the Product Cycle," *Quarterly Journal of Economics,* May 1966. The product life cycle in marketing appears, for example, in Chester Wasson, *Dynamic Competitive Strategy and Product Life Cycles* (St. Charles, Ill.: Challenge Books, 1974).
9. Analogously, the firm may desire the flexibility to test the market using a limited capital commitment, before making expensive, highly illiquid investments in large-scale production runs.
10. Much of the literature on the Leontief paradox is summarized in Baldwin (1971).
11. Before the 1980s, several analysts demonstrated some patterns of innovation among industrial countries: for example, U.S. firms tended to be laborsaving in their innovations; European firms were relatively material- and capital-saving; and Japanese firms were relatively material- and space-saving.
12. See Krugman (1983).

Appendix 3–1

The International Trade and Investment Theory of the Firm

Introduction

We can continue to explore the implications of international trade theory from a managerial perspective by considering the situation of a firm that produces some good A for domestic and possible foreign consumption. The manager is concerned about both the possibility of exporting his product *and* the choice of locations in which to produce it. Following the guidelines of comparative advantage, the firm should produce and export product A in whichever country offers least cost production. Following the international product cycle, the firm should consider foreign markets initially for their potential demand for a new product and later as possible sources of low-cost production (through foreign direct investment) for serving multiple markets. The model presented here enables us to focus on these key strategic issues for the international firm.

Choosing Production Locations

Let us assume that the goal of the firm is long-run profit maximization, subject to a production function in each country of operation and subject to three explicit nonproduction costs, defined below. The decision of interest is the choice among production locations for serving given markets, as well as the kind of output supplied to the market (namely, final or intermediate goods). We are straying well beyond the pure concept of international trade with this view—but the result will enable us to see more clearly how trade fits into a firm's international strategy.

An approach suggested by Hirsch (1976) was to develop a cost function for the firm based on five variables:

P_a = Cost of production per unit in home country, a.

P_b = Cost of production per unit in host country, b.

K = Firm-specific information such as proprietary technology and management know-how (valued in cost/unit of output), whose generation cost is zero (at this time) for the possessor firm, since it already has the capacity on hand, and positive for its competitors.

M = Export marketing cost differential, which is measured as export marketing costs minus domestic marketing costs (valued in cost/unit of output).

C = Additional cost of controlling and coordinating an international company, with production in home and host countries, compared to just operating one facility in the home country (in cost/unit of output).

Each of the variables is measured as:

$$X = \sum_{t=1}^{T} \frac{X_t}{(1 + r)^t}$$

where X is the variable; t is the time period of the project, from 1 to T; and r is the project's cost of capital. Thus, each variable is a present value of a specific cost to be incurred by the firm in a given project. The alternatives available to the firm for serving the host country market can then be evaluated on cost grounds.

Using an extension by Grosse (1981), additional conclusions can be drawn from these variables, and more can be shown by including revenue variables:

$R_a\ R_b$ = Average revenue (i.e., price per unit) in home, host country.

Specifically, the following decision criteria can be established for the firm: Exports should be used to supply the host country market when:

$$R_b - P_a - M > R_b - P_b - C$$

and

$$R_b - P_a - M > R_b - P_b - K$$

Assuming that R_b is given, then the inequalities state that exports should be used to supply a foreign market when the unit cost is lower than the unit cost for undertaking foreign direct investment to set up local production *and* the unit cost is lower than that of another firm obtaining the proprietary knowledge (K) and producing in the host country. (An unstated, but plausible, third alternative would be for a *home country* competitor to obtain the technology and export to the host country. This would be a proprietary advantage that it could use to lower P_a or M for itself.)

A second solution justifies foreign direct investment, and subsequent local production in the host country, when:

$$R_b - P_b - C > R_b - P_a - M$$

and

$$R_b - P_b - C > R_b - P_b - K$$

Again assuming that R_b is given, then the inequalities show that foreign investment, or more exactly, local production in the host country, is the optimal alternative; that is, the delivered cost for using exports is greater than that for using foreign direct investment plus local production.

Notice that the argument, advanced in several empirical studies, that a local production presence generates greater sales than imports through a sales office or a distributor, can be introduced here by allowing R_b to vary. Demand analysis can lead to separate R_b estimates for exports as opposed to local production. Then even if *costs* were lower using exports, the firm might choose local production because expected R_b with the local production presence is sufficiently higher than expected R_b with exports.

The third logical solution leaves us without a clear decision, namely:

$$R_b - P_b - K > R_b - P_a - M$$

and

$$R_b - P_b - K > R_b - P_b - C$$

In this case, if R_b is again held constant, cost conditions show that a local competitor in the host country can obtain the necessary technology and produce the product for sales there more cheaply than the proprietor firm can through exports or direct investment. As far as final product sales are concerned, the proprietor firm will be a relatively inefficient supplier, competitive only if the market is large enough to support both firms—or if R_b is greater for this firm because of a brand name or some other demand-side influence.

This third case illuminates the potential for sale of intermediate goods. That is, the proprietor firm can attempt to sell its proprietary knowledge to the local competitor, in the form of a licensing agreement to produce the product, or perhaps through the sale of intermediate products that embody the proprietary knowledge. Such a solution is not certain, however, since the competitor firm may value the proprietary knowledge differently from the proprietary firm and may be unwilling to pay an acceptable price for it—preferring to re-create the necessary technology or skill internally, using its own scientists and managers.[1] Another strategy for the proprietor firm would be to seek a joint venture with this competitor, though the valuation problem remains unsolved. Magee (1977), Buckley and Casson (1976), and others have explored some of the ramifications of these "externalized" production strategies (i.e., cases in which the firm sells proprietary knowledge, rather than embodying it in final products).

Applying the Formulation

The explanatory power of the above formulation is very broad; for instance, it can be used to analyze the *commodity composition* of both trade and investment. A firm with no affiliates in the host country must rely on exports (or licensing) for all products sold there. A firm that already operates a producing affiliate in the host country can supply that market with some products from local production and other products through exports from the home country, depending on the calculations above for each product. In fact, the local production presence for some products may increase expected R_b for others and also lower the additional C for additional locally produced products—stimulating both more exports to and more local production in the host country.[2]

When firms in the same industry from both countries look at each other's markets as targets of exports or direct investment, the model can be used to help explain *cross-hauling* of products (i.e., export or foreign direct investment plus local production of the same products in both directions between two countries). Each firm can consider the potential competitiveness of its whole product line in the other firm's market. Individual products in a particular aggregate industrial class may be exported or locally produced in both countries, although the products themselves may be different, and thus cross-hauling is apparent but not real. Alternatively, the very same products may be exported (or locally produced) in both directions, when no cost advantage exists, if each firm calculates that its R_b exceeds the price available to its competitor—because of product differentiation, for example. Finally, though not clearly a result of this model, cross-hauling may occur just because each market is large enough to consume both firms' output.

Another aspect of the activities of multinational firms that is conducive to modeling within the above framework is **offshore assembly.** Primarily a cost-reducing strategy, offshore assembly occurs when a firm ships raw materials and components of a product to some foreign (low-cost) site for assembly or formulation and then ships the final products to home or third-country markets for sale. In the context of the inequalities utilized previously, and looking only at the home country market, a firm should use offshore assembly if:

$$R_a - P_a{}^* - M^* - P_b{}^* - C > R_a - P_a$$

and

$$R_a - P_a{}^* - M^* - P_b{}^* - C > R_a - P_a{}^* - M^* - P_b{}^* - K,$$

where $P_a{}^*$, $P_b{}^*$ = unit costs of the parts of total production carried out in each location and M^* = the export/reexport cost differential over purely domestic marketing costs. As with the original specification, each of the three alternatives may be preferable, depending on the firm's estimates of expected costs and revenues.

The second inequality here presents an interesting dilemma to the firm. If another firm can accomplish the offshore assembly more cheaply than the proprietor firm (i.e., if the inequality is reversed), then licensing that part of the production process may be justified. In this case, however, the proprietor firm has a distinct advantage over the other firm, which could be compelled to sell its output back to the original firm. Even if that other firm could obtain the knowledge necessary for assembly without paying the price demanded by the proprietor firm, such an option can be precluded, because the proprietor is a monopoly supplier of components. This means that licensed offshore assembly may be desirable to a firm, since the externalized stage of production is reinternalized for final sales and proprietary knowledge need not be dissipated.

A variety of additional aspects of the behavior of multinational firms can be examined within the framework presented here (e.g., strategy to deal with tariffs and taxes in each country, multimarket assignments of production and exports, and strategies for products that contain greater or lesser contents of K). In each case, the key variables can be modeled explicitly and conclusions drawn accordingly.

The main purpose of this appendix has been to introduce a framework for discussing the activities of multinational firms that is conducive to economic analysis in the neoclassical (or actually the imperfect competition) tradition. The framework that is used offers a very large number of insights into the behavior of such firms with relatively little complexity.

References

Buckley, P., and M. Casson. *The Future of Multinational Enterprise.* New York: Holmes & Meier, 1976.

Grosse, R. *The Theory of Foreign Direct Investment.* University of South Carolina, Essays in International Business, no. 3, December 1981.

Hirsch, S. "An International Trade and Investment Theory of the Firm." *Oxford Economic Papers,* July 1976.

Magee, S. "Information and the MNC: An Appropriability Theory of Direct Foreign Investment." In *The New International Economic Order,* ed. J. Bhagwati. Cambridge, Mass.: MIT Press, 1977.

Mirus, R. "A Note on the Choice between Licensing and Direct Foreign Investment," *Journal of International Business Studies,* Spring-Summer 1980.

Rugman, Alan, *Inside the Multinationals.* New York: Columbia University Press, 1981.

Endnotes

1. Rolf Mirus (1980) explores this issue in some detail, concluding that licensing would generally be preferable but that the foreign direct investment alternative may still be chosen if the two firms cannot find an acceptable licensing fee or if investors in the proprietor firm favor cash flows from foreign direct investment over cash flows from licensing.
2. Viewed from another perspective, the local production presence in country b may enable the firm to obtain funding in the local capital market. This possibility may lower the total borrowing costs for the firm, or improve its foreign exchange exposure position. This issue is implicitly contained in the variable P_b.

4

FOREIGN DIRECT INVESTMENT

This chapter discusses the single phenomenon that most distinguishes the multinational enterprise from other types of firms, namely foreign direct investment (FDI). It explores the reasons why firms undertake FDI and subsequent local production in host countries, and also the effects of FDI on industry structure around the world. Then it shows patterns of FDI, based on countries that are sources and targets of such investment and on companies that engage in FDI. Lastly, it discusses the issue of disinvestment—when a firm sells or closes an FDI project. The main goals of the chapter are to:

1. Define foreign direct investment and show how it fits into the MNE's activities.
2. Explain why firms undertake FDI, especially in comparison with exporting or other kinds of international business ventures.
3. Show patterns of FDI that illustrate the relative size and importance of different countries, industries, and companies—with particular coverage of FDI in the United States.
4. Show how theories of international business, such as the international product cycle and competitive advantage, focus on FDI and discuss additional theories of FDI, such as Dunning's eclectic view.
5. Show how disinvestment fits into company strategy along with foreign direct investment.

Introduction

Foreign direct investment (FDI) has probably been the most-studied aspect of the activities of multinational enterprises during the last three decades. More accurately, the causes and effects of FDI, and the subsequent operations of foreign affiliates, have been areas of extensive academic and public policy studies, which continue today. Similarly, the strategic fit of FDI and foreign affiliates within a company's global activities has become a central concern of more and more managers, as increasing numbers of firms in many countries have looked abroad for markets and supplies. Both of these aspects of FDI are examined here.

The present chapter, after defining key issues, begins with the manager's view: Why should a firm consider FDI, and how does FDI fit into global strategy? Next, patterns of direct investment since World War II are discussed, with regard to the countries that make and receive the investment and the industries and companies most involved. A section is devoted to examining foreign direct investment coming into the United States, the largest single host country. Fourth, explanations are offered for the observed facts and some conclusions are drawn for company managers and government officials. Finally, the analysis covers disinvestment, the sale of an existing affiliate, which is the "final" stage in FDI, though most projects do not reach that stage. Detailed consideration of the operation of a foreign investment project is left for the chapters in Part 3 of this book.

What Is FDI?

Foreign direct investment (FDI) involves ownership of a company in a foreign country. In exchange for the ownership, the investing company usually transfers some of its financial, managerial, technical, trademark, and other resources to the foreign country. The foreign company may be created as a new venture by the investor, or it may be acquired from an existing owner. Essentially, a company can view this kind of investment just as it views domestic investment—but in this case the project is located in another country. Just as a firm chooses among projects in capital budgeting domestically, it can add on foreign projects, which constitute FDI. Some investors bring in substantial funding with them, others borrow locally to finance their new affiliates, and yet others do both; some investors transfer many people to work in the new affiliate, while others simply hire locally for staffing needs (or acquire an existing company that already has full staffing). The point is that although no particular type of resource needs to be transferred to carry out FDI, FDI is usually accompanied by some transfer of money and people.

The main concept behind FDI is the *control* of assets in another country. That is, foreign direct investment is generally undertaken by a firm that seeks to serve a new market for its products or services or that seeks to obtain additional supplies for its existing markets. For example, Du Pont Chemical

An IBM direct investment in Argentina: an office tower in Buenos Aires.
Milton & Joan Mann/Cameramann International

Corporation has used direct investment in 42 countries to market or produce its various products; Texaco, by contrast, has invested in oil exploration projects in dozens of countries, seeking additional petroleum supplies for its markets in the United States and abroad. In each case, the firm wants *control* over the foreign project in order to utilize its competitive advantages through the new facility.

Notice the contrast between this kind of investment and **portfolio investment,** in which the firm buys stocks, bonds, and other financial assets to hold in its portfolio. Du Pont holds a large and diversified portfolio of financial assets, including shares of other companies. However, its holdings of controlling interest in its own subsidiaries, and now of Conoco (an oil company), are *direct* investments that involve management of the activities involved. In balance sheet terms, portfolio investment relates mainly to the firm's holdings of marketable securities, while direct investment relates to the purchase and management of plant and equipment (plus other assets and liabilities of the direct investment project). The conceptual distinction between direct and portfolio investment is that the former requires control by the investor, whereas the latter is passive and requires no management effort by the investor.[1]

To reiterate: Foreign direct investment involves a controlling interest in a new or existing business enterprise in a foreign country. Such investment may be *financed* in many ways: the parent firm can transfer funds to the new affiliate and issue ownership shares to itself; the parent firm can borrow all of the required funds locally in the new country to pay for ownership; and many combinations of these and other alternatives can be followed.The key point here is that *no* international transfer of funds is necessary; FDI requires only transfer of *ownership* to the investor, which may finance the transaction in innumerable ways.

Who Is Concerned about FDI?

Essentially the same business participants and regulators that appeared in Figure 2-1 as actors in the MNE's global dealings are the ones that are concerned about FDI. The MNE itself must view these actors as key parts of the environment in which it operates. Each home and host country **government** views the MNE and its direct investment projects as generators of income, employment, technology, and so on that must be regulated to obtain the best gains for the government (obviously a contradictory goal, since each actor cannot obtain *all* the benefits of the MNE's activities). **Competitors** in the host country worry about added competition, and competitors in the home country worry about the direct investor's strategic gains from the foreign operations. **Suppliers** and **customers** in each country generally view the direct investment as useful because it brings the MNE closer to host country customers and usually leads to increased need for supplies. Finally, inside the MNE, **managers** and **workers** may have several perspectives on an FDI project, ranging from the expectation of new and interesting assignments to the expectation of job losses due to the foreign project's replacement of domestic output.

Toyota Motors' investment in a joint venture with General Motors in Fremont, California, exemplifies these issues.[2] It is a direct investment because Toyota obtained 50 percent ownership and assumed approximately 50 percent managerial responsibility for the project. The U.S. government views the foreign investment as *desirable* because it has created jobs in California but as *questionable* because it has combined two of the largest auto manufacturers worldwide (which raises antitrust concerns). The Japanese government may view the investment as a necessary step to reduce U.S. protectionist pressures against Japanese exports, but the investment could lead to fewer Toyota exports from Japan and to fewer jobs for Japanese workers, a negative result from their viewpoint. Each of the companies involved views the project as an opportunity to learn from its counterpart: GM will try to transfer

Japanese labor relations and productivity skills to its own people, and Toyota will learn much more about the U.S. auto market and GM's operations. There may be fewer jobs for Toyota workers in Japan if the Fremont plant replaces them—or more jobs if more parts, components, and other Toyota vehicles are sent to the United States as a result of the project. Finally, Toyota's suppliers in Japan may have to follow Toyota to the United States in order to maintain their sales, and Toyota's customers in the United States may experience a shorter delay before the delivery of new cars (though perhaps a higher price). Unfortunately, there is no simple way to evaluate beforehand all the implications of such a project.

As companies continue to seek better strategies for their businesses in different countries, and as governments change their views on foreign direct investment (through elections and other changes of power), the forces shaping FDI decisions shift over time. Since companies are the central decision makers in FDI, their views of the investment process are considered first.[3]

The Strategy of Foreign Direct Investment

Why does a firm undertake foreign direct investment? A wealth of studies done during the 1960s and 1970s disclosed that the most important reason for entering a foreign market was to sell products that the firm already sold successfully in its home country.[4] A reason that has grown in importance as international transportation costs have fallen substantially is to lower production costs by producing in a low-cost country for sales in other countries

Table 4-1 **Reasons for Foreign Direct Investment**

Supply Side

1. To lower production costs.
2. To lower delivery costs (costs of transportation, insurance, tariffs, etc.).
3. To acquire a necessary raw material.
4. To do offshore assembly.
5. To establish a "portfolio" of production sources.

Demand Side

1. To explore new markets, and to serve a "portfolio" of markets.
2. Because an export market was closed by a prohibitive tariff or quota.
3. To establish a local presence with service and product availability.
4. To meet "buy national" rules or preferences in the host country.
5. To gain visibility as a "local" firm, employing local people, paying local taxes, etc.
6. To respond to rivals' threats.

(often called "offshore assembly" or "foreign sourcing"). These and other strategic concerns that may be bases for undertaking FDI appear in Table 4-1.

Notice that the reasons are grouped into supply-side and demand-side categories. While a company may focus on a particular reason as the basis for a given FDI decision, both kinds of factors should be considered when making the decision. Beginning with the supply side, each reason is discussed below.

The Supply Side

Lower Production Costs On the basis of national comparative advantage, a company may discover that its product can be produced at less cost in the foreign country than at home, because of lower wages, cheaper real estate, or other differences in cost conditions. One strategy is to import the product from the country in which it can be produced more cheaply. Another strategy is to establish operations in the lower-cost country. Such a foreign direct investment may be used to produce and sell in the local, host country market or to export to the home country and elsewhere.

Lower Delivery Costs The appropriate cost to use in choosing among production locations is **delivered cost**—so the cost of transporting products to the market should be considered along with the production cost. If the distance is long or tariffs are high between the home and host countries, perhaps local production in the host country will minimize the delivered cost, even if the production costs of the home and host countries are equal or somewhat favorable to the home country. Notice that delivery costs are defined to include both the cost of transportation *and* regulatory costs such as tariffs.

Acquisition of a Raw Material If Japanese manufacturers want to obtain a secure source of oil for their plants, they must look offshore to suppliers, since no oil has been found domestically. Rather than contract with other companies for the purchase of oil, the Japanese firms may decide to invest in oil production abroad, through direct investment. Similarly, U.S. aluminum companies have invested in Jamaica and Bolivia to mine bauxite for their manufacturing in the United States. Generally, a firm may look at foreign countries not only as targets for the sale of its products but also as potential sources of needed raw materials.

Offshore Assembly or Foreign Sourcing This category is really a subhead of the first one, focusing on production for sales outside the host country. Like FDI to obtain raw materials, FDI to do **offshore assembly** is used to gain access to a factor of production, namely labor, that is cheaper or more productive than the home country supply. Many U.S. electronics manufacturers utilize offshore assembly in Taiwan, Singapore, or Hong Kong to assemble their radios, TVs, stereos, calculators, and so on. They produce components in the United States, ship them to the Far East for assembly into final products, and then reexport the products to the United States for sale. Alternatively, a firm may choose to carry out its entire production process in the foreign country, using that site as a source from which to sell to the home country (and elsewhere)—hence the second label, **foreign sourcing.**

Portfolio of Production Sources Firms that produce any kind of product or service may discover that it is advantageous to have multiple sources of supply. Having several sources of inputs lessens the danger of problems with any one supplier company or type of material. To reduce the risk of bottlenecks in production or distribution caused by problems that may arise in any one country, (e.g., strikes, civil unrest, poor quality), it also makes sense to have suppliers in different countries.

The Demand Side

New Markets The most common justification for undertaking FDI is to use local production as a means for establishing new national markets for a product. The firm may choose among FDI, export from the home country, or some other strategy of serving the foreign market (e.g., licensing, franchising, a turnkey venture). If the foreign market appears large enough and local production appears feasible, then FDI can be used to enter the market. Even if the firm already sells one product through exports in the host country, direct investment and local production may be used to sell additional products there.

Restriction of Exports If a national market is closed by a prohibitive tariff or a quota, direct investment may provide an acceptable alternative. Because we are talking about a limitation on the quantity that can be sold in the foreign market, this is a demand-side constraint, not a price or cost constraint. Even if production in and export from the home country are less costly, a quota or total embargo will limit or eliminate sales through exports. In such situations, foreign direct investment and local production can fill the demand of the foreign market.

Local Presence Many times, a local production presence will enable a firm to sell greater quantities of its products, because customers have confidence that the firm is accessible for service and additional product supply. A firm that sells only through imports may not provide as good after-sale service or as great availability of additional products. Visibility as a local producer may convince buyers that the firm is seriously committed to the host country market and can be counted on to deliver contracted orders. Also, local production permits the firm to adapt products more closely to local demand conditions—a flexibility that does not exist for firms that simply export.

"Buy National" Rules Under certain conditions, most countries, including the United States, restrict purchases by government agencies to local, home country suppliers. The United States requires government agencies to buy from U.S. suppliers if their product quality is acceptable and if their prices are competitive with those of foreign bidders for the same contract.[5] Many other countries simply close contracts to foreign bidders, regardless of quality or availability. To avoid such restrictions, a firm may choose to establish a local production presence and thus become a local supplier in the eyes of government buyers.

A constraint similar to the "buy national" rules of governments may exist when local customers maintain a preference for buying from local suppliers, again effectively shutting out nonlocal producers from the market. (In the 1960s and early 1970s, many U.S.-based multinationals changed their subsidiaries' names in Latin American countries to local-sounding names, in order to avoid the negative connotation of being North American.)

Good Corporate Citizen Another reason for establishing local manufacture or local provision of services is to gain respectability as a good corporate citizen in the host country by employing local people, paying local taxes, and otherwise participating in the host society. Such respectability may lead to more favorable perception by local buyers, and even to more favorable treatment by the host government.[6] For this reason, sales may be higher through FDI and local production than through exports from the home country. The decisions by Toyota, Nissan, and other Japanese automotive manufacturers to set up plants in the United States in the late 1970s and early 1980s were substantially an effort to present themselves as good corporate citizens in this country (with positive effects, hopefully, on their car sales)—and to avoid having penalizing quotas and other potential barriers placed on their exports from Japan.

Response to Rivals' Threats If a rival firm enters some national market with local production, a firm may respond by similarly entering that market, to avoid being shut out through tariff or other protection by the host government. A firm would also enter that market to avoid giving its rival an advantage from experience in producing locally. By entering the host market in this way, the firm precludes its rival from building a strong, monopolistic position there, from which the rival could expand into other markets as well.

Each of these bases for deciding to undertake foreign direct investment may be used to justify such a decision, but it should not be the manager's sole justification; in every case, a full analysis is needed to compare direct investment with alternatives for accomplishing the same purpose. (The conditions that justify FDI relative to such alternatives as exporting or licensing are shown in the appendix to Chapter 3.) Before we return to the problem of deciding when to invest, we present some empirical evidence on FDI in the next section.

Patterns of Foreign Direct Investment

Direct Investment by Country

The vast majority of foreign direct investment that has occurred historically has been made in the period since World War II. This is the result of the growth in national markets, coupled with the continued willingness of developed-country governments to permit foreign ownership of local companies. In addition, such investment (and exports) has been facilitated by the tremendous decline in international transportation costs and improvement in transportation availability that have occurred in the postwar period.

Table 4-2 shows the distribution of worldwide FDI by country of origin—that is, based on the country from which multinational enterprises

Table 4-2 **Stock of FDI Abroad by Firms from Developed Market Countries** (in billions of U.S. dollars)

Country of Origin	1967	1971	1975	1978	1981	1983
United States	56.6	82.8	124.1	168.1	226.4	226.3
United Kingdom	17.5	23.7	30.4	41.1	65.5	73.8
Germany, Federal Republic of	3.0	7.3	16.0	31.8	45.3	51.8
Japan*	1.5	4.4	15.9	26.8	37.1	45.3
Switzerland	5.0	9.5	17.6	24.6	36.6	39.9
Netherlands	11.0	13.8	19.0	23.7	32.2	35.7
France	6.0	7.3	11.1	14.9	24.6	29.2
Canada	3.7	6.5	10.4	13.6	25.6	30.4
Sweden	1.7	2.4	4.4	6.0	n.a.	n.a.
Belgium-Luxembourg	2.0	2.4	3.6	5.4	n.a.	n.a.
Italy	2.1	3.0	3.3	3.3	n.a.	n.a.
Total above	110.1	163.1	255.8	359.3	493.3	532.4
All other†	4.0	5.0	7.2	10.0	52.3	63.1
Grand total	114.1	168.1	263.0	369.3	545.6	595.5

* Fiscal year beginning April of the year indicated on the basis of cumulative annual flows of direct investment as reported to the International Monetary Fund.
† Includes Austria, Denmark, Norway, Finland, Portugal, Spain, Australia, New Zealand, and South Africa.

Sources: United Nations, *Transnational Corporations in World Development,* (New York: United Nations, 1978), (E/C10/38); International Monetary Fund, *Balance of Payments Yearbook* (Washington, D.C.: IMF, 1984, 1985); and United Nations, *Trends and Issues in Foreign Direct Investment and Related Flows: A Technical Paper* (New York: UNCTC, 1985), CTC/59, p. 25.

undertook foreign direct investment projects. Notice that the United States has accounted for about half of the total investment over the whole period, though the U.S. share has been declining fairly steadily, to less than 40 percent by 1983. Also notice that, after rebuilding their economies from war damage, both German and Japanese firms have shown the most rapid growth in FDI during the postwar period. In fact, both of the traditional powers of the early 20th century, the United States and the United Kingdom, have seen a decline in their shares of global FDI, though firms from both countries continue to invest abroad and their FDI shares still lead those of other countries. (The recent trend has simply been for Japanese and German firms to invest abroad at a greater rate of growth.)

FDI undertaken by all less developed countries combined accounted for less than 10 percent of the total reported in Table 4-2.[7]

So far, only the source countries for FDI have been examined. Now consider the target or host countries. (An implicit point of the preceding paragraphs is that virtually all of worldwide FDI comes from developed market economies—the "first world." Very little comes from the communist countries or from the less developed countries—the "third world.") Again, most of the direct investment flows occur between developed countries, and mostly toward Europe, though the United States has been the largest single target country for FDI in the whole period—and in the 1980s the balance of the flow has shifted toward the United States. Table 4-3 shows these flows for selected years.

Direct Investment in Various Industries

The composition of foreign direct investment across industries has favored a few very large industries. In highly aggregated terms, these industries are: manufacturing, raw materials, extraction, and trade services. Unfortunately, data are not available for many countries by detailed industrial category. Looking just at the United States, Table 4-4 shows several industrial categories of FDI and highlights the fact that the oil industry is the largest single participant in outgoing U.S. FDI. Direct investment by manufacturing industries has been growing at a faster pace than that of the oil industry, but oil still dominated in the mid-1980s. Notice that trade services (e.g., shipping, insurance, banking) have grown at a very fast rate as well, consistent with the growth of the service sector within the United States during the past two decades.

Table 4-5 presents evidence on some more highly aggregated industrial categories of FDI for six of the largest source countries, showing that total manufacturing generally exceeds the other two broad headings of investment. There has been one major shift in FDI among these categories, namely the relative increase in service sector activity, which includes banking, insurance, and other services. FDI has been growing over time in every sector for each country, with the perhaps anomalous exception of service sector FDI

Table 4-3 **Flows* of FDI into and out of Developed Market Countries, 1967–1986** (in millions of U.S. dollars)

Country and Country Group	1967–1969	1970–1972	1973–1975	1976–1978	1979–1981	1982–1984
Outflows of domestic capital (annual average)						
United States	−5,173	−7,651	−11,498	−11,784	−13,653	−1,367
Canada	−222	−316	−703	−1,230	−3,310	−2,915
Western Europe†	−3,427	−6,151	−11,903	−9,087	−15,222	−10,726
Austria	−10	−25	−29	−69	−107	−127
Belgium-Luxembourg	−39	−161	−235	−380	−431	−187
Denmark	−8	−76	−100	−35	−90	−105
Finland	−17	−53	−24	−47	−126	−284
France	−297	−454	−905	−1,196	−2,601	−2,083
Germany	−512	−1,160	−1,856	−2,417	−3,313	−2,733
Italy	−259	−242	−270	−254	−722	−1,617
Netherlands	−382	−543	−1,225	−528	−418	−667
Norway	−3	−21	−129	−116	−127	−379
Spain	−9	−41	−84	−78	−191	−311
Sweden	−131	−218	−384	−520	−389	−928
Switzerland‡	−733	−1,557	−3,243	—	—	—
United Kingdom	−1,027	−1,600	−3,428	−3,447	−6,540	−4,304
Japan	−183	−479	−1,847	−1,770	−2,750	−4,423
Southern Hemisphere§	−96	−140	−305	−301	−865	−1,317
Australia	−74	−115	−209	−176	−410	−1,092
Total†	−9,101	−14,744	−26,256	−24,162	−35,800	−23,748
Inflows of foreign capital (annual average)						
United States	923	926	3,795	4,823	14,573	15,233
Canada	617	807	652	756	−166	627
Western Europe†	3,144	5,694	8,862	7,620	9,560	9,819
Austria	39	84	126	102	203	220
Belgium-Luxembourg	252	386	901	1,017	1,080	984
Denmark	70	131	160	59	82	64
Finland	14	27	41	28	19	19
France	277	611	1,352	1,470	2,205	1,806
Germany	634	1,219	1,952	1,530	640	1,127
Italy	337	976	617	493	562	980
Netherlands	331	576	927	91	143	−92
Norway	63	93	257	472	312	180
Spain	179	233	355	557	1,227	1,624
Sweden	120	86	77	41	144	118
Switzerland‡	197	307	517	—	—	—
United Kingdom	631	965	1,580	1,760	3,024	2,788
Japan	64	157	130	48	19	257
Southern Hemisphere§	786	1,318	1,025	1,199	1,600	1,765
Australia	599	1,027	615	1,105	1,476	1,702
Total†	5,534	8,902	14,464	14,445	25,686	27,701

* Includes reinvested earnings.
† Including countries not listed separately.
‡ Derived from the year-to-year changes of the estimated stock of direct investment assets and liabilities, respectively (estimates of the Union Bank of Switzerland).
§ Includes Australia, New Zealand, and South Africa.

Sources: United Nations, *Transnational Corporations in World Development,* (New York: United Nations, 1978), (E/C10/38); International Monetary Fund, *Balance of Payments Yearbook* (Washington, D.C.: IMF, 1984, 1985); and United Nations, *Trends and Issues in Foreign Direct Investment and Related Flows: A Technical Paper* (New York: UNCTC, 1985) CTC/59, p. 25.

Table 4-4 **Value of U.S. Private Direct Investment Abroad by Industry**
(in billions of current dollars at year-end)

					Manufacturing			
Date	Total FDI	Mining and Smelting	Petroleum	Trade/ Distribution	Total Manufacturing	Chemicals	Machinery	Transportation Equipment
1929	7.7	1.2	1.1	0.4	1.9	n.a.	n.a.	n.a.
1940	7.3	1.0	1.3	0.5	2.0	n.a.	n.a.	n.a.
1950	11.788	1.204	3.671	0.986	3.886	0.512	0.807	0.485
1960	32.744	3.013	10.944	2.397	11.152	1.902	2.251	2.118
1970	75.480	5.405	19.754	6.201	31.049	5.865	7.842	5.058
1980	213.468	6.493	46.920	25.752	89.063	19.044	23.299	12.343
1985	232.667	n.a.	58.347	n.a.	95.586	19.847	18.741	11.787

Source: U.S. Department of Commerce, *Survey of Current Business,* various issues.

Table 4-5 **Value of Private Direct Investment Abroad by Industry by Country of Origin**

Country and Industry	1971 ($ millions)	Percent	1976 ($ millions)	Percent	1985* ($ millions)	Percent
United States						
Total	101,313†	100	137,244	100	256,536	100
Extractive	30,989	31	36,771	27	57,977	23
Manufacturing	44,370	44	61,062	45	95,175	37
Service, of which	25,954	26	39,411	29	90,301	35
Banking and insurance	9,726	10	16,392	12	—	—
United Kingdom						
Total	23,717	100	31,277‖	100	54,464‡	100
Extractive	8,051	34	8,747	28	4,701	9
Manufacturing	10,043	42	14,131	45	30,846	57
Service, of which	5,633	24	8,399	27	18,916	34
Banking and insurance	1,212	5	1,410	5	—	—
Canada						
Total	6,524	100	9,390	100	31,576§	100
Extractive	938	14	1,963	21	7,894	25
Manufacturing	3,437	53	4,729	50	14,525	46
Service, of which	2,149	33	2,698	29	7,926	25
Banking and insurance	405	6	622	7		

Germany, Federal Republic of						
Total	7,277	100	19,915	100	60,050	100
Extractive	350	5	1,419	7	2,342	4
Manufacturing	5,796	80	14,032	71	25,821	43
Service, of which	1,131	16	4,464	22	27,383	46
Banking and insurance	494	7	1,941	10	—	—
Japan						
Total	3,962	100	10,620	100	83,649	100
Extractive	892	23	2,778	26	12,631	15
Manufacturing	1,092	28	3,723	35	24,426	29
Service, of which	1,978	50	4,119	39	43,330	52
Banking and insurance	843	21	2,376	22	—	—
Italy						
Total	3,343	100	2,864	100		
Extractive	849	25	861	30	n.a.	
Manufacturing	881	26	907	32		
Service	1,613	48	1,096	38		

Sources: United Nations, *Transnational Corporations in World Development: A Re-Examination* (New York: UNCTC, 1978); national sources for 1981 data; and United Nations, *Trends and Issues in Foreign Direct Investment and Related Flows: A Technical Paper* (New York: UNCTC, 1985), CTC/59, p. 80; and unpublished UNCTC data.

* 1985 data do not add to totals, due to unallocated "other" category.

† data for 1973

‡ data for 1981

§ data for 1984

‖ data for 1974

Table 4-6 **Average Overseas Production Ratios* of MNEs† from Industrial Countries, 1977** (percent)

	United States	Europe (total)	EEC (total)	Germany	France	United Kingdom	Other Europe (total)	Sweden	Japan	Other Countries (total)	Canada	Total
High research intensity												
Aerospace	7.8	10.2	10.2	47.0	0.0	NAS						8.1
Office equipment (including computers)	42.2	42.5	42.5			NAS						42.2
Petroleum	49.1	66.8	72.8	NAS	54.0	70.2	0.2		1.6	3.5	67.0	50.5
Measurement, scientific, and photographic equipment	35.2	5.6	NAS	NAS			NAS	NAS				33.2
Electronics and electrical appliances	21.2	27.9	20.4	19.6	9.0	31.8	59.1	46.1	4.3	69.6	NAS	22.0
Chemicals and pharmaceuticals (including soaps and cosmetics)	26.6	40.5	36.2	34.2	33.4	39.9	64.7	57.0	4.4	NAS		30.8
Total	37.3	47.1	47.2	27.1	32.4	51.7	46.3	43.9	3.7	17.9	35.4	37.7
Medium research intensity												
Industrial and farm equipment	23.1	30.8	23.1	7.1		40.6	45.5	65.6	2.8			22.4
Shipbuilding, railroad and transportation equipment	5.0	0.1	NAS		NAS		0.2	NAS	7.1			4.8
Rubber	31.6								7.0	NAS		29.3
Motor vehicles (including components)	21.4	21.3	20.4	17.6	21.7	23.2	29.0	29.0	18,2			21.0
Metal manufacturing and products	11.4	17.0	17.4	9.3	25.3	33.6	15.0	8.6	3.4	22.8	39.0	13.1
Total	20.1	20.2	18.9	12.3	21.4	32.9	26.2	29.3	8.6	22.3	39.0	18.4

Low research intensity												
Building materials	21.1	39.5	40.2	NAS	52.0	30.4	NAS	NAS	3.0			30.5
Tobacco	29.0	58.7	58.7	NAS		61.0						44.0
Beverages	23.8	14.3	14.3			14.3			NAS	5.0	5.0	18.3
Food	20.7	56.4	48.0		33.4	36.9	NAS		2.1	6.2	9.3	33.3
Paper and wood products	13.7	33.8	41.8	NAS		50.7	23.2	35.3		32.5	32.5	19.7
Textiles, apparel, leather goods	10.8	38.1	38.1		NAS	41.7			12.4	NAS	NAS	19.2
Publishing and printing	6.3	20.8	22.9			22.9	NAS	NAS				10.4
Total	18.8	48.5	45.0	13.2	44.7	70.9	29.3		5.9	21.5	25.6	28.9
Other manufacturing	16.9	0.8	0.8	1.0	NAS	NAS						6.6
Total	29.2	37.5	36.6	18.5	28.6	41.8	43.0	33.1	6.7	20.4	31.8	29.5

NAS—results not given for reasons of confidentiality and disclosure. The information is, however, included in the appropriate aggregates.
* Sales of overseas affiliates and associate companies (excluding goods imported from parent for resale) divided by total worldwide sales of group. Expressed as a percentage.
† Any firm for which an estimate of overseas production was available from any of the sources described in Dunning and Pearce; 523 of the 866 firms in the sample are covered.

Source: John Dunning and Robert Pearce, *The World's Largest Industrial Enterprises* (Westmead, England: Gower Publishing, 1981), p. 119, table 6.1a. Based on sales data from *Fortune,* May 8 and August 14, 1978. Ratios obtained from survey conducted by Dunning and Pearce and from other sources.

from Italy. The trend in service sector FDI appears to follow the worldwide increase in white-collar, office-type employment, and especially the decreasing growth rate of manufacturing relative to services in the industrial countries.

More disaggregated data for FDI from other countries are much harder to obtain. In a 1979 survey, Dunning and Pearce (1981) found evidence, shown in Table 4-6, relevant to FDI from many of the developed countries of Europe, plus the United States and Japan. Table 4-6 presents the ratio between the sales of foreign affiliates and total worldwide sales, aggregated into 19 industrial categories. Since foreign direct investment is the basis for foreign production, we can conclude from the table that the industries most heavily involved in FDI are petroleum, tobacco, and office equipment. In each of these industries, firms from all countries averaged over 40 percent of their worldwide sales from overseas affiliates, that is, from FDI projects.

Direct Investment by Company

Since ultimately we are concerned about the firms that engage in FDI, let us turn finally to a view of the companies most heavily involved in this activity. Using the *Business Week* and *Fortune* annual surveys of the largest U.S. and non-U.S. industrial corporations, Table 4-7 compiles the leading (in sales) five firms in each of 18 industrial categories. Notice that most of these firms are indeed U.S.-based and that they are all multibillion-dollar enterprises. In addition, though not demonstrated in the table, they are all important multinational enterprises, owning and operating on average over 30 foreign affiliates per firm.

Foreign Direct Investment in the United States

The Pattern by Industry

Looking specifically at foreign direct investment coming into the United States, we see a pattern similar to that in the rest of the industrial countries. That is, the dominant industries are petroleum, manufacturing, and services (mainly trade, real estate, banking, and insurance). The growth has been more rapid in services than in the other major sectors. These patterns can be seen in Figure 4-1, which traces FDI into the United States since the early 1970s. In the 1980s, not only has foreign direct investment grown faster than U.S. FDI going abroad, but it has also grown faster than the U.S. economy overall. That is, incoming FDI has provided a substantial boost to U.S. national income (and also forced U.S. firms to compete even harder in their own domestic market).

Table 4-7 **The Largest Five Firms in 18 Industries** (ranked by annual sales in millions of U.S. dollars, 1985)

	Sales 1985	Sales 1977	Growth of Sales, 1977–1985 (in percent)	Rank Position, 1977
Aerospace				
United Technologies (U.S.)	14,992	5,551	270.1	2
Boeing (U.S.)	13,636	4,018	339.4	3
Rockwell International (U.S.)	11,741	5,858	200.4	1
McDonnell Douglas (U.S.)	11,478	3,545	323.8	4
Lockheed (U.S.)	9,535	3,373	282.7	5
Office equipment				
IBM (U.S.)	50,056	18,133	276.0	1
Xerox (U.S.)	8,732	5,077	172.0	2
Digital Equipment Corporation (U.S.)	7,029	1,059	663.7	—
Honeywell (U.S.)	6,625	2,911	227.6	5
Hewlett-Packard (U.S.)	6,571	1,360	483.2	—
Petroleum				
Exxon (U.S.)	86,673	54,126	160.1	1
Royal Dutch Shell (Netherlands/UK)	81,744	39,680	206.0	2
Mobil (U.S.)	55,960	32,128	174.2	3
Texaco (U.S.)	47,500	27,920	170.1	4
Chevron (U.S.)	41,742	—	—	—
Electronics				
General Electric (U.S.)	28,285	17,519	161.5	1
Matsushita (Japan)	20,749	6,888	301.2	—
Hitachi (Japan)	20,525	8,222	249.6	5
Philips (Netherlands)	18,079	12,702	142.3	3
Siemens (Germany)	17,834	10,641	167.6	4
Chemicals and pharmaceuticals				
Du Pont (U.S.)	29,483	9,435	312.5	2
Bayer (Germany)	15,598	9,220	169.2	3
BASF (Germany)	15,072	9,116	165.3	4
Hoechst (Germany)	14,510	10,042	144.5	1
ICI (UK)	13,895	8,139	170.7	5

Table 4-7 *(continued)*

	Sales 1985	Sales 1977	Growth of Sales, 1977–1985 (in percent)	Rank Position, 1977
Industrial and farm equipment				
Mitsubishi (Japan)	14,112	8,089	174.5	1
Daewoo (Korea)	8,698	851	1,022.1	—
Caterpillar Tractor (US)	6,725	5,849	115.0	3
Mannesmann (Germany)	6,171	5,049	122.2	—
BTR (UK)	5,028	—	—	—
Rubber				
Goodyear (U.S.)	9,585	6,628	144.6	1
Michelin (France)	5,191	3,549	146.3	4
Firestone (U.S.)	3,794	4,427	85.7	2
Dunlop-Pirelli (UK/Italy)	3,650	4,233	86.2	3
Bridgestone (Japan)	3,624	1,556	232.9	—
Motor vehicles				
General Motors (U.S.)	96,372	54,961	175.3	1
Ford Motor (U.S.)	52,774	37,841	139.5	2
Toyota Motor (Japan)	26,040	9,601	271.2	—
Chrysler (U.S.)	21,255	16,708	127.2	3
Nissan (Japan)	18,226	7,677	237.4	—
Metal manufacture and production				
IRI (Italy)	26,758	—	—	—
U.S. Steel (U.S.)	18,429	9,610	191.8	1
Voest-Alpine (Austria)	13,633	2,732	499.0	—
Nippon Steel (Japan)	12,535	8,911	140.7	2
Thyssen (Germany)	11,358	8,325	136.4	3
Building material				
Saint Gobain (France)	7,556	6,477	116.7	1
Owens-Illinois (U.S.)	3,674	2,767	132.9	2
Owens-Corning Fiberglas (U.S.)	3,305	1,480	223.3	3
USG (U.S.)	2,526	1,177	214.6	—
Jim Walter (U.S.)	2,256	1,422	158.6	—

Table 4-7 *(continued)*

	Sales 1985	Sales 1977	Growth of Sales, 1977–1985 (in percent)	Rank Position, 1977
Tobacco				
R. J. Reynolds (U.S.)	15,732	4,816	326.7	2
Philip Morris (U.S.)	12,149	3,849	315.6	3
BAT Industries (UK)	11,397	6,616	172.3	1
American Brands (U.S.)	7,308	2,892	252.7	5
Rothmans International (UK)	3,314	883	375.3	—
Beverages				
PepsiCo (U.S.)	8,057	3,546	227.2	2
Coca-Cola (U.S.)	7,904	3,560	222.0	1
Anheuser-Busch (U.S.)	7,000	1,838	380.8	3
Grand Metropolitan (UK)	6,037	—	—	—
Allied Breweries (UK)	3,369	1,393	241.9	5
Food				
Unilever (UK/Netherlands)	21,627	15,965	135.5	1
Nestlé (Switzerland)	17,159	8,396	204.4	2
Beatrice Foods (U.S.)	12,046	5,829	227.8	3
Kraft (U.S.)	9,942	5,239	189.8	5
Sara Lee (U.S.)	8,080	—	—	—
Paper and wood products				
Georgia Pacific Portland (U.S.)	6,716	3,675	182.7	1
Champion International (U.S.)	5,770	3,442	167.6	3
Weyerhaeuser (U.S.)	5,206	3,283	158.6	4
International Paper (U.S.)	4,502	3,669	122.7	2
Kimberly-Clark (U.S.)	4,073	1,726	236.0	—
Textiles, Apparel, and Leather				
Haci Omer Sabanci (Turkey)	2,934	2,903	101.1	1
Burlington Industries (U.S.)	2,832	2,388	118.6	3
Courtaulds (UK)	2,702	2,618	103.2	2
Interco (U.S.)	2,509	1,566	160.2	5
Kanebo (Japan)	2,162	1,807	119.6	4

Table 4-7 *(concluded)*

	Sales 1985	Sales 1977	Growth of Sales, 1977–1985 (in percent)	Rank Position, 1977
Publishing and printing				
Time Inc. (U.S.)	3,404	1,250	272.3	1
Dai Nippon Printing (Japan)	2,997	1,173	255.5	3
Times Mirror (U.S.)	2,959	1,129	261.6	5
Dun & Bradstreet (U.S.)	2,772	—	—	—
Bertelsmann (Germany)	2,415	1,173	205.9	2
Leisure-time industries				
Eastman Kodak (U.S.)	10,631	5,967	178.2	1
Warner Communications (U.S.)	2,235	1,144	195.4	2
MCA (U.S.)	2,099	878	239.1	3
Walt Disney (U.S.)	2,093	—	—	—
Brunswick (U.S.)	1,539	1,000	153.9	4
Other manufacturing				
Mining Mining (U.S.)	7,846	3,980	197.1	3
Ruhrkohle (Germany)	7,647	4,730	161.7	1
CBS (U.S.)	4,677	2,776	168.5	4
Charbonnage de France (France)	4,384	2,392	183.3	—
PPG Industries (U.S.)	4,346	2,506	173.4	5

Sources: *Fortune,* "The Fortune 500," April 28, 1986; *Fortune,* "The International 500," August 4, 1986; *Business Week,* "International Corporate Scoreboard," July 22, 1985; and John Dunning and Robert Pearce, *The World's Largest Industrial Enterprises* (Westmead, England: Gower Publishing, 1981).

The Pattern by Country of Origin

The main countries whose firms are undertaking this flow of FDI into the United States are, not surprisingly, the same countries that follow the United States in overall FDI worldwide: Great Britain, the Netherlands, Japan, Canada, Germany, Switzerland, and other European countries. Table 4-8 shows a disaggregation of the recent stock of FDI according to both industry and country of origin.

The British lead in overall FDI in the U.S. market is not surprising, given Britain's number two position in worldwide FDI and its colonial ties to this country. Dutch direct investment, especially in petroleum (Royal Dutch/Shell) and manufacturing (Philips and Unilever), surprisingly ranks second,

Figure 4-1 **Foreign Direct Investment into the United States**

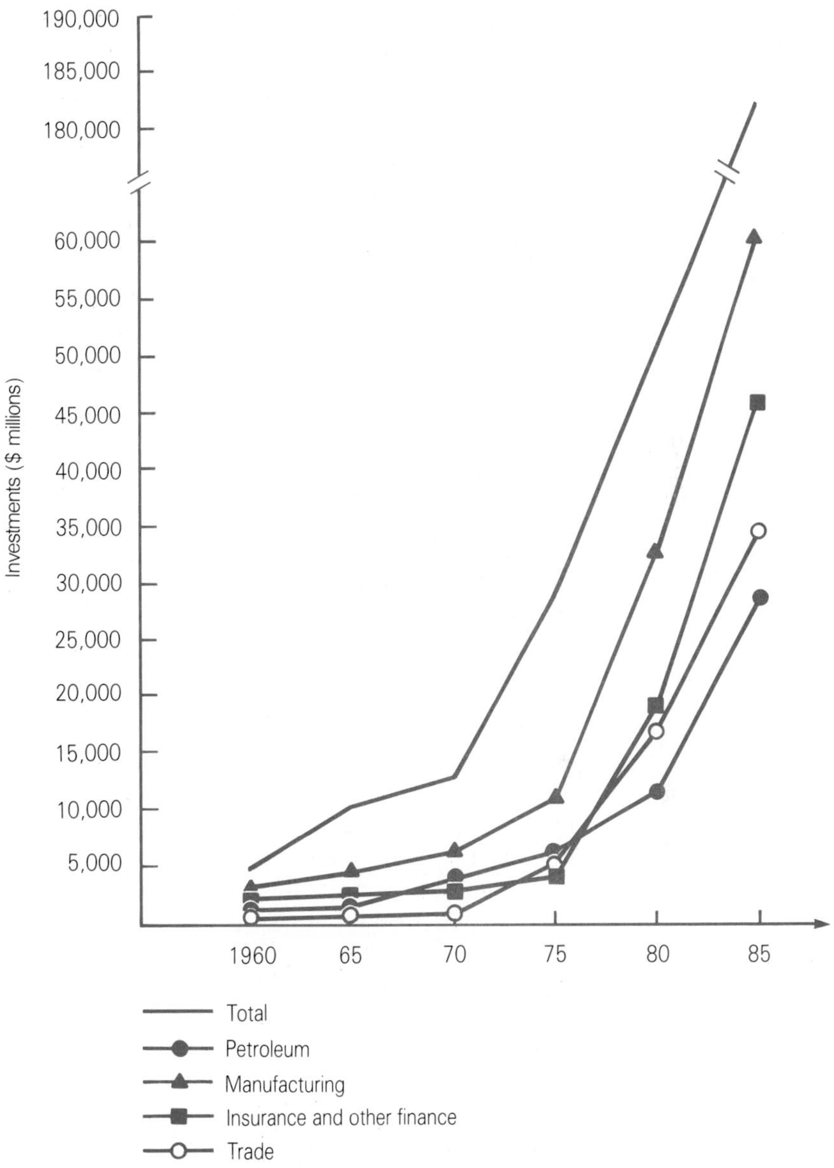

Table 4-8 **Foreign Direct Investment Position in the United States by Industry and Country** (in millions of U.S. dollars)

Industry	United Kingdom	Netherlands	Japan	Canada	Germany	Switzerland	France
Petroleum	12,246	11,315	31	1,659	n.a.	n.a.	n.a.
Manufacturing	11,884	12,986	2,621	5,130	6,198	7,431	5,485
Foods	2,613	n.a.	149	178	31	n.a.	348
Chemicals	4,035	3,488	267	227	3,838	2,185	2,820
Machinery	1,942	1,940	624	1,206	1,066	671	205
Wholesale and retail trade	6,847	2,544	11,822	2,143	4,726	778	581
Banking	2,539	1,570	2,176	1,332	222	88	483
Real estate	4,623	2,325	1,054	2,580	1,049	444	26
Total	43,766	36,124	19,116	16,678	14,417	11,040	6,295

Source: Department of Commerce, *Survey of Current Business,* August 1986.

far ahead of Germany and Japan. Canada, with its proximity to this market, ranks among the leading source countries in virtually every industrial category.

The Major Foreign Investors in the United States

The specific firms that have taken the largest FDI positions in the U.S. economy tend to follow the list of the largest firms in international business throughout the world. Table 4-9 lists the 25 largest foreign direct investors in the United States in 1985, along with some of their characteristics. Note that these firms compete in industries where U.S. competitors are also strong. A fundamental reason for their ability to survive in the U.S. marketplace is simply that demand is large enough to absorb multiple competitors. That is, the foreign firms do not have to outcompete American firms to survive. This is particularly true in the petroleum sector, where 4 of the 25 compete. The competitive advantages that the foreign firms do possess appear to stem largely from proprietary technology, goodwill based on high quality and performance, and lower costs—very similar to those of successful U.S. firms.

Current Trends

FDI in the United States has grown tremendously during the 1980s. This phenomenon may be attributed to a variety of causes, including the recovery of the United States from the early-1980s recession before other industrial nations, the devaluation of the dollar relative to other widely traded currencies in the mid-1980s, and the faster growth of non-U.S. MNEs in the 1970s and 1980s as they caught up to U.S. firms in size and geographic scope. In the

Table 4-9 **The 25 Largest Foreign Investments in the United States**

Foreign Investor	Country	U.S. Company	Percent Owned	Industry	Revenue ($ millions)
1. Seagram Company, Ltd.	Canada	Joseph E. Seagram & Sons	100	Spirits and wine	1,564
		Du Pont	21	Chemicals, energy	33,223
					34,787
2. Anglo American Corporation of South Africa, Ltd.	South Africa	Phibro-Salomon	26	Metal trading, brokerage	26,703
	Bermuda	Engelhard Corporation	27	Metals	2,019
		Adobe Oil & Gasoline	28	Energy	203
		Inspiration Consol Copper	50	Copper	165
		Terra Chemicals	100	Fertilizer	273
	UK	National Mine Service	51	Mining equipment	77
					29,540
3. Royal Dutch/Shell Group	Netherlands	Shell Oil	69	Energy	20,062
	UK	Scallop	100	Energy	
		Billiton Exploration	100	Metals	1,560
		Billiton Metals	100	Metals	
		Ocean Minerals	30	Metals	
					21,622
4. British Petroleum Plc	UK	Standard Oil Ohio	53	Energy	13,152
		BP North America	100	Energy	n.a.
					13,152
5. Mitsui & Co., Ltd.	Japan	Alumax	45	Aluminum	1,004
		Mitsui & Company, USA	100	Multicompany	5,802 (est.)
					6,806 (est.)
6. Flick Group	Germany	W.R. Grace	28	Multicompany	6,128
7. BAT Industries, Plc.	UK	BATUS	100	Paper, retailing, tobacco	5,165
8. Générale Occidentale	France	Grand Union	100	Supermarkets	4,137
		Diamond International	100	Packaging, lumber	781
					4,918

Table 4-9 *(concluded)*

Foreign Investor	Country	U.S. Company	Percent Owned	Industry	Revenue ($ millions)
9. Tengelmann Group	Germany	Great A&P Tea	51	Supermarkets	4,608
10. Régie Nationale des Usines Renault	France	American Motors	46	Automotive	2,878
		Mack Truck	20	Automotive	1,292
					4,170
11. Philips	Netherlands	North American Philips	61	Electronics	3,168
					325
		Signetics	100	Semiconductors	3,493
12. Bayer AG	Germany	Mobay Chemical	100	Chemicals	1,132
		Miles Laboratories	100	Health care	1,076
		Compugraphic	79	Photocomposition	276
		Helena Chemical	100	Chemicals	
		Haarmann & Reimer	100	Chemicals	816
		Agfa-Gevaert	100	Photographics	
					3,300
13. Unilever NV	Netherlands	Lever Brothers	100	Consumer goods	
		Thomas J. Lipton	100	Food	3,132
		National Starch & Chemicals	100	Adhesives, starch	
14. Volkswagenwerk AG	Germany	Volkswagen of America	100	Automotive	2,454
		Triumph-Adler (North America)	100	Office equipment	600 (est.)
					3,054
15. Midland Bank Plc.	UK	Crocker National Corporation	57	Banking	2,894
16. Hongkong & Shanghai Banking Corporation	Hong Kong	Marine Midland Banks	51	Banking	2,412
17. Schlumberger NV	Netherlands Antilles	Schlumberger Technology	100	Oilfield services electronics	2,400

18. Nestlé	Switzerland	Nestlé	100	Food	
		Libby, McNeill & Libby	100	Food	
		Stouffer Corporation	100	Food, restaurant	2,341
		Alcon Laboratories	100	Drugs	
		Beech-Nut	100	Food	
		Other companies	100	Food, drinks, health care	
19. Brascan, Ltd.	Canada	Scott Paper	24	Paper products	2,293
20. Petrofina SA	Belgium	America Petrofina	75	Energy	2,242
		Petrofina Delaware	100	Oil and gas exploration	49
					2,291
21. Canadian Pacific, Ltd.	Canada	Soo Line Railroad	56	Railroad	299
		Canadian Pacific Enterprises US	100	Agricultural products, minerals, china	1,926
					2,225
22. Française des Petroles	France				
	Canada	Total Petroleum	100	Energy	2,200(est.)
23. George Weston, Ltd.	Canada	Interbake, Inc.	100	Biscuits	375
		Stroehmann Brothers	100	Bakery	
		Eastern Fine Paper	100	Paper products	
	Canada	Peter J. Schmitt	100	Food wholesaling	
		National Tea	100	Supermarkets	1,722
					2,097
24. CIBA-GEIGY, Ltd.	Switzerland	CIBA-GEIGY Corporation	100	Chemicals, drugs	1,965
		ILFORD Corporation	100	Photographic products	44
					2,009
25. Grand Metropolitan	UK	GrandMet USA	100	Tobacco, drinks and food	1,347
		Intercontinental Hotels	100	Hotels	449
					1,796

Source: Adapted from *Forbes*, July 4, 1983.

Assembly of Volkswagen automobiles in the New Stanton plant in Pennsylvania.
Courtesy Volkswagen of America, Inc.

late 1980s, the threat of increased protectionism in the United States has encouraged many Japanese firms (such as the auto manufacturers) to set up operations in this country to avoid the possibility of harm due to greater import restrictions.

Because of the very large existing base of U.S. FDI overseas, the *growth rate* of FDI in the United States is likely to exceed that of outgoing FDI into the 1990s. Whether U.S. or non-U.S. firms will be more successful in foreign markets is quite another question—and one that U.S. MNE managers will help resolve in the future. The perhaps even more important question—whether U.S. firms will be able to survive competition *in the United States* from their foreign rivals—also remains to be answered. The grounds on which the competition will take place will almost certainly be the development of sustainable competitive advantages by the successful firms.

Explanations of the Foreign Direct Investment Process

How can the flows of FDI and the shifts in the company and country composition of FDI be explained? There is no single theory that covers all the characteristics of the foreign investment process. Several views have been presented, however, that offer partial explanations of what is observed. The theory of the international product cycle, discussed in Chapter 3, clarifies several of the reasons for FDI. The theory of competitive advantage, presented in Chapter 2, sheds some light on company characteristics that often lead to FDI. The comparative cost view, presented in the appendix to Chapter 3, adds some useful points regarding the choice of FDI versus other market-serving alternatives. Dunning's "eclectic view" focuses attention on three types of variables that play important parts in explaining FDI. Finally, the concept of internalization can be used to tie together several of the other strands of thinking about FDI. This section reviews each of these theories as it relates to foreign direct investment.

International Product Cycle

The theory of the international product cycle hypothesizes that foreign direct investment (*or* host country production by local firms) will take place in countries that originally import a new product from the country where it is developed. That is, once a product has been introduced successfully into one country, subsequent export and foreign manufacture generally follow. If the innovating company chooses to produce overseas, then its establishment of a foreign affiliate is FDI. By the time the product arrives at the standardized stage, cost considerations are foremost and low-cost production locations are sought, perhaps in low-wage areas of developed countries or in less developed countries. The international product cycle has been discussed in some detail in Chapter 3; here an example may offer additional insights.

Radio Corporation of America (RCA), originally a division of General Electric Company, began producing television sets in the late 1920s. Television had been invented and reinvented in various forms during the previous 30 years by scientists in several countries, but RCA was one of two firms to introduce the product into the market successfully, in the early 1940s. (Du Mont Laboratories was the other firm that began marketing televisions, in 1939, along with RCA.) Initially, TV sets and programming were sold primarily in the United States, though sales occurred in Great Britain as well. The market for television remained very small until after World War II.

Domestic competition in television manufacture arose during the late 1940s, from General Electric itself (which had sold RCA) and from American Telephone & Telegraph. The market for television began to grow rapidly, with about 140,000 sets per month sold by 1948. RCA began exporting into the Canadian and European markets in the late 1940s.

Such U.S. competitors as Westinghouse and Admiral entered the market during the 1950s. The Japanese producers Sony and Panasonic introduced competing products in the early 1960s, and by about 1965 television was in the maturing product stage. At that point (in 1964), RCA decided to use direct investment in Canada to serve that market with locally manufactured picture tubes. At about the same time, it established a manufacturing plant in England to serve the European market.

Ultimately, cost conditions became the overwhelming factor in TV competition, and RCA followed several firms into offshore assembly, choosing Taiwan (in 1970) and Ciudad Juárez in Mexico (in 1969) as its bases. Now the firm produces parts and components in more than a dozen countries, including the offshore assembly sites, and sells them in more than 50 countries. RCA has followed the international product cycle through all three stages, producing first in the United States, then in Canada and Western Europe, and now also in less developed countries.[8]

Competitive Advantage

The theory of competitive advantage, presented in Chapter 2, explains foreign direct investment as one of the many ways in which a firm may capitalize on its proprietary assets. RCA was able to use FDI to take advantage of its new technology. Similarly, Texas Instruments and other calculator manufacturers have used FDI to assemble their products in low-cost countries. Of course, not all FDI is based on firms' taking advantage of proprietary technology. Relatively standardized products such as processed foods are produced and sold by foreign direct investors in many countries. Oil companies invest abroad not only to explore for oil but also to operate gas stations and to produce and sell nonproprietary petrochemicals. Producers of farm machinery sell their tractors and other machines through exports to their own sales offices in many countries, and they also assemble many kinds of equipment abroad in direct investment projects.

Consider Beatrice Companies (formerly Beatrice Foods) as an example. This $9 billion company has affiliates in 31 foreign countries, many of which are joint ventures with local partners. Beatrice managers consider one of their firm's major competitive advantages to be brand loyalty, built up over many years with many products. For example, Beatrice subsidiaries make Tropicana juices, Swiss Miss cocoa, La Choy Chinese food, Meadow Gold milk, Fisher nuts, Murray cookies, Samsonite luggage, Culligan water treatment, and many other products. Virtually none of these products would be considered "high-tech," but Beatrice has maintained a highly competitive position in many markets through careful product positioning. One senior Beatrice manager in the international division explains that the company's key advantages are product and country experience, which have resulted in extensive national distribution systems in many countries and in very substantial positive brand recognition. Product technology and economies of scale in production, on the other hand, play very little role in Beatrice's competitive position relative to other firms.

Beatrice has found that foreign direct investment provides a highly successful vehicle for utilizing the firm's competitive advantages. Very little exporting is done among the Beatrice affiliates worldwide, since economies of scale are relatively unimportant, and most products are produced in host countries. A local production presence offers the company the ability to react quickly to shifts in consumer demands—a crucial need in the highly competitive consumer goods businesses in which Beatrice operates.

Comparative Cost

The comparative cost view of FDI follows on the theory of comparative advantage, discussed in Chapter 3. In this case, we look at an individual firm's choice of production locations based on *delivered* cost to its relevant markets. Just as the theory of comparative advantage showed the appropriate *country* to produce and export a given product, based on production costs, the extension to FDI focuses on a *company's* use of this information. If it were really less costly to produce bananas in Honduras and appliances in the United States, then United Fruit Corporation should look at Honduras as a site for FDI to produce bananas, which can then be exported to the U.S. market. (Leave the appliances to another company!) Indeed, this is exactly what United Fruit (whose brand name for bananas is Chiquita) has done—not only in Honduras but also in El Salvador, Costa Rica, Ecuador, and other countries where banana production is very inexpensive, due to climatic conditions and inexpensive labor.

In the final analysis, what counts is *delivered* cost. So United Fruit or any other foreign investor must consider not only the production costs involved in the foreign country but also the transportation costs and tariff or other restrictions that may apply to the product. This differs from traditional comparative advantage theory, which focused only on production costs. Even if bananas could be produced more cheaply in Honduras than in Costa Rica, and exported to Costa Rica, firms probably could not take advantage of this condition, because the government of Costa Rica places tariffs and other restrictions on imports. Similar problems often arise as well from high transportation costs: cement can be produced more cheaply in Colombia than in Venezuela, but the cost of delivering it to the Venezuelan market from a Colombian city such as Bogotá or Barranquilla is much higher than the production cost difference. So each country produces cement for domestic consumption and does not export it. The appropriate way for a company to take advantage of this situation would be to invest directly in each country to produce cement for the local market.

Dunning's Eclectic View

John Dunning (1977) has proposed a multifaceted "theory" of FDI that includes emphases on country-specific variables such as production costs and regulatory constraints, company-specific (ownership) variables such as proprietary skills and scale economies, and internalization variables related to the firm's choice to utilize its proprietary capabilities through its own affiliates or through dealings with other firms. Each of these three kinds of variables has been the focus of theories of international trade and investment.

Dunning's view is "eclectic" in that it packages a number of competitive advantages together and uses the concept of internalization to provide decision-making rules.

Dunning's view is quite useful in forcing the decision maker to consider not only cost factors or demand forecasts but also the other key issues. Thus, the size of the market may well justify entering it, but *location* factors may call for exports rather than FDI. Similarly, local production costs may favor direct investment, but if the company's resources (its *ownership* advantages) are too limited, then FDI may be infeasible and licensing a local firm (that is, *not* internalizing) may offer a viable alternative. By combining three distinct perspectives, Dunning's view enables the decision maker to avoid the trap of narrow-minded focus on only a part of the full picture.

To reiterate, Dunning's **eclectic view** states that the FDI decision should be made on the grounds of these three factors:

1. *Ownership advantages:* the company's competitive advantages, such as proprietary technology, management skills, goodwill, and economies of scale.
2. *Location advantages:* the relevant cost, risk, and regulatory conditions in the countries under consideration. These include national production costs, tariffs, taxes, international transportation costs, and political risks.
3. *Internationalization advantages:* the benefits that the firm would realize by itself operating in the host country versus the benefits of operating through a local distributor, licensee, or other contractee. (See the next section.)

Internalization

Chapter 2 presented the idea that vertical or horizontal integration of a firm across national boundaries was a characteristic of the MNE. In fact, that integration is itself foreign direct investment—the firm that buys a metal mine or an oil well abroad is undertaking FDI, just as the firm that sets up a restaurant abroad similar to its domestic restaurants is undertaking FDI.

Internalization is a very useful concept because it focuses attention on the decision to internalize or not to internalize across national borders—that is, the decision to use or not to use FDI. The optimal decision should be based on the product's stage in the product cycle, the competitive advantages of the firm, and the costs of this alternative relative to others that are available. That is, internalization can be used as a broad label to encompass each of the more precisely focused views discussed above. The foreign investment decision then can be stated as follows: The firm should internalize foreign market and supply opportunities up to the point that the additional costs of internalizing outweigh the additional benefits of doing so.

Other Explanations for Foreign Direct Investment

A number of additional explanations for FDI have come from many different social science disciplines.[9] Two of the more important ones are noted here.

Some political scientists writing about the global spread of capitalism have viewed the process of FDI as the natural tendency of capitalist firms, which need to find new markets for their products once existing ones have been saturated. The "exploitation" of foreign markets, then, enmeshes these markets in the international capitalist system.[10] This view of FDI emphasizes its negative aspects, namely control of part of the local economy by foreign owners and transfers of funds to the parent companies. The view is important because it is held by policymakers in some countries and because it always provides a rationale for penalizing foreign firms when a scapegoat is needed for economic or political problems.

Another view, presented by Jean Boddewyn (1983), looks at FDI in three steps: necessary conditions, motivations, and precipitating factors. This view regards virtually all of the reasons for FDI discussed above as *conditions* that may make FDI desirable. Boddewyn points out that all of these conditions are based on the premise or *motivation* that the firm is managed to maximize profits. Each condition offers a way in which the firm can pursue its central goal of profit maximization—for example, reducing costs, enlarging market share, or creating new products. Finally, there must be some *triggering factor* that induces the firm to take advantage of the conditions to seek its central goal. This last point is quite important. Firms have infinite possible strategies at their disposal; but for FDI to result, a clear definition of goals and acceptable alternatives, plus some precipitating event (such as a period of negative earnings or a change in leadership), are required.

In sum, each of the views of FDI presented above offers insights into the managerial and regulatory issues related to such investment. The company manager can benefit from utilizing the various views in considering the firm's choices for doing business in foreign countries, whether it be market-serving or supply-seeking business. The government policymaker can better understand the motivations of company managers by seeing the key factors that affect company investment decisions.

Disinvestment

This chapter has looked mainly at the process of entry into foreign direct investment, without considering in any detail the operation of the foreign affiliate once it has been established. The termination of a foreign affiliate, that is, **disinvestment** (or divestment), can be seen as almost a mirror image of the entry decision. Using Dunning's three-factor view of FDI, disinvestment can be rationalized when any of the conditions for FDI disappears. If a firm ceases to possess a competitive (or ownership) advantage relative to other firms in the host country, the profitability of operating there may disappear. Or if political or economic changes in the host country make the local project no longer viable, the reason for being there (i.e., locational advantage) may disappear. Finally, the local affiliate may be unjustified if the firm finds it no longer useful to internalize the activity, but may sell or rent it to another firm. In short, disinvestment may be justified once the conditions that originally justified FDI cease to exist.

In Boddewyn's terms, once changes in the conditions make FDI unattractive relative to other alternatives, and profitability would be better served by not operating the affiliate, then all it takes is some precipitating factor to make the disinvestment decision. This precipitating factor may be the assignment of a new manager to supervise the company division in which the project is based; if the project shows poor results in its sales, profits, or costs, the new manager may look to disinvestment as a method to eliminate the problem. Another factor that may stimulate the firm to consider disinvesting is the threat of host government constraints—ranging from expropriation, to higher taxes, to limits on financial transfers. In any of these cases, the decision to disinvest is usually made at the home office of the firm, by a senior decision maker. This contrasts with the FDI decision, which is often proposed by a middle-level manager or division and simply approved by the home office.[11]

The firm can utilize disinvestment strategically in the context of the international product cycle. A product in the innovation stage is generally produced in one country and sold domestically and through exports. As the product enters the maturing stage, market and cost conditions may justify FDI in host countries for local sales. As the product enters the standardized stage, cost conditions may justify closing high-cost production sites in favor of sites located in low-cost regions or countries. So, especially in the standardized product stage, disinvestment may be part of a planned, strategic process of global production and sales in the MNE.

For example, the Monsanto Corporation, a multinational chemical company, operated synthetic fiber plants for many years in several Western European countries. During the early 1970s, these operations became unprofitable due to price competition from firms that faced lower costs of production. After several years of losses, Monsanto decided to sell all of its synthetic fiber business in Europe, divesting the whole set of subsidiaries.[12] Rather than compete in the standardized stage of the product cycle for these products, Monsanto decided to place its resources into other products in earlier stages of the cycle.

Conclusions

FDI is a complex form of international business, necessarily involving the transfer of a company's ownership to foreign owners and typically involving transfers of funds, people, products, and other items. During the post-World War II period, the largest sector in which FDI has taken place has been manufacturing, though the single industry with the most foreign investment has been petroleum. The single largest source country for FDI is the United States, while German and Japanese FDI has been growing at the fastest rate during the past decade.

Firms undertake FDI to serve new markets, to obtain needed inputs for their domestic businesses, and generally for many of the same reasons that they undertake domestic capital investment. The reasons for going overseas also include international diversification, which allows firms to reduce the variability of their earnings. Foreign disinvestment may be a final step in a firm's strategy in a particular country, though it is by no means the logical end of FDI.

Foreign direct investment is *the* activity that makes a company multinational. It should be viewed, however, as one among several alternatives for serving host country markets (or for obtaining necessary factors of production). How can the manager decide when to utilize this alternative? Based on the criteria laid out above, the company manager needs to consider:

1. Incremental cash flows from the project, as with any other capital investment.
2. The costs of undertaking this alternative relative to the costs of other alternatives available to the firm, such as exports or some other contractual form.
3. The strategic fit of the project within the firm's global activities, taking into account the firm's competitive advantages.
4. Related to 3, the issue of whether this type of internalization is preferable to other strategies, such as contracting with outside firms.

Thus, armed with a pro forma capital budget and a statement of the firm's competitive advantages and strategy, the manager can decide whether or not FDI is the appropriate alternative to serve the company's goals in any given situation.

Questions

1. What do you think are the reasons that Imperial Chemicals Industries (ICI) decided to invest in the U.S. market? How would these correspond to RCA's reasons for setting up manufacturing in Singapore?
2. In general, why would a company use FDI rather than exports to serve a foreign market?
3. Are direct investment and disinvestment simply mirror images of each other? What are the key differences between the decision process for direct investment and the decision process for divestment?
4. Compare competitive advantage, comparative advantage, and the international product cycle as explanations of FDI. How are the three theories related?

5. How does the concept of internalization relate to FDI?
6. Why have Japanese automobile manufacturers been setting up operations in the United States in the 1980s? How do your reasons fit with the theories discussed in this chapter?
7. Which countries are the main sources of foreign direct investment in other countries? Why? Which countries are the main recipients of FDI? Why?
8. Which companies have been the main foreign direct investors in the 1970s and 1980s? What enables these companies to compete in the various markets that they serve?
9. Observers note that the United States is becoming a service-based economy. Why has foreign direct investment by service firms not grown dramatically relative to FDI in other sectors?
10. What are the key differences between a domestic direct investment project and a foreign direct investment project? Should both types of project be evaluated similarly?

References

Aharoni, Yair. *The Foreign Investment Decision Process.* Boston: Harvard Business School, 1966.

Boddewyn, Jean. "Foreign and Domestic Divestment and Investment Decisions," *Journal of International Business Studies,* December 1983.

Buckley, Peter, and Mark Casson. *The Future of Multinational Enterprise.* New York: Holmes & Meier, 1976.

Calvet, Luis. "A Synthesis of Foreign Direct Investment Theories and Theories of the Multinational Firm." *Journal of International Business Studies,"* Spring-Summer 1981.

Casson, Mark. *The Theory of Foreign Direct Investment.* University of Reading Discussion Papers, no. 50, November 1980.

Caves, Richard. "International Corporations: The Industrial Economics of Foreign Investment." *Economica,* February 1971.

Dunning, John. "Trade, Location of Economic Activity, and the MNE: A Search for an Eclectic Approach." In *The International Allocation of Economic Activity,* ed. Bertil Ohlin. New York: Holmes & Meier, 1977.

Dunning, John, and Robert Pearce. *The World's Largest Industrial Enterprises.* Westmead, England: Gower Publishing, 1981.

Grosse, Robert. *The Theory of Foreign Direct Investment,* University of South Carolina Essays in International Business, no. 3, December 1981.

Hymer, Stephen. *The International Operations of National Firms: A Study of Direct Foreign Investment.* Cambridge, Mass.: MIT Press, 1976. (Originally published in 1960.)

Vernon, Raymond. *Storm over the Multinationals.* Cambridge, Mass.: Harvard University Press, 1977.

Endnotes

1. This distinction is often difficult to draw when one firm buys partial ownership of another firm. Such an investment may be direct, even if only 5-10 percent ownership is purchased, if the investor is given management control. It may be a portfolio investment, even if 50 percent or more is purchased, if the investor does not exercise management control. For measurement of FDI, the U.S. Department of Commerce arbitrarily defines ownership of 10 percent or more as direct investment.
2. "GM-Toyota Accord to Produce Autos Gets Final Approval," *The Wall Street Journal,* April 12, 1984, p. 10.
3. Governments may also be central decision makers in FDI, because many of the largest third-world multinational corporations are government owned, as are many multinational corporations in Europe (e.g., national oil companies, French banks, and British Steel).
4. See, for example, Grosse (1981), which cites new evidence and several additional studies.
5. United States Code, Section 10A ff.
6. The "obsolescing bargain," discussed in Chapter 22, may wipe out expected profitability once the plant has been built. That is, once the firm has committed its funds and built the local facility, the host government gains a better bargaining position, since the physical investment is in place. The host government may then demand a better sharing of the gains from the investment—through higher taxes, greater local management and ownership, and so on.
7. Some data on FDI from developing countries have been compiled by Louis Wells in *Third World Multinationals* (Cambridge, Mass.: MIT Press, 1982).
8. "Television," *Encyclopaedia Britannica,* 1969; Stanley Kemper, *A History of Television* (Atlanta: Television Encyclopedia Press, 1965); and *RCA: An Historical Perspective* (New York; RCA, 1978).
9. See Grosse (1981).
10. Theodore Moran, "Foreign Expansion as an Institutional Necessity for US Corporate Capitalism," *World Politics,* (April 1973).
11. See Boddewyn (1983); and S. C. Gilmour, *The Divestment Decision Process* (Boston: Harvard Business School, 1973).
12. See "Monsanto to Sell Acrylic Fiber Line in Europe," *The Wall Street Journal,* (March 8, 1983).

Case
International Food Corporation—France

Current Difficulties

The situation at International Food Corporation's (IFC) French subsidiary was driving the home office to distraction by the end of 1986. After 10 years of steady growth and profitability during the 1970s, IFC-France began to lose sales in 1980 and actually to lose money beginning in 1983. The problem was initially attributed to the unprecedented rise in the dollar's value relative to the franc during 1981-84, but the subsidiary's performance did not improve in 1985 or 1986, when the dollar dropped precipitously compared to the franc. (See Figure 1, which depicts the franc/dollar exchange rate during 1970-87. Figure 2 then presents financial statements of IFC-France for 1986.)

The home office staff viewed this situation as a cause for real alarm, since the subsidiary had accumulated losses of over $US 160 million by the end of 1986. In contrast, the subsidiary's managers felt that a series of random events

Figure 1 **The Franc/Dollar Exchange Rate, 1970–1986**

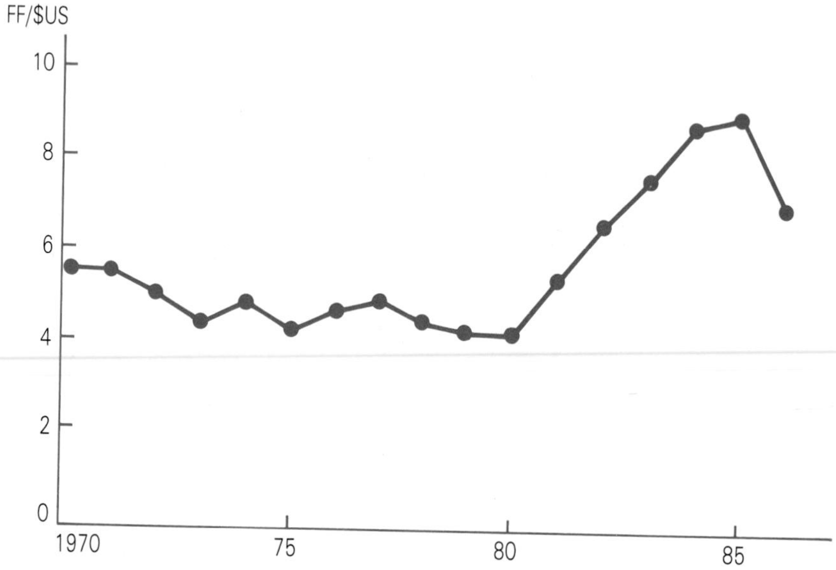

This case was written by Professor Robert Grosse in 1987 as a basis for class discussion.

Figure 2 **Financial Statements of IFC-France for 1986** (in millions of U.S. dollars)

Income Statement

Net sales and operating revenues	6,298
Operating expenses	5,974
Gross operating margin	324
Interest expense	345
Earnings before tax	(21)
Income taxes	0
Net income after tax	(21)

Balance Sheet

Assets		Liabilities	
Cash	163	Short-term debt	660
Short-term investments	411	Accounts payable	410
Accounts receivable	701	Accrued expenses	552
Inventories	709	Long-term debt	1,058
Net property, plant and equipment	1,099	Deferred income taxes	187
		Stockholders' equity	216
Total assets	3,083	Total liabilities	3,083

had combined to produce the red ink, but that profitability would return even in 1987 and performance would be consistent with that of other IFC units within a few years.

In fact, Jean Bedouin, general manager of the French subsidiary, felt so positive that he sought permission to expand the local operation to manufacture a new line of frozen dessert products that had become very successful in the U.S. market. He proposed that $US 15 million more be invested to build the new assembly line and cold-storage facilities needed for this purpose. Since Bedouin had exceeded company performance goals in the previous divisions that he had run, it was quite difficult for the home office to judge him harshly in this case.

Some Background on International Food Corporation

International Food Corporation was founded in 1949 through a merger of three medium-sized U.S. food processing firms. Each of the three had been feeling severe competitive pressure from such market leaders as Kraft, Borden, and Standard Brands. The managers of the three companies chose a strategy of joining forces to reduce distribution costs and carve out a stronger market position in a greater variety of products than any of the companies had been able to achieve previously.

IFC's main product areas include dairy products such as cheeses, yogurt, and ice cream; canned fruits and vegetables and juices; frozen fruit pies and frozen vegetables; and such specialty products as mineral water, nonalcoholic coolers, and diet fruit-based sodas. Two of the founding companies had produced dairy products, and IFC still viewed dairy products as a core business. Frozen produce and specialty products, however, were the fastest-growing IFC businesses during the 1980s. The firm was committed to expansion in these two areas.

International Foods sells primarily to supermarkets and grocery stores in the United States. In fact, until the early 1960s, the firm's activities were confined almost entirely to North America. The United States and Canada accounted for 97 percent of its sales. The only sales elsewhere were exports on request to a handful of European wholesale customers and some cross-border sales from Texas and California into Mexico.

In 1963, IFC first entered the European market directly through a sales office and warehouse operation in Swindon, England, outside London. Based on the existing level of exports of canned produce to one English grocery chain, IFC's management felt that a local presence would enable the firm to sell to many more British customers. IFC began to process fruits and vegetables in the United Kingdom in 1965, when it became clear that lower costs could be achieved by manufacturing locally. IFC sales in the United Kingdom reached $US 30 million by 1968, and the stage was set for further European expansion.

The IFC French subsidiary was opened in 1969 by a senior manager of the British subsidiary. This was done explicitly to diversify IFC's production base into Europe, since at the time Britain was not a member of the European Common Market. The French plant, near Lille, produced most of the same canned fruits and vegetables as were produced in the English plant. A few products were imported from England to fill out the line.

Figure 3 **Pro Forma Income Statements for IFC-France** (in millions of U.S. dollars)*

	1987	1988	1989	1990	1991
Sales	379	517	575	652	748
Operating expenses	371	481	532	603	681
Gross operating margin	8	36	43	49	67
Interest expense	4	7	9	9	9
Pretax earnings	4	29	34	40	58
Income taxes	2	13	14	18	26
Net income after tax	2	16	20	22	32

* These data show the *marginal* impact of the frozen food business.

IFC operations in Italy and Germany were begun in 1975 and 1976, respectively. In each of these cases, IFC chose to license a local food processing firm to manufacture and sell its brand name frozen food products. In return for the use of IFC's processing technology and its brand names, the local firm paid a royalty that amounted to 5 percent of sales. International Foods retained the right to establish quality control standards for these products, but in fact no serious problems arose with either licensee. The home office managers were not sure whether the current arrangements with the Italian and German licensees represented the best strategies for IFC, but since both of them regularly generated profits for the firm, they were left in place.

The Competitive Environment in France

During its entire life, the IFC subsidiary in France never attained a leading market share for any of its products. Although some of the specialty products were relatively novel in the French market when they were introduced, IFC was beaten out by Nestlé in several lines and by a local French producer in others. When price competition became severe at the end of the 1970s, the French subsidiary was unable to match the costs of three of its rivals and began losing market share. A major advertising campaign in 1981 was successful in raising the subsidiary's market share in all of the canned food lines, but recessionary conditions that lasted until 1984 led sales to stagnate all the same.

By the end of 1986, Jean Bedouin felt that the best strategy for escaping the weak market position of IFC-France was to move into local production of frozen fruits and vegetables. He had his corporate treasurer draw up a pro forma capital budget for the expansion needed to enter this segment in a major way. Based on a similar investment in the United Kingdom, he estimated that it would cost $US 15 million to build a modern, highly efficient freezing plant and storage facility. This investment would be repaid within five years. The project would become profitable within two years, assuming no major reaction by rival firms to enter this market segment on a large scale. Bedouin's projections for IFC-France sales and profits, including the new project, appear in Figure 3.

5

THE FOREIGN EXCHANGE MARKET

This chapter focuses on the mechanisms through which one country's currency can be exchanged for the currency of another country. The markets in which such transactions take place are called foreign exchange markets, and the purpose of this chapter is to show how these markets work and how firms can use them. The main goals of the chapter are to:

1. Explain how foreign exchange transactions take place.
2. Examine the main foreign exchange markets that operate in the United States.
3. Discuss the full range of participants in foreign exchange markets and their motives for buying and selling.
4. Consider the various types of exchange arbitrage that take place in the interbank market and between different foreign exchange markets.
5. Explain the fundamental economic factors that determine the exchange rate in the absence of government intervention in the foreign exchange markets.
6. Show how firms can operate successfully in more than one currency without facing unacceptable levels of exchange risk.

Introduction

The truly fundamental differences between international and domestic business are that international business extends domestic concerns to include (1) different rules and practices for doing business abroad or on a globally integrated scale and (2) the different national currencies that are used in different countries. The focus of this chapter is on these currencies and their interrelations.

This first section discusses the central concern in foreign exchange markets, the exchange rate. The next section examines the major institutions and activities that constitute the foreign exchange market in the United States today. The third section looks at the main categories of participants in foreign exchange markets worldwide. Since the exchange rate is the central variable of interest here, the fourth section introduces the issue of exchange rate determination. The final section of the chapter explores the problem of exchange risk and methods for protecting the firm against such risk.

Currencies, like any other products, services, or claims, can be traded for each other. The **foreign exchange market** is simply a mechanism through which transactions can be made between one country's currency and another country's currency. Or, more broadly, a foreign exchange market is a market for the exchange of financial instruments denominated in different currencies. The most common location for foreign exchange transactions is a commercial bank, which agrees to "make a market" for the purchase and sale of currencies other than the local one. In the United States, hundreds of banks offer foreign exchange markets in dozens of cities—though about 40 percent of all foreign exchange business is done through the 10 largest banks in New York.[1]

Foreign exchange is not simply currency printed by a foreign country's central bank. Rather, it includes such items as cash, checks (or drafts), wire transfers, telephone transfers, and even contracts to sell or buy currency in the future. Foreign exchange is really any financial instrument that carries out payment from one currency to another. The most common form of foreign exchange in transactions between companies is the draft (denominated in a foreign currency). The most common form of foreign exchange in transactions between banks is the telephone transfer, generally for transactions of $1 million or more. Far down the list of instruments, in terms of the value exchanged, is actual currency, which is often exchanged by tourists and other travelers.

Since no currency is necessarily fixed in value compared to others, there must be some means of determining an acceptable price, or **exchange rate.** How many British pounds (£) should one dollar buy? How many Brazilian cruzados should be paid to buy a dollar? Since 1973, most of the industrialized countries of the noncommunist world have allowed their currency values to fluctuate more or less freely (depending on the time and the country), so that simple economics of supply and demand largely determine

Figure 5-1 **The Foreign Exchange Market at Bankers Trust Company of New York, January 8, 1987**

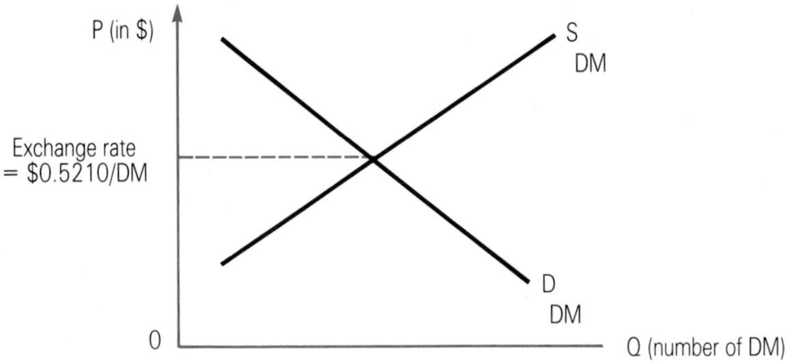

Suppliers of Marks	Demanders for Marks
U.S. exporters	U.S. importers paying in marks
German direct investors	U.S. direct investors in Germany
U.S. foreign investors remitting profits	German foreign investors in the United States remitting their profits
German portfolio investors	U.S. portfolio investors in Germany
Bear speculators	Bull speculators
Arbitrageurs	
Government "interveners"	

exchange rates. In graphic form, Figure 5-1 shows that the intersection of the supply curve and the demand curve for German marks (DM) sets the price, or exchange rate, of marks in terms of dollars. A variety of the participants in the foreign exchange market are listed below the graph: their specific activities are discussed in the following section.

Notice that the exchange rate of $0.5210 per DM is offered by one specific bank. This was the closing exchange rate quoted by Bankers Trust Company of New York for purchases of at least $1 million worth of deutsche marks on January 8, 1987. Another bank in New York may have quoted a slightly higher or a slightly lower rate at the same time; and banks in San Francisco or London or Tokyo probably quoted rates that differed even more. The rates quoted depend on each bank's interest in being involved in foreign exchange transactions and on the varying strategic positions and risks taken by the banks. Thus, the foreign exchange market among banks may be viewed as one large market, or as many small markets with extensive (potential and actual) interrelations. Generally, the interbank market within any country is viewed as one market and intercountry dealings are somewhat segmented by different rules and risks (though in the United States the San Francisco market often offers quotations from various banks that differ noticeably from rate quotations in New York, due partly to the difference in time zones).

The differences in rate quotations may appear to be very small to an outsider. Deutsche marks may be quoted at $0.52109 at Citibank in New York and at $0.52261 at Bank of America in San Francisco. This difference seems small—but for every DM1 million sold, the buyer of dollars in San Francisco receives an extra $1,610. Since the transactions are generally rapid and for values of $5-10 million, such differences may add up to a substantial gain (or cost) to the participant in the foreign exchange market.

The various foreign exchange transactions mentioned above involve large commercial banks and large amounts of money. Most of the companies that do international business also utilize foreign exchange markets, but far less frequently than banks and for transactions that involve less money. Consequently, the access of these companies to foreign currencies differs from that of the banks. (Specifically, banks make the market and companies pay for the use of this service.) The next section explains the various parts that constitute the U.S. foreign exchange market.

Foreign Exchange Markets in the United States

Figure 5-2 presents an overview of the foreign exchange markets operating today in the United States. In this section, each of these markets is discussed in some detail.

The Interbank Market

Although the foreign exchange dealings of most managers involve a company buying from or selling to a bank, it is important for managers to understand the foreign exchange market between banks. This is because, as noted above, the vast majority of large-scale foreign exchange transactions are interbank, and these transactions tend to determine exchange rates—which occasional market participants such as companies must deal with.

Local and regional commercial banks may offer clients a foreign exchange service, which such banks provide on request by dealing through a larger bank, typically in a large city (such as New York, San Francisco, Chicago, Miami, and perhaps half a dozen more U.S. cities). If a local bank receives a request to buy Swiss francs (SF) for an importer in New Jersey, it will call its correspondent bank in New York (say, Chemical Bank) and arrange to buy the SF, say for $0.6213/SF. Then the local bank will add on its service charge, so that the importer pays $0.6313/SF. Thus, the local bank earns $0.01 per SF, or about 1.6 percent on the transaction.

Chemical Bank, in turn, will either take the requested Swiss francs from its own holdings of that currency or will enter the **interbank market** to buy them. Assuming that Chemical does *not* have the SF on hand, one of its foreign exchange traders will call several other major banks (or brokerage

Figure 5-2 **U.S. Foreign Exchange Markets**

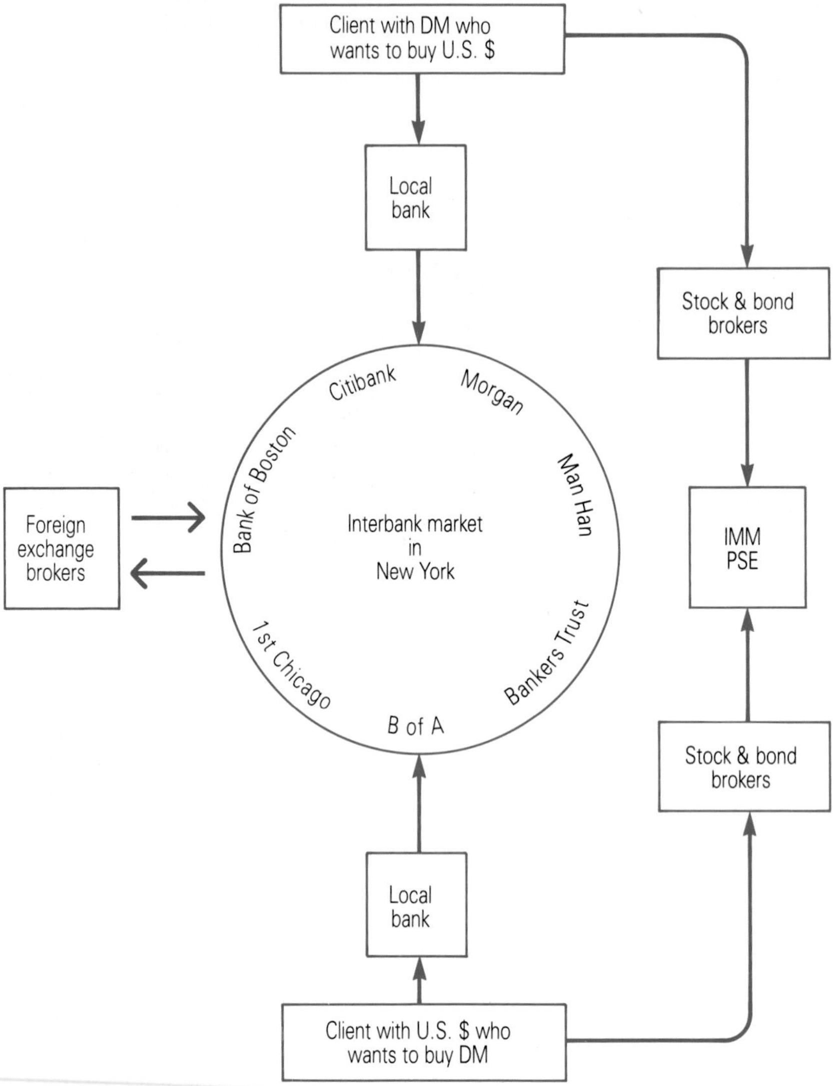

Source: Adapted from St. Louis Federal Reserve Bank *Review,* March 1984, p. 9.

houses, which are discussed below) and contract to buy Swiss francs from the lowest bidder.

The interbank market generally operates with large transactions only—of about $1 million to $10 million exchanged for the equivalent foreign currency. On a typical day in 1983, the 100 members of the main association

Foreign exchange trading on the Tokyo Foreign Exchange in 1986.
Wide World Photos, Inc.

of commercial banks in foreign exchange dealings (called the Clearinghouse Interbank Payments System, CHIPS) transacted roughly $30 billion of currency trades.[2]

The Brokers' Market

Another facet of large-scale foreign exchange dealing in the United States is the **brokers' market.** About half a dozen foreign exchange brokerage companies make markets for foreign currencies in New York (as well as in London and elsewhere), creating trading in many currencies similar to that in the interbank market. In this case, the key differences are that the brokers seek to match buyers and sellers on any given transaction, without taking a position themselves; that they deal simultaneously with many banks (and other companies); and that they offer both buy and sell positions to clients (where a bank may wish to operate on only one side of the market at any particular time).[3] Also, the brokers deal "blind," offering rate quotations without naming the potential seller/buyer until a deal has been negotiated. Brokers play a large part in the total market, as shown in Table 5-1.

Before moving on to other foreign exchange markets, let us consider an example in which the spot market is used by a tourist planning a trip to Japan. This person wants to visit Tokyo to see a friend during Christmas vacation and

Table 5-1a **Foreign Exchange Turnover in Selected Markets for April 1983** (in billions of U.S. dollars)

	Total Turnover			
Transactions	United States	Tokyo	Canada	Singapore
Interbank*	456	183	75	118
Direct with domestic banks	60	—	3	27 (including brokers)
Direct with banks abroad	136	92	21	91
Through brokers	260	90	35	—
Customer	87	65	27	5
Chicago Mercantile Exchange contract turnover	50			

* Data are adjusted to eliminate double-counting of interbank transactions.

Table 5-1b **Foreign Exchange Turnover in the U.S. Interbank Market in April 1983** (in billions of U.S. dollars)

Type of Transaction	Turnover of 119 Banks
Spot	
Direct with banks in United States	93.8
Direct with banks abroad	81.1
Through brokers	224.2
Subtotal	399.2
Swaps	
Direct with banks in United States	22.5
Direct with banks abroad	51.7
Through brokers	130.2
Subtotal	204.4
Outright Forwards	
Direct with banks in United States	3.1
Direct with banks abroad	3.7
Through brokers	4.6
Subtotal	11.4
Total Transactions	
Direct with banks in United States	119.4
Direct with banks abroad	136.5
Through brokers	359.1
Grand Total	615.0

Note: "Turnover" is the value of funds exchanged during the time period shown. Terms are defined in the text.
Source: Quarterly Review, Federal Reserve Bank of New York, Summer 1984.

Rate Quotations

Exchange rate quotations come as two-digit numbers, bid/asked, with the preceding numbers assumed. A deutsche mark quote of 50/70 on January 9, 1987, will mean an actual price of:

DM 1.91950 bid to buy one U.S. dollar.

DM 1.91970 asked for selling one U.S. dollar.

The bank is offering (bidding) to buy dollars for 1.9195 marks per dollar and also offering (asking) to sell dollars for 1.9197 marks per dollar. Of course, the actual transaction will involve $1 million or more, to be exchanged at those prices.

Rates are typically quoted on the **Continental basis,** as units of foreign exchange per dollar, everywhere. U.S. banks have traditionally used the **American basis,** quoting $U.S. per unit of foreign exchange. Clearly, whether the quote is DM 2.0 per dollar or $0.50/DM, the value is the same. *The Wall Street Journal* now offers both types of quotation, as shown in Figure 5-3.

Another means that is used to distinguish the two ways of presenting an exchange rate is to call a quotation of domestic currency/foreign exchange an **indirect quote.** Conversely, a quotation of units of foreign exchange/domestic currency is called a **direct quote.** This system has more general applicability to any pair of currencies, whereas the American Continental system relates only to rates involving the U.S. dollar.

to do some sight-seeing. She is taking $1,000 with her, having already purchased the round-trip airline ticket. Since dollars cannot be used for most purchases in Japan, she needs to buy Japanese yen. How should she do it?

Looking at Figure 5-3, she sees that Bankers Trust is offering to sell large quantities of yen at the rate of 158.1 yen per dollar. At the "retail" level, that is, for small transactions such as this one, she can expect to receive only about 150 yen per dollar. Indeed, when she called Bank of America and Wells Fargo Bank in San Francisco, rates of 151 yen per dollar were quoted. Instead of carrying the cash with her, she wants to get traveler's checks. Upon calling the office of American Express in San Francisco, she found that yen-denominated traveler's checks were available but that they would cost her $1 for every 145 yen, plus a $5 service charge.

The tourist was willing to pay the extra cost to obtain the protection of traveler's checks, but one final problem arose. A friend who worked in foreign exchange dealing at Crocker National Bank told her that the yen would probably decline in value relative to the dollar in the next few days. Since she would not leave for Tokyo for another week, she wondered whether it was worth waiting for the expected devaluation. The answer to this question is that no one knows! She can hope for a devaluation, and delay purchase of the yen for a week, or ignore the potential gain—or loss!—and buy the yen today. In such a short time period, it is probably best to ignore the few days' variability in the exchange rate—since it could be favorable or

Figure 5-3 **Foreign Exchange Rate Quotations**

FOREIGN EXCHANGE

Thursday, January 8, 1987

The New York foreign exchange selling rates below apply to trading among banks in amounts of $1 million and more, as quoted at 3 p.m. Eastern time by Bankers Trust Co. Retail transactions provide fewer units of foreign currency per dollar.

Country	U.S. $ equiv. Thurs.	U.S. $ equiv. Wed.	Currency per U.S. $ Thurs.	Currency per U.S. $ Wed.
Argentina (Austral)	.7955	.7955	1.257	1.257
Australia (Dollar)	.6658	.6635	1.5028	1.5072
Austria (Schilling)	.07402	.07369	13.51	13.57
Belgium (Franc)				
Commercial rate	.02497	.02491	40.05	40.15
Financial rate	.02477	.02452	40.37	40.78
Brazil (Cruzado)	.067304	.067304	14.858	14.858
Britain (Pound)	1.4742	1.4720	.6783	.6793
30-Day Forward	1.4682	1.4662	.6811	.6820
90-Day Forward	1.4567	1.4549	.6865	.6873
180-Day Forward	1.4405	1.4388	.6942	.6950
Canada (Dollar)	.7293	.7286	1.3712	1.3725
30-Day Forward	.7281	.7275	1.3735	1.3745
90-Day Forward	.7258	.7257	1.3778	1.3780
180-Day Forward	.7222	.7217	1.3847	1.3856
Chile (Official rate)	.004964	.004964	201.46	201.46
China (Yuan)	.26933	.26933	3.7128	3.7128
Colombia (Peso)	.004527	.004527	220.90	220.90
Denmark (Krone)	.1372	.1370	7.2875	7.3000
Ecuador (Sucre)				
Official rate	.006847	.006847	146.05	146.05
Floating rate	.006826	.006826	146.50	146.50
Finland (Markka)	.2099	.2099	4.7650	4.7650
France (Franc)	.1564	.1559	6.3950	6.4150
30-Day Forward	.1557	.1552	6.4225	6.4450
90-Day Forward	.1550	.1543	6.4525	6.4800
180-Day Forward	.1540	.1535	6.4925	6.5150
Greece (Drachma)	.007246	.007236	138.00	138.20
Hong Kong (Dollar)	.1285	.1285	7.7820	7.7840
India (Rupee)	.07651	.07391	13.07	13.53
Indonesia (Rupiah)	.0006094	.0006094	1641.00	1641.00
Ireland (Punt)	1.4050	1.4030	.7117	.7128
Israel (Shekel)	.6729	.6729	1.486	1.486
Italy (Lira)	.0007364	.0007396	1358.00	1352.00
Japan (Yen)	.006327	.006323	158.05	158.15
30-Day Forward	.006338	.006335	157.77	157.84
90-Day Forward	.006356	.006353	157.34	157.40
180-Day Forward	.006383	.006382	156.67	156.70
Jordan (Dinar)	2.8985	2.8985	.345	.346
Kuwait (Dinar)	3.4153	3.4153	.2928	.2928
Lebanon (Pound)	.01096	.01096	91.24	91.24
Malaysia (Ringgit)	.3841	.3842	2.6035	2.6030
Malta (Lira)	2.7211	2.7211	.3675	.3675
Mexico (Peso)				
Floating rate	.001078	.001057	928.00	946.00
Netherland (Guilder)	.4620	.4598	2.1645	2.1750
New Zealand (Dollar)	.5430	.5430	1.8416	1.8416
Norway (Krone)	.1356	.1357	7.3725	7.3700
Pakistan (Rupee)	.05797	.05797	17.25	17.25
Peru (Inti)	.071685	.071685	13.95	13.95
Philippines (Peso)	.04868	.04868	20.56	20.56
Portugal (Escudo)	.006920	.006885	144.50	145.25
Saudi Arabia (Riyal)	.2666	.2667	3.751	3.7500
Singapore (Dollar)	.4607	.4607	2.1705	2.1705
South Africa (Rand)				
Commercial rate	.4660	.4660	2.1459	2.1459
Financial rate	.2163	.2163	4.6232	4.6232
South Korea (Won)	.0011609	.0011609	861.40	861.40
Spain (Peseta)	.007590	.007583	131.75	131.88
Sweden (Krona)	.1477	.1477	6.7700	6.7725
Switzerland (Franc)	.6213	.6165	1.6095	1.6220
30-Day Forward	.6228	.6180	1.6057	1.6181
90-Day Forward	.6250	.6202	1.5999	1.6124
180-Day Forward	.6284	.6237	1.5914	1.6033
Taiwan (Dollar)	.028169	.028169	35.50	35.50
Thailand (Baht)	.03825	.03825	26.14	26.14
Turkey (Lira)	.0013196	.0013196	757.80	757.80
United Arab (Dirham)	.27225	.27225	3.673	3.673
Uruguay (New Peso)				
Financial	.005586	.005586	179.00	179.00
Venezuela (Bolivar)				
Official rate	.1333	.1333	7.50	7.50
Floating rate	.04399	.04000	22.73	25.00
W. Germany (Mark)	.5210	.5185	1.9195	1.9288
30-Day Forward	.5217	.5086	1.9168	1.9260
90-Day Forward	.5228	.5204	1.9126	1.9215
180-Day Forward	.5245	.5221	1.9067	1.9155
SDR	1.22535	1.22656	0.816097	0.815288
ECU	1.07241	1.07197	...	...

Special Drawing Rights are based on exchange rates for the U.S., West German, British, French and Japanese currencies. Source: International Monetary Fund.

ECU is based on a basket of community currencies. Source: European Community Commission.

z-Not quoted.

Source: *The Wall Street Journal,* January 9, 1987, p. 36.

unfavorable—and just buy the yen at the most convenient time before departing to Tokyo. (One more point to confuse the matter: she could buy traveler's checks in U.S. dollars and exchange them for yen in Japan when needed. Again, no one can be sure what the yen's value will be during her vacation time in Tokyo!)

While this example does not offer a guaranteed way to make money from foreign exchange dealings, it does illustrate the kinds of problems that beset individuals and companies as they work with foreign currencies. Fortunately, there are some methods to help avoid the uncertainty involved in foreign exchange; they are discussed below in the section "Methods of Protecting against Exchange Risk."

So far, the discussion has focused only on the *spot market,* that is, the market for immediate exchange of one currency for another. An additional, very large part of the U.S. foreign exchange market is the set of instruments that allow contracting today for delivery of currency in the future. The main instruments of this type are forward contracts, foreign exchange futures contracts, and foreign currency options.

The Forward Foreign Exchange Market

The **forward foreign exchange market** at commercial banks in the United States offers banks, companies, and individuals the opportunity to contract *today* for a specific foreign exchange transaction in the *future,* at a fixed price (i.e., exchange rate). Forward contracts are negotiated between the offering bank and the client as to size, maturity, and price. Referring to Figure 5-3, we see that Bankers Trust was offering to sell British pounds for $1.4405/£ in 180 days on January 8, 1987 (for quantities of at least $1 million).

The rationale for forward contracts in currencies is analogous to that for futures contracts in commodities; the firm can lock in a price today to eliminate uncertainty about the value of a future receipt or payment of foreign currency. Such a transaction may be undertaken because the firm has made a previous contract, for example, to pay FF 1 million to a supplier in three months for some needed inputs to its operations. If the firm wants to eliminate the risk that its payment in three months will change in dollar terms (i.e., that the FF 1 million may cost more dollars then), it can contract with a bank to buy FF 1 million three months forward, at a price established today. (From Figure 5-3, we see that that price was $0.1550/FF for a contract with Bankers Trust on January 8, 1987.) Thus, firms can use forward contracts to eliminate the risk of variability in future dollar costs or revenues due to exchange rate changes. This concept, called "hedging," and other motives for using the forward market are discussed below.

Notice that in the above example the forward contract used for hedging does *not* correspond directly to an insurance contract. The forward contract does fix a minimum "loss" for the firm, by setting the guaranteed price of exchange in the future. Even if the dollar devalues to $0.17 per FF in three months, the forward contract holder is still able to buy 1 million FF for $0.1557/FF. However, if the French franc devalues over the next three months to, say, $0.1457/FF, the forward contract holder will have an **opportunity cost** of the difference between the forward rate and the (eventual) future spot rate (a difference of $0.01/FF, or 6.4 percent). Thus, the forward contract

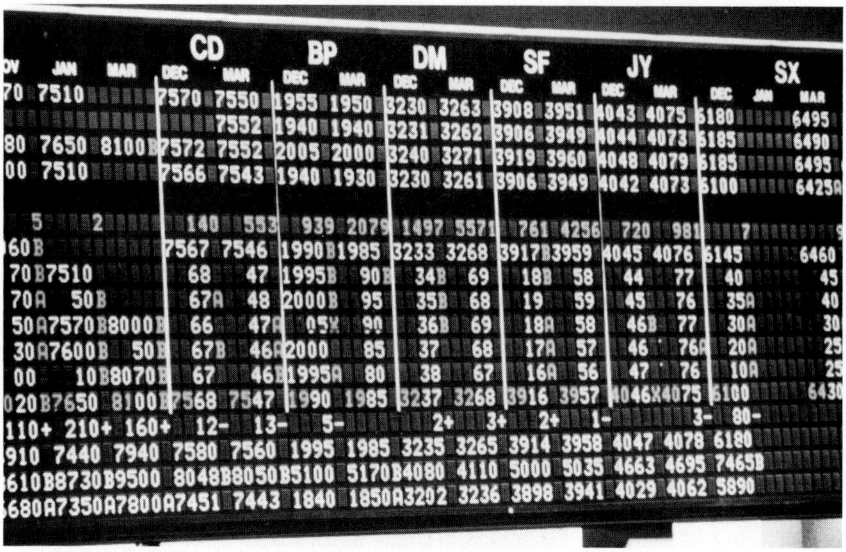

Foreign currency futures quotations on the Chicago Mercantile Exchange.

Courtesy Chicago Mercantile Exchange.

insures against potential losses *and* against potential gains in foreign currency value.

Forward markets exist in any currencies and for any maturities that banks are willing to offer. Most of the forward contracts used in the United States involve exchanges of U.S. dollars for German marks, Japanese yen, British pounds, Swiss francs, Canadian dollars, and French francs. Maturities tend to be six months or less, though single-year and multiyear forward contracts are sometimes available.

The Futures Market in Currencies

A very similar type of instrument is available on several securities exchanges in the United States and abroad. The foreign exchange **futures contract** is an agreement to buy or sell a fixed amount of foreign currency for delivery at a fixed future date at a fixed dollar price. The main difference between futures and forward contracts in the United States is that futures contracts have fixed sizes (about $50,000 to $100,000, depending on the currency) and preestablished maturity dates. (All are 3-, 6-, or 12-month contracts maturing on the third Wednesday of January, March, April, June, July, September, October, or December.) Also, futures contracts are only available for a few currencies (Canadian dollars, German marks, French francs, Swiss francs, British pounds, Japanese yen, Italian lira, and Mexican pesos) and only if a buyer and a seller can be found at the time. The futures market at the Chicago Mercantile Exchange is currently very thin (i.e., few contracts are traded) except for the three-month contracts denominated in Canadian dollars, German marks, and Swiss francs.

Futures contracts are more widely accessible to firms and individuals than forward contracts, because of their smaller value and the margin requirements that enable brokers to obtain collateral from market participants. (However, the currently thin nature of this market does not allow participants the wide range of currencies and maturities that are available for large-scale transactions in the forward market.) The standard contracts available at the Chicago Mercantile Exchange are described in Figure 5-4.

Foreign currency options are an additional instrument of the foreign exchange market in the United States; they are described in the accompanying box.

Foreign Currency Options

The most recently created type of foreign exchange market offers participants the *right* to buy or sell foreign currency in the future, rather than the obligation to do so. Foreign currency options are similar to foreign currency futures in the United States, in that the contracts are for fixed quantities of currency to be exchanged at a fixed price in the future. The key difference is that the maturity date for an option is only the last day to carry out the currency exchange; the option may be "exercised," that is, presented for currency exchange, at *any* time between its issuance and the maturity date, or not at all.

A **foreign currency option** is a contract offering the holder the right to buy (namely, a **call option**) or sell (namely, a **put option**) a fixed amount of foreign currency for a fixed price during a fixed time period. The buyer of a call option on British pounds obtains the right to buy £50,000 at a fixed dollar price (i.e., the **exercise price**) at any time during the (typically) three-month life of the option. The seller of the same option faces a **contingent liability** in that the seller will have to deliver the British pounds at any time, if the buyer chooses to exercise the option.

The market value of an option depends on its exercise price, the remaining time to its expiration, the exchange rate in the spot market, and expectations about the future exchange rate. An option may sell for a price near zero or for thousands of dollars, or anywhere in between. Notice that the buyer of a call option on British pounds may pay a small price to obtain the option but does *not* have to exercise the option if the actual exchange rate moves favorably. Thus, an option is superior to a forward contract having the same maturity and exercise price because it need *not* be used—and the cost is just its purchase price. However, the price of the option is generally greater than the expected cost of the forward contract; so the user of the option pays for the flexibility of the instrument.

Some recent currency option prices from the Philadelphia Stock Exchange are presented in Figure 5-5.

Figure 5-4 **Foreign Currency Contracts at the Chicago Mercantile Exchange***

Contract	Size	Grade	Hours°	Months	Clearing House/	Ticker	Fluctuation in Price	Equals Contract	Limit	Last Day Trading	Delivery Date
Pound Sterling	25,000		7:30°° 1:24 (9:20)	Jan., Mar., Apr., June July, Sept., Oct., Dec., and spot month	B1	BP	0.0005 (5 points) ($2.50/point)	$12.50	0.05 (500 point) ($1.250)	2 business days before 3rd Wed.	3rd Wed.
Canadian Dollar	100,000		7:30°° 1:22 (9:19)	Jan., Mar., Apr., June, July, Sept., Oct., Dec., and spot month	C1	CD	0.0001 (1 point) ($10/point)	10.00	0.0075 (75 point) ($750)	2 business days before 3rd Wed.	3rd Wed.
Dutch Guilder	125.000		7:30°° 1:30 (9:23)	Jan., Mar., Apr., June, July, Sept., Oct., Dec., and spot month	H1	DG	0.0001 (1 point) ($12.50/point)	12.50	0.0100 (100 point) ($1,250)	2 business days before 3rd Wed.	3rd Wed.
Deutsche Mark	125,000		7:30°° 1:20 (9:18)	Jan., Mar., Apr., June, July, Sept., Oct., Dec., and spot month	D1	DM	0.0001 (1 point) ($12.50/point)	12.50	0.0100 (100 point) ($1,250)	2 business days before 3rd Wed.	3rd Wed.
Japanese Yen	12,500,000		7:30°° 1:26 (9:21)	Jan., Mar., Apr., June July, Sept., Oct., Dec., and spot month	J1	JY	0.000001 (1 point) ($12.50/point)	12.50	0.000100 (100 point) ($1,250)	2 business days before 3rd Wed.	3rd Wed.
Mexican Peso	1,000,000		7:30°° 1:18 (9:17)	Jan., Mar., Apr., June, July, Sept., Oct., Dec., and spot month	G1	MP	0.00001 (1 point) ($10/point)	10.00	0.00150 (150 point) ($1,500)	2 business days before 3rd Wed.	3rd Wed.
Swiss Franc	125,000		7:30°° 1:16 (9:16)	Jan., Mar., Apr., June, July, Sept., Oct., Dec., and spot month	E1	SF	0.0001 (1 point) ($12.50/point)	12.50	0.0150 (150 point) ($1,875)	2 business days before 3rd Wed.	3rd Wed.
French Franc	250,000		7:30°° 1:28 (9:22)	Jan., Mar., Apr., June, July, Sept., Oct., Dec., and spot month	K1	FR	0.00005 (5 point) ($2.50/point)	12.50	0.00500 (500 pcint) ($1,250)	2 business days before 3rd Wed.	3rd Wed.

* These were contract characteristics in February, 1985. They are subject to change. For current information, contact the Chicago Mercantile Exchange.
° Times in parentheses indicate close on last day of trading.
°° Central time

Figure 5-5 **Currency Options on the Philadelphia Stock Exchange**

FOREIGN CURRENCY OPTIONS

Wednesday, February 11, 1987

Philadelphia Exchange

Option & Underlying	Strike Price	Calls–Last Feb	Calls–Last Mar	Calls–Last Jun	Puts–Last Feb	Puts–Last Mar	Puts–Last Jun
50,000 Australian Dollars-cents per unit.							
ADollr	...62	r	r	r	r	r	0.69
66.83	...63	r	r	r	r	r	0.97
66.83	...66	0.83	r	r	r	0.66	r
66.83	...67	r	0.48	r	r	r	r
12,500 British Pounds-cents per unit.							
BPound	145	r	r	r	r	0.20	r
151.88	.150	r	r	r	r	1.25	r
151.88	.155	0.05	0.75	r	r	r	r
50,000 Canadian Dollars-cents per unit.							
CDollr	...71	r	r	r	r	r	0.10
74.42	.71½	r	r	r	r	r	0.11
74.42	...72	r	r	2.45	r	r	0.18
74.42	...73	r	1.60	r	r	r	0.48
74.42	.73½	r	1.09	r	r	0.17	r
74.42	...74	0.43	0.73	1.04	0.06	0.35	0.76
74.42	.74½	r	0.46	r	0.15	0.45	r
74.42	...75	0.04	0.25	0.70	r	r	r
74.42	.75½	r	0.19	r	r	r	r
74.42	...76	r	r	0.40	r	r	r
62,500 West German Marks-cents per unit.							
DMark	...50	5.13	r	r	0.01	0.05	0.29
55.06	...51	4.12	4.00	r	r	r	0.48
55.06	...52	r	r	r	r	0.15	0.63
55.06	...53	2.09	2.47	r	0.01	0.30	0.90
55.06	...54	1.03	1.72	2.60	0.06	0.51	1.24
55.06	...55	0.38	1.10	2.16	0.26	0.92	1.71
55.06	...56	0.07	0.64	1.66	0.94	1.45	r
55.06	...57	0.03	0.40	1.28	r	r	r
55.06	...58	r	0.23	1.00	r	r	r
55.06	...60	s	0.09	0.55	s	r	r
125,000 French Francs-10ths of a cent per unit.							
FFranc	.165	r	r	5.45	r	r	r
6,250,000 Japanese Yen-100ths of a cent per unit.							
JYen	...62	3.03	r	r	r	r	r
65.06	...63	2.15	2.40	r	r	0.20	0.58
65.06	...64	r	r	r	r	0.39	0.93
65.06	...65	r	r	r	0.20	r	1.30
65.06	...66	0.04	r	1.37	r	r	1.84
65.06	...67	r	0.25	r	r	r	r
65.06	...69	r	0.09	r	r	r	r
62,500 Swiss Francs-cents per unit.							
SFranc	...60	r	r	r	r	0.10	r
65.08	...61	r	r	r	r	r	0.74
65.08	...62	r	r	r	0.01	r	0.93
65.08	...64	r	r	3.30	0.11	0.80	r
65.08	...65	r	1.34	r	r	r	2.15
65.08	...66	r	0.90	2.26	r	r	r
65.08	...67	r	0.72	r	r	r	r
65.08	...70	r	r	1.03	r	r	r
62,500 European Currency Units-cents per unit.							
ECU	...110	r	r	r	r	r	2.47
Total call vol.		19,862		Call open int.			517,365
Total put vol.		15,962		Put open int.			501,560

Source: *The Wall Street Journal,* February 12, 1987, p. 34.

Who Uses Foreign Exchange Markets?

Participants in the foreign exchange market range from multinational banks to travelers from Detroit to Windsor, Canada, from multinational companies to foreign central banks. Users of foreign exchange markets fall into five basic classes:

1. Traders/brokers.
2. Speculators.
3. Hedgers.
4. Arbitrageurs.
5. Governments (for intervention; that is, participation in the market to set an exchange rate).

Traders and Brokers

Foreign exchange traders work in commercial banks and may deal in spot market transactions or forward market transactions. Their goal in the market is to match up buyers and sellers of foreign exchange, charging an implicit fee (hidden within the exchange rate quotation itself) for providing this service. Such traders *may* buy or sell foreign exchange for the account of their own bank, thus creating foreign exchange risk for the bank. "Positions" of this kind are generally eliminated during the trading day, so that the trader ends up finding a paired buyer/seller for each maturity and amount of foreign currency. (If the trader *does* accumulate one-sided transactions in one currency, so that the bank finds itself with net foreign exchange due or owed, we call this "speculation.") Among the buyers and sellers of foreign exchange that the traders serve are the literally millions of companies and individuals that export, import, or travel internationally, needing foreign currency instruments to make their payments or cancel their receipts.

Foreign exchange brokers work in brokerage firms, which may also deal in spot or forward transactions. As noted earlier, such brokers attempt to match buyer and seller in a single transaction, with the margin between quoted rates plus a fixed fee as their commission. Brokerage firms typically deal only in foreign exchange transactions, not in any other financial instruments.

Both traders and brokers function primarily as *market makers,* profiting from their dealings through fees implicit in their rate quotations. In principle, they do not take one-sided positions in the market, though such speculation does occur and often leads to sizable gains (or losses!) for banks and brokerage houses.

Speculators

Banks, companies, individuals, and governments may all function as speculators in the foreign exchange market at one time or another. A speculator is simply a participant in the foreign exchange market that takes an open position. That is, the speculator buys foreign currency without simultaneously contracting to sell it, or sells foreign exchange without possessing the currency to meet the obligation. Such short (net sale of foreign exchange) or long (net acquisition of foreign exchange) positions subject the speculator to risk that the dollar value of the foreign currency may change before the position is eliminated.

For example, if you feel that the deutsche mark (DM) is going to go up in value relative to the dollar, you may buy 100,000 DM today and deposit them in some interest-earning instrument. You are long in DM. If you don't simultaneously sell 100,000 DM in the spot, forward, futures, or options market, then you have an exposure in DM. If your guess is correct and DM do appreciate relative to dollars, your speculation will be rewarded with a profit when you finally sell the marks for dollars. If you are wrong, however, you will receive fewer dollars from your eventual sale of DM than you could have received otherwise.

Hedgers

Many companies and individuals take long or short positions in the foreign exchange market, not to speculate, but to offset an existing foreign currency position in another market. That is, they engage in **foreign exchange hedging.** For example, a chemical company may agree to sell £500,000 of plastic to a buyer in London, payable in 180 days. This company has a de facto foreign exchange exposure, even though it has not entered the foreign exchange market. By contracting with a bank to sell £500,000 forward for dollars in 180 days, the company eliminates its foreign exchange exposure. Thus, one-sided participation in the foreign exchange market may *not* be speculation, if the contract offsets an existing exposure of the company in some other transaction.

Hedging may be carried out in a variety of ways, many of which do not involve the foreign exchange market at all. The general issue of protecting against foreign exchange risk is discussed in a later section of this chapter.

Arbitrageurs

Foreign exchange arbitrage involves simultaneous contracting in two or more foreign exchange markets to buy and sell foreign currency, profiting from exchange rate differences *without* incurring exchange rate risk. Foreign exchange arbitrage may be two-way, three-way, or intertemporal; and it is generally undertaken by large commercial banks that can exchange large quantities of money to exploit small rate differentials.

Two-Way The simplest form of exchange arbitrage is two-way, between any two currencies and between two places. Quotations for Swiss francs in the spot market on January 8, 1987, were:

At Bankers Trust in New York: $0.6213/SF.

At Bank of America in San Francisco: $0.6218/SF.

At Lloyds Bank in London: $0.6249/SF.

An arbitrageur can buy SF in New York and simultaneously sell them in London, making a profit of $0.0036/SF, or 0.58 percent per transaction. While the percentage gain is small, it translates to $3,600 for every million SF traded, and it involves no exchange risk. By repeatedly arbitraging this price (exchange rate) differential, the arbitrageur will make a profit until the exchange rate differential drops below the transactions cost (i.e., the telephone bill, plus the arbitrageur's salary, plus other relevant costs).

This same two-way arbitrage may also occur in the forward market or between forward and futures markets.[4] From the quotations here, we see that profitable arbitrage opportunities exist between the New York forward market and the Chicago futures market, as well as between New York and San Francisco forward markets:

> At Bankers Trust in New York: 156.7 yen/$ for delivery in 180 days.
>
> At Bank of America in San Francisco: 154.4 yen/$ for delivery in 180 days.
>
> At the Chicago Mercantile Exchange: 160.2 yen/$ for delivery on June 20, 1987.

An arbitrageur can buy yen in New York and sell them in San Francisco, both for exchange in 180 days, and earn 2.3 yen/dollar, or 1.47 percent per transaction. Similarly, an arbitrageur can buy yen in Chicago and sell them in San Francisco, to make 5.8 yen/dollar, or 3.62 percent per transaction. The difficulties with the latter transaction are that contracts may not be available for the desired amount or maturity date and that transactions costs are higher for the intermarket exchanges. Nonetheless, both transactions may be feasible and profitable, even after costs are considered.

Three-Way When the arbitrageur does not wish to operate directly in a two-way transaction, because of restrictions on the market or for any other reason, profits may still be available through triangular or **three-way arbitrage.** In this case, the arbitrageur moves through three currencies, starting and ending with the same one, and incurring no exchange rate risk. Quotations from the London *Economist* and *The Wall Street Journal* on January 12, 1987 show the following two-way exchange rates:

> $1.4742/£ at Bankers Trust in New York
>
> $0.1572/FF at Bank of America in San Francisco
>
> FF 9.350/£ at Lloyds Bank in London

In this case, two-way exchanges are ignored and the transactions will be to (1) buy FF/sell dollars, (2) buy £/sell FF, and (3) buy $/sell £; *or* (1) buy £/sell dollars, (2) buy FF/sell £, and (3) buy $/sell FF.

The optimal transactions can be illuminated by creating **cross rates** from the quotations. For instance, if the arbitrageur wants to compare the London exchange rate with the other two, a pound/French franc rate can be created as:

$$\frac{\$0.1572/\text{FF}}{\$1.4742/\pounds} = \pounds 0.1066/\text{FF in New York and San Francisco (or FF } 9.38/\pounds)$$

Similarly the pound/dollar cross rate is:

$$\frac{\pounds 1/\text{FF}9.350}{\$0.1572/\text{FF}} = \pounds 0.680/\$ \text{ in London and San Francisco (or } \$1.470/\pounds)$$

And the franc/dollar cross rate is:

$$\frac{\text{FF } 9.350/\pounds}{\$1.4742/\pounds} = \text{FF } 6.342/\$ \text{ in London and New York (or } \$0.1577/\text{FF})$$

From these comparisons, the arbitrageur can see that the maximum profits from triangular arbitrage come from (1) buying FF for dollars in San Francisco, (2) selling FF for £ in London, and (3) buying $ for £ in New York; *or* (1) buying £ for dollars through the cross rate exchange, (2) selling the £ for FF through the cross rate exchange, and (3) buying $ for FF through the cross rate exchange. Either of the two procedures will yield the same percentage profit, though it must be ascertained that the cross rates are in fact available as calculated.

Intertemporal

Exchange arbitrage across maturities, or **intertemporal arbitrage,** is similar to the previous two forms, in that it requires starting and ending with the same currency and incurring no exchange rate risk. In this case, profits are made by exploiting *interest rate differentials,* as well as exchange rate differentials. Also, the intertemporal exchange arbitrageur (or interest arbitrageur) must utilize funds for the time period between contract maturities, whereas the two- and three-way arbitrageurs only need funds on the delivery date.*

Consider the following information:

At Bankers Trust in New York, the spot exchange rate is: SF 1.6095/$.

At Bankers Trust in New York, the 180-day forward is: SF 1.5627/$.

At Barclays Bank in London, the dollar (eurodollar) deposit rate is: 6.13 percent/year.

At Barclays Bank in London, the SF (eurofranc) deposit rate is: 3.94 percent/year.

The interest arbitrageur who begins with U.S. dollars has two alternatives for using funds in intertemporal arbitrage. First, the funds may simply be invested in a dollar-denominated instrument, such as a eurodollar deposit at Barclays Bank. This investment pays 6.13 percent per year, or 3.07 percent for the six-month investment. Alternatively, the arbitrageur may buy SF, invest in a franc-denominated instrument, and buy dollars forward. These three transactions create a dollar-denominated instrument, which pays 3.94 percent/year, plus the percentage exchange rate change. The forward premium on Swiss francs (i.e., the implicit exchange rate change in percentage terms) is:

$$\frac{XRf - XRs}{XRs} = 1.143 \text{ percent/year}$$

where:

XR = Exchange rate.
f = Forward.
s = Spot.

This means that the dollar value of the francs increases by 1.1 percent/year between the

* The two foreign exchange contracts in intertemporal arbitrage, spot and forward, are a form of *swap* agreement. (That is, dollars are swapped for francs today and francs are swapped back for dollars in the future.) When the swapped foreign currency is invested in a money market instrument, the full set of three transactions constitutes *interest arbitrage.*

purchase and sale of SF. Thus, the full return on this arbitrage is approximately: (3.94 percent + 1.1 percent) per year = 5.04 percent per year, or 2.52 percent for six months. This is clearly *less* than the return on a dollar instrument, so interest arbitrage should *not* be undertaken here.[5]

The basic relation between interest arbitrage and domestic investment may be shown as:

$$(1 + \text{i domestic}) \overset{e}{=} (1 + \text{i foreign}) \frac{XRf}{XRs}$$

where i = interest rate. This is called the **interest parity** equation. In equilibrium, both sides are equal. Most of the time, either domestic investment or interest arbitrage will be profitable, and such arbitrage tends to push interest and exchange rates to the point where the equation holds.

Because the interest parity relationship is generally close to equality, the percentage gains available to interest arbitrageurs are low. Large banks, which can commit funds to foreign currency investments with low transactions costs (usually in the eurocurrency market), are the main participants in interest arbitrage. (Notice that earnings from interest arbitrage include both interest earnings, which are positive, and exchange rate earnings, which may be positive or negative.)

Governments

Governments participate in the foreign exchange market as (1) buyers and sellers of foreign exchange and (2) the rulemakers. The reader should not become so engrossed in the economics of the foreign exchange market as to ignore the government's ability to change the exchange rate by fiat or to close trading in foreign exchange at any time. Since the major noncommunist developed countries agreed to allow floating currency values in early 1973, most of those 10 to 15 countries have largely allowed the market to determine exchange rates. However, the other 150 countries of the world have fixed their currency values to the dollar, pound, or other currency; and/or they have used exchange controls to limit access to foreign exchange; and/or they have not allowed a foreign exchange market to operate. In virtually all of these countries, no forward, futures, or options markets exist. (Mexico, in which a futures market and some forward contracts in pesos are available, is an exception.) The rationales of governments for intervening in the market are discussed below in the context of the balance of payments (see Chapter 7). Here we need to recognize that government intervention is always a potential concern and often an actual one.

As buyers and sellers of foreign exchange, governments act to influence the exchange rate and to reduce or augment holdings of various currencies in the central bank. If a country has been running a balance of trade deficit, it may be able to reduce the deficit by having the central bank buy foreign currency in the open market. Sufficient purchases will cause the local currency to devalue, making exports cheaper and imports more expensive to buyers. If export and import price elasticities are high enough, this may lead to an improvement in the balance of trade.[6]

Determination of the Exchange Rate

Exchange rates are determined by the activities of the five types of actors described above. If one could calculate the supply and demand curves for each exchange market participant, and anticipate government constraints on the exchange market, then exchange rate determination would be fairly simple. The composite supply and demand for foreign exchange would be as depicted in Figure 5-1.

Lacking this information, the analyst can still rely on two fundamental economic relationships that underlie exchange rate determination. Note that this section considers only economic factors; government restrictions on the exchange market are ignored.

The two fundamental economic relationships are *purchasing power parity* and the *international Fisher effect.* The former posits that shifts in exchange rates will occur to offset different rates of inflation in pairs of countries, and the latter posits that exchange rates will shift to offset interest rate differentials between countries.

Purchasing Power Parity (PPP)[7]

If a standard ton of polyurethane plastic costs $200 in the United States and DM 400 in Germany, then **purchasing power parity (PPP)** requires an exchange rate of 2 DM/$. The same reasoning could be used for all products whose production processes are equivalent in two countries and which are traded between these countries. The exchange rate that comes closest to simultaneously satisfying all of these equilibrium conditions is the PPP rate—a rate that equates the internal purchasing power of the two currencies in both countries.

Assuming that we begin from that exchange rate, what will happen if Germany's inflation is 5 percent and U.S. inflation is 10 percent in the following year? Purchasing power parity requires that the exchange rate adjust to eliminate this differential. Specifically, it requires that:

$$\frac{1 + \text{Infl}_{\text{US}}}{1 + \text{Infl}_{\text{Ger}}} = \frac{\text{XR}_{t+1}}{\text{XR}_t}$$

where:

Infl = Inflation rate.

t = Time period.

This means that inflation in the United States relative to inflation in Germany should be the same as the future exchange rate compared to the spot exchange rate. The relationship can also be written in a form similar to the interest parity equation, by rearranging terms:

$$(1 + \text{Infl}_{US}) = (1 + \text{Infl}_{Ger}) \frac{XR_{t+1}}{XR_t}$$

Purchasing power in each currency will be retained if:

$$XR_{t+1} = \frac{1.10}{1.05} (\$0.32/\text{DM}) = \$0.335/\text{DM, or DM } 2.98/\$$$

International Fisher Effect

The **international Fisher effect** translates Irving Fisher's reasoning about domestic interest rates to the transnational level. Fisher showed that inflation-adjusted (i.e., "real") interest rates tend to stay the same over time; as inflation rises or falls, so do *nominal* (unadjusted) interest rates, such that real interest rates remain unchanged. At the transnational level, nominal national interest rates are expected to differ only by the expected change in the national currency's price (i.e., the exchange rate). The international Fisher effect thus concludes that interest differentials between national markets will be eliminated by adjustments in the exchange rate. In terms similar to PPP, we see that:

$$\frac{1 + i_{US}}{1 + i_{foreign}} = \frac{XR_{t+1}}{XR_t}, \text{ or } (1 + i_{US}) = (1 + i_{foreign}) \frac{XR_{t+1}}{XR_t}$$

If the eurodollar deposit rate is 10 percent/year and the euro-French franc rate is 15 percent/year, the franc will be expected to devalue in the coming year by:

$$\frac{1.10}{1.15} = 0.9565, \text{ or } 4.35 \text{ percent}$$

Notice that the international Fisher effect *will* operate in a free market, because investors will receive a higher return in French francs otherwise. As more and more U.S. investors put their money in eurofrancs, the spot price of FF will rise. Similarly, as U.S. investors return their franc earnings to dollars at the end of the period (year), this increased demand for dollars will cause the franc to devalue (in the future). Thus, dollar and franc earnings will tend to be equalized.

Combined Equilibrium Relationships

The future exchange rate, XR_{t+1}, will be partially determined by both of the above factors (PPP and international Fisher), which can be viewed in a general equilibrium context, as shown in Figure 5-6. This figure also demonstrates the interest parity relationship, which provides another link between current and future currency values. Remember that these relationships are

Figure 5-6 **Exchange Rate Determination**

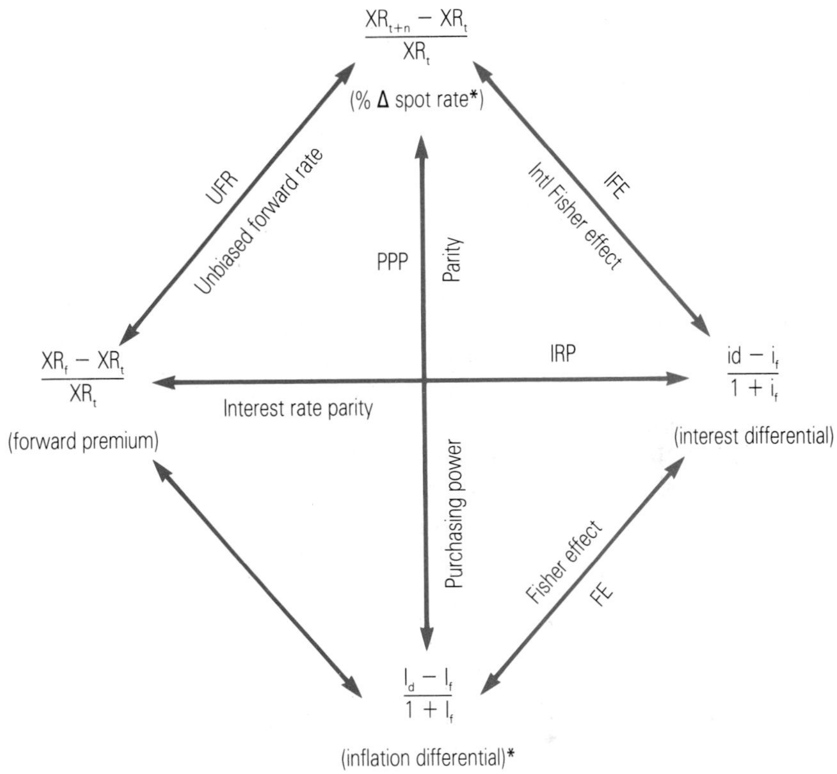

* = Forecasted value

This model ignores government XR controls and transactions costs.

equilibrium economic conditions, which hold only approximately since substantial uncertainty exists about future conditions. Also, if a government intervenes to disallow the market from determining exchange rates, the relationships may diverge substantially from the equilibrium conditions. Figure 5-6 shows the main economic influences that—along with government policies and other factors—combine to determine exchange rates.

A final caveat is in order. Despite the strong relationships among interest differentials, inflation differentials, and exchange rates, there are other important *economic* influences operating in international finance. Pure speculation can cause shifts in exchange rates, despite the fundamental economic conditions that have been described above. A country's balance of payments position (see Chapter 7) may affect the exchange rate, even though that position also affects interest and inflation rates as well. Since the abandonment of the Bretton Woods system of fixed exchange rates, exchange rate determination has been extremely uncertain—perhaps similar to the determination of future values of stock exchange indexes.

Methods of Protecting against Exchange Risk

Exchange risk is a very real concern for financial managers, whether or not their firms are directly involved in international business. The fact that the prices of imported products and services often vary with the exchange rate means that a local firm's costs may be dependent on the exchange rate. Similarly, if any of the firm's sales are exported, its earnings may vary as foreign sales change due to exchange rate changes. Even a purely domestic firm is faced with these problems, since suppliers and competitors that *are* doing international business will adjust to exchange rate changes—and this will affect the domestic firm.

From this perspective, exchange risk is *not* the risk that a local currency will decrease in value (devalue) relative to the dollar. *Exchange risk **is** the possibility that a firm will be unable to adjust its prices and costs to exactly offset exchange rate changes.* Thus, if a U.S. importer faces 10 percent higher costs because of a dollar devaluation from DM 2.5/US$ to DM 2.25/US$, he still has no exchange risk as long as he can raise his own prices by 10 percent without lowering total sales. (This result is the microeconomic version of purchasing power parity.) The problem may be viewed as one of "passing through" cost increases to the firm's customers via higher sales prices.

Similarly, the appropriate measure of exchange risk for financial instruments is the firm's possible loss or gain in purchasing power from exchange rate-adjusted interest rates. Investing in a U.S. dollar account that pays 10 percent per year is better than investing in a French franc account that pays 20 percent per year if during the year the franc devalues by 12 percent.

Alternatives to Minimize Exchange Risk

Exchange risk exists whenever the firm's prices and costs cannot be exactly adjusted to offset changes in the exchange rate. Let us now consider a group of alternatives that will allow a firm to minimize (or at least reduce) its exchange risk. These alternatives fall into four categories:

1. Risk avoidance.
2. Risk adaptation.
3. Risk transfer.
4. Diversification.

The Strategy of Risk Avoidance **Exchange risk avoidance** is the strategy of trying to escape foreign currency transactions. A purely domestic firm can try to make all of its purchases from local suppliers of locally produced goods and to make all of its sales to local buyers in competition only with other domestic firms. Obviously, this strategy is impractical, if only because all firms are affected by goods priced in foreign currency—automobiles, chemicals, steel, and so on. Also, there are very few industries that do not use imported materials, or export some of their output, or compete with imported products.

The Strategy of Risk Adaptation **Exchange risk adaptation** offers a more realistic alternative for protecting the firm against exchange risk. This strategy includes all methods of "hedging" against exchange rate changes. In the extreme, exchange risk calls for protecting all liabilities denominated in foreign currency with equal-value, equal-maturity assets denominated in that foreign currency. An illustration can best clarify this point.

Assume that a French firm has contracted to buy $100,000 of machinery from a foreign supplier for use in its manufacturing operations. The purchase is payable in six months in U.S. dollars. To eliminate foreign exchange risk completely, the firm may do two things. First, it may raise its own prices to customers once the six months pass, in order to equate franc devaluation to price increase. (Note that this does *not* involve a foreign currency hedge.) If this option is not available, which is often the case, the firm may look to its other option: obtain some equal-value *dollar asset* maturing in 180 days. This may be as simple as depositing funds in a dollar-denominated bank account for six months or as arcane as arranging a swap of the dollar liability for some other firm's franc liability. Fairly standard methods of hedging an exposed dollar liability include:

1. Obtaining a dollar-denominated financial asset (e.g., a time deposit or a CD) that matures when the liability comes due.
2. Finding a buyer for your firm's products and agreeing to receive payment in U.S. dollars for the same value and time as the liability.
3. Finding a bank that will contract to buy francs from you and sell you dollars at a price fixed today for exchange when the liability comes due. (This is called a "forward contract.")
4. Agreeing with another (e.g., North American) firm to exchange your dollar liability for that firm's (i.e., its French subsidiary's) franc liability.
5. Contracting for any other equal-value, equal-maturity dollar-denominated asset that will offset the exposed liability.

The firm's goal in choosing among these methods is to minimize the cost of protection against exchange rate risk.

The Strategy of Risk Transfer The third strategy for reducing exchange risk is **exchange risk transfer.** This strategy involves the use of an insurance contract or guarantee, which transfers the exchange risk to the insuror or guarantor. In many countries, the central bank offers exchange risk guarantees to importers and exporters of some products, according to the bank's policies. Technically, though perhaps not realistically, any firm or government agency could issue a guarantee covering exchange rate changes to a local importer—at a price that would presumably reflect the risk.

The Strategy of Diversification The final strategy for reducing exchange risk is **currency diversification.** That is, a firm can reduce the risk of unexpected local currency devaluations by spreading its assets and liabilities across several currencies (e.g., deutsche marks, Swiss francs, and pounds, in addition to U.S. dollars). This strategy simply means, "Don't put all of your eggs in one basket." Domestically, a firm should deal with several suppliers and a variety of customers in order to reduce risk through diversification. Internationally, a firm should hold assets (and liabilities) in several currencies in order to reduce the impact of unexpected exchange rate changes.

The strategy that is probably most useful to the majority of firms is risk adaptation, or hedging. A key point of this section is to recognize that other alternatives may be used in many instances when hedging would be more expensive or otherwise less desirable. Nonetheless, the central problem in exchange risk management is hedging, and corporate treasurers should always be on the lookout for new instruments and techniques.

Conclusions

The foreign exchange market is a central part of international business. That market is really several distinct markets, including spot transactions as well as forward contracts, futures, options, and other instruments that may vary from country to country.

The participants in the foreign exchange market include commercial banks—the most important participants in terms of the value of transactions undertaken—and many other actors in the private and public sectors, such as corporations, individuals, and governments. The main forces determining exchange rates tend to be the large banks that trade billions of dollars worth of currencies daily.

Exchange rates are determined by government choice in each country. When, as in most industrialized, noncommunist countries today, the government allows the free market to operate, such economic factors as inflation differentials and interest rate differentials tend to determine exchange rates. Even so, forecasting exchange rates is a highly uncertain activity today, because of the wealth of factors that influence these rates.

Finally, protection against exchange rate variations is possible through many kinds of hedging strategies. Generally, companies, banks, and individuals want to find foreign currency liabilities to balance against their existing foreign currency assets, and vice versa. The ultimate decision to hedge or not hedge (i.e., speculate) is a matter of policy for the firm; there is no "right" answer.

Questions

1. Who are the main participants in the foreign exchange market in the United States? How does each of these participants affect the exchange rate?
2. Based on Figure 5-1, would you expect interest rates in Japan to be higher or lower than those in the United States? Why?
3. Given that France's inflation is about 15 percent per year at present, while U.S. inflation is about 4 percent per year, what do you expect to happen to the franc/dollar exchange rate in the next few months? Why?
4. Explain the business of interest arbitrage. How can a bank profit from it?
5. What is the difference between the forward exchange rate and the future spot exchange rate?
6. How do foreign exchange brokers function in the U.S. foreign exchange market?
7. Explain the influence of the U.S. government in determining the exchange rate between the dollar and the Japanese yen. How does the Japanese government affect this rate?
8. Currently, the interest rate on U.S. dollar deposits in London is 10.375 percent per year and the rate on German mark deposits there is 5.6875 percent per year. The spot exchange rate is US$0.3254/DM. What do you expect the exchange rate to be in one year?
9. How would you hedge the value of your export sale of FF 10 million of computers to a French customer? You will be paid in 180 days in francs. On what basis would you choose among hedging methods?
10. Why do the exchange rates of the forward market and the futures market differ for similar maturities?

References

Andrews, Michael. "Recent Trends in the U.S. Foreign Exchange Market," *Quarterly Review,* Federal Reserve Bank of New York, Summer 1984.

Giddy, Ian. "Foreign Exchange Options." *Journal of Futures Markets* 3, no. 2 (1983).

Kindleberger, Charles, and Peter Lindert. *International Economics.* 7th ed. Homewood, Ill.: Richard D. Irwin, 1982.

Kubarych, Roger. *Foreign Exchange Markets in the United States.* Federal Reserve Bank of New York, 1981.

Shapiro, Alan. *Multinational Financial Management.* Boston: Allyn & Bacon, 1982.

Endnotes

1. "Evolution and Growth of the United States Foreign Exchange Market", *Quarterly Review,* Federal Reserve Bank of New York, Autumn 1981.

2. The clearing member banks of the New York Clearinghouse Association are: Bank of New York, Bankers Trust, Chase Manhattan Bank, Chemical Bank, Citibank, European American Bank, Irving Trust, Manufacturers Hanover Trust, Marine Midland Bank, Morgan Guaranty, National Westminster Bank, and U.S. Trust.
3. "Taking a position" means purchasing an asset (or liability) denominated in a foreign currency without simultaneously matching it with a liability (asset) of the same value and maturity in the same currency. If a U.S. bank buys Swiss francs, it has taken a position in Swiss francs. When the bank sells those Swiss francs to a client, it has eliminated the position.
4. Ian Giddy has shown how similar arbitrage can be used between a forward market and an *options* market, since the combination of a put and a call option on the same currency is analogous to a forward contract. See Giddy (1983).
5. Notice that analogous conditions face Swiss arbitrageurs, who *should* buy dollars, invest in a eurodollar deposit, and buy SF forward under these conditions. (Check the results mathematically.) Thus, interest arbitrage *will* occur in the example, though not by dollar-holding arbitrageurs.
6. The Marshall-Lerner condition requires that the export elasticity of demand plus the import elasticity of demand is less than one in order for a devaluation to improve the balance of trade. See, e.g., Kindleberger and Lindert, 7th ed., pp. 292-96.
7. This entire discussion refers to *relative* purchasing power parity (PPP). The stronger, absolute version refers to parity in the values of factor inputs used in the production of products whose prices reflect relative factor productivities. Relative PPP considers only *changes* in the relative price levels between countries, not the initial (absolute) levels.

Case

Fred's Furniture, Ltd.

Fred Fox walked out of his Piccadilly Circus store one afternoon in August 1986, shaking his head and wondering whether there was any solution to the foreign currency game. He had just contracted for the third time with his good friend Jean Marnier in Paris for an export shipment of FF 2,000,000 of tables, chairs, and sofas that would be sent in November and paid for in February 1987. The past two times that Fox had dealt with Marnier on similar shipments, he later discovered that devaluations of the franc relative to the pound had left him with virtually no profit on the sales. This time he had been able to get Marnier to accept a 15 percent markup in the price quote (payable in francs) to offset the expected devaluation of the franc between now and next February. Unfortunately, he had been unable to persuade Marnier to pay in British pounds! The exchange rate risk still existed, and despite the price markup Fox was very unhappy about living with it.

A second, related problem compounded Fox's frustration. He had just agreed to buy a large supply of polyvinyl chloride (PVC) plastic, from which one of his local furniture suppliers would construct the ultramodern tables that currently made up about one fourth of Fox's sales in England. He had already given a price quotation to his manufacturer, so there was no flexibility at that end. The supplier of this PVC was in Germany, and demanded to be paid in German marks (in 120 days). Once again, Fox had tried to anticipate the possible impact of currency changes on this DM 200,000 transaction, but he had been unable to figure out a solution.

Fred sometimes thought that he was blessed with good fortune because he lived within the European Community, since the member countries had eliminated almost all restrictions on exports of furniture among the 12 countries in the Community. His export sales were growing very satisfactorily, except for the foreign currency problem. That problem, however, was a curse to his business, since Fred made no claim to be a "finance man," and he was truly baffled by the fluctuations among pounds, marks, francs, lira, and other currencies.

A trip to the local Barclays Bank office cleared up some of the issues for him. First, he discovered that he could contract for a forward sale or purchase of any of the currencies that he dealt with. By accepting a small premium or discount relative to the current exchange rate, Fox could guarantee a fixed exchange rate for his future purchases of marks (for pounds) and his future sales of francs (to buy pounds). The rate quotations relevant to the two transactions described above are listed in Table 1.

The Barclays banker also suggested that Fox consider financing his French franc receivable with a loan in francs, rather than using British pound financing during the period from now until payment by Marnier's firm. This

This case was written in 1986 by Professor Robert Grosse as a basis for class discussion.

Table 1 Exchange Rate Arrangements as of March 31, 1985[1]

Pegged: Single Currency: U.S. Dollar	Pegged: Single Currency: French Franc	Pegged: Single Currency: Other	Pegged: Currency Composite: SDR	Pegged: Currency Composite: Other	Flexibility Limited vis-à-vis a Single Currency or a Group of Currencies: Single Currency[2]	Flexibility Limited vis-à-vis a Single Currency or a Group of Currencies: Cooperative Arrangements	More Flexible: Adjusted According to a Set of Indicators	More Flexible: Managed Floating	More Flexible: Independently Floating
Antigua and Barbuda	Benin	Bhutan (Indian rupee)	Burma	Algeria[3]	Afghanistan[3]	Belgium	Brazil	Argentina	Australia
Bahamas	Burkina Faso	Gambia (£)	Burundi	Austria	Bahrain[4]	Denmark	Chile[3]	Costa Rica[3]	Canada
Barbados	Cameroon	Lesotho (South African rand)	Guinea[3]	Bangladesh[3]	Ghana	France	Colombia	Ecuador[3]	Dominican Republic
Belize	Central Africa Republic	Swaziland (South African rand)	Iran	Botswana	Maldives	Germany, Federal Republic of	Peru[3]	Greece	Jamaica
Bolivia	Chad		Jordan	Cape Verde	Qatar[4]	Ireland	Portugal	Guinea-Bissau	Japan
Djibouti	Comoros		Kenya	China, People's Republic of	Saudi Arabia[4]	Italy[6]	Somalia[5]	Iceland	Lebanon
Dominica	Congo		Rwanda	Cyprus	United Arab Emirates[4]	Luxembourg[3]		India[8]	New Zealand
Egypt[3]	Equatorial Guinea		São Tomé and Príncipe	Fiji		Netherlands		Indonesia	Philippines
El Salvador[3]	Gabon		Seychelles	Finland[7]				Israel	South Africa
Ethiopia	Ivory Coast		Sierra Leone[3]	Guyana				Korea	Uganda
Grenada	Mali		Vanuatu	Hungary				Mexico[3]	United Kingdom
Guatemala[3]	Niger		Vietnam	Kuwait				Morocco	United States
Haiti	Senegal			Madagascar				Nigeria	Uruguay
Honduras	Togo			Malawi				Pakistan	Zaire
Iraq				Malaysia				Spain	
Lao People's Democratic Republic[3]									
Liberia									
Libya									
Nicaragua[3]									
Oman									
Panama									
Paraguay[3]									
St. Christopher and Nevis									
St. Lucia									
St. Vincent and the Grenadines									
Sudan[3]									
Suriname									
Syrian Arab Republic[3]									

Trinidad and Tobago	Malta	Sri Lanka
Venezuela[3]	Mauritania	Turkey
Yemen Arab Republic	Mauritius	Western Samoa
Yemen, People's Democratic Republic	Mozambique	Yugoslavia
	Nepal	
	Norway	
	Papua New Guinea	
	Romania	
	Singapore	
	Solomon Islands	
	Sweden	
	Tanzania	
	Thailand	
	Tunisia	
	Zambia	
	Zimbabwe	

[1] No current information is available relating to Democratic Kampuchea.

[2] All exchange rates have shown limited flexibility vis-à-vis the U.S. dollar

[3] Member maintains dual exchange markets involving multiple exchange arrangements. The arrangement shown is that maintained in the major market.

[4] Exchange rates are determined on the basis of a fixed relationship to the SDR, within margins of up to ±7.25 percent. However, because of the maintenance of a relatively stable relationship with the U.S. dollar, these margins are not always observed.

[5] The exchange rate is maintained within overall margins of ±7.5 percent about the fixed shilling/SDR relationship; the exchange rate is reevaluated when indicative margins of ±2.25 percent are exceeded.

[6] Margins of ±6 percent are maintained with respect to the currencies of other countries participating in the exchange rate mechanism of the European Monetary System.

[7] The effective exchange rate, measured by a basket of currencies of the main trading partners, is maintained within margins of ±2.25 percent.

[8] The exchange rate is maintained within margins of ±5 percent on either side of a weighted composite of the currencies of the main trading partners.

Source: International Monetary Fund, *Exchange Arrangement and Exchange Restrictions: Annual Report, 1985* (Washington, D.C.: IMF, 1985).

Table 2 **Interest Rate and Exchange Rate Quotations Offered to Fred Fox, August 1, 1986**

Spot exchange rates:	FF 10.34 per £ DM 3.19 per £
180-day forward rate:	FF 10.22 per £
120-day forward rate:	DM 3.15 per £
120-day or 180-day British pound deposit interest rate: 9.8125% per year 180-day euro-French francs deposit interest rate: 7.375% per year 120-day euro-German mark deposit interest rate: 4.50% per year Fred's Furniture would pay the deposit rate plus 2% per year for a loan.	
Six-month put options on French francs at FF 10.20 per £ have a premium of £300 per contract; each contract is for FF 100,000. Six-month call options on German marks at DM 3.20 per £ have a premium of £200 per contract; each contract is for DM 50,000.	

Note: Each exchange rate can be used as a bid or offered rate as needed; ignore the difference.

would enable Fox to balance out his furniture sale in francs with the loan repayment and also give him funds today that could be used in his ongoing business. Unfortunately for Fox, the young Barclays banker also suggested that he consider taking out an option on future marks in the London International Financial Futures Exchange. Since Fox could not follow the banker's explanation of the way this instrument works he determined to eliminate options as an alternative. All of the rate quotations given by Barclays to Fox are listed in Table 1.

Beyond the short-term problem of dealing with the two transactions described above, Fred wants to establish some kind of system for handling future foreign-currency business. He is highly risk averse when it comes to exchange rate risk, and his primary objective is to avoid large losses due to currency fluctuations.

6 INTERNATIONAL FINANCIAL MARKETS AND INSTITUTIONS

This chapter considers foreign and international financial markets that allow firms to find sources of funds outside their home countries and to place available funds in portfolio-type investments outside the home country. These markets include national money and capital markets in different countries, plus the euromarkets, both short and long term. Since the eurocurrency and eurobond markets are widely used even by purely domestic firms, a knowledge of the instruments and institutions involved will benefit financial decision makers in almost any kind of firm. The main goals of the chapter are to:

1. Review the basic characteristics of all the financial markets that may be available to a firm in international business.
2. Give insights into domestic money and capital markets that exist around the world.
3. Give insights into the functioning of the euromarkets.
4. Show how firms can take advantage of the opportunities available in all of these markets.
5. Explain how the international monetary (IMF) system functions and how it relates to both private sector firms and governments.

Introduction

Whether or not a company becomes directly involved in international business through exports, direct investment, and the like, there is still an important international market to consider, even for domestic business: the market for borrowing and lending abroad. Many times, companies find that borrowing funds abroad is less expensive than borrowing domestically, in the United States or in any other home country. The relatively unrestricted "euromarkets" generally offer better terms to borrowers (and lenders) than do domestic financial markets in any country. This chapter explores the various foreign and international financial markets (except the foreign exchange market, which was discussed in Chapter 5) and examines ways to utilize them for domestic and international business.

Table 6-1 presents an overview of international financial markets. It should be emphasized that the final market to consider in conducting financial transactions in these markets is the market for real goods and services, or

Table 6-1 **International Financial Markets**

Market	Instruments	Participants	Regulator
International monetary system	Special drawing rights; gold; foreign exchange	Central banks; International Monetary Fund	International Monetary Fund
Foreign exchange markets	Bank deposits; currency; futures and forward contracts	Commercial and central banks; firms; individuals	Central bank in each country
National money markets (short term)	Bank deposits and loans; short-term government securities; commercial paper	Banks; firms; individuals; government agencies	Central bank; other government agencies
National capital markets (long term)	Bonds; long-term bank deposits and loans; stocks; long-term government securities	Banks; firms; individuals; government agencies	Central bank; other government agencies
Eurocurrency market	Bank deposits; bank loans; eurocommercial paper	Commercial banks; firms; government agencies	Substantially unregulated
Eurobond market	Bonds	Banks; firms; individuals; government agencies	Substantially unregulated

consumption. That is, the ultimate use of financial instruments in each of these markets is to claim goods and services, today or in the future. Table 6-1 sketches some of the important characteristics of the six types of international financial markets.

International Financial Markets

The **international monetary system** is a market among the central banks of the countries that belong to the International Monetary Fund (IMF). This organization functions as a kind of central banking system for the national governments of its 137 members. Each member country deposits funds at the IMF, and in return each may borrow funds in the currency of any other member country. This system is *not* open to private sector participants, so it is not directly useful to company managers. However, agreements made between member countries and the IMF often lead to major changes in government policies toward companies and banks (such as exchange rate changes and controls and trade controls), so an understanding of the international monetary system may be quite important to managers. Regulation in this system comes through rules passed by the IMF's members. The major financial instruments used in the international monetary system are national currencies, gold, and a currency issued by the IMF itself, called the SDR (special drawing right). These points are defined more clearly, and the IMF system is discussed in detail, in a later section of this chapter.

A **foreign exchange market,** as seen in the previous chapter, is a market in which financial instruments denominated in one currency can be exchanged for market instruments denominated in another currency. Typically, most foreign exchange is sold through the commercial banking system of a country, in the form of bank deposits. Cash exchanges by traveling business people and tourists are quite common—but nearly all of the vast quantities of money exchanged goes between banks, as account transfers, and in large amounts. Regulation of foreign exchange markets comes primarily from the national government of the country where the markets are located, through the central bank. The main instruments used in foreign exchange dealings include account transfers by telephone, wire, or otherwise; bank drafts; forward and futures contracts; and currencies.

National money markets and national capital markets are simply the national financial markets of countries other than the home country of the firm. So, for a U.S.-based company, the money and capital markets of France are international (really foreign) financial markets. Access to such markets is often limited to "domestic" firms, which usually include locally incorporated subsidiaries of multinational enterprises. Thus, foreign money and capital markets are additional potential sources and users of funds for the MNE.

Short-term national financial markets, or national money markets, generally offer the MNE some opportunities to obtain or place funds. Typically, local bank deposits and short-term investments in Treasury securities give the firm an interest-earning opportunity for its locally available funds. A variety of additional instruments can also be found in many of the developed countries and a number of LDCs. Commercial paper, promissory notes, and short-term government obligations are just a few of them. MNEs can often borrow from local banks or through the issue of some form of promissory notes—or sometimes directly from the government. For short-term funding and investing decisions, the MNE manager needs to be aware of the wide variety of money market instruments that are available in host countries.

Similarly, **long-term national financial markets,** or national capital markets, offer additional opportunities to MNE financial managers. A number of countries have national securities markets in which the MNE can issue its own securities (stocks and bonds) or invest in the securities of other firms. In most countries, long-term bank loans provide a source of funds and national treasury issues provide investment possibilities. Regulation in both of these national financial markets comes from the national government, through such agencies as the central bank, the treasury, and the securities exchange.

The fifth and sixth markets for financial instruments are the **euromarkets**—The short-term eurocurrency market and the long-term eurobond market. Each of these financial markets is characterized by the issuance of instruments (i.e., deposits or bonds) denominated in some currency other than the one of the country where the instruments are issued. The euromarkets are generally unrestricted by governments and establish their own pricing and other conditions.

The **eurocurrency market** is a largely short-term market for bank deposits and loans denominated in any currency except the currency of the country where the market is located. In London, for example, the eurocurrency market is a market for bank deposits (and loans) denominated in dollars, marks, yen, and any other currency except British pounds. In Paris, the eurocurrency market is a market for similar instruments denominated in dollars, marks, yen, pounds, and any other currency except French francs. Most of the transactions in this market have maturities of less than one year, although some deposits and loans are long-term. The main instruments used in the eurocurrency market are certificates of deposit and time deposits, and bank loans. During the past few years, euro-commercial paper has become a significant short-term instrument as well.

The **eurobond market** is a long-term market for bonds denominated in any currency except the currency of the country where the market is located. It is basically the long-term counterpart of the eurocurrency market (though there are also other important differences). The only instruments used in the eurobond market are bonds, denominated in various currencies, typically with a floating interest rate. Since regulation is minimal in the countries that permit eurobond issue, participants in this market depend for protection on the reputations of the other participants rather than on national securities laws.

Advantages of Euromarkets

The euromarkets offer investors and borrowers in one country the opportunity to deal with borrowers and investors from many other countries, purchasing and selling deposits, bonds, and loans denominated in many currencies. Euromarkets may be entered through affiliates of "eurobanks"—banks that participate in the euromarkets—in virtually any country. For instance, a eurodollar loan may be taken by a U.S. company, dealing through the local office of a U.S. bank that legally books the transaction in London. Similarly, a U.S. investor may place a deposit in the eurodollar market simply by instructing a local U.S. bank to create the deposit in its foreign branch in London, Panama, or any one of more than a dozen euromarket centers worldwide. Finally, eurobonds and euro-commercial paper may be issued by investment banking firms on behalf of company or government clients in several national markets simultaneously to many types of investors. In all, the euromarkets offer substantial opportunities to virtually any large or medium-sized firm that deals in financial markets for either borrowing or lending.

The last market of interest here is the market for goods and services, which is the ultimate destination of the financial instruments used in the other markets. Either at present or in the future, the various financial instruments will be utilized to purchase real goods or services from suppliers in one country or another. The key *social* benefits of the various international financial markets are that they facilitate the processes of matching borrowers and lenders in all parts of the world and that they facilitate payments through widely accepted media of exchange.[1]

Let us consider first the local money and capital markets of the host countries where multinational firms establish their affiliates.

Foreign Money and Capital Markets

In each country that the MNE enters, it will be able to obtain some degree of access to local financial markets. The MNE will generally utilize such markets to perform necessary local financial transactions and often to hedge its local asset exposure through local borrowing (or its local liability exposure through local deposits or investments). But the MNE can also utilize local financial markets to obtain additional funding (or place additional funds) for its nonlocal activities. A Mexican firm, for example, may choose to borrow funds through its Houston affiliate to finance its local needs in Texas *and* to finance some of its needs in Mexico.

Usually national financial markets are not fully accessible to foreign firms, being reserved for domestic borrowers and lenders to a large degree. In these cases, use of local financial markets must be supplemented by use of the financial markets in the country of the parent company or elsewhere.

Table 6-2 **Characteristics of Selected National Money and Capital Markets**

Issue Country	Limits on Access to Market	Foreign Exchange Market	Borrowing Instruments Available	Size of Stock Market	Size of Bond Market
Argentina	Same treatment as local firms	Austral fixed to U.S. dollar; large black market; no forward market	Short-term bank loans; limited overdrafts; discounted A/R*; long-term bank loans	Buenos Aires bolsa has about 65 issues actively traded	Thin market exists; high cost
Brazil	75% of bank credit limited to British firms; FDI not limited	Cruzado highly regulated; official and parallel markets; no forward market	Discounted A/R; short-term bank loans; overdrafts; limited long-term loans	São Paulo bolsa has 608 firms, of which about 100 are actively traded	Very thin and limited to Brazilian firms
Canada	FDI not limited, except for banks and natural resources	Spot, forward, futures, options in Montreal and Toronto	Short-term bank loans; trade credit; commercial paper; B/A**; long-term loans	Toronto exchange has 300 companies	Large and liquid
France	Same treatment as local firms	Spot and forward markets, especially in Paris	Discounted A/R; overdrafts; trade credit; factoring	Paris bourse has 1,100 firms listed	In 1983, FF 145 billion issued
Germany	Same treatment as local firms	Very liquid spot and forward markets, especially in Frankfurt	Short-term bank loans; discounted A/R; overdrafts; trade credit	650 firms listed in Frankfurt exchange	Very deep market for domestic DM and euroDM
Hong Kong	Same treatment as local firms	Active spot market in Hong Kong dollars, fixed to U.S. dollar	Short-term bank loans; overdrafts; discounted A/R	247 stocks listed; few foreign ones	None

Typically, such problems arise in countries that impose exchange controls, which limit the MNE's capability to put needed funds in the affiliate. Selected information about national short- and long-term financial markets in a number of countries is presented in Table 6-2. Notice that the developed countries in the table have far fewer restrictions on their money and capital markets and that the United States has the fewest of all. Exchange controls are the rule in LDCs and are fairly common in developed countries as well.

MNEs and National Money Markets

The advantages that MNEs obtain from entering national money markets as *borrowers* of funds stem from the portfolio effect of holding liabilities in more than one (fluctuating) currency and from the local risk hedging that occurs as the MNE moves to balance local assets such as plant and equipment

Table 6-2 *(concluded)*

Issue Country	Limits on Access to Market	Foreign Exchange Market	Borrowing Instruments Available	Size of Stock Market	Size of Bond Market
India	Most FDI limited to maximum of 40% foreign ownership	Only licensed banks and dealers; spot market only; rupee controlled	Short-term bank loans; overdrafts; discounted A/R; *no* factoring	Active markets in several cities, especially Bombay	None
Japan	Not restricted by law but by discrimination	Limited to registered banks and brokers; spot and forward	Short-term bank loans; discounted A/R; trade credit; factoring	Tokyo exchange second to New York	Very large, including Samurai
Mexico	51% local ownership required	Official and free markets; highly limited; floating peso; no forward market	Short-term bank loans; discounted A/R; trade credit; factoring	200 firms in Mexico bolsa, of which about 50 are actively traded	Mostly limited to government issues
United States	Same treatment as local firms	Spot, forward, futures options in New York City and Chicago	Almost unlimited	New York Stock Exchange has 1613 firms listed	In 1984, $45.5 billion issued
United Kingdom	Same treatment as local firms	Spot, forward, futures options in London	Overdrafts; short-term bank loans; many others	2,738 firms listed in London exchange	Europound common

* Accounts receivable
** Bankers acceptance
Sources: Business International Corporation, *Financing Foreign Operations*. New York: Business International Corporation (1986 edition); and various national sources.

with local liabilities, such as local-currency borrowing. Additional benefits may occur if the local government subsidizes such loans through interest rate reduction, tax breaks, or otherwise; a policy of this kind may be offered to attract the MNE's investment. This may lower the whole MNE's cost of capital if the subsidy does not disappear and if the interest rate remains below the comparable home currency rate during the borrowing period.

The advantages that MNEs obtain from entering national money markets as *lenders* of funds stem from the portfolio effect of holding financial instruments in more than one currency. There may also be a gain from balancing local-currency assets and liabilities if an excess of local liabilities was held previously. In addition, local financial investments may be a necessary strategy when exchange controls or profit remittance limits exist—such investments offer the firm an outlet for retained earnings that yields interest. Sometimes an exchange control policy may make the local-currency interest rates higher than those available in other currencies (after adjusting for expected exchange rate changes). In these cases, higher than normal profits can be earned by investing funds in local instruments, although exchange controls may limit conversion of the profits into the home country currency or a government-imposed exchange rate change may wipe out the advantage.

MNEs and National Capital Markets

The advantages that MNEs obtain from entering national capital markets as *borrowers* are similar to those obtained from entering short-term national markets. However, the opportunities are generally much more limited. Very few countries have substantially developed stock markets, and those that do usually restrict the issuance of shares by foreigners. A few exceptions exist, such as the United States, the United Kingdom, Germany, and France, but even they serve only the largest and most creditworthy MNEs.[2] National bond markets, when they exist at all, are also very restrictive. Thus far, virtually all of the foreign bond issues have taken place in New York (called "Yankee bonds"), London, Switzerland, Germany, and Japan (called "Samurai bonds"). Table 6-3 gives some idea of the size of the foreign bond market and the eurobond market. (The foreign bond market is simply the national bond market of any country as it relates to foreign institutions that seek to issue bonds in that market.)

Notice that all of the foreign bond issues combined do not account for nearly as much funding as the eurobond market. Also notice that the eurobond market is dominated by U.S. dollar issues, while the foreign bond market is far less concentrated in any one currency. (Swiss franc foreign bonds have dominated such issues in the 1980s.) The amount of foreign bonds denominated in currencies other than dollars is more than 80 percent of the total. In contrast, the eurobond market, mostly functioning outside the United States, is dominated by dollar issues, which constitute about three fourths of that total. In all, dollar-denominated issues account for about 60 percent of all international bonds.

Finally, the advantages that MNEs obtain from entering national capital markets as *lenders* come mainly from diversification and from higher returns that may be protected by exchange controls, just as in the short-term market. Since the national capital markets are generally small, opportunities to use them are quite limited for foreigners as well as domestic investors.

Regional Money and Capital Markets

Until recently, the scope of financial markets and instruments was predominantly domestic or fully international, but not regional. In the past decade, however, the European Community (i.e., the European Common Market, which is discussed in Chapter 9) has designed both a regional monetary system (the **European Monetary System, EMS**) and a regional currency

Table 6-3 **Foreign Bond and Eurobond Market Characteristics** (in millions of U.S. dollars)

	1981	1982	1983	1984	1985
(Eurobonds)					
Total euro	31,616	51,645	48,501	79,458	136,731
U.S. dollar	26,830	43,959	38,428	63,593	97,782
German mark	1,277	2,588	3,817	4,604	9,491
British pound	501	748	1,947	3,997	5,766
Japanese yen	368	374	212	1,212	6,539
European currency units	309	1,960	2,019	3,032	7,038
Other	1,697	795	2,078	3,020	10,114
(Foreign bonds)					
Total foreign	21,369	26,397	27,828	27,953	31,025
U.S. dollar	7,552	5,946	4,545	5,487	4,655
German mark	1,310	2,952	2,671	2,243	1,741
British pound	746	1,214	811	1,292	958
Swiss franc	8,285	11,432	14,299	12,626	14,954
Japanese yen	2,457	3,418	3,772	4,628	6,379
Other	538	479	1,730	1,677	2,339
Grand total	52,985	78,042	76,329	107,411	167,756

Source: *World Financial Markets,* Morgan Guaranty Trust Company, various issues.

unit (the **European Currency Unit, ECU**) for intergovernmental financial transactions in the Community. While it seems unlikely that either of these institutions will achieve a position of serious rivalry with the private markets in the United States or the eurocurrency market, they have begun to establish a major presence in Europe. In 1984 a handful of banks began to offer deposits denominated in ECU, and a few years earlier some international lenders offered loans denominated in ECU.[3] Within two years, ECU-denominated eurobond issues became a multibillion-dollar market segment. (See the "tombstone" advertisement of an ECU-denominated bond issue shown in Figure 6-1. Undoubtedly, the possibility exists that this regional financial market will become even more influential in the years ahead.

Historically, financial markets developed among the countries comprised by the colonial empires of England and France. The **sterling area** refers to Great Britain and a group of former British colonies that still deal among themselves in British pounds. Similarly, the **franc area** refers to France and its former colonies, which also continue to denominate a substantial amount

Figure 6-1

EUROPEAN INVESTMENT BANK

ECU 125,000,000

7¾ per cent. Bonds due 1993

Issue Price: 101 per cent.

Bank of Tokyo International Limited

Credit Commercial de France — **EBC Amro Bank Limited**

Merrill Lynch Capital Markets — **Morgan Guaranty Ltd**

Morgan Stanley International — **Orion Royal Bank Limited**

Privatbanken A/S — **Société Générale**

S.G. Warburg Securities

NEW ISSUE — *All these Bonds having been sold, this announcement appears as a matter of record only.* — NOVEMBER 1986

Source: *Europe,* The European Communities, December 1986, p. 22.

of business among themselves in French francs. While substantial financial transactions are conducted within the sterling and franc areas, the eurocurrency market now dominates the total volume of financial flows among the countries in these areas.

The Eurocurrency Market

Definition

A **eurodollar** *is a dollar-denominated bank deposit located outside the United States.* This simple statement defines the basic instrument called the eurodollar. (Eurodollars are *not* dollars in the pockets of people who live in Europe! They are deposit liabilities of banks.) The widely discussed eurocurrency market is just a set of bank deposits located outside the countries whose currency is used in the deposits. Since almost 80 percent of the deposits are denominated in U.S. dollars, it is reasonably accurate to call this the **eurodollar market.** Notice that the eurodollar market is not limited to Europe; very large eurodollar markets exist in Hong Kong, Bahrain, Panama, and other cities throughout the world. For this reason, the eurodollar market is sometimes called the international money market.[4]

This financial market grew from its inception sometime in the late 1950s to a size of about $US 2,833 billion at the end of 1985, as shown in Table 6-4.

Significance

What is the significance of the international money market? Since the eurocurrency market rivals domestic financial markets as a funding source for corporate borrowing, it plays a key role in the capital investment decisions of many firms. And since this market also rivals domestic financial markets as a

Table 6-4 **Eurocurrency Market Size and Growth** (measured by foreign currency liabilities at end of period, in billions of U.S. dollars)

	1971	1973	1975	1980	1983	1985
Gross market size	150	310	480	1,524	2,278	2,846
Nonbanks	30	55	80	327	478	585
Official monetary institutions	15	40	70	150	91	112
Other banks	105	215	330	1,047	1,645	2,149
Eurodollars as a percentage of total	76	73	78	75	90	89

Source: *World Financial Markets,* Morgan Guaranty Trust Company (various issues).

deposit alternative, it absorbs important amounts of savings from lenders (i.e., depositors) in many countries. In fact, the eurocurrency market complements the domestic financial markets, giving greater access to borrowing and lending to financial market participants in each of the countries where it is permitted to function. Overall, the eurocurrency market is now the world's single most important market for international financial intermediation.

This market is completely a creation of the regulatory structures placed by national governments on banking, or more broadly, on financial intermediation. If national governments allowed banks to function without reserve requirements, interest rate restrictions, capital controls, and taxes, then the eurocurrency market would just involve the transnational deposits and loans made in each country's banking system. Instead, national governments heavily regulate national financial markets, in efforts to achieve various monetary policy goals. Thus, the eurocurrency market provides a very important outlet for funds flows that avoid many of the limitations placed on domestic financial markets. Many national governments have found the impact of the eurocurrency market on their firms and banks to be favorable, so they have allowed this market to operate.[5]

Bases

Since the eurocurrency market is a creation of the regulatory structure, it may be helpful to think about the key underpinnings of the system that allows eurodollars. There are essentially three conditions that must be met for a eurocurrency market to exist. First, some national government must allow foreign currency deposits to be made, so that, for example, depositors in London can obtain dollar-denominated time deposits there. Second, the country whose currency is being used—in this example, the United States—must allow foreign entities to own and exchange deposits in that currency. Third, there must be some reason, such as low cost or ease of use, that prompts people to use this market rather than other financial markets, such as the domestic ones. The eurocurrency market has met these conditions for the past three decades, and its phenomenal growth testifies that the demand for such a market has been very large.

A wide range of countries allow foreign-currency deposits to be held in their banking systems. Many of them impose restrictions (interest rate limits, capital controls, and so on) on these as well as on local-currency deposits, so that a free market does not exist. Other countries, including most of the developed countries and many of the newly industrializing countries, allow foreign-currency deposits that are not subject to the regulations placed on domestic deposits. In such countries, participants find more favorable interest rates, greater availability of funds, and greater ease of moving funds internationally. These countries tend to be the euromarket centers.

Only a few currencies have become popular as eurocurrencies. Generally, these are the ones that are used widely in international trade—the U.S. dollar, the British pound, the French franc, the German mark, and a handful of others. The governments of all the nations whose currency is being used have consented (or, more accurately, have not objected) to allow foreign banks, companies, and individuals to hold and use deposits denominated in that currency. This may appear to be a trivial point, but any limitation on nonresidents' use of dollar (or other eurocurrency) deposits would quickly eliminate that currency from the euromarket. The U.S. government's temporary freeze on Iranian assets held in U.S. banks in 1979 caused a tremendous crisis in the eurodollar market, because other participants saw the possibility of losing use of their eurodollars at the whim of the U.S. government. The potential problem will continue to exist, but on the whole participants in the euromarket expect that full freedom to use the (dollar-denominated) deposits will continue indefinitely.

The third condition that is fundamental to the success of the euromarket is that it must possess advantages that will attract participants to the market. Those advantages include the ability to carry out dollar-denominated transactions outside the United States and the availability of favorable interest rates relative to rates in the domestic market. The first advantage clearly exists, because eurodollar account owners can sell their accounts to pay for other transactions, without any need to deal directly in the United States. The second advantage also exists, primarily because lack of regulation of the euromarket allows banks to reduce their costs and pass on the savings to clients in the form of lower loan rates and higher deposit rates. Figure 6-2, shows that the eurodollar interest rates have a very small spread over the domestic deposit rate.

Eurocurrency Interest Rates

The base interest rate paid on deposits between banks in the eurocurrency market is called **LIBOR,** the London interbank offered rate. (Outside London, which is the center of the entire euromarket, the base rate on deposits is generally slightly higher.) LIBOR is determined by the supply and demand for funds in the euromarket for each currency. Because participating banks could default (and, infrequently, do default) on their obligations, the rate paid for eurodollar deposits is always somewhat above the domestic Treasury bill rate. Also, because domestic banks must comply with Federal Reserve requirements, they offer slightly lower deposit rates than unregulated eurobanks, as shown in Figure 6-2.

The lending rate has no name comparable to the prime rate, but it is determined as LIBOR plus some margin, or spread, charged to the borrower. Banks generally do not require compensating balances or other implicit charges in addition to the spread over LIBOR in the euromarket. This also helps reduce the cost of using the euromarket for borrowers. The total cost of borrowing in the euromarket for a prime U.S. corporation historically was marginally below the domestic U.S. prime rate. Since the early 1980s, prime borrowers have been able to obtain the same rate in both markets.

Interest rates on other eurocurrencies generally follow the same pattern,

Figure 6-2 **Interest Rates on Domestic and Eurodollar Deposits and Loans**

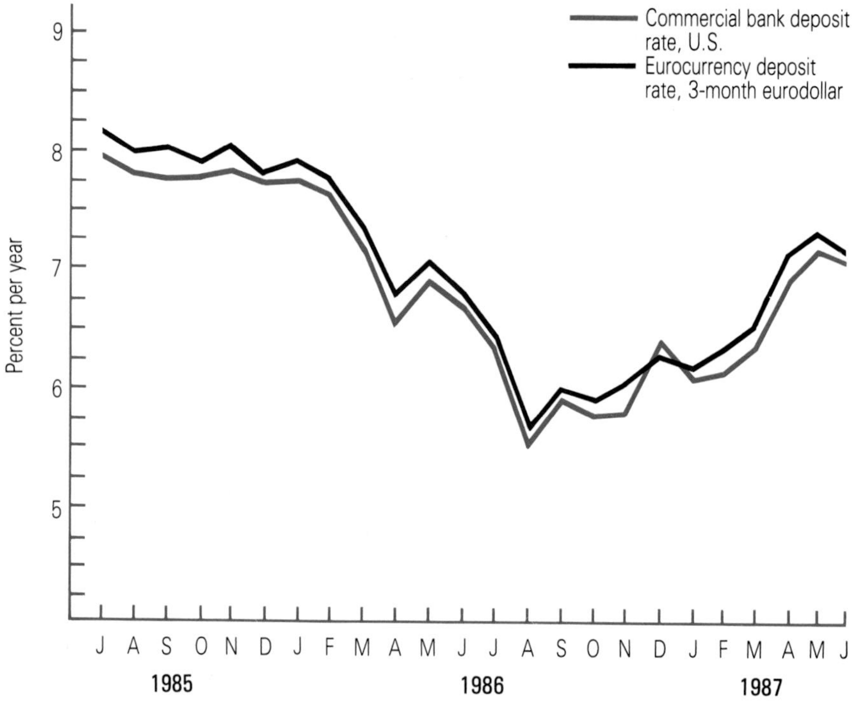

Source: Gunter Dufey and Ian Giddy, *The International Money Market* (Englewood Cliffs, N.J.: Prentice Hall, 1978, p. 51). Data for this figure were carefully selected to achieve a high degree of comparability. U.S. lending rates were prime rates adjusted for the prevailing compensating balance requirements of 15 percent. Regarding eurodollar deposit rates, the premiums over London interbank offer rates were obtained from Morgan Guaranty Trust Company, *World Financial Markets.* As for deposit rates, U.S. CD rates were used as counterparts of eurodollar deposit (bid) rates. U.S. prime rates, London interbank deposit and offer rates, and U.S. CD rates were taken from the *International Reports* weekly reporting service.

though when capital controls exist in a particular country (e.g., France), borrowing rates may be higher in the euromarket (which is not restricted) than in the domestic market. Figure 6-3 traces three-month eurocurrency deposit rates during the past decade. Notice that the countries whose currencies have tended to decline relative to other currencies during this period (such as France and Great Britain) show generally higher eurocurrency deposit rates than the "strong currency" countries (such as Germany and Japan).

Other Market Characteristics

Transactions in the eurodollar market generally involve $US 1 million or more, although in the past several years many deposits of $50,000 to $100,000

Figure 6-3 **3-Month Eurocurrency Deposit Rates** (yearend)

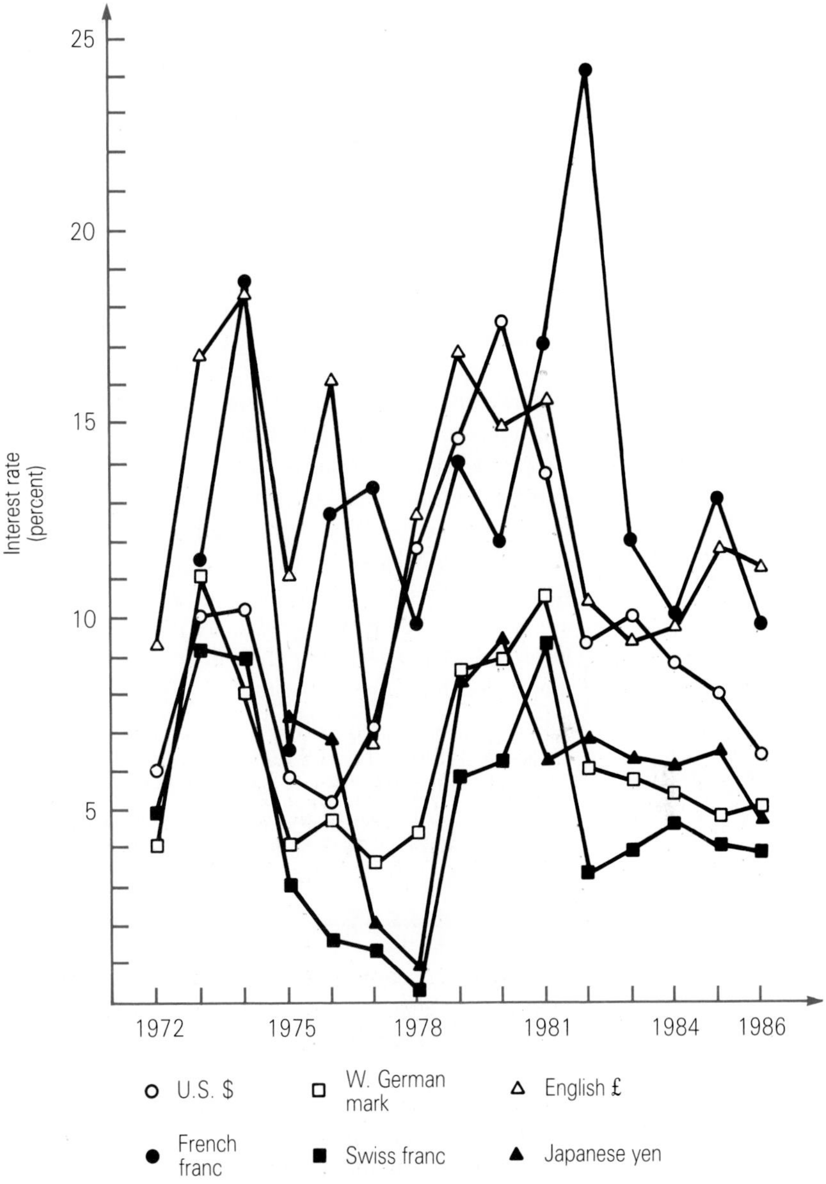

Source: Morgan Guaranty World Financial Markets.

have been given at LIBOR, and loans of similar amounts have been offered at the analogous lending rates. The market is directly accessible to banks, which carry out about three fourths of the total volume of transactions among themselves. Companies and individuals participate through their banks, generally at interest rates slightly less favorable than those offered between banks. (Investors may also participate in the euromarket indirectly by purchasing money market funds in the United States, when the funds themselves place large portions of their pooled investments in eurodollar accounts.)

Criticisms of the Euromarkets

The eurodollar market has been criticized over the years as contributing to worldwide inflation and as creating major new risks in the international banking system. While neither of these claims has been proven (or disproven) conclusively, they are worth considering here.

Because the eurodollar market adds to the worldwide volume of dollar-denominated assets, it has been accused of increasing the global money supply beyond the control of the U.S. authorities. This may be true to some extent, but a number of factors mitigate the total impact of eurodollars. First, eurodollars exist only as time deposits and certificates of deposit, never as demand deposits or cash. Hence, in the narrow definition of money that includes only cash and demand deposits, eurodollars do not even appear at all. Second, as already noted, about three fourths of all eurodollars are interbank deposits rather than new credit to companies or individuals that may use it for capital investment and thus economic growth. The interbank transfers (sometimes called "pyramiding") do not create any new credit, however measured. And finally, the eurodollar deposits that are used by companies and individuals for investment and consumption probably replace other (e.g., domestic) bank deposits that would have been used for the same purposes anyhow. That is, because the eurodollar deposits pay interest rates higher than domestic deposits, they often substitute for domestic deposits, and thus they are used for the same purposes that those deposits would have served. All in all, eurodollars probably add slightly to the total volume of economic activity worldwide because they provide a form of financial intermediation between depositors (savers) in many countries and borrowers (investors or spenders) in many countries that is more efficient than that of individual domestic financial markets.

On the issue of increased risk, it has been argued that the eurocurrency market has led to much greater extension of loans to troubled borrowers, such as the governments of less developed countries that were facing virtual impossibility of repayment in the early and mid-1980s. Unquestionably, the eurodollar market provided the mechanism through which these governments borrowed most of the money that was loaned to them in the 1970s. It is not clear, however, that any other financial markets would have fared any differently in the absence of eurodollars. Essentially, participation in the euromarket has opened one more type of business to international banks, and these banks must manage this business with the same prudence that they manage the other businesses in which they participate.

Eurobonds

Eurobonds are the long-term analogue of eurocurrencies. They are issued in countries of convenience and denominated in currencies other than the local one. With eurobonds, *taxation* of the interest income received by investors is a key concern, so most of them are issued in tax jurisdictions that do not impose taxes on such interest payments (e.g., Luxembourg). Eurobonds, like domestic U.S. bonds, are issued by corporations and government agencies. They may be convertible into equity, and they may have fixed or floating interest rates.

Borrowers (i.e., issuers of eurobonds) utilize this market for these main reasons: (1) no regulatory agency establishes rules for disclosure by issuers, so that substantial red tape is avoided—though this generally limits participation to blue-chip corporations and governments; (2) the interest rates can be marginally lower than those on domestic issues because investors can usually avoid taxes on their interest income; and (3) the issuer gains access to potential investors in many countries simultaneously because the investment banks that place the issue offer it internationally. From time to time, eurobond issue is stimulated by additional reasons, such as domestic bond market restrictions that lead issuers to seek overseas funding. In 1964, for example, the United States established capital controls that made foreign bonds less attractive to U.S. investors (the Interest Equalization Tax was effectively a tax on interest received by U.S. citizens from foreign bond investments) and that limited lending by U.S. parent companies to their foreign subsidiaries. As a result, both U.S. and foreign issuers that were trying to place dollar-denominated bonds turned to the fledgling eurobond market for their funding.

For the investor, the eurobond market offers these advantages: (1) all issues are structured to allow exemption from interest withholding tax on the income earned; and (2) the terms of eurobond issues are more varied than those of domestic bond issues. For example, eurobonds usually have shorter maturities than domestic bonds (five to eight years), and eurobonds often have floating-rate interest payments.

During the 1970s and early 1980s, the growth of the eurobond market was fairly similar to that of the eurocurrency market. In the early 1980s, the vast majority of eurobonds were being issued in U.S. dollars and the market continued to grow in both size and diversity (as shown in Table 6-3).

The IMF System

The last international financial market that we will examine here may be viewed as either the most important of all or as one that is generally irrelevant

The International Monetary Fund's headquarters building in Washington, D.C.

Photri, Inc.

to private business managers. The international monetary system is a financial market in which only central banks and the **International Monetary Fund (IMF,** or the Fund) operate; so private business has no active role in it. On the other hand, rules for international financial dealings among countries are often set at the IMF and substantial international loan decisions are made between governments and the IMF—so that the rules of the game in the other international financial markets are greatly influenced by IMF activities.

The international monetary system determines the exchange rate regime that prevails among the major developed countries, whose currencies are used for the vast majority of international payments. The IMF negotiates with governments of debtor nations for loans directly from the Fund and for loan conditions that are used as a basis for lending by private banks to these same borrowers. In addition, the IMF serves as an intermediary for emergency loans between member governments to cope with the capital flow or exchange rate crises that occur from time to time due to speculation in foreign exchange markets or other causes. All in all, the international monetary system plays a substantial role in determining the rules of the game for private companies and banks in international business—so its functioning should be understood by managers.

Brief History

The International Monetary Fund was designed in 1944 at a conference of the Allied nations held at Bretton Woods, New Hampshire. Its general purpose was to provide a multilateral framework for avoiding international financial crises by establishing rules for national exchange rate policies and for adjustment to balance of payments disequilibria (discussed in the following chapter), and it was specifically intended to avoid the disastrous financial contraction that had occurred during the 1930s. As originally negotiated, and as implemented in 1946 when the Articles of Agreement were signed by the initial 46 member countries, the IMF system required *fixed* exchange rates among member countries, with gold as the basis for currency valuation. The U.S. dollar was initially fixed at a value of $35 per ounce of gold, and all other currencies were fixed at values expressed in both dollars and gold.

Fixed exchange rates were a fundamental base of the Bretton Woods system. Under the Articles of Agreement, each country was obligated to maintain its currency value at the initially set value (the "par" value), with a band of ±1 percent of flexibility around the par value. If a foreign central bank demanded to sell a country's currency back to the issuer, that country was required to pay the equivalent amount of gold, U.S. dollars, or some other acceptable currency.

In order to join the IMF, a country was required to make a deposit of gold (25 percent) plus its own currency (75 percent), such that each member country's total deposit was roughly in proportion with its share of world trade. Then each member country received the right to borrow up to 200 percent of its initial deposit at the Fund in any currency to help pay for imbalances such as the one mentioned above. If a country borrowed more than its original deposit, the IMF would stipulate economic policies that the borrower had to follow in order to receive more financial support.

While the IMF sought to provide assistance for nations facing balance of payments problems, its only resources were the contributions of its member countries: quotas based on each country's part in world trade, which initially constituted about $9 billion. This relatively small amount of liquidity was not sufficient to support the post-World War II economic recovery, or specifically, the payments imbalances, of even the European countries.[6] Ultimately, the U.S. Marshall Plan injected the needed funding into the international financial system, and specifically into Europe, during 1948-52.

In fact, the IMF provided very little funding to its member countries in its early years. During the Suez crisis in 1956, it loaned $1.7 billion to Great Britain, France and India. Later, during speculative runs on the British pound (i.e., periods when speculators sold large quantities of pounds for other currencies, in expectation of a devaluation of the pound) in 1961 and 1964, it extended loans to Great Britain. By the end of the 1960s, the IMF was regularly providing credit to member countries, though still not at the levels that many analysts believed necessary to stabilize the system. (The alternative view is that the IMF should not provide credit to the member countries at all, but rather that these countries should be forced to adjust their economies to escape balance of payments problems. Balance of payments adjustment is discussed in Chapter 7.)

At the end of the 1960s, the U.S. dollar began to be the object of speculative pressure. The problem was severe, since the dollar constituted the base for the entire system of value (through its formal link to gold at $35 per ounce). The United States was unable to devalue to stop the speculation, and later it was unwilling to continue to sell its gold holdings to foreign central banks that wanted to redeem their dollars. In August 1971 President Nixon announced that the United States would no longer sell gold to foreign central banks in exchange for dollars; and in December 1971 he announced a devaluation of the dollar to $39 per ounce of gold.

These events essentially destroyed the Bretton Woods system of fixed exchange rates. Many initiatives to repair the system were presented during the following two years, but the United States would no longer accept the responsibility of providing the dollar as a fixed base for other currencies. In February 1973 the dollar was again devalued, this time to $42 per ounce of gold. In subsequent months, the IMF system was changed de facto to a floating exchange rate system that allowed each country to leave the value of its currency free to change with market forces or to fix that value to some other currency. Since that time, the United States has allowed the dollar to float in value relative to all other currencies, with occasional efforts by the Fed (the Federal Reserve System) to influence the dollar's relationship to particular currencies, such as the German mark and the Japanese yen.

The Current IMF System

Under the current IMF system, no limitations are set on each member country's decision either to fix its currency value relative to some other currency or to allow it to fluctuate as supply and demand dictate. (Notice that it is impossible to keep any one currency fixed relative to all others, if the others are changing at the same time.) In 1976, an accord called the Jamaica Agreement altered the IMF charter to allow formally for floating exchange rates. Today, the exchange rate regimes used by each nation are substantially unrestricted and government strategies to influence exchange rates are altered as desired.[7]

At about the time that the link between the dollar and gold was broken, the IMF's members agreed to create a new currency that the Fund would issue when authorized to do so by a vote of the members. This currency, called the **special drawing right (SDR),** allows its holder to obtain (or draw) other currencies from the IMF (or from other members) when desired. SDRs have been created and issued on six occasions to date; their total value is about $21 billion. In each instance, the SDRs were allocated to Fund members according to their quotas. This new "international money" has served to support a number of countries that encountered financial crises since 1971, allowing these countries to finance their imbalances, but it has not been a solution to imbalances in international financial flows. During the international debt crisis of the early 1980s, SDR use was wholly inadequate to deal with the more than $350 billion of dollar debt owed by Latin American countries to foreign lenders.

Special Drawing Rights and the Private Sector

During the 1980s, SDRs have been fairly widely used as a currency of denomination for private sector financial instruments such as bonds and long-term bank loans. Because the SDR has a value based on five currencies (see Figure 6-4), it is more stable as a borrowing or lending tool than any individual currency.

When the dollar devalues relative to other widely traded currencies, so also does the SDR—but only 42 percent of the SDR's value is affected negatively. The other 58 percent of the SDR's value is based on marks, pounds, yen, and French francs—and these currencies may rise or fall relative to the dollar in such a situation. Overall, the changes must net out over all currencies, and an instrument such as the SDR changes relatively little in value compared to any single currency. The SDR is really a "basket" of currencies whose value is generally more stable than that of any one of its components.

Since the SDR is nothing more than an accounting convention, it cannot be used in final settlement of private sector accounts. That is, no such thing as an SDR bill or coin exists. However, since the SDR does have a value measurable in terms of any other currency, it can always be settled in dollars, marks, or any other currency (e.g., in so many "SDRs worth of dollars.") Financial instruments can be purchased in SDRs worth of different currencies and later paid out in SDRs worth of the same or other currencies at maturity.

Just as the ECU has gained wide acceptance as an instrument for denominating international financial transactions, so too the SDR promises to gain wide acceptance as a risk-reducing instrument. (The SDR has the advantage of including the U.S. dollar in the group of currencies that determine its value, whereas the ECU is based only on European currencies.) At present, however, private sector investors and borrowers are using a much greater volume and value of ECU-denominated instruments than SDR-denominated instruments.

Unresolved Problems with the IMF System

The IMF system today differs dramatically from the model established at Bretton Woods in 1944. Flexible exchange rates have been substituted for fixed ones; gold has been greatly reduced as an international monetary asset, and its link to the dollar has been severed; a new reserve currency, the SDR, has been used to increase world liquidity; and perhaps most important, the U.S. dollar is no longer the single base for the IMF system of value. These major changes have come in response to problems and crises that have occurred during the past 40 years—yet the IMF system itself survives. While few people would argue that the IMF has led directly to greater international

Figure 6-4 **The Special Drawing Right** (in 1986)

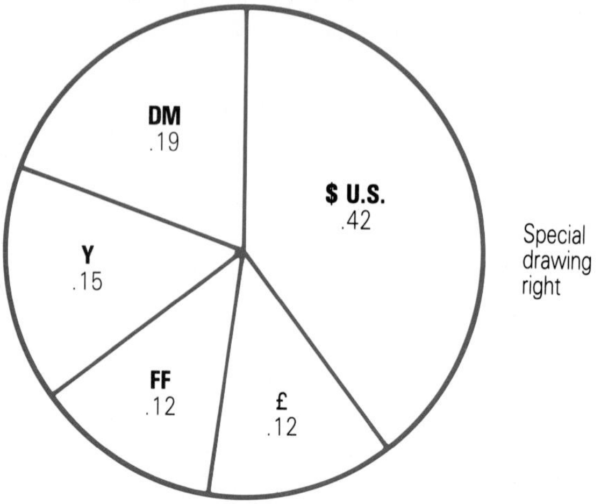

Distribution of value of the SDR,
Basic monetary unit of the International Monetary Fund

E.G., in dollars: $1 \text{ SDR} = \frac{\$\_\_}{\text{DM}}(.19) + \frac{\$\_\_}{\text{FF}}(.12) + \frac{\$\_\_}{\text{Y}}(.15) + \frac{\$\_\_}{£}(.12) + \frac{\$\,1}{\$}(.42)$

financial stability over its history, at least the system has been flexible enough to accommodate the various crises that have threatened it.

Several problems that remain in the system deserve note. First, there has always been an uncomfortable tension between the countries that want to utilize the IMF simply as a bank for reducing the negative impacts of balance of payments difficulties and the countries that want to utilize it to subsidize economic development. The "link" between the IMF and development finance was originally relegated to the World Bank (the IMF's sister institution). Traditionally, the IMF has loaned funds only for short-term uses, sometimes extending to two or three years. Many borrowing countries, especially the less developed ones, have repeatedly called for greater use of IMF resources to finance development projects. While there are often no clear differences between financing payments imbalances and financing development projects that may later reduce those imbalances, the IMF has not substantially widened its scope. In the early 1980s, under the cloud of multiple national loan renegotiations by Latin American countries, the Fund began to extend longer-term loans and to reconsider its strategy. The ultimate result of this crisis remains to be seen.

A second problem that continues to plague the Fund is the issue of exchange rate regimes. Even as the flexible rate system moves through its second decade, there are repeated calls for a return to fixed, or more tightly constrained, currency values. The great instability of international financial dealings during the entire period since the OPEC oil crisis of 1973–74 has led some analysts to argue for a return to fixed rates. The evidence during the entire 20th century tends to suggest that no matter what exchange rate regime prevails, if international trade relations are unstable and payments imbalances are substantial, no exchange rate regime will be able to solve the problem. Thus, this problem most likely cannot be eliminated.

On the whole, the international monetary system plays an extremely important role in all international financial dealings, simply by being the focal point for establishing rules on exchange rates, exchange controls, intergovernmental loans, and other official transactions.

Conclusions

Whether or not a company or bank is involved in international trade, investment, or other international business, it is important for its managers to understand some of the key aspects of international financial markets. The eurocurrency market may offer a low-cost borrowing opportunity; or the eurobond market may provide an outlet for selling new debt to a wider group of investors. The international monetary system establishes a framework within which governments set international financial policies that may affect many firms. The money and capital markets in foreign countries may offer opportunities to multinational firms that operate in those countries. The foreign exchange market determines the cost and availability of foreign currencies, used in business by many firms. Finally, all of these markets influence the functioning of the markets for real goods and services, the ultimate use for all financial claims.

Questions

1. How can a firm such as Ajax Steel in Peoria, Illinois, utilize the eurodollar market to minimize its financing costs? This firm is a medium-sized manufacturer with no foreign sales.
2. How may the International Monetary Fund affect companies' activities in international business?
3. What is the difference between a eurobond and a domestic bond in the United States? Which one would you prefer to issue as a company manager? Which one would you prefer to buy as an investor? Why?
4. Does the eurodollar market add to world inflation? Explain why or why not using the material in this chapter and your knowledge of macroeconomics.
5. As a French resident, would you prefer to deposit your $1 million inheritance in a U.S. bank or in the eurodollar market? Why?
6. If you were offered the opportunity to establish a deposit in London

denominated in ECU, would you choose that rather than a deposit in British pounds or dollars? Why or why not?

7. What are the important differences between the Bretton Woods system and the current IMF system? How do these differences affect the MNE manager?
8. If your firm had a subsidiary in Japan and about 100 million yen in exposed assets (i.e., plant and equipment), how would you protect it against exchange risk?
9. Explain the role that the IMF plays in the international debt crisis. Use outside information as well as that which appears in this book.
10. What are the necessary conditions for existence of a euromarket? Do you expect the eurodollar to exist 10 years from now? Why or why not?

References

Argy, Victor. *The Postwar International Money Crisis.* London: Allen & Unwin, 1981.

Dufey, Gunter, and Ian Giddy. *The International Money Market.* Englewood Cliffs, N.J.: Prentice Hall, 1978.

Dufey, Gunter, and Rolf Mirus. *International Finance.* New York: McGraw-Hill, 1987.

Einzig, Paul, and Brian Scott Quinn. *The Eurodollar System.* 6th ed. New York: St. Martin's Press, 1977.

Feiger, George, and Bertrand Jacquillat. *International Finance.* Boston: Allyn & Bacon, 1982.

Pennant-Rea, Rupert. "International Monetary Reform: A Survey," *Economist,* October 5, 1985.

Endnotes

1. Dufey and Mirus (1987), chap. 1, presents this point clearly and discusses its importance.
2. Some information about the rules on access to national stock markets by foreigners appears in Business International Corporation, *Investing, Licensing, and Trading Conditions* (New York: Business International Corporation, 1984).
3. See *The ECU* (Luxembourg: European Communities, 1984). Also see "European Currency Units," *International Banking Report,* February 17, 1984, published by the London *Financial Times;* and "Edging Closer to a Common Currency," *Euromoney,* September 1985, pp. 19-28.
4. See, for example, Dufey and Giddy (1978).
5. Realistically, if any one government disallows the euromarkets, they can still function almost as effectively in other countries and currencies. At

present, the U.S. government has the most important role, since about 80 percent of eurodeposits are denominated in U.S. dollars.

6. See the Economic Cooperation Act of 1948 (Public Law 472, 80th Congress), U.S. Code Congressional Service, 1948.
7. Exchange rate policies *are* constrained by the IMF if a country seeks to borrow more than its quota from the Fund.

Case

Bell South—Borrowing in International Financial Markets

Introduction

One of the major changes in the business system of the United States in the 20th century occurred on January 1, 1984, when American Telephone & Telegraph (AT&T) was forced to sell its operating telephone subsidiaries. The U.S. Department of Justice decided to deregulate long-distance telephone service by allowing other companies to compete with AT&T. To reduce AT&T's competitive advantage over other companies, the Justice Department required that AT&T sell all of its 22 regional telephone operating companies (i.e., the companies, such as Southern Bell, that actually provided telephone service in 22 regions of the United States). Now AT&T owns only a long-distance operating network of telephone service, its research division (Bell Labs), its manufacturing division (Western Electric), a new data processing division (AT&T Information Systems), and an equipment manufacturing division.

The "breakup" of AT&T left the operating companies regrouped into seven corporations, with responsibility for providing local telephone service in seven areas of the United States. This change was truly dramatic. AT&T had been the largest private corporation in the world, and before 1984 each operating company had functioned only as a division of the national company and each division had made decisions only about telephone service in its area. Now each operating company had to make *all* decisions as an independent corporation, including decisions on financing, investing, and general business strategy.

The decision of interest in this case is the financing decision. How should a company finance its business activities? More specifically, how should a major capital project be financed? For any large corporation, and for many medium-sized ones as well, the eurocurrency market offers very attractive financing opportunities. Bell South was chosen because its managers do not have experience in dealing with the eurocurrency markets and because it definitely should take advantage of the opportunities available there. Additional financial markets available to corporations in the United States are noted for comparison.

This case was written by Professor Robert Grosse as a basis for class discussion. The specific borrowing situation is fictitious, and references to Bell South are based on a publicly available information.

The Case

In the aftermath of the decision by the U.S. Department of Justice to dismantle (*organizationally) the national telephone system in 1982, individual operating subsidiaries of AT&T were beginning to face major new decisions as soon-to-be-independent companies. Each of the operating companies was very large by current industrial standards—Bell South alone had assets worth more than $21 billion and employed over 100,000 people. None of the operating companies had had experience in large-scale financing, research and development in telecommunications, or the design of a marketing strategy, since all of these functions had previously been performed by AT&T (or Bell Labs) at the national level.

One of the first priorities established by Bell South's senior management in 1983 was to initiate a research program with a laboratory facility in either Raleigh, North Carolina, or Melbourne, Florida (near major concentrations of electronics companies). Since the company would not become independent until January 1, 1984, no actual investment could take place until then. Nonetheless, Bell South's managers wanted to be ready to go with their plans on "independence day."

Among the more difficult problems facing David Green as treasury manager for Bell South was the issue of financing the research lab, which was estimated to cost about $25 million. While this level of funding was not large compared to AT&T's total borrowing, it would present some difficulties for a newly independent Bell South (primarily because of this firm's inexperience in such negotiations). Green was discussing the problem with his recently hired assistant, who had just graduated from a prestigious school of business administration.

The assistant (i.e., you) was proposing to consider the idea of eurocurrency financing, for which lower interest rates were available and fewer restrictions existed on loans. Specifically, the assistant recommended the use of a euro-deutschemark loan, which could be obtained for close to one half of the interest cost that had been offered for a domestic, dollar-denominated loan by NCNB (North Carolina National Bank). Other alternatives should also be considered, of course. Table 1 shows various borrowing options and their costs in August 1983.

The research facility has an expected life of 10 years. It will be financed separately each year, so that every year the lowest-cost source of funds should be chosen. For the first year (effective on January 1, 1984), funding will be available at the interest rates shown in Table 1. Each type of lender also charges fees on the loan. The fees are paid one time, at the beginning of the loan period, and they are some percentage of the total loan value (as shown). Right now, the only task is to choose the funding source for the first year; subsequent borrowing decisions will be made at the end of each year.

Table 1 **Possible Sources of $25 Million, One-Year Borrowing for Bell South**

Type of Funding	Interest Cost* US$	C$	FF	DM	SF	Fees (paid up front)
Syndicated euro-currency loan (LIBOR)	11.13	10.31	16.50	6.13	5.00	2.00
Eurobond issue	12.25	12.00	—	8.36	—	1.75
U.S. domestic bank loan (prime rate)	11.50					3.00
U.S. domestic bond issue	12.65					2.25
U.S. domestic equity issue (required rate of return)	18					2.25
Spot exchange rate (fx/$)	1	1.23	8.0	2.6	2.10	
One-year forward XR	1	1.29	9.1	2.3	1.95	

* All interest costs are stated as annual percentage rates. Since one-year loans are being used, the rates must be renegotiated every year during the project. Bell South can be expected to pay a "spread" of ⅜ percent over LIBOR quotes and ¼ percent over prime, plus onetime, up-front fees, based on the value of the loan. Assume for simplicity that all interest is paid at the end of the full loan period.

In addition to a bank loan in the eurodollar market, Bell South can consider using a domestic bank loan. In either case, the company will pay the base interest rate plus some additional margin to the bank lender. If the company issues new bonds, it will have to pay the interest rate shown plus the up-front fee. If it issues new stock, investors would expect a return of about 18 percent per year, much higher than the bank charges. Many other financing sources exist, but the choices shown are very commonly used in the U.S. market.

LIBOR is the London interbank offered rate, the interest rate offered by banks in London for large deposits (eurocurrency deposits) from other banks. The lending rate does not have a name; it is just called "LIBOR plus the spread," and it varies depending on the creditworthiness of the borrower.

Questions

1. What is the cheapest way to finance the research facility without incurring exchange risk? [*Hint:* To do the calculations, assume that interest rates remain constant during the life of the project.]
2. Should the company use long-term financing, such as a bond issue, so that it would not have to refinance every year?

Appendix 6–1
Eurodollar Expansion and Contraction

Eurodollars are *not* money in the same way that checks and cash are. Eurodollars are time deposits or certificates of deposit, some of which have maturities of as little as one day. Hence, eurodollar deposits with very short terms are "quasi money" and can be used by their holders in very much the same way as demand deposits. Other eurodollar deposits can be used in much the same way as domestic time deposits and CDs. This appendix explains the process of eurodollar creation, expansion, and contraction, so that the reader can understand the basic mechanics of the market and of the not-so-arcane transactions that take place.

Let us begin with Metalworks, Inc., a company in Cleveland that produces small metal fittings for auto manufacturers. This company has an interest-earning checking account at Ohio Bank & Trust that regularly contains about $1 million more than the company uses for its operations. Rather than leave the money in a low-interest deposit, the financial manager of Metalworks decides to place the excess $1 million in an alternative, still very liquid, investment. The manager of Ohio B&T suggests a eurodollar negotiable certificate of deposit, placed at the bank's branch in London.

The eurodollar deposit would pay the interest rate, LIBOR, to Metalworks for three months, after which Metalworks could roll over the deposit at the new LIBOR or withdraw the funds and use them otherwise. Metalworks could hold the eurodollar CD for the entire three-month period or sell it at any time in the market for eurodollar CDs at whatever price buyers offered. Ohio B&T guaranteed that it would buy back the CD at a small cost in reduced interest if Metalworks chose to sell it during the three-month period. At this time, LIBOR was at 10.75 percent per year on three-month dollar deposits and Ohio B&T was paying 5½ percent per year on the checking account in Cleveland.

Having made the decision to go ahead, Metalworks deposited $1 million in the eurodollar deposit in London. That is, Ohio B&T created an account on the books of its branch in London payable to Metalworks, even though all of the discussions took place in Cleveland. The three T-accounts below summarize this transaction, which constitutes the creation of 1 million eurodollars. (Note that DD means "demand deposit" and CD means "certificate of deposit.")

Metalworks, Inc.

A	L
−DD at Ohio B&T +CD at B&T London	

Ohio B&T, home office

A	L
	−DD owed to Metalworks +DD owed to B&T London

Ohio B&T, London office

A	L
+DD at home office	+CD owed to Metalworks

So far, no credit has been extended, even though a million eurodollars have been created. There was simply an exchange of one bank account for another. At this point, Metalworks is satisfied with its position. Ohio B&T, however, has accepted a new deposit that is costing it 10.75 percent per year, so it needs to find a use for the funds that will bring in more than that. Typically, the bank will look to other banks in the London market to purchase the funds. If Ohio B&T can find another bank that offers a slightly higher interest rate, it may lend the funds to that bank. Let us assume that Crédit Suisse needs funds for a loan that it wants to make in Switzerland, so its London branch offers Ohio B&T 10.90 percent per year for $1 million for three months. This second transaction appears as follows in the T-accounts of the participants:

Ohio B&T, home office

A	L
	−DD owed to B&T London +DD owed to Crédit Suisse

Ohio B&T, London office

A	L
−DD at B&T home office +CD at Crédit Suisse	

Crédit Suisse

A	L
+DD at B&T home office	+CD owed to B&T London

In this step, Crédit Suisse has exchanged a CD payable to Ohio B&T, London, for a demand deposit at Ohio B&T, Cleveland, each for $1 million. Now Ohio B&T has solved its problem of finding a borrower for the funds, but Crédit Suisse has taken on the same problem.

Crédit Suisse next uses the funds to make a loan to Nestlé Corporation, at an interest rate of 11.45 percent per year for the three-month period. Thus, Nestlé is paying a spread, or margin, over LIBOR of 0.75 percent per year.) The final transaction in eurodollar expansion looks like this:

Ohio B&T, home office

A	L
	−DD owed to Crédit Suisse +DD owed to Nestlé

Crédit Suisse

A	L
−DD at B&T home office +Loan to Nestlé	

Nestlé

A	L
+DD at B&T home office	+Loan due to Crédit Suisse

Now there are $2 million of eurodollars in existence (the CD of Ohio B&T's London office owed to Metalworks and the Crédit Suisse CD owed to B&T London) plus a eurodollar loan of $1 million. Assuming that both deposits and the loan are held to maturity, these eurodollars will have a life of three months. All of the participants are in "equilibrium" in the sense that they are all earning a satisfactory return on their eurodollar dealings (assuming that Nestlé has invested the money in some activity that pays more than 11.45 percent per year).

Eurodollar contraction occurs when the deposits mature and must be paid out. If each depositor simply redeposits the funds in another eurodollar deposit and Nestlé rolls over its loan, then the accounts are rolled over and no change in the total number of eurodollars occurs. However, if any participant does not redeposit the funds in a eurodollar account, then there is a decline in the number of eurodollars (though *not* in the number of dollars in the B&T home office account.)

Assume now that Nestlé pays back the loan after three months and that Metalworks shifts its deposit back to a demand deposit in Cleveland. In this case, Nestlé will pay Crédit Suisse $1 million plus interest ($28,625); Crédit Suisse will pay Ohio B&T, London, $1 million plus interest ($27,250); and Ohio B&T, London, will transfer $1 million plus interest ($26,875) to the account of Metalworks in Cleveland. At this point, no eurodollars remain and each euromarket participant is left with a profit (if Nestlé did indeed earn more than 11.45 percent per year on its use of the funds).

Because much of business activity is refinanced repeatedly, the eurodollar market generally does not decline in volume. And because more and more firms and banks are entering the eurodollar market, the volume of eurodollars has tended to grow over the years.

7 THE BALANCE OF PAYMENTS

This chapter covers the measurement and interpretation of all international transactions between one country and the rest of the world: that is, the balance of payments. Since the system of recording these transactions is fairly complex, a major part of the chapter consists of an explanation of that system. Examples of countries in different balance of payments situations illustrate the use of the system and the implications of deficit and surplus balances. The remainder of the chapter explains what happens when imbalances of payments exist and shows why company managers involved in international business need to understand the balance of payments. The main goals of the chapter are to:

1. Explain how the double-entry bookkeeping system of measuring balances of payments works.
2. Look at recent balances of payments for the United States and discuss their implications.
3. Show how balance of payments adjustment takes place.
4. Discuss the many implications of balance of payments problems from the perspective of private sector managers whose firms do business across national boundaries.

Introduction

How well do we keep track of the millions of transactions that take place annually between exporters and importers, international banks and multinational companies? The bankers who tabulate the foreign exchange dealings of their own banks are only a part of the picture. How well can we account for the part of direct investment that occurs through overseas borrowing, yet affects the home country's international economic position? Even more simply, how well can we measure "international" transactions that are just transfers of funds from the account of an importer to the account of a foreign exporter in the same bank?

The answer to these questions, realistically, is "not very well." National governments create elaborate accounts for the transactions between their residents and foreigners, but it is often very difficult to obtain full and accurate information. Putting that problem to the side for the moment, let us consider the methods that governments use to record each country's international transactions.

The most widely used measure of international economic transactions for any country is the balance of payments (BOP) statement. This record attempts to measure the full value of the transactions between residents of one country and residents of the rest of the world for some time period, say one year.[1] The balance of payments is a *flow* concept, in that it records flows of goods, services, and claims between countries over a period of time, rather than a stock of accumulated funds or products. It is a *value* concept, in that all the items recorded receive a monetary value, denominated in the given country's currency at the time of the transaction.[2] *The* **balance of payments (BOP),** then, *is a record of the value of all the economic transactions between residents of one country and residents of all other countries during a given time period.*

Why do we worry about measuring these transactions? Because if a country records a substantial imbalance between inflows and outflows of goods and services for an extended period of time, some means of financing or adjusting away the imbalance must be found. For example, when oil prices rose dramatically in 1973-74 and again in 1979, Brazil continued to import much the same quantity of oil but had to pay a much higher bill (total cost = price times quantity). Given no major change in Brazil's exports, the country ended up spending a lot more foreign currency on imports than it received from exports. This imbalance could have been financed, if Brazil borrowed funds from abroad—with the eventual obligation to repay the loans. The imbalance could also have been adjusted away, if Brazilians bought less of other imported goods or increased their own exports. Finally, the Brazilians could have done nothing and just paid out more cruzados, if OPEC countries were willing to accept this currency and hold onto it. (Technically, this would have been borrowing from OPEC, since OPEC would eventually spend the cruzados.) Anytime an imbalance occurs between a country's imports and exports of goods and services, it must be covered by an equal and opposite imbalance in flows of claims (e.g., money, bonds, official reserves.)

Still, the manager may wonder why he or she should be concerned about this issue. So far, the problem is macroeconomic, referring to a *country's* international transactions. The problem becomes much more important if we realize that national governments are likely to set their regulatory policies to reduce BOP imbalances. Thus, in the above example of Brazil, foreign *firms* may discover themselves faced with new tariffs or quotas; companies operating in Brazil may find that access to foreign exchange for imports or for profit remittance is limited, while subsidies are offered on exports; and foreign *bank* lenders may find new loan requests coming in from Brazil. All in all, the manager should recognize that the balance of payments is an *indicator* of subsequent government policy changes.

In another equally important vein, the manager should be interested in national balances of payments because of their direct importance in determining exchange rates. Since the collapse of the fixed exchange rate system in 1971, most of the world's developed countries and many of the LDCs have been allowing the values of their currencies to fluctuate in the market (usually with some degree of government intervention). This means that, other things equal, when the supply of a country's currency in foreign exchange markets exceeds the demand, the currency will devalue. Such an excess supply could have occurred in the Brazilian example, unless some demand for cruzados arose for another purpose (e.g., for direct investment). Although it is the total demand and supply of the currency in foreign exchange markets that leads to exchange rate determination, many analysts discuss a trade imbalance as being likely to affect the rate, ignoring other sources of currency demand or supply. One must be careful to include all of these sources when attempting to judge exchange rate changes.

The next section looks at the full set of transactions that constitute the balance of payments and explains the system of BOP accounting that is used to create the records used by governments. The third section presents the various account aggregates that are balances of payments. The BOP of the United States is discussed in some detail in the fourth section. Because the BOP is a dynamic concept, changing daily as transactions occur, the adjustment mechanisms leading from surplus and deficit balances toward equilibrium points are then examined. Finally, the last section presents implications of the BOP for managers and shows how managers can use BOP information to make decisions.

Balance of Payments Accounting

There is no such thing as "*the* balance of payments," since the accounts are organized in a double-entry bookkeeping system and for every debit entry there is a credit entry of equal value. There are seven or eight BOP measures; these group some international transactions together and leave others in a

Table 7-3 *(continued)*

	1981	1982	1983	1984	1985
34. U.S. official reserve assets, net	−5,175	−4,965	−1,196	−3,131	−3,858
35. Gold		(*)	...	...	...
36. Special drawing rights	−1,824	−1,371	−66	−979	−897
37. Reserve position in the International Monetary Fund	−2,491	−2,552	−4,434	−995	908
38. Foreign currencies	−861	−1,041	3,304	−1,156	−3,869
39. U.S. government assets, other than official reserve assets, net	−5,137	−5,766	−5,013	−5,516	−2,628
40. U.S. credits and other long-term assets	−9,710	−10,123	−9,931	−9,619	−7,219
41. Repayments on U.S. loans	4,370	4,326	4,969	4,483	4,435
42. U.S. foreign currency holdings and U.S. short-term assets, net	204	32	−52	−380	156
43. U.S. private assets, net	−98,982	−107,535	−43,281	−11,800	−31,697
44. Direct investment	−8,691	2,198	−4,881	−4,503	−19,091
45. Foreign securities	−5,429	−7,772	−7,676	−5,059	−7,871
46. U.S. claims on unaffiliated foreigners reported by U.S. nonbanking concerns	−331	n.a.	−5,333	6,266	n.a.
47. U.S. claims reported by U.S. banks, not included elsewhere	−84,531	−106,711	−25,391	−8,504	−5,926
48. Foreign assets in the United States, net (increase/capital inflow [+])	**77,921**	**84,494**	**81,722**	**97,319**	**123,108**
49. Foreign official assets in the United States, net	4,785	3,043	5,339	3,424	−1,908
50. U.S. government securities	6,272	5,046	6,502	4,857	−939
51. U.S. Treasury securities	4,983	5,716	6,989	4,690	−610
52. Other	1,289	−670	−487	167	−329
53. Other U.S. government liabilities	−69	−12	199	453	148
54. U.S. liabilities reported by U.S. banks, not included elsewhere	−4,083	−1,713	433	663	372
55. Other foreign official assets	2,665	−278	−1,795	−2,549	−1,489
56. Other foreign assets in the United States, net	73,136	81,451	76,383	93,895	125,016
57. Direct investment	21,301	9,424	11,299	22,514	16,254
58. U.S. Treasury securities	2,932	6,945	8,731	22,440	20,910
59. U.S. securities other than U.S. Treasury securities	7,109	5,973	8,612	12,983	50,712
60. U.S. liabilities to unaffiliated reported by U.S. nonbanking concerns	532	n.a.	−1,318	4,284	n.a.
61. U.S. liabilities reported by U.S. banks, not included elsewhere	41,262	62,869	49,059	31,674	40,610
62. Allocations of special drawing rights	**1,093**	...	...	...	...
63. Statistical discrepancy (sum of above items with sign reversed)	**25,809**	**41,864**	**9,331**	**30,486**	**32,739**
63a. *Of which* seasonal adjustment discrepancy	...	...	...	...	...
Memoranda:					
64. Balance on merchandise trade	−27,889	−36,331	−61,055	−114,107	−124,289

Table 7-3 (*concluded*)

	1981	1982	1983	1984	1985
65. Balance on goods and services	11,079	−225	−32,912	−95,945	−102,880
66. Balance on goods, services, and remittances	8,975	−2,680	−35,503	−98,836	−106,418
67. Balance on current account	4,471	−8,093	−41,563	−107,358	−117,664
Transactions in U.S. official reserve assets and in foreign official assets in the United States:					
68. Increase (−) in U.S. official reserve assets, net	−5,175	−4,965	−1,196	−3,131	−3,858
69. Increase (+) in foreign official assets in the United States	4,854	3,055	5,140	2,971	−2,056

Source: U.S. Department of Commerce, *Survey of Current Business* (March issue, various years).
* The United States no longer includes official holdings of gold in its official reserves measures.

in 1985—a merchandise trade deficit (which also appears in the memoranda in line 64).

Actually, if lines 2-13 and 16-27 are placed side by side, the entire balance on goods and services has been reconstructed, with lines 1 and 15 as total exports and total imports (and line 65 as the balance itself). Notice that while the U.S. merchandise trade balance recorded a persistent deficit in the face of higher oil prices in the early 1980s, the balance on goods and services showed more mixed results. This balance was in surplus in 1981, as a result of the huge amounts of income generated by U.S. direct investment abroad. That is, in 1981 the entire trade deficit of about $28 billion was washed away by almost $32 billion of "receipts of income on U.S. [direct investment] assets abroad" (line 11), before considering other service flows, which approximately balanced out. By 1985, however, the merchandise trade deficit was so large that it overwhelmed direct investment income and had to be financed by massive borrowing from abroad.

In order to understand the main factors contributing to the U.S. flows of merchandise and services, a disaggregation of the accounts would be useful. The same annual article in the *Survey of Current Business* presents industry-level data concerning the merchandise trade flows. Looking at the 1985 BOP as shown in Table 7-4a, we see that the main sectors contributing to U.S. merchandise exports were nonelectrical machinery ($45.7 billion), agricultural products ($29.4 billion), automobiles ($22.9 billion), and chemicals ($18.0 billion).[4] Before drawing conclusions about the U.S. comparative advantage, we need to look at imports too. Table 7-4b shows that the largest categories of merchandise imports in 1985 were automobiles ($65.0 billion), petroleum and products ($50.4 billion), nonelectrical machinery ($38.7 billion), and consumer durable goods ($33.1 billion). While a careful examination of the underlying reasons for the various flows is beyond the present

Table 7-4a **U.S. Merchandise Trade** (in millions of U.S. dollars)

Line		1984	1985
D	Merchandise trade by end-use category. Census basis, including miltary grant shipments		
1	Merchandise exports. Census basis, including military grant shipments	218,744	212,373
2	Agricultural products	38,145	29,447
3	Nonagricultural products	180,599	182,926
4	Excluding military grant shipments	180,577	182,909
5	Foods, feeds, and beverages	31,353	23,883
6	Agricultural	30,397	22,751
7	Grains and preparations	18,050	12,676
8	Wheat	6,672	3,866
9	Soybeans	5,420	3,878
10	Other agricultural goods, feeds, and beverages	6,926	6,196
11	Nonagricultural (fish, distilled beverages, etc.)	957	1,132
12	Industrial supplies and materials	61,761	58,299
13	Agricultural	7,303	6,298
14	Raw cotton, including linters	2,488	1,611
15	Tobacco, unmanufactured	1,541	1,499
16	Other agricultural industrial supplies (hides, tallow, etc.)	3,274	3,188
17	Nonagricultural	54,458	52,001
18	Fuels and lubricants	9,718	10,164
19	Coal and related fuels	4,239	4,543
20	Petroleum and products	4,735	5,016
21	Paper and paper base stocks	4,597	4,065
22	Textile supplies and materials	2,521	2,476
23	Chemicals, excluding medicinals	18,834	18,004
24	Other nonmetals (minerals, wood, rubber, tires., etc.)	8,558	8,170
25	Steelmaking materials	1,174	1,185
26	Iron and steel products	1,769	1,536
27	Other metals, primary and advanced, including advanced steel	7,287	6,401
28	Precious metals (gold, silver, platinum)	2,294	1,646
29	Capital goods, except automotive	72,484	73,615
30	Machinery, except consumer-type	61,072	59,138
31	Electrical and electronic, including parts and attachments	14,985	13,460
32	Generators, transformers, and accessories	1,685	1,519
33	Broadcasting and communications equipment	7,762	6,494
34	Telephonic and other electrical apparatus	5,538	5,447
35	Nonelectrical, including parts and attachments	46,087	45,678
36	Construction machinery and nonfarm tractors	6,436	6,638
37	Textile and other specialized industry machinery	3,799	3,649
38	Other industrial machinery, n.e.c.	13,210	12,900
39	Agricultural machinery and farm tractors	1,602	1,555
40	Business and office machines, computers, etc.	15,982	15,907

Table 7-4a (*concluded*)

Line		1984	1985
41	Electronic computers and parts	14,347	14,436
42	Scientific, professional and service industry equipment	5,056	5,030
43	Civilian aircraft, engines, parts	9,738	12,986
44	Civilian aircraft complete, all types	4,098	6,689
45	Other transportation equipment	1,674	1,492
46	Automotive vehicles, parts, and engines	20,869	22,867
47	To Canada	15,492	17,234
48	To all other areas	5,377	5,633
49	Passenger cars, new and used	4,922	6,071
50	Trucks, buses, and special vehicles	2,443	2,744
51	Bodies, engines, parts and accessories, n.e.c.	13,504	14,052
52	Consumer goods (nonfood, except automotive)	13,411	12,563
53	Consumer durables manufactured	5,057	4,490
54	Consumer nondurables manufactured	7,908	7,597
55	Unmanufactured consumer goods (gem stones)	446	476
56	Special category (military-type goods)	5,019	5,362
57	Exports n.e.c. and reexports	13,848	15,784
58	Domestic (low-value, miscellaneous)	8,012	9,568
59	Foreign (reexports)	5,836	6,216

Source: U.S. Department of Commerce, *Survey of Current Business,* March 1986.

Table 7-4b **U.S. Merchandise Trade** (in millions of U.S. dollars)

Line		1984	1985
	D Merchandise trade by end-use category. Census basis including military grant shipment		
60	Merchandise imports. Census basis	330,514	335,127
61	Foods, feeds, and beverages	21,345	21,280
62	Coffee, cocoa, and sugar	4,859	4,421
63	Green coffee	3,098	3,076
64	Cane sugar	1,291	848
65	Other foods, feeds, and beverages	16,487	16,858
66	Meat products and poultry	2,119	2,276
67	Fish and shellfish	3,694	3,884
68	Vegetables, fruits, nuts, and preparations	3,009	3,235
69	Whiskey and other alcoholic beverages	2,874	2,873
70	Industrial supplies and materials	122,582	111,588
71	Fuels and lubricants	62,259	54,877
72	Petroleum and products	57,323	50,414

Table 7-4b (*concluded*)

Line		1984	1985
73	Paper and paper base stocks	7,340	7,170
74	Materials associated with nondurable goods and farm output, n.e.s.	16,234	16,062
75	Textile supplies and materials	3,573	3,460
76	Tobacco, unmanufactured	640	549
77	Chemicals, excluding medicinal	8,441	8,502
78	Other (hides, copra, materials for making photos, drugs, dyes)	3,579	3,552
79	Building materials, except metals	5,250	5,752
80	Materials associated with durable goods output, n.e.s.	31,499	27,727
81	Steelmaking materials	1,679	1,497
82	Iron and steel products	10,551	9,010
83	Other metals, primary and advanced, including advanced steel	14,515	12,726
84	Precious metals (gold, silver, platinum)	4,889	4,590
85	Nonmetals (oils, gums, resins, minerals, rubber, tires, etc.)	4,754	4,494
86	Capital goods, except automotive	60,757	62,790
87	Machinery, except consumer-type	56,561	56,801
88	Electrical and electronic and parts and attachments	19,032	18,106
89	Nonelectrical and parts and attachments	37,528	38,694
90	Construction, textile, and other specialized industry machinery and nonfarm tractors	6,166	6,745
91	Other industrial machinery, n.e.s.	9,966	10,937
92	Agricultural machinery and farm tractors	1,893	1,670
93	Business and office machines, computers, etc.	14,028	13,076
94	Scientific, professional, and service industry equipment	5,475	6,296
95	Transportation equipment, except automotive	4,197	5,994
96	Civilian aircraft, engines, parts	3,799	5,632
97	Civilian aircraft complete, all types	1,310	1,822
98	Automotive vehicles, parts, and engines	56,789	65,046
99	From Canada	22,993	24,624
100	From all other areas	33,796	40,422
101	Passenger cars, new and used	30,717	36,063
102	Trucks, buses, and special vehicles	8,200	9,419
103	Bodies, engines, parts and accessories, n.e.s.	17,872	19,564
104	Consumer goods (nonfood) except automotive	61,299	65,060
105	Consumer durables manufactured	31,249	33,104
106	Electric household appliances, radio, television	10,762	11,218
107	Consumer nondurables, manufactured	26,273	27,983
108	Textile products, except rugs	13,847	14,849
109	Unmanufactured consumer goods (gems, nursery stock)	3,777	3,973
110	Imports, n.e.s. (low value, U.S. goods returned, military aircraft, movies, exhibits)	7,742	9,358

Source: U.S. Department of Commerce, *Survey of Current Business,* March 1986.

One of the important categories of U.S. exports are electrical appliances such as those produced by Sunbeam Appliance Company.

Courtesy of Sunbeam Appliance Company

scope, it can be seen that the U.S. is clearly a net exporter of agricultural products as well as technology-intensive nonelectrical machinery and chemicals. (This situation occurs for two reasons. First, the United States simply produces a surplus quantity of agricultural products that other countries need. Second, the U.S. agricultural industry is technology- and capital-intensive relative to that of the rest of the world). It is likewise clear that the United States is a huge oil importer because of insufficient domestic supply, as well as a net importer of autos and consumer durables. Notice that, with the service category eliminated, the U.S. has a large merchandise trade deficit in each year shown and that oil imports have contributed the largest single value to that deficit.

Returning to the summary BOP (Table 7-3) and moving down the column, we find unilateral transfers (gifts) in lines 29-32. In this case, all entries are *net* values—credits minus debits. Since only one column is being used, the total addition to or subtraction from each type of claim is recorded, netting total flows during the given year. Line 29 sums all nonmilitary gifts into and out of the United States for the year, showing a net debit value of $14,784 million for 1985. For most advanced industrial countries, in fact, unilateral transfers are a persistent net debit entry because of foreign aid and private gifts going abroad. Conversely, in many LDCs, with the exception of the OPEC countries, unilateral transfers persistently add up to a net credit entry. The "thank-you notes" pile up in the industrial countries, while the aid itself goes to LDCs. When unilateral transfers are added to trade in goods and services, we obtain the current account balance, which appears in line 67.

The U.S. presentation separates military aid from other gifts, recording the unilateral transfer in line 28 and simultaneously showing the equal value of the goods and services transferred in line 14 (i.e., as exports).

It is the U.S. capital accounts that are extremely different from our conceptual presentation. In the official presentation, assets in foreign countries that are bought or sold by U.S. residents are recorded in lines 49-62 and summed in line 48. This aggregation of all claims in the U.S. BOP emphasizes the individuals and institutions that generate these flows, but it obscures the long-term/short-term dichotomy of the conceptual view.

It is fairly easy to separate official reserves flows from the other capital accounts. Lines 35-38 list the four categories of official reserves, and line 34 shows the net change in reserves. These entries can be placed at the bottom of the table, after eliminating them from the summary line 33. Thus, in 1985, U.S. asset flows abroad were $84,925 million (i.e., an outflow of assets), but they were only $81,067 when official reserves are segregated out. The official reserves gain (inflow) was − $3,858 million, which already appears in line 68.

Because the data collection process is so difficult, with literally billions of transactions among millions of entities to record each year, the U.S. BOP (or that of any other country) unquestionably lacks complete coverage. Some international transactions simply do not get recorded, and thus the total volume of transactions is understated. Also, because banks, exporters, and foreign investors, etc., report to different agencies and on different forms, the entities that *are* recorded may not balance overall. Thus, "statistical discrepancy," a special category to account for errors and omissions, is placed in line 63. As the ability to record more and more of the transactions that occur improves, the size of this entry should decline. Considering just the few most recent years, however, the discrepancy is often huge—$32,739 million in 1985 for example.

For additional discussion of the U.S. balance of payments format and specific entries, see *Survey of Current Business,* June 1978, part 2; Stern et al. (1977); and Maldonado (1980).

Implications of the U.S. Balance of Payments for International Firms

What do all of these transactions mean to business managers operating in the United States? First of all, the persistent and increasing balance of trade deficits during the 1980s portend increasing restrictions on U.S. imports and a tendency for the dollar to devalue relative to the currencies of the major trading partners with which the United States has bilateral deficits, such as

Canada, Britain, Japan, and Germany. While protectionism grew during the period from 1980 to 1987, the value of the dollar shifted wildly from revaluation of about 40 percent in the early 1980s to devaluation of a similar magnitude by early 1987, leaving its value relative to the value of other industrial country currencies about the same in 1987 as it had been in 1980.

Initially, the U.S. merchandise trade deficit was financed largely by income on U.S. assets abroad, such as remittances from foreign subsidiaries and interest on foreign loans. By 1983 even these flows had become inadequate to balance the excess of imports over exports, and by 1985 the negative balance on goods and services had jumped to over $100 billion per year. This situation would have presented a major crisis for any other country. The United States benefited from the fact that the U.S. dollar was the base currency for international business transactions and was viewed as a relatively stable store of value. Thus, the huge deficits were financed by massive capital inflows—investments by foreign nationals who wanted to hold U.S. securities or invest in U.S. businesses. As a result, by 1986 the United States had become a major net capital importer for the first time since the last century.

This situation has created major concern among U.S. policymakers, who realize that any important shift in investors' confidence away from the United States could trigger even greater dollar devaluation and serious economic recession. If incoming foreign direct and portfolio investment do not finance the trade deficit, then either official reserves must be used to make payment (i.e., buy back dollars from foreign central banks) or expenditures on imports must be constrained (and/or exports must be subsidized) by policy to move closer to a balance. Continuing dollar devaluation is expected to improve the trade balance automatically, as exports become cheaper to foreign buyers and imports more expensive to U.S. buyers—but as of 1987 this adjustment has been wholly inadequate to equilibrate exports and imports. Let us consider the adjustment process in more detail.

The Adjustment Process

Balance of payments adjustment may occur through any sequence of events that leads from a situation of net positive or negative official reserve flows to a balance, in which no official reserves flow. Such adjustment takes a country from an initial deficit (or surplus) to equilibrium. The means for achieving BOP adjustment are numerous, ranging from trade and capital controls for restricting each of these accounts, to interest rate policy aimed at influencing capital flows, to exchange rate change, which affects all accounts. Tracing the intricacies of each policy or event and its impact on a country's internal and external balance goes far beyond the scope of the present text.[5] Let us consider, therefore, the simple adjustment process in the actual world of flexible exchange rates.

The **automatic adjustment mechanism** for a country that allows the value of its currency to fluctuate in the foreign exchange market is based on the exchange rate itself. When a country runs a balance of trade deficit, importing more than it exports, that country's currency will begin to accumulate in the hands of foreign exporters (or their banks). At some point, those foreign firms and banks will view their holdings of this currency as an excess and will begin to sell it off and bid its price down. As in any market with a situation of excess supply, the price of the product (namely, the currency) will fall to eliminate the excess. (This is exactly the same mechanism that was discussed in Chapter 5 as the adjustment process for the foreign exchange market.) When the price of the home currency falls, exports become cheaper to foreign purchasers and imports become more expensive to domestic consumers, leading to a tendency toward trade equilibrium as exports increase and imports decline.[6]

The automatic adjustment mechanism also responds to imbalances in the capital accounts; however, such interactions are substantially more complex. As noted earlier, interest arbitrageurs will operate to equate interest differentials and forward premiums (discounts) among major convertible currencies. Since the forward exchange rate is a good estimator for the future spot rate between any two countries' currencies, we can see that any change in either country's interest rate or the spot exchange rate will have an impact on the forward rate (and hence the future spot rate). Now if for some reason our domestic interest rates rise, foreign arbitrageurs and investors will purchase our assets now and sign forward contracts to convert back to their own currencies in the future. The net result will be that the initial outflow of claims (i.e., ownership of home country assets) causes the spot exchange rate to revalue (home currency/foreign currency ↓) and the forward rate to devalue (home currency/foreign currency ↑). Foreign interest rates may also rise as other countries try to lure back investors. In addition, the initial inflow of investment may cause home country interest rates to fall as demand for home country assets rises. Initially, the home country will export additional financial claims, pushing the basic BOP toward surplus; once the exchange rate changes (and interest rates adjust), there will be a reverse flow of claims.

A clearer and no less important phenomenon relates to the long-term capital account. If home country investors and banks invest/lend more abroad than foreigners lend to the home country, we will face a deficit on long-term capital. Other things equal, this will lead to a devaluation of the home currency, because there is an excess demand for foreign exchange to buy foreign long-term assets. The devaluation will make foreign assets more expensive, thus enticing both foreign and home country investors to buy home country assets. The final tendency is toward equilibrium in capital flows, with the final exchange rate being an equilibrium rate.

All of the above description of the adjustment process is intended to demonstrate the *automatic* steps that would occur without government intervention. Once a deficit or surplus occurs, the government may impose controls on various BOP accounts—or it may "finance" the deficit by borrowing from foreign banks and other foreign lenders. For example, when copper prices fall and Chile faces a BOP deficit on the current account, Chile's

A major source of Chile's exports, the copper mine at Chuquicamata.

Photri, Inc.

government may borrow from the IMF or from a private bank. By borrowing foreign currency in exchange for a loan commitment, Chile obtains an inflow of official reserves (the foreign exchange) that may exactly offset the outflow needed to pay for the trade deficit. Chile's BOP returns to equilibrium, with the commitment to repay the loan eventually (and lose official reserves in the future).

Chile could avoid the need for future repayment of the loan by aiming instead to control specific balance of payments accounts. For example, Chile could place restrictions on imports and offer incentives to exports, thus pushing the trade balance in a favorable direction. Similarly, Chile could offer incentives to foreign direct investment, in this case improving the capital account and leading toward a basic balance surplus. These policies can be used separately or together by a country to avoid letting the automatic adjustment mechanism function, with the problem that ending the policies may lead to the automatic adjustment anyway. At any given time, however, a country may prefer to utilize these policies rather than accept a currency devaluation or a need to borrow more from international lenders.

Even from this brief view, it can be seen that BOP adjustment may be a very complex process—though one that has important implications for a company or bank dealing with any given country. The main concern of this chapter has been to sketch the components and determinants of the BOP itself, not to investigate the adjustment process in detail. The conclusions then relate to the *pressures* on a country to adjust—which may be alleviated by automatic adjustment or by government policies on foreign exchange, trade, and investment (or by both).

Evaluating the Balance of Payments

How can one interpret a deficit (or surplus) on any given balance of payments? That is, what should one expect, in terms of exchange rate changes or government policies, when a particular balance of payments is not balanced?

Consider, first, the trade balance. Table 7-5 shows a substantial trade surplus for Mexico in 1982. This $6,795 million surplus provided Mexico with the ability to pay some of its outstanding debt service (i.e., interest and principal coming due for the year). However, the total debt service due, plus other service imports, totaled over $19 billion in 1982—so there was a $6,514 million deficit on goods and services, which had to be "financed" by an outflow of claims of equal value. If the only other BOP category had been money, then Mexico would have ended up creating a large additional supply of pesos in the world market. This would have probably led to a peso devaluation and/or government policies to restrict imports and stimulate exports.

Table 7-5 **An Overview of Mexico's Balance of Payments, 1982** (in millions of U.S. dollars)

	Debits −	Credits +		BOP Measures	
Merchandise imports	14,435	21,230	Merchandise exports	6,795	Merchandise trade balance
Other imports	19,753	6,444	Other exports	−6,514	Goods and services balance
Gifts given		296	Gifts received	−6,218	Current account balance
Long-term capital inflows		10,404	Long-term capital outflows	+4,186	Basic balance
Short-term capital inflows	3,658		Short-term capital outflows		
Errors and omissions	5,318				
Official reserves		3,470			

Source: IMF, *International Financial Statistics,* 1986 yearbook, p. 346.

In reality, the continued substantial oil exports in that year, plus people's expectations about Mexico's future economic strength (among other factors), led to huge long-term investment flows (both direct investment and long-term loans), which more than offset the current account deficit. Thus, the basic balance showed a surplus of $4,186 million—and this implied a future revaluation of the peso, other things being equal.

Finally, the inflow of short-term capital plus errors in recording that turned out to be a debit entry in 1982, more than balanced the outflow of goods, services, gifts, and long-term claims. Thus, Mexico recorded a net outflow of official reserves for the year of $3,470 million. This "bottom line" implied a pressure toward peso devaluation during the year (which did occur) in the absence of any additional government policy. Even this last balance did not tell how much of the flows were due to existing regulations and policies and how much to market forces.[7]

What is needed to interpret the Mexican balance of payments position more accurately is substantial additional information. First, several years of BOP records can provide help in interpreting trends toward deficit or surplus (or just instability). Second, disaggregation of trade accounts to see which products or services dominate the accounts would add to an understanding of how sensitive Mexico's trade may be to world prices and demand. Clearly, Mexico's main export sector is petroleum, and its balance of payments is extremely sensitive to changes in international oil prices. Third, some measure of the national economy's condition, over time and relative to that of other countries, can illuminate problems or opportunities that affect the BOP but do not appear directly in it. For example, the huge external debt of Mexican public and private sector borrowers caused a major crisis of confidence in Mexico as a target for international investment during the 1980s, and this problem appears likely to hinder Mexico's ability to finance current account deficits in the future. (Interest payments on the external debt do appear in the BOP, but it may not be clear that the debt burden is growing and intractable.)

Hopefully, this example has demonstrated (1) that it is possible to obtain valuable insight into a country's economic position through the BOP and (2) that the BOP accounts alone provide a very imperfect view, one that needs to be supplemented with other information.

The company manager can utilize BOP information in planning strategy for exchange risk management and financial flow policy. When a country faces a persistent deficit on the current account or on the basic balance, it can fairly safely be assumed that the currency will devalue and/or the government will set up restrictions on imports and on currency outflows, such as profit remittances. If the imbalance appears primarily on the capital account, as was true in the case of Mexico, capital controls are even more likely. Appropriate strategy may entail hedging with financial instruments or adjusting the firm's activities to reduce the assets exposed to this kind of risk.

Conclusions

The balance of payments is a very complex subject for managers. Managers should understand BOP accounting, so that they can use BOP data in company strategy formulation. Generally speaking, BOP data for several years are needed in order to draw useful conclusions. Because automatic adjustment to BOP imbalances is limited by governments, no simple management decision rules can be derived from BOP data alone. Also, because governments intervene in different ways and at different times to alter exchange rates and exchange policies, BOP analysis can only enable a company manager to understand the key influences involved—the timing of government policies remains fairly unpredictable. Understanding these influences can help the manager to create a business plan that minimizes the risks associated with likely BOP conditions in a given country.

Balance of payments accounting is similar to financial accounting for a company, especially to the financial statement called "statement of net change in financial position." It is a flow concept, measured over a period of time. It includes all transactions between residents of a country and residents of all foreign countries during a given period.

There is no such thing as *the* balance of payments. The debits and credits in the total set of entries in a BOP account must add up to the same amount. If only certain entries are included, the BOP may not balance—for example, if the BOP is confined to exports and imports of merchandise, the trade balance. The official reserves balance is the final balance in a BOP account, and even this one may not provide a clear picture of a country's position. Borrowing of official reserves which must be paid back later, adds to the official reserves balance surplus, and the country may use such a loan to try to hide its BOP problems.

Balance of Payments Problems

Instructions:

1. Make the proper entries for the following transactions on the accompanying worksheet.
2. Calculate the basic balance of payments surplus or deficit.

ROW = Rest of the world.

1. Residents of the United States exported $5,000 of merchandise to residents of ROW, who paid by drawing on their accounts with the Chase Manhattan Bank.
2. U.S. tourists spent $120 for goods and services while traveling in ROW.

They paid in ROW currency, which they obtained by cashing American Express traveler's checks at ROW banks.

3. Diplomatic missions of foreign governments spent $150 in the United States, drawing on their deposits in U.S. banks.
4. The U.S. government made cash grants of $1,000 in economic aid to less developed countries. The governments of these countries utilized $300 of the grants to buy machinery in the United States. They held the remainder on deposit in a U.S. bank.
5. Residents of the United States imported $7,200 of merchandise from ROW residents, of which $4,000 was paid by drafts drawn on deposits of U.S. banks in ROW banks and $3,200 was paid through an increase in the deposits of ROW banks in U.S. banks.
6. The ROW central bank bought $200 of gold from the U.S. government, paying for it by check drawn on its deposit with the Federal Reserve Bank of New York.
7. U.S. ships carried goods for ROW merchants. The shipping charges of $300 were paid through a draft drawn on the ROW merchants. (ROW merchants paid their bank, the ROW bank increased the deposits of U.S. banks, and U.S. banks paid the shipping companies.)
8. Private citizens in the United States received merchandise gifts from foreigners valued at $60.
9. U.S. residents bought $400 of bonds issued by a Japanese utility and paid for the bonds with checks drawn on their accounts in U.S. banks. The Japanese utility held the proceeds in U.S. banks.
10. U.S. residents sent $250 of U.S. currency through the mail as gifts to persons in ROW.
11. The U.S. government donated $1,000 of surplus wheat to needy countries in ROW.
12. A U.S. multinational firm set up a factory in ROW, sending $50,000 in cash and $100,000 in machinery to the ROW location.
13. Bank of America made a $75,000 loan, payable in one year, to an ROW businessman (who had a deposit of $25,000 at Bank of America).
14. The U.S. Fed floated a $100 million bond, denominated in SDRs and payable in two years. The bond was purchased by the ROW central bank and paid for in SDRs.

Worksheet

	Debit	Credit
A. Goods and services		
1. Merchandise		
2. Transportation		
3. Travel		
4. Miscellaneous, government		
B. Unilateral transfers		
1. Private		
2. Government		
C. Long-term capital		
1. Foreign direct investment		
2. Private portfolio investment		
3. Government investment		
D. Short-term capital		
1. Private		
2. Government		
E. Official reserves		
1. Gold		
2. SDRs		
3. Foreign exchange		
4. Position in the IMF		

Questions

1. What, exactly, is measured in a balance of payments? In a double-entry BOP accounting system, how can the accounts fail to balance?
2. Explain how the trade account in a country's BOP may be related to the short-term capital account.
3. Of what importance is the BOP of a host country (such as Mexico in the text example) to the MNE manager? Of what importance is the home country's BOP?
4. How can a country's balance of trade be in a deficit, while its current account is in a surplus?
5. Explain why the balance of payments is organized into trade, gifts, long-term capital, short-term capital, and official reserve accounts. Why is it useful to draw these distinctions?
6. As a company manager in Great Britain in 1983, when oil prices have fallen 25 percent compared to 1981 prices, what would you expect the trade balance to show? What government policies would you expect? What automatic adjustment would you expect to occur, other things being equal?
7. If interest rates are higher in the United States than in Japan, what would you expect the capital accounts to show? (*Note:* What if the interest rates in both countries have not changed from last year?) Does the exchange rate make any difference?
8. What impact does the IMF have on balances of payments when it creates new SDRs and distributes them to member countries? (The Chapter 6 discussion of SDRs may help you in answering this question. SDRs are the liabilities of the IMF itself, and they are reserve assets to the countries that receive them.)
9. Looking at the U.S. BOP in Tables 7-3 and 7-4, what automatic adjustments and policy changes do you anticipate for the next year?
10. How can a country such as Brazil finance its foreign debt, which was about $100 billion in 1987? Specifically, use balance of payments categories to show what kinds of transactions would generate foreign currency for Brazil.

References

International Monetary Fund. *Balance of Payments Manual.* 4th ed. Washington, D.C.: IMF, 1977.

Kemp, Donald. "Balance-of-Payments Concepts—What Do They Really Mean?" *Review,* Federal Reserve Bank of St. Louis, July 1975.

Maldonado, Rita. "Recording and Classifying Transactions in the Balance of Payments." *International Journal of Accounting,* 1980.

Stern, Robert. *The Balance of Payments.* Chicago: Aldine Publishing Co., 1973.

Stern, Robert, et al. *The Presentation of the U.S. Balance of Payments: A Symposium.* Princeton University Essays in International Finance, no. 123, August 1977.

"U.S. International Transactions." *Survey of Current Business,* various issues.

Endnotes

1. A "resident" for balance of payments purposes is generally defined as an entity or person residing in the country for one year or more.
2. This valuation scheme then leads to a summary BOP which includes home-currency values of transactions from different dates, when exchange rates may have been different. Because the BOP is a flow measure, no end-of-period adjustment is made for asset/liability valuation changes.
3. The distinction between stock ownership as portfolio investment and stock ownership as direct investment is not easy to draw. The U.S. Department of Commerce defines FDI as 10 percent or more ownership of a firm (see Chapter 4) for most purposes. Other governments often use 25 percent ownership as the dividing line.
4. These categories involve different levels of aggregation of subindustries, so the full table should be used to draw inferences, rather than just trying to compare, say, automobiles with agricultural products.
5. The various views of BOP adjustment are presented very clearly in Stern (1973).
6. This result will occur only if the devaluation causes export quantity to rise enough so that export *value* (price × quantity) increases, and vice versa for imports. The mathematical condition that underlies this reasoning is the Marshall-Lerner condition.
7. For example, the government could have borrowed extensively to obtain foreign exchange through long-term bank loans from abroad. This strategy appears in the BOP as an inflow of official reserves and an outflow of long-term capital, each of which improves the basic balance. Yet this may be pure "window dressing" to avoid showing a deficit—and in any event the loans must eventually be repaid.

8 BARRIERS TO INTERNATIONAL TRADE AND INVESTMENT

This chapter begins the direct consideration of government policies that affect international business transactions. In particular, it analyzes the rules on imports and exports that restrict trade flows. In addition, it discusses rules on investment flows. The implications of government trade and investment policies for national welfare, and for company managers, are presented in some detail. The main goals of the chapter are to:

1. Examine six major types of trade and investment barriers and note why they exist.
2. Explain the reasons that governments use barriers to imports and capital outflows.
3. Show the economic impacts of three specific trade barriers—tariffs, subsidies, and quotas.
4. Discuss current U.S. trade policies.
5. Note some of the current government policies that limit international capital flows.
6. Suggest some strategies for company managers to deal with barriers to trade and investment.

Introduction

Thus far, our attention has focused primarily on the activities of companies and on the functioning of the markets they compete in. Little emphasis has been placed on the regulatory restrictions that companies face. Direct investment (plus local production) and exports have been seen as substitutes when barriers disallow or restrict one or the other—but the barriers themselves have not been discussed in any detail. This chapter covers some of the major types of restrictions that exist on company exports (on *imports,* from the receiving country's view) and international capital flows.

In the next section, some of the most common forms of restrictions are discussed and analyzed. Then we consider the host government's point of view on trade and investment policies. The economic impacts of three major types of trade barriers are laid out in the fourth section. With these basics in place, we then discuss actual policies, looking specifically at U.S. commercial policy. Home and host country *investment* controls are discussed in the sixth section. Finally, suggestions for corporate strategy in light of the barriers are offered, followed by conclusions.

Common Forms of Barriers

Barriers to international flows of goods and services can be grouped into six broad categories for convenience of discussion:

1. Price-based constraints (e.g., tariffs, subsidies).
2. Quantity limits (e.g., quotas, embargoes).
3. Buyers' or sellers' cartels (e.g., OPEC, the International Sugar Agreement, the MultiFiber Agreement).
4. Other **NTBs** (nontariff barriers) on trade.
5. Financial limits (e.g., exchange controls, profit remittance limits).
6. Limits on FDI entry and operations.

Each of these categories is described in this section and discussed in more detail in subsequent sections.

Tariffs and Subsidies

All countries in the noncommunist world use price-based constraints, i.e., **tariffs,** on their imports. In fact, tariffs are a form of tax, paid on goods shipped internationally. Tariffs are generally charged on imports, as a tax that raises the cost of importing goods. They are usually charged as a percentage of the value of the goods shipped, that is, on an *ad valorem* basis. The United States, for example, has a long list of tariff rates charged on imports, ranging from zero to 117 percent (on tobacco), with an average of about 3.7 percent *ad valorem.*[1] Clearly, tariffs are intended to raise the cost of importing into a country. This accomplishes three goals: (1) it makes local production more competitive; (2) it generates revenue for the government; and (3) it reduces the quantity of imports. Tariffs present a cost to consumers, who must pay a higher price for protected goods than they would have paid if there were no tariffs.

Following similar reasoning, most countries also offer **subsidies** to some domestic companies, so that their products can compete better with imports. In this case, domestic producers are aided directly, typically through low-cost loans or tax breaks that lower their cost of doing business, while imports are not aided and may still be faced with additional tariffs. The federal government of the United States does not offer much of this type of support, though some individual states and local governments offer incentives that constitute subsidies for local producers.[2] The main cost of a subsidy is that someone must pay for it—generally the taxpayers of the subsidizing country.

A second form of subsidy is the export subsidy, which a government may offer to stimulate the exports of domestic firms. In this case, the government provides financial aid to exporting firms through, for example, tax breaks or low-interest loans. These firms in turn export more and stimulate national income. This form of protectionism also has a cost: the country receiving the exports will face unfair competition from the subsidized firms.

Quotas and Embargoes

Quantity limits, such as **quotas,** are also used to restrict international trade. Here the limitation is on the number of units of a product that may be imported or on the market share allowed to imports. Quotas are sometimes imposed on exports as well. For example, a "voluntary" quota on Japanese auto exports to the United States allowed the Japanese automobile producers to export 2.4 million cars to the United States from April 1986 through March 1987, leaving the rest of the market to domestic producers (*and* to imports from other countries). In a slightly different policy, Canada allows foreign banks to hold a total of not more than 16 percent of bank deposits in the country—a limit on market share rather than a limit on the amount of deposits. A quota can be established at any level of import quantity. The particular type of quota that sets the limit at zero imports is called an **embargo.** Often an embargo is placed on imports for clearly political reasons (e.g., to penalize an adversary during a war) rather than to stimulate domestic production or serve any strictly economic goal. The main economic costs of quotas are that they limit access by consumers to otherwise available products and that they tend to raise the prices of the protected products.

Cartels

Cartels operate in international trade to fix prices or quantities sold in various markets. The restrictions function in much the same ways as the controls of individual governments that were noted above, however they are imposed, not by individual governments, but by a group of producers or consumers of a particular product. Virtually all of the cartels in operation today are associations of countries, because in most countries company cartels have been outlawed by antitrust policies. The OPEC cartel is a group of oil-producing countries that restrict both the quantity and the price of the oil that its members sell. (See Chapter 24 for a detailed look at the international oil industry.) The International Sugar Agreement establishes a base price for exports of sugar and market shares for the exporting countries that participate in the agreement. Cartels constrain the market for international trade in individual products in many of the same ways as the controls of individual governments.

Nontariff Barriers

Other **nontariff barriers** (NTBs) to international trade appear in national regulations and practices. These include a wide variety of barriers, ranging from bureaucratic delays in processing requests for import permits, to quality standards that preclude foreign-produced goods, to buy-national programs that require governments to purchase from domestic suppliers. In each case, the NTBs raise the cost of importing and thus tend to reduce the country's total imports. Consumers in the protected country generally find that NTBs lead to lower availability and higher prices of protected products.

A second set of restrictions that relate to the trade controls discussed above are capital controls. These government policies are used to limit flows of funds or other financial instruments across national borders. Capital controls can also restrict trade as well, by limiting exporters' and importers' access to foreign exchange.

Exchange Controls

Financial limits, such as **exchange controls,** are generally used to limit outflows of foreign exchange. A country may choose this policy in order to avoid devaluation of its currency, which would otherwise take place through the free market for exchange rate determination, because of an excess supply of the currency in the foreign exchange market. A country may also limit access to foreign exchange in order to curb importers' ability to pay their suppliers—thus restricting imports. Another purpose of exchange controls is to stimulate exports, by simply offering exporters a more favorable rate of exchange (so that they can sell their foreign-currency receipts for more local currency). For example, most Latin American countries allow exporters to exchange their dollars at the unrestricted exchange rate, which gives more local currency for each dollar sold. Brazil, among other countries, then restricts importers' access to dollars by requiring a large deposit of funds several months before an import shipment has been received—a very costly process. Brazil and other countries have also frequently limited the number of dollars that Brazilian travelers are allowed to purchase for trips abroad.

Exchange controls may be used specifically to regulate capital markets, rather than aiming at exports or imports. Many times, a country has discovered that speculators have begun to push down the value of its currency; and to stop this activity, the country may limit access to foreign exchange or otherwise restrict financial transactions that tend to devalue the currency. Such controls undoubtedly have an impact on exports and imports as well.

The main forms of exchange controls in use today include fixed exchange rates, with limited access to foreign exchange; different exchange rates for different categories of market participants; and bureaucratic controls, such as "red tape," that require the expenditure of substantial time and effort to get access to foreign exchange. Each of these forms of exchange controls can be used both to restrict imports and to control capital flows. The main costs of exchange controls are the loss of trade and investment that would have taken place in their absence.

Foreign Investment Controls

Foreign investment controls range from the rejection of all foreign direct investment, as in several communist countries, to limits on the activities of foreign-owned firms, such as limits on profit remittances and other financial transfers. Controls of this kind include both price-based policies, such as taxes or price controls, and quantity restrictions, such as limits on the entry of foreign investment. In South America, the Andean Pact countries require that foreign investors sell 51 percent ownership to local investors over a 15-year period of time after an investment has been made; they limit profit remittance to 20 percent of accumulated capital per year; they prohibit royalty payments to parent companies; and they restrict various other activities of foreign investors. Until the end of 1984, Canada limited the quantity of foreign direct investment through a screening of potential investors carried out by the Foreign Investment Review Agency.[3] Foreign investment controls generally create competitive conditions that favor local firms competing with foreign-owned firms within the country. The costs of foreign investment controls are the lost FDI that they deter; these costs are difficult to measure, though Chapter 10 looks carefully at this issue.

Altogether, the barriers to international trade and investment examined above create tremendous limitations on the ability of market participants to determine the prices and quantities of products sold in international business. The purpose of this chapter is not to criticize the barriers but to understand them and to see how to deal with them. Let us look next at governments' reasons for utilizing the various barriers.

Reasons for Barriers: The Host Government's View

Tariff, subsidy, quota, and other policy constraints on trade vary, literally from month to month, not only between countries but also in individual countries, as economic and political conditions, and even governments, change. While there is no single main reason for imposing these barriers, it is possible to construct an overview of the government concerns that lead to them. Figure 8-1 presents the reasons that underlie much of the trade and investment policy in use today.

The principal goals of controls on trade or direct investment flows are to promote national economic growth (usually the primary objective of less developed countries) and to forego balance of payments adjustment (and save jobs—usually the primary objective of industrial countries). These goals can be approached in many ways. For example, the classic strategy of CEPAL (the United Nations Economic Commission for Latin America) has been to replace imports with local production; this calls for raising tariffs to cut imports. In contrast, the strategy of Japan and ASEAN (the Association of South East Asian Nations) has been not to restrict imports, but to subsidize exports and thus help them compete in world markets. Altogether, the reasons for imposing trade controls that appear in Figure 8-1 can be traced to the goals of stimulating or preserving national economic output or to the goal of improving the balance of payments. (An additional goal that should be noted is protection to achieve political ends, such as penalizing unfriendly countries.)

Improving the balance of payments may mean eliminating a deficit or reducing a surplus. For the most part, countries facing a balance of trade surplus simply acquire financial claims on deficit countries, without encountering any pressure to "improve" the situation toward a balance. Countries with a trade deficit, on the other hand, spend their available foreign exchange to pay for imports, and ultimately they must either eliminate the deficit or run out of foreign currency with which to finance it (unless recurring loans can be used to finance the deficit indefinitely). Thus, for balance of payments purposes, governments use trade controls most often in efforts to eliminate trade deficits.

Consider separately each of the reasons for controls listed in Figure 8-1.

Figure 8-1 **Reasons for Trade and Investment Controls**

1. To protect import-competing domestic firms (includes saving jobs).
2. To promote import substitution.
3. To promote infant industries.
4. To reduce reliance on foreign suppliers.
5. To encourage local and foreign direct investment.
6. To achieve health and safety standards.
7. To reduce balance of payments problems.
8. To promote export-based growth.
9. To restrain foreign firms from dumping.
10. To serve political goals.

Protest by U.S. garment workers in Philadelphia against imported clothing.
Wide World Photos, Inc.

Protecting Import-Competing Domestic Firms

This rationale is used virtually everywhere. The United States imposes tariffs on imported steel, uses "voluntary" quotas on imported TVs and autos, and subsidizes domestic exporters to improve their ability to compete with foreign producers. Such measures are used widely because, among other reasons, the companies and people hurt by the foreign competition make strenuous efforts to convince the government that restrictions would be beneficial to them. For example, the United Auto Workers and the Big Three auto manufacturers (GM, Ford, and Chrysler) in the United States are highly visible groups that can lobby relatively effectively for protection against foreign competition. Similar conditions exist in every country for some industries, and various forms of protection exist everywhere to protect import-competing firms.

Promoting Import Substitution

Using this justification, many less developed countries have established very high tariffs on selected products. In this way they hope to encourage local or foreign investors to inaugurate local production of formerly imported products. This would both reduce a trade balance deficit and provide additional jobs for local workers. Import substitution policy has not proven effective for any country trying to achieve an "economic miracle," such as Japan in the 1950s and 60s or Singapore and Hong Kong in the 1970s, but it can be part of a development strategy aimed at fostering new capital investment in specific industries. In this sense, the import substitution argument can be compared to the infant industry argument.

Promoting Infant Industries

Virtually every developed country raised tariffs and NTBs during its period of development, to enable new industries to start up without overwhelming competition from established firms abroad. Wide acceptance has been given to a policy of imposing a tariff or other barriers for a limited period of time to enable an infant industry to begin operation. Unfortunately, there is no clear measure of the appropriate time period for infant industry protection, so that such policies often tend to continue indefinitely. Brazil, for example, has recently established an embargo on imports of microcomputers. All microcomputers must now be produced by Brazilian firms. This policy excludes IBM, Burroughs, Apple, and other companies from the Brazilian market for an indefinite period of time, since it is not clear when Brazil's infant industry will be mature enough to allow elimination of the protection. The infant industry argument for protection rests completely on the premise that the protection will be eliminated when the new industry has achieved competitive status—a status that is often difficult to define.

Reducing Reliance on Foreign Suppliers

Most national governments prefer to obtain domestically whatever goods and services may be needed for protection against a foreign political power. With few exceptions, most countries supply their own armed forces, their own defense systems (though equipment may be imported) and their own supplies of many critical materials, such as food. The types of controls usually imposed to achieve this objective are not tariffs but government contracting agreements, under which the government buys the required products or services only from domestic suppliers or produces them through government agencies. The U.S. government, for example, must buy its supplies from domestic suppliers, unless foreign competitors offer substantially lower prices and acceptable quality.[4] It purchases some products, epecially defense-related ones, *only* from domestic suppliers.

Encouraging Local and Foreign Direct Investment

Tariffs and NTBs are sometimes used to encourage the replacement of imported goods with locally produced goods. Often Latin American governments raise tariffs on specific goods that they want to see produced locally, as part of a development strategy. Many governments raise barriers on imports of specific products in order to foster local production of those products—regardless of the nationality of the companies that produce them. In an often cited case, the Mexican government negotiated with John Deere Company and several other tractor manufacturers to allow four of them to produce their products locally, while denying other tractor manufacturers access to the Mexican market.[5]

Achieving Health and Safety Standards

National health and safety requirements for products and services are generally applied to imports *and* locally made goods or services. The process of verifying that imported items meet these standards may be used as a barrier to entry. Imports may be discouraged by simple red tape that forces the potential importer to expend much time and money to obtain proof of qualification. Or rules may be set that require expensive alterations of foreign-made goods to meet domestic product norms. The U.S. requirement that imported cars be modified from their home country configurations to meet the pollution control standards of the Environmental Protection Agency are a barrier that substantially raises the prices of these cars.

Reducing Balance of Payments Problems

All of the points made up to now have related directly or indirectly to the attempts of governments to increase domestic economic activity. These attempts *also* affect the balance of payments. Some restrictions on trade and investment, however, are imposed specifically to improve the BOP. These restrictions are generally not product or industry specific; rather, they limit broad classes of imports or all imports or they support exports or local production generally. Moreover, restrictions aimed at improving the BOP may be placed on capital flows as well as imports and exports.

Promoting Export-Based Growth

The strategy of export-led growth is based on a combination of the two basic economic reasons for trade and investment barriers. By encouraging exports through subsidies of some type, a government can foster greater production (and employment) at the same time that it reduces a balance of payments deficit, *without* limiting other countries' access to the national market. During the period since World War II, this strategy has vied for acceptability among less developed countries with the CEPAL strategy of import substitution (though there is no concep[illegible] why both strategies cannot be followed simultaneously).

Restraining Foreign Firms from Dumping

A monopolistic practice often seen in business is the attempt by one firm to cut prices temporarily in order to take sales away from competing firms. When the competing firms leave the market or go bankrupt, that firm controls the market and is free to raise its prices. In international trade, the practice of selling into a foreign market at a price below the firm's cost is called **dumping.** Because dumping tends to harm local firms and strengthen foreign competitors, it is restricted in most countries. While dumping is widely agreed to be "unfair" trade, it is quite difficult to measure a firm's actual costs or arrive at some "fair" market price. Very little consensus exists on any measure of dumping that would be appropriate for use as a standard for limiting the practice; and "dumping" is often used unjustifiably to criticize the practices of foreign low-cost producers that enter a home market. (The steel imports case in this chapter provides a useful example of the problems in defining and coping with dumping.)

Serving Political Goals

This last rationale may in fact be a part of the basis for many protective policies that are ostensibly pursued for other reasons, but here we focus on restraints that are imposed for specifically political reasons. For example, the motives for the U.S. embargo on exports to the Soviet Union after the Soviet invasion of Afghanistan were essentially political. Similarly, political motives have given rise to the various limitations on trade that the U.S. government has imposed on communist countries from time to time. The policies adopted to pursue a noneconomic goal may actually cause some degree of economic hardship.

The foregoing discussion has simply explained some of the reasoning behind trade and investment barriers. Next, let us consider some of the economic problems raised by the use of three trade barriers.

An Economic Comparison of Three Trade Barriers

A Simple Graphic Analysis

Typically, when a government seeks to protect a domestic industry, it implements a tariff on imports, or a quota on imports, or a subsidy of domestic producers. Let us consider the economic implications of each of these policies in a hypothetical situation. Figure 8-2 compares the three policy choices for Bhagwatia, a country that wants to protect its steel industry.

Figure 8-2 **The Bhagwatia Steel Industry**

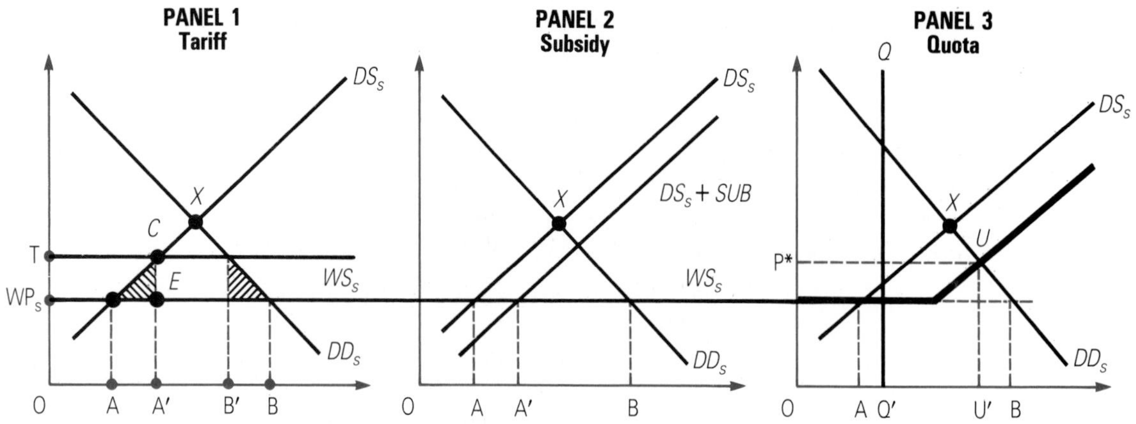

DS_S and DD_S are the domestic supply and demand for steel, respectively. WS_S is the production of steel available from all other countries combined—the world supply of steel. If the home country's supply of and demand for this product are relatively small compared to the world supply, then the world price is essentially a "given" to Bhagwatia and the world supply curve is perfectly elastic, a horizontal line across the figure. The price charged by foreign suppliers is WP_S, the world price of steel. Under conditions of free trade, producers in the home country will supply OA of steel and importers will sell AB of steel, so that total sales equal OB of steel. Notice that the figure is drawn so that domestic consumers would gain by importing, because they could consume more steel at a lower price than if the country simply produced all steel locally (at point X on the figure).

If the government wants to raise domestic output of steel to OA′, then it could use a *tariff* of size CE (which is an *ad valorem* percentage of CE/A′E), as shown in panel 1 of Figure 8-2. This raises the import price for domestic consumers to OT. Domestic producers of steel will sell OA′ of their output at the new, higher price, while foreign suppliers sell only A′B′. The initial effects of this policy are:

1. Increased domestic production and employment, assuming no retaliation by foreign governments.
2. Decreased domestic consumption of steel at the new, higher price.
3. Improved balance of trade, because of reduced imports (from AB to A′B′).
4. Increased government revenue from the tariff receipts (CE times A′B′).
5. Loss of consumer welfare (equal to the two shaded areas in panel 1).

The tariff alters consumers' marginal allocations of income, since it raises the price of steel relative to the prices of other goods and services sold in the country. If the country began in free-market equilibrium, then this represents a misallocation of income. A tariff may be easy to impose politically, since it appears to penalize "foreigners" relative to domestic producers, and the true costs are not readily apparent.

If the government wants to raise domestic output to OA′ using a *subsidy,* then the subsidy must push domestic supply out to A′ at price WP_S. This is shown by the new supply curve, DS_S + SUB, in panel 2. In this case, the domestic price stays at WP_S, and imports are reduced by only AA′. (To cut imports by as much as the tariff did, the government would need a subsidy large enough to shift out the supply curve by AA′ + BB′.) The subsidy shown in the graph has the following initial effects:

1. Increased domestic production and employment, assuming no retaliation.
2. No change in total domestic consumption of this product; no change in price.
3. Improved balance of trade, because of reduced imports (from AB to A′B′).
4. New government revenue needed to pay for the subsidy.
5. Loss of consumer welfare, because consumption is reduced by BU′.

Subsidies do not alter consumers' marginal allocations of income, because they leave prices unchanged. When a government chooses a revenue-generating policy (such as raising taxes) to pay for a subsidy, taxpayers can see clearly the impact of the policy; thus, a subsidy is more visible than a tariff to consumers and taxpayers. In conceptual terms, a subsidy is generally preferable to a tariff, because although they both have economic costs, the subsidy does not affect relative prices. In pragmatic political terms, and in the United States in particular, subsidies are viewed as "handouts," not to be distributed freely to companies without clear and substantial justification; so tariffs tend to be more readily acceptable.

If the government of Bhagwatia wants to raise domestic output to OA′ using a *quota,* then the quota must be less than OQ′, where Q′U′ is equal to OA′ from panel 1, as shown in panel 3. The quota will delegate OQ′ to imports, leaving the rest of the market at any given price to domestic producers. Essentially, this can be viewed as a case with a supply curve shaped as shown in heavy lines in panel 3. The imports take OQ′ at price P*, and domestic producers sell Q′U′. This quota has the following initial effects:

1. Increased domestic production and employment, assuming no retaliation.
2. Decreased domestic consumption of steel at the new, higher price.
3. Improved balance of trade, because of reduced imports.
4. No change in government revenues or expenditures.
5. Loss of consumer welfare, because consumption is reduced by BU′.

The initial impact of a quota is as obvious as that of a tariff. Like a tariff, a quota misallocates income by altering the relative price of the product being protected. A quota does not generate revenue for the government—a tariff does—or require government expenditure to pay for it.

All of these results will be somewhat different if domestic demand is very price elastic, or if domestic supply is very price elastic, or if the world price is not perfectly price elastic. The results will also be different if the country began in an already biased position—that is, with some trade barriers already being used. In that case, the value of the new barrier must be compared with the situation under the previous conditions—a kind of second-best problem.

Empirical Estimates of the Costs of Protectionism

A number of estimates have been made of the impact of trade restrictions on the U.S. economy in recent years. Table 8-1 presents a summary of findings from several studies concerning the economic impact of U.S. tariffs on U.S. consumers; and Table 8-2 presents findings from several studies on quantitative restrictions used by the United States to limit imports. Each of these estimates is intended to measure the net cost to consumers in terms of higher prices, reduced availability of imports, and spillovers into other parts of the economy. Notice that virtually every protectionist policy has a very large cost associated with it, in terms of losses incurred by consumers. For instance, quotas on textile imports under the Multifibre Agreement cost U.S. consumers over $3 billion per year; tariffs on imported iron and steel cost U.S. consumers over $4 billion per year. Estimates from the same sources showed that the average cost of protection *per U.S. job saved* in the steel and autos industries was about $100,000 per year! The next section describes the various protectionist policies used by the United States in international trade.

U.S. Commercial Policy

The basic tariff structure of the United States remains as outlined by the Smoot-Hawley Act (the Tariff Act of 1930) and amended to change tariff rates from time to time. In 1934, for example, the Reciprocal Trade Agreements Acts amended Smoot-Hawley, allowing the president to negotiate tariff changes. More recently, the Trade Reform Act of 1974 spelled out detailed provisions for aiding U.S. industries harmed by imports, ranging from additional protection to financial assistance for the injured firms and employees.

The attempts to lower trade barriers since World War II have been largely *multilateral* rather than bilateral. That is, the objective has often been to set tariff treatment that applies to many trading partners rather than only two. In 1946, the General Agreement on Tariffs and Trade (GATT) was formed by 22 countries as a forum for negotiating multilateral tariff reductions. (GATT is discussed in more detail in Chapter 9.) The United States has participated in seven rounds of negotiations since that time, with the result

Table 8-1 **Costs of Tariffs, by Product Category**

Product	Annual cost to U.S. consumers (in millions of 1980 U.S. dollars)	Source	Year of Estimate
Selected agricultural	317	a	1980
Aluminum	286	b	1980
Chemicals	829	b	1980
Copper	1,589	c	1979
Flatware (stainless steel)	31	c	1979
Footwear	1,037	b	1980
(Footwear, nonrubber)	(14)	d	(1977)
Furniture and fixtures	926	b	1980
Glass and glass products	906	b	1980
Jewelry	83	a	1980
Leather products	183	b	1980
Iron and steel	4,047	b	1980
Machinery (electric)	5,646	b	1980
Machinery (nonelectric)	5,324	b	1980
Metal products	386	b	1980
Miscellaneous manufacturing	1,005	b	1980
Paper, paper products	129	b	1980
Printing and publishing	466	b	1980
CB transceivers	57	d	1977
Sugar	1,742	d	1977
Textiles	3,160	b	1980
Transport equipment	4,955	b	1980
Wearing apparel	11,795	b	1980
Wood, wood products	710	b	1980
Zinc	175	c	1979
Total cost of tariffs listed	45,784		

[a] International Trade Commission, statistical services.
[b] Authors' estimate.
[c] Charles Pearson, "Adjusting to Imports of Manufacturers from Developing Countries," in *The International Economy: U.S. Role in a World Market,* prepared for the Joint Economic Committee of Congress, December, 1980.
[d] Morris E. Morkre and David G. Tarr, *Effects of Restrictions on United States Imports: Five Case Studies and Theory,* (Washington, D.C.: Federal Trade Commission, Bureau of Economics, June 1980).
Source: Michael Munger, "The Costs of Protectionism," *Challenge* (January-February 1984), p. 55.

Table 8-2 **Costs of Quantitative Restrictions to U.S. Consumers**

Product	Restriction	Annual cost to U.S. consumers (in millions of 1980 U.S. dollars)	Source	Year
Apparel, textiles	Quotas	3,416	a	1982
Ball bearings	OMA	N.E.		
Batteries	OMA	N.E.		
Coffee	OMA	720	b	1975
Footwear	OMA	1,634	c	1977
Footwear	OMA	681	d	1979
Footwear (plastic)	OMA	197	d	1977
Meat	Quota	816	e	1977
Meat	OMA	1,362	e	1977
Mushrooms	OMA	N.E.		
Steel (carbon)	OMA	1,706	f	1977
Steel, alloy tool	OMA	N.E.		
Steel, stainless	OMA	N.E.		
Sugar	Quota	1,000	g	*1980
Televisions	OMA	600	h	1977
Televisions	OMA	251	i	1980
Televisions	OMA	0	d	1979
Televisions	OMA	0	j	1980
Tin	OMA	N.E.		
Total costs of quantitative restrictions listed*		11,532		

N.E. = Not estimated.
* Assuming television OMA cost is zero.
[a] "Talking Business: With (Martin) Wolf of the Trade Policy Research Center," *New York Times,* January 1, 1982.
[b] General Accounting Office, "International Commodity Agreements."
[c] International Trade Commission, in CWPS-217.
[d] Morris E. Morkre and David G. Tarr, *Effects of Restrictions on United States Imports: Five Case Studies and Theory* (Washington, D.C.: Federal Trade Commission, Bureau of Economics, June 1980).
[e] Council on Wage and Price Stability, TA-201-25.
[f] Robert W. Crandall, "Federal Government Initiatives to Reduce the Price Level," in *Brookings Papers on Economic Activity,* 1978.
[g] Consumers for World Trade, Newsletter, "Special Issue Trade Roundup," Fall 1982.
[h] International Trade Commission, in CWPS-227.
[i] Charles Pearson, "Adjusting to Imports of Manufacturers from Developing Countries," in *The International Economy: U.S. Role in a World Market,* prepared for the Joint Economic Committee of Congress, December, 1980; and International Trade Commission statistical services.
[j] Victor Canto and Arthur Laffer, "The Effectiveness of Orderly Marketing Agreements: The Color TV Case," *Business Economics,* January 1983.
Source: Michael Munger, "The Costs of Protectionism," *Challenge* (January-February 1984), p. 56.

that U.S. tariffs today average only about 3.7 percent *ad valorem* to most countries of the world.

Additional U.S. commercial policy takes a wide variety of forms, such as:

1. Trigger-price penalties on steel imports.
2. An orderly marketing agreement for color TV imports.
3. A "voluntary" quota on imports of Japanese automobiles.
4. A Caribbean Basin Initiative that eliminates tariffs on a wide variety of goods imported from Caribbean countries.
5. A Trading-with-the-Enemy Act that forbids trade with a small number of communist countries (e.g., Cuba and North Korea).
6. An Export Sales Company Act that subsidizes U.S. exports.
7. "Buy American" requirements for government purchases.
8. Trade adjustment assistance, which compensates firms and workers whose income has been harmed by imports.

Each of these policies serves to "distort" the free-market process of international trade. However, since the initial situation was *not* one of free trade, each of the policies should be evaluated as a second-best alternative, compared with other choices.

The **trigger-price mechanism** on steel imports from 1978-82 (see the case on the steel imports problem at the end of this chapter) required the U.S. International Trade Commission to judge whether the pricing of imported steel was "fair" (i.e., whether it reflected cost conditions in the exporting country) and not just **dumping** (i.e., selling at a low price to get rid of excess steel output). The trigger-price mechanism was used to place penalties on steel imports from Japan, European countries, and even newly industrializing countries such as Korea and Brazil. The objective of this program was to protect U.S. steel manufacturers against unfair foreign competition, which may be either steel production subsidized by the foreign government or steel sold below a fair price to help the foreign producer use up excess inventory. The trigger prices actually used in this instance were all based on *Japanese* production costs.

The **orderly marketing agreement** for color TV imports follows reasoning similar to that of the trigger-price mechanism. In 1977, the U.S. government negotiated an orderly marketing agreement with the government of Japan that established a quota on TV imports from Japanese companies and an additional quota on imported unassembled TVs from Japanese companies. Much of the TV imports then began to come from Korea and Taiwan. So in 1980, the orderly marketing agreement with Japan was extended to TV imports from those two countries as well. By the end of 1981, color TV imports had leveled off and U.S. domestic production had increased substantially—though much of the additional U.S. production was just assembly of unfinished TVs from the restricted countries.[6]

The **voluntary quota** on Japanese auto imports can be viewed as a form of orderly marketing agreement. It established annual limits on total Japanese auto exports to the United States. If these "voluntary" limits are not followed, then the U.S. government is expected to impose mandatory constraints on auto imports. Thus, the implication is that the limits are actually mandatory. As of 1987, a maximum of 2.4 million cars per year were permitted to be imported from Japan.[7]

The **Caribbean Basin Initiative** simply eliminates tariffs on most imports from countries in the Caribbean region (including Central America). This policy was proposed in 1982 as a measure to improve the economic conditions of U.S. allies in the region, and thus to help ensure their support for U.S. political policies. The tariff part of the initiative was implemented in January 1984. While some major exports from the region are excepted (e.g., sugar, coffee, tin, textiles), thousands of manufactured products and other goods are covered. Obviously, this is a free-trade policy, not a restriction on trade.[8]

The **Trading-with-the-Enemy Act** disallows exports to and imports from countries that have been determined to be enemies of the United States by the U.S. government. North Korea has been included among such countries since 1950; Cuba, since 1961; and Vietnam, since 1975. Depending on the particular year and circumstances, other communist countries have also been included. Immediately after the Soviet invasion of Afghanistan in 1979, for example, U.S.-Soviet trade was severely limited. Most of the restrictions imposed at that time were terminated in 1980.[9]

In 1984, the U.S. policy of encouraging exports through income tax deferral (the DISC legislation) was replaced by the **Foreign Sales Corporation Act.** This act allows U.S. exporters to establish overseas affiliates to manage their export sales, and these affiliates are legally exempt from current U.S. taxation on the income from such sales until the earnings have been remitted to the parent firm in the U.S.[10] This policy offers a direct subsidy to U.S. exports, by reducing the taxes paid by exporters.

For some purchases, when bids from domestic suppliers are competitive with bids from foreign suppliers, the federal government of the United States is required to **buy American.** This policy has not been clearly implemented, and individual government agencies appear to be following it in a relatively uncoordinated way.[11] As previously noted, however, purchases of defense-related materials by the U.S. government are carefully restricted to reliable, U.S.-based suppliers.

Finally, **trade adjustment assistance (TAA)** is offered to aid U.S. firms and individuals that have been harmed by competition from imports. This assistance takes such forms as loans to help companies retool so that they can compete with imports; direct unemployment compensation to individuals, who are expected to seek new jobs in other industries during the period of compensation; and counseling to help individuals find alternative employment.[12] In late 1985 the unemployment benefits were cut from TAA and placed in the broad U.S. policy of unemployment compensation. Retraining and relocation benefits still are offered.

In sum, U.S. commercial policy is a patchwork of regulations, most of which are intended to promote free trade and economic growth, but a small number of which are highly visible programs to aid specific (politically powerful) industry sectors. The trade adjustment assistance program is intended to help companies and workers shift to more competitive activities, thus allowing comparative advantage to work, yet not ignoring the burden of adjustment felt by the less-competitive parts of the economy.

Home and Host Country Investment Controls

Though often not as clearly linked to international trade as trade barriers, **investment controls** do play a part in restricting trade flows. In this case, the controls are placed on the movement of money or other financial instruments between countries. A simple control such as limited access to foreign exchange can cut imports just as effectively as a tariff, if it disallows importers from obtaining the needed means of payment for their purchases. In addition, **capital controls** generally intend to help a country's balance of payments deficit, by limiting capital outflows. This policy goes beyond improving the trade balance and includes the possibility of improving the basic balance (which includes direct investment and long-term loans), or even the official reserves balance (which includes short-term capital flows).

For example, since 1982 Venezuela has used a system of multiple exchange rates both to reduce imports and to encourage capital inflows. Importers, in most cases, are required to buy foreign exchange at the market rate, which in mid-1984 was about 9 bolivars per U.S. dollar. Most existing loans from abroad, on the other hand, could be repaid at a rate of 4.3 bolivars per dollar—a much more manageable cost for the local borrowers. New loans and remittances on direct investments could be exchanged at a rate of 6 bolivars per U.S. dollar, still a favorable rate relative to the market rate. (Exporters could sell their foreign exchange receipts at the market rate, thus receiving more bolivars for their domestic needs than what the official rate would give.)

The United States has not used exchange controls, though it has imposed some financial controls. The most widely discussed U.S. controls were the capital controls imposed on U.S.-based multinational firms in the mid-1960s. Initially (in 1965), these controls were voluntary, requesting that MNEs finance their foreign subsidiaries through foreign borrowing, rather than through financial transfers from the United States. In 1968 the controls were made mandatory, requiring that affiliates in Europe and a few non-European countries not receive additional financing from the U.S. parent firms, while allowing limited funds transfers to affiliates in less developed countries. The MNEs found so many ways to circumvent the controls (not the least of which was a tremendous expansion of the eurodollar market) that the ultimate effect on the U.S. balance of payments was probably minimal. The controls were dismantled in 1974.[13]

Investment controls may be defined to include limits on foreign *direct* investment. This type of control is the rule rather than the exception today. Almost every country restricts foreign direct investors of some kind from doing business in the domestic market. The limits range from total disallowance (in several communist countries) to selective permission of investors (in many less developed countries). Direct investment controls generally do *not* seek to improve the balance of payments; their purpose is to maintain domestic ownership and control over key segments of the economy.

Company Strategies for Dealing with the Barriers

The fundamental strategy for coping with trade and investment barriers is to utilize the firm's competitive advantages to best function under them. Since methods for using trade and investment to overcome constraints on either were presented in Chapter 2, there is no need to discuss them here. However, a few specific strategies that may be appropriate when additional barriers to imports are imposed are worth considering.

Each time the cost of importing a product is raised, the relative advantage of producing it locally increases. This points toward the alternatives of direct investment, licensing of a local firm, use of a turnkey venture, or some other organizational strategy that employs local production. The multiproduct firm may consider negotiation with the government to produce or just assemble a small number of products locally in return for permission to import other products without prohibitive tariff barriers. The increase in import cost due to the new barrier may force the firm to consider the other alternatives for the first time—and it may actually have been less costly (i.e., more profitable) to produce locally even before the new barrier was in place.

Another strategy that the firm should consider is the establishment of production in more than one country, to remove the "hostage" problem, in which the firm is dependent on supply from one national source for sales in perhaps several countries. By using a portfolio of production sources, the firm can reduce the bargaining power of any one national government over its multicountry operations. Even though costs would probably be minimized by producing in just one country, the risk of regulatory change or other problems may make using a portfolio of production sources a better solution. The trade barriers discussed in this chapter should remind the manager that each national operation of the firm is subject to the national rules of that country—rules that can be altered at any time.

Many countries allow relatively unrestricted importation of intermediate goods (e.g., unassembled TVs or autos) but impose substantial tariffs and NTBs on final products. Such a regulatory environment may favor local assembly of a product, while the vast majority of the product's value is produced elsewhere. This strategy is widely used in Latin America, where most countries want to encourage the growth of domestic manufacturing and to reduce dependence on imports. Pharmaceutical firms, auto companies, and other manufacturers have found that local assembly (formulation in the case of drugs) enables them to avoid very high tariffs and NTBs without committing a large capital investment to a small or politically unstable country.

The major Japanese producers of cars and trucks have already chosen to set up local production in the United States to reduce the expected impact of increasingly restrictive U.S. policy on auto imports. Nissan manufactures both cars and trucks in South Carolina; in 1984, in a joint venture with General Motors, Toyota began producing a compact car in California; Honda produces cars and motorcycles in Ohio and lawn mowers in South Carolina; and other Japanese firms are following close behind. This strategy is clearly political, since the costs of delivering a car to the U.S. market are far lower for Japanese producers than for U.S. producers. (See the auto industry analysis in Chapter 24.)

The appropriate strategy in any situation, of course, will be dependent on the specific conditions involved. However, it is possible to conclude that, as suggested in Chapter 2, the approach to thinking about alternative strategies is to evaluate the firm's competitive advantages and to compare the ownership strategies on that basis.

Conclusions

This chapter has covered a wide range of aspects of barriers to international trade and investment. We defined the most common forms of barriers first, and then we looked at the reasons that governments utilize them. Economic analysis of the barriers showed that they generally harm an economy more than they help it, but strong conclusions in any case depend on the situation faced by the country. An economic loss may well be justified in the face of political gain. Most of the evidence regarding U.S. barriers appears to show that they have not benefited the U.S. economy as a whole, though they may have helped firms protected by them. The U.S. policy of trade adjustment assistance attempts to reduce the burden of adjustment borne by workers and companies that become noncompetitive vis-a-vis imported products.

Company strategies for dealing with protectionist policies follow the same criteria noted previously. Firms can shift between such alternatives as foreign direct investment and imports when barriers make one alternative preferable to the other. They can diversify their international operations to avoid the hostage problem that occurs when they are dependent on one national market or supply source, and thus one national government has sovereignty over their activities. And, of course, they can simply pass on the costs of trade and investment controls to their customers.

Questions

1. How can a French clothing manufacturer cope with a new increase in the tariff on its shipments of garments to the United States, its biggest export

market? Present your answer in terms of cost conditions, competitive market conditions, and strategic goals.

2. What are the basic principles of U.S. trade policy today? Explain how specific policies follow these principles.
3. What is the difference between a tariff, a quota, and a subsidy, in terms of their economic impact. (Assume that all three limit imports to achieve a given increase in domestic production and sales.)
4. Assume that South Korea's government offers low-cost loans to exporters as a way to stimulate the economy. How would you, as a company manager of a U.S. firm competing with Korean firms, react in your activities? That is, how would you alter your present business, which is 100 percent domestic production and sales? Also, would you try to influence the U.S. government or to utilize its programs in this situation? How and why?
5. What is a solution to the steel imports problem in the United States, viewed from the perspective of a U.S. steel company? (Use the case at the end of this chapter for additional information.)
6. What should the U.S. government do to deal with the current problems of the steel industry? Why?
7. What is the probable impact of direct investment controls on the flow of FDI into a country? Does the United States use any such controls? Which countries do?
8. Is there any industry in which the United States could justify using an infant industry tariff? What justifications are used for U.S. tariff policy?
9. Explain the idea of dumping. What is an appropriate policy that a national government might adopt to deal with the dumping of foreign products?
10. What would you do, as manager of Toyota Motors Company in Japan, when faced with a "voluntary" limit on the number of cars you can export to the United States? Give details.

References

Canto, V., and A. Laffer, "The Effectiveness of Orderly Marketing Agreements: The Color TV Case". *Business Economics,* January 1983.

Hufbauer, Gary, and Howard Rosen. *Trade Policy for Troubled Industries.* Washington, D.C.: Institute for International Economics, 1986.

Kindleberger, C., and P. Lindert. *International Economics.* 6th ed. Homewood, Ill.: Richard D. Irwin, 1978.

Munger, M. "The Costs of Protectionism," *Challenge,* January-February 1984.

Endnotes

1. According to the U.S. International Trade Commission, U.S. tariffs in 1983 averaged 5.4 percent on *dutiable* items. Many items enter the United States with no tariff at all—including thousands of goods imported from

less developed countries under the generalized system of preferences (GSP). Overall, the average U.S. tariff in 1983 was about 3.7 percent *ad valorem.*

2. The program of trade adjustment assistance (TAA) does support U.S. firms hurt by import competition, but this support is paid mainly as unemployment compensation to laid-off workers. See *United States Code Annotated,* Title 19, Custom Duties, Sections 2271-2298. The compensation arrangement lapsed in December 1985 and was passed into the general federal program of unemployment compensation. In March 1986, the compensation arrangement was reinstated for six years, retroactive to December 1985.
3. In 1984, Canada switched from a policy of using the Foreign Investment Review Agency to limit FDI coming into the country, to a policy of promoting inward FDI to stimulate economic growth, with a change in the agency's name to Investment Canada.
4. The requirements for U.S. government purchases from domestic suppliers appear in the *United States Code Annotated,* Title 41, Public Contracts, Sections 10a-10d.
5. John Deere de Mexico, S.A. de C.V. Harvard Business School case 9-313-239.
6. Canto and Laffer (1983).
7. *Automotive News,* February 16, 1986, and March 10, 1986.
8. The Caribbean Basin Initiative was passed into law in 1983. In January 1985, the tariff provisions of the initiative were finally enacted.
9. The Trading-with-the-Enemy legislation appears in the *United States Code Annotated,* Title 50, War and National Defense Appendix, Emergency and Post-war Legislation, Sections 1-43.
10. The Foreign Sales Corporation was established as part of the Trade and Tariff Act of 1984.
11. See note 4 above.
12. See note 2 above. See also Hufbauer and Rosen (1986).
13. A very useful discussion of the U.S. capital control program appears in Gunter Dufey and Rolf Mirus, *International Finance* (New York: McGraw Hill, 1987), Chapter 10.

Case
The Steel Imports Problem

Competitive Conditions in the Industry

"The U.S. steel industry was hard hit by the deep recession of 1974-75 and the sluggish recovery of world steel demand that followed. . . . Current capacity utilization rates in the industry are near 80 percent compared to a peak of 97 percent in 1973. Profit rates are less than half of 1974 peak levels." In addition, "the U.S. balance of trade in steel has shifted. In 1955, the U.S. exported more steel than it imported; today, imports are supplying nearly 18 percent of domestic requirements, and our exports of steel are negligible." (1977)[1]

"The large U.S. steel producers are running out of time . . . . If we have no desire as a government to have a viable, strong steel industry . . . then we will not have one. . . . From 1978 to 1981 the real cash flow of six major U.S. steelmakers fell to minus $7.4 billion. . . . Last year (1982) when only 48 percent of the nation's steel capacity was operating, imports accounted for 22 percent of the U.S. market. If current trends continue, they could grow to 40 percent within the next decade." (1983)[2]

Both of the statements above reflect the continuing crisis in the United States steel industry in the 1980s. Many of the major firms have gone into bankruptcy or have been acquired by remaining firms in the industry so that in 1987 only half a dozen major steelmakers remain. Average return on equity in the industry has been negative for the past decade. Even the leading firm, U.S. Steel, has diversified such that about half of its business is now in the oil industry (from the acquisition of Marathon Oil Company). This case presents a perspective of the industry that focuses on the possible strategies domestic steelmakers and the U.S. government can take to deal with the crisis.

The difficulties encountered by U.S. steel producers in the 1970s arose because of (1) increases in the cost of producing steel products, and (2) increases in steel imports, especially from Japan. The cost increases from 1972 to 1977 occurred mainly because (a) coal prices rose 138 percent, (b) iron ore prices rose 76 percent and (c) steel scrap prices rose 133 percent. Additionally, from 1973 to 1977 hourly employment costs rose 66 percent while productivity rose at only 1.9 percent per year.[3] Profitability in the steel industry was 3.5 percent in 1976, well below the average for all manufacturing.

The difficulties that continue into the late 1980s include relatively high

A teaching note by Professor Robert Grosse, October 1978 (revised 1987).

wage costs; relatively low productivity, a strong dollar until 1985, which led to higher U.S. prices compared to major trading partners such as Japan and Germany; increasing competition from such newly industrializing countries as Brazil and South Korea; and finally, worldwide overcapacity in the industry, which is leading to widespread losses and government subsidies to local steel industries in many countries. Profitability for the U.S. industry has been negative in almost every year during this decade. Table 1 compares some of the industry conditions in the United States with major trading partners such as Japan, West Germany, and the United Kingdom.

Table 1 **Steel Industry Operating Conditions in Four Industrial Countries, 1976 and 1986** (US$/metric ton)

	United States	Japan	West Germany	United Kingdom
1976				
Labor costs				
Manhours per ton shipped	11.12	9.47	9.53	18.27
Employment cost per hour	12.18	5.62	8.17	4.44
Employment cost per ton	135.37	53.09	77.90	81.03
Materials costs				
Iron ore per ton	48.78	32.77	38.29	38.30
Coal cost per ton	44.54	57.39	62.18	58.95
Total materials cost	190.26	159.42	203.21	188.91
Total cost/ton	350.61	262.50	308.22	306.38
Total revenue/ton	352.52	280.59	333.97	301.67
1986				
Labor costs				
Manhours per ton shipped	6.41	6.05	7.21	6.49
Employment cost per hour	24.14	14.16	15.96	12.12
Employment cost per ton	154.64	85.73	115.06	78.69
Materials costs				
Iron ore per ton	69.35	42.18	61.98	60.24
Coal cost per ton	51.63	64.79	73.31	60.22
Total materials cost	289.82	251.14	269.48	264.75
Total cost/ton	481.71	426.47	428.97	366.67
Total revenue/ton	603.89	553.55	508.38	470.74

Source: Paine Webber, Inc., *World Steel Dynamics* "Cost Monitor #9," New York: Paine Webber, Inc. 1987.

The Perspective of the U.S. Government

The U.S. government's policies will reflect basic views of international economics. Since World War II, the United States had been the champion of free trade. This position has clear theoretical implications—that free trade leads to increased world output and employment and increased economic interdependence. Empirical studies tend to support the view that output, employment, and interdependence all increase with freer trade. Free trade, however, requires free competition in the markets for production factors in each country, and adoption of a laissez-faire policy by each national government, in order to satisfy the theoretical assumptions and generate the expected benefits. If a government subsidizes exports, then retaliation by the government of the importing country may be justified, since such subsidies interfere with free-market operations, thus altering the distribution of benefits from trade. The facts of the present case need to be clarified on three counts:

1. What are the costs of production in each country?
2. What subsidies are offered by Japanese and European governments?
3. What existing U.S. policies are available?

See Table 1 on the first point. Since we lack the time and resources to do further analysis, let us accept the U.S. government conclusions on the second point: "Recent evidence suggests that the value of the various subsidies offered by governments to their steel producers does not represent a significant share of total production costs. Unpublished FTC figures place the value of these subsidies at less than 1 percent of total cost for Japan, West Germany, and Italy." With respect to the third point, the U.S. government has used tariffs, voluntary restraints, trigger prices and subsequent fines, and trade adjustment assistance to remedy the problems created by imports.

If we wish to pursue the free-trade ideal, and disallow "cheating" that may occur through government subsidies, we need to evaluate the Japanese steel prices versus Japanese steel production costs, adjusted to exclude subsidies. Graphically, we need to see whether the Japanese price is less than the average total cost (of production *plus* delivery).

As long as the Japanese sell steel in Japan at prices high enough to pay for total fixed costs plus variable costs, they can sell any excess abroad at prices that cover only the variable costs and still remain profitable. As far as our data are concerned, it does *not* appear that the Japanese are dumping the steel products shown.

The "trigger price" system, which allowed the United States to penalize Japanese (or other) importers if dumping occurred, offered a highly visible means of protection for U.S. steel producers. Unfortunately, this system did not improve the efficiency of these manufacturers.

Any real solution to this problem will require the U.S. steel producers to become cost competitive. Perhaps this competitiveness could occur if U.S. producers specialized in some steel products and left others to be sold by importers. Trade adjustment assistance, which is consistent with the goal of free trade, will allow workers to be retrained and factories retooled so that U.S. employment is not seriously harmed. Consumers will benefit, of course, from the lower prices of steel imports.

This brief commentary certainly does not "solve" the steel imports problem. It does provide, however, some factual information necessary for taking an informed position and carrying out an analysis of many of the major issues involved in the controversy. There are two key questions: (1) What are the potential strategies for U.S. steelmakers; and (2) What is an optimal policy for the U.S. government?

Endnotes

1. Taken from the Council on Wage and Price Stability (COWPS) report to President Carter, October 5, 1977.
2. Taken from the article, "Time Runs out for Steel," *Business Week,* June 13, 1983.
3. All data from the report to the President from the Council on Wage and Price Stability.

9

ECONOMIC INTEGRATION AND INTERNATIONAL BUSINESS

This chapter continues the discussion of government policies that affect international business, focusing on multinational agreements among governments to reduce business barriers among member countries. The European Community is the most important regional example of such an agreement. In addition, the worldwide General Agreement on Tariffs and Trade (GATT) is discussed. This chapter is institutional in nature; it describes the rules and institutions in the various integration groups and notes implications for company managers operating in these groups. The main goals of the chapter are to:

1. Note the basic economic costs and benefits of economic integration (such as trade creation and trade diversion).
2. Explain the structure and functioning of GATT.
3. Present a panorama of types of economic integration and discuss country groups that illustrate each type.
4. Explain the structure and functioning of the European Community.
5. Explain the structure and functioning of the Andean Pact and other integration efforts of less developed countries.
6. Explore company strategies for dealing with integration rules.

Introduction

Economic integration involves the establishment of transnational rules on economic activity that lead to greater trade and economic cooperation between countries. That is, a group of nations can (often painstakingly) negotiate a set of commonly accepted rules on intragroup trade and other economic relations that lead to increased (more beneficial) commercial dealings among them. By creating a multicountry market, the group encourages larger-scale (lower-cost) production and greater competition among firms in the group, promoting efficiency in each of the national economies involved. Generally, economic integration efforts have been made at the regional level, encompassing 5-10 countries in close geographic proximity—though one of the most important transnational agreements is the General Agreement on Tariffs and Trade (GATT), which now involves 90 nations throughout the world.

The most visible results of regional economic integration at present are two groups of countries in Europe—the European Community and the (communist) Comecon bloc. Both of these groups were formed after World War II, and they each sought to pool resources to promote reconstruction and generate rapid economic growth after the destruction caused by the war. The European Community (often called the Common Market) is discussed below in some detail, as are Comecon, the Andean Pact (among five Latin American countries), ASEAN (among five Asian countries), and Caricom (among more than a dozen Caribbean islands).

Economic integration efforts among less developed countries (LDCs) tend to pursue the goals of increased economic ties and growth, plus a goal of increased political power in dealing with the developed countries. Countries within Latin America, the Caribbean, Africa, and Asia have joined together in almost a dozen regional integration agreements. Each of these agreements has sought to raise the level of economic development of the member countries and to create a better bargaining position with the developed countries. Thus far, the accomplishments of the LDC integration efforts have been small, but the goals remain important and such efforts are likely to continue.

Economic integration involves a sharing of the costs and benefits that result from reducing barriers to commerce and financial dealings among member countries. Each member of an integration group must agree to give up some national policy prerogatives to a transnational (regional) authority, typically on such issues as tariffs and movements of labor and capital among the countries in the group. Each of these countries expects this to generate gains from increased trade and other business activity, such as foreign direct investment, that will exceed the costs of adjusting to the new rules.

The noncommunist groups that have implemented regional economic integration affect company activities in a number of ways, but primarily by altering the rules on exports and imports among members of the group.

Additional effects include changes in tax rates and policies, removal of restrictions on movements of money and people among member countries, and other regulatory changes. These effects are discussed below in the context of specific economic integration efforts.

The basic economics of regional economic integration concern the shifts in business activity that occur as a result of the integration process. Two fundamental principles relate to the trade effects of integration. First, if the integration group causes member countries to alter their production toward greater efficiency (i.e., toward their comparative advantages) and to trade more extensively with one another, then **trade creation** occurs. Trade creation is the result of reducing trade barriers among member countries, whose firms subsequently compete more freely with one another. More efficient, lower-cost producers in member countries will gain markets from less-efficient producers, thus creating more exports among the countries in the group. The creation of new trade is demonstrated in Figure 9-1.

S_1S_1 and DD are the supply and demand curves for any good that may be traded between countries 1 and 2. The graph assumes that country 2 is the more efficient producer of the product, as shown by its supply curve S_2S_2. The trade barriers before economic integration are depicted by the vertical distance between country 2's supply curve and the supply-plus-tariff curve labeled TT. When countries 1 and 2 agree to eliminate tariffs between themselves, then country 1's consumption of the product increases from B to

Figure 9-1 **Trade Creation in Product X between Countries 1 and 2**

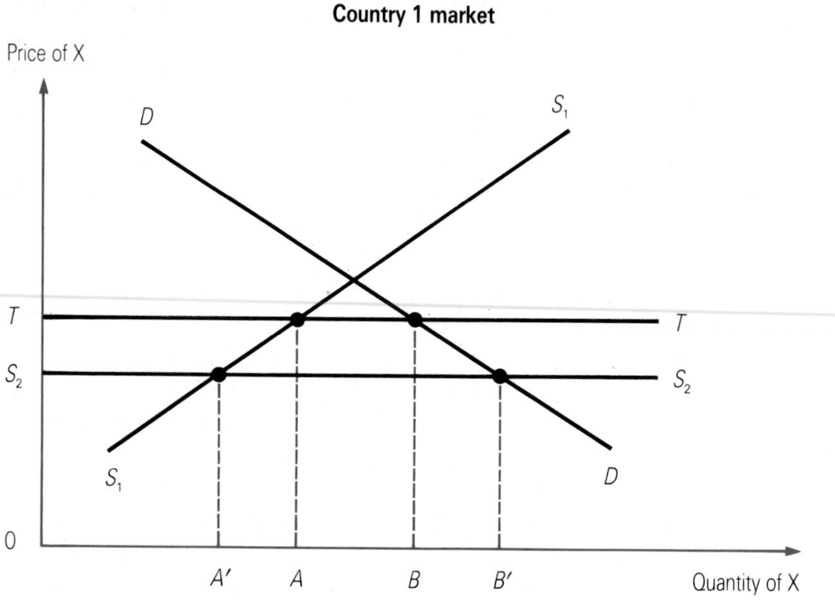

B′. Consequently, country 1's firms supply only OA′ (instead of OA) amount of the product, and the rest, A′B′, is imported from country 2. This trade creation benefits country 1 by lowering the price of the product to consumers and by enabling productive resources to be shifted to more efficient uses.

Second, if the integration group causes member countries to decrease their trade with nonmember countries, then **trade diversion** occurs. Trade diversion would occur in the above example if the tariff reduction caused imports from country 2 to replace other imports from the rest of the world, which is more efficient but which still faces the unreduced tariff of country 1. Thus, trade diversion is the loss of production and exports from more efficient nonmember countries to less efficient member countries that are protected by tariffs or other barriers against nonmembers.

Empirical studies of these effects in regional integration groups have tended to demonstrate substantial trade creation and little trade diversion within developed-country groups, but less impressive results among less developed countries. Table 9-1 presents measures of the trade creation effects of regional economic integration in both industrial and developing country groups. Notice that among the LDC blocs, only the Central American Common Market demonstrated a large percentage of intragroup trade (over 20% of total trade)—and that group virtually ceased to operate after the fall of the Somoza regime in Nicaragua in 1979. The European Community countries have moved from about one third intra-group trade to over 50%, though membership has increased importantly as well.

From a conceptual point of view, the total economic gains generated by the formation of an integration group tend to be larger when (1) the member countries initially have very high trade barriers among themselves, so that more trade creation occurs; (2) the member countries possess relatively similar comparative advantages, so that less trade diversion occurs; (3) the number of member countries is larger, so that more comparative advantages can be exploited; and (4) the tariffs imposed on nonmember countries are lower, so that less trade diversion occurs.[1]

Before turning to *regional* integration examples, we discuss the most important *global* agreement on the reduction of trade barriers.

The General Agreement on Tariffs and Trade (GATT)

GATT is an institutional structure that the industrialized countries established just after World War II to promote expanded trade among its members and to avoid the protectionism practiced during the prewar depression years. Initially, in 1948, GATT had 23 member countries. In the late 1980s, there were 90 members, including industrialized, less developed, and communist nations. Clearly, GATT is more than a regional effort to share trade benefits among a small group of countries; it is a global effort to enhance the gains generated by trade.

Table 9-1 **Trade Creation Effects of Regional Integration**

A. Intratrade of Developed Countries by Region

Economic Groupings (regions)	Value of Intratrade[a] (US $ billions)					Share of Intratrade in: World Exports (%)					Total Group Exports (%)				
	1960	1970	1975	1980	1982	1960	1970	1975	1980	1982	1960	1970	1975	1980	1982
EEC (6)	10.3	43.4				8.0	13.9				34.6	48.9			
EFTA[b]	2.9	9.4				2.3	3.0				15.7	21.8			
EEC (expanded)[c]			145.9	347.0	303.0			16.7	17.3	16.4			49.4	52.8	51.9
Trade in manufactures between expanded EEC and residual EFTA member countries			45.1	105.9	85.1			5.2	5.3	4.6			12.9	13.7	12.4
Intratrade in manufactures of residual EFTA member countries			8.5	14.8	12.4			1.0	0.7	0.7			16.1	12.8	12.0
USA-CANADA[d] (preferential)	—	5.1	11.1	15.7	19.6	—	1.6	1.3	0.8	1.1	—	8.7	8.0	5.7	7.2
CMEA[e]	8.1	18.4	44.4	79.0	82.3	6.3	5.9	5.1	4.0	4.5	62.3	59.4	57.4	51.0	49.8
Total	21.2	76.1	225.0	562.4	502.4	16.6	24.4	29.2	28.1	27.2	34.6	34.5	45.2	46.7	44.7

[a] Based on exports (f.o.b.) data.
[b] Excluding goods shown in annex D of the Stockholm Convention.
[c] The expanded nine-country EEC.
[d] Trade under the U.S.-Canada Automotive Products Agreement negotiated in 1965.
[e] Council for Mutual Economic Assistance.

Source: UNCTAD, (1984), p.38.

B. Intratrade of Developing Countries and Territories by Region

Economic Groupings (regions)	Value of Intratrade (US $ millions)					Exports to Developing Countries as Percent of Total Group Exports					Intratrade of Group as a Percent of Total Exports of Each Group				
	1960	1970	1976	1979	1982	1960	1970	1976	1979	1982	1960	1970	1976	1979	1982
ASEAN[a,b]	839	860	3,619	8,658	16,109	32.8	31.7	30.3	33.6	36.5	21.7	14.7	13.9	17.0	23.3
Bangkok Agreement[c]	—	47	142	444	688	—	20.4	25.7	27.5	31.8	—	1.5	1.0	1.8	2.1
CACEU[d]	3	33	75	132	150	8.3	11.9	15.0	23.7	14.5	1.6	3.4	3.9	4.0	3.6
CACM[e]	33	299	653	896	820	10.0	29.6	29.2	27.6	30.3	7.5	26.8	21.6	19.3	21.8
CARICOM[f]	27	73	212	256	414	12.2	16.6	17.6	19.9	23.2	4.5	7.3	6.7	6.6	9.0
ALADI[g]	564	1,290	4,434	8,289	10,400	19.4	21.2	26.9	29.6	30.3	7.7	10.2	12.8	13.7	13.2
Of which: Andean Group[h]	25	109	594	770	1,167	28.8	29.3	36.2	31.2	39.2	0.7	2.3	4.2	3.3	4.5
WAEC[i]	6	73	117	247	374	14.8	15.1	13.6	17.2	21.0	2.0	9.1	6.7	6.7	10.7
Total Excluding ASEAN and Bangkok Agreement	633	1,768	5,551	9,820	13,325	18.1	21.0	25.2	28.1	28.9	7.2	10.8	12.3	12.9	14.1
Total	—	2,675	9,313	18,922	30,122	—	19.8	26.8	29.8	32.1	—	8.8	11.0	12.5	15.4

[a] Association of Southeast Asian Nations, 1967.
[b] Figures adjusted to exclude entrepot trade. Figures for Singapore exports to Malasia and Thailand are derived from import statistics of these two trading partners.
[c] Bangkok Agreement.
[d] Central African Customs and Economic Union, 1964.
[e] Central American Common Market, 1960.
[f] Caribbean Community, 1968; Eastern Caribbean Common Market is not included.
[g] Asociacion Latino Americana de Integracion, formerly LAFTA, 1960.
[h] Andean Group, 1969.
[i] West African Economic Community, 1959 (initially West Africa Customs Union).

Source: UNCTAD, (1984), pp. 39, 40.

GATT maintains a permanent secretariat of about 300 people located in Geneva, Switzerland. The main functions of the secretariat are to collect information and to carry out studies of trade issues that are relevant to the governmental negotiations held under GATT's auspices. Decision making is reserved for the representatives of the member countries, who approve exceptions to the basic rules that favor global free trade (e.g., permission for the European Community to extend tariff reductions only to its members).

GATT has been used as a forum to negotiate mutilateral reductions in trade barriers. Since 1948, there have been eight "rounds" of negotiations, ending with the Uruguay Round, which was under way in 1987. In each round, tariff levels among GATT's members have been reduced and other trade-liberalizing steps have been taken. The Tokyo Round, in the 1970s, was the first to focus specifically on reducing nontariff barriers, namely customs valuation (which can be used to overassess imports), government procurement, import licensing, subsidies, antidumping measures, and technical barriers to trade. By the end of the Tokyo Round, tariffs among GATT member countries averaged less than 10 percent *ad valorem* on all products, though greater tariffs and other restrictions still exist in some countries, and on agricultural products more than on manufactured goods.

GATT was formed as a multilateral institution for improving trade relations among its members, specifically seeking to avoid bilateralism, in which pairs of countries negotiate trade agreements that exclude other countries. A fundamental concept in GATT negotiations is the **most-favored-nation** (MFN) principle, which requires that any tariff reduction negotiated between any two members of GATT be extended to all members of GATT. Thus, if the United States and Canada agree to reduce tariffs on their trade in electrical appliances, the same reduction must be passed on to the other members of GATT. Most-favored-nation treatment has ensured the continued multilateralism of a large part of international trade negotiations since World War II.

Many exceptions have been made to GATT's basic rules. Since sovereignty ultimately rests with national governments, any transnational agreements such as GATT are of course subject to the continued willingness of countries to participate and accept the rules. The main exceptions to adherence to GATT's rules have been allowed to countries facing a balance of payments crisis. Such countries are generally permitted to erect temporary restrictions on imports until the balance of payments crisis ends. In addition, countries that form a regional bloc for economic integration are allowed to create trade policies that are more favorable to members of the bloc than to outsiders, as long as the bloc does not raise new trade barriers against other members of GATT. Each of the regional blocs discussed below has tried to eliminate trade barriers among its members and to leave in place barriers to the imports of other countries.

In 1986, a conference was held in Punta del Este, Uruguay, to discuss the formal opening of a new round of GATT. The Uruguay Round began in 1987, but it is not expected to conclude until 1990 or later. This round of negotiations is intended to focus on four previously neglected areas: trade in agricultural products; trade in services, such as banking and data processing; constraints on foreign direct investment that limit trade; and protection of intellectual property, such as patents, copyrights, and trademarks.[2]

Regional Economic Integration—The Basic Typology

Economic integration in its broadest sense signifies the expansion of commercial and financial ties among the nations of the world. This process has been going on for centuries, making rapid advances as transportation and communication among nations become easier and less costly. Various political empires of the past pursued economic integration as a policy for economic development, seeking in this way to realize gains from trade and specialization. Since World War II, economic integration has been pursued by small groups of countries that wanted to expand their national markets, increase their economic and political power, and realize the economic gains of greater intragroup trade. Half a dozen regional blocs were established in the 1950s, and several more have been established since then. To understand the rationales behind these blocs and to see their impacts on business activities, it will be useful to present a typology of integration forms.

Though no regional bloc fits perfectly into any of the following categories, each can be placed reasonably accurately in one or another, and the categories are quite distinct. Five increasing levels of **regional economic integration** can be distinguished:

1. Free-trade area.
2. Customs union.
3. Common market.
4. Economic union.
5. Political union.

Each succeeding level of integration involves greater cooperation among the bloc's member countries, and at the ultimate level the bloc members become unified into a single political entity, a new country. Countries need not follow the steps sequentially until political union has been achieved—most regional blocs remain at some level of integration without seeking to attain closer ties. Some analysts do argue, however, that the greatest integration yields the greatest gains from integration—so underlying pressures toward greater ties may exist.[3] (These pressures were certainly seen as Great Britain debated entry into the European Common Market from its inception and in 1973 eventually joined that regional group.)

Free-Trade Area

The first level of economic integration, the **free-trade area,** involves the elimination of tariffs on trade among the countries in the regional group. Most of the integration efforts in the post-World War II period have begun from this base. Following the reasoning of Chapter 3 concerning the benefits of free trade, each participant in the free-trade area expects to gain by specializing in the production of goods and services in which it possesses comparative advantages and by importing from other countries in the group products and services in which it faces comparative disadvantages. Thus, trade should be *created* among member countries, giving them less-expensive access to more goods. (Note that this trade may take place between unrelated firms or within MNEs that operate in more than one member country.)

A cost of free-trade areas to member countries is trade diversion from outside countries. Since tariffs remain on imports from nonmember countries, some trade may be diverted from the most efficient producers outside the area to less-efficient producers inside the area, who are still protected by tariffs. In the extreme, if every country belonged to one free-trade area, then the gains to all would be maximized. Given the numerous and complex reasons for trade barriers that exist today, regional blocs have formed free-trade areas to obtain a kind of second-best gain, since full free trade appears unattainable.

Among the free-trade areas is the European Free Trade Area (EFTA), formed at about the same time as the Common Market (in 1960) and comprising those Western European countries that did not become Common Market members. Today, the members of the EFTA are Austria, Norway, Sweden, and Switzerland. (The United Kingdom and Denmark left EFTA to join the Common Market in 1973.) The Latin American Free Trade Association (LAFTA), originally composed of the Spanish-speaking countries in South America plus Brazil and Mexico, has evolved into a group called ALADI (Asociación Latinoamericana de Integración), which includes the same countries. Even after 25 years of existence, this group has *not* been able to eliminate tariffs or other trade barriers among its members. It has, however, led to a reduction of trade barriers and an increase in economic cooperation.[4]

Customs Union

The second level of regional economic integration, the **customs union,** involves the elimination of tariffs among member countries *plus* the establishment of a common external tariff structure toward nonmember countries. As with each succeeding form of integration, member countries are required to give up control over more economic policies to the group than they gave up at the previous level—in this case the regulation of imports from outside countries. The additional benefit from this policy is intended to be the avoidance of bias in attracting imports to the group; if external tariffs differ from country to country, then outsiders will favor importing into the lowest-tariff member country in order to sell in the whole group. In this way, the lowest-tariff member of the group would benefit at the expense of the other members. The common external tariff takes away that possibility.

None of the regional integration groups in existence today has been formed specifically to achieve a customs union. Most of these groups aim for even greater economic ties among their members—that is, a common market or even economic union. In fact, because of slow progress in attaining further levels of integration, several of the regional integration groups can be categorized as customs unions. The Caribbean Common Market is one such group, and the Andean Pact is another. The former group includes 12 of the English-speaking islands of the Caribbean (all former British colonies), and the latter includes Bolivia, Colombia, Ecuador, Peru, and Venezuela. In both of these groups, efforts are under way to reduce trade barriers and increase intragroup business, but thus far neither has achieved the regulatory harmonization of a common market.

Common Market

This third level of economic integration, the **common market,** is characterized by the same tariff policy as the customs union *plus* freedom of movement for factors of production (i.e., labor and capital) among member countries. A common market is perhaps the ultimate feasible step in multicountry associations for permitting individuals and firms to carry out their transnational business activities in member countries without facing barriers to movements of products, people, or money. This level of integration avoids the intercountry regulatory bias on trade and direct investment, both of which are thus left to determination by market factors.

The best example of a regional group that constitutes a common market is the European Common Market, also known as the European Community. This bloc of 12 countries includes Belgium, Denmark, France, Germany, Greece, Ireland, Italy, Luxembourg, the Netherlands, Portugal, Spain, and the United Kingdom. It is discussed in some detail below.

A regional group that possesses some of the characteristics of a common market is the Council for Mutual Economic Assistance, or COMECON, which includes the Soviet Union and most of its allies (Bulgaria, Cuba, Czechoslovakia, the German Democratic Republic, Hungary, Mongolia, Poland, Romania, and Vietnam). These countries are all communistic, so their economic systems do not permit free trade in the first place. However, they do utilize agreements to stimulate reciprocal exchanges of materials, technical assistance, and specialization of production, while limiting participation by outsiders in the members' economies.[5] Moreover, they do not harmonize their national monetary and fiscal policies substantially enough to constitute an economic union.

Economic Union

An **economic union** is characterized by harmonization of economic policy beyond that of a common market. Specifically, an economic union seeks to unify monetary and fiscal policy among its member countries. A common currency, or a permanently fixed exchange rate, is one aspect of an economic union. Harmonized tax rates and tax rate structures are other aspects. To a large degree, national governments participating in an economic union relinquish control over much of national economic policy to the group.

As one might expect, due to these major policy constraints, there are not many economic unions in existence. At present, only the Belgium-Luxembourg Economic Union (BLEU) fits into this category. Belgium and Luxembourg maintain a fixed exchange rate (1 Belgian franc = 1 Luxembourg franc) and a highly coordinated set of monetary policies. Their tax rates and structures are virtually identical. They reach their other political decisions on a largely separate basis, and they each maintain a quite distinct political existence. These two countries are the smallest in the Common Market, and they have allied themselves with each other primarily to gain a larger voice in European affairs.

Political Union

The highest level of regional economic integration is **political union,** under which all economic policies are unified. Countries that unite under a common government lose their national identities and become parts of a single state. Important examples of political unions are Canada, the Soviet Union, and the United States, each of which combined independent states into a single country. In fact, since the members of a political union cease to be separate countries, perhaps political union should not be considered a part of economic integration at all. Political union, however, does form the logical end point of increased economic cooperation among a group of nations.

In sum, the five levels of economic integration do not necessarily represent a sequence of steps toward political and economic union. But they do present strategic alternatives for groups of countries that seek to increase their international (intragroup) trade and thus to benefit from the larger market created by the integration group. Examples of integration groups are shown in Table 9-2.

The European Community

History

Soon after the end of World War II, various policymakers and analysts began promoting the idea of a Western European union of some sort.[6] One goal of the union would be to assure the cooperation of the countries in the region and thus avoid another cataclysmic war. A second goal was to create another economic and political force to deal with the Soviet Union and the United States, which arose from World War II as the leading world powers. U.S. policy has broadly supported these goals from the beginning, and through the Marshall Plan it provided substantial funding for European reconstruction

Table 9-2 **Levels of Economic Integration**

Level	Examples	Members
1. Free-trade area	European Free Trade Area	Austria, Norway, Sweden, Switzerland
	Latin American Free Trade Area (ALADI)	Argentina, Bolivia, Brazil, Chile, Colombia, Costa Rica, Ecuador, El Salvador, Guatemala, Honduras, Mexico, Panama, Paraguay, Uruguay, Venezuela
2. Customs union	Andean Pact	Bolivia, Colombia, Ecuador, Peru, Venezuela
	Caricom	Antigua and Barbuda, Bahamas, Barbados, Belize, Dominica, Grenada, Guyana, Jamaica, Montserrat, St. Kitts-Nevis, St. Lucia, St. Vincent, Trinidad and Tobago
3. Common market	European Community	Belgium, Denmark, France, Greece, Ireland, Italy, Luxembourg, Netherlands, Portugal, Spain, United Kingdom, West Germany
4. Economic union	Belgium-Luxembourg Economic Union	Belgium, Luxembourg
5. Political union	United States, Soviet Union, Canada	

(about $200 billion) from 1948 to 1952. Several regional organizations were formed in the early postwar years, including the Organization of European Economic Cooperation (OEEC), in 1948, which later became the Organization for Economic Cooperation and Development (OECD), and the Council of Europe, in 1949, which focused more on political issues than on economic issues.

The European Coal and Steel Community, a cooperative venture among Belgium, France, Germany, Italy, Luxembourg, and the Netherlands, began operating in 1952. This organization removed barriers on intragroup shipments of coal, iron, steel, and scrap. In 1957, the same six countries established Euratom to regulate and monitor the production of nuclear energy. Finally, also in 1957, they formed the European Economic Community (EEC). The combination of these three integration efforts has become known as the **European Community (EC).**

The Treaty of Rome, which established the European Economic Community, laid out a schedule for the elimination of intragroup tariffs, the creation of a common external tariff, and guidelines for additional harmonization of such economic policies as tax structures, exchange rates and controls, immigration among member countries, and agricultural support programs. Although the objectives of the integration process were not achieved exactly as scheduled, all of them have been realized—even with the expansion of the EC to include Denmark, Ireland, and the United Kingdom in 1973. (Greece entered the EC in 1981; Portugal and Spain, in 1985. As of late 1987, these additional countries had not been fully assimilated.) Thus, the European Community is truly a common market; and its members are continuing to pursue harmonized and joint economic policies that could lead to the further level of economic union.

Institutions

The European Community operates through four main institutions:

1. The Council of Ministers, which has one plenipotentiary representative from each member country.
2. The Commission, which has 17 members chosen by agreement of the member governments.
3. The European Parliament, which has 518 members who are elected directly by the voters in each member country.
4. The Court of Justice, which has one judge from each member country.

The *Council of Ministers* is the ultimate decision-making body of the European Community. Its 12 members are the foreign ministers of each country, though other representatives are often used when specific issues are under discussion—for example, the agriculture ministers when agricultural policy is being debated. With the exception of the budget, which is handled primarily by the Commission and the Parliament, the Council makes all the final decisions of the EC. It meets and has staff in Brussels, Belgium.

The Council of Ministers makes decisions only on proposals presented to it by the Commission. The main technical analysis and consensus building take place in the Commission, which is generally viewed as being relatively Europe-oriented and not biased toward the national interests of any individual country.

The *Commission* functions mainly as the executive branch of the European Community, drafting legislation for proposal to the Council, overseeing the implementation of Community policies, and carrying out studies of key policy issues. Although the Council retains the ultimate authority to adopt Community legislation and policies, the Commission prepares the decisions and regulations and does most of the technical work. The approximately 10,000 members of its staff form the main body of EC employees. The Commission's staff, like that of the Council, is located in Brussels.

The *European Parliament,* consisting of 518 members who are elected directly by voters in the 12 member countries, has been developing its range of functions only in the past few years. Although established by the Treaty of Rome in 1957, the Parliament did not become a directly elected body until 1979. At present, the Parliament serves mainly as the watchdog on Community expenditures, though it also evaluates other decisions of the Council. It meets in Strasbourg, France, but its secretariat of over 2,000 people is located in Luxembourg.

Finally, the *Court of Justice* serves as the official interpreter of European Community law. Most of its cases have related to interpretation or application of the Treaty of Rome, based on actions by member countries, individuals, and companies. As EC rules have become more closely interwoven with national laws in the member countries, the Court has been serving increasingly as a court of appeals for national courts when EC issues are concerned. The Court's 460 staff members and 11 judges have offices in Luxembourg.

Impact on Business

The European Community's impact on business activity in and among the member countries has been widely debated over the years. Most of the empirical studies on that impact have shown that on balance the EC has created much more trade than it has diverted from the rest of the world. Table 9-3 summarizes a number of such studies that appeared in the 1960s and 1970s. Similar conclusions have been drawn concerning the effects of the accession of Denmark, Great Britain, and Ireland to the EC.

As far as foreign direct investment is concerned, the conclusions are somewhat different. Studies have shown that the EC played an insignificant role in the growth of FDI in its region; what mattered most appears to be the size of the individual national markets (Scaperlanda and Mauer 1969). A recent study of both trade and direct investment impacts on national incomes in each EC member country showed across-the-board favorable effects. Table 9-4 presents detailed results of the study. Denmark is the only country to show a negative net impact of integration during 1974–1981, mainly because of very little trade creation.

The impact of the EC on other business activities have not been studied in as much detail as its impact on trade and direct investment. Most likely, some additional transnational business activity in Europe has resulted from the establishment of the European Community, given the Community's focus on creating a regional market. For example, efforts to create regional MNEs to compete with U.S.-based firms have led to the formation of Airbus Industries, which currently competes actively with such firms as McDonnell Douglas and Boeing. An intra-EC effort to create a globally competitive semiconductor and electronics consortium recently produced a pooling of resources by several European electronics companies (although IBM is seeking to be included in the group). The regional MNEs are expected to gain economies of scale and access to additional technology (and perhaps other competitive advantages) that would not be available to any one firm. Overall, Community-wide ini-

Table 9–3 **Estimates of Trade Creation and Diversion in the EEC**

		Trade Created				Trade Diverted†			
Author	Period Studied	All Goods ($ billions)	(%)*	Manufactures ($ billions)	(%)*	All Goods ($ billions)	(%)*	Manufactures ($ billions)	(%)*
Prewo	1970	19.8	23	18.0	34	−2.5	6	−3.1	15
Truman	1968								
Unadjusted		—	—	9.2	26	—	—	−1.0	7
Adjusted		—	—	2.5	7	—	—	0.5	4
Balassa	1970	11.3	13	11.4	21	0.3	1	0.1	0
Kreinin (unweighted average of three estimates)	1969–70	—	—	8.4	—	—	—	1.1	—
Williamson and Bottrill	1969	—	—	11.2‡	25	—	—	0	0
Aitken	1967	9.2	14	—	—	0.6	2	—	—

* Percentages relate to total and extra-area imports of all goods and of manufactured products.
† Numbers with negative signs represent external trade creation.
‡ Unweighted average of alternative estimates.

Source: Robson (1980), p. 177.

Table 9-4 **Integration Effects on the Growth Rate of Member Countries, 1974–1981**

Contributions to Growth	Germany	France	Italy	Nethl.	Belg-Lx.	UK	Ireland	Denmark
Actual growth rate	2.65	2.66	2.74	1.99	2.03	1.24	3.84	1.98
1-Growth due to EC [1 = − 2− 3 + 4 + 5 + 11 + . . . + 16]	0.91	1.57	0.42	0.53	0.71	0.37	0.31	−0.64
Made up of								
2-Terms of trade changes	−0.01	−0.39	0.05	0.07	−0.22	−0.31	0.32	−1.51*
3-Change in propensity to import	0.88	0.79	0.40	0.29	0.57	0.32	3.28	0.21
4-Growth of exports of manufacturers	0.02	0.30	0.07	2.33	0.27	0.79	2.38	−0.08
5-Change in the trade balance of manufacturers	0.74	0.66	−0.83	−2.66	0.74	0.50	−1.72	−2.86
6-Growth of exports of food products and beverages	0.50	1.35	0.14	1.28	0.42	0.65	1.12	0.78
7-Change in the trade balance of food and beverages	−0.44	−1.20	−0.35	−0.47	0.01	−1.98	−0.50	−0.46
8-Export gains due to increased prices of food	0.02	−0.07	−0.10	−0.63	−0.13	−0.03	−0.38	−0.17
9-Change in the balance of price effects of total imports on agricultural goods	−0.24	0.08	0.09	0.07	−0.12	−0.04	0.36	0.12
10-Net CAP—budget payments†	−0.05	0.08	0.06	0.26	0.06	−0.32	0.86	0.19
11-total CAP effects [11 = 6 + 7 + 8 + 9 + 10]	−0.21	0.23	−0.15	0.51	0.24	−1.72	1.47	0.45
12-Net non-CAP—budget payments	0.06	0.02	0.20	0.03	0.09	0.08	0.54	−0.04
13-Labour remittances	..	..	.08	..	..	..	..	..
14-Direct foreign investment	0.35	0.03	−0.04	−2.53	−0.02	0.09	0.20	0.89
15-Interdependence effect	−0.25	0.01	0.47	1.71	0.19	−0.48	1.37	−0.73
16-Residual + errors [16 = (1 + 2 + 3) − (4 + 5 + 11 + . . . + 15)]	1.06	0.72	1.06	1.49	−0.45	1.14	−0.32	0*

* Estimated jointly and without considering total capital flows.
† CAP = Common Agricultural Policy

Notes: As defined in the model a negative sign of the terms of trade means an improvement. The total may differ from the sum of its components due to rounding. Appropriately the CAP total should also include effects on the terms of trade and propensity to import. The total CAP effects are therefore likely to be upward/downward biased. Trade estimates for the Netherlands are upward biased due to entrepot trade.

Source: A. J. Marques Mendes, "The Contribution of the European Community to Economic Growth," *Journal of Common Market Studies* (June 1986), p. 269.

tiatives to stimulate additional business activities appear to be generating more than just trade and direct investment in the EC.

These initiatives have included efforts to facilitate the movement of working people among member countries. As a result, in the late 1960s the labor markets of each member country were opened up to the residents of other member countries, but additional policies were needed to harmonize health and pension benefits for workers who moved between member nations (and also to harmonize licensing requirements for various professions, which are somewhat different in each member country). Another

Hensies Customs Post, Highway E10, French/Belgium Border

Milton & Joan Mann/Cameramann International

initiative is the European Monetary System (discussed in Chapter 6), which is part of the EC's attempt to facilitate capital movement among its members. Although this system has not eliminated the problems of exchange rate fluctuations and speculative capital flows, it has improved the ability of EC member countries to deal with intraregional financial problems.

To balance the optimistic tenor of the preceding discussion, it should be noted that many difficulties continue to hinder the EC's functioning. Primary among these difficulties is the Common Agricultural Policy, a system of subsidies and other support for EC farmers, which currently uses up over half of the EC budget. As new members join the EC, the problems presented by agricultural policy become even greater.

The Andean Pact

This section focuses on the **Andean Pact,** an economic integration effort among LDCs in Latin America. The institutional structure and goals of this group are largely based on those of the EC, but its impact on international business has been vastly different. The experience of the Andean countries is instructive with respect to the results of transnational LDC integration in general and with respect to policies toward foreign direct investment in particular.

Case
Masasi Corporation

The Masasi Corporation is a British multinational chemical company with operations in eight countries and annual sales over $500 million in 1983. Most of the firm's business until now has been oriented toward Europe and North America. Because of the slow growth rates of sales in those markets, and the economic crisis in Latin America, Masasi's managers have decided to consider expansion into Asian countries. The first step was to consider entering the largest market, Japan. Assessment of competitive conditions there showed a very dynamic market with strong price competition. Subsequent looks at Hong Kong, Singapore, Taiwan, and other Asian countries showed greater possibilities of profitable expansion there, but no one country appeared large enough to absorb the output of a local plant for the polyethylene that Masasi wants to produce.

Three of the company's top managers flew from London to several cities in the region in 1983, trying to narrow down the choices for a facility and an Asia strategy. The size and liberal trade policies of the ASEAN group (viz., Malaysia, Indonesia, Singapore, Thailand, and the Philippines) led to plans to set up a plant to manufacture polyethylene in Southeast Asia to serve primarily that regional market. The company's officials had had preliminary talks with government officials from the various countries in the region and finally decided to set up a plant either in Indonesia or Malaysia. Both countries are producing natural gas, a necessary production input, and possess known reserves that will last for at least another 30 years. The problem is to choose where the company should set up its plant and how it should raise the $4 million needed to finance this project.

The following is some of the information available on each country and the requirements likely to be demanded by each government.

Malaysia is basically an agricultural country, with about 30 percent of its population in the industrial sector. The government encourages the local private sector and foreign firms to set up businesses in line with its economic policy of utilizing local resources in both agriculture and manufacturing industries. The education standard in the country is high and is enabling Malaysia to modernize with fewer difficulties than in many other less developed nations. Moreover, Malaysia has much of the infrastructure needed to accommodate industrialization.

The local currency of the country is fairly stable, with an exchange rate around 2.30 Malaysian dollars per U.S. dollar. As an incentive for foreign manufacturing investment, the government gives foreign investors an income

This case was written by Margarita Siman and Ahmad Sabri Ismail, with revisions by Professor Robert Grosse. It is intended for use in class discussion, 1984 (rev. 1987).

Numerical Solution to Masasi Case (in $ millions)

	Malaysia	Indonesia
Sales	$10	$10
Labor cost	3	2
Materials	3	2.5
Indirect cost	3	4
Net income before taxes	1	1.5
Tax	0 (for 3 years) 0.55 (after 3 years)	0.675
Net income after taxes	1 (for 3 years) 0.45 (after 3 years)	0.875

tax holiday for three years, provided that the manufacturing facility is set up in a designated location.

By comparison, *Indonesia,* which is also an agricultural country, has a larger reserve of natural gas. The labor cost in the country is 33 percent lower than in Malaysia. The government requires that 90 percent of company managers be local nationals; the Malaysian government demands only 80 percent. Both governments require that local resources be used when available and that a minimum of 50 percent of the output be exported. Indonesia demands that at least 80 percent of capital be raised abroad, whereas Malaysia stipulates that a minimum of 40 percent of the capital come from foreign sources. The Indonesian rupiah is devaluing at the rate of 25 percent per year. Currently, the rupiah exchanges at the rate of 100 rupiahs per U.S. dollar. Indonesia also has a 45 percent corporate tax rate and charges a further 20 percent tax on remittance of profits. Malaysia imposes a corporate income tax of 55 percent after the tax holiday period, with no dividend withholding tax. The interest rate for loans to Masasi in Indonesia is 17 percent, whereas the Malaysian rate is 15 percent.

Masasi would be able to secure a loan in the international (eurodollar) loan market at a rate of 13 percent. The opportunity cost of capital used by the Indonesian government to evaluate foreign investment projects is 20 percent, whereas the Malaysian officials use a rate of 30 percent. The company expects to sell about $10 million worth of polyethylene in a typical year's operation. Annual labor cost is expected to be $2 million in Indonesia and $3 million in Malaysia. Cost of materials is estimated to be $2.5 million in Indonesia and $3 million in Malaysia. The indirect cost in Indonesia would be about $4 million, while in Malaysia it is expected to be $3 million. Transportation is cheaper and faster in Malaysia. Both countries propose to allow the company to operate for 10 years without permitting other foreign firms to enter the market for polyethylene.

PART 3

MANAGING THE MNE

11

DEALING WITH THE CULTURAL ENVIRONMENT

Culture can be an elusive concept. It is difficult to define, and yet everyone knows it's really there. For the MNE, understanding host country and home country cultures is important. But there is more to the situation than just this. Companies, MNEs included, have "corporate cultures" of their own—and the challenge for the MNE is to integrate across country-based cultures within a corporate culture of its own. Not an easy task! This chapter looks closely at culture, both country and corporate, and examines culture in action—as evidenced in communication and education, achievement motivation, attitudes toward work, group identification, concepts of time, and hierarchical relationships. The chapter also discusses the effects of culture on the competitive advantages of MNEs and what managers can do to reduce cultural risk. The main goals of the chapter are to:

1. Raise the level of cultural awareness and understanding regarding the potential effects, either good or bad, of culture on business practices.

2. Define country culture and corporate culture.

3. Examine how home country, host country, and corporate cultures interact and how the competitive advantages of MNEs are influenced by cultural variables.

4. Examine how MNEs can manage cultural risk from the perspective of both strategic management and operating management.

Introduction

What is culture? Why is it important in international business? These questions have become increasingly important over the past few years. They have to do with the implementation of strategy, or how firms accomplish their business objectives. "Culture" can either facilitate or hinder business effectiveness. In the purely domestic firm, there are two dimensions to culture—the home (environmental) culture, which provides homogeneity and a basic consistency affecting all firms and other parties involved in business, and the corporate culture, which is peculiar to each business organization. In the MNE, there is a very important third dimension: the host country culture.

Culture and the MNE

Operationally, the MNE straddles the home and host country cultures, and does so within a corporate culture of its own. The MNE's objective here is to accommodate cultural differences (among these three cultures) and to manage the situation, whatever it implies, so as to maximize profitability and attain other objectives. "Culture" is often viewed as constraining management options—but this need not be the case. Culture, country or corporate, often provides opportunities for business success. Look, for an example of country culture, at what the Japanese commitment to quality meant for the competitive advantage of its firms in several U.S. markets, such as consumer electronics and automobiles. For an example of corporate culture, note Henry Ford's accomplishments in assembly line technique, an innovation exported by the Ford Motor Company on a global scale in its early days. Ford's ideas reflected a set of management values that separated the factory worker from any responsibilities (and benefits) related to improving production technology. Ford's ideas also involved wage payments that were high enough for workers to be automobile purchasers and were based on time worked rather than "pieces" of product produced. (This was a substantial departure from the prevalent piece rate payment system and worker involvement in job and task definition.)

Cultural variables, within the MNE setting, actually are considerably more complex than the **tricultural setting** noted above. Considering that MNEs do business across and within different environments, successful MNE operations must often accommodate diverse cultural complexities. But what is culture?

Culture, Cultural Environment, and Corporate Culture

Culture consists of behavioral patterns, values or beliefs, art forms, institutions, or whatever else might be characteristic of a "community of social expression." This community may be a town or city (Fort Worth, Texas, for

Figure 11-1 **Cultural Variables and the MNE**

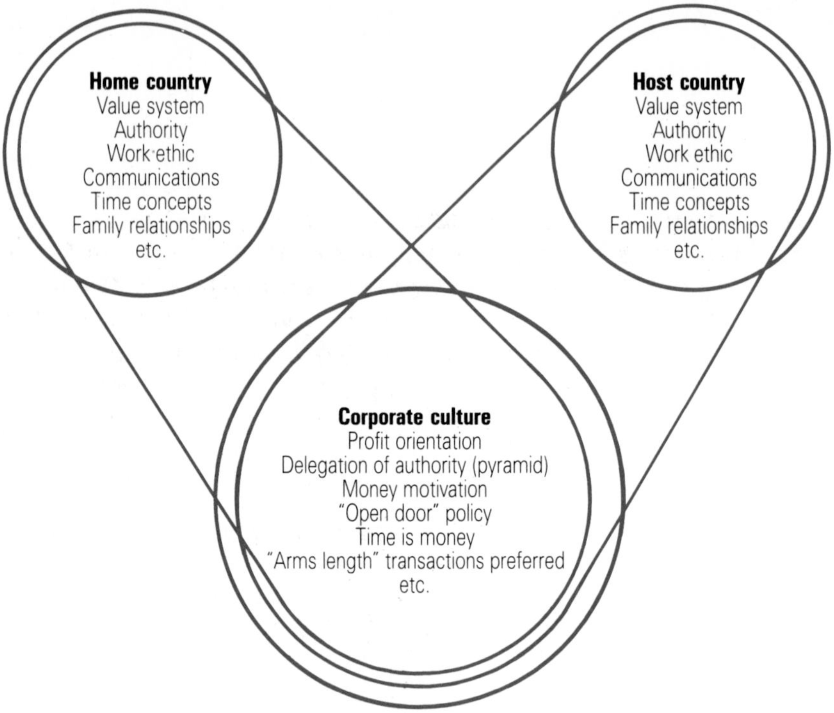

example, in contrast to Little Rock, Arkansas), a region (e.g., Southern California compared to New England), a country (e.g., the People's Republic of China compared to West Germany), a company (e.g., your local bank versus Sears Roebuck), or even a family. Consider for a moment how each of these examples provides contrasts in terms of internal community behavior. Southern California conjures up images of youthfulness, mobility, a willingness to try new things, and so on. New England appears more traditional, older, more settled, and so on. Similar comparisons could be made regarding the cities and countries mentioned. The implications for business of even the few items noted, however, could be many. Japanese cars became popular in California early on—then their popularity spread eastward. "Made in the USA" probably reflects special value interests that are more prevalent in the Midwest than along the Pacific or Atlantic seaboards. There are reasons for these phenomena. Their genesis can be found in how people live and how they perceive life itself.

Societal Culture

That culture is an important aspect of social life everywhere was confirmed decades ago by Bates, whose research concluded that there is nothing natural to man and that human behavior reflects social influences and expectations.[1] Ronen's more recent research concluded that "culture defines and expresses both attitudes and behavior . . . [and] represents a shared way of being, evaluating, and doing that is passed from one generation to the next."[2]

Although **societal culture** is ubiquitous, there is, nonetheless, no such thing as a universal culture. Every place has its culture, but culture is not the same everywhere. But while cultural environments serve to differentiate the behaviors of culturally segmented groups, they also serve to ensure behavioral consistencies within culturally homogeneous groups. Differences among cultures give areas or groups distinctiveness, while cultural homogeneity gives areas or groups definition. The cultural environment determines the nature and extent of the homogeneity, and differences in culture characterize the environments within and across which the multinational firm operates.

Corporate Culture

Corporate culture is a subset of what has been identified thus far. The Management Analysis Center has defined corporate culture as

> *the way an organization performs a given set of tasks. It is the set of traditional and habitual ways of thinking, feeling, and reacting to opportunities and problems that confront an organization. It is rooted in the past successes and failures of the organization—and successes provide models to follow in the future. Culture is an emotional bond that holds an organization together. . . . Culture . . . is a pattern of beliefs and expectations shared by members of an organization. These beliefs and expectations produce rules for behavior—norms—that powerfully shape the behavior of individuals and groups in the organization.*[3]

Corporate culture is thus much more than management style. It goes beyond any individual and reflects an operational ambience. For example, some business organizations are production driven; that is, key strategic and operational decisions reflect production considerations, and the organization's power center is in production. By definition, then, market staying power is product or process centered. Imagine what happens to such a business when market staying power is successfully challenged by a competitor—say a foreign multinational. Marketing and service factors now move up on the list of priorities for competitive success. How quickly can a production-dominated organization define and implement the institutional response needed for a more sophisticated assessment of customers' needs? How quickly (and effectively) can internal control and the locus of decision making be altered to reflect less generous operating margins, the need to reduce production costs, an accelerated pace of new product introductions, and so on? These become crucial issues—issues that are deeply identified with the corporate culture. The magnitude of change confronting the business means that its corporate culture will probably be redefined. As Lucas suggests, this redefinition process is likely to be political-cultural in nature and to substantially reflect influences internal to the firm.[4] Hopefully, the result—a renegotiated order—will be achieved without too much difficulty.

The interplay and diversity among home country, host country, and corporate cultures define the extent of the cultural risk that exists in a business situation. The definition and management of such risk are obviously important and will be specifically addressed later in the chapter. At this point, some details are presented on the nature of home/host country cultural differences and their importance for management.

Doing Business in a Foreign Culture

What Can We Say with a Gift?

It's dangerous for any executive to extrapolate home country values and practices and apply them to foreign countries and cultures. As a case in point, consider the simple idea of gift-giving. Reardon's recent *International Business Gift-Giving Customs: A Guide for American Executives* presents survey findings that involved a polling of 125 business leaders at large U.S. multinationals.[5] As the following observations illustrate, even the simple act of gift-giving is substantially culture-bound!

> Red roses for a German lady mean "I'm in love with you!"
>
> In Latin America, a gift of cutlery signifies that you want to cut off a relationship; a handkerchief means that you wish the recipient tears.
>
> When in Japan, never open a gift in front of the giver unless you are asked to. In the People's Republic of China, business gift-giving is not a common practice, and if a gift is given, it should be given only after all business negotiations have been completed—and not in front of others.
>
> Generosity and reciprocity are two hallmarks of gift-giving in Arab countries. Gifts of quality are exchanged in nearly ritualistic fashion. Food or drink should never be brought to an Arab's home—they would imply that the host is not generous. An Arab's wife or wives are not to be given gifts, or even acknowledged in conversation.
>
> Frenchmen prefer gifts that compliment their intellectual interests. Germans find social entertainment quite acceptable. The British prefer not to discuss business at dinner.
>
> To Latin Americans, time is not especially important and embracing on meeting and parting establishes a sense of trust and rapport. Gift-giving is

viewed as an enjoyable pastime, but it is never done during the course of business.

Communication and Education

Gift-giving, which is a form of communication, can be quite culture-bound—as are other forms of communication. Cordiality and friendliness, for example, are expressed via the handshake of Westerners when people meet. Respect and social position are dominant in the greetings of Japanese, who bow before each other. Indeed, the angle of the bow will vary by the amount of respect due. The point to remember, according to Ronen, is that language (either spoken or silent) conveys social reality as well as providing for communication.[6] This is clearly evident in the dialogue presented in Figure 11-2.

Formal education is also typically viewed as culture-bound. It is not valued in some societies, possibly little valued in certain subgroups within societies, and highly valued in others. Educational systems and vehicles also vary widely across countries and cultures. Business schools, for example, are not too prevalent outside the United States and Canada. They are a fairly recent addendum to the educational systems in other countries. Literacy levels and social/technical competences usually correlate positively with the value placed on education.

Figure 11-2 **Communication Perceptions—Beware!**

Behavior	Perception
American: How long will it take you to finish this report?	**American:** I asked him to participate. **Greek:** His behavior makes no sense. He is the boss. Why doesn't he tell me?
Greek: I don't know. How long should it take?	**American:** He refuses to take responsibility. **Greek:** I asked him for an order.
American: You are in the best position to analyze time requirements.	**American:** I press him to take responsibility for his actions. **Greek:** What nonsense: I'd better give him an answer.
Greek: Ten days.	**American:** He lacks the ability to estimate time; this time estimate is totally inadequate.
American: Take 15. Is it agreed? You will do it in 15 days?	**American:** I offer a contract. **Greek:** These are my orders: 15 days.

Source: From *Interpersonal Behavior* by H. C. Triandis. Copyright © 1977 by Wadsworth Publishing Company, Inc. Reprinted by permission of Brooks/Cole Publishing Company, Pacific Grove, California 93950.

Milton & Joan Mann
Cameramann International

La Casa del Whopper

Consider Burger King's experience in adjusting to Venezuelan tastes and preferences at its five restaurants in Caracas. The hamburger buns don't come with sesame seeds on them anymore; the Venezuelans kept brushing them off. Catsup is sweeter, and milk shakes are sweeter and creamier. The menu includes soft ice cream—which is everyone's favorite dessert in Latin America. Latins are late diners, so the Caracas Burger Kings stay open as late as 1:30 A.M. Everything else, however, is standard Burger King. For example, frozen french fries (which are imported, since Venezuela doesn't grow the "right kind" of potatoes) are prepared according to parent company specifications.

The managing director of the Venezuelan Burger Kings feels that the Latin American fast-foods markets are at the stage reached by the U.S. markets in the 1950s. But he expects the Latin American markets to develop fast, especially over the next 10 years, and he feels that Burger King's best growth opportunities are in international markets. At the start of 1987, about 10 percent of Burger King's 5,012 restaurants operated outside the United States. Small as this number may be, Burger King has more restaurants in Latin America than its "archrival," McDonald's.

Burger King has learned that cultural adaptation must relate to business enhancement and that simply adapting to local cultures may be counterproductive. For example, Burger King originally served wine in its French restaurants, but customers tended to linger and visit over their glasses of wine. This affected table turnover and revenues. You can't buy wine at a French Burger King anymore!

Source: Mimi Whitefield, "La Casa del Whopper Goes South," *Miami Herald*, November 29, 1982, p. 5; and information provided by Burger King Corporation, Miami, Florida, January 22, 1987.

The cultural peculiarities of any group of people are extensive and affect business operations in ways too numerous to discuss here in detail. However, some cultural characteristics are more important to management than others. Such characteristics probably include achievement motivation, attitudes toward work, group identification, concepts of time, and hierarchical relationships.

Achievement Motivation

McClelland's benchmark study *The Achieving Society* provided a host of basic insights into **achievement motivation.**[7] McClelland reported that behavior patterns follow thought patterns—that is, people behave according to how they think. If people think about achievement, they have a desire or need for achievement and will seek to be achievers. McClelland noted that achievers universally exhibited three distinguishing characteristics: taking personal responsibility for solving problems, setting moderate achievement goals and taking moderate risks, and needing performance feedback. These characteristics, according to McClelland, position achievers as likely business executives.

The competitive, entrepreneurial business environment provides achievers with opportunities to "take command" by setting a strategy and implementing it, to be aggressive and take chances in the marketplace, and to value profits—which are, in fact, market-generated feedback on the appropriateness of the achiever's actions. Taking a broader perspective, a society whose business function responds to the needs of achievers will attract achievers to the enterprise sector and will thus be an achieving society. Moreover, a society that responds in this way to achievers creates an environment conducive to the economically effective application and growth of achievement motivation in general. The whole system feeds on and favors itself.

In support of his conclusions, McClelland observed and recorded the incidence of achievement orientation in different societies and found a strong, positive correlation between a high need for achievement and high economic growth. He found such a correlation when analyzing a society through time and when comparing different societies at a given point in time. For a business manager in an MNE context, achievement orientation is very important. It correlates with economic growth and expanding profit opportunities and with societal interests in economic achievement. It identifies foreign markets that are likely to be more accommodative of business success and, conversely, less antagonistic toward business in general.

Attitudes toward Work

Attitudes toward work are closely related to achievement motivation. The ideas are slightly different, however. Attitudes toward work include the "work ethic," the allocation of different types of work among different groups within the society, and even the relationship between labor and capital.

The **Protestant work ethic** is often cited as one of the driving forces in the development of the U.S. economy. This contention rests on the fact that in its early days the United States was populated via a large influx of immigrants from the United Kingdom, Holland, and other European countries. Many of these immigrants reflected a sociocultural heritage based on Puritan, Calvinist, or Lutheran doctrines that differed from Catholicism in several important relevant respects. In a classic essay written near the end of the large-scale European immigration into the United States, Fullerton noted that in Protestantism the person-God relationship is direct and individualism is emphasized in the struggle for salvation. The idea of work in this view pertains to discipline—that is, the fortification of the individual against temptation. Work is commanded by God and an end in itself. Fullerton contrasted this perspective with the situation he saw in Catholicism, where the church mediates, as it were, between a person and God (e.g., via the sacrament of penance) and is itself populated by religious clerics who establish standards for the laity. The result was, in the Protestant view, that the daily living of Catholics was too casual and that the work of Catholics did not directly equate with prayer.[8]

Given these differences, one might expect that the commitment to work will differ considerably between societies embracing the Protestant view of work and those embracing the Catholic view. Management in a U.S. MNE operating in a Latin country may be well advised to temper its expectations, and structure its operations, to accommodate the different concept of work likely to be held by its Latin employees.

Attitudes toward work, to be sure, are also influenced by factors other than religion. Geography and climate, for example, are important influences. Temperature extremes, whether hot or cold, affect living patterns—including work-related activities. Attitudes toward work may also differ between private sector and public sector employment and may vary with the size of the enterprise. Harris and Moran report, for example, that in France there is little incentive to be productive in the government bureaucracy and in public concerns but that French workers in the private sector

> *have the reputation of being productive. Part of the explanation . . . may lie in the French tradition of craftsmanship. A large proportion of the French work force has been traditionally employed in small, independent businesses where there is widespread respect for a job well done. Many Frenchmen take pride in work that is done well because traditionally they have not been employed in huge, impersonal industrial concerns.*[9]

Further evidence of the productivity differences between privately owned and publicly owned enterprises is seen in "privatization" trends, especially in the United Kingdom and in some of the continental European countries, where some public enterprises that have become noncompetitive and required government subsidies have been sold to private interests.

Attitudes toward work reflect the distribution of different kinds of work among different segments within a society. Social class distinctions may well determine who does manual labor—indeed, they may even bestow a "right" over such work by a specific class. In England, for example, class consciousness has greatly influenced labor-management relations. Historically, the factory-level work group was quite independent. It had its own leadership and its own allocation of effort and income, and it contracted with management on piece payment rates and production schedules.

Attitudes toward work are readily seen as affecting a variety of management decisions, such as staffing, production scheduling, equipment utilization, and process technology, as management seeks to work efficiently and competitively within whatever constraints society presents. The links among attitudes, constraints, and the choice of management options may be more direct, however. Some options may just be ill-advised, if not downright unacceptable. In the Hindu culture, for example, the use of laborsaving machinery was opposed early on by Mahatma Gandhi, who noted:

> *Men go on "saving labour" till thousands are without work and thrown on the streets to die of starvation. I want to save time and labour, not for a fraction of mankind, but for all.*[10]

Moreover, if the Hindu's goal in existence is the liberation of the soul from the body, and this in turn is accomplished through the development of "wantlessness," can Hindus embrace an economic system stressing wants and the satisfaction of wants or appreciate technology and machinery whose function is solely to satisfy material wants?[11] If you plan to do business in India, you might well read up on Gandhi and Hinduism (among other things).

Group Identification

Group identification, a hallmark of the "Japanese management style," which both fascinated and perplexed European and U.S. managers in the 1970s and 1980s, is generally credited with delivering substantial productivity gains. Japanese workers are seen as intensely loyal to their work groups and as committed to group success. Individual interests and values give way to those espoused by the group. Harmony and hard work characterize the workplace. Labor-management relations are essentially nonadversarial in this model. New equipment and work methods are introduced without workers fearing for their jobs. Some roots of the model—including the development of communities and the difficulties of living off the land—can be found in the social structure of imperial Japan. Other roots are more recent—such as the paternalism that developed among the business class in response to the emigration of farmers into industrial centers.

In contrast, **social Darwinism** and the **rugged individualist** are often used to typify the keys to economic growth in the United States. Concepts of opportunity and entrepreneurship go hand in hand with "survival of the fittest." The Protestant ethic, the "frontier," and an abundance of natural resources (including fertile land) all favored the growth of individualism. It's not difficult to see why Americans have a hard time understanding Japanese business.

There are also other dimensions of group identification that are important to the international manager. For example, different ethnic groups, or subcultures, often exist within a society (e.g., the Flemish and Walloons in

Belgium), and relations among these groups may not be harmonious. Staffing problems may result from the existence of such groups, as may difficulties in crossing market segments.

Concepts of Time

Cultures vary considerably in how they view time. In the United States, punctuality is valued. Typically, time is of the essence. Executives are often "time driven." Their day is defined in terms of a series of time slots through which they are programmed. Some executives even take courses in "time management." Other societies hold quite different views of time. In some African cultures, for example, time is not a constraint. Lateness is considered acceptable behavior. Time bends to accommodate behavior. People who are pressed by time are not trusted. Latins are famous for their "tomorrow" attitude. The stereotype is one of laziness, but in fact the origin of the attitude is an uncertain future. Why stress a timely behavior when the circumstances of tomorrow may well require a different behavior?

Time orientation is important in understanding people and how they behave—as Figure 11-3 illustrates. Many Americans, for example, are future oriented. Peasant-dominated societies are more concerned with the here and now. The Chinese and other Oriental cultures are very concerned with the past. Different views of time affect interpersonal relationships, the pace with

Figure 11-3 **Time and Conflict** (a continuation of the dialogue in Figure 11-2)

Behavior	Attribution
In fact, the report needed 30 days of regular work. So the Greek worked day and night, but at the end of the 15th day he still needed to do one more day's work.	
American: Where is the report?	**American:** I am making sure he fulfills his contract. **Greek:** He is asking for the report.
Greek: It will be ready tomorrow.	[Both make the attribution that the report is not ready.]
American: But we had agreed it would be ready today.	**American:** I must teach him to fulfill a contract. **Greek:** The stupid, incompetent boss! Not only does he give me the wrong orders, but he doesn't even appreciate that I did a 30-day job in 16 days.
[The Greek hands in his resignation.]	*[The American is surprised.]* **Greek:** I can't work for such a man.

Source: From *Interpersonal Behavior* by H. C. Triandis. Copyright © 1977 by Wadsworth Publishing Company, Inc. Reprinted by permission of Brooks/Cole Publishing Company, Pacific Grove, California 93950.

which business can be conducted—and even product definition. Where time is valued, you'll probably see timesaving products. Household appliances generally originate in the United States, where family members, not household servants, perform the routine cleaning and cooking chores and where the demands on these people are typically seen as endless. "Time" influences business decisions in a variety of ways.

Hierarchical Relationships

Culture also affects **hierarchical relationships.** Vertical organization structures of six or more layers are often evident in the United States, and decision-making and authority levels are allocated by hierarchical standing. In Japan, functional organizations are typically flatter and communication is more horizontal. Participation in decision making is less a function of responsibility than it is of knowledge. Figure 11-4 illustrates the difference between American and Japanese organization structures. In the Latin cultures, people and personalities dominate. Key people, the chiefs (or "jefes") control decision making. The worker's task is to perform routine jobs and to call on the jefe for decisions. This leads to an inordinate amount of paper-shuffling and to a lack of initiative among employees at the lower skill levels. It also leads to economic and social dependences of workers on their jefes and therefore to paternalism.

Hierarchical relationships are thus seen to affect reporting and control, communication, documentation, attitudes toward paternalism, the locus of initiative, and so on. Interestingly, workers at a Spanish subsidiary of a U.S. multinational, in a dispute with management, refused to eat the lunch provided by the company or to use company-provided transportation to get

Figure 11-4 **Responsibility and Decision-Making Stereotypes of American and Japanese Firms**

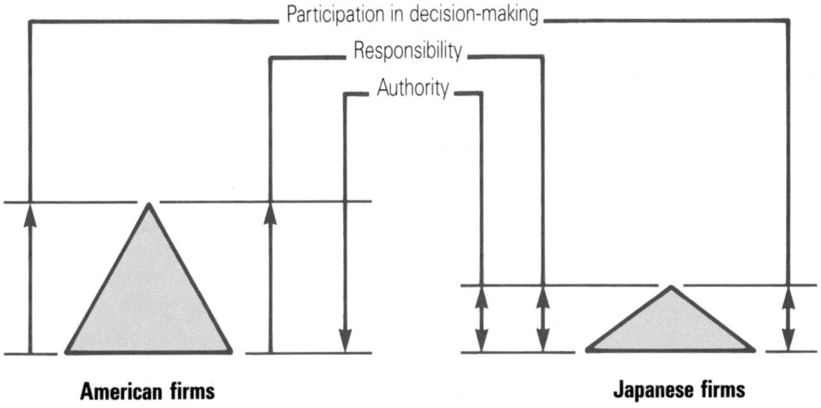

home. These actions, which the workers took at some cost, registered the workers' denial of their jefes' paternalism. They were a slap in the face of the Spanish management. Managers in the U.S. parent had a hard time understanding their significance.

It should be fairly obvious that cultural characteristics vary considerably across different societies and that their potential for affecting business decisions and business success is significant. Both of these conclusions have been illustrated in the preceding discussion of just five cultural characteristics. The important points here are that multinational firms are confronted with cultural risk by definition and that this risk can be substantial. The following section discusses this risk as it relates to the competitive advantages of MNEs. Also, since the MNE cannot avoid cultural risk, the *management* of cultural risk is the basic issue. The last section of this chapter addresses this matter.

Cultural Risk and the Competitive Advantages of MNEs

In Chapter 2, considerable attention was given to the concept of competitive advantages. Thirteen such advantages were listed and discussed. Comments on how to "take advantage" of these competitive advantages were made, and alternative methods for exploiting competitive advantages through alternative forms of foreign involvement were analyzed. Let's return to some of these topics of Chapter 2 and put them into a cultural perspective.

Proprietary Technology

The competitive advantage of **proprietary technology** relates to culture in several ways. As noted earlier, the cultural characteristics of a particular society affect product design itself, for example, by determining use conditions and expectations regarding product longevity (i.e., useful life). Witness the trend toward "low maintenance" products in the United States and the Western European countries. Note how Europeans, in general, have a more evident "lifetime of value" standard, especially for big-ticket items, than do Americans. Culture affects process technology too. Recall Gandhi's outlook toward the use of machinery. One could argue that the incidence of innovation in product and process technologies is also culturally affected. In the United States, the market-oriented entrepreneur is intrinsic to the decentralized, capitalistic economic system. Historically, the U.S. environment has been the most prolific spawning ground of new products that the world has ever known. In contrast, Japan has traditionally purchased advanced technologies and then worked to perfect them in terms of product quality and cost minimization via process technology enhancements.

Cultural risk is certainly important to both the development and the transfer of product and process technologies. Some products can be successful in one foreign market and not another—or substantial product adaptation may be required to make them successful. Process technology may have to be adjusted to reflect a cultural nuance—such as the three-hour midday lunch break and the effect it would have on the operation of a printing company or any other business in which extensive setup time is required prior to a production run. Firms that overlook the need to adapt to the local culture do so at considerable risk to their competitive potential. Successful adaptation may also be difficult to accomplish in firms whose corporate culture is monolithic or ostensibly risk averse.

Goodwill

Regarding **goodwill,** cultural risk is probably most evident in the potential for misreading the extent and durability of the franchise allegedly developed via time and experience in the home market as that franchise is commercially exploited in the foreign market. Mistakes can be made in market segmentation strategy, pricing strategy, and so on. The franchise may or may not be transferable. Products bearing labels of the European fashion houses—such as Pierre Cardin and Gino Pompeii—sell in upscale market segments around the globe. Chrysler, on the other hand, eventually withdrew from direct participation in European markets. Why couldn't Chrysler transfer its U.S. franchise successfully? The answer lay, in part, in the production cost increases associated with its need to move quickly in upgrading process technologies at its (former) European subsidiaries—as illustrated in the United Kingdom, where Chrysler (i.e., its subsidiary Rootes) "bought out" the old piece rate practice by paying workers time-measured wages well in excess of industry norms. Also, the Chrysler brand name had no special appeal for Europeans.

Scale Economies in Operations and Finance

Scale economies in production, purchasing, distribution, and financing were listed in Chapter 2 as potential sources for competitive advantages. The first of these is probably the most vulnerable to cultural risk. Large-scale production operations may be bound by product market limitations, such as extensive segmentation reflecting, for example, cultural diversities within the customer base that affect product use, or resource market limitations, such as the lack of an industrial plant-oriented culture among the workers. On this latter point, there is a famous case involving a Colombia-based textile manufacturer that established a modern plant in a rural area near Medellín and encountered numerous problems involving personnel behavior, such as widespread instances of fathers beating daughters who were employed at the plant, because the daughters brought home more money than the fathers did. People living in rural/peasant communities had difficulty in adjusting to an industrial setting, and the company had difficulty in adjusting to the rural/peasant setting. The period of transition was very costly.

There is some exposure to cultural risk in purchasing and distribution. Lot sizes may be affected by changes in process technology. The availability, price, and quality of raw materials and vendor-supplied components may be culturally influenced. The propensity of dockworkers, or perhaps miners, to go on strike may be relevant here—as may be the work ethic or the industrial culture. Shopping habits affect distribution and are often culturally influenced. For example, people living in the smaller towns and villages of Europe prefer almost daily shopping. This leads to a more atomized distribution channel structure and possible losses of scale economies.

The scale economy that is probably least vulnerable to cultural risk is financing. Money is generally fungible internationally. Some funds-sourcing strategies relate to impersonal international capital and money markets and are thus generally not exposed to cultural nuances. Others, however, can relate to a wide range of types of funding sources, such as "building societies" in Great Britain and the *financieras* prevalent in Latin America. Such financing can vary considerably country by country, reflecting local values and practices. The use of debt can also reflect local values and practices. In Japan, for instance, a 4-to-1 debt to equity ratio—unheard of in the West—is not at all unusual.

Government Protection

Perhaps surprisingly, **government protection** can be substantially culture-bound. Witness the free-market philosophy so predominant in the United States and the difficulties some industries and unions have had in convincing the U.S. government to protect domestic markets through import restrictions. The idea of protectionism is foreign to the culture of numerous American citizens. On the other hand, developing countries often agree to erect import restrictions to protect growing domestic industries. Multinationals setting up plants in such countries can often expect this kind of support for local production. Those investing in developing countries might also expect to find varying degrees of hostility among host country personnel, including government officials. For U.S. MNEs, the "ugly American" syndrome can be very real—and nearly impossible to overcome.

Human Resource Management

Because it deals directly with people, **human resource management** is significantly culture-bound. For example, personnel practices and policies concerned with promotion, compensation, layoffs, and unionization vary considerably across (and even within) countries. In Japan, promotions are often based on age and seniority; in the United States, on seniority and equivalent capability (if the company is unionized) or or merit (if the company is not unionized). Compensation is likewise based on age and seniority in Japan and on seniority or merit in the United States. As a form of employee compensation, profit sharing is frequently found and substantial in Japan but hardly evident in the United States and Western Europe. Layoffs of workers fly in the face of management's commitments and self-esteem in Japan; they are commonplace in the United States. Unions are often company specific in Japan, industry specific in the United States, trade specific in the United Kingdom, and politically specific in France. Thus, it is nearly impossible for the MNE to generalize cross-culturally regarding human resource management. However, there has been some movement recently toward similarities in practices as markets have become increasingly competitive in the open, global economy.

The challenge for the MNE is to learn not only how to accommodate differences in practices within the technological, financial, marketing, and managerial constraints facing them but also how to transfer practices that have been found especially productive in one locale to other locales—a difficult but potentially rewarding initiative.

Scale Economies in Advertising

Technology (e.g., the media available), government regulation, and culture all influence **scale economies in advertising.** Such economies rely on the repetition of standardized advertising appeals. The amount, content, and delivery of advertising messages may well have to accommodate cultural nuances, however. Advertising is much less prevalent in Iran under the ayatollah, for example, than it was in the days of the shah. Some messages may be irrelevant, or perhaps even offensive, depending on the cultural setting. The "Coke adds life" theme, which is designed to promote consumption by showing how Coke fits in nearly everywhere, would probably be ineffective in Buddhist settings—which typically value the suppression of desires.

Message delivery involves the use of media. Some media are culturally inappropriate for promoting certain types of products. Feminine hygiene products are advertised on television in the United States, for example, but not in Latin America. In some countries, the use of particular media may have important political implications. Terpstra reports, for example, that the two leading newspapers in Colombia, *El Tiempo* and *Espectador,* support different political groups and that the smart promoter might do well to advertise in both.[12] The "bottom line" here is that purchase decisions are made by people, and therefore the motivation to buy may well reflect people-specific characteristics. Such characteristics sometimes manifest a transnational homogeneity—when they reflect income level, for instance. Often, however, cultural influences are dominant in defining them. Only when the former situation exists can scale economies in advertising be realized.

Multinational Sourcing and Marketing Capabilities

Culture also affects multinational sourcing and marketing capabilities, two competitive advantages that are distinctive to MNEs. The **multinational sourcing** advantage implements a set of intermediate production, purchasing, and/or logistic relationships. The establishment of these relationships (e.g., purchase contracts) incorporates management's appraisals of the performance risks it has identified. As time unfolds, events with a low probability of occurrence may indeed take place. There might be a civil war, for example, or U.S. longshoremen might refuse to unload cargo from Soviet or Iranian ships. Similarly, unanticipated events may occur that change the basic premises underlying the production, sourcing, or marketing patterns originally defined (e.g., U.S. consumers may again prefer big, or small, cars), thus denying the benefits expected from those patterns. Such events could result from cultural change or from management's misreading of the cultural environment. Similar comments might be made regarding **multinational marketing** networks.

The key point is that sourcing and marketing capabilities relate to both resource and sales markets and how these are linked through the MNE. These capabilities allow the MNE to locate the most profitable resource and sales (product) markets and to link them systematically. Culture is a concern relevant to the ongoing, efficient operation of these linkages.

Managerial Experience

Managerial experience in several countries, another competitive advantage distinctive to MNEs, is both dependent on and constrained by cultural variations. Being able to understand different cultures and being able to conduct effective cross-cultural operations are the competitive requirements unique to MNEs. The cultural differences evidenced internationally can provide the very basis for an MNE's ability to generate a competitive position. The learning curve effect, which energizes the MNE system and provides the competitive edge, is itself predicated on the successful transfer of management know-how among parent and subsidiaries. Cultural heterogeneity, however, complicates the transfer of such know-how and adds a special risk dimension to the transfer process. Some firms avoid this risk by not transferring management know-how to certain areas. For example, Kujawa reports that not all Japanese firms operating in the United States bring in Japanese systems of people management because they often have less risky alternatives (e.g., unique process technologies) for achieving the competitive success of their U.S.-based subsidiaries. On the other hand, some Japanese firms were successful in the U.S. market because of their ability to take advantage of the management expertise developed at home. For these firms, the cultural disparity between the United States and Japan relevant to industrial relations provided the very opportunity they needed for competitive success.[13]

International Diversification

International diversification is essentially a portfolio concept used to reduce risk and cost. It is pertinent to the global, MNE level; that is, it is the corporate headquarters that manages the "portfolio." The strategy is not culturally neutral, however. Its success ultimately turns on the profitable

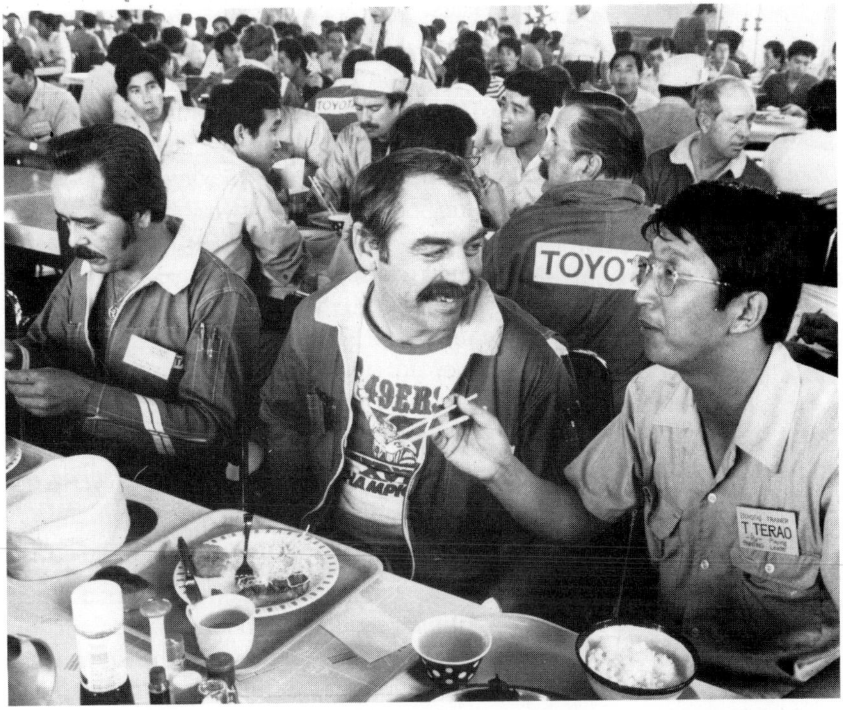

Ed Hollbrook, center, who lost his job when GM closed its Fremont, California, plant in 1981, talks with his Japanese trainer during lunch at Toyota's Homi training center, western Japan. Two dozen American employees from a Toyota-GM joint venture train in Japan, staying in the training center, where they share Japanese-style communal baths and a diet of western and Japanese food. At left is Sam Gonzales, another trainee from California.

Wide World Photos, Inc.

operation of the units contained in the portfolio. This situation returns us to the whole host of considerations regarding culture and competitiveness that have already been discussed.

The earlier part of this section focused on how cultural differences could generate problems for MNEs. Toward the close of the section, cultural differences were seen as providing both problems and opportunities. The key to the firm's success or failure was seen in how its management perceived and accommodated these differences. The next section deals with this topic in more depth.

The Management of Cultural Risk

The management dimension of dealing with the cultural environment focuses on three basic points (which were identified earlier in the chapter):

1. Firms that operate multinationally are by definition confronted with cultural risk.
2. Since cultural risk cannot be avoided, it must be managed.
3. The MNE's objective is to accommodate cultural differences among home country, host country, and corporate culture and to manage this process so as to maximize profitability and achieve other objectives.

From an operational perspective, cultural risk arises from but two roots: (1) unawareness of culture-based differences that affect the effective functioning of the enterprise and (2) management insensitivity toward these differences. The MNE can reduce cultural risk through diversification and effective risk management techniques.

Fortunately, or perhaps unfortunately for some, the marketplace often drives home an awareness of cultural differences by means of operating mistakes—errors that educate but are also often costly. Similarly, management insensitivity to cultural differences is typically readily reversed by a business flop. The question arises, then, as to what means management might use to avoid such disasters and forewarn the firm of potentially excessive cultural risk. This question, in turn, hinges on two others. How extensive are the cultural differences among the home and host countries and the company? How dependent is the competitive viability of the firm on culture-influenced factors? Answering these questions raises the firm's awareness of cultural differences in ways very specific to management's needs. But answering these questions also requires perhaps expensive prior analysis. This can be difficult to justify in the absence of costly prior experience. In the absence of such experience, success in anticipating and appreciating cultural risk requires enlightened and proactive management.

Reducing cultural risk involves both strategic and operational management considerations. The portfolio approach to risk reduction is a strategic concept; dealing with cultural differences day-by-day is an operational concept. The portfolio approach is germane to management at the corporate level; the operational approach is germane to management at the strategic business unit (SBU) level.

The Strategic Management Perspective

The portfolio concept is based on the assumption that if the firm's operations in one environment provide it with information useful in another environment, it benefits because of its multinationality. Where cultural similarities exist among different environments, the MNE's ability to transfer experience gives it a stronger competitive presence. Where cultural differences exist, the mature MNE may still be competitively advantaged if its experience has resulted in increased awareness of cultural differences and an enhanced ability to define the operational importance of these differences.

An intermediate posture is probably the one that is most commonly found. Many products (including services) comprise components—some of which are readily standardized and afford significant scale economies in research, production, or distribution and others of which are customized to meet specific needs (culturally determined or otherwise), so that scale economies and low production costs are less important to market success than uniqueness in product design or appeal. The packaging of these components represents the final product. For an MNE to have a competitive edge in these products, there must be an opportunity for component commonality, which, in turn, allows for scale economies. This means that if the MNE is to be competitively successful, it must find intermarket product commonalities that are culturally neutral.

The Operating Management Perspective

Managing cultural differences in the operational context is quite a different story. Here the problems and issues are much more people specific. Setting strategy at the MNE level results in positioning; implementing strategy at the SBU level means making the enterprise system function effectively. Staff input at the MNE level is probably critical as strategy formulation unfolds. Implementation at the SBU level, however, is clearly the responsibility of line management. The key is the manager!

At the implementation level, the manager is responsible for identifying and harmonizing differences among the host country, home country, and corporate cultures. If the predominant philosophy of the MNE is ethnocentric, the manager's task will probably be one of communicating parent company directives to subsidiaries with little concern for accommodating the interests of the subsidiaries. If the predominant philosophy is polycentric, managers will have little need to communicate with one another. The corporate culture will be fragmented. If the predominant philosophy is geocentric, the parent company will be concerned principally with adjusting operations to fit local conditions so as to maximize total return to the MNE system. Unlike the ethnocentric MNE, the geocentric MNE gives the manager considerable latitude for accommodating cultural nuances. In fact, MNE success in the geocentric mode requires such accommodation. In the commentary that follows, the assumption is that geocentricity prevails.

Harris and Moran characterize the multinational manager as a cosmopolitan, an intercultural communicator, an agent of change, and a cultural transmitter. Keys to success in these diverse roles include an understanding of and commitment to global leadership; an appreciation for cross-cultural studies; an understanding of the cultural factors affecting communication; and knowledge of the relationships between communication and change, human factors and change, culture and change and the development and management of change strategies.[14] There are two important points here. Management success in implementation is a function of attitudes—which, in turn, are substantially conditioned by the corporate culture itself. It is also a function of expertise—the application of talent affected by training. Several useful training methodologies have been developed, including intercultural communication workshops and cross-cultural simulations. (Chapter 17, "Personnel Management," delves further into cross-cultural training needs and approaches.)

Conclusions

This chapter acknowledged the significant impact of culture on the operations of multinational enterprises. Culture was identified in terms of home country, host country, and corporate roots. The objective of the firm in international business is to address the inevitability of cultural risk and to manage that risk. Culture was defined as distinctive—that is, as behavior patterns, values or beliefs, art forms, or whatever else might be characteristic of a "community of social expression." It was shown that although culture is ubiquitous, a common, global culture does not exist.

Doing business in a foreign environment requires management adaptation. Home country values and practices will probably not suffice. Cross-cultural differences in achievement motivation, work attitudes, group identification, time perceptions, and hierarchical relationships were discussed, especially as these differences affect business decisions and business success.

All of the MNE's 13 potential competitive advantages are affected, in varying degrees, by diversity in cultural environments. Culture can influence *proprietary technology*, for example, as related to product design by affecting product use conditions. Process technology may need adaptation as it is transferred from one country to another. Different cultural environments were identified as giving rise to competitive advantages—the United States, for example, has traditionally been very receptive to product innovations. Americans, according to the stereotype, are typically willing to try new things. It was noted that the transferability of *goodwill* is dubious and depends on homogeneous strands of cross-cultural similarities between markets.

Of the five advantages related to scale economies, the advantages in production and advertising are probably the most susceptible to cultural risk. To the extent that culture affects market size and segmentation or the behavior of in-plant personnel, it has an impact on *scale economies in production*. The amount, content, and delivery of advertising messages, and hence *scale economies in advertising*, are affected by cultural nuances. Culture may also affect the availability, price and quality of raw materials or vendor-supplied components, and thus *scale economies in purchasing and distribution*. *Scale economies in financing*, when related to the international money and capital markets, are not generally vulnerable to cultural risk. Financial institutions, however, can vary substantially country by country and often reflect cultural attitudes to savings and lending. The use of debt itself may be regarded as highly desirable in some cultures and as socially unacceptable in others.

Government protection, which is a public policy statement and should reflect public interests and values, is typically culturally influenced. The United States, for example, has eschewed trade protectionism for at least the past 50 years.

Human resource management, which deals directly with people and their behavior in the workplace, is obviously culturally affected. If, for example, a group of production managers were transferred from either Italy or Germany to a factory in Japan or Canada, the adjustments required of all parties would be fairly extensive.

Multinational sourcing and marketing capabilities lead into the establishment by the MNE of transnational purchasing, intermediate production, and/or logistic relationships and marketing patterns that are themselves dependent on the given set of existing or anticipated conditions. Many of these conditions can be influenced by people and are culture-bound.

The competitive edge provided by *managerial experience in several countries* is rooted in cultural differences. If all environments were totally homogeneous, the ability of MNE management to bring in superior (e.g., more productive) practices would give it no advantage over local management. It is the differences in experiences internationally and the capacity to learn from one situation to be more effective in another that can give the MNE an advantage over purely local firms. Similarly, *international diversification*, to be an effective strategy, requires success in simultaneously operating in different political, economic, and cultural environments.

The last section of the chapter dealt with the management of cultural risk. The roots of cultural risk were identified as managers' unawareness of or insensitivity to cultural differences. Such management behavior, unfortunately, can lead to costly mistakes, which, fortunately, are educators and motivators in themselves. Managers are advised to develop and maintain assessments of the cultural differences among home and host countries and an awareness of the dependence of the firm's competitiveness on culturally based factors.

Both strategic management and operational management can work to reduce cultural risk. The strategic management focus is on portfolio techniques implemented at the corporate level. However, this approach rests not only on balancing offsetting situations but also on building expertise from similar situations. Cultural commonalities among the different operating environments provide the MNE with the ability to transfer lessons learned in one environment to other environments. Also, the mature MNE often deals with cultural risk and is experienced in accommodating cultural differences. At the operational level, the problems and issues related to risk reduction are much more people specific. The MNE's corporate philosophy is pertinent here. The purely ethnocentric firm offers little latitude for accommodating cultural differences, but this is not the case in the geocentric firm. Training in cross-cultural communication, cultural awareness, cross-cultural change, and so on finds fruitful ground in the geocentric firm.

Questions

1. Define the term *culture.* How can culture be ubiquitous and yet distinguishing?
2. Give an example of a business practice that you feel reflects cultural origins.
3. How does the cultural context confronting an MNE differ from the one with which a domestic firm deals?
4. Give an example of a cultural difference between two environments and show how it affects business.
5. After initially transferring its operating policies from the United States to France, Burger King (*a*) adjusted them to suit its own needs in light of the local cultural environment or (*b*) adjusted them to accommodate the local environment. With which of these two explanations do you agree? Could you agree with both?
6. How does culture relate to competitive advantage? Give an example of cultural differences destroying an MNE's competitive advantage. Give an example of cultural differences enhancing an MNE's competitive advantage.
7. What is cultural risk?
8. Show how strategic management deals with cultural risk.
9. Show how operational management deals with cultural risk.
10. In the predominantly geocentric MNE, why is training (of the proper type) pertinent to the reduction of cultural risk? Can you give examples of such training?

References

Austin, Lewis. *Saints and Samurai: The Political Culture of the American and Japanese Elites.* New Haven, Conn.: Yale University Press, 1975.

Brislin, R. W. *Cross Cultural Encounters: Face to Face Interaction.* Elmsford, N.Y.: Pergamon Press, 1981.

Jamieson, I. "The Concept of Culture and Its Relevance for an Analysis of Business Enterprise in Different Societies." *International Studies of Management and Organization* 12, no. 4 (1982-83), pp. 75-105.

Ronen, Simcha. *Comparative and Multinational Management.* New York: John Wiley & Sons, 1986.

Terpstra, Vern. *The Cultural Environment of International Business.* Cincinnati: South-Western Publishing, 1978.

Wright, P. "Organizational Behavior in Islamic Firms." *Management International Review* 21, no. 2 (1981), pp. 86-94.

Endnotes

1. Marston Bates, *Gluttons and Libertines: Human Problems of Being Natural* (New York: Random House, 1968).
2. Simcha Ronen, *Comparative and Multinational Management* (New York: John Wiley & Sons, 1986), p. 17.
3. Paul J. Stonich, ed., *Implementing Strategy: Making Strategy Happen,* written by the staff of Management Analysis Center, Inc. (Cambridge, Mass.: Ballinger Publishing, 1982), p. 34.
4. Bob Lucas, "Political-Cultural Analysis of Organizations," *Academy of Management Review,* (January 1987), pp. 144-56.
5. Kathleen Reardon, *International Business Gift-Giving Customs: A Guide for American Executives* (Janesville, Wis.: Parker Pen Company, 1984). The book may be ordered from the Public Relations Department, Parker Pen Company, P.O. Box 5100, Janesville, WI 53547.
6. Ronen, *Comparative and Multinational Management,* p. 97.
7. David C. McClelland, *The Achieving Society* (Princeton, N.J.: D. Van Nostrand, 1961).
8. Kemper Fullerton, "Calvinism and Capitalism," *Harvard Theological Review* 21 (1928), pp. 163-91. Reprinted in Ross A. Weber, ed., *Culture and Management* (Homewood, Ill.: Richard D. Irwin, 1969), pp. 91-111.
9. Philip R. Harris and Robert T. Moran, *Managing Cultural Differences* (Houston: Gulf Publishing, 1979), p. 223.
10. D. P. Mukerji, "Mahatma Gandhi's View on Machines and Technology," in *Culture and Management,* ed. Ross A. Weber (Homewood, Ill.: Richard D. Irwin, 1969), p. 113. Reprinted from *International Social Science Bulletin* 6, no. 3 (Paris: UNESCO, 1954), pp. 411-23.
11. *Ibid.,* p. 114.
12. Vern Terpstra, *International Dimensions of Marketing* (Boston: Kent Publishing, 1982), p. 162.
13. Duane Kujawa, "Technology Strategy and Industrial Relations: Case Studies of Japanese Multinationals in the United States," *Journal of International Business Studies,* Winter 1983, pp. 9-22.
14. Harris and Moran, *Managing Cultural Differences,* passim.

Case
NUMMI

NUMMI stands for New United Motor Manufacturing, Inc., a 50–50 joint venture between Toyota Motor Corporation and General Motors Corporation—automobile companies that are, respectively, the third largest and the largest in the world. NUMMI, which began production in late 1984, assembles smaller-sized cars designed by Toyota. It is located in Fremont, California and employs about 2,500 people. The plant receives components and parts from Toyota plants and suppliers in Japan and from suppliers in the United States. The cars it assembles are sold to marketing organizations belonging to each of its parent companies.

Why a "NUMMI"?

NUMMI was conceived during the early 1980s, an admittedly tumultuous time for the auto industry in America. High energy prices and changing consumer preferences had resulted in an expanding demand for smaller, high-quality, more fuel-efficient cars. Japanese auto producers, Toyota among them, were operating under a program of Japanese export quotas on cars shipped to the United States, a program intended (1) to give U.S.-based producers "breathing time" to adjust their production to meet market needs and federal standards on increased fuel efficiency and (2) to encourage Japanese auto companies to establish production in the United States.

One could speculate at length about the factors that motivated Toyota and General Motors (GM) to join together to form NUMMI. At the time, however, articles in the press focused on two important considerations.

Toyota found the idea of producing in the United States attractive for short-term reasons, such as the quota, and for long-term reasons, such as its own business philosophy and the global competitive environment facing the auto industry. At the same time, it was interested in lowering the risks associated with beginning U.S. production by bringing in a partner knowledgeable about U.S. marketing and labor-management practices and by learning how to manage successfully in the United States. General Motors, on the other hand, was comparatively inexperienced in small-car production and in the shop floor, worker-management, and vendor-supplier relationships that were needed to make such production cost competitive. It saw the joint venture with Toyota as an opportunity to participate, in a substantial way, with one of the world's foremost cost-competitive producers of high-quality, small

This case was written by Professor Duane Kujawa. Information on NUMMI's operations was obtained by the author during on-site research in September 1986. The research was part of a larger research project directed by Professor Tetsuo Abo at the University of Tokyo's Institute of Social Science and funded by the Toyota Foundation in Japan. The support from Professor Abo and the Toyota Foundation is gratefully acknowledged, as is the cooperation of New United Motor Manufacturing, Inc.

cars—and to learn from the experience and transfer what it learned to other GM operations. From this perspective, General Motors' participation in NUMMI would serve to enhance GM's potential for future success in small-car production.

Thus, there were sound business reasons for creating NUMMI. Lowering the risks associated with possible future financial and operating commitments of impressive magnitudes motivated both Toyota and GM to come together in NUMMI.

But NUMMI involved other risks—risks that were intrinsic to its very nature. Could Toyota's Japan-based management system be implemented successfully in the United States? NUMMI would be breaking new ground and creating a distinctive, hybrid corporate culture reflecting both Japanese and American culturally based traits and culturally influenced institutions. At the beginning, neither GM nor Toyota was really sure that an experiment like NUMMI could succeed.

The GM-Toyota Contractual Relationship and Toyota's Responsibility for Running the Plant

The joint-venture agreement between GM and Toyota gave Toyota the responsibility for operating the plant and established an eight-person board of directors consisting of four Toyota representatives and four GM representatives. Although the board is the ultimate decision-making body, it cannot by itself change the joint-venture contract. Toyota runs the plant, and this situation can be changed only if both Toyota and GM agree.

In implementing its responsibility for running the plant, Toyota has drawn on its experience with its production system in its Japanese plants, an experience that reflects substantial and compelling Toyota-specific and "Japanese" influences and characteristics. Those influences and characteristics determine the entire NUMMI system, a system that differs noticeably from that found in "traditional" U.S. auto plants. To enable us to place differences in perspective, let us note first some of the fundamental features of the traditional U.S. system as seen in auto and other types of plants over the years.[1]

The "Traditional" U.S. System

The automobile assembly line concept was built around the idea of engineering the production job down to a series of discrete worker tasks. The simpler these tasks were, the better, since that made it possible to use less expensive workers. Production engineering made these workers more productive by providing them with specific operating methods and tools, many of special design. Production engineering also determined output standards and time standards against which to measure worker "efficiency." The quality control department checked to see whether the product produced was within what was felt to be a tolerable quality range. Training was limited to what was necessary to make the worker more effective on his or her present job.

The traditional U.S. auto plant was a unionized plant, and its work practices reflected a variety of influences regarding workers' and unions' interests in job control and income protection. For example, there were typically a large number of job classifications and wage levels reflecting the various tasks that workers performed. An employee usually worked strictly within his or her job classification.

Critics of the traditional system felt that it was "dehumanizing" and that it permitted no personal identification between the worker and the job, the product, or the company.

Relationships with suppliers were typically subject to periodic review and "rebidding." This meant that vendors would prepare proposals, which might or might not be accepted, to supply certain components, made to the buyer's specifications and design configuration, for a particular model year. The relationship was tenuous and often temporary. If a new vendor came in with a lower price and was deemed reliable, a new supply relationship was created. Critics saw this behavior as denying the benefits of experience and promoting an orientation toward short-term profit on the part of vendors. Both of these effects were seen as impairing product quality. Vendors shipped on a periodic basis, and buyers routinely performed receiving inspection and testing before putting these shipments into their inventory.

Before leaving the U.S. system, it is important to note that many of its practices have distinctively American roots. Scientific management principles have long been part of the U.S. industrial culture. They pertain to the procedures for engineering a job down to its simplest tasks. Social Darwinism (the "survival of the fittest") comes into play when workers' interests and vendors' interests are constantly subjected to competitive and impersonal market tests. "Extended hierarchical relationships" come into play when workers are just "hands" that need to be managed and supported from above. The distribution of power reflects these relationships.

Toyota's Plant Management Approach at NUMMI

Visualize an automobile assembly line such as that shown in the photo of the line at NUMMI. As the line moves along, teams of employees work together on the car, installing, for example, the battery and battery cables or certain dashboard components.

Each team is responsible for its increment of work on each car. Quite importantly, each team is also responsible for assigning specific tasks among its members, and these assignments may rotate hourly, daily, weekly, or whatever—as the team may wish. Each team sets its own task sequence and is responsible for the quality of its work.

If a team is having difficulty with the number of tasks it has to complete during the time it has the car, the allocation of tasks within the team or among teams may be changed. The key is to have each team working productively on each car during its allotted time.

The members of each NUMMI team generally get together about 10 or 15

Introduction

Strategy and structure pertain to the making and implementing of decisions. In the organizational setting, decision making is a complex process—a process affected by perceptions, communications, values, issues, priorities, external pressures, personalities, and so on. It is unrealistic to streamline this process into a rigid set of authority and reporting relationships. Decision making is a dynamic process. The better decisions are made when the process is constrained only by the needs of the current situation, including the need to apply the appropriate expertise. Nonetheless, hierarchical structures do exist in business. Such structures formally define the allocation of authority and responsibility, especially regarding the flow and control of funds.

Complementarity of Strategy and Structure

Typically, as a firm grows, its structure becomes increasingly complex. There is also increasing concern that the firm be organizationally competent enough to carry out competitive strategies and flexible enough to accommodate changes in strategies. Pan Am, for example, sold its Pacific routes (and some equipment) to United Airlines in late 1985 for $750 million. This allowed United to integrate domestic and international flights, especially through its already existing hub in San Francisco. United figured that its domestic system would feed passengers into its international flights and make for higher profits than Pan Am was able to generate in the Pacific. Pan Am, on the other hand, did not have a substantial domestic feeder system into the Pacific area. Developing one was beyond its financial capability at the time. The $750 million would help Pan Am buy new equipment and strengthen the Atlantic (United States/Europe) routes that it fed off its substantial East Coast domestic system. Strategy and structure are thus seen to be mutually complementary. What United had in place in the United States gave it the basis for being competitive internationally. What Pan Am got strengthened its overall competitive posture. Given their different route systems, equipment, and strategies, United and Pan Am both improved their global business positions through this transaction.

Topics to Be Analyzed

Strategy formulation and implementation are typically studied in considerable depth in the "capstone" business policy course. However, an international business course oriented toward managerial issues and management decision making must also deal with concepts of strategy and structure—an especially rewarding experience, since the evolution of the MNE itself richly illustrates the interplay between these two important topics. In the materials that follow, strategy and structure are first defined. The relationships between strategy and structure as the MNE evolves are then characterized and highlighted. Next, the three fundamental organizational and behavioral orientations peculiar to the MNE—ethnocentric, polycentric and geocentric—are examined. Following that examination, some of the basics on strategic planning and management and on the strategic issues faced by the MNE are discussed. This draws the material of the present chapter to a close and sets the stage for the more detailed look at strategy formulation in Chapter 20, "Developing a Global Strategy."

Strategy and Structure Defined

Strategy

Strategy involves goal setting and the planning needed to attain goals.[1] It also involves translating plans into programs and monitoring programs to make sure they remain goal directed. Strategy is pertinent to two levels within the enterprise: the corporate level and the strategic business unit (SBU) level.

At the corporate level, two primary considerations in setting strategy are synergy and balance. The different SBUs in the corporate "portfolio" must realize some operational benefit, or **synergy,** derived from their common corporate parentage. For example, automatic welding technology (including the use of robots) developed for use in Nissan's plants in Japan is also used at the Nissan plant in Tennessee.

Alternatively, or in addition, different SBUs may complement, or **balance,** one another in terms of cash needs or cash flows. For example, stable and profitable cigarette sales produce substantial revenues for the tobacco operations at RJR Nabisco that provide the financial resources needed to implement the firm's current global product diversification strategy. In this sense, tobacco sales in the United States can be seen as enabling Del Monte (an RJR Nabisco subsidiary) to expand in Europe or Latin America.

For the corporate level to serve some competitively meaningful role, either synergy or balance must be present. If synergy or balance were not present, the SBU would bear the burden of sustaining the corporate level without receiving any benefit in return. In such circumstances, the corporate structure, serving no economic or commercial purpose, would be forced by a competitive marketplace to disintegrate.

Strategy at the SBU level is operations driven. It is concerned with competition, technology, production, logistics, marketing, taxes, and so on. Scale economies, learning curve effects, and similar phenomena are especially pertinent. Managers at the SBU levels are more market driven, more concerned with the typical management functions, and are typically responsible for the "bottom line." Consider the Burger King franchisee in Venezuela. Management there is on the "firing line" day in and day out, but it relies heavily on Burger King U.S., the franchisor, for direction on product quality control, production techniques, new products, and so on.

Figure 12-1

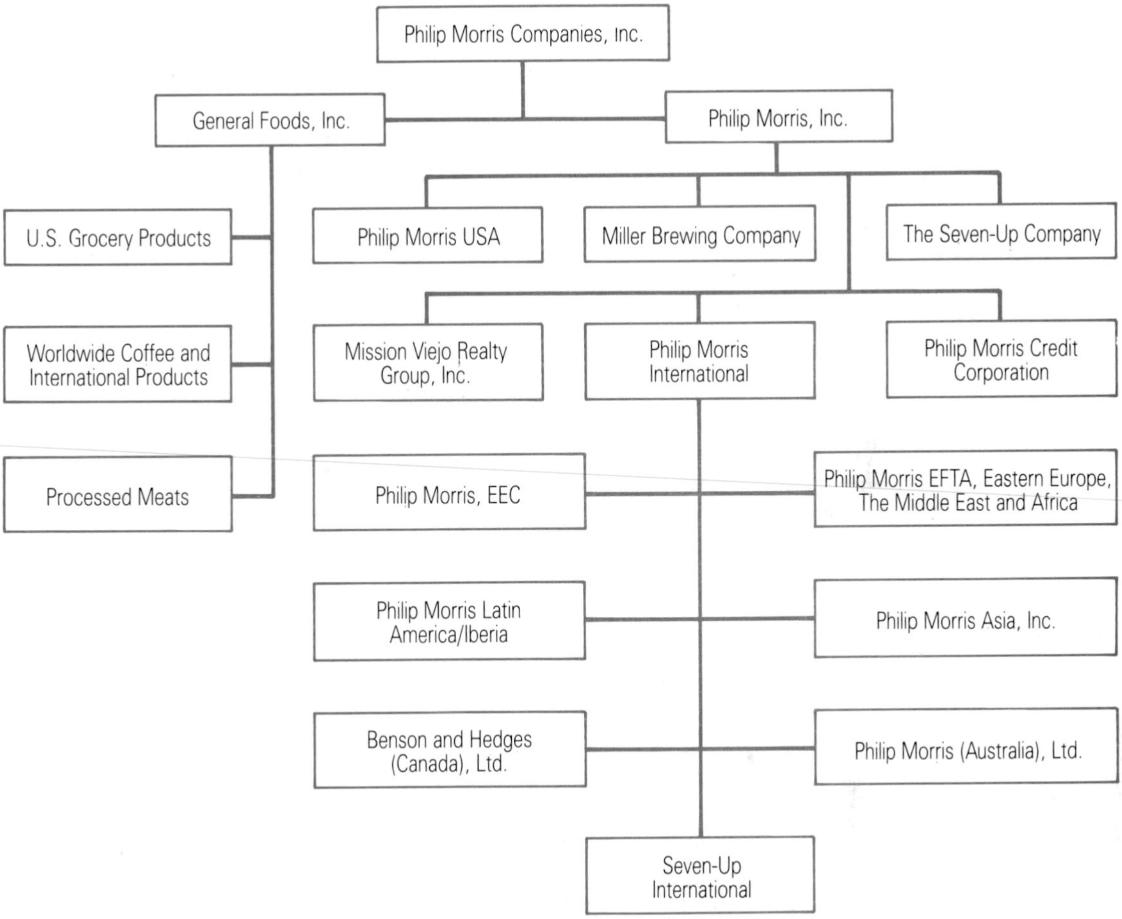

"We believe it is a fallacy to think that being bigger will ensure our continued prosperity.—Hamish Maxwell, chairman of the board and chief executive officer, 1985 *Annual Report,* Philip Morris Companies, Inc., p. 5.

The first steps toward ensuring success is to define Philip Morris into a set of smaller business units—each with profit and loss responsibilities.

Structure

Strategy, as already noted, operates through structure. **Structure** embodies all the operational attributes of the enterprise and can be extremely complex. At its best, it is the institutional embodiment of strategy implementation. Several of the chapters in this book deal with the different elements of structure, thus broadly defined. This chapter will look at structure in terms of organizational relationships and, to some extent, the locus of power as these have changed and developed with the maturing of the MNE itself.

Structural Change and the Evolution of the MNE

Much of the growth of multinational enterprises in the manufacturing and service sectors has taken place in the past four decades. The pattern of that growth was traced to some extent in the earlier chapters, especially Chapters 2 and 3, in the discussions of the *international product cycle* relative to international trade and foreign direct investment. Further consideration of the product-life-cycle (PLC) model, as it illustrates organizational change and key strategy points, would certainly be useful in the present context. Let's turn back the clock to the mid-1950s or so and examine, from the starting point, the roots and growth process of what has become the modern MNE. (To facilitate discussion, the following focuses only on firms in the manufacturing sector.)

Setting the Stage

Following World War II and into the 1950s, income levels advanced substantially in the United States—giving rise to significant and expanding levels of discretionary spending by U.S. citizens. Producers increasingly responded by offering products that were destined to satisfy new and expanding market segments of distinctive tastes and preferences. This, in turn, led to product differentiation as a basis for competitive strategy and to market segments in which income levels were important determinants of demand characteristics. These market segments, almost by definition, were not initially highly competitive, and for these and other reasons oligopolistic market structures were spawned—a small number of producers served (shared) the market and enjoyed above-average returns.

At this point, there was nothing international about the firm. It was busy learning about and responding to domestic market opportunities. Organizations were often structured on a product or functional basis, with power

Functional Structure

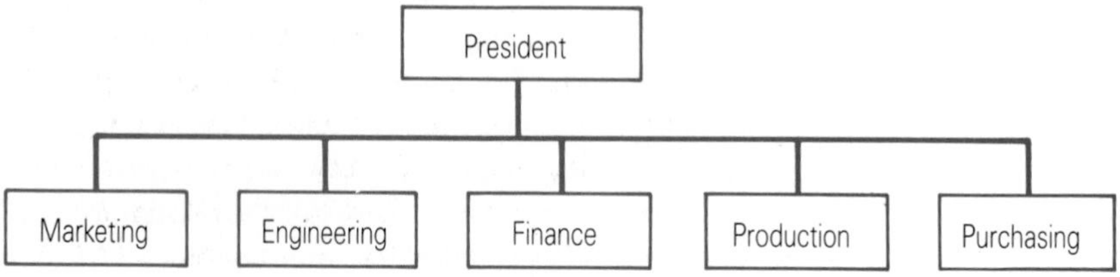

Product Structure

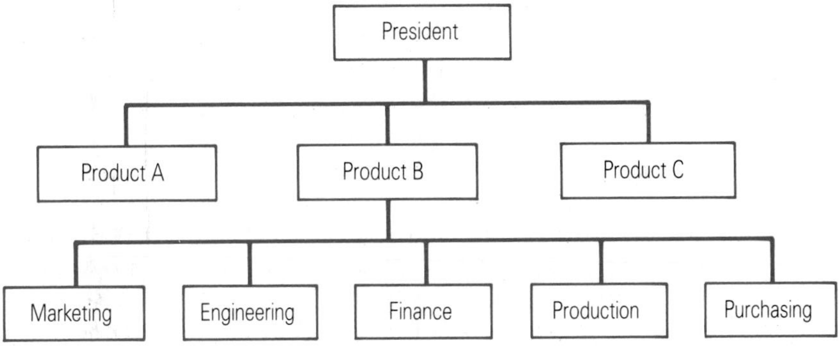

centers likely to be located in engineering and manufacturing, or perhaps even marketing. Organization charts were typically like those presented here. The **functional structure** was usually the first one to be implemented. There was a single product or product line, and management power clearly ascended the pyramidal organization structure. The functional structure facilitated internal technical and marketing coordination. As more numerous and more distinctive market niches developed, so too did product lines and the need for the firm to move to a **product structure.** This organizational form allowed the firm to segmentize internal operations so as to match them with product and market differences. It continued to facilitate internal coordination. As with the functional structure, power in the product structure was hierarchically defined.

Fortuitous Exports

At this time, products that were successful in the U.S. market were also found to be in demand in foreign markets, such as in Canada and Western Europe, where income levels and income-related tastes and preferences were similar to those in the United States. Research showed that exports to these markets were often unsolicited—which implied that intermediaries, typically either foreign or domestic firms that were specialists in exporting, with knowledge of what U.S. producers were bringing to markets and what would sell overseas (mainly in advanced industrial societies) were creating export markets by requesting products from U.S. suppliers.[2]

Firms were not systematically exploiting export markets during this period. Exports were handled by the domestic divisions and frequently were just viewed as orders placed by yet another customer—that happened to be located in New York, London, or some other port city—and was handling the shipping of products to customers in foreign markets. At this point, there was still nothing international about the firm from the organizational perspective.

But from the operational and financial perspectives, the firm began to become dependent on exports.

Deliberate Exports

As **accidental exports** attracted the attention of management, firms became involved in direct exporting. Exports had become important. They accounted for a goodly share of production and profits. Company sales representatives began calling on overseas customers, but product modifications to secure foreign sales were minimal and sales contracts were typically denominated in dollars. In these earlier times, exports by U.S. pharmaceutical companies, for example, typically involved products packaged for the U.S. market and were priced in dollars.

By now, the firm had established an **export department,** often within marketing, which was initially concerned with logistics—packaging, shipping, letters of credit, insurance, and so on. The customers of this department were often viewed as less familiar and less reliable than those of the domestic divisions, so that to some extent the department had to negotiate with the domestic divisions to secure product for export sales. Thus, foreign sales were not given as high a priority as domestic sales. In fact, during periods of robust home demand when production was pushing capacity limits, it was not unusual for exports to be cut so that domestic customers could be satisfied. A modern-day illustration of this greater emphasis on the domestic market is provided by the steel minimills in the United States, which often export excess supply rather than sell off inventory at depressed prices at home—a practice that would spoil their domestic market.

But with the continued expansion of foreign sales, often accompanied by intensifying home front competition as other domestic producers cut into the firm's innovative lead, corporate attitudes began to change. In some cases, the result was the establishment of an **international division** (still concerned only with exports) that operated on a par with the domestic divisions and had

The Export Department—Exports Worthwhile but Not Significant

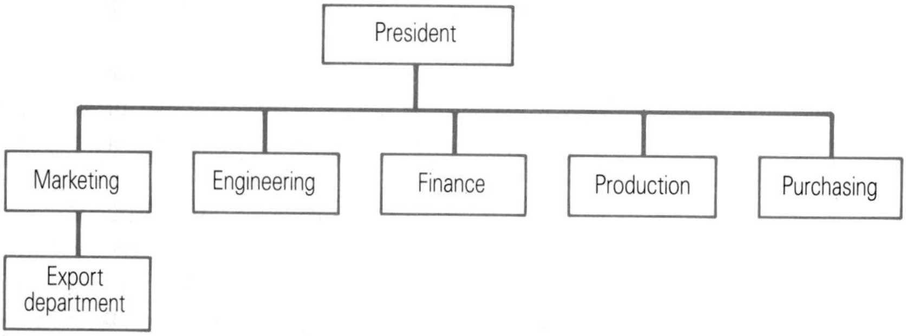

The International Department—Exports Important: A Substantial Part of Company Sales

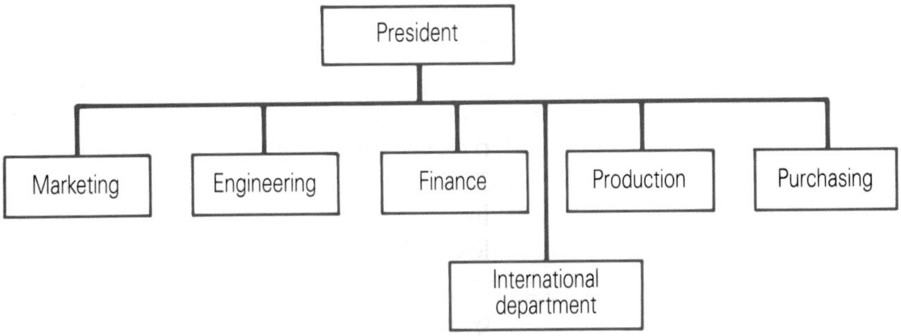

some influence over product design, availability, and price in the export markets. Gradually, the international division accumulated some power. From being a product and schedule "taker," this division now had influence over production schedules and product allocation and was able to justify minor product modifications necessary to export success. The Singer Company and its famous sewing machine operations grew this way. The accompanying organization charts typify this evolution.

The conclusions at this point are several. Perhaps the most important is that exports are affecting the bottom line in a measurable way. Organizationally, the international division has credibility. Now the firm's strategy is to serve both domestic and foreign markets with domestically based production. Both domestic and export markets are valued for their profit contributions. This means that more funds are available for R&D, for capital investment, and for dividends. These funds strengthen the firm regardless of where it operates. Thus, success in the export market is seen as important for success in the domestic market. Serving both domestic and foreign markets rather than just domestic markets often results in scale economies in production or research and engineering and thus lower product unit costs. Export market success enhances domestic market success in this regard too.

Expanded Competition and the Competitive Response

Competition continued to build in the domestic market as other firms imitated the success formulas of the original firms. For the same reason, competition developed in the export markets too. Domestically, the innovative firms had responded by defining market segments more precisely and by bringing more varied products to the marketplace. The result was that product lines grew, enabling these firms to enjoy some level of monopoly profits over a now extended period of time. In the foreign markets, the vulnerability of the MNE, in this earlier period, was enhanced because far-flung logistic and management networks were costly and because products

Table 12-1 **Product Lines Manufactured at Foreign Subsidiaries of 180 U.S. MNEs**

Foreign Subsidiaries	Number of Product Lines		
	1955	1965	1975
In all locations	294	674	1,633
In Canada	62	115	263
In Europe	82	246	647
In Latin America	69	120	211
Elsewhere	81	193	512

Source: Raymond Vernon, *Storm over the Multinationals* (Cambridge, Mass.: Harvard University Press, 1977), p. 65. Reprinted by permission.

sold overseas were not fully adapted to the consumer preferences of the foreign market. Competitors producing in Western Europe and Canada, for example, were able to imitate the competitive essence of a product and yet package the product to meet distinctive preferences of foreign consumers. They produced and marketed within their local markets (which were export markets to the MNE). The U.S. MNEs were at a product *disadvantage*—and possibly a cost disadvantage too, since they faced tariffs, shipping costs, and other changes not experienced by the foreign competition. They responded by opening plants in their export markets.

These direct foreign investments were significant in many ways. They allowed the U.S. MNEs to get inside tariff barriers, and they eliminated transcontinental shipping and insurance costs. Perhaps more important, they facilitated significant product adaptation—a fine tuning of product design in response to distinctive use conditions in foreign markets. Quite important too, as these overseas subsidiaries gained experience, the "new" products developed to meet increasingly competitive domestic markets were channeled into overseas markets. This gave the subsidiaries competitive strengths reflective of the positive synergistic effects associated with multinational enterprise. Evidence on the growth of the overseas product lines of U.S. MNEs is presented in Table 12-1.

Structural Implications of Foreign Direct Investment

Putting plants overseas affected the "mind-set" of MNE management in several important ways. The balance sheet exposure of having assets placed in foreign countries required closer attention to foreign operations by top management. The transfer (export) of product and/or process technologies, required initially to get the foreign plant on line, and the ongoing transfer of component parts between the parent and the **foreign subsidiary** meant, in some cases, substantial attention to foreign operations by lower-level man-

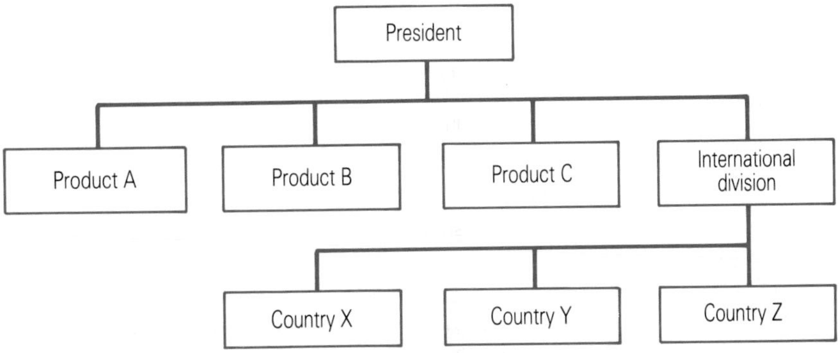

agement and technical staff. The firm's marketing activities, which began with exporting, were adapting now to new logistics patterns and enhanced sales potentials. The production and distribution pipeline was shorter now, and the firm was able to be more price competitive. The subsidiary's sales revenues were definitely denominated in local currency, as were many of the costs of its operations. Parent company nationals were probably on assignment at the subsidiary. Local management had considerable control now over production, marketing, and other functions and had more flexibility to respond effectively to competitive opportunities in the marketplace. The firm's strategic objectives at this time were to establish a solid market presence by building on the technical, financial, and managerial expertise provided by the parent, and eventually to expand market share.

Organizationally, these early days of foreign direct investment saw a group of geographically defined subsidiaries reporting to the parent through an international division. Often this international division was organizationally parallel to the product or functional divisions. The structure was a hybrid, with responsibilities allocated between domestic and international via a set of nondistinctive categories. It was a logical structure, though, in terms of historical evolution. The international division was already in place before the subsidiaries were established. Its roots went back to the days of deliberate exports. The accompanying organization chart typifies the international division within a general product division structure with manufacturing subsidiaries in several countries.

The Drive to Structural Maturity

As scale economies in production grew and as markets were developed outside the traditional geographic domain of each subsidiary, the business effectiveness of the geographically defined subsidiary declined. (In some MNEs, subsidiaries in different countries could even be found competing

The Global Structure—Narrow Product Line

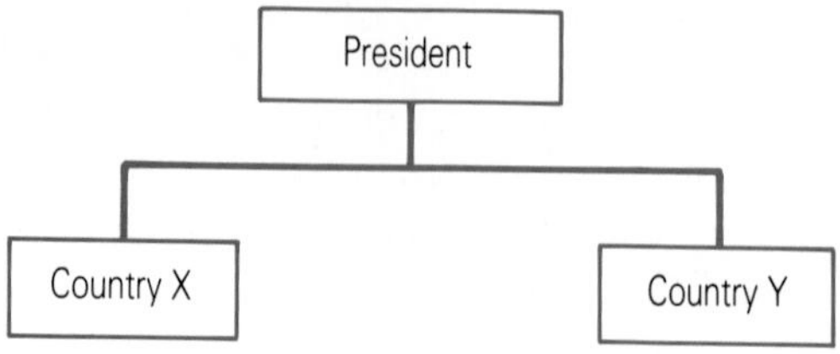

with one another in some third markets—note the discussion presented below in the highlighted feature "What Went Wrong at Westinghouse?") If product lines were fairly narrow, product groups with both domestic and foreign jurisdictions were typically formed. If broad product lines were the rule, the **matrix structure** was the answer. In this case, country- or subcountry-level managers reported to both area and product managers. It was their job to balance global or regional rationalization needs against local market needs or nuances. They were "company specialists" rather than just market or technical specialists.[3] The organization charts on this page illustrate these two structures.

Some companies, it should be noted, do not prefer the matrix-type structure—and rightly so. Single-product companies and companies with a dominant, distinctive product (such as Coca-Cola) need not evolve into the matrix structure. Product proliferation, on the other hand, leads almost invariably to a matrix organization. The strategy implications here are fairly straightforward. The subsidiary is an extension of the parent, and it benefits

The Global Matrix Structure

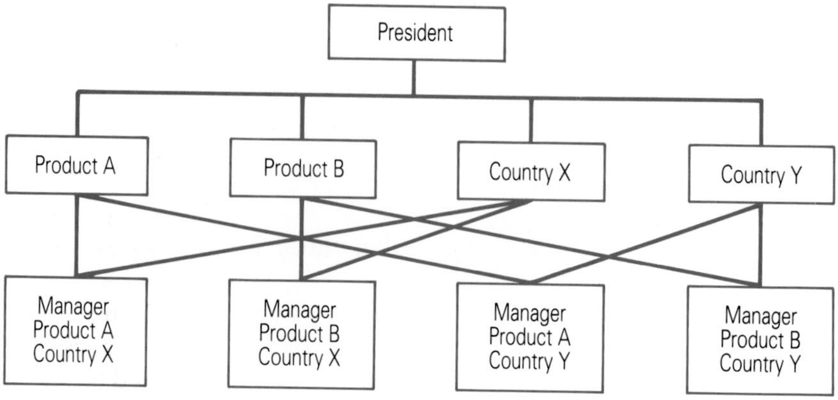

from the parent's market dominance in a single or narrow product line. The multiproduct firm, on the other hand, must find the niche that requires product uniqueness but still allows it to gain from positive linkages among its products and markets. Success here involves fine tuning and considerable knowledge of both company capabilities and market opportunities. The matrix structure makes possible the "team" response required for success in situations where no one person has all the knowledge or all the information needed.

The Driving Force of the Market—The Rationale of Change

The preceding discussion on the evolution of the MNE and the accompanying structural changes might appear to imply that management is consistently reactive, that it merely adapts to changes in its competitive environments—at times, even begrudgingly. This conclusion would be fairly accurate for the emergent MNE. It does not mean, however, that change is made without intelligence or that management's behavior is without a rationale. The marketplace conveys a lot of information!

By participating in and paying attention to the market, management receives important feedback on the commercial propriety of its behavior. Accidental exports, for example, give the firm important information—not only on the marketability of the product overseas, but also on market potential, pricing strategy, characteristics of customers (including their motivations for buying), locations of customers, distribution channels, and so on. Also, quite importantly, most business organizations are justifiably cautious. They just don't throw funding into projects unless there is a reasonable expectation of success. Success in an initially limited market justifies (and helps fund) expansion. It gives the project, and the project team, credibility. It allows management to compete intelligently with other potential users of the firm's limited funds. Put somewhat differently, it would be fair to say structure does not change without reason. Changes in the marketplace provides a rationale for changing structure. The successful (lasting) firm responds properly to those changes.

Three Classic Strategies/Structures—Ethnocentric, Polycentric, and Geocentric

Rutenberg sees the "two economic reasons that sustain most international diversification" as experience curves and risk spreading.[4] Experience curves, in the extreme, would lead to globally centralized power—or ethnocentric organization. Risk spreading, on the other hand, requires a portfolio of reasonably unrelated, globally distributed subsidiaries—a polycentric organization.[5] Why do these two strategies lead to these particular structures, and what do the strategies mean operationally?

The Ethnocentric Organization

The Rationale for Ethnocentrism Experience curve effects result in declining costs of operations (e.g., production, marketing, and distribution). These effects require standardization, which allows repetition to result in increased efficiency. In the aerospace industry, an 80 percent experience curve seems to be the historical standard in manufacturing. This means that every time cumulative production doubles, costs of production decline to 80 percent of the previous level. The **experience curve effect** is thus readily seen as an important competitive weapon. Standardized production lowers costs of production and enhances profit margins and competitiveness. For the MNE, competitive success entails effectively transferring what was learned in one location to other locations. Doing this positions the MNE further down the experience curve and gives it a competitive advantage over firms operating only in local markets. In Chapter 2, this effect was labeled "managerial experience in several countries".

Ethnocentrism in Operation The strategy/structure implications here are fairly straightforward. The multinational enterprise operates on global product mandates and is typically organized at the top on a product division basis. This is a niche strategy made viable by the presence of a globally identifiable market segment that allows for standardization in production (for example) and, for the MNE able to transfer experience internationally, the delivery of a competitive edge.

Ethnocentrism, as a management core strategy, carries with it distinctive organizational and operational characteristics.[6] As already noted, the organization is divisionalized at the top on a product basis. The divisions manage their own inventories and logistic flows internationally. Products are designed for the home (parent company) market and manufactured in large factories located where costs are lowest. These factories serve both domestic and export markets. In this environment, products are not likely to be adapted, in any substantial way, to reflect foreign market differences. Both internal and external pressures exist for uniform, global product pricing. The finance function is typically controlled at the MNE level, and profits remitted to the parent company are the bottom line in evaluating foreign investment opportunities.

Ethnocentrism, like any strategy, has the potential for generating certain kinds of problems as it is being implemented. In its eagerness to take advantage of experience effects, management may overlook market niches that are best served by products adapted to satisfy localized preferences. Moreover, these overlooked niches may be where future market growth is concentrated—to the potential detriment of the firm's predominant position in its well-established market. That experience curve benefits are proportionately larger in the earlier stages of production (i.e., with newer products) magnifies the significance of this problem.

perspective, and it seeks to maximize total global returns to the MNE and all its units. It is especially relevant to the global matrix structure, identified earlier as especially pertinent to the multiproduct firm with a niche strategy turning on the firm's ability to deal successfully with distinctive markets that require unique products—all of this balanced against the firm's multiproduct capabilities and its desire to benefit from scale economies.

Geocentrism in Operation The geocentric organization is typically a matrix organization. The markets of the MNE are distinctive enough to require a distinctive product response from it. This denies the opportunity to benefit from ethnocentrism. On the other hand, enough commonalities exist—for example, in the customer base or in component parts or product cores—to permit scale economies and experience curve effects. This denies the opportunity to benefit from polycentrism. Geocentrism, then, is a global concept attuned to local market needs.

The geocentric organization is often defined as a hybrid that includes elements of geographic and product structures. Its objective is to blend these two elements into a competitive, profitable market presence. Hence the matrix structure—and a critical need for internal communication and for a corporate-wide perspective on what constitutes success. These are difficult needs to address—especially if the MNE has traditionally been ethnocentric (centralized power) or polycentric (dispersed power). Often the need for geocentrism evolves as product markets mature. Market trends are, in a sense, forcing that evolution. The transition from ethnocentrism or polycentrism to geocentrism is thus typically a real phenomenon addressed by many MNEs, but a totally geocentric firm may be hard to find. The transition is certainly not a simple one.

The above commentary on ethnocentrism, polycentrism, and geocentrism in MNEs is highlighted in Figure 12-2 on the next page.

Strategic Management and Planning in the MNE

As noted at the beginning of this chapter, strategic management and planning are typically covered in the "capstone" business policy course. To enhance understanding of the chapters that follow, however, some introductory comments on strategic management and planning and on the nature of the key strategic issues facing MNEs are required now. Chapter 20, "Developing a Global Strategy," will revisit strategic management and put an integrated, operational perspective around it.

Strategic Management—The Basics[8]

Strategic management is a process that can be conceptualized in terms of six fundamental steps, as shown in Figure 12-3.

Formulating the mission statement defines why the organization exists.

Figure 12-2 **The Three Classic Strategies/Structures Compared**

Basic Rationale	Key Features/Implications
The Ethnocentric MNE	
Cost cutting via learning curve effects transmitted by parent to subsidiaries	Company strives for globally standardized products and production processes
	Company targets on market niches that are similar internationally
	Strong headquarters involvement at all levels
	Company too often overlooks new markets—extensive communication needed (hard to provide cross-culturally and over long distances)
The Polycentric MNE	
Cost/risk reduction via portfolio effects at the parent level	Company (including subsidiaries) thrives on product and market distinctiveness in different countries
	Company enjoys maximum freedom in product pricing (because markets are separate and distinctive internationally)
	Internal communication not important; few internal transfers of knowledge internationally
	Long-term prognosis for the polycentric MNE is negative—product markets becoming increasingly similar internationally
The Geocentric MNE	
Ethnocentric and polycentric pressures balanced in favor of optimizing the MNE system	Company is typically organized on a matrix basis—product and geographic divisions
	Best structure for handling changing market preferences and new products
	Internal communication critical
	Key personnel developed over the long term and on a *global* experience basis

Business organizations exist to make profits, but typically their mission statements go beyond this purpose and indicate how the firm will pursue profits compared to how other firms might do so. "Flying the friendly skies of United" suggests, for example, that United Airlines wants to compete on the basis of high-quality service. The **mission statement** thus begins to define the firm.

Determining strategic objectives and *formulating the master strategy* answer three basic questions:[9] Where are we? Where do we want to be? How do we get there? These answers, in turn, build on a detailed analysis of the firm's internal *s*trengths and *w*eaknesses and of the external *o*pportunities and *t*hreats that confront it. (The literature refers to this as the **SWOT analysis.**) Consistent with the mission statement and in light of the SWOT

Figure 12-3 **The Strategic Management Process**

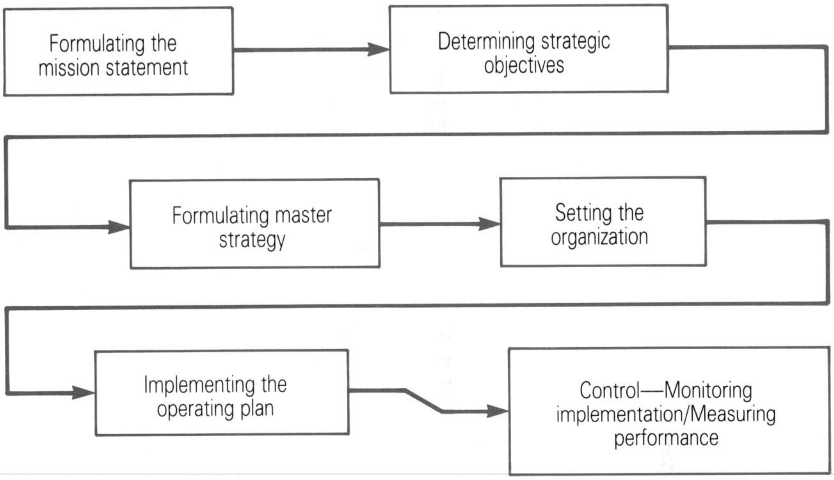

analysis, the firm then sets its **strategic objectives** and its **master strategy**—the basic blueprint on how to accomplish the strategic objectives.

Setting the organization and *implementing the operating plan* constitute the implementation phase of the strategic management process. Setting the organization involves organizational structuring. It allocates the tasks that must be done to implement the master strategy, and it defines responsibilities and allocates power within the organization. Implementing the **operating plan** involves short-term planning, setting operating targets, determining budgets, and so on.

Matsushita's Mission—and the Beginning of Strategy Implementation

Mission statements and master strategies can be vague concepts at first. To clarify the concepts a bit, let's look at what Matsushita, the maker of Panasonic and Quasar products, is and what it says about its mission.

Today, Matsushita is "home" to 150,000 employees worldwide. It produces and sells over 14,000 products in more than 130 countries. Its global sales total over $22 billion. Traditionally Matsushita manufactured consumer electronic products, but as a result of its pursuit of new products and technologies, it now serves industrial, office, and communications markets as well.

Matsushita's basic mission statement is its creed:

Through our industrial activities, we strive to foster progress, to promote the general welfare of society, and to devote ourselves to furthering the development of world culture.

Matsushita's more specific mission is to focus on "key areas of technological growth which will have a tremendous impact on society in the near future." These are communications and information processing technologies, semiconductor components and materials technologies, advanced video and audio technologies, and production engineering technologies, such as robotics and factory automation.

Visualize Matsushita as the high-tech, R&D-oriented company that it is, and from a global perspective, try to identify broadly the strengths and weaknesses a company of this kind might have in addressing such issues as new product development and the understanding of specific market segments.

Source: Information abstracted from *Matsushita Electric Corporation of America*, an undated brochure provided by company officials in September 1986.

Control, the final step in the strategic management process, consists of monitoring strategy implementation, measuring performance against pre-established standards, and taking corrective action when necessary .

Strategic Issues in the MNE

Dymsza identifies a variety of strategic management/planning issues germane to the multinational enterprise. Some of these issues are unique to the MNE; others are extensions of issues pertinent to firms in general. Dymsza poses the issues as follows:

In what region and what countries and when should a company expand its international commitments in funds, technology, management, know-how, and personnel?

Should the MNE enter a new country? What type of entry should it undertake . . . : exporting, licensing, direct investments, management contracts, other arrangements?

What are the opportunities/risks in various countries in different modes of entry?

In what countries should the MNE expand its existing plants, undertake new investments, make acquisitions?

What product adaptations should the MNE make, and what new products should it introduce in various countries? To what extent should it change its marketing and product mixes in different countries?

What should the MNE do about exchange risk, political vulnerability, and adverse government controls and regulations? Should it disinvest or phase out business in certain countries?

Where should the MNE raise funds for its worldwide operations?

Should the MNE go into joint ventures with private firms or government enterprises abroad, and under what conditions?

What management development programs should the MNE undertake at headquarters and its affiliates abroad?[10]

These questions generally pertain to the geocentric multinational. In light of the preceding discussion, several other questions are certainly suggested:

How distinctive, or universal, are the market determinants of product, promotion, distribution, and other policies?

What products, product cores, and component parts can be produced most economically on an internationally integrated basis? On a country or regional basis?

If scale economies in production and marketing are optimal for relatively small markets, what opportunities for product differentiation and competitiveness exist?

How can the product and the production and marketing functions be disaggregated to allow for an effective blending of scale economies and learning curve effects and the differentiation necessary to respond to market peculiarities?

These questions and the questions posed by Dymsza cover a variety of fundamental issues. Some of these issues are pertinent to the MNE because they involve crossing country, market, or cultural boundaries; others, because they involve dealing in international markets (e.g., foreign exchange or capital markets). One thing is certain: these issues surely present the MNE with a more complex business environment. But they also provide the MNE with business opportunities that it alone is strategically poised to benefit from.

Conclusions

Strategy consists of two components: formulation and implementation. Formulation is based on SWOT analysis. Implementation requires people, money, organization, and so on—the structure through which strategy operates. Strategy involves setting goals and doing the planning necessary to attain goals. It operates at the corporate and SBU levels. At the former level, the main concerns are synergy and balance; at the latter level, operating effectiveness and efficiency are the main concerns. Structure, at its best, is the institutional embodiment of strategy implementation.

The evolution of the MNE provides an illustrative, and relevant, example of the interplay between strategy and structure. Highlights of this evolutionary process included fortuitous exports and the development of an operating and financial dependence on foreign markets. Deliberate exporting followed, which meant that foreign sales had become an objective in their own right. By this time, an export department had probably been established to facilitate logistics matters. Afterward, in many cases, exporting became more significant and product modifications, special pricing strategies, and the like were developed to enhance foreign sales. The export department then gave way to the international division—a more internally influential unit. Exports were now affecting the bottom line in a substantial way.

As competition expanded in both domestic and foreign markets, firms implemented several defensive strategies, including product line expansion at home (and later abroad) and direct investment in foreign markets. This latter strategy enabled the MNE to produce within tariff walls and to eliminate heavy shipping costs. Very importantly, it allowed product modification—the fine tuning of product specifications to the incomes, tastes, and use conditions peculiar to the foreign market. Drastic organizational change accompanied foreign direct investment. Within the MNE, not only were marketing and logistics changed, but production, engineering, personnel, accounting, finance, and so on were redefined to include multinational operations. Initially, the geographic definition of operations gave rise to geographically defined organizational structures.

As the mature multinational evolved, as product lines expanded overseas (in the same way that they expanded domestically), and as competitive conditions became increasingly difficult, many firms moved to the global matrix structure—a team-based approach to blending company capabilities with market opportunities.

Three classic strategies/structures were discussed. The ethnocentric organization relies on scale economies and learning curve effects to develop and sustain a low-cost competitive strategy. The polycentric organization, on the other hand, lacks opportunities for scale economies and learning curve effects because it has to deal with diverse and distinctive geographically defined markets. This often results in multiple power centers within the MNE and, as time and technology unfold, in resistance to changes that are necessary to meet competitive threats. The geocentric organization is an alternative to both ethnocentrism and polycentrism. It balances market needs favoring distinctive approaches against the firm's multiproduct capabilities and its desire to benefit from scale economies and learning curves. The geocentric organization is typically a matrix organization.

The strategic management process was defined as consisting of six components: formulating the mission statement, determining strategic objectives, formulating the master strategy, setting the organization, implementing the operating plan, and applying a control system. Various strategic issues pertinent to the MNE were identified. Some of these issues arose because the MNE crossed country, market, and cultural boundaries—such issues as market selection, entry strategy, and ownership strategy. Others arose because the MNE was operating through international markets with characteristics peculiar to themselves, such as the foreign exchange and capital markets. The complexity of operating multinationally presents the MNE with both a challenge and an opportunity. It makes success difficult, but it also makes success defensible (at least over some intermediate period).

Questions

1. Is the statement that structure follows strategy justified? Could the opposite hold true—that is, could strategy follow structure?
2. Of what relevance to strategy are synergy and balance? Can you give some examples of synergy in MNEs? Of balance? If neither synergy nor balance were present in a particular MNE, could the corporate level be justified? Could it be sustained?
3. What were the internal, organizational effects of fortuitous exports? Of deliberate exports?
4. Why would the international division have more power than the export department? In this context, what is "power"? What does power mean in terms of the firm's future direction?
5. Why does direct foreign investment affect the organization structure so significantly? How does it affect the organization structure?
6. What went wrong at Westinghouse?
7. What is the driving force behind the ethnocentric organization? Give three examples of companies that behave ethnocentrically.
8. What is the driving force behind the polycentric organization? Give the theoretical argument behind the statement that global profit maximization is most likely to occur in the polycentric organization.
9. How does geocentrism differ from ethnocentrism and polycentrism? Is geocentrism the strategy/structure of the future?
10. What are the six components of the strategic management process? How do these components relate to Matsushita and to the text discussion of Matsushita? Why are they important?

References

Abegglen, James C., and George Stalk, Jr. *Kaisha: The Japanese Corporation.* New York: Basic Books, 1985.

Doz, Yves L. "Strategic Management in Multinational Companies." *Sloan Management Review,* Winter 1980, pp. 27-46.

Garland, John, and Richard Farmer. *International Dimensions of Business Policy and Strategy.* Boston: Kent Publishing, 1986.

Gates, Stephen R., and William G. Egelhoff. "Centralization in headquarters-subsidiary Relationships." *Journal of International Business Studies,* Summer 1986, pp. 71-92.

Kujawa, Duane. *Japanese Multinationals in the United States: Case Studies.* New York: Praeger Publishers, 1986.

Mascarenhas, Briance. "International Strategies of Non-Dominant Firms." *Journal of International Business Studies,* Spring 1986, pp. 1-26.

Endnotes

1. For an extensive report on strategic management, especially as it pertains to the MNE, see William H. Davidson, *Global Strategic Management* (New York: John Wiley & Sons, 1982).
2. Claude L. Simpson, Jr., and Duane Kujawa, "The Export Decision Process: An Empirical Inquiry," *Journal of International Business Studies,* Spring 1974, pp. 107-17.
3. David P. Rutenberg, *Multinational Management* (Boston: Little, Brown, 1982), p. 23.
4. Ibid., p. 12.
5. For the original presentation on ethnocentric, polycentric, and geocentric MNE structures and strategies, see Howard V. Perlmutter, "L'Entreprise internationale—trois conceptions," *Revue Économique et sociale,* May 1965. (A translation appears in *Quarterly Journal of AISEC International,* August 1967.)
6. See, for example, Rutenberg, *Multinational Management,* pp. 16-18.
7. See, for example, International Labour Office, *Social and Labour Practices of Some US-Based Multinationals in the Metal Trades* (Geneva: ILO, 1977); and Rutenberg, *Multinational Management,* passim.
8. This account of the strategic management process was adapted from James M. Higgins, *Organizational Policy and Strategic Management,* 2nd ed. (Hinsdale, Ill.: Dryden Press, 1983).
9. Ibid., p. 65.
10. William A. Dymsza, "Global Strategic Planning: A Model and Recent Developments," *Journal of International Business Studies,* Fall 1984, pp. 169-70.

Case
Windmere Corporation

Windmere manufactures and markets a diversified line of consumer electrical products through its Consumer Group. It also owns and operates a chain of Save-Way stores—its Professional Group—that supply barbers and beauticians, as well as the general public, with personal care appliances, liquid products, and hair care accessories. The combined sales of both groups in 1985 were about $91 million—nearly double their sales in 1980.

The 1985 product line of Windmere's Consumer Group was fairly broad. It included several models of hair (blower) dryers, hair curlers, curling irons, lighted makeup mirrors, shavers and related personal beauty products, electronic air cleaners, oscillating fans, nail dryers, and wand-type massagers. These products are marketed under a variety of brand names, such as Signature, Pro, Windmere, Boss, Solid Gold, Prelude, Mirror-Go-Lightly, Fabergé, Brut, and Ronson.

Time and Change

In 1973, Windmere marketed only two products: "permanent lash clusters" and the 1,000-watt Pro hairstyling dryer. From 1973 to 1985, its product line expanded enormously and its sales (of consumer products) grew 200-fold—from $306,000 in 1973 to about $51 million in 1985. Indeed, Windmere's Consumer Group grew at a rate nearly 10 times that of the consumer electrical products industry in general. This was an impressive accomplishment.

The Hong Kong Connection

From the very beginning, Windmere sourced its electrical personal care products in Hong Kong. Indeed, from the early 1970s on, the company purchased products from different factories and trading companies in the old British crown colony.

Windmere's founder and current board chairman, Belvin Friedson, personally developed this strategy and personally established the commercial contacts in Hong Kong. The idea was really quite simple. Hair care consumer products were fairly standardized and could be produced quite cheaply in Hong Kong, with its comparatively low labor costs. In fact, many producers there were capable of making such products. They sold directly to buyers and also through Hong Kong-based trading companies.

This case was written by Professors Duane Kujawa and Harold Strauss. School of Business Administration, University of Miami, Coral Gables, Florida. The authors gratefully acknowledge the cooperation and assistance of Windmere Corporation, and especially Windmere's president, David Friedson, in providing company-specific information.

The arm's-length buying arrangement was a learning experience for Windmere. It soon became evident to Friedson that quality control, scheduling, and other considerations, including Windmere's developing satisfaction with sourcing in Hong Kong and its desire to expand its activities there, required that it secure a longer-term relationship with its suppliers. Accordingly, Durable Electrical Metal Factory, Ltd., a Hong Kong-based, independent manufacturer that had emerged as one of Windmere's more important suppliers, joined Windmere in establishing several joint ventures. Durable-Belson, for example, was set up in 1975 as a manufacturing joint venture. In 1977, two other joint ventures were established: Dubel Industrial, Ltd., an injection molding operation, and Kamwon Electrical Factory, Ltd., an electrical products manufacturer. Subsequently, Windmere acquired 50 percent ownership of Durable itself.

Similarly, K. C. Lau & Co., Ltd., a trading company with which Windmere had developed a good working relationship, was acquired in 1978. This too was done for control reasons—but there were also reasons that went beyond scheduling, documentation, and financial considerations.

Windmere had learned that operating without the aid of a Hong Kong-based trading company resulted in higher prices and poorer goods and services. It worked with several trading companies, but was displeased with nearly all of them. This was because Windmere was dissatisfied with certain Hong Kong "business practices," such as paying trading companies or their key personnel "face money" or kickbacks that were over and above the normal commissions earned. The company felt that operating through a controlled trading company would ensure a more honest, dependable relationship. It also felt that a controlled trading company could help expand Kamwon's and Durable's businesses more effectively. Subsequently, K. C. Lau & Co. was merged into PPC Industries, Ltd., another trading company and a wholly owned subsidiary of Windmere.

By 1980, Windmere had thus put into place the basic operating structure that it felt was necessary to be competitive and to grow as a provider of low-cost, high-quality consumer electrical products to markets in the United States.

Establishing Production in the People's Republic of China

As Windmere's marketing success and its sourcing needs expanded, the company began to look beyond Hong Kong—where labor was becoming increasingly expensive and seasonally scarce. Lai Kin, the managing director of its Durable joint venture, set up an assembly operation in Canton in the People's Republic of China (PRC) in 1980. Labor rates were much lower there—but so were productivity and product quality. David Friedson, Windmere's president, put it this way:

> *At this time, the modernization of China had begun, but it was in a rudimentary form. The authorities in Canton could not understand our needs, and the workers had no concept of what [factory] work meant. Productivity was*

extremely low; the defect rate of products was extremely high; and the experiment was doomed to failure. At the insistence of Mr. Lai we allowed the experiment to continue because we thought we would lose face with the Chinese if we withdrew.[1]

Lai's persistence led to a second attempt to establish operations in the PRC. Man Fung Village, which is in the Shenzhen Special Economic Zone and lies about 35 miles north of Hong Kong, was the scene of a special challenge in 1981. Durable transferred a production line, complete with workers and equipment, from Hong Kong to an old theater in Man Fung Village to demonstrate what the Hong Kong Chinese could do in terms of efficiency and productivity. The mayor and people of Man Fung Village were impressed with this demonstration. They committed themselves to duplicating what they saw in that old theater.

Early the next year, the village put up some facilities and about 100 workers signed up to work there. Durable provided equipment, middle management, supervision, and training.

The rest is history!

Within a few years, the operation employed 2,700 workers and was the largest employer in the Shenzhen Zone. Moreover, Durable's workers were making about double the standard wage for government jobs in China. They were able to build large two-story villas that were beyond the reach of the average Chinese worker. Compensation typically totaled over $65 a month, including bonuses, which, even with transportation costs factored in, resulted in a cost savings of about 50 percent compared to Hong Kong-based production.[2] Interestingly, with the success of the Man Fung operation, Durable felt that it could close its Canton plant without "losing face."

Windmere's president, David Friedson, states that, in the company's opinion,

China provides us with the best value in labor for producing the kinds of products that we produce. This is based on the actual cost of labor as well as other benefits, such as free land and buildings the Government provides and the close proximity to our Hong Kong facilities.[3]

By 1986, nearly 60 percent of Durable's output was produced in China. This was expected to grow to 70-80 percent in 1987.[4] It would probably be capped at that level, however, since Windmere didn't want to "become wholly dependent on a single source."[5] An organization chart depicting the relationships among Windmere's major affiliates and divisions is presented in Figure 1.

Recent Developments

In the last few years, Windmere has added several products that can take advantage of its low-cost production in Hong Kong and the PRC. In 1986, for example, Windmere acquired the Mirror-Go-Lightly line from Jerdon Industries. It expected sales to be $3 million or more that year. In early 1987,

Figure 1 **Organization Structure—Windmere Corporation**

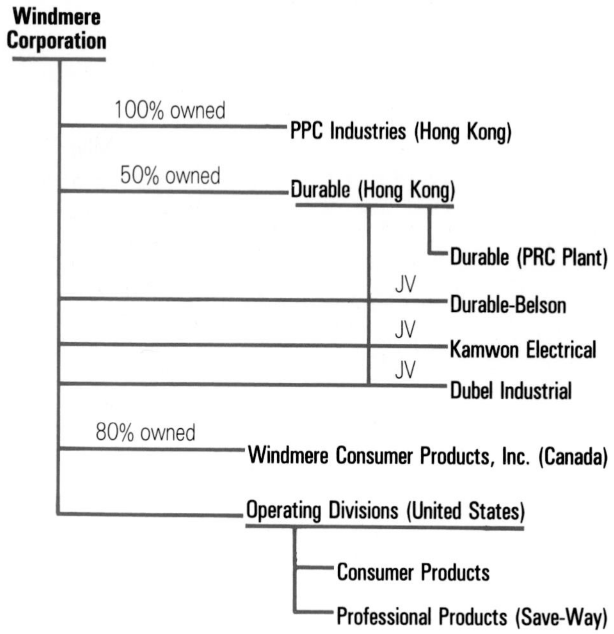

Note: The structure depicted here pertains to the material presented in the case and is useful in understanding the relationships discussed in the case. It is not an "official" organization chart provided by the company.

Windmere introduced the Clothes Shaver (a device to remove lint and fuzz from wools and linens), which was expected to add another $3 million in sales. The Crimper, a heated styling element introduced in late 1986, was expected to generate yet another $3 million in sales.

In 1985, Windmere established a Canadian sales subsidiary, whose results to date have been worthwhile. On the other hand, the performance of Hairflayre, Ltd., its 50 percent-owned British marketing joint venture, proved unsatisfactory and Windmere withdrew from the British market in 1985.

Endnotes

1. Letter from David M. Friedson to Dr. Harold Strauss, dated August 13, 1984.
2. Michael Browning, "Dade Capitalist Brings Holiday Joy to Chinese," *Miami Herald,* January 30, 1984, pp. 1A and 11A.
3. Letter from Friedson to Strauss.
4. "Strong Rebound: Windmere Back in the Black after Heated Court Battle," *Barron's/Investment News & Views,* February 9, 1987, p. 45.
5. Ibid.

13

MARKETING MANAGEMENT

Marketing management in the MNE has two major kinds of concerns. At the operations (business unit) level, it addresses the traditional "four Ps" (product, price, place, and promotion) as they operate in different environments—technical, social, legal, economic, and so on. At the MNE level, it addresses the MNE's potential for competitive strengths in marketing and what the MNE must do to benefit from that potential. This chapter focuses on these concerns. The main goals of the chapter are to:

1. Develop an appreciation for the complexity of marketing management in the MNE—especially with regard to the effects of environmental nuances on the MNE's internal operations and competitive strengths.
2. Review the evolution of marketing management within the MNE.
3. Examine how the international marketing environment provides opportunities for MNEs, specifically in connection with:
   a. Product influences and pressures for product adaptation or standardization.
   b. Pricing concerns and the basis for setting an optimal pricing strategy.
   c. The transferability of experiences among markets and the importance of place.
   d. Promotion influences and promotion as an MNE competitive advantage.

Introduction

As suggested in some of the earlier chapters, marketing in the multinational enterprise can be especially challenging and complex.

The Extractive Industries

For MNEs in the extractive industries dealing with commodities that follow global pricing trends, marketing will probably involve long-term contracts with provisions stipulating consistency in product quality, timely delivery, and periodic price adjustments based on changes in some price index. For example, Intercor, the coal mining joint venture of Exxon and the Colombian government, sells premium-quality bituminous coal, mainly to electric utility companies in Europe. Sales contracts, which specify quality standards, quantities, and delivery dates, are typically for five or more years. Prices are keyed to spot market prices—which will probably vary during the term of the contract.

The Service Industries

In services, the product is "produced" at the time of sale or consumption. The buyer/seller relationship is personalized, and therefore substantially influenced by environmental, including cultural, factors. Thus, an advertising agency such as J. Walter Thompson would approach potential clients in Japan with considerable deference to age and seniority and an appreciation for the participative, consensus-style decision making typically found in larger Japanese firms. This would require an extensive and patient selling effort.

The Manufacturing Industries

In manufacturing, the MNE is also often quite marketing intensive. On the one hand, it may seek to maintain competitiveness by extending product life cycles through advertising, packaging, branding, distribution, and the like. On the other hand, it monitors changing market needs and may respond to them by introducing new products. Heinz catsup, for example, has been around for nearly a century, but its plastic, squeezable bottle is less than five years old. The new sales generated by this ostensibly simple packaging innovation have helped Heinz capture over 50 percent of the U.S. catsup market. Over a third of the company's revenues now come from products new to Heinz in the past decade—such as Weight Watchers frozen dinners and Chico-San rice cakes. Heinz has capitalized on recent trends toward nutritious dieting and natural foods.

Complexity of Marketing Management in MNEs

Marketing management is typically seen as involving functional expertise that is especially pertinent at the SBU level. But there is more to this in an MNE context. At the international level, the MNE/SBU tries to identify and implement marketing strategies and programs that benefit in one area from experiences gained in other areas or that can effect positive scale economies by allocating fixed costs (for example, in R&D related to product development) over two or more markets. At this level, marketing management can be dealing both with a number of products that are in various life-cycle stages in a single market area and with single products that are in various life-cycle stages, depending on the market area. This means that strategies, staffing, and other functions are more complicated and demanding both within individual markets and internationally.

The key points here are that marketing management is more complex in the MNE than in the non-MNE and that MNE/SBUs with global marketing responsibilities must respond to two major issues—one dealing with the environmental variations and similarities that affect marketing strategies and programs, the other focusing on the internal operations that can give rise to competitive strengths unique to the MNE (see Figure 13-1). Responding to these issues effectively is marketing management's challenge.

This chapter considers both issues. The environmental analysis is especially important to the MNE in dealing with the unification or fragmentation influences[1] that affect product, place, price, or promotion—the traditional four Ps of marketing. The internal analysis is important in implementing marketing programs that successfully utilize opportunities to benefit from scale economies in production, R&D, and so on, as well as opportunities to benefit from experiences in one market that make the firm more effective (profitable) in other markets. First, we discuss marketing management and the expanding importance of environmental and internal analyses as the MNE evolves from emergent to mature. Then we examine the four Ps, fairly extensively, in the context of the international marketing environment.

Marketing Management and the Evolution of the MNE

Accidental Exporting

As noted in Chapter 12, "Strategy and Structure," many of today's large MNEs began their international involvement via accidental, or fortuitous, exporting in the 1950s and early 1960s. In those days, export marketing management was fairly simple. The product was determined to suit the domestic market, as was the price. There was no deliberate promotional program aimed at foreign markets, and often distribution was either the buyer's responsibility

Figure 13-1 **Marketing Management in the MNE**

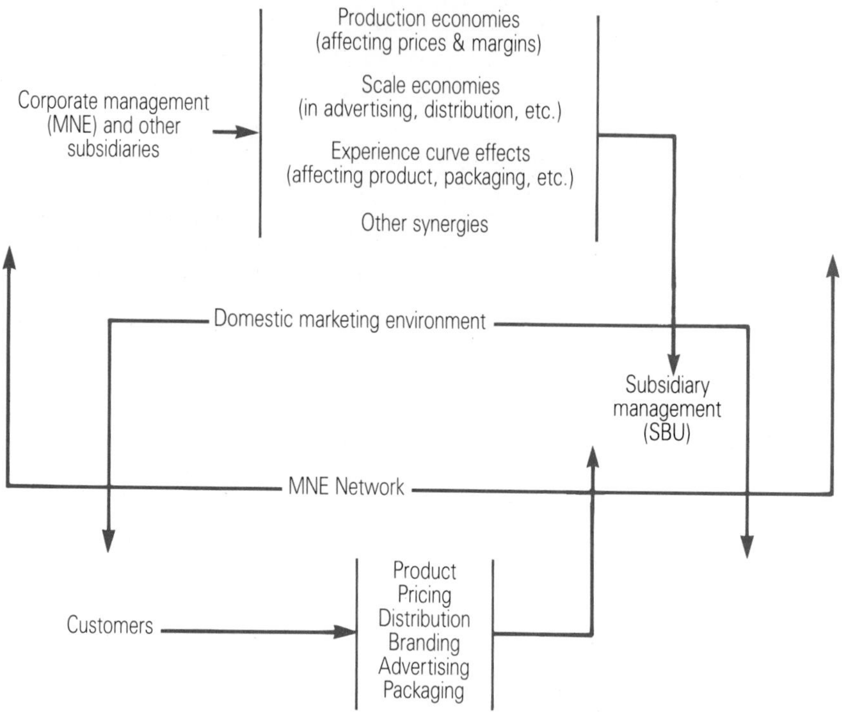

or just involved shipment to the domestically based exporter that was buying the product. The same packaging and warranty policies that were used in domestic sales were also used in foreign sales.

Deliberate Exporting

As foreign sales grew, deliberate exports displaced accidental exports and the producer's participation in international marketing began to expand. Sales representatives were assigned to foreign markets and producer-developed distribution channels were now used. Logistics received increasing management attention. Product pricing strategies became more market based, but this presented some special problems. One of these problems concerned the cost add-ons associated with exporting, such as shipping, insurance, tariffs, and packaging; another concerned the currency required. (In these times, exports were nearly always denominated in dollars. This put currency risk on the foreign customer.) Operating margins were required to cover the cost add-ons. Prices had to be high enough to do this while still leaving room for profits. What product adaptation there was at this time generally centered on technical modifications to meet foreign use conditions. Foreign marketing research was embryonic. Follow-up service was just being developed, and its absence presented a real barrier to more successful market penetration—a situation not unlike the one facing many of the U.S. firms that sought to export to Japan in the mid-1980s.

When a firm established an international department, marketing management grew in importance. Extensive foreign sales offices were set up, as were warehouses and repair centers. Exports were now a substantial portion of total sales and there was increasing integration between domestic and foreign marketing groups on product planning, production scheduling, and so on. Foreign marketing research expanded, and the firm was beginning to look for synergies in product design and promotional appeal between the domestic and foreign markets.

Producing in Foreign Markets

With the onset of foreign direct investment, marketing activities and the importance of marketing management increased dramatically. (For many firms, this took place in the late 1960s.) The defensive nature of this initial investment (recall the discussion on this subject in Chapter 12) meant that foreign markets were becoming very competitive for firms that were merely exporting to them. Producing overseas gave rise to new products that were designed to closely fit foreign market needs. Marketing research for foreign markets blossomed. Distribution channels were shortened and redefined. Given the heightened competition, promotional activities (including advertising) expanded. Competitive pricing strategies became commonplace, as did pricing in local currencies. Margins were tighter. Firms began looking for competitive advantages through scale economies in marketing via product R&D, distribution, advertising, and so on.

Marketing and the Mature MNE

Over time, the management response to these kinds of competitive pressures culminated in what by the mid-1970s had come to be called the **mature MNE.** In this organizational form, effective international marketing management is crucial. Such management involves coordinating, among the parent and its subsidiaries, product development and new product introduction strategies, taking advantage of experiences in one market to improve positions in other markets, benefiting from scale economies in production and marketing, and so on—while paying close attention to the distinctiveness of some markets and what this implies with regard to decentralized, market-specific strategies and operations.

This discussion of marketing and the MNE underscores the effect of the environment on the MNE's marketing strategies and decisions. The changing environment facing the MNE results in both structural and operational changes within the MNE. Understanding international marketing management requires a more detailed knowledge of these varied environmental influences—our next subject.

The International Marketing Environment and Its Challenges to MNEs

The world is indeed complex, and a review of each market—nuance by nuance—would be impossible to accomplish in a text such as this. The decision-oriented nature of management suggests that a more appropriate approach to the environment would be to focus on decision topics and to center on concepts. Marketing's **four Ps**—product, price, place, and promotion—require management decisions and make up the **marketing mix,** a term that identifies marketing both strategically and operationally. Our discussion of the environment centers on the four Ps.

Product

Producers view products as having a distinctive configuration that is definable and reproducible. The **product** can be anything from an American Express card, which is governed by a set of policies determining its use while limiting the company's exposure and risk, to a Nissan 300 ZX sports car, which is produced by means of a deliberate and controlled process to guarantee product quality and costs. Consumers, however, view products as satisfying needs. To many, the American Express card provides global liquidity and connotes a sense of personal financial maturity and the 300 ZX reinforces a self-image of youthfulness and excitement. Marketing management's first task is to identify consumer needs and define their product impact (e.g., how these needs influence product design).

Is consumer electronics a global industry or not? From the consumer's viewpoint, what gives rise to such global uniformity regarding product design and performance?

Click/Chicago/Mark Segal

Research indicates that consumer needs are usually determined by economic (e.g., income) and sociocultural (e.g., legal, religious, cultural) factors. The American Express card and the 300 ZX, for example, are popular with high-income consumers and have a sort of "universal," cross-country appeal. Within country markets, consumers and nonconsumers of these products would correlate well with high and low income levels, respectively. In contrast, some products—foods, clothing, shelter, and the like—are more culture based. To some extent, **culture-based products** tend to be "necessities" and **income-based products** tend to be "discretionary" purchases. Given these market-based characteristics of consumer buying behavior, rising or high income levels facilitate a product policy that transcends country or cultural barriers. Cultural characteristics, on the other hand, make for a variety of discrete markets, which, in turn, leads to a fragmented product policy—that is, the design of different products to serve different markets.

Cultural Change and the Youth of Today

Japanese youth like to munch on Big Macs. Russian youth love blue jeans. American youth jog along with their Sony Walkman radios. They all idolize the same rock stars and drool over the same "hot" cars. The youth of today seem to have a lot in common—no matter where they live.

Not so with the older folk! They value "tradition" more. In fact, in some societies the young and the old even see themselves as belonging to different cultures. The young are always seen as a problem. There is genuine concern over what the future holds for them and with how the different generations "get along."

Two conditions come to mind. First, young people are not yet settled in their ways. They are just establishing their own identities and are therefore generally quite open to change. Second, income has been advancing in almost every society, so that many of the youth of today are concerned only with discretionary spending—they get the necessities at home. These two conditions favor both homogeneous, cross-cultural behavior and products that are truly multinational. Do you agree or not? Why?

Actually, a variety of factors—some compelling, others not—exert fragmentation, or decentralization, influences on product design and packaging. *For discussion purposes,* let us begin with the idea that a product can be the same (i.e., standardized) in the foreign market as it is in the home market, and put the burden of justifying **product modification** on foreign market factors. What could justify product modification?

Technical Factors All products must be technically consistent with their environments. A classic example is the voltage of electric current which may vary (e.g., from 110 volts in the United States to 220 volts in Europe). Another is the use of different measurements by different countries, such as feet and pounds instead of meters and kilograms. Production technology may differ from one country to another. The availability of capital equipment or highly skilled workers may also vary country by country. These differences, in turn, may affect product design or quality. Certain raw materials may be unavailable locally. Import restrictions or economic factors may force products and production processes to be altered so that available raw materials can be utilized.

Use Conditions Products may be used in drastically different conditions from one market to another. Western Europe's long history of urban development, with villages and cities having narrow roads to accommodate the horses and buggies of days gone by, has certainly influenced automobile size. The bumpy brick roads often found in older towns and the often poorly maintained roads in rural areas mean that more durable autos and tires have to be built. Climatic conditions, transportation capabilities, and storage facilities all influence product configuration.

Legal Environment The variations in laws from country to country affect products in numerous ways. Many countries have safety and pollution control standards. Products must be modified to meet these standards—for example, automobiles imported into the United States since the mid-1960s, when special safety regulations went into effect. (It might be noted that British Leyland Motor Corporation's Austin-Healey sports car was withdrawn from the U.S. market at that time because management decided not to adjust its classic design to meet the new safety requirements.) Foods and drugs are also usually heavily regulated areas, as is noise abatement. Terpstra reports, for example, that British lawn mowers are kept off the German market because they do not meet Germany's stringent noise control laws and that countries differ considerably in the amount of sugar, fruit, and juice they allow in jam, the amount of water they allow in canned fruit and vegetables, and the preservatives they allow in cereals.[2] Developing countries frequently limit the number of models of a product and the prices at which products may be sold. Any of these legally imposed constraints obviously affect product design.

Use conditions and the technical and legal environments leave a firm that wants to serve a particular market little room for discretion. Other factors—both economic and sociocultural—allow firms varying degrees of discretion with regard to product adaptation. These factors include income levels and income dispersion, educational levels, and consumer tastes and preferences.

Income What people earn determines what they can afford. Regardless of overall income level, many countries are similar in that they all have a high-income stratum that has the discretionary income to afford the big-ticket item. Certain items, then, such as French perfumes, are used in all of these countries by persons with high incomes. Key variables here, aside from income levels and income structure, include the size of the various income groups and their effective purchasing power. Country markets may, in some cases, be dominated by higher or lower-income classes. In such cases, the kinds of products or product variations that will sell in the high-income countries differ considerably from the kinds that will sell in the low-income countries.

It is not unusual, for instance, for stripped-down versions of products sold in high-income areas to be marketed in low-income areas. For example, Singer sells a line of sewing machines in parts of Africa that are often simple and handpowered; in Europe, it sells a line of electrical machines with insertable cams to automate complicated patterns. Income levels and the dispersion of income help define market size, which, in turn, influences the selection of process technology and product configuration.

Education The general level of education affects product decisions both directly and indirectly. A highly literate market, for example, would typically demand more complex products. Product sophistication should match consumer sophistication. Computers and other electronic apparatus find limited markets where illiteracy prevails, as, in general, do products with complicated maintenance requirements, such as chain saws.

Consumer Tastes and Preferences What consumers desire is often related to culture—as discussed in Chapter 11, "Dealing with the Cultural Environment." Toyota learned this the hard way in 1956, when it designed a small car for the Japanese market that it thought would be adaptable to the U.S. market.[3] The home market version had a 20-horsepower engine and a top speed of 62 miles per hour. It weighed nearly three quarters of a ton, and it was not fuel efficient as compared to other small cars being sold in the United States. The lack of fuel efficiency turned off small-car lovers, the smallness was unappealing to consumers who wanted style, and the performance characteristics were just not attractive. The car, which was marketed under the name Toyopet (a self-deprecating name at best), presented a confused message to American consumers and flopped. No firm can afford to ignore consumer tastes and preferences.

The history of the MNE, brief as it is, contains numerous examples of firms that have misread local market preferences for products of certain sizes, configurations, colors, and so on.[4] For example, Campbell Soup, an American company, had difficulty in adjusting its products to suit the tastes of its European consumers. Knorr Soup, a European company, found it difficult to break into the U.S. market with its dehydrated soups in the face of the preference of U.S. consumers for soup in liquid form.

MNEs' Responses Firms must decide whether or how they want to respond to the aforementioned economic and sociocultural factors. What would Campbell sell in Europe if it had not sweetened its tomato soup? Marginal analysis would be the appropriate method to employ here. What would be the sales revenues and costs if the product were not adapted to accommodate local influences? What would they be if it were? What alternative approaches might be taken? Which alternative is the most profitable?

Interestingly, one could argue that product analysis by the MNE should always seek to favor standardization, since it is in standardization that the MNE has competitive strengths vis-à-vis other firms. In this sense, MNEs can be seen as market leaders in market segments where tastes and preferences are converging internationally and where products (or product cores) are thus being standardized internationally.

Price

Setting a product price is a difficult task at best. Ideally, the firm prefers as few constraints as possible on its product pricing. The only constraint that most firms want to accept is that imposed by competition, but even then the typical corporate strategy is to reduce or eliminate the effect of competition on pricing, for example, through the implementation of a strategy involving product differentiation. Firms want to set prices so that they can maximize profits under the given market conditions. Multinationals have more than this to deal with, however. Price strategy for a global market must accommodate considerations that would not exist otherwise, or at least would be less pressing. These considerations include price escalation when exporting, transfer pricing, dumping, price controls, and price differentials among segmented markets. Each of these considerations is explained in the text that follows.

Price Escalation when Exporting The term **price escalation when exporting** refers to the percentage add-ons to the ex-factory price of a product by the middlemen that make up the distribution network and by tariffs, as the product goes from domestic producer to foreign customer. The ex-factory price is amplified by the combined amount of these add-ons, multiplied by one another. Distribution channels are typically lengthier when exporting than when selling domestically. For the MNE exporting an end product, price escalation cuts into sales and profits by biasing the product's final price upward. For the MNE exporting component parts or subassemblies, on the other hand, although price escalation still exists, it is not as big a problem. There is less price escalation for components and subassemblies than for end products, and the effect is thus less than otherwise. The value added by the foreign-based production is not exposed to price escalation. Also, the MNE typically handles the international distribution of components and subassemblies in-house (via commercial shippers), where costs are not subject to percentage add-ons.

Transfer Pricing What a subsidiary is charged by another subsidiary or the parent company for the intracompany sale of a product or part is termed the **transfer price.** For the exporting unit, the transfer price affects sales revenues; for the importing unit, it affects costs. The transfer price also affects the amount of money that flows between the exporting and importing units (the goods transferred have to paid for), the amount of the tariffs paid on the transferred items, and the amount of the profits (or losses) realized at each unit (since transferred goods are part of the cost of goods sold at the importing unit and part of the total income received at the exporting unit). If firms were totally free to set transfer prices as they wished and were not concerned about where funds were accumulated in the MNE network, they would probably do the following on parts sent to subsidiaries:

1. Set prices high in countries where income taxes are high.
2. Set prices low where imports come in at high tariffs.
3. Set prices high where the parent company has a problem in getting profits out of the country where a subsidiary is located.
4. Set prices low if income taxes in the parent country are high.

In reality, the MNE is not really free to set transfer prices in whatever manner it wishes, because governments are generally concerned about the amounts of income taxes and tariffs collected. At best, the price set by the company is justifiable, reasonable, and acceptable to the government. Typically, an arm's-length price, one that would be set between two unrelated firms in a competitive marketplace, is deemed acceptable. Alternatively, the price may be negotiable between the company and the government agency involved—and be pegged at a justifiable and reasonable level. At worst, from the company's perspective, the government sets the price at whatever level it wants to and collects taxes and tariffs accordingly. Deliberate attempts by MNEs to present their records in a fraudulent manner to evade taxes or tariffs are, of course, illegal—criminal acts. For internal accounting and control

---

Amway's Tariff Troubles

In 1982, Amway Corporation's board chairman, president, executive vice president, and vice president were charged with criminal fraud by the Canadian government. The case involved allegations by Canadians that imports into Canada by Amway of Canada, Ltd. were deliberately undervalued for years to avoid payment of the proper Canadian customs duties. In addition to the criminal case, the Canadian government filed a U.S. $122 million civil suit against Amway Corporation to recover the alleged lost duties.

In the criminal court case the following year, the prosecution contended that Amway presented hundreds of false invoices and fictitious sales lists to Canadian customs officials. The case ended with an agreed-upon arrangement between the government and Amway that included the dropping of criminal charges against the four Amway executives and the payment of a C$25 million fine.

In 1986, the civil case went to court and Amway lost a C$113 million judgment as the government sought to claim lost customs revenues.

Source: "Amway's 4 Top Aides Fail to Show in Canada to Face Fraud Charges," *The Wall Street Journal,* December 1, 1982, p. 18; "Amway and Unit to Pay $25 Million Fine on Canadian Government Fraud Charges," *The Wall Street Journal,* November 11, 1983, p. 8; and "Amway Will Appeal Four Canadian Orders in a Customs Battle," *The Wall Street Journal,* June 20, 1986, p. 35.

---

purposes, however, a company can use whatever transfer prices it wants to use.

Dumping Another major concern that affects the pricing strategies of MNEs is **dumping.** The General Agreement on Tariffs and Trade (GATT) forbids selling products in export markets at less than the prices for which they are sold in the home market. This restriction is meant to preclude the introduction of disruptive, predatory pricing practices whereby, for example, an exporter could establish a monopoly in a foreign market by pricing deceptively low to drive competitors out of that market—and then increase its prices at will. Under GATT, a country can erect a retaliatory tariff to offset dumping. (Chapter 8 discussed some of these issues.)

Dumping and Protectionism Put Pressure on the Japanese

GATT's dumping regulations and Japan's protectionist policies on the home front are an "odd couple" pressuring Japanese VCR manufacturers to open U.S. plants. What makes the situation even stranger is that the Koreans are really behind it all.

Korean-made videocassette recorders, manufactured under license from the Japanese, are competing head-on with Japanese VCRs in the American market. (*Note:* There are no U.S. VCR manufacturers. Even RCA, General Electric, and Zenith buy their VCRs from the Japanese.) So far, the Koreans have not undercut the Japanese prices—but pressures are building for a price tumble. The problem is that no such competitive pressures are being applied by the Koreans in the Japanese home market. The Japanese would be in violation of GATT if they lowered their prices in the United States while maintaining their present prices in Japan. Consequently, industry watchers expect Japanese VCR makers to move rather quickly in setting up U.S.-based VCR production. This would free them to price according to market conditions in both Japan and the United States.

Source: This highlighted feature is based on "Japanese VCRs May Soon Say 'Made in the U.S.A.,'" *Business Week,* August 5, 1985, pp. 36–37.

Price Controls Governments, especially governments in developing countries, have been known to set product prices. But from time to time, **price controls** also appear even in developed countries—in the United States, for example, in the early 1970s. Price controls can present some real problems. Some MNEs have abandoned foreign markets because of their inability to price products at profitable levels. Price controls are typically evident in markets where there are inflationary pressures, and they are usually applied in both product and resource markets. As a result of local political pressures, wages are sometimes allowed to advance, while the firm is not allowed to pass this cost increase along in the form of a higher product price. Profits

Canada, and the Caribbean Basin. The U.S. subsidiary, Aerospatiale Helicopter Corporation (AHC), also maintains spares and maintenance bases in Mexico and Canada—where parts from both the parent and AHC are inventoried. The U.S. subsidiary purchases engines and avionics from U.S. suppliers (Lycoming and Collins, respectively) and manufactures and installs its own interiors. A similar sourcing pattern exists at the Brazilian subsidiary. The French parent markets fully assembled helicopters throughout Western Europe and parts of Asia. Sales in Eastern Europe are accomplished through licensees in Rumania and Yugoslavia and in parts of Asia through licensees in India and Indonesia. These licensees import components and subassemblies, including engines and avionics, from France and provide locally manufactured interiors.

More complicated patterns of logistics networks could be presented, but the conclusions would remain the same: (1) intracorporate product transfers combined with local sourcing can be intricate and costly to establish and maintain, and (2) their efficient management is essential to the competitiveness of the firm. Viewed slightly differently, one could conceptualize that geographically distributed production facilities provide the MNE with cost efficiencies that enhance competitiveness and profitability but that the movement of parts and products among these facilities results in distribution costs that diminish the cost savings resulting from these location advantages. The value of effective, internal communication pertains to both the establishment and the operation of geographically distributed facilities. The whole "problem" is best resolved through linear programming, with the optimal solution considering not only direct shipping and packaging costs but also inventory charges and the scale economies realized in production when a single production site serves multiple markets.

On this last point, an interesting illustration was provided by Ford Motor's international sourcing patterns on four-cylinder engines. Early in the 1970s, Ford-Britain put a new four-cylinder engine plant on-stream to serve both the British and U.S. markets. As demand in the UK grew, production for the U.S. market was shifted to a new Ford-Brazil plant. Eventually, as both Brazilian and U.S. demand grew, production was shifted to a new Ford-U.S. plant.[7]

Decisions regarding distribution systems within countries must consider a set of variables totally different from those related to global logistic networks, where costs and timing are the key concerns. With **in-country distribution,** cost and timing are again important, but local conditions, institutions, and cultural influences are also important.

One approach to in-country distribution is to secure the services of distributors outside the firm which are, in turn, responsible for the selling of the product in their respective countries or local markets. In this instance, the MNE is accessing the foreign market through indirect exporting. It is effectively buying local expertise, but it can no longer determine distribution costs, ensure product quality, and maintain timely delivery schedules. (The classic case of the French wine producer that exported to the United States through local agents comes to mind here. The U.S. importing company let thousands of bottles sit in a New York warehouse during a winter freeze. The wine was ruined, but the importer sold it anyway—at depressed prices. It took the French vintner several decades to overcome the bad product image caused by this importer's indiscretion.)

Indirect exporting may be the only sensible approach, however, for smaller MNEs or for MNEs serving smaller markets. Moreover, the loss of control will vary, depending on just which form of indirect exporting is selected. The loss is greatest when ownership of the product is transferred to a buyer that, in turn, exports the product to the foreign market. Examples here include **export commission agents,** which buy on behalf of foreign clients; **export merchants,** which buy for their own account and then sell to foreign customers; and **international trading companies,** which, like export merchants, buy for their own account but then often sell in the foreign market through their parent companies. The Japanese *sogo sosha,* such firms as Mitsui and C. Itoh, are classic examples of international trading companies. More recently, however, such firms as General Electric and K mart have established international trading companies. In the United States, the Export Trading Company Act, passed in 1982, enables small and medium-sized U.S. firms—companies that are often too small to go after foreign markets—to combine export operations in a separate **export trading company,** exempt from antitrust law so long as this does not adversely affect their competitive practices in the domestic market. Bank holding companies are permitted to hold stock in export trading companies—a privilege that is designed to make financial services more readily available to potential customers.

Indirect exporting may also involve using agents that export on behalf of a supplier without taking title to the exported goods. Such agents include **manufacturer's export agents** and **export management companies**—firms that represent several noncompeting manufacturers overseas and often even provide shipping and promotional services. (International trading companies and export management companies, it should be mentioned, may buy and sell for their own account and may operate on a commission basis.)

Most MNEs serve their major foreign markets through direct exporting or foreign-based production. During direct exporting, these firms may or may not procure logistics support, such as that offered by freight forwarders, customs brokers, and distributors. Similarly, foreign-based production to serve foreign markets would probably involve local distributors, wholesalers, and retailers. Whether or not to use such intermediaries is essentially a "make or buy" decision that turns on comparative costs, operating margins, or other expectations related to sales or profits. These factors are, in turn, likely to be influenced by local conditions, institutions, and culture.

For example, the average size of wholesalers and retailers is considerably smaller in the markets of smaller countries than in the markets of larger countries.[8] Also, both wholesaling and retailing are generally more atomized outside the United States than within the United States. This may require the MNE to work with several, parallel channels within a country market, and to stand prepared to provide channel participants with inventory and technical support on a timely basis. If the firm were a U.S. MNE, this would represent a different way of doing business than it was accustomed to at home.

Promotion

When a firm is dealing with the four Ps of marketing, **promotion** is probably the one in which the environmental influence is greatest. Promotion seeks to activate the motivation to purchase by conveying the information that the firm needs to get across the desirability of its product. Promotion typically deals with advertising, personal selling, and sales promotion—which usually involves brochures, displays, exhibitions, samples, and so on. However, promotion does not exist alone. Place and price, for example, are often closely related to promotion, as are product design features and product quality. How often have we heard that a product "sells itself" or that there is a 20 percent price discount during a special promotional period? Promotion, as noted, more often just relates to advertising, personal selling, and sales promotion. Promotion is normally place specific and therefore very culture-bound.

Promotion Practices Vary Internationally In many countries, legislation or industry practices significantly affect advertising. In the United States, for example, such products as liquor and cigarettes cannot be advertised on television, and advertising messages, regardless of media, are subject to "truth in advertising" standards. In Sweden and Great Britain, among other countries, advertising is subject to a "purchase" tax just like that paid on a product purchased in a store. In some countries, governments must preapprove advertisements for certain kinds of products. In yet others, certain media, such as television, may not be available for advertising. Restrictions of these kinds often lead to what the MNE may consider creative forms of advertising, such as billboard advertising at local soccer fields.

Global surveys related to advertising show considerable differences among countries in both media selection and per capita advertising outlays.[9] In the United States, for example, 38 percent of all advertising outlays are spent on print media; in Jamaica, 47 percent; and in Peru, 14 percent. In the United States, 20 percent of all advertising outlays are spent on the TV media; in Jamaica, 15 percent, and in Peru, 42 percent. In Jamaica, advertising expenditures absorb about 1.0 percent of GNP (gross national product), which is about half of advertising's share of GNP in the United States but nearly seven times its share in India. Among the factors affecting these distributions are literacy, living standards, infrastructural development, and regulation.

Because of language, ethnic, and religious differences among customers, **personal selling,** by its very nature, is largely country- or subcountry-bound. This is especially true for consumer goods firms, whose personal selling is mainly concentrated among the wholesalers and retailers with

From Picadilly to Prague, Coca-Cola's logo blends in with youthfulness and vitality.

Click/Chicago/D and J Heaton
Click/Chicago/Bob Brudd

which the firm deals. For firms dealing with intermediate goods, economic factors typically become more important in the purchase decision. Such firms often put together selling teams so that all the relevant expertise—marketing, technical, financial, and so on—can be brought to bear on the purchase decision. One could also argue that mature intermediate products will involve personal selling that is more culture- or country-bound than the selling of innovative products, whose producers have more control or influence over the purchase decision.

The Promotion Strategies of MNEs For the multinational enterprise seeking to obtain and implement competitive advantages, the question of the global standardization of promotional strategies and campaigns is quite important. To some extent, scale economies do exist, for example, in advertising—that is, in advertising research, copy preparation, and so on. The big plus, however, is the experience effect. A successful promotional campaign in one market may indeed bode well for similar successes in other markets. As mentioned earlier, income-related influences on consumers' tastes and preferences often override cultural and country-related influences in the product-specific areas that are more likely dominated by MNEs. Cross-cultural and cross-country similarities that correspond to similarities in income levels provide a rationale for similarities in promotional campaigns. To the extent that an MNE can transform a promotional program in one country into a competitively superior or more timely program in another country, it will be benefiting from an experience effect. The business world is replete with examples of this process. Marketing-intensive firms such as Coca-Cola, Heinz, Ford Motor, and Exxon have successfully developed and implemented international promotional programs.

Conclusions

International marketing management varies considerably, depending on the product and the market. For the global MNE, the challenge is to create and sustain a competitive edge based on experiences elsewhere or on scale economies that are unavailable to other firms.

International marketing management has changed considerably within the MNE as the MNE has grown and matured. In the early years, product and price were set by domestic demand conditions and exports were mainly fortuitous. Later, firms became more deliberate regarding exports. Technical adaptation to foreign product markets began, as did more direct involvement in the logistics function. As export markets grew, international departments, foreign marketing activities, and production integration between foreign and domestic markets evolved. Direct foreign investment, itself occasioned by the need for enhanced competitiveness in foreign markets, expanded the nature of the marketing function dramatically. New products were introduced. Pricing strategies became more market specific, and promotion and distribution were subjected to closer local control. In today's mature MNE, the keys to success are parent-subsidiary coordination on production and marketing issues and close attention to the distinctive characteristics of local markets. This contention was examined more closely as each of the major decision-making areas of marketing management—categorized in terms of marketing's traditional four Ps—was discussed.

Product is defined by the nature of consumers' needs and is substantially influenced by both culture and income levels. Culture and the local economic and institutional settings make for the fragmentation of products; higher and rising income levels generally make for the unification of products. More specifically, technical factors often result in product modifications to meet local market needs. Use conditions, climate, transportation capabilities, and storage facilities, which may differ from market to market, also lead to product adaptations—as do legal, income, educational, and consumer influences and maintenance requirements.

Most firms, including MNEs, want as much freedom as possible with regard to *price*, so that they can price according to market conditions and, hopefully, maximize revenues and profits. The product pricing of the MNE must accommodate a set of considerations broader than the set of conditions that must be accommodated by the exclusively domestic firm. Price escalation when exporting—the result of the percentage add-ons of channel participants and tariffs—multiplies ex-factory price increases. Transfer pricing on items that move between units within the MNE can affect overall revenues, the direction of revenue flows, and the taxes and duties paid in different countries. Transfer prices are generally closely scrutinized by governments. Dumping, which involves selling at unfairly low prices in foreign markets, is prohibited by GATT. Price controls are another concern of the MNE. At one time or another, many countries set product and resource prices—leaving the MNE with few short-run options. Finally, the problem of maintaining price differentials among markets that are otherwise segmented is also germane to the MNE. While markets maintain a geographic separation, certain segments across geographic boundaries may be developing into homogeneous markets. This presents the MNE with a pricing problem as it seeks to maintain price differentials among location-specific and product-specific markets.

Place is important to the MNE as both a strategy variable and an operations concern. In the strategic context, MNEs have the capability to identify lead markets that provide them with internationally transferable experiences and integrated production practices that result in competitive advantages. As an operations concern, global logistics networks can be very complex in mature MNEs and their efficient and timely operation can contribute to the competitive advantages of MNEs. In-country distribution systems are similarly important, but they are influenced to a greater extent by local conditions, institutions, and cultures. Firms may engage in indirect exporting—thus buying local expertise at the cost of losing control. They may export directly and they may produce and distribute within the foreign market—thus requiring flexibility and adaptation as operational hallmarks and management characteristics.

Promotion is probably the most environmentally influenced of the four Ps. It can take on many forms, and it can follow from decisions made regarding product, price, and place. However, promotion generally pertains to advertising and personal selling—both of which are substantially influenced by market-specific factors. Personal selling, by its very nature, is fairly culture-bound. For the MNE, the challenge is to find promotional strategies and programs that are transferable internationally. Cost savings is one incentive here, but the experience effect as related to the potential effectiveness of programs is considerably more important.

Questions

1. What are the two major issues confronting marketing management in the MNE? How does marketing management in the MNE differ from marketing management in a purely domestic firm, if at all?
2. How have the emergence and maturation of the multinational enterprise influenced the development of the international marketing management function? The domestic marketing management function?
3. Rising personal income generally expands discretionary purchasing power. How does this fact benefit the global marketing presence of the MNE?
4. Identify the main factors influencing product design among MNEs—especially the factors that exert fragmentation pressures. What should the MNE be doing in the face of such pressure?
5. Identify the main factors influencing the pricing strategy of MNEs. Is the maintenance of price differentials among segmented markets unique to

MNEs? What similarities and differences might exist between a domestic firm that is trying to maintain a market segmentation strategy via product differentation and an MNE that is trying to maintain a market segmentation strategy across geographically segmented markets for a single product?

6. How has the desire of Japanese VCR manufacturers to maintain price differentials in geographically segmented markets (e.g., Japan and the United States) led to allegations of dumping, a practice disallowed by GATT, and to subsequent pressures on the Japanese to manufacture VCRs in the United States?
7. What are the major features of the lead market concept as a tool for strategic marketing planning?
8. How does the operations variable "place" affect the competitive strategy of MNEs? Characterize the importance of logistics in MNE competitive strategy as the MNE has evolved from emergent to mature.
9. What are the main points with regard to in-country distribution that an MNE must consider? What are the trade-offs with regard to in-country distribution strategy that the MNE has to evaluate?
10. Why is the question of the globally standardized advertising campaign relevant to an MNE?

References

Boddewyn, Jean J. "Comparative Marketing: The First 25 Years." *Journal of International Business Studies,* Spring-Summer 1981, pp. 61-80.

Cateora, Philip. *International Marketing.* Homewood, Ill.: Richard D. Irwin, 1983.

Doyle, Peter; John Saunders; and Veronica Wong. "A Comparative Study of Japanese Marketing Strategies in the British Market." *Journal of International Business Studies,* Spring 1986, pp. 27-46.

Kaynak, Erdener. *Marketing in the Third World.* New York: Praeger Publishers, 1982.

Levitt, Theodore. "The Globalization of Markets." *Harvard Business Review,* May-June 1983, pp. 92-102.

Majaro, Simon. *International Marketing: A Strategic Approach to World Markets.* London: Allen & Unwin, 1984.

Walters, Peter G. P. "International Marketing Policy: A Discussion of the Standardization Construct and Its Relevance for Corporate Policy." *Journal of International Business Studies,* Summer 1986, pp. 55-70.

Endnotes

1. Unification and fragmentation influences refer to concepts initially identified by John Fayerweather. A unification influence facilitates the global strategy and competitive distinctiveness of MNEs. A fragmentation influ-

ence requires a location-specific response from the firm. See John Fayerweather, *International Business Strategy and Administration* (Cambridge, Mass.: Ballinger Publishing, 1982), pp. 300-327.

2. Vern Terpstra, *International Dimensions of Marketing* (Boston: Kent Publishing, 1982), p. 89. Some of the other examples in this section are also noted in this reference.
3. "Toyota Concern to Build Car to Sell for $1,250," *New York Times,* February 9, 1956, p. 2.
4. For numerous examples, see David Ricks, *Big Business Blunders* (Homewood, Ill.: Richard D. Irwin, 1983).
5. David P. Rutenberg, *Multinational Management* (Boston: Little, Brown, 1982), chap. 1, "Organizational Structures and Tensions" (First National City Bank case), pp. 1-9.
6. This concern was first expressed in Jean-Jacques Servan-Schreiber, *The American Challenge* (New York: Atheneum Publishers, 1968).
7. Information obtained during interviews with Ford Motor Company's world headquarters staff, Dearborn, Michigan, in 1971 and 1972. See also "Cleveland Plant to Manufacture Pinto Engine Castings," *Iron News,* November 1971, p. 4; and "Ford to Build Mavericks in Brazil; Plans $150 Million Investment," *The Wall Street Journal,* March 3, 1972, p. 3
8. Terpstra, *International Dimensions,* pp. 125 and 127, as derived from *Statistical Yearbook* (New York: United Nations, 1979), table 147.
9. Terpstra, *International Dimensions,* p. 159.

Case
Monster Chomp Cookies in Brazil

Beatrice Companies, Inc. is a highly diversified producer of processed foods, beverages, consumer products, chemicals, and other products in 30 countries, with sales offices and licensees in over 120 more. In 1984, Beatrice's sales were about $12 billion worldwide, with U.S. sales accounting for about three quarters of that amount. In that year, less than 5 percent of Beatrice's sales were made in Latin America, although the company was then a market leader in most of the products it sold in the region.

Beatrice Enters Brazil

Beatrice entered the Brazilian market in 1983, through its acquisition of 80 percent ownership in an existing local firm, Ailiram, S.A. Ailiram was a local manufacturer of cookies and candies in the São Paulo state, selling mainly to retail stores outside the city of São Paulo. Ailiram's cookies were very similar to those sold by dozens of other Brazilian firms—plain, fairly undifferentiated, round cookies and biscuits made of wheat flour and sugar. The company was formed in 1945, and by 1983 it had grown to include two manufacturing plants and 1,000 employees. Beatrice intended to use Ailiram as a base for entering the national Brazilian market, first by pursuing sales to supermarkets—a fast-growing segment for food product distribution—in the city of São Paulo, then by expanding product lines and distribution throughout the whole country.

Soon after the acquisition, managers of the subsidiary were planning a strategy to break into the highly competitive market for sales of cookies to supermarkets. A survey showed that about a dozen other companies already sold similar products to leading supermarkets and that Ailiram would have very little chance to displace any of them unless it produced a new type of cookie.

The Creation of Monster Chomp

On a trip to the United States, one Ailiram executive noticed the highly successful Monster Chomp cookies that were sold there. She felt that this product would have good sales potential in Brazil since cookies of this kind were not being sold in that country. Ailiram's attempt to sell to supermarkets would be greatly enhanced by the appealing packaging of Monstrinho Creck cookies. These would sell at the top end of the cookie market, where only a

This case is reprinted from *Case Studies in International Business for ESL*, by Christine Grosse and Robert Grosse, Prentice-Hall, 1988. Reprinted by permission of Prentice-Hall. Eleven additional cases on international business are available in this same source.

few other brands were competing. By successfully selling Monstrinho Creck cookies, Ailiram would establish an image of high-quality, innovative products and demonstrate to supermarkets that it knew how to mass-market cookies. Both of these goals had been set by Beatrice, which wanted to compete nationally throughout Brazil in both cookie and candy markets.

The Monster Chomps sold in the United States were much thicker and softer than the cookies normally sold in Brazil. Ailiram's managers felt that cookies had to be hard and flat in order to meet Brazilian children's tastes—but that their shape could be unusual. Thus, they decided to produce a hard, flat cookie that looked as if a monster had taken a bite out of it. The flavors initially chosen were chocolate, vanilla, and coconut.

A completely new package design was chosen to appeal to children between the ages of 5 and 12. (A survey showed that children up to the age of 10 accounted for almost 50 percent of Brazilian cookie consumption.) The

Table 1 **Monstrinhos Creck Cookies—Eight-Month Forecast, 1984**

	May	June	July	Aug.	Sept.	Oct.	Nov.	Dec.
Price index	100							166
Retail price (200 grams)	600							
Ailiram sales price (net, 200 grams, Cr$)	400	423	456	484	512	545	578	615
Ailiram sales price (net, 1 kilogram, Cr$)	2,000	2,115	2,280	2,420	2.560	2,725	2,890	3,075
Ailiram sales (tons)	120	350	280	300	330	350	330	300
Net trade sales (Cr$ millions)	240	740	638	726	845	954	954	923

package, shown in the accompanying illustrations, depicts a friendly monster with a chomp out of a cookie on its front. On the back of the package, some child's game is shown and a lesson about safety or some other constructive message is presented. Thus, the package provides both an appealing, funny advertisement and an educational lesson.

The advertising campaign to introduce Monstrinho Creck in the São Paulo area was quite expensive. Initial estimates were for a total marketing cost of about US$500,000. As shown in Tables 1 and 2, this expense would virtually eliminate any profit for the first year of sales. Subsequently, prospects appeared very good for a growing profit margin and greater sales. The expected return on sales of 13-15 percent is similar to that of other Beatrice products, but this expected return does not take into account for the high risk of doing business in Brazil at present (i.e., during the debt crisis of the 1980s).

Table 2 **Monstrinhos Creck Cookies—Three-Year Forecast**

	1984 (8 mos.)	1985	1986
Price index	100	180	260
Exchange rate (average, Cr$)	1,600/US$	2,880/US$	4,160/US$
Avg. Ailiram sales price (net, 1 kilogram, Cr$)	2,551	4,592	6,631
Ailiram sales (tons)	2,360	6,065	7,670

	1984 (8 mos.)		**1985**		**1986**	
	Cr$ mil.	Percent	Cr$ mil.	Percent	Cr$ mil.	Percent
Net trade sales	6,020	100.0	27,850	100.0	50,860	100.0
Cost	3,492	58.0	15,875	57.0	28,990	57.0
Gross margin	2,528	42.0	11,975	43.0	21,870	43.0
Advertising	491	8.2	1,453	5.2	2,107	4.1
Sales promotion, trade	122	2.0	29	0.1	—	—
Sales promotion, consumer	50	0.8	111	0.4	51	0.1
Sales promotion, merchandising	71	1.2	278	1.0	334	0.7
Market research	49	0.8	79	0.3	51	0.1
Total marketing expenses	783	13.0	1,950	7.0	2,543	5.0
Gross contribution	1,745	29.0	10,025	36.0	19,327	38.0
Sales expense	1,264	21.0	5,292	19.0	9,663	19.0
Administrative expense	289	4.8	1,114	4.0	2,034	4.0
Total sales and administrative expense	1,553	25.8	6,406	23.0	11,697	23.0
Profit contribution	192	3.2	3,619	13.0	7,630	15.0

14 ACCOUNTING AND TAXATION

Accounting systems vary considerably country by country. This presents problems for MNEs that have to report operations on a consolidated basis in the system of the parent company's country. Moreover, parent companies must account for foreign purchases and sales and report foreign operations on their own books. Tax systems differ country by country, and MNEs want to avoid being "double-taxed" on profits that subsidiaries earn and send home. This chapter covers such issues. The main goals of the chapter are to:

1. Explain how and why accounting and taxation are different in MNEs than in domestic companies.
2. Explore why countries differ regarding accounting systems.
3. Describe how MNEs account for foreign purchases and sales and report foreign operations on the parent's books.
4. Describe how MNEs report foreign and domestic operations on a consolidated basis, including
   a. The definition and handling of conversion and translation gains and losses.
   b. U.S. financial standards on consolidations and disclosures.
5. Examine how income deferral and foreign tax credits work to the benefit of the MNE.
6. Examine accounting/management information systems in MNEs.
7. Explain how MNEs achieve compliance with the U.S. Foreign Corrupt Practices Act.

Introduction

Accounting and tax matters are typically seen as administrative concerns. Financial reporting requires adherence to a set of prescribed procedures and standards. Tax laws mandate a certain type of record-keeping and reporting and the payment of taxes to the appropriate authorities. For the purely domestic firm, accounting and tax matters do not usually result in competitive advantages—although every manager certainly wants to keep as much profit as possible by minimizing taxes.

Accounting Differences of MNEs

For the MNE, the situation is somewhat different. Accounting and tax matters are obviously more complex, and they can have a direct effect on the MNE's profitability and competitiveness. The astute handling of taxes can, for example, result in legitimate tax avoidance and increased profits or deferred taxes. Why locate profits in Greece, which has a 49 percent tax rate, in contrast to Taiwan, where the rate is 12.5 percent? Also, timely and accurate MNE system-wide financial reporting can lead to more informed management (and better management decisions) and more informed investors (which, hopefully, makes the firm a more attractive investment). Enhanced profits and more effective management should make the firm more competitive. Relationships among competitiveness, multinational operations, international accounting, and taxation will be visited at various points in this chapter.

Financial accounting systems differ country by country, and managers in multinational firms must be aware of these differences to know what information their accounting records are really conveying. For similar reasons, managers must be aware of the special circumstances and rules affecting the handling of international transactions and the parent company's consolidated statements reporting on the MNE's global situation. Financial accounting at the subsidiary and parent levels reflects not only traditional accounting practices but also laws and regulations regarding disclosure (with publicly held companies) and taxation. Variations in accounting practices and in exchange rates, which alter the unit of measurement, complicate the financial accounting systems of MNEs.

In addition to financial accounting systems, most firms utilize managerial accounting systems or managerial information systems that reflect, in some cases, slight modifications to financial accounting data already generated or, in other cases, the collection and presentation of additional data useful for managerial control purposes. This chapter deals with managerial accounting when the firm is operating cross-nationally and cross-culturally. (In general, management control systems are discussed in Chapter 15 in the section on control.)

Tax Differences of MNEs

Tax laws also differ country by country. Moreover, tax laws must address the location of income and define the territorial extent of the jurisdiction of the taxing authorities. Taxation at just the domestic level can be quite complex. It can be even more complex at the international level. This chapter presents some highlights regarding taxation in the MNE. It discusses key tax topics relating to multinational operations, such as deferral, Subpart F income, and foreign tax credits. It also discusses the tax advantages of using a foreign sales corporation. A final section of the chapter deals with management responsibilities under the U.S. Foreign Corrupt Practices Act.

Accounting

Because accounting systems deal with numbers, they are perceived as being precise. And in the sense that they report specific numerical measurements, they are precise. But the purpose of an accounting system is to convey information—and measurement of activity in monetary terms is simply the mechanism used to achieve this purpose. What is to be measured, how it is to be measured, and how often it is to be measured are important questions that an accounting system must address. Answering them involves people and judgments. An **accounting system** is thus a contrived system. Its objectives, rules, and methods are established by people with needs that they hope the system will fulfill. It is, in brief, place specific.

Country Differences in Accounting Systems

Consistent with this perspective, Zeff's classic *Forging Accounting Principles in Five Countries* demonstrated that such influences as theory, practice, and social, political and economic conditions come together to determine an accounting system.[1] Choi and Mueller identified 15 such conditions, some of which follow:[2]

1. *Type of Economy Involved.* Inventory methods, audit functions, and cost accounting techniques are affected by whether the economy involved is agrarian, extractive, or industrialized.
2. *Legal System.* Code law countries favor codification of accounting principles and procedures; common law countries are typified by private, professional organizations that establish accounting policies.
3. *Political System.* In centrally controlled economies of communist states, profit and the private ownership of fixed assets and land may not even exist. Political systems are also known to have exported accounting practices, as in the British Commonwealth countries and in former Dutch and French possessions.

4. *Social Climate.* Concepts of public disclosure and social responsibility have had considerable influence on accounting practices in the United States; in Switzerland, which requires substantially less public disclosure than the United States, the influence of such concepts is far smaller. In some Latin countries, accounting is equated with bookkeeping and seen as socially unimportant.
5. *General Levels of Education and Facilitating Processes.* People need to know mathematics if the quantitative information in an accounting system is to be used effectively. Computerization requires the presence of electronic data processing installations.

As expected, accounting practices are found to vary country by country. For example, disclosure of the cost of sales is a reporting requirement in Brazil and the United States, a minority practice in the United Kingdom, seldom found in Sweden, and not permitted in West Germany.[3] (Periodic reports published by major accounting firms and available in most university libraries present highlights of accounting practices in selected countries.)

Accounting for International Transactions

Firms active in international business often deal in foreign currencies. Exports and imports, for example, may well be denominated in foreign currency and entail trade credit of 30, 60, or 90 days or longer. Dividends paid by a foreign subsidiary are denominated in the home currency of that subsidiary and are usually declared weeks prior to actual payment. Debt denominated in foreign currency entails predictable servicing requirements that involve purchasing foreign currency for delivery at some known future date. Such **international transactions** have to be reflected in the company's accounting records.

Three alternative situations may be involved in accounting for transactions denominated in foreign currency. To understand these alternatives, consider the export sale illustrated in Figure 14-1.

Alternative 1: Immediate Payment The exporting firm does not hold the foreign currency beyond the date of its receipt, which is also the date the sale is made. Financial accounting standards in the United States require that assets, liabilities, sales, and expenses denominated initially in foreign currency be reflected in the accounts in the dollar equivalent on the date they arise. In the present case, the foreign currency would be converted into dollars in the exporter's accounts on the date the sale is made. The exporter's accounts would also reflect the net dollars received when the foreign exchange is sold.

To illustrate, consider an export sale to a German buyer for 3,000 deutsche marks (DMs). On the date of sale, the DM is trading at 3 DM per dollar. Neglecting bank charges for selling the DMs, the sale generates $1,000 in revenues for the exporter. Excluding the credit to finished goods inventory

Figure 14-1 **Accounting for Foreign Currency Transactions: The Three Alternative Situations—Export Sale Illustration**

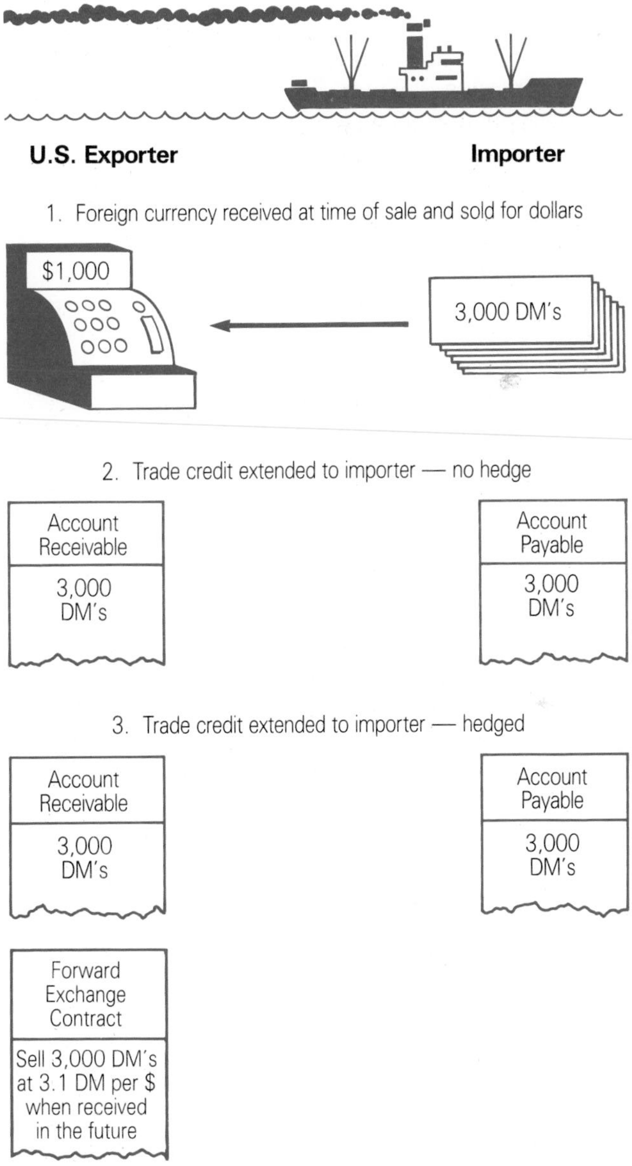

and the debit to cost of goods sold, the debit and credit entries are simply as follows:

Dr: Cash	$1,000	
Cr: Sales Revenues		$1,000

Alternative 2: Trade Credit In this case, the exporter is willing to accept payment for the goods in foreign currency at some future date *and* does not cover this exposure with a forward market transaction. The accounting principle identified in alternative 1 would still hold as far as initial entries are concerned. Thus, the entries on the date of sale are as follows:

Dr: Account Receivable	$1,000	
Cr: Sales Revenues		$1,000

(Note that the account debited is Account Receivable and not Cash. This reflects the fact that the sale was made on trade credit.)

During the period of time for which the trade credit was extended, the DM depreciates to 3.2 DM per dollar. This lowers the dollar value of the sale of the export to $938 at the time the receivable is collected. (Don't forget that the sale, by contract, is for precisely 3,000 DMs.) Settlement of the account thus involves a **conversion loss** (that is, a loss when an account is settled), which is reflected on the exporter's books in this way:

Dr: Cash	$938	
Dr: Foreign Exchange Transactions	$62	
Cr: Account Receivable		$1,000

The Foreign Exchange Transactions account is debited for foreign exchange losses and credited for foreign exchange gains. It is an income statement account that is closed out to profit and loss at the end of the accounting period.

To complicate matters a bit, consider the same case but with the exporter's accounting period ending during the time period in which the trade credit is extended—and after the DM depreciation. To reflect conditions as factually as possible, the foreign exchange loss is reflected in the end-of-period reports as follows:

Dr: Foreign Exchange Transactions	$62	
Cr: Account Receivable		$62

The foreign exchange loss in this case is termed a **translation loss** (that is, a loss on a transaction that has yet to be settled). Later, when the export is paid for, the following accounting entries are made:

Dr: Cash	$938	
Cr: Account Receivable		$938

Can You Figure This One Out?

On December 15, 1986, Saks Fifth Avenue, a wholly owned U.S. subsidiary of the British-American Tobacco Company, Ltd., declared a dividend of $2 per share, payable on January 15, 1987. The British parent holds 1 million shares. (All of these figures are hypothetical.) Assuming that the applicable accounting rules are like those described for the U.S. exporter in the accompanying text, that British-American Tobacco closed its fiscal year on December 31, that from December 16 to December 28, 1986, the British pound went from $1.45 to $1.50, and that there was no forward market hedge on the dividend receivable, what accounting entries would British-American Tobacco show on its books on December 15, 1986, December 31, 1986, and January 15, 1987? What entries would Saks Fifth Avenue show on these same dates?

Alternative 3: Trade Credit—Hedged This alternative is like alternative 2, except that the exposure of the foreign exchange receivable because of the export is exactly offset by a forward exchange contract requiring the sale of 3,000 DMs. The initial entries related to the sale of the goods and the account receivable would remain precisely as shown above. However, subsequent entries will reflect the forward market transaction. No accounting entries are made to record the forward contract at the time the contract is made (i.e., at the time of the sale). Assuming that the forward contract rate is 3.1DM per dollar, the dollars collected by the exporter (when the DMs are received per the export sale and paid out to complete the forward contract) total $968. The accounting principle is that forward contracts offsetting specific foreign currency receivables or payables are included in the dollar basis of the original foreign currency transaction. Hence, the subsequent accounting entries are as follows:

Dr: Cash	$968	
Dr: Foreign Exchange Transactions	$32	
Cr: Account Receivable		$1,000

In this instance, the foreign exchange loss (debit) has been reduced to $32 because of the forward exchange contract. If the contract had been written at a rate of 3 DM per dollar, there would be no foreign exchange transactions loss at all.

In their 1979 international survey of accounting practices, Fitzgerald, Stickler, and Watts reported that the U.S. accounting practices described in connection with alternatives 1, 2, and 3 are consistent with the accounting practices followed in most other advanced industrial societies.[4]

Consolidations

A **consolidated statement** is a single balance sheet or income statement that combines the financial accounts of the parent and its subsidiaries. All

MNEs, U.S. or otherwise, prepare consolidated statements, so that managers, lenders, investors, and others can understand the overall financial situation of the firm. **Consolidation** is required of publicly held U.S. firms. It is a tedious process requiring adherence to specific procedures and is performed at the parent company level. Before consolidation is discussed in more detail, some basic definitions and concepts must be understood. (Recall that we are mainly concerned with the situation pertinent to the *U.S.* MNE.)

A consolidated statement pertains only to a parent and its subsidiaries. For accounting purposes, a **subsidiary** is a foreign corporation more than 50 percent of whose common stock is owned by the parent (implying parental control). Technically, if the parent owns 50 percent or less of the foreign entity's common stock, that entity is an **affiliate,** not a subsidiary. The foreign entity is considered a **branch** if it is not incorporated in the foreign country but exists as an office or extension of the parent and is legally constituted as a branch. If affiliates and branches are not consolidated per se, how are they handled at the MNE level? This question is important, and answering it necessitates a brief digression from our discussion of consolidation.

The parent company's books (nonconsolidated) carry any foreign entity (subsidiary, affiliate, or branch) as an investment reflected on the asset side of the balance sheet. A branch is reflected in the plant and equipment accounts, for example, depending on what buildings, furniture, and so on are physically in place at the foreign entity. An affiliate or subsidiary is shown in a specific investment account, such as Investments in Foreign Companies.

Income from a foreign branch is considered the same as income to the parent since the branch is simply an extension of the parent. Income from an affiliate can be handled by either the cost method or the equity method, depending on the level of parent company ownership. If parent ownership is below 20 percent, the **cost method** must be used—that is, the affiliate's income is recognized on the parent's books only when the parent receives it in the form of dividends. When such income occurs, income is credited and cash is debited. If parent ownership is 20 percent or more (meaning the foreign entity can be an affiliate or a subsidiary and is not just a financial investment), the **equity method** is used—that is, the parent's investment account is increased by the income that the foreign entity earns, in proportion to the parent's ownership share, whether or not that income is paid out in dividends. In this case, income at the affiliate, as allocated to the parent, is credited and the investment account is debited. When a dividend is paid out of the earnings, the investment account is credited and cash is debited. Figure 14-2 illustrates these alternative methods for handling income.

Preparing a Consolidated Report

A **consolidated report** involves the line-by-line summary of the balance sheet and income statement accounts of both the parent and its subsidiaries.

These adjustments offset the net effect or residual resulting from the inequality between assets and liabilities and from the fact that all of the subsidiary's asset and liability accounts are translated to the consolidated balance sheet at the same rate of exchange. These are translation gains/losses resulting from consolidation. There are thus two sources of adjustments to consolidated net worth—those resulting from *conversion gains/losses* as the subsidiary adjusts its own books to reflect changes in the subsidiary's own local-currency value of assets and liabilities based on currencies other than its own and those resulting from *translation gains/losses* as the structure of accounts (i.e., assets exceed liabilities) and the translation rules regarding the use of a single exchange rate result in residuals that have to be recorded in the consolidated statement.

Consolidation Illustrated

Let's proceed by illustrating these principles in our case with Friendly Industries. As a first step, Sympático's balance sheet, changed to show the situation where Sympático actually earned 5 million pesos profit during FY1987, appears below. (For simplicity, the 5 million peso increase in net worth is balanced by a similar increase in cash.)

SYMPÁTICO, S.A.
Balance Sheet
December 31, 1987
(thousands of pesos)

Assets	
Cash	11,000
Accounts receivable (total)	18,000
Plant and equipment	24,000
Liabilities	
Accounts payable	12,000
Bank loan	10,000
Parent company loan	7,500
Net worth	23,500

Before consolidation, any intracompany transactions are netted out. For example, Sympático's parent company loan, a liability, is offset by an asset on the parent's books reflecting the loan due from Sympático. Similarly, Friendly's investment account showing its ownership of Sympático is netted out against Sympático's net worth account balance reflecting Friendly's ownership position. Assuming that Friendly, the parent, had a flat year in 1987, the consolidated balance sheets for FY1986 and FY1987 might thus look as follows:

FRIENDLY INDUSTRIES, INC.
Consolidated Balance Sheets
(thousands of dollars)

	End of Fiscal Year 1986	1987
Assets		
Cash	$ 815	$ 822
Accounts receivable	3,040	3,036
Plant and equipment	16,060	16,048
Liabilities		
Accounts payable	630	624
Bank loans	825	820
Long-term debt	10,000	10,000
Net worth		
Common stock	3,600	3,600
Earned surplus	4,860	4,860
Cumulative translation adjustment	0	2

The net result of the consolidation is a onetime $2,000 credit to the net worth account Cumulative Translation Adjustment. The $2,000 credit can be explained by looking at the changes in the dollar basis of each individual account at the end of FY1986 and FY1987. Recall that such changes can be caused by exchange rate changes resulting in (1) conversion gains or losses and (2) translation gains or losses, and (3) changes in the subsidiary's accounts owing to operations during the period (the 5 million peso increase in cash in the present example). The changes in Friendly's accounts can be explained as follows:

Account	Change	Comment
Cash	$ 7,000 dr	Gain of 5 million pesos during fiscal year yields a dollar gain of $10,000. Translation loss on 6 million pesos is $3,000.
Accounts Receivable	4,000 cr	Conversion gain of $4,000 on 2 million peso write-up on dollar-based receivables. Translation loss on 16 million pesos is $8,000.
Plant and Equipment	12,000 cr	Translation loss on 24 million pesos is $12,000.
Accounts Payable	6,000 dr	Translation gain on 12 million pesos is $6,000.
Bank Loan	5,000 dr	Translation gain on 10 million pesos is $5,000.
Cumulative Translation Adjustment	2,000 cr	Entry to balance out net effect of conversion and translation gains/losses.

Note that the sum of the debit changes equals the sum of the credit changes, so that the net effect of the changes is zero. This follows since the entry to Cumulative Translation Adjustment is a balancing entry. This is always the way in which residual gains or losses derived during consolidation are handled.

Statement of Financial Accounting Standards No. 52

Foreign Currency Translation

December 1981

Financial Accounting Standards Board

Financial Accounting Standards Board

U.S. Financial Accounting Standards on Consolidation and Disclosures

The accounting procedures just discussed regarding consolidations are those required of U.S. MNEs by Financial Accounting Standard 52. Specifically, FAS 52 requires that

1. A subsidiary's books be kept in the **functional currency** of the subsidiary, that is, its home currency (pesos, in Sympático's case).
2. Changes in a subsidiary's foreign-currency assets and liabilities be reflected in changes in its functional currency records.
3. The exchange rate on the balance sheet date be used to translate assets and liabilities from the subsidiary's functional currency accounts into the parent's **reporting currency** accounts (dollars, in Friendly's case).
4. A **weighted-average exchange rate** be used to translate income statement accounts from the functional currency into the reporting currency.
5. Net gains or losses arising from consolidation be reported directly as charges or credits to a special account in stockholders' equity (that is, to Cumulative Translation Adjustment in the Friendly case).

An exception to these rules occurs, however, when the subsidiary is operating in a hyperinflationary environment or when its operations, financing, and cash flow are highly dependent on the parent. The parent's currency then serves as both the functional currency and the reporting currency. In such a situation, assets carried at historical costs—fixed assets and, in some instances, inventories—are translated at historical rates of exchange. Other balance sheet items continue to be translated at current rates.

Income statement accounts similarly differentiate between accounts that are carried at historical costs and those that are not. In the former instance, such accounts use historical costs and the historical exchange rates that were in effect when the purchases were made. In the latter, such accounts continue to use the average exchange rate for the period. Translation gains or losses are taken as periodic charges or credits to income. They are not taken directly to equity.

The importance of understanding FAS 52 is underscored by Choi's observation that the current-rate translation basis (notwithstanding the exceptions noted) required by FAS 52 in the United States is also the method that is used most frequently in Japan and Europe.[5]

Financial accounting disclosure, including disclosure of foreign operations, is accomplished by means of the consolidated statements reporting just discussed. Reporting just on foreign operations is another matter. For U.S. firms, FAS 14 is the controlling policy statement. FAS 14 requires financial reporting by business segments, including geographic segments. To illustrate, Table 14-1 presents a financial report pertaining to Bank of America's foreign operations.

Table 14-1 **Bank of America: 1984 Performance by Geographic Profit Centers** (in millions of U.S. dollars)

	Average Assets	Gross Revenue	Total Expense	Operating Income
Asia	$ 12,168	$ 1,405	$ 1,306	$ 99
Europe, Middle East, and Africa	19,701	2,436	2,353	83
Latin America and Caribbean	8,334	1,450	1,437	13
North America (international)	3,788	656	629	27
Total international	43,991	5,947	5,725	222
Total domestic	76,196	8,450	8,219	198
Total BankAmerica Corporation	$120,187	$14,397	$13,944	$420

Source: BankAmerica Corporation, 1984 *Annual Report*, p. 51.

Accounting practices and standards could be treated in considerably greater depth. Here, however, we have confined ourselves to presenting some important concepts that should help managers better understand some of the fundamental accounting implications of multinational operations.

Managerial Accounting/Information Systems

Accounting information systems pertaining to management decision making can be varied and complex. Such systems are conditioned by many influences—the nature of the financial reports; the records needed to prepare the financial reports and the usefulness of such records (or the ease with which they can be modified) for decision-making purposes; product configuration; process technology; local financial practices; the legal, cultural, and social environments; and so on.

The key issue regarding an appropriate **management information system (MIS)** is essentially similar to the issue already discussed on product configuration and advertising in Chapter 13. That issue is to determine the appropriate balance between a **universal MIS**—uniform, easily understood at all management levels, and efficient to produce—and an MIS that is substantially adapted in each instance to fit the nuances of discrete, local environments.

For the ethnocentric MNE, the universal MIS is the ideal. Decisions at the parent level dominate the MNE network, and the parent generally imposes operating standards that determines operations everywhere. Parent company managers insist on information flows that are easily understood and consis-

Management information systems in MNE are especially complex and are a challenge to design. Often special consultants are called in to help put the right MIS "on-line."
Click/Chicago/Jon Riley

tent in their measurement of activities at all subsidiaries. Note that this is not a bad MIS policy for the ethnocentric MNE. It is in agreement with the firm's corporate strategies and functional policies. The fact that the firm dominates a global market, and that the parent is the source of this dominance, allows it to disregard local influences on operations. Production, marketing, and other functions are carried on in the same way at both the parent and subsidiary levels. For example, IBM's recently built personal computer plant in Mexico operates under production standards and an MIS similar to those that are in place in its U.S. personal computer plants.

For the polycentric MNE, a universal MIS makes little sense. Operations decisions and key managerial decisions are made at the subsidiary level. There is little need to accumulate information for use at the parent level. For example, Ford-Germany's cars have differed substantially from Ford's U.S. cars and Ford's U.S. and German markets have been geographically segmented. Installing a global MIS would be of questionable value to Ford—and, in fact, the parent and its European subsidiaries were fairly autonomous, with infrequent information exchanges below the board of directors level, until some product integration policies came on line in the early 1970s.

For the geocentric MNE, the need is to find the balance between an MIS that consistently portrays operations at all subsidiaries and one that accommodates local nuances giving real meaning to the data and information transmitted. For example, H. J. Heinz has manufactured powdered baby food in Italy which was packaged in the United States and sold in the People's Republic of China (PRC). (This was an interim arrangement pending completion of a baby-food processing and packaging plant in the PRC.) In this case, Heinz had to transmit a lot of information internationally and also to develop the information base it needed in order to successfully market a product in China. For the geocentric MNE, such as Heinz, finding the appropriate balance between global information needs and local market information needs is a compelling necessity.

The theory of the MNE discussed in Chapter 2 revealed that MNEs have several competitive advantages over purely local firms. The effective transmission and implementation of these advantages within the parent-subsidiary MNE network gives the MNE units their competitiveness. This means that management at all levels must have some fundamental, universal understanding regarding technology, operations, and so on. This, in turn, requires information feedback, effective management communication, and the like. The MIS must contain some measurements that are common to all locales. Where local nuances obviate this possibility, extra care must be taken to train managers in what their MIS is really telling them.

Taxation and the MNE

The issue of taxation is especially important to the MNE since the MNE operates in multiple taxing jurisdictions (i.e., countries) and has options for avoiding or deferring taxation in certain countries. Income, which is typically taxed at the source, has more than a single source when it is generated at the subsidiary level. The country in which the subsidiary is located views the subsidiary as a source; the country in which the parent is located views the MNE structure as a source. In some cases, U.S. MNEs can defer U.S. income taxes by retaining profits at the subsidiary level; in other cases, they cannot. Through foreign sales corporations, U.S. firms can defer taxes. In all cases, however, the U.S. Internal Revenue Service has the upper hand. It has the final word on how much a firm's taxes are. This section discusses these and related topics.

Income Taxes—The General Case

The after-tax income to the parent generated by profits at the subsidiary can vary considerably, depending on the handling of foreign taxes in the country of the parent company. The payment of the foreign tax by the subsidiary can be ignored, acknowledged as an income deduction (as it is in the United States for income taxes paid to state governments), or recognized as a dollar-for-dollar tax credit. Table 14-2 illustrates the use of these alternative approaches and their bottom-line results.

Table 14-2 **Alternative Methods for Recognizing Taxes Paid at the Subsidiary by the Parent Company's Home Country**

Item	Double Taxation	Income Deduction	Tax Credit
Operating income	$100,000	$100,000	$100,000
Subsidiary's taxes	30,000	30,000	30,000
After-tax income	70,000	70,000	70,000
Parent's taxes	50,000	35,000	20,000
Net after-tax income to parent	$ 20,000	$ 35,000	$ 50,000

Note: The applicable income tax rate at the subsidiary is 30 percent; at the parent, 50 percent.

The example in Table 14-2 gives quite different results, depending on how the taxes paid by the subsidiary are handled by the tax authorities at the parent company level. The net, after-tax income to the parent ranges from $20,000 to $50,000! Fortunately for business executives who want to minimize taxes, bilateral tax treaties between the United States and a large number of other countries (including West Germany, France, the United Kingdom, and other countries where large amounts of U.S. direct investment are in place) allow for a U.S. tax credit for foreign income taxes paid by subsidiaries. It seems reasonable too that if the parent company's country is to allow tax credits for taxes paid by subsidiaries in other countries, the books of those subsidiaries should be "reconstructed" to conform to the depreciation and other tax-related rules of that country. Most tax authorities, including the U.S. Internal Revenue Service (IRS), reserve the final word on taxes, and Section 482 of the U.S. Tax Code allows the IRS to reconstruct a company's records, if necessary, and to assess the tax due. This assessment, of course, can be appealed to the U.S. Tax Court. Assuming that the tax accounting rules have already been accommodated, let's look at a concrete example to illustrate how tax credits work.

Taxation Illustrated

Magna Corporation's wholly owned French subsidiary, Monser, S.A., has closed its fiscal year with pretax profits of 8 million francs. Monser's dividend payout ratio is 50 percent, and the French income tax rate is 25 percent. Magna's U.S. federal income tax rate is 34 percent, and the rate of exchange is FF 8 per dollar. To complicate matters a little, let's also assume that there is a 10 percent French tax on dividend remittances to foreigners. The actual funds received by Magna can be determined in this way:

Monser's pretax profit	FF 8,000,000
French income taxes	2,000,000
Monser's after-tax profit	6,000,000
Dividends declared (50 percent)	3,000,000
Less: Dividend remittance tax	300,000
Dividends received by Magna	
In French francs	2,700,000
In U.S. dollars	337,500

Since Magna prepares its own income statement, dividends received from a subsidiary represent taxable income, and since there is a tax treaty between the United States and France that allows for a tax credit on foreign taxes paid, the taxes that Magna was imputed to have paid in France on its portion of Monser's income can be deducted from Magna's U.S. tax bill. (Recall that in the absence of a tax treaty, there would be no tax credit for foreign taxes paid.) This may sound more complicated than it really is. Let's return to our example.

Magna received a net-of-all-taxes dividend of $337,500 from Monser. The taxes that this $337,500 bore were the $37,500 (FF 300,000) that Monser paid in dividend remittance taxes, *plus* the French income taxes of $125,000 (FF 1,000,000) that Monser paid on the FF 4 million that it had to generate in pretax income in France to fund payment of the dividend. These taxes are important since if local taxing authorities give a credit for foreign taxes paid, the dividend at the parent's level must be "grossed up" to include these taxes. The **grossed-up dividend** thus represents the total taxable income imputed to have been received by the parent. The system has to work this way if the foreign taxes are subsequently credited against U.S. taxes due. Let's return again to our example.

Net dividends received by Magna	$337,500
Plus: Dividend remittance tax	37,500
Plus: French taxes paid by Monser on dividend received by Magna	125,000
Grossed-up dividend to Magna	500,000
U.S. income tax on grossed-up dividend	170,000
Less: Foreign tax credit	162,500
U.S. taxes payable—preliminary determination	$ 7,500

The last line, U.S. taxes payable, is a preliminary determination in that this amount can still be offset by unused foreign tax credits on income from Magna's subsidiaries in other countries or by unused foreign tax credits generated from foreign operations in the past seven years. In no instance, however, can unused foreign tax credits be used to reduce taxes on domestically produced income. The rationale for grossing up the dividend to include the foreign taxes paid on it is that if one tax is to be a credit against the other, they both have to be applied to the same income base. If this were not the case in our example, Magna's initial tax determination would be 34 percent of $337,500, or $114,750. A U.S. tax of $114,750 would be wholly offset by French income taxes of $125,000. That all U.S. taxes could be eliminated in the face of a foreign income tax rate lower than the U.S. rate (i.e., 25 percent/34 percent) is irrational.

Income Taxes—A Special Case

Income tax rates for businesses vary considerably country by country—as Table 14-3 illustrates. In fact, some countries don't tax business income at all and other countries don't tax income from foreign sources. The former include Bermuda and the Cayman Islands; the latter include Panama and Liberia. Wouldn't the astute MNE set up a holding company in one of these countries to receive the dividends of its subsidiaries, which it could then divert (as investments) to other subsidiaries? (If such a holding company never paid a dividend to the U.S. parent, the parent company could defer U.S. income taxes forever.) Many U.S. MNEs pursued this practice prior to the passage of the Revenue Act of 1962. President Kennedy was outspoken in his opposition to the practice, which, although legal, effectively exempted multinationals from paying U.S. income taxes on foreign earnings (for the time being). The provisions of the Revenue Act of 1962 that eliminated the practice were the policy response to his initiatives.

Table 14-3 **Corporate Income Tax Rates in Selected Countries as a Percentage of Taxable Income***

Country	Tax Rate	Country	Tax Rate
Denmark	50%	Philippines	35%
France	50	United Kingdom	35
Venezuela	50	United States	34
Turkey	46	Argentina	33
Belgium	46	Japan	33
Mexico	42	Taiwan	25
Singapore	40	Liechtenstein	15
Italy	33		

* Data are for the end of 1986, except for the United Kingdom and the United States, which are for 1-1-87 and 7-1-87 respectively. Tax and tax rates may vary with definitions of "Taxable Income," which may differ according to sources and deductibles allowed, with levels of earnings and with uses of earnings, e.g., distributed as dividends or undistributed. Rates shown are maximums.

Source: Data, except for the United States, were collected from various sections in Price Waterhouse's *Corporate Taxes: A Worldwide Summary,* 1986 Edition. (The U.S. rate is that contained in the Tax Reform Act of 1986.)

The act specifically defined a **controlled foreign corporation (CFC)** and Subpart F income to isolate and tax holding company earnings. A CFC is a foreign corporation that is 50 percent or more owned by U.S. "shareholders"—defined as U.S. citizens (including corporations) holding 10 percent or more of the common stock. (Thus, a U.S. citizen that owned less than 10 percent did not qualify as a U.S. "shareholder" for the purposes of this act.)

Subpart F income is defined as the income received by a foreign-base company. A **foreign-base company,** in turn, is a CFC that derives income from investments, sales, services, or shipping. Subpart F income is deemed to have been received by the U.S. parent of the CFC. It is not deferred, unlike the operating income that a subsidiary derives from the actual conduct of a business and does not pay to the parent as dividends—as with Monser and Magna. There is one exception, however—the **10/70 rule.** This rule recognizes that subsidiaries may have income from numerous sources: production and sales, investments, and so on. The 10/70 rule stipulates that if less than 10 percent of a CFC's income is Subpart F income, then full deferral applies. If more than 70 percent (but less than 100 percent) of a CFC's income is Subpart F income, then none of it is deferred. (If Subpart F income constitutes between 10 percent and 70 percent of the CFC's income, then the CFC's income is allocated between deferred and not deferred in the same ratio as its origin.)

If Monser were a holding company and if its 8 million franc income were from dividends, management fees, and royalties, those 8 million francs, equal to $1 million, would immediately be taxable income to Magna—whether or not Monser declared any dividend. The initial U.S. tax would be $340,000, but $250,000 of this would be offset by income taxes paid in France by Monser. (Note that there would be no U.S. tax credit for dividend remittance taxes, since in this instance Monser paid no dividend to Magna.)

The Foreign Sales Corporation

Several countries have established schemes for subsidizing exports by "relieving" export profits or revenues of taxes. In many European countries, for instance, firms that export are rebated by governments for the taxes their export products carried. A major business tax in Europe is the **value-added tax (VAT).** This tax is applied to the value added by each producer/processor/distributor as a product progresses through the stages of production and distribution. It is applied to both intermediate products and final products. The total value-added taxes paid on a product are returned by the government to the exporter, thus making exports more price competitive in world markets than they would be otherwise.) In the United States, channeling exports through a **foreign sales corporation (FSC)** has distinctive tax advantages.

A U.S. company can establish an FSC to handle its exports and to accumulate profits on its export sales. Approximately 65 percent of the profits of the FSC will be tax exempt. Certain procedures and restrictions apply, however. The FSC, for example, must be physically located outside the United States or in a U.S. possession other than Puerto Rico, and it must actually participate in the conduct of export business. It cannot be a mere "shell." It must maintain an office, keep records, participate in sales solicitations and negotiations, and handle order processing, billings, and collections. The parent and its FSC are free to establish transfer prices on export goods as they see fit; however, profits at the FSC are limited to the larger of 1.83 percent of the total revenues generated by exports or 23 percent of the total income of the FSC and its parent.[6]

Dividends remitted by the FSC to its parent are totally tax-free at the parent level. At most, therefore, 65 percent of the profits at the FSC (which equals 65 percent of 23 percent of the combined, total corporate profits, or 15 percent of the total corporate profits) are tax exempt. Since countries where an FSC is located can also tax the FSC's profits, the preferred location for FSCs is the U.S. Virgin Islands, where U.S. tax laws are in effect.

There are other special situations where tax laws authorize tax benefits—for example, the FSC for small businesses, which does not require an offshore location, and the **domestic international sales corporation (DISC),** which can enjoy a tax deferral on some export earnings. Inquiries on these and other tax-related issues should always be directed to a competent authority, such as a tax accountant.

Taxation—The Management Impact

How do the tax matters just discussed relate to management? In many ways, tax considerations are one of several important inputs into management decision making. They are certainly relevant to the strategic management function at the corporate, MNE level, especially with regard to decisions on ownership structures, plant location, production allocation, target market selection, and financing. The astute manager will incorporate tax effects on cash flow projections when building the data base appropriate to the planning function.

At the SBU level, tax concerns need to be addressed (perhaps jointly in some cases by both SBU-level and corporate- level managers) in decisions on intracorporate product transfers and transfer prices, personnel assignments, cash management and short-term financing arrangements, dividend policy, export strategy, profit planning, and accounting systems.

To illustrate the pervasiveness of tax considerations, *The Wall Street Journal* reported these responses of MNE managements to the Tax Reform Act of 1986:[7]

1. Managements will have to make decisions on "whether or not to repatriate to the United States billions of dollars in profits from their foreign subsidiaries."
2. In the face of lower U.S. corporate income tax rates and the specter of unused foreign tax credits, MNEs will probably be "loading up foreign

subsidiaries with more debt and less equity" to locate more profits at the U.S. parent.

3. "Foreign subsidiaries may find themselves being billed for services that headquarters used to provide free, such as accounting, planning, marketing, proprietary technology and product development"—payments on which raise the costs of subsidiaries and the income of the parent company.
4. Investment location decisions will be reconsidered, and MNEs may well "begin to shun such high-tax countries as Germany."

Management Responsibilities under the Foreign Corrupt Practices Act

During the 1970s, there was considerable public concern in the United States (and elsewhere) over unethical business practices—bribes to secure sales contracts, falsification of corporate records, and so on. Many of these practices, engaged in outside the United States, involved dealings between representatives of U.S. corporations and officials of foreign governments. In response, legislation was enacted in 1977 to mandate corporate control over firms' activities in this regard.

The **Foreign Corrupt Practices Act** (Public Law 95-213) forbids bribes and similar questionable conduct, requires that funds not be made available for the payment of bribes and other questionable financial activities, and mandates that companies develop and apply internal accounting and control procedures to support the requirements of the act. A compelling feature of the act is that its penalties for noncompliance include not only fines for both companies and company officials but also *imprisonment of company officials.*

Although the internal accounting and control procedures mandated by the act are costly, they may save money too by reducing the potential for fradulent activities. When the act was first passed, many observers felt that its antibribery provisions would put U.S. firms at a competitive disadvantage overseas. A recent study, however, suggests that this has not been the case. The act has caused no loss of foreign sales by U.S. firms.[8]

Conclusions

Accounting and tax matters are especially challenging to MNE management. They are both complex and rewarding. Properly approached and implemented, accounting systems and tax strategies—especially those that pertain to the transfer and evaluation of management expertise and the minimization of cash outflows stemming from taxes—can support the competitive presence of MNEs both at home and abroad.

Accounting systems were seen to reflect environmental influences, such as the legal climate and levels of education, and to vary somewhat country by country. Accounting for international transactions was discussed, as was consolidation accounting. The rules germane to each of these activities are fairly complex, and the record-keeping is tedious. Management's responsibility is to acquire knowledge of the rules and to ensure that they are followed.

The taxation of MNEs varies, depending on the answers to a variety of questions. Is there a tax treaty between the home and host countries? What are its provisions? Is the foreign entity an operating company, or is it simply a holding company? What are the levels of taxes abroad, and of the dividends remitted to the parent? What is the overall foreign tax credit limitation? Can export income be channeled through a foreign sales corporation? The questions can go on and on.

Management has special responsibilities under the Foreign Corrupt Practices Act. The most difficult one to address is the requirement for internal accounting and managerial controls to ensure compliance with the act. Managers who fail to comply can face a jail sentence.

Questions

1. Explain how accounting and tax matters can affect the competitiveness of an MNE.
2. Distinguish between financial accounting and managerial accounting/information systems; between accounting for international transactions and accounting for consolidations.
3. Identify three environmental factors that have influenced the development of indigenous financial accounting systems. Identify specific results of these influences.
4. Explain the differences between the "trade credit" and the "trade credit—hedged" cases when accounting for international transactions.
5. Distinguish between a parent company's financial statements and the consolidated statements. Where does an investment in a subsidiary appear on the parent's books? On the consolidated statements?
6. What is FAS 52? What are its major provisions?
7. Distinguish between a conversion gain/loss and a translation gain/loss. Of what significance is the difference between the two?
8. In the Magna Corporation example, change the French income tax rate to 30 percent. What will Magna's U.S. taxes then be?
9. Distinguish between Subpart F income and ordinary income. Why is this distinction necessary?
10. Identify some management problems that must be resolved when a foreign sales corporation is established. Of what benefit is a foreign sales corporation?

References

Arpan, Jeffrey S., and Lee H. Radebaugh. *International Accounting and Multinational Enterprises.* New York: John Wiley & Sons, 1985.

Evans, Thomas G.; Martin E. Taylor; and Oscar Holzmann. *International Accounting and Reporting.* New York: Macmillan, 1985.

Fox, Samuel, and Norlin G. Rueschoff. *Principles of International Accounting.* Austin, Tex.: Austin Press, 1986.

Gray, S. J.; J. C. Shaw; and B. McSweeney. "Accounting Standards and Multinational Corporations." *Journal of International Business Studies,* Spring-Summer 1981, pp. 121-36.

Walter, Ingo. *Secret Money: The Shadowy World of Tax Evasion, Capital Flight, and Fraud.* Lexington, Mass.: Lexington Books, 1985.

Endnotes

1. Steven A. Zeff, *Forging Accounting Principles in Five Countries: A History and an Analysis of Trends* (Champaign, Ill.: Stipes Publishing, 1977).
2. Frederick D. S. Choi and Gerhard G. Mueller, *An Introduction to Multinational Accounting* (Englewood Cliffs, N.J.: Prentice-Hall, 1978), pp. 24–28.
3. Konrad W. Kubin, "Comparative Accounting Systems," in *Handbook of International Business,* ed. Ingo Walter, (New York: John Wiley & Sons, 1982), chap. 23, pp. 22-4 and 22-5.
4. R. D. Fitzgerald, A. D. Stickler, and T. R. Watts, *International Survey of Accounting Principles and Reporting Practices* (New York: Price Waterhouse International, 1979).
5. Frederick D. S. Choi, "Accounting for Multinational Operations," in *Handbook of International Business,* ed. Ingo Walter (New York: John Wiley & Sons, 1982), chap. 23, pp. 23-9 and 23-14.
6. Detailed information on foreign sales corporations can be found in analyses of the Tax Reform Act of 1984 prepared by most major accounting firms and by Commerce Clearing House.
7. Douglas R. Sease and Thomas Kamm, "Tax Bill May Force New Practices Abroad," *The Wall Street Journal,* August 22, 1986, p. 20.
8. J. L. Graham, "The Foreign Corrupt Practices Act: A New Perspective," *Journal of International Business Studies,* Winter 1984, pp. 107-23.

Case
Hurricane Canoe Corporation

Hurricane Canoe Corporation (HCC) is a major U.S. canoe manufacturer located in Orlando, Florida. The firm is not large by overall U.S. industrial standards, but it is the second largest canoe builder in the world. With annual sales of about $200 million and assets of nearly $100 million in North America and Europe, HCC is clearly beyond the small-business stage. Its sales growth has exceeded 20 percent per year since 1978, and its prospects for continued success appear good.

Most of HCC's growth has come through expansion of its distribution network. The firm's main products have remained basically the same over the years: canoes, paddles, safety and camping gear, and some specialty clothing. Its diversification has been primarily geographic (rather than through new products), though some of its sales outlets have added other firms' canoes and canoe rentals to their functions. HCC's U.S. operations reported sales of $72.7 million and profits before taxes of $11.4 million in 1986 (exclusive of management fees and royalties from foreign operations).

Hurricane Canoe began its foreign operations in the late 1960s by establishing a sales office in Montreal, Quebec, Canada. Canoeists in Canada rank among the most avid in the world, and HCC had great expectations for Canadian sales of its high-performance Kevlar and ABS boats. These expectations were borne out by sales of hundreds, then thousands, of boats in the first eight years of the Canadian operation. Subsequently, HCC established a wholly owned assembly operation in Windsor, Ontario, Canada, which currently produces one third of HCC's North American output. At present, 75 percent of the Windsor operation's output is sold in Canada and the balance is exported to the United States at a price to HCC-owned distributors of cost plus 10 percent. Pretax profits in Canada last year were $5.8 million on sales of $45 million.

After several years of small-volume exports to European purchasers, Hurricane Canoe established a regional sales office in Frankfurt, West Germany, to serve the Common Market. This wholly owned subsidiary established ties with unaffiliated distributors throughout Western Europe and even arranged continuing contracts with purchasers in East Germany. Selling canoes and peripheral equipment manufactured in both the United States and Canada, the Frankfurt office showed a pretax profit last year of $16.8 million on sales of $48.8 million. During the past five years, sales of the Frankfurt office have been growing phenomenally—25 percent per year.

This case was written by Professor Robert Grosse.

In 1978, HCC formed a joint venture with Kirk and Steuergard, S.A. (K & S), of Denmark, the world's leading manufacturer of Olympic-style canoes. In return for a 49 percent contribution of capital, technology, and management, HCC received 49 percent ownership and exclusive distribution rights for K & S boats in North America. This $5 million investment in Copenhagen was a sizable commitment of funds, but the investment was paid back within three years and profits continue to grow rapidly. Last year, the joint venture's sales and pretax profits were $25 million and $6.9 million, respectively. Currently, this affiliate is capitalized at $9.7 million.

Hurricane Canoe's most recent foreign venture is a 100 percent-owned assembly plant near Barcelona, Spain. HCC saw low-cost assembly, plus tariff-free access to the Common Market, as adequate justification for the investment. HCC spent $4.5 million during the start-up phase of operations, and at year-end 1986 it had assets worth $2.9 million in the Barcelona plant. In the past year, the sales of this plant were a modest $6.5 million and initial operating problems led to a loss of $1.2 million.

Hurricane Canoe's policies require that each subsidiary remit 50 percent of its after-tax earnings to the parent company. Each affiliate—that is, the German joint venture—pays out 50 percent of pretax earnings in dividends. A management fee totaling 2 percent of sales is charged to all wholly owned subsidiaries. A royalty totaling 5 percent of sales is charged to all manufacturing affiliates.

Tax-rate data for the countries within which Hurricane Canoe operates are presented in Table 1. Using these data as necessary, complete Table 2 to figure Hurricane Canoe's U.S. income taxes last year. From a total tax perspective, what costs is HCC bearing to maintain its ethnocentric 50 percent dividend payout ratio from overseas operations in the face of rapid growth and high cash needs in its European operations? (As a basis for comparison, assume that no dividends are paid out by the operations in Germany and Denmark and that the Canadian subsidiary requires that two thirds of its after-tax profits be reinvested in Windsor.)

Table 1 **Tax Rates** (percent)

	United States	Canada	Germany	Denmark	Spain
Corporate income tax	34	45	56/36*	50	35
Dividend withholding tax	0	25	25	30	15
Royalties and fees withholding tax	0	30	25	0	15

* In Germany, the corporate income tax rate is 56 percent on undistributed profits and 36 percent on distributed profits (i.e., dividends paid out).

Table 2 **U.S. Income Tax Calculations** (in millions of U.S. dollars)

	United States	Canada	Germany	Denmark	Spain
Country level					
Sales	72.7	45.0	48.8	25/12.3	6.5
Pretax profit	11.4	5.8	16.8	6.9/3.4	−1.2
Income tax	____	____	____	____	____
After-tax profit	____	____	____	____	____
Dividends		____	____	____	____
Parent level (consolidated, except as noted)					
Gross dividends		____	____	____	____
Less: Dividend withholding tax		____	____	____	____
Net dividends	____	____	____	____	____
Management fees		____	____	____	____
Royalties		____	____	____	____
Total fees and royalties		____	____	____	____
Less: Fee/royalty withholding tax		____	____	____	____
Net fees and royalties	____	____	____	____	____
Grossed-up income		____	____	____	____
U.S. tax—initial		____	____	____	____
Less: Foreign tax credit		____	____	____	____
U.S. tax due (by country)	____	____	____	____	____
Total U.S. tax due	____				

15

FINANCIAL MANAGEMENT AND CONTROL IN THE INTERNATIONAL FIRM

This chapter discusses the opportunities and problems that face multinational firms because they operate in a multicurrency world. Basically, it is an extension of corporate finance to the international level. The capital budgeting process is reviewed, with attention given to foreign exchange risk and political risk and also to opportunities for financing with nondomestic sources of funds. Short-term asset management is similarly covered, with emphasis on centralized international cash management. The choice of debt versus equity for financing the MNE's activities is considered, and the special financing advantages available to the international firm are pointed out. Finally, a more comprehensive look at foreign exchange risk management complements the one in Chapter 5. The main goals of the chapter are to:

1. Elaborate the differences from traditional capital budgeting analysis that occur because of the international nature of the firm.
2. Explain the concept of political risk and discuss methods for dealing with it.
3. Show how the MNE can make financial structure decisions based both on its total capitalization and on market conditions in the countries where it operates.
4. Elaborate the differences from traditional working capital management that occur because of the international nature of the firm.
5. Define transaction, translation, and economic exchange risk and present methods for dealing with each.
6. Show how financial controls can be established in the MNE.

Introduction

Any firm with affilitates in at least two countries (or even with a simple sales office abroad) is faced with the need to deal with differences in the financial environment of these countries—differences in their tax systems, their currency systems, and numerous other differences. Can you imagine trying to keep the books of a company such as Johnson & Johnson, which is required to maintain financial records according to the different accounting standards in the dozens of countries where it operates, plus records for use in internal control? Beyond the chores of record-keeping, the firm operating at this level obtains opportunities to transfer funds (and products) between countries, to utilize financial markets in each country to serve its global needs, and to diversify its risks internationally. Increasing numbers of MNEs, such as Sears and General Electric, are building internal financial institutions so that they can take advantage of these opportunities around the world. This chapter explores the opportunities and problems of firms in such an environment.

The issue of measuring an MNE's tax liabilities was covered in the previous chapter; what matters here is the firm's ability to arbitrage tax jurisdictions (that is, to reduce global taxes paid by incurring expenses in high-tax countries and showing higher profits in lower-tax countries) and in general to deal with taxation in each country of operation. Similarly, national financial markets and the euromarkets were discussed in Chapter 6; here the emphasis is on using these markets to optimize the financial position of the multinational firm. The issue of exchange risk was treated in Chapter 5; what remains is to consider such risk in the context of a firm that does repeated international business and maintains long-term assets abroad. Finally, consideration is given to the full set of financial issues in a firm whose subsidiaries in different countries are competing for use of the available financial resources. This chapter treats the topic of multinational financial management as a whole.

The chapter is structured to cover major issues in corporate finance as they are relevant in the international context. Basic financial management can be divided into two broad headings: (1) choice and management of *sources* of funds and (2) choice and management of *uses* of funds. At the international level, exchange risk management must be added. Figure 15-1 depicts the topics that constitute the substance of the chapter. Overall financial management requires *control* over each type of decision depicted in the figure—especially since financial managers in each affiliate may be making decisions that affect the total corporation's financial position.

The next three sections explore some aspects of long-term asset and liability management. Then working capital management is covered. Next, a section is devoted to a more extensive presentation of exchange risk management than that given in Chapter 5. Finally, the problem of financial control is discussed.

The main uses of funds in a business can be divided into long-term

Figure 15-1 **Financial Management in the MNE**

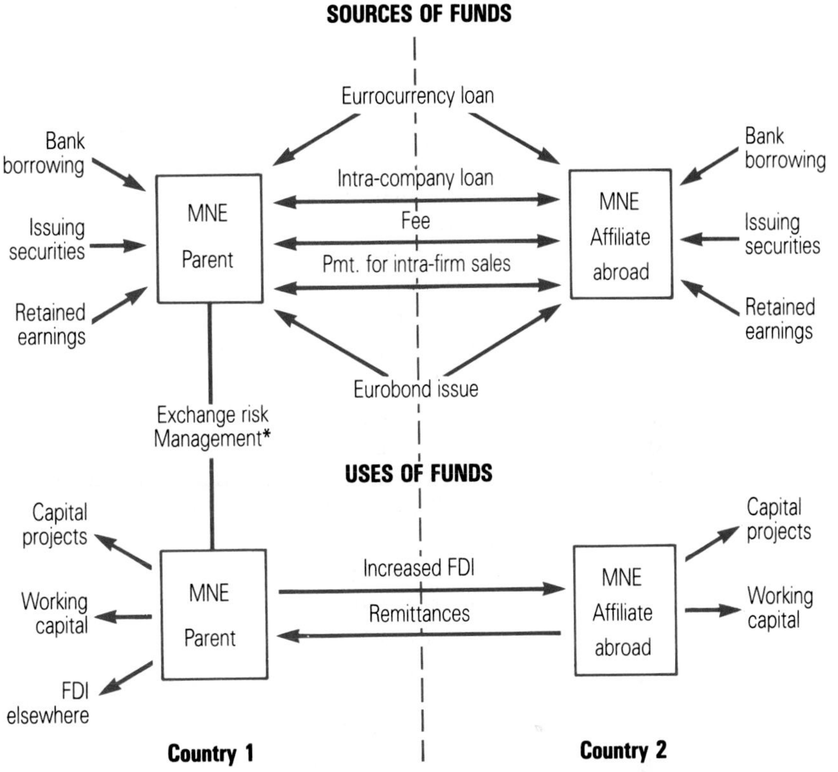

* Exchange risk management is a company-wide concern that relates to all of the issues shown above.

capital projects and such short-term assets as cash, securities, accounts receivable, and inventories. Long-term overseas projects are our first subject for discussion.

Capital Budgeting in the Multinational Enterprise

Capital project evaluation follows much the same reasoning in an international firm as in a domestic firm, though additional variables and risks must be considered. Specifically, foreign projects must be evaluated for exchange risk, political risk, different financing costs, and any problems associated with the transfer of products, services, or funds due to government controls in any of the relevant countries. To see how these factors appear in the analysis, consider the following example of a food processing plant to be constructed by a U.S.-based company in Shapironia.

The company has developed the following pro forma income statement for the proposed investment project:

Proposed Shapironia Processing Plant
Pro Forma Income Statement, Typical Year
(in local currency)

Sales	10,000,000
Cost of goods sold	
Local materials	1,000,000
Imported materials	2,000,000
Labor	3,000,000
Overhead expenses	600,000
Interest on loan from parent firm	400,000
Net income before tax	3,000,000
Local tax—50%	1,500,000
Net income after tax	1,500,000

Assuming that the investment made by the parent firm is 4 million in local currency, the project appears to have a simple return on capital of about 38 percent per year (1,500,000/4,000,000). As long as the firm's cost of capital is less than 38 percent, the project is worth undertaking.[1] The normal, domestic concerns apply to this project evaluation—that is, the estimate is only as good as the forecasts of costs and sales. In addition, this foreign project faces potentially important considerations, such as exchange risk, currency inconvertibility and other political risks, and preferential local-borrowing opportunities.

Exchange risk will affect the U.S. dollar value of the profits earned, potentially raising or lowering them substantially. For example, if the local-currency value rises by 10 percent in relation to the dollar, net income after tax will rise (in dollar terms) by 10 percent, other things equal. However, if imported materials come from the United States, then that cost (in local currency) will fall. Similarly, if the loan is made in dollars, then interest cost (in local-currency terms) will fall. Sales, if any are exported from Shapironia, may decrease due to the exchange rate change.[2] In sum, a rise in the value of the local currency relative to the U.S. dollar will tend to cause an increase in dollar profits from the affiliate—and such profits will tend to fall if the local currency devalues relative to the dollar.

Political risk constitutes another concern in the attempt to evaluate this project properly. If the host government decides to restrict profit remittances, then no matter how profitable the project, the MNE will not be able to utilize its earnings elsewhere in the firm or to distribute them to shareholders. This problem is known as **currency inconvertibility,** regardless of whether the cause is a political decision or simply an economic reality. If discontent with the Shapironia government leads to strikes or to violent confrontation between the government and opposition groups, then the plant may be damaged or its production curtailed. Not all political risk is negative—if the government chooses to reduce corporate taxes to stimulate greater investment, then the project may generate greater profitability than that shown above. In sum, political risks need to be considered when the full set of the project's financial implications is being judged.

Borrowing costs may not be the same in Shapironia and the United States. Thus, if the firm uses its weighted-average cost of capital in capital budgeting decisions, this project should be adjusted to account for any locally subsidized borrowing opportunity that may exist. Many countries (and states or provinces within countries) offer low-interest loans to corporate investors in order to attract production facilities and jobs. If this is true in Shapironia and if the firm chooses to borrow some funds locally, then the subsidized capital cost should be reflected in the capital budget.[3] The project as shown uses an intracompany loan, whose interest may be charged at the parent's actual cost of funds or marked up (or down) to achieve greater (or lesser) transfer of funds to the parent.

Finally, it should be recalled that the capital budget measures the project's **incremental impact** on the whole firm. Thus, if there are export sales from the parent to this new affiliate, those new sales must be counted in the evaluation. If the project replaces sales that were formerly exported to Shapironia, those lost sales must be counted. Any other intracompany impacts should also be measured in the project evaluation. This means that the project should be judged in comparison with other alternatives available to the firm for serving the Shapironia market (as discussed in the appendix to Chapter 3). If exports from the United States offer a greater incremental profitability than the proposed plant, then that alternative should be chosen. In summary, the incremental gains to the firm from the proposed project should be compared with the potential gains from other international business alternatives that may also be available.

Political Risk Management

Definition

Political risk is the increase or decrease in a firm's value that may occur because of unexpected changes in the external, political environment.

Political risk generally refers to a full range of environmental factors that may affect the firm's performance in a particular country. Normal business risks are excluded from this category, but most of the other factors that are outside the firm's control are included. Thus, political risk includes the risk that a government may alter its policies toward the firm or its products (e.g., through price controls), thus lowering or raising profitability or asset values. Political risk also includes the risk of civil war, foreign war, riots, strikes, and other violent social acts that disrupt business. Efforts to harm foreign firms or the particular firm through kidnappings, assassinations, sabotage, or other means fall into this category. Although expropriation of the firm's assets by the host government occurs very infrequently, it constitutes a major political risk. Remember that political risks are not only negative—when a government changes its policies to the firm's advantage (e.g., by lowering taxes or providing some kind of subsidy), this positive outcome also constitutes political risk.

All of these factors are considered political risks because they can all lead to losses (or gains) by the firm for reasons unforeseeable and uncontrollable by it and because they all constitute discontinuities in the firm's external environment. In other words, political risks must involve *changes* in the environment that can affect the firm. Therefore, an *existing* government policy that disallows profit remittances is not a political risk; it is a business condition in the particular country. The possibility of expropriation can be considered virtually a nonrisk for most manufacturing investments in most countries; almost all expropriations since World War II have taken place in extractive industries (e.g., oil, copper, bauxite) and in a handful of less developed countries (primarily in Latin America and the Middle East).

Political risks may be "macrorisks" or "microrisks." A **macrorisk** applies to all foreign firms doing business in a particular country. For example, the changes in taxation or profit remittance rules that often occur in LDCs generally apply to all the foreign firms in those countries. A **microrisk,** on the other hand, applies specifically to one firm or one group of firms. For example, Saudi Arabia's decision to nationalize its oil industry in 1974 constituted a risk for foreign oil companies there, but that risk did not carry over into the manufacturing sector. Similarly, ITT's reported involvement in attempts to overthrow the Allende government in Chile in the early 1970s caused substantial government reprisals at that time in Chile and continuing wariness on the part of Latin American governments with respect to ITT activities.[4] This political risk is company specific.

What exactly is at risk? The answer to this question clearly depends on the type of firm and on its activity in the country. A manufacturing plant typically exposes physical facilities, people, and money to political risk. A sales office may leave only a small number of people and a small amount of equipment at risk. An international bank loan may expose only money to political risk. The correct measure of exposure is that part of the firm's worldwide business that could be affected by unexpected political events or policies in the given country. To determine an appropriate strategy for dealing with this risk, the firm must establish the importance of the risk to its operations.

The full scope of the issues involved in political risk is so broad that it cannot be presented in detail here. Kobrin (1982) encompasses the range of "potentially significant managerial contingencies generated by political events and processes" in his definition of political risk. Brewer (1985) sees political risk as "uncertainty about the political environment of business and its effects on individual firms," that is, as a measure of the effects of politics on business. Every definition of political risk focuses on the potential impact of political factors on company performance.

meet the entire company's needs and then distribute funds to affiliates as required. Also, the group should develop detailed knowledge of financial opportunities worldwide, thus enabling the firm to borrow at lower cost or lower risk than firms without such expertise.

If the MNE reduces its total assets through centralized cash management, it also reduces both its exchange risk and its political risk, in that fewer assets are at risk worldwide. The political risk of a country does not change, but the exposure of the company to that risk decreases. Political risk may also be hedged or transferred by the decision makers in the cash management group, who have greater access to protection tools than do managers in any one affiliate.

Whether or not actual cash is placed in a central location, such a location can be used to keep track of financial flows within the MNE. When accounts among affiliates lead to partially or totally offsetting transfers, the cash management center can *net* the transfers and move only the final sum required. For example, if Beatrice France sells $1 million of products to Beatrice U.S., it will incur an account receivable, say in 180 days. Simultaneously, Beatrice Switzerland may borrow $1 million from the home office. If Beatrice Switzerland sells some products to the French affiliate, the bill could be denominated in dollars, to partially or completely offset the other two liabilities. Thus, this fourth kind of gain from international cash management involves (and is called) **multilateral netting of accounts.** Figure 15-5 shows these three transactions, as well as other methods of shifting funds

Figure 15-5 **Some Methods of Moving Funds in the MNE**

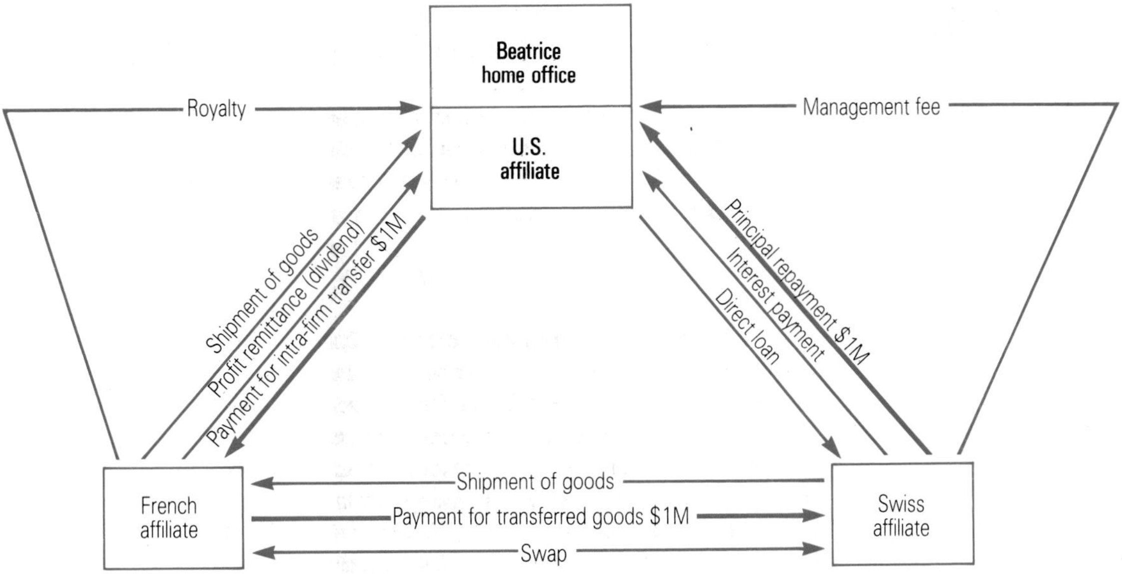

among affiliates in the MNE. Notice that the funds transfer methods depicted in the figure may be used not only to carry out the transactions discussed above but also to transfer funds to a desirable location in order to minimize taxes or to avoid exchange and political risk in any country. If Beatrice wants to shift more funds to Switzerland in order to expand its operations there, it can lend or invest more from the home office, swap assets between affiliates (e.g., accounts receivable from Switzerland for cash from France), remit less from the Swiss affiliate, and even use Switzerland as a cash management center, shifting available cash from other affiliates to that central location for redistribution as needed.

The fifth kind of gain from centralized cash management relates to business strategy. Placing the cash management function in one location, either at the home office or at a location closely monitored by the home office, makes better control possible. In this way, the firm can assure that cash management decisions are made to meet global corporate needs rather than to improve an affiliate's position, possibly at the expense of the rest of the company. This is especially true with respect to hedging, which should be decided at the corporate level, since virtually every affiliate is likely to have assets or liabilities in another currency that are partially or totally hedged by balance sheet items of other subsidiaries.

While the benefits of centralized cash management are easy to see and potentially very large, it also presents some problems. Most important, if freedom to manage cash is taken away from the affiliate manager, some of the affiliate's ability to improve its performance is also taken away. The evaluation of each affiliate must recognize this point. (This idea is discussed further in the section on controls.)

Another problem with internationally centralized cash management arises when national rules restrict financial transfers into or out of some countries. Virtually all less developed countries and many developed ones limit funds outflows through exchange controls or taxation. Some countries specifically disallow international netting of payments. Because of such restrictions, international cash management today requires a great deal of knowledge about national financial constraints, and often a decentralized strategy of funds transfers because of these constraints.

Accounts Receivable

Accounts receivable (A/R) management may be divided according to the type of customer: A/R due from outside customers and A/R due from other affiliates of the firm. Receivables due from outside customers are the typical source of exchange risk, which can be handled as discussed in Chapter 5. Receivables due from other affiliates can be priced and timed to maximize the gains for the MNE, if a central policy is devised.

To deal with the exchange risk created by contracts with outside customers, the MNE can use any number of hedging strategies. In addition, the MNE can substantially reduce the expected cost by setting appropriate credit terms (to discourage late payments, or penalize them to account for expected devaluation of the receivable) and by pricing to account for expected exchange rate changes. The key to managing foreign-currency accounts receivable is to plan the currency and price *before* contracting, that is, before creating the receivable. One way to eliminate exposed accounts receivable is to discount them by creating banker's acceptances, factoring, or forfaiting. (These three discounting methods are discussed in Chapter 18.)

Intracompany accounts receivable can be managed to serve a variety of company goals. Assume, for example, that the firm wants to move as much money as possible from a foreign affiliate to the home office. One way to do this is to have the foreign affiliate prepay any intrafirm purchases, and conversely to have the parent delay any payments due to the affiliate. Another is to price the intrafirm shipment so that greater profit is shown at the home office. (Some legal limitations on the use of these transfer strategies exist in most countries; for example, prepayments are limited to at most 90 days in many countries.)[10]

To move funds from a foreign affiliate to the parent firm, the parent can charge a high **transfer price** for sales to the affiliate. The transfer price is simply the price paid by the affiliate for an intrafirm sale of some product or service. If the product is a computer that costs the firm $1,000 to manufacture, the transfer price might be $1,000—in which case the manufacturing affiliate earns no profit. If the foreign affiliate is just a sales office, it might sell the computer to an outside customer for $3,000. Figure 15-6 depicts the transactions involved. Now, ignoring transportation costs and taxes, the foreign affiliate shows a profit of $2,000 on the sale. The firm could just as easily have charged $3,000 to the foreign sales office for the computer, leaving the entire $2,000 profit in the manufacturing affiliate. Or the firm could have charged some transfer price between $1,000 and $3,000, to share the profits between affiliates. The "optimal" transfer price would move the funds wherever the firm desires, subject to government constraints and the costs of carrying out the transfer. Important criteria for choosing transfer prices are the tax rates in each country, government-imposed price restrictions, and the risks of holding funds in a given currency and country. This simplified example is intended to offer a view of the basic issue in transfer pricing, rather than to say that either of the two extreme prices is "optimal," or even legally possible.

All in all, the management of accounts receivable is an area of great opportunity for the MNE, and one in which the purely domestic firm does not have the same options.

Inventories

Inventory management in an MNE parallels inventory management in a domestic firm. In addition, its concerns include physical risk reduction through diversification of location (if inventories are held in more than one country) and exchange risk increase due to denominating inventories in different currencies. Like centralized cash management, centralized inventory

Figure 15-6 **Transfer Pricing in the MNE**

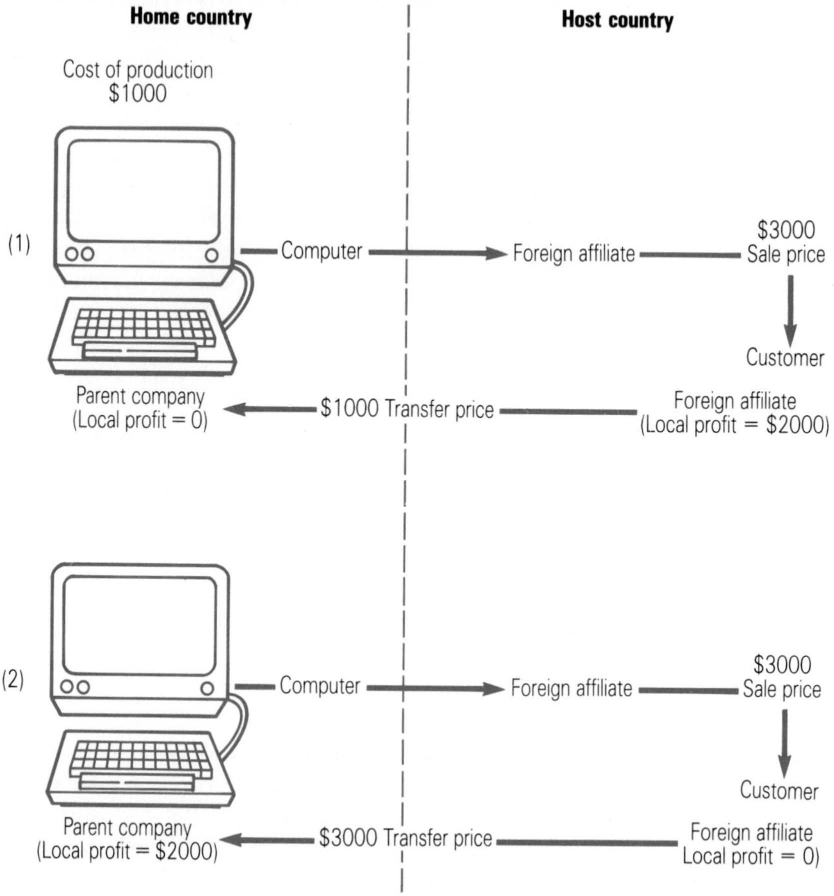

management offers cost-reducing opportunities to the MNE. If the firm produces the same product in more than one country, it can reduce the level of the inventories it needs globally by shipping products from locations where extra inventory exists to locations where inventory is drawn down.

Diversification of inventories across countries cannot be overemphasized as a potential advantage of the MNE. If for any reason the firm's production or shipment in one country is curtailed, the MNE with multiple production sites can serve various markets from other sources. Financially, the firm's costs would be lowest at one particular site at any given time. Strategically, its ability to ship from several sites reduces its risk of sales losses due to the strikes, other production problems, and adverse political developments that may arise in any one country.

Accounts and Notes Payable

To some extent, accounts and notes payable can be managed in the same way as accounts receivable. That is, for accounts and notes payable from one affiliate of the firm to another, the firm can use the timing and pricing of transfers to move funds where and when desired. Payables to outside suppliers and lenders are a key source of foreign exchange risk, which can be managed as discussed previously. Except for dealing with exchange risk, foreign payables can be managed as in the domestic firm, with the aim of minimizing the cost of making necessary payments.

Exchange Risk Management

Exchange risk has been discussed primarily in relation to transactions denominated in foreign currency. In addition, exchange risk exists in the translation of financial statements and, in principle, for future, yet unspecified activities of the firm. Three kinds of exchange risk should be differentiated: (1) transaction risk, (2) translation risk, and (3) economic risk. Each of these kinds of risks is important to the MNE, and each leads to somewhat different conclusions for hedging strategies.

Transaction Risk

When a specific contracted asset or liability is denominated in a foreign currency, it is subject to **transaction risk,** or the risk of change in its home-currency value during the time to maturity. Accounts payable and receivable, loans, and bank deposits denominated in foreign currencies are examples of items that are subject to such exchange risk. Each foreign-currency transaction can be hedged (or not) with some offsetting transaction in the same currency and with the same maturity.

Translation Risk

Translation risk is the risk of value changes in foreign-currency assets and liabilities on the balance sheet—whether or not the transactions occur during the accounting period. For example, the plant and equipment of foreign subsidiaries is subject to valuation change even if no purchase or sale of such facilities takes place during the accounting period. Because balance sheet information is reported to U.S. securities regulators and in financial statements published in the United States, valuation changes in the foreign operations of U.S. firms become public knowledge. Loss in the values of foreign-currency assets, regardless of its impact on company earnings, may negatively affect investors' perceptions of a firm. To avoid the appearance of weakness due to the devaluation of foreign assets, firms often try to hedge their balance sheets through financial contracts (such as forward contracts or money market hedges). This issue has been discussed in Chapter 14; conclusions as to the desirability of **balance sheet hedging** are ambiguous. On the one hand, since investor decisions may be based on valuation changes in foreign-currency assets, the firm should hedge to avoid investor preoccupation with such changes; on the other hand, since the valuation of foreign-currency assets may not affect the economic viability of the project, it would be a waste of effort for the firm to deal with such changes.[11]

Economic Risk

Economic risk is the risk of unexpected changes in future cash flows from foreign operations (and from activities denominated in foreign currencies, wherever they occur). Such risk is most important to the firm, since future cash flows are the basis for the firm's value. Unfortunately for the MNE manager, it is not possible to know with certainty the full set of future cash flows that will occur. So a hedging strategy cannot be perfectly matched with such cash flows. To deal with economic risk, the firm may choose to follow a generalized strategy of hedging transactions when they are contracted and trying to balance foreign currency assets and liabilities as they appear on the balance sheet. Or the firm may choose not to hedge at all, on the assumption that future currency fluctuation will be approximately offset by price changes in each country (i.e., that purchasing power parity will approximately hold). Despite the inherent difficulty of predicting future foreign exchange exposures, ultimately the firm should be concerned about economic (foreign exchange) risk as the key variable in exchange risk management.

In fact, all three kinds of foreign exchange risk play important parts in the management of an international firm. No single hedging strategy can cover them all, so the MNE manager must devise plans for dealing with each. Fortunately, both transaction and economic risk deal with future cash flows, so the management of these two kinds of risk can be combined fairly readily. For example, the firm can hedge all occasional exports denominated in foreign currencies and seek local-currency financing for the entire production of its foreign affiliates. Then, if it does not employ balance sheet hedging (as suggested above), it can follow a consistent and simple hedging strategy. Judging from the immense volume of material dealing with corporate foreign exchange management strategies, it is safe to say that MNEs generally do *not* follow such simple strategies. Instead, they combine some hedging with some speculation in an effort to maximize their results from foreign exchange dealings.[12]

Control: Identifying Objectives, Evaluating Affiliate Performance, and Making Performance Consistent with Goals

Control is the fundamental part of management that involves developing profit plans for the firm and its divisions, then deciding what to do when actual operating results differ from those planned. For a foreign investment project, the financial control process generally begins with putting together a set of pro forma financial statements (income statement, balance sheet, cash flow report), such as the income statement shown at the beginning of this chapter. Then detailed budgets are developed for individual divisions, allocating the full capital budget to the specific purposes for which it will be used. During the time period after the creation of these plans, the firm's management observes the results and any deviations from the budgets. Usually, of course, actual results differ from budgeted ones. Finally, the firm develops a management plan for dealing with the deviations and implements it. The process is cyclical—as each planning period ends, another begins—and new budgets and managerial contingencies may be developed.

In the multinational firm, the potential for substantial home office control over affiliates exists because major capital budgeting usually requires more resources than those available in an affiliate—and home office assistance is needed to carry out capital projects. In addition, financial reporting to the parent company provides an informational basis for controls, which may or may not be exercised, depending on the extent of the firm's decentralization. And finally, because the people assigned to manage foreign affiliates are usually well known to the home office managers, there is an informal, personal contact that ties affiliates to the home office. All of this goes to say that the home office has the potential to impose substantial controls on the activities of foreign affiliates.

The process described so far is substantially equivalent to the one used to evaluate and control domestic divisions in a firm. But foreign affiliates face a wide range of additional factors that may affect their performance, and these factors should be taken into consideration when setting the goals and judging the performance of affiliates. How should the managers of foreign affiliates be evaluated for their financial performance? If they are evaluated in local-currency terms, then the home office must worry about hedging foreign-currency exposures and about remitting or reinvesting profits. If they are evaluated in home-currency terms, then their managers must deal with exchange risk and remittance policy. If they are limited in their financial dealings due to centralized cash and foreign exchange management policies, but they are evaluated in home-currency terms, then it must be recognized that their options are limited. On another issue, if transfer prices are set to move funds to the home office, then foreign profitability will look worse than it would if these prices were set to keep more funds in the affiliates. Correct evaluation of the performance of affiliate managers must take into account the constraints imposed on the affiliates.

Most managers and outside analysts agree that foreign affiliates must be evaluated in home-currency terms, since home-currency investors judge the firm as a whole. What the firm must do is create an evaluation scheme that produces home-currency performance measures, adjusted to account for the limitations placed on the affiliate by the home office.[13]

Conclusions

Financial management in a multinational firm encompasses concerns and opportunities greatly expanded from those encompassed by financial management in a domestic firm. Foremost among these concerns and opportunities is foreign exchange risk management, which is considered in several chapters of this book. Ultimately, foreign exchange risk management seeks to maximize the value of future cash flows into the firm, just as most other aspects of financial management seek to do.

The issue of political risk arises when the firm operates in more than one national legal jurisdiction. The MNE possesses the ability to avoid total dependence on national authorities for its ability to operate; when the national government in one country, places limitations on the MNE, the MNE can turn to other countries for sales, production, and so on. This asymmetry in bargaining power will be seen again when the government/business relationship is explored in Chapters 21-23. The MNE cannot avoid political risks completely, but it can reduce them through hedging, insuring, and diversifying strategies.

The capital structure of a multinational firm is limited primarily by the existing norms in the firm's home country, but that does not stop the firm from using different structures in host countries, as local conditions dictate. Extensive borrowing may be used in high-risk countries, to reduce political and economic exposures of assets. It may also be used in low-interest countries whose currencies are not free to adjust to eliminate interest differentials. This strategy may create highly leveraged affiliates, but it can be used to finance many other parts of the MNE more cheaply than local borrowing elsewhere. Also, locally subsidized financing often presents opportunities for borrowing that may lower the MNE's average cost of capital.

Working capital management presents a wealth of opportunities for minimizing financing costs and maximizing returns on available funds through the use of foreign markets and euromarkets. From centralized cash management, to multilateral netting of accounts payable, to pooling inventories, the MNE has far more flexibility than purely domestic firms. Because of its ability to move funds internationally, the MNE can arbitrage tax and other regulatory jurisdictions to minimize taxes and other costs of operation.

All in all, international finance is one of the most exciting, dynamic areas of corporate management at the international level—but it is also one of the most complex.

Questions

1. What are the main pros and cons related to the centralization of cash management in a multinational enterprise?
2. Define political risk. How may it affect a multinational firm?

3. Explain the difference between transaction and translation risk in foreign exchange risk management.
4. What competitive advantages does an MNE possess relative to local firms in terms of international financing opportunities?
5. How can a firm such as United Technologies, which has subsidiaries in Mexico and Argentina, protect these affiliates against both political and foreign exchange risk?
6. How can an MNE utilize intracompany accounts (such as loans, fees, and product shipments) to deal with exchange risk?
7. What is a transfer price? In dealing with its American affiliates, what transfer pricing policy should Nissan use to keep more funds in its Japanese affiliates?
8. What does it mean to say that the cost of capital is lower in Japan than in the United States? If this is true, how can U.S.-based MNEs that have affiliates in Japan take advantage of the situation?
9. Explain why economic risk, not translation or transaction risk, is the measure of foreign exchange risk that the MNE manager should be concerned about.
10. Should the managers of an MNE's foreign affiliates bear the responsibility for exchange risk management, or should this task be centralized? Explain your choice carefully.

References

Brewer, Thomas, ed. *Political Risks in International Business.* New York: Praeger Publishers, 1985.

Business International Corporation. *Financing Foreign Operations.* New York: Business International Corporation, current edition.

Grosse, Robert, and John Stack. "Noneconomic Risk Evaluation in Multinational Banks," *Management International Review* (1/1984).

Hekman, Christine. "A Financial Model of Foreign Exchange Exposure," *Journal of International Business Studies,* Summer 1985.

Kobrin, Steven. *Managing Political Risk Assessment.* Berkeley; University of California Press, 1982.

Lessard, Donald, and Peter Lorange. "Currency Changes and Management Control: Resolving the Centralization/Decentralization Dilemma," *Accounting Review,* July 1977.

Mascarenhas, Briance, and Ole Christian Sand. "Country-Risk Assessment Systems in Banks: Patterns and Performance," *Journal of International Business Studies* (Spring 1985).

Robins, Sidney, and Robert Stobaugh. *Money in the Multinational Enterprise.* New York: Basic Books, 1973.

Rutenberg, David. "Maneuvering Liquid Assets in a Multinational Company:

Formulation and Deterministic Solution Procedures," *Management Science,* June 1970.

Shapiro, Alan. *Multinational Financial Management.* Boston: Allyn & Bacon, 1982.

Endnotes

1. A full set of the measures used in capital budgeting appears in basic finance texts, such as Weston and Brigham, *Managerial Finance,* 7th ed. (Hinsdale, Ill.: Dryden Press, 1981).
2. However, if the local-currency price goes up due to the currency revaluation and demand is price inelastic, then the total revenue received may go up even if the quantity sold declines.
3. Low-cost financing may be available locally even without government subsidy. In most countries, capital controls limit the ability of foreigners to borrow locally. Thus, in Japan, where interest rates are below those in the United States, a firm with local operations may take advantage of these rates.
4. See, for example, "The ITT Affair," in Prakash Sethi, *Up Against the Corporate Wall* (Palisades, Calif.: Goodyear Publishing, 1976).
5. Useful surveys of political risk models appear in Kobrin (1982) and Brewer (1985).
6. See, for example, Shapiro (1982), chap. 9.
7. *Eximbank Program Summary* (Washington, D.C.: Office of Public Affairs, Export-Import Bank of the United States, n.d.).
8. See Alan C. Brennglass, *The Overseas Private Investment Corporation* (New York: Praeger Publishers, 1983); and Business International Corporation, "Investment Guarantees," in *Financing Foreign Operations* (New York: Business International Corporation, current edition).
9. Calculated from *Business Week,* March 22, 1985, p. 134; and Ravi Sarathy and S. Chatterjee, "The Divergence of Japanese and U.S. Corporate Financial Structure," *Journal of International Business Studies,* Winter 1984.
10. See Business International Corporation, *Financing Foreign Operations,* for information about restrictions on financial transfers in over 50 countries.
11. See, for example, Dennis Logue and George Oldfield, "Managing Foreign Assets when Foreign Exchange Markets Are Efficient," *Financial Management,* Summer 1977.
12. See, for example, Nick Gilbert "Hedging Trims the Costs," *Euromoney,* February 1985, pp. 141-44; and Derek Bamber "How SKF International Keeps a Grip on 18 Currencies," *Euromoney,* September 1982, pp. 341-51.
13. See, for example, Lessard and Lorange (1977) and Robins and Stobaugh (1973).

Case
Bill Smythe & Co.

Introduction

A firm from any country that decides to set up a foreign subsidiary for manufacturing, sales, shipping, or other business activity, generally faces an important challenge in dealing with the foreign-currency aspects of the business. American firms in particular tend to have difficulty with this situation, because they often operate in dollars exclusively in their U.S. operations. European firms, on the other hand, commonly are used to working in at least two or three currencies, and in many cases with the European Currency Unit as well. So, especially for American firms, the need to understand and deal with foreign currencies is a fundamental business problem of the 1980s.

One industry that has long been associated with international business is the production of textiles, for example, men's and women's clothing. From the ancient silk trade that formed an important part of the activities of the British East and West India Companies to modern offshore assembly of blue jeans in Taiwan, trade in textiles has extended throughout the world. Even with this international component, the production of clothing in most countries remains primarily domestic. That is, due to differences in costs, tastes, and government regulations, clothes sold locally are generally also produced locally.

The clothing business in the United States historically has been a very inward-looking industry. Most clothing is made from domestically produced fibers, either natural (such as cotton or wool) or synthetic (such as nylon or polyester). Although a large percentage of the natural fiber is imported today, most clothing is still made of primarily domestically manufactured material. Very little of the United States' domestic production is exported; several American companies, however, have foreign subsidiaries that produce locally in various foreign markets.

One way that domestic firms have been able to survive international competition is through successful lobbying for protection against imports. The textile industry in the United States has been one of the most adept at gaining government protection, mainly through the international Multifibre Agreement. This accord among producing and consuming nations gives the importing companies essentially unlimited power to restrict imports of both raw materials and assembled clothing in order to protect domestic producers. The Multifibre Agreement is a major exception to the rules of the General Agreement on Tariffs and Trade (GATT) that promote freer trade among such member nations as the United States and its European trading partners.

This case was written by Professor Robert Grosse as a basis for class discussion, 1987.

About the Company

Bill Smythe & Co. was founded in 1951 by a Philadelphia shop foreman, Bill Smythe. He had spent five years working for a small men's shirt manufacturer in Yeadon, Pennsylvania, that went out of business due to inadequate sales and rising costs. With his knowledge of the manufacturing process and his determination to succeed through better marketing than his predecessor, Smythe set up his shop in a West Philadelphia industrial district and began to produce a line of high-quality men's shirts and women's blouses. His initial customers were many of the same clients served by the previous company.

Within a year of opening the shop, Smythe decided to expand his marketing efforts. Sales were fairly stable but barely enough to pay the bills until he set up a licensing agreement with one of the leading designers of high-fashion women's clothing. This agreement enabled him to produce blouses under the designer's name and to obtain access to several large department stores as clients. Even after paying the licensing fee, Smythe's earnings rose substantially.

By 1960 Bill Smythe & Co. was selling over 200,000 shirts and blouses per year. The original 5 employees had grown to 11, and the shop now took up 4,000 square feet of operating space. At this point Smythe had licensing agreements with three fashion designers for making both shirts and blouses. The branded lines made up over three fourths of his total sales. In looking over the business, Smythe decided that his next step should be to expand into additional product lines.

The process of growth continued during the 1960s. The firm added lines including handkerchiefs, undergarments, and jackets—though the last line was discontinued in 1968 when consistently poor sales led Smythe to drop it. By the end of the decade, Bill Smythe & Co. had become a fairly large producer of shirts and blouses in the northeastern United States, with export sales into Canada. Despite the efforts to diversify, sales were dominated by Smythe's two original lines.

By that time, competition from foreign producers was beginning to affect sales. Smythe found that Italian and Spanish firms, in particular, were making unbranded shirts that undercut his prices by almost 30 percent, and some of these firms were producing brand-name shirts at a similar price advantage. By coincidence, Smythe discovered that one of the Italian firms was run by a high school classmate, Joe Todarello, who had returned to his parents' native country and entered the business there. When his friend mentioned that his father wanted to sell the firm, Smythe quickly offered to buy it and keep his friend as general manager. This arrangement was concluded in 1977. It turned out very well, with the Italian subsidiary bringing in about 22 percent of total company sales within four years of the acquisition.

Although he had never thought about the problem in any detail, Smythe began to realize that changes in the lira/dollar exchange rate were altering his costs and profits in a serious way in the early 1980s. He was especially unhappy with the loan that he had used to finance most of the purchase of the Italian firm. The loan was made in dollars to the Italian subsidiary with Smythe & Co.'s guarantee, but the subsidiary was paying it off through profits earned. With the demise of the Bretton Woods system of fixed exchange rates in 1971, the lira had been devaluing in spurts against the U.S. dollar (thus raising the financing cost with each devaluation). Figure 1 shows this situation. When the dollar began to decline relative to the deutsche mark and the Japanese yen in 1985, the lira strengthened somewhat, but the downward trend seemed likely to continue. Smythe found that his earnings in Italy declined precipitously from 1981 to 84 (due to depressed sales as well as currency devaluation). In 1985 sales rose, but operating profits remained weak. In 1986 earnings (counted in dollars) rose sharply as operating costs in Italy stabilized and the U.S. dollar weakened.

Current Concerns

Bill Smythe sat uncomfortably in his living room in December of 1986, looking over the projected earnings statement (Table 1) drawn up by Joe Todarello. While the numbers in lira appeared clear and justifiable, Smythe was totally unable to come to grips with the problem of exchange risk and

Figure 1 **Lira/Dollar Exchange Rates*, 1970–1986**

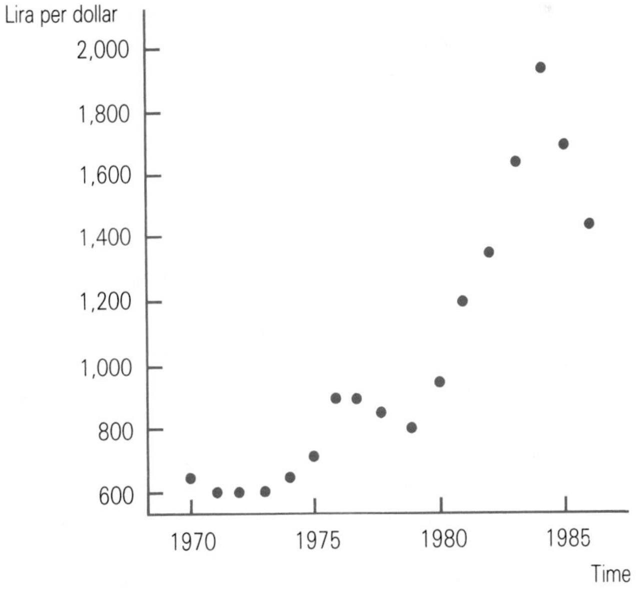

* Lira per dollar, end-of-year market rate.

Table 1

SMYTHE ITALIA
Pro Forma Income Statement
1987 to 1991
(in billions of lira)

	1987	1988	1989	1990	1991
Revenues:	21	27	36	46	60
Local sales	15.8	20.4	28.5	35.7	49.2
Export sales	2.3	3.9	4.5	6.8	8.2
Earnings on investments	3.1	2.7	3.4	3.4	3.0
Expenses:	18	22	28	35	47
Labor	5.2	6.8	8.8	11.5	14.9
Local materials	6.1	7.9	10.3	13.4	17.4
Imported materials	1.9	2.1	2.9	3.5	4.2
Licensing fees	0.9	1.1	1.4	1.8	2.4
Supervisory fees	0.7	0.9	1.1	1.4	1.9
Operating overhead	1.5	1.8	2.3	2.9	3.9
Interest expense	2.1	2.3	2.5	2.8	3.1
Net income before taxes	2.8	4.1	7.1	8.6	12.6
Corporate income tax (45%)	1.3	1.8	3.2	3.9	5.7
Net income after taxes*	1.5	2.3	3.9	4.7	6.9

**Note:* Tax of 30 percent is payable on any profit remitted to the U.S parent.

projecting dollar values of the various cash flows. Moreover, he felt that some attention should be paid to the possibility of restrictions on the firm's shipments of materials and finished shirts and blouses between Italy and the United States. He had asked Todarello to describe the currency situation in 1985 and 1986. Table 2 was Todarello's response.

Table 2

SMYTHE ITALIA
Flow of Funds Statement
December 1986
(values in $ U.S. equivalents)

	Currency		
Cash flow	**Lira**	**Dollars**	**Marks**
Next month	82,000	−39,000	8,000
In 2 months	79,000	−43,000	8,000
3 to 6 months	360,000	−195,000	34,000
7 to 12 months	540,000	−295,000	52,000
13 to 18 months	570,000	−295,000	57,000
19 to 24 months	580,000	−310,000	57,000
Year 3 and after (per year)	1,180,000	−600,000	120,000

The projections show a stable growth of lira earnings and cash flow. Dollar cash flows are negative, reflecting the continued purchase of materials and equipment from the U.S. parent company. Profit remittances are *not* included in the calculations. Export sales to a German department store, which began in 1984, are listed as German mark cash inflows, also growing at a stable rate. Export sales from the Italian subsidiary to the U.S. parent company are shown as lira cash inflows, since they are billed in lira by the subsidiary.

16 INDUSTRIAL RELATIONS

Industrial relations are often regarded as place specific and therefore not especially relevant to MNEs and their competitive strategies. This perspective is inaccurate. MNEs possess internal strengths that they can use to improve their industrial relations management at the levels of both the parent and the subsidiary. Moreover, MNEs must consider the effects of industrial relations environments on some of their key strategic management concerns. This chapter examines these topics. The main goals of the chapter are to:

1. Explore the international aspects of industrial relations from the standpoints of MNEs, labor, and society.
2. Present the industrial relations systems approach to characterizing industrial relations environments.
3. Describe the international activities of trade unions.
4. Examine the management of industrial relations within MNEs.
5. Explain how industrial relations concerns affect certain strategic management decisions, such as those pertaining to production allocation, production smoothing, and disinvestment.

What Are Industrial Relations?

In the following chapter, "Personnel Management," the focus is on the relationship of individual employees to their employers. In this chapter, the focus is on collective employee-employer relationships. Such relationships vary considerably country by country and industry by industry, and this variability can provide the MNE with important problems and opportunities. These will be discussed later. Let's begin, however, by reviewing some key aspects of **industrial relations,** especially in the United States. Knowledge of the U.S. industrial relations system will provide us with a basis for noting and understanding differences between U.S. industrial relations and industrial relations in other countries.

Industrial Relations in the United States

In the United States, we typically view industrial relations within the context of union-management relations and of a collective agreement or **labor contract.** Industrial relations, then, involve both substance (i.e., the terms of the contract) and procedure (i.e., determining and administering the contract).

Among the topics usually covered in labor contracts are job classifications, wages, wage supplements (such as shift differentials and overtime pay premiums), fringe benefits (such as health insurance and the retirement program), holidays, vacations, promotion and layoff procedures, a no-strike/no-layoff commitment, union recognition and security, and management rights. Other topics, such as cost-of-living wage supplements and the procedures to follow with regard to plant closings, may also be covered. Typically, the contract includes rules regarding its administration. These rules identify the structure of the in-plant union representation and the procedure to be followed in handling complaints (or grievances)—so as to resolve them in a timely fashion consistent with the substantive provisions of the contract.

Laws enacted by the U.S. government have established rules regarding bargaining unit determination (whom will the contract cover?), union recognition, and the conduct of the parties during collective bargaining. The size or scope of the **bargaining unit** is usually decided by the National Labor Relations Board (NLRB) in an administrative ruling based on employee and employer petitions, historical precedents relating to the common interests of groups of workers, the nature of the tasks identified in the proposed unit, and so on. Voting by the employees in the proposed unit decides whether there will be a union and, if so, which union it will be. If there is strong employee support for a union and management concurs, the NLRB may determine a bargaining unit and then certify a union without an election.

U.S. law also requires that both management and union bargain in good faith (this means, for example, that information necessary to the successful conduct of the bargaining must be shared and that there must be give-and-take during the negotiations) and that bargaining be conducted only over topics related to the terms and conditions of employment. Overall, the thrust of U.S. labor law has been to lower the potential for labor-management conflict by establishing rational, democratic procedures related to union recognition; by limiting the substance of collective bargaining to worker-related interests and issues; and by requiring the parties to the collective bargaining process to be reasonably open, accessible, and forthcoming.

Perceptions of the Stakeholders

We see from this that industrial relations are important in several respects. From management's perspective, industrial relations determine labor costs, the facility with which work processes are changed, and the potential for conflict in resolving differences held by the union, the firm, or the employees. From the union's perspective, industrial relations determine the extent of shared decision making on matters that concern workers and on the level of income and financial security enjoyed by those whom the contract covers. Government and society value successful industrial relations too. Such issues as the frequency and duration of strikes that interrupt commerce, the cost-push pressures of wages on product prices, and worker participation in decision making typically relate to broader social interests in productivity, competitiveness, inflation, employment growth, and industrial democracy.

In the following section, the international dimension of industrial relations pertinent to MNEs and their operations will be discussed, as will important public policy issues regarding the effects of MNEs on employment and industrial relations. Subsequent sections cover key features of the industrial relations environment—worker representation, the nature of the labor-management agreement, wage determination, industrial conflict, and so on—that are evidenced in several countries. In addition, the activities of unions and government-related organizations at the transnational level are characterized and discussed. The chapter concludes with a section on the management of industrial relations in an MNE context and on the impact of industrial relations on strategic management.

What's International about Industrial Relations?

Like industrial relations at the national or domestic level, industrial relations at the international level are important to companies, management, unions, workers, society, and government.

Ethnocentric, Polycentric, and Geocentric Views

The ethnocentric MNE, which mandates the behavior of subsidiaries, typically has problems regarding industrial relations. The cultural, legal, and factual contexts that drive industrial relations are too crucial to be managed from the distance of the parent company. As a result, local management is usually given, perhaps begrudgingly at first, considerable autonomy in its industrial relations.

If one considers the multinational enterprise (MNE) to be simply a collection of reasonably freestanding, national production and marketing units, then industrial relations would, at a minimum, be as important to the MNE as to a purely domestic company. This is the polycentric view. Key elements in the competitive success and profitability of either type of firm—production wages, work methods, benefit levels, and so on—would be determined by means of the industrial relations process. But there is really more to industrial relations than this for the MNE—as will be shown later.

The mature multinational enterprise is more than a collection of free-standing, national subsidiaries. Because of its transnational linkages in terms of technological (including management expertise) and financial flows and because of its ability to identify and utilize product and resource markets advantageously, the geocentric MNE is quite different from the non-MNE in its industrial relations. Here are some illustrations:

Opel (General Motors' German subsidiary) negotiates an *increase* in the basic workweek hours with Belgian unions as it adds a second shift at its Belgian assembly plant. The intent of management is to keep the costs of production there competitive with the costs of production at a similar Opel plant in Germany. The intent of the Belgian workers is to expand employment and enhance job security.

A U.S. electronics firm cuts back its U.S. manufacturing output 10 percent by laying off a like percentage of its U.S. workers. Its French subsidiary picks up the resulting product market slack. By cutting back employment in the United States, the firm avoids the large payments to workers that French law would have required if the cutback had been made by the French subsidiary.

Workers at a German company's British subsidiary go out on strike to support their demand for improved wages. Operations at the company's German plants continue, providing substantial cash inflows (revenues) to the entire MNE system. The British workers completely forgo their cash inflows—their wages—during the strike. The company is less severely pressed financially than these workers are and can sustain a long strike if need be.

Ford of Europe integrates production among several European subsidiaries. For certain models of cars, the engines are British-made, the power train and some stampings German-made, the wheels and other stampings Belgian-made, and so on. A strike by workers in Belgium could shut down plants in Britain, Germany, and elsewhere. This gives the Belgian workers operational leverage vis-à-vis management and enhances their power in collective bargaining. Figure 16-1 illustrates this point.

Figure 16-1 **How Vulnerable is Ford to a Strike in Belgium? Transnational Sourcing in Ford of Europe**

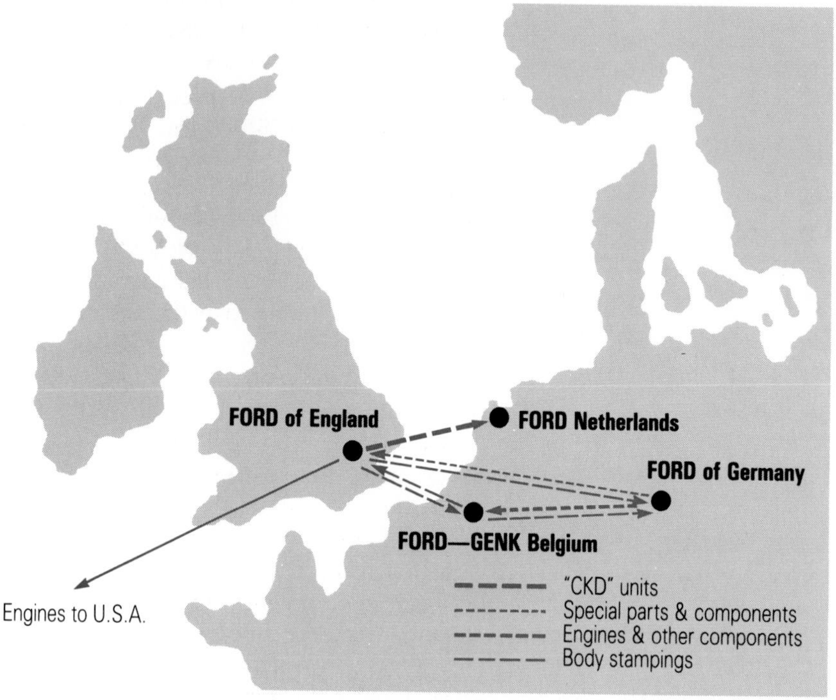

Note: The patterns depicted are for two car models produced in the 1970s. "CKD" ("completely-knocked-down") refers to packages of components from which a complete car could be assembled.

These examples show how the multinationally distributed operations and markets of the MNE affect the economics and stability of the workplace and the relative bargaining power of the parties involved in industrial relations. These effects, in turn, can have a significant impact on unions and on worker-related social issues.

Labor's View of MNEs

Organized labor usually operates within the context of a nationally defined industrial relations system. It is the product of a specific cultural and legal heritage. As the above examples indicate, the MNE may determine or influence labor's interests transnationally, but unions and workers are less transnationally mobile than the MNE. They see the MNE, then, as having options that they do not have. They see it as having the potential for:

Forcing workers in one country, faced by competition from workers in other countries, to "bid down" their wages and benefits in order to get or keep jobs.

Taking advantage of differences in legally required benefits for workers by adjusting operations in countries where the costs of such adjustments are lowest and thus forcing excessive dislocation burdens on workers in these low-benefit countries.

Outlasting workers in the event of a strike in one country because cash inflows to the MNE are at least partially maintained by operations in countries where there is no strike.

In the Ford of Europe example above, the bargaining leverage gained by the unions because of transnational production integration may be only a short-run benefit, as the company might position future production facilities in worker and union environments that are less threatening to it.

Social Issues and MNEs

From a broad public policy perspective on the international dimensions of industrial relations, the MNEs have been both criticized and praised. Critics contend that by opening plants abroad, the MNEs have exported jobs from the United States and destroyed the diverse industrial base that it needs to sustain its economic well-being.[1] They argue that MNEs have compromised the national security of the United States by locating high-technology operations overseas and by licensing foreign firms to produce high-technology products. It has also been argued that MNEs, by the very nature of their operations, negate the national interest expressed in the U.S. National Labor Relations Act, in maintaining the balance of power between management and unions that successful collective bargaining requires.[2] On the other hand, supporters of the MNEs contend that overall employment has grown faster in MNEs than in non-MNEs[3] and that workers in MNEs receive higher salaries than workers in non-MNEs.

A key issue in the public policy area arises from the ability of MNEs to respond quickly to new market opportunities wherever they arise, whereas workers are unable to suddenly relocate geographically or acquire new needed skills. This is the adjustment problem. Most industrialized countries offer adjustment assistance funds to retrain and relocate workers affected by changes in products and markets. This says that these countries value the economic benefits that are realized when firms develop new products and markets and that society in general should provide a "cushion" to workers adversely affected by such developments. Some countries, as noted earlier, penalize firms for laying off workers by requiring large severance payments. This says that these countries do not want workers and society to be forced into a costly adjustment process unless the threshold value of the economic benefits realized in this way is above a legally defined minimum. A problem here is that marketplace competition may make adjustment compelling anyway. What could result from penalizing layoffs is "hidden unemployment" as workers are kept on the job in the face of declining production or product prices and state-provided subsidies keep firms afloat and jobs intact. This is a problem today in some of the state-owned enterprises in France and the United Kingdom. Finally, the more aggressive countries underwrite or legislate benefits to firms that invest in them or trade internationally so that they may get to keep jobs and earn foreign exchange. These benefits take such forms as tax rebates on exports, low-interest loans, government-funded R&D, and special purchase agreements. Policies of this kind distort comparative advantage and raise the specter of free versus fair trade and investment flows. They also politically distort economic considerations and invite a desire for political retaliation.

The Diversity of the Industrial Relations Facing MNEs

Since MNEs have generally concentrated their manufacturing[4] investments in the more industrialized countries, where larger markets and higher income levels exist, two of these countries—the United Kingdom and West Germany—have been contrasted with the United States to illustrate the diversity among country-bound industrial relations systems. Japan's industrial relations system has also been considered, because of the positive influence of its work force management techniques and industrial relations on its industrial prowess and its competitive successes. To help us focus on the business-related features of these industrial relations systems, our discussion is organized around selected key industrial relations issues as evidenced in each system.

Worker Representation

United States In the United States, the union, if certified, becomes the exclusive bargaining agent for the employees in the bargaining unit. It negotiates with the company on the contract terms, and it monitors management's compliance with the contract. Depending on what the contract stipulates and on what state law may require, workers may or may not have to join the union or pay union dues as a condition for continued employment. Collective bargaining typically occurs at the company and plant levels, with some notable exceptions involving multicompany bargaining, for example, in trucking and the building trades, where the level is regional, and in the steel industry, where it is national.

United Kingdom Work groups within a plant often express a sense of solidarity and negotiate with management on matters that they feel are important. They elect someone from their ranks to be their chief spokesperson, or steward. Workers also often belong to a union, which is organized on a geographic basis and includes members at many firms in a local area. Collective bargaining is conducted with a company's representatives by a council of representatives of the unions in the area. It may also be conducted by a **stewards' council** representing only workers at the company. This dualism, which is in sharp contrast with the exclusive jurisdiction that prevails in the United States, allows for conflict between the unions and the stewards. For example, the union council may accept an agreement with management and the company stewards may reject it. Major work stoppages have resulted in cases of this kind. Labor negotiations are conducted at the company level with the larger firms in an area, or at the industry level for an area if the firms are fairly small.

Germany Union membership is purely voluntary, and there is only one union for laborers in each major industry. Collective bargaining, conducted between the union and the employers' federation for the industry, covers major terms of employment, such as wages. Firms that are federation members apply the labor agreement to their workers. Nonfederation firms may or may not implement their industry agreements, depending on a variety of factors—the tightness of the labor market, the desires and solidarity of their workers, and so on. Secondary conditions of employment (such as the scheduling of vacations and workshifts) are negotiated at the company and/or plant levels between management and legally established **works councils**—whose members are elected by the company's workers and may or may not be union members.

Works councils in Germany are legally empowered to "codetermine" with management issues related to worker safety procedures and other in-plant practices. These works councils are made up of management and employee representatives. Some employees are also elected to serve as employee representatives on **boards of supervision.** These boards, which operate in some respects like boards of directors, appoint and evaluate top management. Works councils and the presence of employees on boards of supervision are the results of the widespread German codetermination movement.

Japan Unions in Japan are typically characterized as **enterprise unions.** There are over 70,000 of them, and they usually include all the hourly and salaried employees of the firm. Workers view themselves as employees first—and because they are employees, they belong to the enterprise union. Collective bargaining is accomplished at the enterprise level. Enterprise unions in the same industry affiliate to form industrial federations, which are generally loosely knit and do not themselves engage in collective bargaining. The federations typically coordinate the bargaining policies and timing of enterprise unions during *Shunto,* the so-called Spring Offensive.

Labor-management relations in Japan reflect the often close, mutually supportive identification between the worker and the company. The larger firms, for example, offer "lifetime" employment (i.e., up to retirement age) and structure their operations, and changes in operations, to accommodate that commitment. Workers, on their part, dedicate themselves to the company. They seldom change employers in mid-career.

The Labor Agreement

United States The **labor agreement** is a contract that can be enforced in court, if need be. It is in effect for a fixed period of time, and its terms and conditions apply to all of the workers covered by it. Therefore, the employees of an individual bargaining unit have no individualized right to bargain with management for their own wages and benefits. Legislation at the national level abolishes this right for such workers.

The content of the contract, which is typically fairly extensive, covers the various topics identified earlier. Disputes regarding the proper application of the contract's provisions are typically resolved by means of the grievance system specified in the contract itself. This usually means that binding arbitration, where an impartial, outside party makes the final decision, is the last step in the grievance procedure.

United Kingdom The labor agreement is not a legally binding contract. It is an "understanding" among the parties that basically means, given the present circumstances, these are the acceptable terms and conditions of employment. Violations of the agreement by unions or stewards' groups carry no legal penalties since these entities are not recognized in law. They have no legal status or identity.

The content of the United Kingdom labor agreement is generally less extensive than that of the U.S. contract. Such agreements may contain provisions defining the structure of the relationships among the parties. Separate wage provisions are then negotiated; their duration is effectively open-ended. Procedures for handling complaints are often spelled out in the labor agreement, but there is no provision for arbitration. In fact, complaints are typically handled by the shop steward, who was probably not formally involved in the negotiations establishing these procedures, and resolved, if need be, by industrial action (i.e., a strike) before the procedures have been completed.

Germany Workers in an industry may be covered by several fixed-term contracts, each of which has a different expiration date. There is typically a wage structure agreement that spells out the job classifications and the relative wage levels for the different jobs. The tariff, or wage, agreement sets out the actual wages to be paid. Another agreement may specify the amount of indemnification paid a worker who loses his job because of automation or a sales decline. Yet another agreement covers general working conditions, such as work times, personal leave, vacations, and overtime pay. The provisions of each agreement are limited to the issues that it alone addresses.

Conflicts over the application of an agreement can be negotiated between management and the individual involved, perhaps with the participation of a union representative and/or the works council. The final resolution of complaints is handled in German labor courts, if necessary. In contrast to the U.S. situation, individual workers covered by labor contracts may still negotiate individually or collectively with management to secure wages and benefits superior to those defined in the contract. By statute, their individual rights here are not preempted.

Japan Union and company representatives review annually the labor agreement and it is changed if the parties agree that this should be done. Typically, labor agreements cover wages, bonuses, working conditions, grievances, personnel affairs, and welfare issues. **Shunto,** the Spring Offensive, is an annual, enterprise-level bargaining over wages and the summer bonus that is coordinated closely at the industry level. The practice of *Shunto* acknowledges that wage gains at the enterprise level are constrained by the labor costs of a firm's competitors. *Shunto* attempts, in effect, to extend wage bargaining to cover all of the firms in an industry. There may be yet another round of bargaining when unions negotiate the year-end bonus.

The provisions of the Japanese labor agreement are often general and vague, and they even include employment conditions that are legally required. Disputes about the rights conveyed in such agreements are often settled between the parties in an amicable manner featuring compromise. The disputes can be taken, however, to an agreed-upon private third party for mediation and, if necessary, arbitration. Japanese labor law establishes labor relations commissions that can also mediate and arbitrate disputes, and the courts can do this too.

Industrial Conflict

The two most common forms of industrial conflict are strikes and lockouts. **Strikes** can result from two types of disputes: those relating to rights that workers feel are theirs because of contracts or past practices and those relating to interests that workers have regarding the setting of wages, benefits, and other terms and conditions of employment. **Lockouts,** in which employers close the plant and thus keep employees from working, don't occur nearly as often as strikes. Other forms of industrial conflict include "work to rule" (i.e., a slowdown, "going by the book"), industrial sabotage, and the occupation of plants by workers.

United States As noted, most labor agreements contain provisions barring strikes. The very existence of the agreement signifies that both management and the union have defined their mutual interests. The contract conveys certain rights to both parties (e.g., the wages to be received and the ability of management to reassign workers). The grievance system, which typically includes binding arbitration, is also defined in the contract. This procedure resolves whatever disputes over rights may arise.

Strikes and lockouts during the term of the contract are usually forbidden. One effect of all this is that once a contract is in place, strikes and lockouts are typically illegal and rare. Such actions, however, are not rare after a contract expires and when a new contract is being negotiated. They

West German employees who were barred from jobs in their home country talk with French communist-led CGT union delegates during a meeting here after holding a news conference on West Germany's labor interdictions (Berufsverbote).

Wide World Photos, Inc.

then involve the entire bargaining unit. At such times, the parties are seeking to define their interests. Typically, "wildcat" strikes—strikes that occur during the term of a contract—result from allegedly onerous management practices or working conditions related to specific work groups and are not endorsed by the union. Such strikes are usually brief. Other forms of industrial conflict seldom occur.

Business unionism, which characterizes the pragmatic, enterprise-oriented focus of the U.S. labor movement, acknowledges that an ongoing, hopefully profitable, firm is in the best interests of the union and the workers. Likewise, socially accepted values, such as those relating to private property and the concept of the contract, help explain U.S. labor's reluctance to destroy equipment, occupy a factory, or provide less in the way of labor services than the labor agreement calls for.

United Kingdom Labor in the United Kingdom is typically more strike prone than labor in the United States. The social philosophy of **voluntarism,** a keystone concept of the British labor movement, asserts that workers alone will define and pursue their self-interest. From this, it follows that the right to "industrial action," such as a strike or "work to rule," must be unconstrained (e.g., by law). Labor agreements do not prohibit the right to strike, and strikes

Keystone Press Agency

often occur during impasses in bargaining and in support of workers' grievances. Such strikes are typically brief, and they often involve small work groups.

The dual worker representation structure (i.e., the ship stewards and the unions) has been known to complicate both collective bargaining and grievance handling in the United Kingdom and to result in fragmented bargaining relationships—and, in so doing, to enhance the propensity of workers to strike and to extend the duration of strikes. Lockouts, especially those involving company workers other than those in a work group that is out on strike, are not uncommon. Workers extend the idea of voluntarism to mean not only that they will take care of themselves but also that management will take care of itself. There is more class consciousness on the part of both labor and management in the United Kingdom than in the United States, and the work environment is probably more adverse to the efficient settlement of labor-management disputes.

Germany Labor laws prohibit strikes and lockouts when an agreement is in effect. This means that conflicts (such as strikes) over rights are illegal. Conflicts over interests, which occur when an old contract has expired and a new one is being negotiated, are legal. Focus and clarity are given to the issues in collective bargaining and the potential for strikes is reduced by the fact that there are several labor agreements in an industry, with different termination dates and covering different terms and conditions of employment.

This structure is apparently consistent with the preference of Germans for orderly, well-defined work relationships. Nevertheless, during recent years some strikes have occurred when an existing contract was in effect. These strikes were illegal. The issues, however, were usually not rights but interests. Unanticipated inflation was damaging workers' living standards, and strikes were conducted to increase current wages accordingly—even though a current wage agreement was in effect.

Japan Strikes and lockouts at the enterprise level are rare. Strikes of exceedingly brief duration (perhaps a half-day or so) are typically scheduled during *Shunto* to demonstrate workers' support for their representatives' demands in industry-wide negotiations. The issues over which there may be industrial conflict between management and the union are also fairly limited. For one thing, the provisions of the labor contract supersede an individual worker's terms and conditions of employment that are not equal to or better than what the contract mandates. For another, the law establishes standards for minimum wages, hours, overtime, rest periods, vacations, sick leave, sanitary conditions, and discharge notice that are set at the comparatively high levels of other advanced societies.

One result of all this is that the overwhelming majority of strikes are over economic issues, brief, and, since they usually relate to *Shunto,* anticipated. The Japanese social philosophy of *Wa* implies that individuals subordinate individual interests and identities to those of the group. Social harmony and teamwork are derived from this. Significant (i.e., other than ceremonial) conflict is the antithesis of *Wa*.

Cross-Country Comparisons

Management in the multinational enterprise is concerned with several aspects of the industrial relations systems in and across which it operates. These aspects are basically the same as those with which management in the domestic enterprise is concerned, but the MNE can treat them as variables in its strategic planning since its operations transcend typically place-bound industrial relations. This management perspective will be developed more fully toward the end of this chapter. However, some of the groundwork can best be put in place now. The key question is: How do the countries compare on certain issues important to management, such as wages and benefits, the potential for productivity improvement, and production continuity?

Wages and Benefits The importance of the level of wages and benefits is obvious. Major business decisions and significant financial commitments often turn on a comparative analysis of wage and benefit costs. But what about the propensity of these costs to change? What about the pace of these changes relative to inflation in general?

Wages in the United States have traditionally been among the highest in the world. Changes in basic wage rates, within the union-management context, are reflected in labor contracts. Such changes are programmed over a period of time—most often a three-year period. Cost-of-living wage increases must by definition lag inflation, and typically they do not fully offset the amount of inflation. Cost-of-living formulas defined in the labor contract define and control such increases.

In the United Kingdom, wages are almost constantly subject to scrutiny, and if workers or unions feel that higher wages are necessary or desirable, a new round of wage bargaining can occur at any time. The structure of the work force representation may be a factor here too. In the UK, shop-level work groups can initiate new wage demands and attempt to make them effective. In comparable U.S. industrial settings, the more broadly constituted union bargaining unit is the single collective bargaining entity. Wage escalation within that unit is not constantly at issue, as it is in the United Kingdom where a militant and aggressive work group may secure higher wages, which, in turn, leads to demands from other work groups within the firm for the reestablishment of the parity differentials that they have traditionally merited and enjoyed. The potential for a firm to be caught in a wage cost/product price squeeze appears to be substantially higher in the United Kingdom than in the United States.

In West Germany, wages set in industry-wide negotiations are paid by all firms in the industry. The firms also pay wage increments, depending on the labor market conditions they face, their profitability, or the intensity of their workers' demands. Strikes in support of wage increments are illegal when an industry-wide agreement (which covers wage minimums at firms party to industry-wide bargaining) is in effect. Moreover, the social and cultural environment is not usually supportive of random strikes over economic issues by small, shop-level groups. German labor contracts do not contain provisions for cost-of-living wage increases. Wage increases lag inflation.

In Japan, industry-wide wage bargaining occurs during *Shunto* and the unions' wage increase targets reflect the recent inflation experience. Pattern-setting unions in each industry lead the way during *Shunto*. These unions are usually in firms with strong financial positions, and other unions in other firms push to imitate the wages they negotiate. Cost-of-living increases are part of *Shunto's* wage targets. These increases lag inflation, but the pattern wage, which is based on the most profitable firm's ability to pay, may, if extended, put other firms at a cost disadvantage. **Pattern-bargaining,** incidentally, is also common in some U.S. industries (e.g., automobiles and aerospace).

Productivity Improvements The use of new and better tools and equipment, changes in the way the work force is managed, and so on are intended to enhance productivity. A crucial element here is the management incentive to innovate, or take risks, for this purpose—for example, by spending large sums of money for new machinery that management foresees as lowering production costs. Here the prospects for increasing profits justify the cost of the new equipment. Management's right not to share decision making on such changes with unions becomes relevant, as do the timing and the methods by which the firm's workers come to share in the benefits of the productivity improvements.

In the United States and West Germany, management can initiate process improvements, peg the affected workers' wages according to the prescribed job evaluation system, and benefit (profit) substantially from the new equipment. In Japan, a similar situation obtains, but wages, which to a greater extent reflect age and seniority considerations, are not likely to be increased because of a new job assignment. In all three countries, unions bargain for higher wages based, among other things, on the firm's profitability. But the profitability must be demonstrated first. The company does profit from productivity improvement, at least for a while—probably for a year or two.

In contrast, in the United Kingdom, an equipment change is often accompanied by the negotiation of a **gain-sharing agreement** acceptable to the work group affected. A wage increase for this group can lead to demands for wage increases by other groups that seek to maintain parity, or customary wage differentials, among the firm's workers. The overall costs of these wage increases must be measured against the cost saving anticipated if new equipment is installed. In this case, the benefits of the productivity improvements are immediately shared with the workers and the firm's incentive to innovate is dampened.

Strikes and Lockouts Because they interrupt production, strikes and lockouts are costly. Whether or not a firm produces, its fixed costs, such as rent, interest on loans, and management salaries, continue. Without production, sales revenues are reduced (either immediately or eventually, depending on inventories). Industrial conflict per se has costs (to all parties) associated with it. If such conflict can be anticipated, these costs can sometimes be reduced by building up inventories of the firm's product or, if the conflict is expected at a supplier, by building up inventories of the supplier's product. Cross-country comparisons on strike experiences are difficult to interpret.[5] For example, if work stoppages per 100,000 employees in the United States and the United Kingdom are compared, it is found that the United Kingdom has twice as many work stoppages but that the number of lost workdays because of such stoppages in the United States is about double the number in the United Kingdom. The random or unplanned-for strike is, however, widely recognized as being more evident in the United Kingdom than in the United States.

Although the intent of the above data on work stoppages is not to malign the British industrial relations system, when compared to Japan, West Germany, or the United States, the United Kingdom does appear less attractive to

How Would You Handle This One?

A few years back, a large U.S.-based automaker sent some financial auditors to its British subsidiary. During the course of their audit, they found that the compensation paid some in-process inspectors was being charged to quality control instead of to production. They then reallocated that compensation to production. Had the inspectors not been "in-process" but "final" inspectors, charging their compensation to quality control would have been OK.

When the in-process inspectors heard of this reallocation of costs, they walked off the job in protest. This was because the pay for production inspectors was less than the pay for quality control inspectors and they felt their pay would be cut. In support of the inspectors, other workers walked out and the entire plant had to close down.

---

enterprises on three counts. This conclusion is not the purpose of our discussion, however. The point we wish to make is that industrial relations environments can vary substantially and can thereby affect a firm's profitability differently. The management challenge is to align the firm's operations with the industrial relations environment that offers the best fit.

Theories on Industrial Relations Systems

Industrial relations systems vary so much country by country that it is difficult to see what commonalities exist among them. One of the first widely accepted attempts to conceptualize a cross-country theory of industrial relations was presented by Dunlop in the 1950s.[6] In his theory, Dunlop identifies elements common to all industrial relations systems and a schematic framework on the interactions among these elements. Figure 16-2 presents this framework. Dunlop identifies rules, or outputs, as common to all industrial relations systems. They have to exist—and they have to be determined by someone or some group, that is, the *actors*. In some societies, such as the communist countries, government may unilaterally determine these rules. In others, such as the industrial democracies in the West, all three actors—workers, management, and government—participate. The influence of each actor may vary, however, depending on the *rules* at issue. For example, safety rules usually receive special attention by workers, management, and government alike. Installing new equipment and work methods will probably be management's prerogative.

The nature of the rules is also affected by the *contexts* within which they are expected to operate. Variations in product and process technologies, market structures relating to both product and resource markets, and ideology or culture relevant to the workplace may affect the kinds of *rules* as well as the intensity of the actors' interests regarding them. Substantive rules define the nature of the outputs (wages, vacations, etc.). Relational rules define how the actors behave toward one another (e.g., no strikes or lockouts).

Figure 16-2 **Dunlop's Industrial Relations System: Elements and Relationships**

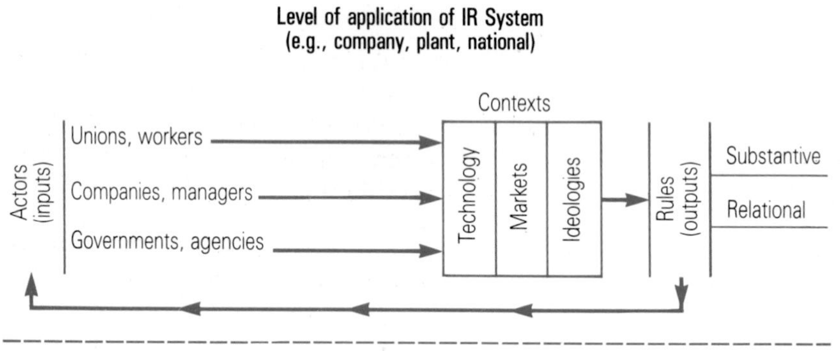

Dunlop's framework is a fairly static one, but it is useful in sorting out and developing an initial understanding of how any system operates. Other theories have been presented, such as that by Clegg, who sought to identify trade union behavior within the context of a systematic behavior pattern.[7] His "trade unionism under collective bargaining" theory rationalizes such aspects of unionism as membership, structure, and governance in terms of the nature and scope of the collective bargaining in which the union participates. Clegg's theory is also useful in understanding the workings of an industrial relations system.

The International Structure of Trade Union Activities

Trade unions are active internationally via three basic avenues—tripartite intergovernmental organizations, affiliation with unions from other countries, and an extension of their contacts with domestic firms and their home country government.

Intergovernmental Organizations

ILO The **International Labour Office (ILO)** is a United Nations affiliate (located in Geneva) composed of government, industry, and union representatives. Through the years, the ILO has sought to define and promote fair labor standards regarding safety, health and other working conditions, and freedom of association and other workers' rights. Through its research and publishing programs, it reports on wages and working conditions by country and industry.

In the early 1970s, the ILO published a study on the social policy implications of the global activities of MNEs.[8] Among the topics covered by the study were investment concentration by area and industry, capital and technology transfers, international trade, manpower effects, working conditions, and industrial relations effects. The study concluded by noting the different views and concerns of employers and workers and recommending that the social problems and benefits specific to MNEs, as opposed to those of national firms, be identified and studied further.

In the latter 1970s, the ILO conducted a series of industry-specific studies on U.S. and non-U.S. MNEs in Western Europe to document these views and concerns. In 1980–81, it published a series of country studies on the employment effects of MNEs—jobs lost and gained because of MNEs and the quality of jobs (e.g., skill levels) within MNEs.[9] It concluded that MNEs were significant employers in many countries, and for a few countries, including the United States, the data implied that employment was growing faster in MNEs than in non-MNEs and that the internal structure of employment was shifting more quickly toward white-collar workers in MNEs than in non-MNEs. The tendency of MNEs to be more R&D intensive than non-MNEs was seen as a key factor affecting the differences between them in employment growth and stability.

OECD In 1976, the **Organization for Economic Cooperation and Development (OECD),** a government, industry, and union group located in Paris, established a set of voluntary guidelines for MNEs. These guidelines note that MNEs are obliged to respect the laws, regulations, and administrative practices of member countries and that countries are obliged to provide national treatment to MNEs within their borders. These mutual obligations of MNEs and countries appear simple, but they can become quite complex. A case in point, which occurred in 1976, involved a disagreement between the Belgian government and the Belgian subsidiary of the Badger Company over whether Badger's parent, the U.S.- based Raytheon Corporation, was responsible for the legally required indemnification payments to Belgian workers who were laid off (permanently) when Badger's Belgian office was closed.[10] The government contended that Badger's Belgian subsidiary lacked sufficient funds for this purpose because of the parent's transfer pricing and transnational work allocation patterns. Here the obligation to respect national laws provided Belgium with a rationale for extending its influence to the parent company in another country.

Transnational Union Affiliations

Windmuller classifies international trade union affiliations into four categories: global, regional, specialized, and industrial internationals.[11] The global international category includes trade union organizations that cut across regional, specialized, and industrial groups. Such organizations, which can be found in nearly every country, are mainly concerned with political and missionary activities.

The International Confederation of Free Trade Unions (ICFTU) is the most important **global international** for MNEs, since its membership is heavily concentrated in North America and Western Europe—areas that are also significant to MNEs. Most of the **regional internationals** are subdivisions of the globals, and their activities are regional applications of what the globals do. **Specialized internationals**—for example, the Worker Group in the ILO, the Trade Union Advisory Committee in the OECD and the European Trade Unions Congress, which represents workers' interests at the European Community level—function as components of intergovernmental agencies and lobby within these agencies.

The **industrial internationals** are also affiliates of the global internationals. In the ICFTU, they are termed the International Trade Secretariats (ITSs), and there is a separate ITS for each major industry group—for example, the International Metalworkers' Federation (IMF) in the metal trades. Unions at the country level in the metal trades belong to the IMF and to industry-specific departments in the IMF—for example, the Automotive Department.

Of special interest to the MNE, **worldwide company councils** have been formed under the auspices of the ITSs. A case in point is the General Motors Council in the IMF, which consists of union representatives from GM plants all over the world. The GM Council meets periodically to share information about working conditions, collective bargaining, and so on. Unions can use this information to push for comparable treatment in country-level bargaining. The international structure of the ITS provides a union vehicle that parallels the international structure of the MNE. On occasion, an ITS representative has sought to intervene at the global headquarters of an MNE on behalf of a member union having difficulty in its dealings with a subsidiary of the MNE at the national level.

During the 1970s, when the worldwide company councils were developed, there was considerable speculation that these councils would be vehicles for transnational collective bargaining with MNEs. However, transnational bargaining is precluded by such factors as the diverse legal and cultural environments affecting national unions.

Extension of Domestic Contacts

Some U.S. unions have responded to the U.S. MNE by trying to bargain with it as a global, headquarters operation. The International Union of Electrical Workers (IUE), for example, invited union representatives from General Electric's foreign plants to participate with it in its collective bargaining. These representatives were just observers, however, and were not directly party to any negotiations. U.S. labor law is the controlling factor here, since it limits collective bargaining to matters related to the U.S. bargaining unit.[12]

Similarly, during collective bargaining several years ago, the IUE proposed that General Electric cease transferring work from its U.S. operations to its foreign operations. The company contended that this proposal was without merit and refused to consider it or to provide the union with details on its foreign operations. The union then filed an unfair labor practice charge with the NLRB. The board's general counsel denied the charge and noted that the union had not substantiated its allegation that work transfers were in fact occurring.[13] Overall, unions have not been successful in their attempts to prohibit or limit, through collective bargaining, the foreign sourcing practices of MNEs (i.e., manufacturing abroad for the U.S. market).

The AFL-CIO has been active in promoting U.S. public policy changes that would limit the ability of U.S. MNEs to export capital and technology and to import production. However, this effort has not been particularly successful.

The U.S.-Canada situation is a special case in the extension of U.S. union activities internationally. A Canadian region is an integral component of many U.S. **international unions.** This binationalism in union structure has facilitated the binational coordination of collective bargaining with MNEs having U.S. and Canadian operations and of subsequent contract administration activities.

The Management of Industrial Relations in the Multinational Enterprise

Earlier material substantiated the view that industrial relations systems differ considerably country by country and are place-bound. Successful MNE management recognizes this and allows subsidiaries considerable autonomy in managing their worker relationships. This approach is consistent with generally accepted management principles regarding line/staff relations and decentralization of decision making supportive of operating responsibilities at the subsidiary level. Thus, Frank Angle, an industrial relations executive at General Motors Overseas Operations Division notes:

> *Management in General Motors has always been based on the line-and-staff principle. Line executives, whether based in the United States, Canada, or overseas, have full operating responsibility and authority . . . to ensure the flexibility necessary to adapt individual operations to local conditions.*[14]

One MNE's view on the flexibility needed in industrial relations is provided by George McCullough, an industrial relations executive at Exxon.

> *My company operates in 137 countries. The variations in our labor relations processes, the manner in which we go about collective bargaining, and the differences in items included in collective agreements are staggering. Even in two countries like Holland and Belgium, where the proximity between Rotterdam and Antwerp has caused us to consolidate some management functions, the labor relations processes are totally independent of each other and the contracts bear little resemblance.*[15]

Studies on the locus of decision making in MNE industrial relations operations invariably conclude that the local management makes the operating decisions and is responsible for implementing those decisions. Even in the Japanese multinationals, industrial relations, in the context of a union-management relationship, is the subsidiary's responsibility. Japanese management frequently defers to the expertise and opinions of local management. A single exception to such local autonomy is the handling of pension issues by MNEs. Approval of pensions, which may involve a future liability of the parent company, is often required at the parent level prior to acceptance at the subsidiary.

Most large MNEs have an **industrial relations staff** at the parent company level. The activities of this staff relate to both operational and strategic matters. These activities include advising and participating in personnel selection and development at both the subsidiary and headquarters levels.

Advising—The Subsidiary Level

The MNE industrial relations staff represents a pool of expertise that is available to subsidiary management. It is not only experienced in industrial relations per se but also knowledgeable about plant operations and workplace management. It can be called on for opinions and suggestions on such local matters as bargaining strategies and tactics or the development of a new job evaluation system.

The MNE industrial relations staff also monitors industrial relations at the subsidiary to ensure that wages, benefits, and working conditions relate solely to local labor market needs—thereby guarding against the emergence of a global settlement pattern, which would probably saddle the company with greater labor costs than those of its competitors. A related function of the headquarters staff is to provide information useful to subsidiary management during labor negotiations—especially when the local union supports its claims by citing ITS-generated data on company-specific conditions in other countries.

Advising—The Headquarters Level

The MNE industrial relations staff counsels the production, marketing, finance, and similar groups at the headquarters level. Budgeting and financial pro formas of subsidiary operations include estimates of labor costs. Forecasts of changes in these labor costs are often provided by the MNE industrial relations staff in consultation with local management. In the event of strikes or lockouts at a subsidiary, the industrial relations staff can provide advice to the MNE-level production, logistics, purchasing, and marketing groups on the anticipated duration of the conflict. If the MNE's production pattern is transnationally integrated, such advice would be especially significant, since operations at other subsidiaries are affected by such a conflict. Alternatively, if headquarters management is weighing the possibility of replacing production at a struck subsidiary by production at another subsidiary, it would probably value an appraisal of the anticipated duration of the conflict.

Senior line management at the MNE level often solicits interpretations by the industrial relations staff of significant events at the subsidiaries. Such interpretations prepare it to participate with and respond to subsidiary management in the making of line management decisions.

Personnel Selection and Development

Management personnel are typically selected by the person to whom they will report. Typically, the person above the one who makes such a selection approves or rejects the selection decision. The top industrial relations executive at a subsidiary would be selected by the subsidiary's managing director, and that selection would be approved or rejected by the headquarters-level executive to whom the managing director reports. Typically, the head of the MNE industrial relations staff consults with senior line management at the MNE on such selection decisions.

The involvement of the MNE industrial relations staff is even more extensive than this, however. Career path and progression planning for key personnel is a fairly continuous process that includes individual development programs, identification of training needs, and so on. The MNE industrial relations staff participates in such planning as it affects key industrial relations personnel at the subsidiaries. Indeed, it may on occasion organize and conduct special training seminars for industrial relations managers from several of the MNE's subsidiaries.

The Industrial Relations Component in Strategic Decision Making in the Multinational Enterprise

Strategic decisions are often regarded as those that establish the longer-run direction of the firm and that provide the basis for operating decisions. From the industrial relations perspective, four strategic decision-making areas appear especially relevant—foreign direct investment, production allocation, production smoothing, and disinvestment.

Foreign Direct Investment

Historically, the foreign direct investments of U.S. MNEs (in the manufacturing sector) were defensive in nature. They were made to protect a foreign market presence originally obtained through exports. As foreign competition developed and profit margins were eroded, the firm sought to establish a plant within the market that it intended to continue serving. Its success often depended on its ability to transfer established management and production techniques from the parent to the subsidiary and to minimize overall production and marketing costs.

Of special importance, then, were those labor-related elements in the foreign environment that affected production costs and product availability. Critical assessments of alternative production sites typically included data on present and anticipated employee compensation costs and days worked per year (exclusive of holidays, vacations, and absenteeism). Wages and benefits are higher in Holland than in Spain, for example. Days worked per employee per year may be lower in West Germany than in the United Kingdom. All of these factors affect (product) unit labor costs. Potentially relevant factors are worker militancy and management's ability to initiate changes in workplace technology and work force organization. In these respects, West Germany might be favored over the United Kingdom or France.

The key here is for management to identify all of the pertinent industrial relations factors and to evaluate its foreign direct investment alternatives in light of those factors. The final outcome may well involve more than just a go or no-go decision. It may involve the nature of the work to be performed at the proposed plant or the kind and amount of production equipment that will be used. It may involve participation by the local government in securing attractive financial support or trade union concessions that will render the proposed facility more profitable. When Ford Motor opened a plant in Belgium in the mid-1960s, for example, the provincial government helped secure a written five-year peace commitment from the local trade unions. When Volkswagen decided to open a plant in Pennsylvania in the mid-1970s, the United Auto Workers (UAW) agreed that Volkswagen's wages could be lower than those of other U.S. automakers.

Production Allocation

With respect to industrial relations, **production allocation** decisions are similar to foreign direct investment decisions. Indeed, some might contend

---

Who's the Culprit in This One?

Because of the global economic recession that occurred in the mid-1970s, a large MNE in the electronics industry had to cut back production in all of its major markets. It ordered a 10 percent employment reduction at all of its plants in those markets.

Some subsidiaries, however, were faced with paying large "redundancy" or discharge payments to workers that were let go. Management at these subsidiaries complained about this. The parent then changed its order and allocated cutbacks at the plants in different countries to minimize the total MNE-system costs resulting from discharge payments. As a result, most of the cutbacks in employment were made in the United States, where no such payments were required. In Western Europe, where the required payments were quite high, there were small cutbacks or none at all.

---

that the latter are, in effect, initial production allocation decisions. New product and equipment cycles, however, do afford MNEs the opportunity to reevaluate, and perhaps renegotiate, their industrial relations environments. In some instances, unions have, in effect, bargained down on wages and benefits to keep jobs or governments have offered special incentives.

Offshore production decisions by MNEs are also production allocation decisions. However, such decisions are special in some ways. They are made largely because of labor cost differences, and they result from the MNE's unique resource market scanning capabilities. The selection of the specific operations to be performed offshore turns substantially on the labor intensiveness involved. The parent-subsidiary logistics involved are usually inventory intensive and time consuming. Thus, the offshore production concept, including the labor element, is not especially flexible. Labor, which is usually the most flexible factor of production, is not so in this context. The firm that engages in offshore production may do well to also maintain a domestic production capability that can respond more quickly to demand changes and competitive conditions in the domestic product market.

Before transferring production to an offshore facility, the firm is required by U.S. labor law to negotiate with the union over the effects of the relocation decision on the workers who constitute the bargaining unit. Since that decision apparently turns on economic factors, and since collective bargaining is concerned with economic factors, enlightened management may well negotiate with the union over the relocation decision and not just over its effects. Negotiations of this kind could well result in the weakening or elimination of the relocation rationale.

Production Smoothing

Rutenberg identifies **production smoothing** as a special variation on production allocation and notes:

> *In each nation, production smoothing problems and opportunities are different. A unique feature of the multinational corporation is that headquarters can alter the flow of products between nations to smooth production . . . [that is, force a] reallocation of markets to factories to achieve optimal production smoothing for a multiproduct, multifactory corporation.*[16]

He identifies three types of factories that are crucial to a production smoothing strategy and relevant to industrial relations: lowest unit cost factories, flexible multi-item factories, and seasonal factories.

The **lowest unit cost factory** produces standardized items and operates at full capacity. In such factories, productivity is the key consideration. Lowest unit cost factories can be either capital intensive or labor intensive. If they are capital intensive, the union enjoys some leverage vis-à-vis management since comparatively high fixed costs will continue in the event of a strike. In such factories, one management strategy is to treat workers as salaried staff to encourage their closer identification with the company; another is to pay workers on a piece rate basis. If they are labor intensive, the offshore manufacturing plant becomes a viable consideration.

The **flexible multi-item factory** is one in which new items are produced. The equipment in such factories is general purpose, and the work force is usually highly skilled. Job enrichment, Rutenberg suggests, appears appropriate to factories of this sort. Worker assignments and job categories cannot be rigidly defined. Some industrial relations environments, such as Japan, seem well suited to the flexible factory.

The **seasonal factory** probably operates a few months out of the year. In such factories, a work force buildup is followed by layoffs. Rutenberg suggests that seasonal factories be located in areas accustomed to seasonal work—in northern Finland, for example, where variations in weather conditions have preconditioned society to accept seasonal changes in labor demand. In such cases, even unions tend to accommodate the cyclical employment pattern.

Disinvestment

A **disinvestment** decision—that is, a decision to close or sell off a plant—is not easily or routinely taken. The prevailing wisdom, however, is that management should move swiftly and decisively in such matters, that it is best not to have a difficult situation linger. This wisdom must confront the reality that in many countries, especially in Western Europe, legally constituted works councils have the right to be informed on the subsidiary's economic health and prospects and that substantial indemnification payments to laid-off workers are often legally required. Therefore, any disinvestment proposal should be carefully analyzed and its attractiveness discounted by the anticipated indemnification costs. The disinvestment procedure should be planned carefully, and the legal rights of workers to information must be addressed. Contingency plans should be developed to cover the adverse publicity that usually accompanies disinvestment decisions, and even the possibility that workers may forcibly occupy the plant and attract additional headlines.

Conclusions

International industrial relations are more complex and diverse than industrial relations in a single country. Industrial relations are not necessarily more difficult to manage at the subsidiary level than at the domestic level, however, and the very diversity of international industrial relations may present opportunities to the MNE—especially in terms of strategic management.

The role and function of the MNE industrial relations staff require a special awareness and sensitivity. The personnel of this staff must be knowledgeable about the different foreign industrial relations systems and the critical trends and events that affect subsidiary operations, and they must be sensitive to the effective allocation of authority and power between the MNE and subsidiary management levels. Sometimes only a fine line separates advising from controlling.

Different as industrial relations systems are, they all share a common general structure. They are all concerned with the determination and application of workplace rules. The basic actors—management, union, and government—participate in varying degrees in this rule-setting. Models, such as those developed by Dunlop, are useful starting points in learning about any specific industrial relations system.

Questions

1. Are industrial relations more or less significant to an MNE than to a purely domestic company?
2. What options or advantages not possessed by a purely domestic counterpart might the subsidiary of an MNE have in its industrial relations?
3. Compare the productivity incentives for management in the British and Japanese industrial relations systems.
4. Compare the productivity incentives for management in the British and American industrial relations systems.
5. If you could pick specific features (rules, practices, etc.) from the American, German, and Japanese industrial relations systems and put them into one "ideal" system, which would you pick, and why?
6. What purposes are served by an MNE industrial relations staff?
7. Why should industrial relations operating decisions be made by subsidiary-level management?
8. What do industrial relations imply for strategic management decisions regarding production allocation?
9. With regard to a plant location decision, what key characteristics of the industrial relations environment would an MNE take into consideration? Which of these characteristics would be of concern to an MNE but not to a purely domestic company?
10. How does industrial relations management in MNEs relate to the competitive advantages of MNEs?

References

Bean, R. *Comparative Industrial Relations: An Introduction to Cross-National Perspectives.* New York: St. Martin's Press, 1985. See, especially, "Industrial Relations in Multinational Enterprises," chap. 8, pp. 184–207.

Dunlop, John T., and Walter Galenson, eds. *Labor in the Twentieth Century.* New York: Academic Press, 1978.

Hanami, Tadashi. *Labor Relations in Japan Today.* Tokyo: Kodansha International, 1979.

Kujawa, Duane. "U.S. Labor, Multinational Enterprise and the National Interest," *Law and Policy in International Business,* 1978 (no. 3), pp. 941-68.

———. "Technology Strategy and Industrial Relations: Case Studies of Japanese Multinationals in the United States," *Journal of International Business Studies,* Winter 1983, pp. 9-22.

Martin, Benjamin, and Everett Kassalow, eds. *Labor Relations in Advanced Industrial Societies.* Washington, D.C.: Carnegie Endowment for International Peace, 1980.

Spalding, Hobart A. *Organized Labor in Latin America.* New York: New York University Press, 1977.

Endnotes

1. An early summary of these views is presented in Nat Goldfinger, "An American Trade Union View of International Trade and Investment," in *American Labor and the Multinational Corporation,* ed. Duane Kujawa (New York: Praeger Publishers, 1973), pp. 28-53.
2. Duane Kujawa, "U.S. Labor, Multinational Enterprise, and the National Interest: A Proposal for Labor Law Reform," *Law and Policy in International Business,* 1978 (no. 3), pp. 941-68.
3. For a general review of the evidence on these issues, see *Employment Effects of Multinational Enterprises in Industrialized Countries* (Geneva: International Labour Office, 1981).
4. The reader should note that workers' and unions' interests in MNEs focus more on firms in the manufacturing sector than on firms in the mining or extractive industries. The foreign situs of a mine may merely reflect the simple fact that that is where the ore is. Locating a plant abroad, however, is seen as a decision that turns on less absolute considerations.
5. The observations on strike effects in this paragraph are based on data presented in Hugh Clegg, *Trade Unionism under Collective Bargaining* (Oxford: Basil Blackwell & Mott, 1978), p. 69.
6. John Dunlop, *Industrial Relations Systems* (New York: Henry Holt, 1958).
7. Clegg, *Trade Unionism,* passim.
8. *Multinational Enterprises and Social Policy* (Geneva: International Labour Office, 1973).
9. For the summary study, see *Employment Effects of Multinational Enterprises in Industrialized Countries* (Geneva: International Labor Office, 1981).
10. R. G. Blainpain, *The Badger Case and the OECD Guidelines for Multinational Enterprises* (Deventer, the Netherlands: Kluwer, 1977)
11. John P. Windmuller, "International Trade Union Organizations: Structure, Function, Limitations," in *International Labor,* ed. Sol Barkin et al., (New York: Harper & Row, 1967).

12. Herbert R. Northrup and Richard L. Rowan, *Multinational Collective Bargaining Attempts* (Philadelphia: Industrial Research Unit, Wharton School, University of Pennsylvania, 1979), p. 120.
13. Duane Kujawa, "Foreign Sourcing Decisions and the Duty to Bargain under the NLRA," *Law and Policy in International Business,* 1972 (no. 3), pp. 523-24.
14. Frank Angle, "The Conduct of Labor Relations in General Motors Overseas Operations," in *International Labor and the Multinational Enterprise,* ed. Duane Kujawa (New York: Praeger Publishers, 1975), p. 138.
15. George B. McCullough, "Comment," in *Multinationals, Unions, and Labor Relations in Industrialized Countries,* eds. Robert F. Banks and Jack Stieber (Ithaca, N.Y.: New York State School of Industrial and Labor Relations, Cornell University, 1977), p. 150.
16. David P. Ruthenberg, *Multinational Management* (Boston: Little, Brown, 1982), p. 182.

Case
Volkswagen of America

Volkswagen of America (referred to hereafter as Volkswagen) is the U.S. subsidiary of Volkswagenwerk A.G., headquartered in Wolfsburg, West Germany. Volkswagenwerk is Germany's largest automobile manufacturer. Its worldwide production capacity is about 2.5 million units—about one third of which it produces outside Germany.[1] In addition to its U.S. operations, Volkswagenwerk has assembly plants in Nigeria, Belgium, and Yugoslavia and produces motor vehicles and components in Brazil, Mexico, Argentina, Peru, and South Africa.

During the 1980s, labor-management relations at Volkswagen of America have generally been quiescent and constructive. But this was not always the case—especially in the start-up years. Let's take a look at what happened then.

Investment Considerations

Volkswagenwerk's first plant in the United States opened in 1969. It produced air conditioners for German-made VW "beetles" sold in the United States. In January 1976, Volkswagenwerk's Supervisory Board (analogous, to some extent, to a U.S. firm's board of directors) authorized management to begin negotiations on establishing an assembly plant in the United States.

The issue over opening such a plant had been debated in the German company for several years. There was concern by worker representatives and others on the Supervisory Board about the employment effects in Germany if cars then being made in German plants and exported were assembled abroad.[2] The timing of the decision coincided with an investigation by the U.S. Treasury Department of an allegation pressed by the United Auto Workers (UAW) that Volkswagenwerk had dumped cars in the United States in 1974 and 1975—that is, priced cars cheaper in the United States than in Germany. Commenting on both the decision and the Treasury Department's investigation, a spokesman for the Supervisory Board noted:

> *We all realize that Volkswagens made in Germany are just too expensive, after repeated dollar devaluations, to meet the American and foreign competition in the United States. If we don't assemble there, we'll lose the American market. [Regarding the dumping complaint,] such a finding could force a reconsideration of the decision to go to the United States—and it would have enormous political repercussions in the Government too. . . . If a special penalty duty were assessed on every Volkswagen, . . . the company would be forced to raise prices by so much that sales in the United States would collapse and our dealer network would fall apart.*[3]

This case was written by Duane Kujawa using publicly available information provided in discussions with Volkswagen company and union officials.

The deterioration of Volkswagen's U.S. market position was also ascribed to higher fuel prices that were reflected in higher shipping costs associated with exporting from Germany, higher German labor costs, and the upward revaluation of the German currency during the 1971-75 period. Labor costs for Volkswagenwerk advanced 40 percent from 1973 to 1976.[4] This brought German labor costs, consisting of wages and benefits, up to parity with those of U.S. auto workers. Moreover, because of differences in vacations, holidays, and so on, German workers spent considerably less time on the job in a typical year than did their U.S. counterparts. The result was that a U.S. Volkswagen plant could operate with direct labor costs about 10 percent lower than labor costs in Germany.[5]

Later in 1976, Volkswagenwerk's Supervisory Board approved a decision to manufacture autos in Westmoreland County, Pennsylvania. The chairman of the Management Board stated that a U.S. assembly plant would "lower manufacturing costs, neutralize the effect of international currency changes, and attain greater flexibility in supplying . . . American dealers."[6]

Obtaining a Labor Contract at Westmoreland

When Volkswagenwerk invested in the Westmoreland plant, it adopted a neutral approach toward the organizing of that facility by the UAW. The German parent had had a long-lasting, constructive relationship with the German union in the metalworking industry (I G Metall), and union members sat on its Supervisory Board. The parent had advised Volkswagen's management not to oppose the UAW's organizing efforts. The parent management did not deal directly with the UAW, however, and avoided giving further direction to Volkswagen's management on the conduct of its labor relations.

In May 1978, the UAW petitioned the National Labor Relations Board (NLRB) to conduct a representation election for hourly workers at Westmoreland. The hourly employment level was then about 900, and nearly 80 percent of the hourly workers had signed petition cards. No other union competed with the UAW, and Volkswagen's management did not oppose the UAW's organizing efforts. The election was held in June, and the UAW received 98 percent of the 885 ballots cast.[7]

Volkswagen immediately commenced collective bargaining with the UAW, and a tentative contract was soon agreed upon. A UAW spokesman noted that the proposed contract included lower wage rates than those paid by the "Big Three" automakers but that most of the other items in the contract were "nearly identical to existing contracts with Detroit automakers."[8] The UAW president hailed the tentative contract as "an excellent example for other foreign auto manufacturers who may open manufacturing or assembly operations in the United States."[9]

But members of UAW Local 2055 at the Westmoreland plant rejected the proposed contract overwhelmingly. Moreover, they began a "wildcat" strike and moved immediately to picket the plant site. The key issue was that the wages called for would be substantially lower than those paid by the Detroit auto firms. The Westmoreland workers were also reportedly of the opinion that the proposed agreement shortchanged them on vacations, delayed for too long (one year) the start of Volkswagen's payments to a layoff fund, and denied workers the right to refuse heavy overtime.[10]

Endnotes

1. "Volkswagenwerk, AG," in *The World Directory of Multinational Enterprises,* ed. John N. Stopford, John H. Dunning, and Klaus O. Haberich (New York: Facts on File, 1980), pp. 1126-27.
2. "Inflation and Jobless Rate Stir West German Concern," *New York Times,* May 19, 1976, p. 64.
3. "Volkswagen Said to Plan Assembly Plant in U.S.," *New York Times,* April 23, 1976, p. 1.
4. "Volkswagen Is Investigating Two Sites in the Northeast for an Assembly Plant," *The Wall Street Journal*, October 6, 1976, p. 3.
5. Ibid.; "VW Delays Start-Up Date at Its Facility in New Stanton; Parts Problems Develop," *The Wall Street Journal,* January 8, 1976, p. 2; and interview with the industrial relations director, Volkswagenwerk, AG, San Diego, California, June 1976.
6. "VW Delays," p. 2.
7. "Volkswagen Workers in Pennsylvania Pick UAW as Their Union," *The Wall Street Journal*, June 12, 1978, p. 21.
8. "VW's American Unit, UAW Agree to Terms of Tentative Contract," *The Wall Street Journal*, October 6, 1978, p. 31.
9. Ibid.
10. "Strike at VW Disturbs Foreign Auto-Makers Weighing U.S. Plants," *The Wall Street Journal,* October 13, 1978, p. 1.

17

PERSONNEL MANAGEMENT

Personnel management within the MNE shapes the conduit through which the implementation of competitive advantages flows. For the mature MNE, which relies on timely and accurate transnational flows of information and directives, the effectiveness of the personnel management function is crucial. The mature MNE requires personnel skilled in the company's operations, in the environments across and within which the MNE functions, and in the art of cross-cultural communication. This chapter examines these needs and covers the entire range of interests and issues pertaining to international personnel management. The main goals of the chapter are to:

1. Describe how and why personnel management in MNEs differs from personnel management in purely domestic firms.
2. Examine the relationship between personnel management and the competitiveness of MNEs.
3. Examine the statistics on the use of foreign nationals (expatriates).
4. Explain the criteria for choosing between local and foreign nationals.
5. Explore issues pertinent to expatriates, such as selection, training, compensation, taxation, repatriation, and promotion.
6. Discuss the present demand for foreign assignments.

Introduction

All businesses function through people, and the effective management of people has become increasingly recognized as fundamental to business success. For the domestic, unicultural firm, people management embodies a varied set of activities. Typically, it includes such personnel practices as recruitment, selection, compensation, career-path planning, promotion, training, and performance motivation. These practices are important to the multinational, multicultural firm too. But they are more complicated in the MNE setting, and there are other personnel practices that are unique to MNEs.

Personnel Management Issues in MNEs

Selection, for example, involves questions at both the parent and subsidiary levels as to whether local nationals or home country nationals should be used. Should Nestlés, for example, rely primarily on Swiss nationals in its home office and on American nationals at its U.S. subsidiary? Are there positions at the subsidiary that Swiss nationals would probably be more suited for? Are there positions from which Swiss nationals should be excluded? Compensation for persons assigned outside their home countries

Managers placed on foreign assignments share a lot of concerns. How will they be evaluated? How about housing? Taxes? Schools for the children?

Click/Chicago/Jon Feingersh

involves packages that cover the added costs of living abroad—for housing, taxes, and so on. People who accept overseas assignments are concerned about how the home office views such assignments and about the advancement opportunities that will be open to them upon their return. Is an overseas assignment an "out of sight, out of mind" situation? Training for a foreign post may well involve an introduction to the cultural, social, and political conditions in the country of assignment. It may well involve training for the entire family of the assignee.

These and other differences between foreign and domestic assignments will be discussed in this chapter. The topics covered include the relationship between the personnel function and the competitiveness of MNEs, the definition of expatriate management, the extent to which expatriates are used and the purposes for which they are used, the use of local nationals versus the use of expatriates, selection and training for foreign assignments, the repatriation and promotion of expatriates, and, quite important, compensation and taxation issues pertinent to an overseas assignment.

Personnel Management and the Competitiveness of MNEs

Traditional View Being Challenged

The traditional view has been that personnel management is a "facilitative" function—something that has to be done well to accommodate the more important success-related strategies pertaining to marketing, production, finance, and so on. Today, this view is being seriously questioned. One challenge to the traditional view originates from the emergence of high-tech companies that value highly skilled employees as human capital assets. Another challenge originates from our growing understanding of and ability to adapt Japanese management practices that view employees as key ingredients in attaining low-cost, high-quality product strategies.[1] Indeed, several industries are totally revamping their personnel practices to utilize the brain power as well as the muscle power of their workers. General Motors' Pontiac Fiero Plant, for example, departs radically from GM's historical management-labor relations in this regard. At Fiero, "operating teams" (workers) are responsible for defining and solving production problems and for quality control as they work to assemble a car.

A third challenge to the traditional view originates from the emergence of the mature, *geocentric* MNE, which relies on the effective, transnational flow of information and directives—accomplished by people—that balance local competitive needs and strengths with those required or available elsewhere in the MNE system. Such information flows require personnel who are skilled in the company and its way of operating, in the environments within and across which the MNE functions, and in the art of communication—including cross-cultural communication.

Personnel Management and the Competitiveness of MNEs

Since personnel management in the MNE shapes the conduit through which the implementation of competitive advantages flow, it has a great impact on the effectiveness of the firm in the marketplace. The challenge of personnel management is to ensure effectiveness at minimum cost by finding the right balance between the parent's people needs and the subsidiary's people needs and to staff these needs at both the parent and subsidiary levels with a continuing flow of knowledgeable, motivated personnel. Reaching these objectives is no easy task—and mistakes can be costly. The personnel manager in the MNE is thus seen as a special kind of person—a specialist in legal matters, such as equal employment opportunity and taxation related to foreign assignments; an expert regarding the personnel functions, such as recruitment, motivation, and compensation; and a highly knowledgeable person on company-specific matters, such as technology and competitive strengths and even the values and preferences of key executives.

Definition and Use of Expatriates

Parent company nationals and third-country nationals assigned to subsidiaries and foreign nationals assigned to parent companies are typically referred to as **expatriates.** They are the major focus of this chapter. Expatriates are generally found in technical and managerial assignments, and their numbers have historically been significant. For example, Hays reported that over 200,000 U.S. citizens worked abroad in the early 1970s, and the U.S. Department of Commerce's 1984 "benchmark" survey on direct foreign investment in the United States reported that an estimated 50,000 foreign citizens were employed by foreign firms in the United States.[2] While the numbers of expatriates working abroad are not tracked on a routine basis and there are no official figures regarding them, the rapid growth in foreign direct investment in the United States during the latter 1970s and the 1980s and the continued expansion of U.S. MNEs abroad during this period suggest that the numbers of foreign nationals working outside their home countries have probably increased during the 1980s. Indeed, Britain's ICI and Holland's Philips alone employed a total of 2,300 expatriates in early 1984.[3]

Variations in the Use of Expatriates

Studies by Franko indicate that an MNE's use of expatriate personnel is high during the initial stages of foreign operations to accomplish technology transfers, including production and management technologies. The number of expatriates declines as the firm's local managers and technical staff assimilate this knowledge. It expands again as local operations become increasingly integrated into a global operational framework.[4] These views suggest that as a product's life cycle evolves, the need for expatriates expands (at the subsidiary level) in the early stage and then diminishes in the later stages. Finally, with the mature MNE the need for expatriates arises at both the subsidiary and parent company levels. These views are also consistent with the staffing needs of those MNEs that develop from *ethnocentric* to *geocentric* as the intrafirm relationship evolves from a parent-to-subsidiary technology transfer process to an integrated, system-wide need for the development and application of MNE-specific competitive advantages. These views also imply an expanding need for an awareness at the global management level based on country-by-country knowledge pertaining to a variety of employment-related concerns, such as laws regarding race, age and sex discrimination, compensation practices, and taxes.

Incidence of the Use of Expatriates

Studies of foreign MNEs in the United States have shed some light on the incidence of the use of expatriates. Of 100 foreign MNEs studied by the U.S. Department of Commerce in 1975-76, about one third reported that their CEOs were expatriates and that, at levels below the CEO, expatriates often occupied one to four management positions. In addition, expatriates held technical positions. Moreover, mode of entry and parent nationality were found to be factors affecting the use of expatriates. Expatriates were more likely to be used in start-up cases than in takeover situations and at Japanese-owned subsidiaries.[5] Kujawa, in a 1980-83 study of Japanese multinationals in the United States, reported extensive use of Japanese expatriates. These expatriates, at Honda in Ohio and at Murata in Georgia, for example, were needed to implement and monitor Japanese management practices related to statistical quality control techniques and continued technology transfers from the Japanese parent to the U.S. subsidiary.[6]

While we can demonstrate that the use of expatriates is fairly extensive and that their use can often be seen as essential for successful MNE operations, the issue of balance remains. Where should the line be drawn between the use of local nationals and expatriates? To this the discussion turns.

Local Nationals versus Expatriates

The question of using local nationals or expatriates can be asked at both the parent company and subsidiary levels. The answer invariably turns on the perceived benefits to be gained by using expatriates balanced against the added costs required to maintain expatriate staff. Benefits are usually derived by bringing in technical or managerial expertise not available locally, including special knowledge about the firm itself. More effective communication and more consistent, trustworthy management behavior may be other objec-

Table 17-1 **Factors Affecting the Choice between Local Nationals and Expatriates**

Factors Favoring Expatriates
Expatriates possess technical and managerial skills.
Using expatriates enhances communications between the parent and the subsidiary.
The presence of expatriates promotes the foreign or MNE image.
Parent/subsidiary relations are facilitated by the presence of expatriates familiar with the corporate culture.
The assignment of expatriates is part of their professional development program, and it improves senior management's decision making.

Factors Favoring Local Nationals
The total compensation paid to local nationals is usually considerably less than that paid to expatriates.
No host country cultural adaptation is necessary when local nationals are used.
Using local nationals is consistent with a promote-from-within policy.
No work permits are needed with local nationals.
Using local nationals promotes a local image.
Using expatriates with special employment contracts rather than local nationals may run afoul of local equal employment opportunity regulations.*

* C. Itoh & Co.'s U.S. subsidiary was alleged by certain key (U.S.) employees to have violated their civil rights by having Japanese expatriates on special employment contracts not available to non-Japanese employees. See S. Prakash Sethi and Carl L. Swanson, "Hiring Alien Executives in Compliance with U.S. Civil Rights Laws," *Journal of International Business Studies,* Fall 1979, pp. 37-50.

tives in assigning expatriates overseas. Measured against these benefits are differing types of costs. Table 17-1 lists some of the pros and cons associated with choosing between local nationals and expatriates.

Cost Considerations

Studies have shown that it can be very expensive to use expatriates. Most firms use the rule of thumb that an expatriate costs at least three times as much as a local national. The reasons for the higher costs are several. Expatriates may be taxed twice on their income, especially their unearned income—in both the home and host countries. They may have home leave, family maintenance, and extra educational expenses. Also, and quite important, some areas just cost more than others to live in, especially if the expatriate's consumption pattern is not consistent with local, or native, supply patterns. For an expatriate, living costs among the different cities of the world are reasonably high and can vary substantially. Table 17-2 shows what it would cost for an American family of four, with a base salary of $40,000 and a

Table 17-2 **Living Costs of American Expatriates: For a Family of Four in Selected Cities, 1984**

City	Housing	Transportation	Taxes	Goods and Services	Total
Hong Kong	$52,360	$15,878	$8,100	$12,713	$89,051
Tokyo	39,487	6,233	15,650	18,435	79,805
Geneva	22,667	5,674	19,983	17,397	65,721
Brussels	9,193	5,228	36,883	13,502	64,806
Frankfurt	12,345	5,518	25,989	14,628	58,480
Buenos Aires	19,103	4,854	21,016	10,596	55,569
Sydney	12,192	9,620	17,860	13,268	52,940
Paris	15,199	4,786	18,886	13,098	51,969
Amsterdam	11,014	5,081	19,723	13,508	49,326
London	15,269	6,254	10,681	13,846	46,050
Rio de Janeiro	13,703	4,216	14,748	11,125	43,792
Mexico City	8,175	2,893	12,480	10,139	33,687

Source: Data prepared by Runzheimer & Co., Rochester, Wisconsin, and presented in *Business Week,* January 16, 1984, p. 99.

rented home, to live in selected cities outside the United States. Not only do the overall costs vary considerably (at the limits), but the individual cost components also vary considerably. For example, the cost of housing ranges from $8,175 in Mexico City to $52,360 in Hong Kong and taxes range from $8,100 in Hong Kong to $36,883 in Brussels! Clearly, expatriates are expensive to put in place and to maintain. The contributions they make while on foreign assignments have to justify such expenditures.

In addition to out-of-pocket costs and the reasons suggested in Table 17-1, there are other reasons why firms use expatriates only when necessary. These reasons and some of the positive aspects of overseas assignments are discussed in the sections that follow.

Effectiveness Considerations

Several final points, however, should be noted regarding the use of local nationals versus the use of expatriates. First, when an expatriate is assigned overseas to fill a skill void, be it technical or managerial, it is often a prime responsibility of that person to train a local national to take his or her place. Second, some overseas positions are appropriate only for local nationals since these positions are highly culture-bound. Industrial relations management is an example. Other positions, such as the senior management position, seem to favor the use of an expatriate in order to facilitate communication and ensure control. Third, as MNEs are maturing into truly global enterprises, the need to integrate top management on a cross-national basis is expanding. Global firms need a global perspective at the top. The fact is, however, that top management and boards of directors have been slow to change and typically are not becoming multinational in their composition.

Host Country Considerations

Host countries, especially developing countries, generally favor the use of local nationals. Their reasons include increasing employment in general (jobs), advancing skill levels via on-the-job training and experience, and saving foreign exchange (where relevant). Nonetheless, these countries accept the use of expatriates when this is justified by legitimate business need. At times, though, MNE-host country friction can make securing local work-permits for expatriates difficult and time consuming.

Even without such friction, regulations regarding the use of expatriates can be complex and costly to the MNE. The Bahamas, for example, will not approve the use of any expatriate until the position to be filled has been advertised and it can be demonstrated that no qualified person is available locally. The MNE also pays an annual work permit fee that can amount to thousands of dollars for each expatriate on assignment in the Bahamas.

To cite another situation, Brazil requires that the MNE document the need for an expatriate with the Ministry of Labor and submit to the ministry a copy of the expatriate's résumé, university diploma, and employment contract (between the MNE and the expatriate). Moreover, Brazil limits the number of foreign nationals employed to one third of the total number of employees and limits the compensation paid to foreign nationals as a group to one third of the compensation paid to all employees.

Selection and Training of Expatriates

An overseas assignment that ends traumatically for an expatriate hurts both the individual and the firm. A valued employee may be demoralized. Crucial time may be lost. Important supplier, customer, or governmental relations may be soured. Recognizing that an expatriate's job is likely to be more demanding than a similar job at the home base, the firm usually takes extra care in the selection and preparation of an expatriate for a foreign assignment. Nonetheless, a study reported in the *Economist* in 1984 noted that one in three American expatriates assigned abroad returned home sooner than originally planned. For European expatriates, the ratio was one in seven.[7] A 1981 study of 80 *American* MNEs found that at half of these companies 10 to 20 percent of the expatriates were called home or fired because of their inability to perform effectively on a foreign assignment.[8] A similar study, focusing on expatriates in 35 *Japanese* MNEs, reported that at over three quarters of these companies less than 5 percent of the expatriates were called

Working effectively in a foreign environment involves knowing what it takes to get the job done within a very different cultural context.

Click/Chicago/Don Smetzer

home.[9] It appears that some companies, especially American MNEs (and perhaps others), have something to learn.

The talents and skills that are needed in an overseas assignment include those typically identified with a domestic assignment—technical competence, educational achievement, initiative, creativity, independence, emotional maturity, ability to communicate, and so on. In an overseas assignment, several other talents and skills can be added to this list—for example, knowledge of a foreign language, cultural adaptability and empathy, and social flexibility (of the expatriate, and the expatriate's spouse and family). When the talents and skills required for a foreign assignment are lacking, special training programs are used. Studies generally confirm these points, but as Tung reports, the selection and training of expatriate personnel depend on just what their overseas positions are—chief executive officer (CEO), other manager, technical specialist, or operative.[10]

Selection

In her 1980 study of 80 U.S. MNEs, Tung found that the importance of certain key attributes related to the selection decision varied considerably, depending on the position being filled at the subsidiary. Selected data regarding these findings are presented in Table 17-3. In the selection decision for a

Table 17-3 **Selection Criteria for Expatriate Personnel: 1980 Survey of U.S. MNEs** (n = 80)

Criterion	CEO	Other Manager	Technical Specialist	Operator
Experience in company	83%	68%	58%	37%
Managerial talent	96	86	16	18
Initiative, creativity	84	82	82	52
Technical knowledge of business	79	91	89	68
Maturity, emotional stability	94	98	75	86
Knowledge of language of host country	26	42	25	46
Adaptability, flexibility in new environment	83	76	46	62
Spouse's and family's adaptability	61	63	40	49

Note: The percentages reflect those respondents who felt that the criterion was used and that it was very important in the selection decision.
Source: Data abstracted from Rosalie L. Tung, "Selection and Training of Personnel for Overseas Assignments," *Columbia Journal of World Business,* Spring 1981, p. 75.

CEO, the criteria emphasized managerial talent, maturity and emotional stability, initiative and creativity, experience in the company, adaptability and flexibility in a new environment, and technical knowledge. For managers other than CEOs, maturity and emotional stability, technical knowledge of the business, managerial talent, and initiative and creativity were emphasized over other criteria.

The criteria were considerably less extensive for technical specialists, where technical knowledge and initiative and creativity were emphasized; and for operators, where only maturity and emotional stability were emphasized. In general, CEOs and other managers were more often seen as needing managerial experience and skills, personal and family flexibility, company experience, and communicative ability. Technical specialists and operatives were generally scored less frequently on all of these points. All four categories were scored quite frequently (that is, in over 70 percent of the MNEs surveyed) regarding technical skills, maturity, and emotional stability. Except for technical specialists, expatriates were required to display an interest in overseas work by a majority of the companies studied.[11]

Training

Training programs seek to prepare potential expatriates for the situations and problems unique to an overseas assignment. For this reason, such programs are country specific and are quite often tailored to individual needs and time constraints. Among the topics typically covered are a cultural orientation, the social and religious setting, political and social issues, language training, home country/host country relations, and the legal environment.

Operations management or industrial engineering in different geographic segments can pool expertise and develop, for example, operating systems with global applicability. Ciba-Geigy, a large Swiss chemical company with major operations in the United States and Europe, routinely integrates operations technology between the two areas. Process engineers and managers in both areas communicate continuously, and often U.S. personnel are on assignment in Europe and European personnel in the United States.

A Global Service Product Brings People Together at Bank of America

Bank of America's System Engineering group (BASE) is responsible for aligning technical expertise with overall business strategies and is providing the bank's World Business Division with managerial and technical support in the development of International Banking Systems (IBS), an on-line computer system that supplies current financial information to account officers and corporate customers, facilitates electronic global monetary transfers, provides treasury department support for foreign exchange and money market activities, and so forth.

The IBS was originally developed in England, Germany, Holland, and Belgium. It is now operational in all overseas divisions and in the United States. Bank of America regards its implementation of the IBS as one of its "most significant strategic decisions." The IBS allows the bank to deliver comprehensive, integrated electronic banking services to customers worldwide.

BASE, headquartered in San Francisco, coordinates closely with the bank's strategic planning and control functions there. The IBS was originally developed in only a few European countries, and was extended to cover global operations. Applications specialists who are already using the IBS were instrumental in implementing it elsewhere. BASE and IBS personnel with experience in the new system assisted colleagues in other countries in getting on-line while streamlining their own operations. IBS allows bankers around the world to coordinate activities with a single global customer, such as an MNE.

Source: BankAmerica Corporation, 1984 *Annual Report,* pp. 2-8.

The point here is that people from different countries with different experiences are valuable at the global level of the MNE. The situation today is very different from what it was in the earlier years, when subsidiaries were appendages. The globally integrated MNE is a different entity and has different personnel needs.

Foreign Assignments in High Demand

People are certainly aware of the increasing potential for professional success associated with overseas assignments. The expatriate assignment is becoming increasingly attractive to many executives. Kenny, Kindler & Hunt, a New York executive recruiting firm, reports that fast-track executives are seeking overseas assignments to show that they can operate effectively at the general management level. In a survey that it conducted in 1983, 37 percent of the 125 managers polled were willing to take overseas jobs—up from 10 percent a decade earlier[27] Heidrick & Struggles, another executive recruiter, reported that managers who in the past had shunned overseas jobs that got them "two-yeared into oblivion," or forgotten at the parent, were now seeking such jobs.[28] These findings comport well with a statement by the vice president of Pepsico's international division that "his group is the primary farm team for top company talent."[29]

Traits of the Modern International Manager

Jacques Maisonrouge, president of IBM World Trade Corporation, expressed some fairly strong beliefs about today's international manager:

> One major consequence of this internationalization of business has been the increased need for international managers; that is, for managers who, aside from having all the qualities that make good managers of national companies, are also mobile, adaptable, and at ease in cultures other than their own. In addition, because they will undoubtedly work outside their home countries at some point in their careers, they should have one or two foreign languages; an understanding of the sociopolitical environment in which they will be working; and a world view that inhibits the growth of chauvinism.
>
> . . . tomorrow's managers will have to demonstrate more awareness of the world around them [and] more flexibility of mind . . . than ever before. In a world where new knowledge continues to accumulate rapidly, the most valuable managers of all will be those who have learned *how* to learn.

Source: J. G. Maisonrouge, "Education of a Modern International Manager," *Journal of International Business Studies,* Spring-Summer 1983, pp. 143-44.

Conclusions

Many important personnel management issues are pertinent to the MNE. One of these is the use of expatriate managers and technical specialists.

Benefits/Costs

Many pros and cons are associated with the use of expatriates. Two pros seem especially relevant, however. Expatriates can provide special expertise that is not otherwise available at a specific location—and they can often provide it quickly and in a manner consistent with company mores. Using expatriates, however, is very costly. Obviously the benefits derived from their special expertise must exceed the added costs of using them.

Historically, a fairly large percentage of expatriate assignments have ended in failure—with the expatriate returning home prematurely. This expensive experience raises questions as to the adequacy of the standards that have been used to select and train them.

Selection

The criteria used in selecting expatriates have varied considerably, depending on the overseas position involved. CEOs and other managers have been required to possess managerial experience and skills, personal and family flexibility, company experience, and communicative ability. Highly valued traits of technical specialists and operatives have included emotional stability and maturity. Training for expatriates has often been country specific, with topics including cultural, religious, political, and social issues; language proficiency; home country/host country relations; and the legal environment. Training for CEOs and other managers has been more extensive than that for technical specialists and operatives. Larger firms have typically employed more sophisticated selection procedures and training programs than those employed by smaller firms.

Compensation

The compensation paid expatriates must be competitive with what they would receive if they were employed at home. It must also cover the added costs of living abroad and of maintaining both a domestic and a foreign presence. Examples of the former are housing, educational expenses, forgone income that might be earned by a spouse or by children, and security expenses. Examples of the latter are travel expenses, the extra costs of maintaining investments at home, and extra taxes. The compensation of expatriates is also complicated by split payroll policies that result in partial compensation payments in both home and host country currencies, by inflation in the country of assignment and by changes in exchange rates.

Taxes

Expatriates always pay income taxes where they work, in the countries that have income taxes. Special considerations derived from their expatriate status may lower their tax bills, however. A U.S. national on assignment abroad is allowed a substantial foreign earned income exemption by the Tax Reform Act of 1986. An expatriate's unearned income is never exempt from U.S. taxation. Foreign taxes paid on such income by an expatriate, however, can be credited against any U.S. taxes due. To be eligible for the foreign earned income credit, an expatriate must meet certain residency requirements.

Repatriation

In the early days of the MNE, expatriate repatriation was often a disappointing experience. Firms were inexperienced in dealing with expatriates, and the competitive pressures of the times allowed for no hesitancy in moving needed people overseas. Mistakes were made. Those who had been on assignment overseas often fared miserably upon their return to the home operation. For these and other reasons, especially reasons related to the taxation policies then in effect, the incidence of expatriate assignments declined.

The Increased Importance and Attractiveness of Expatriate Assignments

As MNEs matured and their operations and marketing became more globally integrated, the status and value of the expatriate were enhanced. Career-path planning and other MNE activities reduced the uncertainties associated with expatriate assignments, especially the uncertainties related to repatriation. Perhaps more important, the attractiveness of expatriate assignments increased as MNEs became more dependent on personnel with multinational experiences that would contribute to strategies of global competitive effectiveness. Consequently, larger numbers of executives and technical personnel have come to view overseas assignments as positive aspects of their professional development.

Questions

1. Identify the links between personnel management and the competitiveness of MNEs. How do expatriate personnel relate to the transfer of management-based technologies, such as those pertaining to experience curves, and product and process technologies?
2. What is an expatriate? Does the use of expatriates correlate with the product life cycle? If so, how? How would the use of expatriates vary among ethnocentric, polycentric, and geocentric MNEs?
3. What are the main pros and cons of using expatriates as compared with using local nationals?
4. What are the most important selection criteria for selecting expatriates for overseas positions? How and why do these criteria vary with the nature of the overseas position?
5. What special training programs might be beneficial for expatriates and their families pending an overseas assignment? What is the likelihood that such programs would be found in a U.S. multinational? Why?
6. What major factors affect the compensation paid to expatriates? With regard to influences on compensation, how do expatriates differ from local personnel?
7. How are exchange rate changes accommodated in the compensation packages of expatriate personnel? How might such packages be administered in the face of currency nonconvertibility?
8. Describe the provisions of the U.S. tax law that pertain to foreign earned income and unearned income. What is the rationale for these provisions?

9. Why did U.S. MNEs have difficult early experiences in the handling of their expatriate personnel?
10. Compare the role and significance of the expatriate in the competitive strategies of the emergent MNEs and the mature MNEs. What role do expatriates play in the competitiveness of MNEs today? What effect does this role have on the desires of personnel to include overseas experiences in their career ladders? Why?

References

Adler, Nancy J. *International Dimensions of Organizational Behavior.* Boston: Kent Publishing, 1986. See, especially, chap. 5, "Multinational Teams"; chap. 8, "Cross-Cultural Transitions: Expatriate Employee Entry and Reentry"; and chap. 9, "A Portable Life: The Expatriate Spouse."

Edstrom, Anders, and Jay Galbraith. "Transfer of Managers as Coordination and Control Strategy in Multinational Organizations." *Administrative Science Quarterly,* June 1977, pp. 248-63.

Grub, Phillip D.; Fariborz Ghadar; and Dara Khambata, ed. *The Multinational Enterprise in Transition.* Princeton, N.J.: Darwin Press, 1986. See chap. 5, "International Personnel Management."

Maisonrouge, J. G. "The Education of the Modern International Manager." *Journal of International Business Studies,* Spring-Summer 1983, pp. 141-46.

Ronen, Simcha. *Comparative and Multinational Management.* New York: John Wiley & Sons, 1986. See chap. 12, "Staffing the MNC Foreign Subsidiary."

Endnotes

1. For evidence, see Duane Kujawa, "Technology Strategy and Industrial Relations: Case Studies of Japanese Multinationals in the United States," *Journal of International Business Studies,* Winter 1983, pp. 9-22; and Duane Kujawa, *Japanese Multinationals in the United States: Case Studies* (New York: Praeger Publishers, 1986), pp. 40-88.
2. Richard D. Hays, "Expatriate Selection: Insuring Success and Avoiding Failure," *Journal of International Business Studies,* Spring 1974, p. 25; and U.S. Department of Commerce, *Foreign Direct Investment in the United States,* vol. 1 (Washington, D.C.: U.S. Government Printing Office, 1976), p. 20.
3. As reported in "Mad Dogs and Expatriates," *Economist,* March 3, 1984, p. 69.
4. Lawrence G. Franko, "Who Manages Multinational Enterprise?" *Columbia Journal of World Business,* Summer 1973, pp. 30ff.
5. U.S. Department of Commerce, *Foreign Direct Investment,* vol. 5, appendix 1, "Management and Employment Practices of Direct Foreign Investors in the United States," pp. I-63-I-64.
6. Kujawa, *Japanese Multinationals,* pp. 40-59.

7. "Mad Dogs and Expatriates."
8. Rosalie L. Tung, "Selection and Training of Personnel for Overseas Assignments," *Columbia Journal of World Business,* Spring 1981, pp. 68-78.
9. Rosalie L. Tung, "Human Resource Planning in Japanese Multinationals: A Model for U.S. Firms?" *Journal of International Business Studies,* Fall 1984, p. 141.
10. Tung, "Selection and Training," pp. 69.
11. Ibid., p. 75.
12. Ibid., p. 76.
13. Tung, "Human Resource Planning," p. 142.
14. See, for example, Hays, "Expatriate Selection," pp. 30-36.
15. Ehrenfried Pausenberger, "The Conduct of International Enterprises in Developing Countries," *Intereconomics,* November-December 1980, p. 297.
16. N. Shehzad, "The American Expatriate Manager's Role and Future in Today's World," *Human Resource Planning,* 1984, pp. 55-61.
17. Llewellyn Clague and Neil B. Krupp, "International Personnel: The Repatriation Problem," *Personnel Administrator,* April 1978, pp. 29-33; and Cecil G. Howard, "Integrating Returning Expatriates into the Domestic Organization," *Personnel Administrator,* January 1979, pp. 62-65.
18. Ibid.
19. Lee Smith, "The Hazards of Coming Home," *Dun's Review,* October 1975, pp. 71-73.
20. Howard, "Integrating Returning Expatriates."
21. "How to Ease Reentry after Overseas Duty," *Business Week,* June 11, 1979, pp. 82-83.
22. Smith, "Hazards of Coming Home."
23. D. W. Kendall, "Repatriation: An Ending and a Beginning," *Business Horizons,* November-December 1981, pp. 21-25.
24. Published evidence on such a point is difficult to find. However, the authors have conducted a considerable number of company-specific case studies in which expatriate executives have attested to these views. One example, involving expatriate management at Chrysler Corporation's then Spanish subsidiary and the parent's desire to wrest managerial control from a local team consisting of both local nationals and expatriates, is briefly reported in Duane Kujawa, *International Labor Relations Management in the Automotive Industry* (New York: Praeger Publishers, 1971), p. 31.
25. For evidence, see Lawrence G. Franko, *The European Multinationals* (Stamford, Conn.: Greylock Publishers, 1976), pp. 187-98.
26. U.S. Department of Commerce, *Foreign Direct Investment,* vol. 5, appendix 1, "Management and Employment Practices," pp. I-60-I-65.
27. "Overseas Work Appeals to More U.S. Managers as a Wise Career Move," *The Wall Street Journal*, July 19, 1983, p. 1.
28. Ibid.
29. Ibid.

Case
Ernesto Gracias por Nada

Ernesto Gracias por Nada had served as president of Ace Synthetics Caribbean (ASYNCA) for two years, and today was his "big day. He was resigning his position with Ace to join Plasticos, S.A. as executive vice president, strategic planning. Ernesto had been working on this move for over a year.

Plasticos was Ace's major customer in the Caribbean and Central America. It bought petrochemical-based feedstocks from Ace that it molded, extruded, or otherwise fabricated into plastic piping, conduit, and sheet used in the construction industry. Both ASYNCA and Plasticos were subsidiaries of U.S. multinationals long active in Latin America. Both were known to be progressive companies. But how often does the president of a major subsidiary resign? What happened at Ace that made Ernesto want to leave? What could Plasticos do for him that Ace couldn't?

Ernesto joined Ace in 1972, nearly 15 years ago. He had just completed his MBA at ESAN, a graduate business school in Lima, Peru. He was 32 then. Ernesto also held a bachelor's degree in chemical engineering from a university near his boyhood home in Rosario, Argentina. Prior to attending ESAN, he had worked for several engineering consulting firms on projects in Argentina, Ecuador, Jamaica, the Dominican Republic, and Peru. The people he worked with were quick to recognize his technical competence and his strong interest in management. Most of them believed that a distinguished career lay ahead of him.

Ace's Organization Structure

Ace Synthetics organized its Latin American Division in 1965 to enhance its focus on several growing, important markets in that region. During the latter half of the 1960s, Ace Synthetics Latin America (ASYNLA) was essentially a marketing organization selling intermediate products produced in upscale, highly capital-intensive plants in the United States. Its marketing success resulted in local production where market size—from a regional, multicountry perspective—could justify direct investment. During the 1970s, Ace put up plants in Brazil, Mexico, Argentina, Chile, and Colombia.

In the early 1980s, ASYNLA "spun off" several operating companies whose responsibilities included both producing certain products locally and marketing all Ace products within their respective countries. Hence, Ace Synthetics Brazil (ASYNBRA), Ace Synthetics Mexico (ASYNMEX), Ace Synthetics Argentina (ASYNAR), Ace Synthetics Chile (ASYNCHI), and Ace Synthetics Colombia (ASYNCO) came into being. ASYNCA was also formed then and was

Note: This case is based on a real person and real companies and events known to the case-writer, Duane Kujawa. Fictitious names have been used for all the parties, however, for purposes of anonymity.

given marketing responsibilities for all Ace products in all the Caribbean and Central American countries. ASYNLA was restructured to perform as a regional headquarters organization responsible for all of Latin America and as a marketing organization covering those Latin American countries where no other subsidiary had responsibility—for example, Ecuador, Bolivia, Uruguay, and Peru. At this time, ASYNLA was relocated from its New Jersey-based parent company office to Coral Gables, Florida.

Ace relied on a matrix structure to provide it with operational flexibility and market continuity. Its major organizational units were product based as well as geographic. The Organic Chemicals Group, for example, had worldwide responsibility for organic chemical production, and it was also responsible for the sale of all Ace products (regardless of their production situs) wherever organic chemical plants were located. (Recall that plants were located in major markets.) Area-specific marketing groups such as ASYNCA handled all of the Ace products marketed in their regions.

In this structure, business plans were developed via a committee process involving those responsible for the production of certain products and those responsible for the territories in which those products were marketed. Decisions on production level, production allocation, and pricing, for example, were recognized as interdependent and as requiring diverse managerial inputs. The matrix structure also allowed for the ongoing close coordination among all the organizational subunits, including production, marketing, R&D, and finance, that was required for maximum long-term profitability.

Ace's Key Personnel Policies

Ace's matrix structure required the internal development of managerial/technical personnel. Committee decisions rested not only on accurate inputs from each member but also on knowledge of the broader, system-wide considerations on which decisions were ultimately based. These considerations, in turn, required personnel who were knowledgeable about Ace's overall operations and committed to maximizing returns at the overall corporate level.

For these reasons, Ace hired in only at the lower-level entry positions. Individuals needed to grow within the organization by accepting diverse and increasingly responsible positions that expanded their knowledge of how Ace operated overall, while allowing for progressively stringent testing of their technical and managerial mettle.

Every year, Ace evaluated the performance of its key personnel and forced a rank-ordering of these people reflecting their performance effectiveness. The top 20 percent were given substantial merit pay increases and positioned for subsequent promotion into even more responsible and rewarding positions. The middle 60 percent were given average raises. The bottom 20 percent got no raise and were often encouraged to leave. Ace's compensation policy was to reward performance while encouraging performance improvement.

Ace preferred to use cash compensation as much as possible. It felt that this was a stronger performance motivator than indirect payments, such as fringe benefits. Many viewed Ace's retirement bonus as the ultimate cash reward. Key employees received a cash bonus equal to three years' salary when they retired. This typically amounted to several hundred thousand dollars and was in addition to the regular retirement program benefits.

Ernesto's Case

Ever since Ernesto joined Ace, he had received superior performance ratings. He was always in the top 20 percent, and he had progressed fairly rapidly up the company's hierarchy. He was initially a technical sales representative in an Argentina-based group responsible for polymer sales. He was appointed head of the polymer marketing group in Peru within two years, and two years after that appointment, he was put in charge of polymer sales for all of Argentina. Two years later, he moved to the Coral Gables regional office as director of polymer sales at ASYNLA. In 1980, he was promoted to director of marketing, Organic Chemicals Group, at ASYNLA. As before, his performance was outstanding.

By 1983, Ernesto had spent five years at Coral Gables. Company policy now required that he return to Latin America since he was not on the Ace-U.S. payroll. During his five years at Coral Gables, he was treated like all Ace-U.S. management personnel in terms of pay scale and basic benefits. In addition, as an expatriate manager, he was given extra compensation to cover schooling costs for his children, travel during an extended annual home leave, and so on.

The five-year limit was imposed for several reasons. One reason was that five years seemed more than adequate from a professional development standpoint. A second was that expatriates were expensive, so there had to be good grounds for continuing to pay the added costs associated with their status. Yet another was that such expatriates from Latin American countries were ultimately more valuable to the company if they returned to Latin America, where their assets, including their linguistic and cultural affinities, could be put to optimum use.

Ernesto was first offered a position as executive vice president at ASYNVEN. He turned it down, claiming hardship on his family if he were to relocate just then. A month later, he requested advancement into the Ace-U.S. organization. His request was denied. Shortly thereafter, Ernesto was offered and accepted the president's position at ASYNCA. Within three months, he and his family had relocated to San Jose, Costa Rica.

Ernesto felt that he had been treated unfairly by Ace. Other Latin American executives confided that they too felt that Ace had treated them as "second-class citizens," since their career paths had been essentially confined to Latin America. Ernesto and others like him were highly result-oriented and had been compensated handsomely over the years. They had all developed substantial investments in the United States. (These investments reflected a variety of concerns, not the least of which was the long-term currency hedge that such investments provided in the face of nearly continuously declining Latin American currency values.) Moreover, a Latin American on assignment in a Latin American country did not receive the special three-year salary bonus upon retiring.

Ernesto arrived in San Jose determined to recover what he felt was a financial loss occasioned by Ace's failure to recognize him on an equal basis with parent country nationals. It took him a year to identify Plasticos as his "target" and to negotiate his salary and benefit package.

18

EXPORT-IMPORT MANAGEMENT

This chapter describes how export-import transactions are carried out and demonstrates how a firm can benefit from being involved in international trade. It illuminates the main participants, instruments, and practices in international trade. The perspectives of small firms, large MNEs, and importers are presented in separate sections, to show the opportunities available to each. The main goals of the chapter are to:

1. Explain how relatively simple export-import transactions, including documentation, work.
2. Show how domestic and multinational firms can benefit from exporting.
3. Demonstrate the gains available to the firm from using imports in its business strategy.
4. Explain a wide variety of the most important trade financing procedures.

Introduction

International trade was probably the first form of international business, and it certainly involves the largest number of participants in international business today. The value of international banking transactions far surpasses that of trade, whose value in turn exceeds that of foreign direct investment, foreign portfolio investment, contractual arrangements such as licensing, intergovernment transfers, and other forms of international business. The participants in many of these business activities tend to be large, established companies and banks. In the area of exports and imports, on the other hand, there is a huge variety of participants, ranging from one-person companies that buy products from manufacturers for export, all the way to major multinational enterprises such as General Electric, which constructs and exports nuclear power plants and a large variety of other products to many countries.

Exporting can be used as a marginal activity by a company that sells some product in one country and agrees to ship that product overseas on request. Similarly, importing may be used to obtain an input needed for manufacturing when domestic supplies are inadequate. In each of these cases, the international aspect of the business may be relatively unimportant to the firm, but it exists anyway. Then if the firm discovers that overseas sales (or imported parts) begin to count for a major part of total sales, it may place some specific focus on developing a strategy for exports and imports.

This entry into international business through exporting or importing is not a *necessary* condition, since a firm may just as well decide to invest overseas in a low-cost location, in order to maintain its market share for a product facing serious price competition. In this case, initial international business occurs through foreign direct investment. The key point is that, generally speaking, exporting or importing is a type of international business open to virtually any size or kind of firm, whereas other types of international activity, such as foreign direct investment and overseas franchising, tend to demand greater capital, management time, and other company resources.

Multinational firms have the potential for using exports and imports both to move products among their affiliates in different countries and to deal with outside customers and suppliers. MNEs that do this face many opportunities for benefiting from low-cost overseas suppliers (including their own affiliates), for selling excess inventories from an affiliate in one country to customers in another, and even for shipping some products to a subsidiary that produces others, in order to offer a full product line to local customers. On the whole, MNEs can use international trade to pursue many business goals more efficiently or effectively than do purely domestic firms.

Many companies fail to consider *imports* as a means of supplying their needs for parts, components, and even finished products. Perhaps this bias is due to the managers' main focus on sales (and hence on potential exports). Or perhaps it follows the typical government-led emphasis on exports to improve a country's balance of trade. Since imports as well as exports may contribute to a company's business success, they should not be ignored. Reducing the cost of production inputs (through importing) adds to the bottom line, just as increasing the volume of sales does.

This chapter is organized to illuminate the main participants, instruments, and practices in international trade first and then to explore managerial issues. The next section lays out the basic export/import transaction. Then the perspectives of small firms, MNEs, and importers are considered in separate sections. After that, the specific issue of financing exports and imports is discussed. Finally, the ways in which exporting and importing can utilize (or create) the firm's competitive advantages are reconsidered.

A Basic Export-Import Transaction

The Participants

Although there is probably no such thing as a "typical" **export-import transaction,** we can consider a number of frequently used instruments and features of such transactions as a basic model, to which other alternatives can be attached or compared. Figure 18-1 depicts a transaction in which an importer and exporter agree on a sale and they each use a bank to handle the financial arrangements. Other intermediaries—an insurance company, a transportation company, and customs in the importing country—are also shown.

The transaction would probably take place somewhat as follows. First, the exporter would look for a foreign buyer for its products. (Alternatively, a foreign buyer might come to the exporter and request a shipment.) When the exporter finds a buyer—not necessarily an easy task—the transaction can proceed. The two firms negotiate for terms, such as the price, the quantity to be delivered, the delivery date, and the payment date. When an agreement is reached, some kind of bill of sale can be drawn up, depending on what the two parties determine. The negotiations will probably include a demand by the exporter to have some guarantee of payment made on the importer's behalf—for example, a letter of credit from a bank that the exporter chooses. (The financial aspects are discussed at length in the "Trade Financing" section.) These negotiations, if successful, result in an export-import transaction.

In addition to the payment documents, the transaction usually involves an insurance contract on the goods shipped (to protect against losses from damage in shipping) and a contract with some transportation company to ship the goods from the exporter to customs in the importer's country. The goods must be cleared by customs inspectors in the receiving country, after which the importer or another transportation company may pick them up for delivery to the importer's facility.

Figure 18–1 **A Simple Export-Import Transaction**

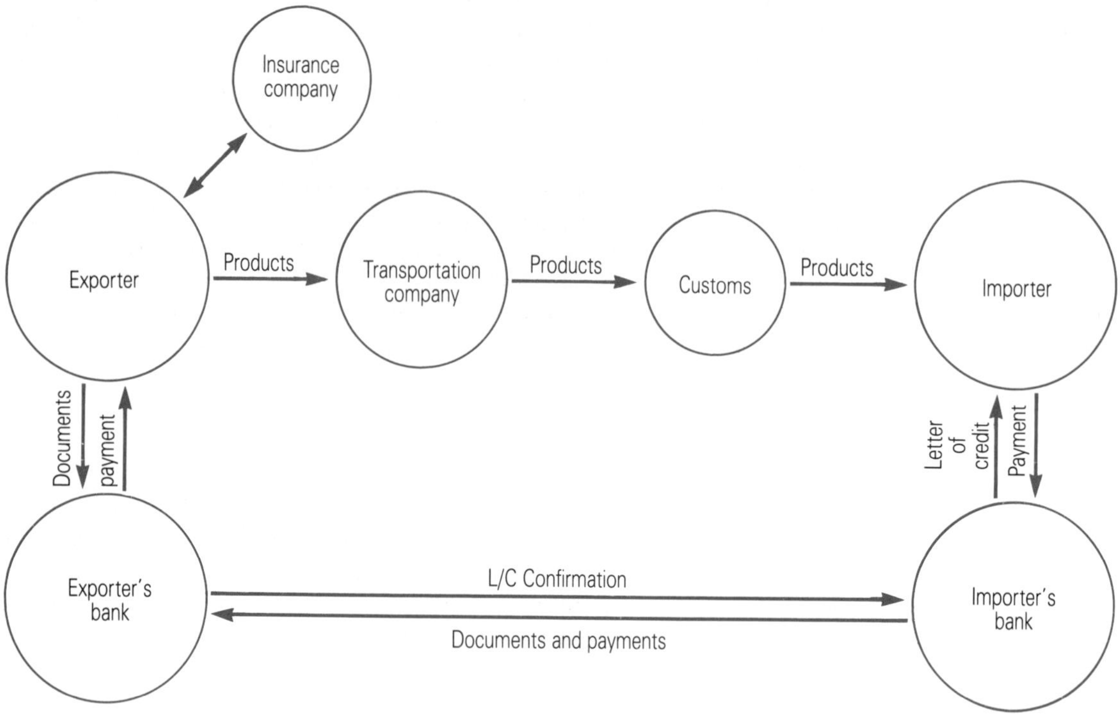

Oil from Latin America being unloaded at EXXON's Baytown, Texas refinery.

Milton & Joan Mann/Cameramann International

This highly simplified transaction illustrates some central concerns of the parties involved in international trade. The exporter wants to assure payment as soon and as certainly as possible. The importer wants to make sure that the goods arrive on time and in good condition. Each bank wants to make sure that payment takes place on time and, of course, that it earns its fees for providing the letter of credit or other services (in addition to any financing that it offers). The insurance company wants to make sure that the cargo is delivered as contracted in the sale. And finally, the transportation company wants to make sure that the exporter (or importer) pays for the shipment as contracted. These concerns are listed in concise fashion in Table 18-1. Notice that the concerns are more or less inverse for the exporter (which wants earlier payment and later shipment) and the importer (which wants later payment and earlier delivery). The other parties mainly want to see the transaction completed as contracted, since their income generally comes from fees based on the value of the shipment.

The Documentation

To carry out the export-import transaction already described, a substantial amount of documentation is required. The documents most often used include the letter of credit, the bank draft, the bill of lading or combined transport document, the commercial invoice, the insurance certificate, and the certificate of origin. Let us consider each of these documents in turn.

Table 18-1 **Export-Import Participants and Their Concerns**

Participant	Concerns	Items Affecting Income	Risks
Exporter	Early payment, guaranteed payment	Revenues, production costs, transport costs	Nonpayment, delays, damage to goods
Importer	Timely arrival of goods, safe arrival of goods, latest payment allowable	Product cost, import-related fees and expenses	Delays, fraud, damage to goods
Exporter's bank	Documents in order, payment received from importer's bank	Fees, contract-processing costs	Nonpayment, incorrect documents
Importer's bank	Documents in order, payment received from importer	Fees, contract-processing costs	Nonpayment, incorrect documents
Insurance company	Payment of premiums, safe arrival of goods	Premiums, contract-processing costs	Damage to goods, incorrect documents
Transport company	Payment of shipping charges	Fees, contract-processing costs	Damage to goods, delays

An (export) **letter of credit (L/C)** is a contract between an importer and a bank that transfers liability for paying the exporter from the importer to the (supposedly more creditworthy) importer's bank. From the issuing bank's point of view, the L/C represents a contingent liability: if the terms stated in the letter of credit are met, then the bank agrees to pay the exporter. As seen in Figure 18-2, the terms of the L/C specify the presentation of appropriate documents (in this case, a commercial invoice, a customs invoice, a packing list, a bill of lading, and a 60-day bank draft) but do not refer to the quality (i.e., acceptability) of the merchandise.

As long as the bank that issues the L/C (Marine Midland International Bank) is presented with the required documents before expiration of the L/C, the bank is obligated to pay the exporter. If the importer fails to pay the bank, then the bank must deal with that problem as a separate contract. Similarly, if the importer fails to receive acceptable merchandise for any reason, that problem must be dealt with as a separate contract not involving the bank (e.g., damages to merchandise are covered by insurance and fraud by the exporter is a failure to uphold the initial commercial contract). Multiple contracts are involved in the simple export-import transaction; the L/C in particular requires only that the specified documents be in order for the exporter to receive payment from the bank—all other contractual obligations are generally separate from this one.[1]

Notice that the document shown in Figure 18-2 is called an "irrevocable commercial letter of credit." The word *irrevocable* refers to the fact that, once drawn up for the importer and accepted by the exporter, the L/C may not be amended by either party without prior approval by both. The L/C is also "commercial," because it refers to a commercial transaction. This type of L/C is called "documentary," because it requires that documents be presented in order to carry out payment. It is the most commonly used means of guaranteeing payment in international trade between unrelated firms. If the paying bank is not in the exporter's country, the exporter may demand that a bank in that country offer a "confirmation" of the L/C. In that event, the responsibility for paying the exporter falls on the confirming bank, which in turn will seek payment from the importer's bank, which in turn will seek payment from the importer. (In this example, the Hongkong & Shanghai Banking Corporation only offers "advice" to the exporter, XYZ Trading Company. This bank could be asked to confirm the transaction and take responsibility as noted.)

The **bank draft,** also called a bill of exchange, is similar to a simple check in its use as the means of payment for an export-import transaction. If the transaction is payable on sight, the draft becomes a check when the exporter presents it (plus the L/C and other documents). If the transaction is payable at some fixed time after acceptance of the documents, the draft is akin to a postdated (delayed-reaction) check, cashable only at the specified date. The latter is called a **time draft,** and the former a **sight draft.** Figure 18-3 is a time draft, payable in 60 days from the account of ABC Company at Marine Midland International Bank.

Figure 18-2

APPLICATION & AGREEMENT FOR IRREVOCABLE COMMERCIAL LETTER OF CREDIT

L/C NO. ______ (For Bank Use Only)

DATE: June 19, 19

To: MARINE MIDLAND INTERNATIONAL BANK
777 Brickell Avenue, Suite 1201
Miami, Florida 33131

Please issue for our account an irrevocable Letter of Credit (herein called Credit) as set forth below by:
☐ AIRMAIL ☐ AIRMAIL, WITH SHORT PRELIMINARY TELEGRAPHIC ADVICE ☒ FULL TELEGRAPHIC ADVICE

Advising Bank (Please leave blank unless Advising Bank has been specified)	**For Account of**
The Hongkong & Shanghai Banking Corp. 18 Rue de la Paix 75002, Paris France	ABC Company 100 Madison Street New York, New York
In Favor of (Beneficiary) XYZ Trading Co., Ltd. P.O. Box 260-09 Paris, France	**Amount** In Numbers: US$45,000.00 In Words: Forty five thousand and 00/100) U.S. Dollars Drafts must be presented for negotiation or presented to drawee on or before Expiration Date. September 1, 19

Available by drafts at 60 days sight (Please indicate Sight or Tenor) drawn, at your option, on you or your correspondent for 100 % of the invoice value.

When accompanied by the following documents, as checked:

CHECK REQUIRED DOCUMENTS

- ☒ Commercial Invoice 1 original and 2 copies.
- ☒ Customs Invoice 1 original and 2 copies.
- ☐ Insurance Policy and/or Certificate ______
- ☐ Including War Risk ______ (If other insurance is required, please state risks)
- ☒ Other Documents Packing list in duplicate
- ☐ Air Waybill consigned to ______
- ☒ On Board Ocean Bill of Lading (if more than one original has been issued all are required)
  Issued to Order of **MARINE MIDLAND INTERNATIONAL BANK**
  Marked: Notify: ABC Company, 100 Madison Street, New York, N.Y.

Freight: ☒ Collect ☐ Paid

Covering: Merchandise described in the invoice as: (Mention commodity only in generic terms omitting details as to grade, quality, etc) Purse accessories

Shipping Terms (Check One) ☐ FAS ☒ FOB ☐ C&F ☐ CIF ☐ OTHER: ______ (Specify City, Port or Airport)

Shipment From: Paris, France **To:** New York, USA **Latest:** August 21, 19	**Credit Transferable** ☐ Yes ☒ No	**Partial Shipments** ☒ Permitted ☐ Not Permitted	**Transshipments** ☐ Permitted ☒ Not Permitted

(Please check appropriate boxes)

☒ Documents and/or Draft(s) must be presented to negotiating or paying bank within 10 days after the date of issuance of documents evidencing shipment but on or before the expiration of the Credit. (*NOTE: If number of days left blank it will automatically be considered 21 days.*)

☒ Insurance effected by ourselves. We agree to keep insurance coverage in force until this transaction is completed.
All banking charges outside the U.S.A. are for ☒ Beneficiary's account ☐ Our account

☐ Other instructions ______

Disposition of Documents: ☒ To Us ☐ Other ______

Unless Otherwise Instructed You May Authorize Your Correspondent To Forward All Drafts and Documents In One Airmail.

MMIB-60(Rev. 8/85)

Figure 18-3 **A Commercial Draft**

Exchange for US$45,000.00 July 23, 19

At 60 days ---------------- *sight pay this* **FIRST**

of Exchange (Second unpaid) to the order of

XYZ TRADING CO., LTD.

US DOLLARS FORTY FIVE THOUSAND AND 00/100----------------------------------

Value received and charge the same to account of

ABC Company
100 Madison Street
New York, New York

To The Hongkong & Shanghai Banking Corp.
Paris, France

No. 002

XYZ TRADING CO., LTD.

MMIB - 132

When a letter of credit is used to guarantee payment to the exporter, the draft remains the vehicle through which payment is made, but it becomes relatively unimportant because the bank issuing (or confirming) the L/C has taken responsibility to pay the exporter, whether or not the importer's account contains sufficient funds. If the draft is used alone (i.e., without a letter of credit), it becomes all-important as the means of payment. (Payment by draft alone, of course, is less expensive to the importer than using an L/C as well.)

When a draft is used without a letter of credit, some form of instructions must accompany it to explain to the various parties involved what other documents and goods are involved in the transaction. (This type of transaction is called a **documentary collection.**) If the draft is payable on sight, then the instruction letter specifies that documents will be released to the importer upon payment of the draft (abbreviated D/P). If the draft is payable at a later date (i.e., a time draft), then instructions specify that the documents will be released to the importer upon acceptance of the draft (abbreviated D/A). Notice that in the case of a sight draft, the importer actually pays the exporter before receiving the goods—so the exporter's main risk is that it may ship the goods to customs in the importer's country and subsequently need to retrieve them if the importer fails to complete the transaction by paying the draft. (Payment on sight occurs when the importer receives the documents, after the exporter ships the goods and sends the documents to the importer.) In the case of a time draft, once the draft is accepted by the importer (it becomes a "collection"), the exporter surrenders the merchandise, with only the draft as its claim on future payment. Both sight and time

The first shipment of Hyundai automobiles from Korea being unloaded at the port of Los Angeles, California.

Wide World Photos, Inc.

drafts accompanied by instructions and other documents (but no L/C) are called **documentary drafts.**

A **bill of lading** issued by a shipping company or its agent is used as evidence of a contract for shipping the merchandise and as a claim to ownership of the goods. The exporter owns the goods until the importer accepts the documents, at which point ownership shifts to the importer. The bill of lading serves as a receipt of the exporter, showing that it delivered the merchandise to the shipping company for transportation to the importer. The bill of lading does *not* require the carrier to inspect the merchandise; it only requires that the carrier accept the containers stated by the exporter to contain the specified merchandise.

If the goods are shipped by airplane or by more than one means of transport, alternative documents may replace the bill of lading. An **air waybill** is used in shipment by air. A **combined transport document** is used for shipments that involve more than one mode of transportation (eg., a truck to the port, then a ship).[2]

Another document usually involved in an export-import shipment is the **commercial invoice,** which is written by the exporter to describe precisely the merchandise and terms of the sale. This document resembles the shipping invoice used in domestic shipments.

Some proof of *insurance* is generally included. The **insurance certificate** will explain what type of coverage is being used (e.g., fire, theft, water) and will name the insuror and the exporter whose property is being insured.

In order to assess tariffs and other government-imposed restrictions on trade, the shipment may require a **certificate of origin,** stating the country in which the goods were produced. This document is necessary when shipping to European Community countries, where tariffs are charged on goods originating outside the Community but not on goods produced in member countries.

Table 18-2 summarizes the documents discussed above, noting the parties involved and the reasons for their use. The above discussion is not intended to cover all the documents used in export-import transactions, but rather to point out the ones that are most widely used. In every transaction of this kind, it is necessary to check with each country's government before shipping, in order to verify what documents are necessary.

Export Management for the Domestic Firm

This section examines exporting as a part of the business of a nonmultinational firm. Such a firm may be large or small, but it is one that does not do substantial international business—that is, its competitive advantages do not include experience in foreign markets. This type of firm must consider exports to be a kind of new business, just like production of a new product or entry into a new market segment in the domestic market. The appropriate products must be selected, buyers must be found, production and transportation costs must be estimated, promotional strategy must be created, and the

Table 18-2 **Common International Trade Documents**

Instrument	Seller or Issuer	Buyer	Reason for Use
Letter of credit (L/C)	Commercial bank	Importer	To guarantee payment to the exporter
Bank draft	Drawn on a commercial bank	Payable to exporter	It is the means of payment.
Bill of lading	Shipping company	Exporter	To prove that the exporter delivered the goods as agreed
Combined transport document	Shipping company	Exporter	To prove that the exporter & each transport company delivered the goods as agreed
Commercial invoice	Exporter	Importer	To describe precisely the merchandise and terms of sale
Insurance certificate	Insurance company	Exporter	To prove that the shipment is insured and on what terms
Certificate of origin	Government of shipping country	Exporter	To prove the country where the merchandise was produced, for customs purposes

business must be incorporated into the organization effectively. While each of these matters deserves detailed study, they are discussed here only to point out some of the most important considerations.

Exporting within Corporate Strategy

Figure 18-4 offers a view of **exporting** in a corporate strategy context. It depicts exporting as a means of entry into foreign markets. Other alternatives include foreign direct investment and contractual arrangements such as licensing and franchising. The company can set its strategy by assessing its competitive advantages and disadvantages (step 1), then proceeding to explore foreign markets that offer a potential for sales.

Figure 18-4 **Foreign Business Strategy**

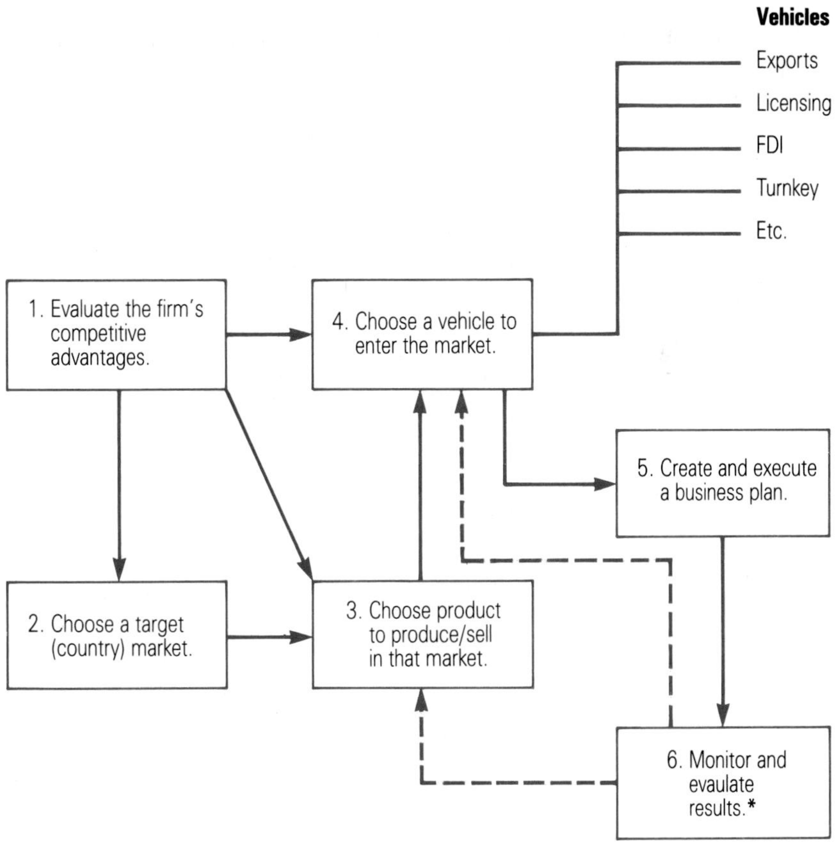

*The dashed lines show that performance evaluation may lead to changes in the products selected or in the market entry vehicle (or even to exit from the market) if the results justify such strategic shifts.

The target markets can be chosen on the basis of expected sales, competition from other suppliers, government restrictions, costs of getting the product to those markets, and any other factors that may be relevant. Although there are over 160 countries in the world, it is most likely that the firm will be able to limit its initial search to a very small number of markets—probably based not only on income but also on proximity and cultural affinity.

Once a country has been chosen (step 2), the strategy must be developed to select products and a market entry vehicle. If the firm makes only one product or a narrow product line, then product selection is not an issue. For the diversified firm, it may be appropriate to introduce different products into different national markets. Product selection is based on competitive conditions in the chosen market for the range of products made by the firm, the costs of making and transporting the products, and the risks involved (step 3). In any event, once a product has been selected, the firm can proceed to explore ways of getting that product to the foreign market.

Depending on the firm's set of competitive advantages and the conditions in a given national market, each of the market-serving alternatives can be evaluated (as discussed in the appendix to Chapter 3). Because the firm presumably has no experience with other international business and because the costs and risks of exporting are usually low, exporting most likely will be chosen (step 4). Assuming that exporting does appear superior to the other choices and that the company does decide to pursue the given market (rather than eliminate it from consideration), a detailed business plan can be created and executed (step 5, as discussed below).

Finally, after observing the results of the strategy for some period of time (step 6), adjustments can be made or the strategy can be rejected in favor of another. Altogether, Figure 18-4 presents a logical structure for thinking about foreign market entry, through exports or other means that may be available to the firm.

The Business Plan

The detailed business plan mentioned above as step 5 should cover the usual marketing considerations such as pricing, promotion, and distribution—and also the organization of the firm to handle this new business.

Pricing may be aimed to cover the incremental costs of producing extra products for export, or to cover the full costs of production (including fixed costs), or to equate marginal revenue to marginal cost. Other goals, such as revenue maximization or loss minimization, could be sought too. The point is that pricing for overseas sales may be based on criteria different from those used in pricing for domestic sales.

Another consideration to keep in mind is that if the exchange rate changes, prices in domestic currency will change in terms of the foreign currency. Such a change may be helpful or harmful to the firm, but it definitely should be taken into account when a pricing strategy for export sales is being set. For a target country whose currency is devaluing relative to the home country currency, the firm's export prices will need to be lowered if it wants to maintain the same host country prices. For a country whose currency is revaluing relative to the home country currency, the firm's product will become less expensive unless export prices are raised to offset the exchange rate change.

A firm exporting to several foreign markets would like to price separately in each market, charging higher prices in markets that will bear them. This strategy can create problems, however, since customers in a low-price country could try to resell the product in high-price countries—competing with the firm itself! Also, this type of price discrimination may lead the authorities in high-price markets to penalize the firm for monopolistic practices.

Promotion may be extended abroad or adapted to the host country environment, as discussed in Chapter 13. If exports are solicited from abroad, then initially no promotion is required. If the firm wants to expand its export business, then some promotional effort will be required. If the market entry mode chosen is exporting through distributors, then promotion must be done among potential distributors, rather than focusing only on final customers.

Distribution to the foreign market will require new arrangements with transportation companies, insurers, and so on, because the transactions will cross national borders and thus cross national legal jurisdictions. While no single distribution method can be singled out as best for all cases, the pros and cons of each method can be evaluated, just as in the domestic market. The key differences are that costs are generally higher because distances are longer and risks are greater because of the additional national economies and legal jurisdictions involved.

Organizational issues relate to the fit of international sales into the company's total business (as discussed to some extent in Chapter 12). Generally, exports are handled by an existing division when they are small in value. As exports grow, at some point it may make sense to assign responsibility elsewhere for foreign sales—by establishing an international division or otherwise reorganizing the firm. Basically, the goals are to communicate with prospective customers in the host country about product availability and to control the export activity so that it does not disrupt other company business.

Export Management Strategy for the MNE

Once the company has become multinational, or is willing to consider establishing overseas operations, a new set of alternatives arises. Now it may be possible to export some products from the home country to the target country and to produce other products in the target market. When the MNE introduces new products at home, it may simultaneously introduce them in the host market, through either exports or local production in the existing facility there. When cost or regulatory difficulties arise in one country, it may be possible to move production to the less-constrained country, resulting in either imports or local production for each market served. The MNE may also export parts or other production inputs from an affiliate in one country to another affiliate in another country for assembly—in this case serving the host country market only indirectly, through products manufactured by the host country affiliate. In general, the MNE possesses a greatly expanded set of choices in comparison with the domestic firm in any country.

Returning to Figure 18-4, the MNE again begins with an inventory of its competitive advantages and disadvantages to see what products and markets are worth exploring. Now it can divide target markets into those where it already has some operations—and thus where additional products can be introduced—and those that are new to it. In a market where the MNE already has operations, it has a competitive advantage (relative to other foreign firms) in knowledge of demand conditions and in knowledge of the legal, cultural, and cost barriers to serving that market. In a market where the MNE does not yet have operations, it faces barriers similar to those confronting the non-MNE, except that the MNE has had experience in dealing with new entry in other markets (such as dealing with tariffs and import licensing) that may be transferable to the new market. The knowledge advantage from previous international business gives the MNE an edge over other firms in market entry in both situations. Thus, the MNE's choice of a target market depends both on market characteristics in potential host countries and on the firm's existing array of foreign affiliates.

The MNE's choice of products to sell in the target market once again depends on the firm's previous activities in that market. Some products may have already been introduced there. Others may be appropriate for local production rather than export from the home country (or from an affiliate in another country). Having considered such factors, the firm can choose products based on expected demand in the target market, on the costs of getting the products to customers, and on the risks involved.

The choice among exports, local production, and other market-serving alternatives has already been discussed. For the MNE, it is important to note that some products may be supplied to a particular country through one vehicle and other products through other vehicles.

When the MNE manager arrives at step 5 of the decision-making process, a specific business plan must be designed, once again recognizing the interrelations between the new project and the firm's existing activities. The new export venture must be evaluated on the basis of its incremental contribution to the firm's sales and profits. If the exports simply replace products previously manufactured by the company in the target country, then they are justified only if they lower the costs or risks of producing and delivering the products to customers. If the exports represent entry into a new market, then they may be evaluated as in the case of the non-MNE.

If the exports are sold from one affiliate to another in the same firm, the issue of **transfer pricing** arises. By pricing intrafirm shipments higher or lower, the firm may transfer more or less funds to the shipping affiliate. While

4. What competitive advantages does a multinational enterprise gain by operating a network of affiliates that export among themselves?
5. What benefits does the domestic firm gain from exporting? How do these benefits differ from the benefits gained by an MNE?
6. What benefits does the domestic firm gain from importing? How do these benefits differ from the benefits gained by an MNE?
7. Explain how forfaiting works. Why would a firm use forfaiting rather than other means of financing an export sale?
8. Countertrading has become quite popular in East-West trade. Why is it *not* likely to replace traditional bank financing as the main source of trade finance?
9. Create a market entry strategy for Nabisco Brands Corporation, which wants to enter the market for cookies in Japan. Assume that the company does not have any affiliates in Japan. Discuss the choice of entry mode, product selection, and business plan.
10. What reasons might a U.S. company have for exporting its electronic products to customers in Mexico even though production costs are lower there and tariffs are fairly high there?

References

Crédit Suisse. *Forfaiting.* Zurich: Crédit Suisse, n.d.

Eiteman, David, and Arthur Stonehill. *Multinational Business Finance.* 3rd ed. Reading, Mass.: Addison-Wesley Publishing, 1982.

Guild, Ian, and Rhodri Harris. *Forfaiting.* London: Euromoney Publications, 1985.

International Chamber of Commerce. *Guide to Documentary Credit Operations.* Paris: ICC, 1978.

Khoury, Sarkis. "Countertrade: Forms, Motives, Pitfalls, and Negotiation Requisites," *Journal of Business Research,* June 1984.

Morgan Guaranty Trust Company. *Financing Exports and Imports.* New York: Morgan Guaranty, n.d.

Organization for Economic Cooperation and Development. *East-West Trade: Recent Developments in Countertrade.* Paris: OECD, 1981.

Endnotes

1. Letters of credit are frequently subject to legal action by parties involved in the export-import process. Much of the terminology and conditions in L/Cs has been standardized and codified in *Uniform Customs and Practices 400,* published by the International Chamber of Commerce.
2. Examples of each of these documents and of the others can be found in International Chamber of Commerce, *Guide to Documentary Credit Operations* (Paris: ICC, 1978).

3. Exports can lower risk by replacing local production in a country that experiences political or economic upheaval. They can also supplement local production, providing a portfolio of supply sources and thus again reducing risk.
4. The banker's acceptance is considered "eligible" if it matures in less than 270 days. That is, the acceptance may be discounted at any Federal Reserve bank by the paying bank or any secondary purchaser of the acceptance.
5. An overview of federal export subsidy programs appears in Business International Corporation, *Financing Foreign Operations,* "Commercial Banks" (New York: Business International Corporation, latest edition). Also see Robert D. Frazer and Associates, *International Banking and Finance,* vol. 1 (Washington, D.C.: R&H Publishers, latest edition).
6. See the Foreign Sales Corporation Act of 1984, which appears in the *Internal Revenue Code* (Washington, D.C.: U.S. Government Printing Office, 1984), sections 921-27.
7. See, for example, *EXIMBANK Program Summary* (Washington, D.C.: Export-Import Bank of the United States, current edition).
8. The factor's fee can be viewed as a charge for accepting the risk of nonpayment, and the discount can be viewed as a charge for making funds available immediately to the exporter; but both charges really contribute to the total cost, which the factor receives to cover the two needs of the exporter.
9. All costs are as estimated by Crédit Suisse, *Forfaiting* (Zurich: Crédit Suisse, 1979).
10. Organization for Economic Cooperation and Development, *East-West Trade: Recent Developments in Countertrade* (Paris: OECD, 1981), pp. 10-11.
11. U.S. International Trade Commission, *Assessment of the Effects of Barter and Countertrade Transactions on U.S. Industries,* publication no. 1766 (Washington, D.C.: USITC, October 1985).

Case

EXIM Company (comparative advantage in international trade)

A. Introduction

A very important factor in determining trade patterns between countries for many products is the cost of production. If this cost is lower in one country than another, then the first country will benefit from producing and exporting the product to the second. For example, if steel costs $300 per ton to make in Japan and $400 per ton to make in the United States, then (all other things being equal) U.S. customers should buy (import) steel from Japanese companies. By the same reasoning, if airplanes cost $4 million to produce in the United States and $5 million in Japan, then Japanese customers should buy (import) airplanes from the U.S. In this example, the U.S. produces and exports airplanes, while Japan produces and exports steel. Each country has a *comparative advantage* in producing one product relative to the other country.

Obviously, countries do not export and import, *companies* do. For any company, the choice of products to export and import depends to some degree on the cost of production in the various countries where the company does business. The company should utilize comparative advantage to decide where (in which country) to produce its products and where to buy its inputs. In the case below, a U.S.-based company sells many products in several different national markets. The problem is to choose whether to obtain computer memory chips in the United States or Japan, and perhaps to consider buying other components and peripheral equipment for resale as well.

B. The Case

EXIM Company is a Connecticut-based corporation involved in assembling computer circuit boards for use in personal computers manufactured by IBM, Apple, Compaq, NEC, and other original equipment manufacturers. During its six-year history, the company has gone from a two-person operation assembling memory expansion boards to a 30-person manufacturing business, now making a wide variety of multiple-function boards and other peripheral hardware used in the burgeoning personal computer market. The firm's annual sales have grown by about 40 percent per year to just over $8 million in 1985.

This case was written by Professor Robert Grosse as a basis for class discussion, 1986.

EXIM was founded by an electrical engineer (Hans Klauser) and a recent M.B.A. graduate of a local business school (Dwight Sutherland). These two entrepreneurs were able to combine basic knowledge of microcomputer hardware with an aggressive marketing strategy for the circuit boards. After borrowing $50,000 from a commercial bank and adding their life savings, EXIM's founders were able to generate enough sales to break even in the second year of operations and to repay their entire loan by the end of the third year. Today EXIM uses 80 percent equity financing (that is, earnings reinvested in the firm by the two owners who continue to own all the stock shares) and 20 percent bank financing, mostly for working capital. The entire operation is housed in a rebuilt factory just outside of West Haven, Connecticut.

Most of EXIM's sales go to the thousands of retail stores that have sprung up in the United States during the 1980s to sell microcomputers and peripheral equipment to businesses, individuals, and other customers. In addition, similar stores in Canada and the United Kingdom have become important customers in the last two years. Export sales to individual customers have been fairly insignificant thus far, but an advertising campaign in two microcomputer magazines has led to sales in Mexico, Ireland, and even in Pakistan.

Figure 1 **Yen/Dollar Exchange Rates**

Date	U.S. Dollar/Japanese Yen Exchange Rates, 1973–85 (in yen / $)	Inflation Rates in Japan and the United States, 1973–85 (in annual percent rates, ΔCPI)	
		Japan	United States
1973	280.00	11.7%	6.1%
1974	300.95	24.4	10.9
1975	305.15	11.8	9.2
1976	292.80	9.3	5.8
1977	240.00	8.0	6.5
1978	194.60	3.8	7.6
1979	239.70	3.6	11.2
1980	203.00	8.0	13.5
1981	219.90	4.9	10.4
1982	235.00	2.7	6.1
1983	232.20	1.8	3.2
1984	251.10	2.3	4.3
1985	200.50	2.1	3.5

Recently, competition from lower-priced boards, many of them imported from Asia, has begun to reduce EXIM's rate of growth in sales. Having read about the problems of the automobile industry and others in the United States due to their competition with Japanese and Korean firms, EXIM's general manager, Hans Klauser, was considering the idea of establishing an assembly operation somewhere in Asia. Klauser felt that his products were essentially "commodities," embodying technology that is readily available from several suppliers in the United States, Germany, and Japan. Therefore, his competitiveness would need to be based to some degree on the prices charged to customers. Superior quality and service could be used to improve sales somewhat, but the key factor would be price.

He was particularly concerned about the cost conditions in each country, which were subject to substantial shifts due to differences in national inflation rates and exchange rate changes. The Japanese yen, for example, had devalued by over 30 percent relative to the dollar in the early 1980s; then it revalued by more than 20 percent in 1985 alone. Japanese inflation, by contrast, had paralleled U.S. inflation during most of the 1980s. Figure 1 depicts the yen/dollar exchange rate during 1973–85 and the inflation rates of each country during the same period.

Table 1 **Production Costs of Computer Components in U.S., Japan, and Korea***

	Comparative Costs		
Component	United States	Japan	Korea
64 K RAM chips (cost per chip)	$ 1.50	$ 1.10	$ 0.90
256 K RAM chips (cost per chip)	$ 7.80	$ 6.60	not available
Internal clock/calendar	$ 9.75	$ 9.70	$ 10.50
Serial port and RS232 cable to attach peripheral equipment	$ 24.00	$ 24.50	$ 23.50
Parallel port and RS232 cable to attach peripheral equipment	$ 23.00	$ 23.50	$ 22.80
Software-in-a-chip to run ramdisk	$325.00	$345.00	not available
Internal modem (300 baud)	$340.00	$335.00	$332.00
Internal modem (1200 baud)	$455.00	$460.00	$470.00

* Data are listed in US dollars at the current exchange rate, December 1985.

Labor costs favored the Asian locations, but not necessarily by enough to overcome a severe dollar devaluation that might occur. Total production costs of several relevant components in 1985 appear in Table 1.

Although the table presents only production costs of EXIM's potential suppliers, these are fairly close to the full delivered cost for almost all of the products, since transportation, insurance, and other costs are minimal for such small, lightweight, manufactured goods. Tariffs currently are less than 5 percent *ad valorem* on these electronic products coming into the United States.

19

TECHNOLOGY AND THE MNE

This chapter focuses on technology—the single most important competitive advantage in business today. It begins by defining technology according to its product, process, and managerial applications. It then considers both company management and government regulatory views concerning the transfer of technology within the firm across national borders. Most of the chapter is devoted to demonstrating how technology can be a competitive advantage and how firms can obtain, utilize, and protect a technological advantage. The main goals of the chapter are to:

1. Define technology and technology transfer.
2. Show how firms can benefit from the use of product, process, and management technology.
3. Analyze the choice of whether to exploit technology within the firm or sell/license that technology to other firms.
4. Explain how a firm can protect its proprietary technology.
5. Point out the concerns of governments in industrial and less developed countries with respect to the use of technology by MNEs.

Introduction

Technology is the single most important competitive advantage of firms in the noncommunist world today. From new products, to knowledge of markets, to industrial processes, technology is a fundamental factor in the success of both domestic and multinational firms. This chapter begins by defining technology itself, and then it explores the use of technology as a competitive advantage of the MNE. Firms need to select technologies that provide optimal competitive gains, then decide how to implement those technologies, and then try to protect their technological advantages. A fundamental problem is deciding how to obtain desired technology—through R&D or through acquisition from another firm.

The transfer of technology among countries within the MNE network and through markets outside the firm is a second focus of our analysis. Dealing with governments in both industrial countries and LDCs on the issue of technology transfer has become a major problem for MNE managers. In industrial countries, technology protection and the generation of new technology are the main areas of concern. In the LDCs, on the other hand, restrictions on technological transfers through limits on royalties, lack of patent protection, and other legal constraints on company activities compel MNE managers to seek strategies that overcome or at least recognize these constraints and incorporate ways of accommodating them.

Definition[1]

The business literature generally refers to at least three types of technology: product, process, and management.[2] **Product technology** is the knowledge used to produce any product—the information that specifies the product's characteristics and uses. **Process technology** is the knowledge used in production to organize the inputs and operate the machinery—it relates to the process by which a given product or service is produced. **Management technology** is the knowledge used in operating a business—the managerial skills that enable a firm to compete by using its resources effectively. Each of these types of technology can create a competitive advantage for the firm that possesses it. That is, although all firms possess each type of technology, an advantage accrues to firms that are able to obtain *superior* technology.

Given that technology is industrial knowledge, we want to consider its creation, its introduction into markets, and its spread into different markets and applications. These three stages of technology development may be labeled invention, innovation, and diffusion. **Invention** is the creation of new knowledge that may have application to business or industry. An invention may be as extraordinary as the light bulb or as commonplace as a new type of laundry soap. **Innovation** is the introduction of the new knowledge into the marketplace. A fairly recent innovation is the microcomputer-based spreadsheet capability that allows financial forecasting for business (e.g., by using the Lotus 1-2-3 program). Most inventions never become innovations, that is, they never reach the stage of commercialization. For every successful innovation, there are hundreds of inventions that never become commercialized. **Diffusion** is the spread of the new knowledge throughout the market, including markets in different countries, and to different product applications. It may take place through a company's affiliates in different locations and businesses or through purchase or copying by competitors. Proprietary drugs are typically diffused by the initiating firm's sale of the product through its affiliates and distributors around the world.

An aspect of technology that should be noted at the outset is its nature as a **public good**—a good that can be used repeatedly without being used up. Technology is a form of knowledge that is not destroyed when it is transferred between people or firms. This aspect of technology is the source of both competitive strength for a firm that successfully innovates and of social concern for countries that wish to have the benefits of innovation made available to their populations at as low a cost as possible. The cost of creating a technology is not zero, and that cost is borne by the innovating firm;[3] the cost of diffusing that technology is generally relatively low—and innovating firms do not like to let their hard-earned technological gains be given away to the public without earning a good return. This issue of social versus private valuation of technology is discussed below.

Technology Transfer

Technology transfer is the diffusion of technology from the place of its introduction to other markets around the world. This diffusion may take place through market transactions, with one firm selling a product, process, or skill to another, or it may be carried out within a firm through its network of affiliates. Since technology has become recognized as an extremely important base for competition worldwide, governments are quite concerned with obtaining up-to-date technology at the lowest possible cost. Innovating companies, on the other hand, wish to protect their technology as much as possible so that they can reap its benefits. Clearly, the interests of firms and governments may diverge in this matter, so technology transfer has become a major issue of debate with respect to the MNE.

Within the multinational firm, technology transfer is also an internal managerial concern. Informing managers, technical staff, and workers in different locations about new technologies is far from costless; and the firm must carry out such transfers efficiently and adjust structurally and operationally in order to derive maximum benefits from the exploitation of these technologies. Part of corporate strategy must be the determination of and the effective transmission of key technology to the people, subsidiaries, and locations that can use it best.

Technology Appropriability

Technology may well represent the key competitive advantage that the innovating firm possesses. After having invested human and financial capital in developing proprietary technology, such a firm will naturally seek to protect it. Looking at the effort of the innovating firm to maximize its returns from proprietary technology (viz, knowledge possessed by the innovating firm that is unavailable to other firms in the marketplace), Magee (1977) coined the term *appropriability*. **Appropriability** is the ability of the innovating firm to protect its technology from competitors and to obtain economic benefits from that technology. The knowledge required to construct a nuclear power plant is very specialized and therefore highly appropriable. On the other hand, the knowledge required to produce a certain food flavor is often quite simple once the ingredients are known—so the innovating firm seeks protection such as a patent, or, as with Coca-Cola, it tries to keep the "formula" secret from competitors. Such knowledge is appropriable only if it can be hidden from rival firms or denied to them through legal means such as patents. The more appropriable the technology, the better able the innovating firm will be to guard it and transfer it internally (that is, to *internalize* the technology).

Technology as a Competitive Advantage

The success of multinational firms during the 20th century has very often depended on a base of **proprietary technology.** In this section, we look first at some empirical evidence about the importance of technology in international competition. Second, we consider the problem of obtaining technology that could give the firm competitive advantages. Third, we consider ways in which a firm can utilize the advantages generated by proprietary technology.

Success of MNEs Based on Technological Advantage

Technology was demonstrated to be a key production factor in international business through a large number of research efforts conducted during the 1960s. The search for an explanation of Leontief's paradox (namely, that although the United States was relatively capital rich, its manufactured exports were less capital intensive and more labor intensive than its import-competing goods) led several investigators to focus on the **technology intensity** of U.S. exports. The studies of Gruber, Mehta, and Vernon (1967), Hufbauer (1966), and Keesing (1965) were discussed in Chapter 3. Those studies concluded that technology intensity was an important explanatory variable for U.S. exports; that is, technology was highly positively correlated with U.S. exports and thus that U.S. exports were technology intensive and not paradoxically labor intensive.

The result of telecommunications research: A new central switching system for long-distance telephone calls developed by AT&T in the late 1970s.

Click/Chicago/Jim Pickerell

Studies of U.S. foreign direct investment have produced similar results: U.S. firms with a higher degree of technology intensity (measured, for example, as R&D expenditures or as the number of scientists and engineers employed relative to the total number of employees) tend to establish more affiliates abroad than do less technology-intensive firms. Gruber et al. (1967), Horst (1972), Caves (1974), and others have lent support to this point. Hence, greater technology intensity seems to lead to greater multinationality. (This correlation was shown clearly in Chapter 2, Table 2-2, which lists top-performing U.S.-based firms, almost all of which are highly multinational and most of which are more or much more technology intensive than the U.S. industry average.)

Each of the preceding measures of the importance of technology in international business supports the general principle that technology is a fundamental "factor of production" that enables firms to compete successfully against foreign and domestic competitors. This does not mean that all firms must be technology intensive in order to succeed; rather, it means that technology is one factor that can create a sustainable competitive advantage for its possessor. The next step is to explore when and how technology can be used in competition. This is something that the studies mentioned above failed to do, since their emphasis was macroeconomic. We want to know how to obtain the technology that leads to an advantage and how to utilize that advantage in business activities. Our next step, therefore, is to focus on these microlevel (company-specific) concerns.

How to Acquire a Technology Advantage

The basic decision for a firm when it is considering the acquisition of any needed input is whether to make that input internally or to buy it from an outside supplier (or to do both). When the input is a known machine or a component, the choice will be whether or not to manufacture it. When the input is a skill, such as knowledge of a particular market, the choice will be whether to hire a specialist or to sell to an intermediary firm that deals with final customers. When the input is process or product technology, the choice will be whether to try to create the knowledge by carrying out R&D or to buy the knowledge from another firm through a license or some other contractual form.

The last of these choices is much more difficult than the first two because so much uncertainty is involved. If the firm chooses to undertake R&D to create product or process technology, there is no way to ensure that the result will meet the need. R&D is risky by its very nature, since it requires creativity on the part of the research person or team and since it leads to output that may be very efficient, very inefficient, or of no use at all in dealing with the problem at hand. So, while the **make-versus-buy decision** can be made on a fairly concrete basis for inputs whose technology and costs are known, the decision to produce technology by carrying out R&D has a much less concrete basis and necessarily leads to substantial uncertainty.

Moving a step further, when a firm depends on technology as a key competitive advantage, the need to generate new technology on a continuing basis becomes paramount. In such industries as pharmaceuticals, computers, and telecommunications, R&D is a critical function in each firm. In industries of this kind, the question becomes: How much R&D should the firm do? Since there is no simple, direct relation between R&D expenditure and successful new product development, there is no simple answer to the question. However, since products in these industries do become obsolete, the firm that does not introduce new products will in all likelihood be unable to compete. Then what level of R&D is in some sense "optimal"?[4]

The best answer is, "It depends." It depends on how large the firm is, how diversified its products and markets are, how financially sound it is, how appropriable its technology is, and many other factors. A small firm that competes on the basis of its ability to create new products must carry out extensive R&D. A very large MNE, on the other hand, may be able to use a comparatively small research team, aimed mainly at learning about new technology developments and deciding whether to incorporate them into the firm's business. If such a firm chooses a particular innovation as one to acquire, then the decision becomes whether to buy it from the producer, or to undertake R&D in an effort to copy it, or even to try to buy the innovating firm. This kind of **follow-the-leader strategy** has been pursued successfully by many firms in a variety of industries. Of course, a firm that pursues the follower strategy loses the opportunity to take full advantage of innovations achieved by other firms. Hoffmann-La Roche, for example, would have earned far less if it had depended on another firm to develop its highly successful tranquilizers, Valium and Librium. Also, there are spillover effects of R&D efforts that may lead to the creation of additional new products or processes. These benefits would be lost to a firm that chose not to carry out the basic research itself and pursued the follow-the-leader strategy. (Internal "new venture teams" are used by 3M to carry out R&D on projects proposed by company employees—projects that are then pursued as relatively independent efforts until results are achieved and the decision to go to market is made.)[5]

Pfizer, a U.S.-based pharmaceuticals firm, chooses to invest in its own R&D for the creation of new ethical drugs (i.e., proprietary pharmaceuticals). Pfizer's choice is to internalize the entire process of R&D, production, and sale as much as possible, and thus to reap maximum revenues and profits. This firm sets limits on its research spending by comparing the expected costs of research projects with the size of the potential market for the new product being sought.

In the area of antiarthritic drugs, for example, Pfizer sought to develop a product that could be administered once a day rather than every few hours. In the pharmaceuticals industry, the process of R&D plus product testing and submitting to regulatory approvals until a new drug is commercialized is generally believed to cost at least $100 million. Only after forecasting that its expected sales would substantially exceed this amount did Pfizer choose to undertake the research that led to the product Feldene. Pfizer does not become involved in R&D for a product whose potential market it judges to be smaller than $100 million. (Notice that the R&D being considered is fairly well targeted on a potential product, rather than open-ended as in the case of university research, which depends largely on the preferences of the individual researchers.)

From Pfizer's perspective, a second limitation on R&D spending is the shortage of highly qualified research scientists to work on possible projects. Even if dozens of the new products that Pfizer is considering for development appear viable, the number of people—inside the firm, in universities, and in other firms—who are qualified and available to do the necessary research is quite limited. This also limits the amount of R&D spending done by Pfizer.

For these two practical reasons (expected market size and availability of research scientists), an optimal amount of R&D can be proximately established despite the claim that research results are unpredictable. That overly simple claim obviously fails to come to grips with the problem, whereas pragmatic reasoning defines the problem clearly and focuses on the real limitations that exist on R&D.

Notice that the multinational firm gains an advantage in R&D because of

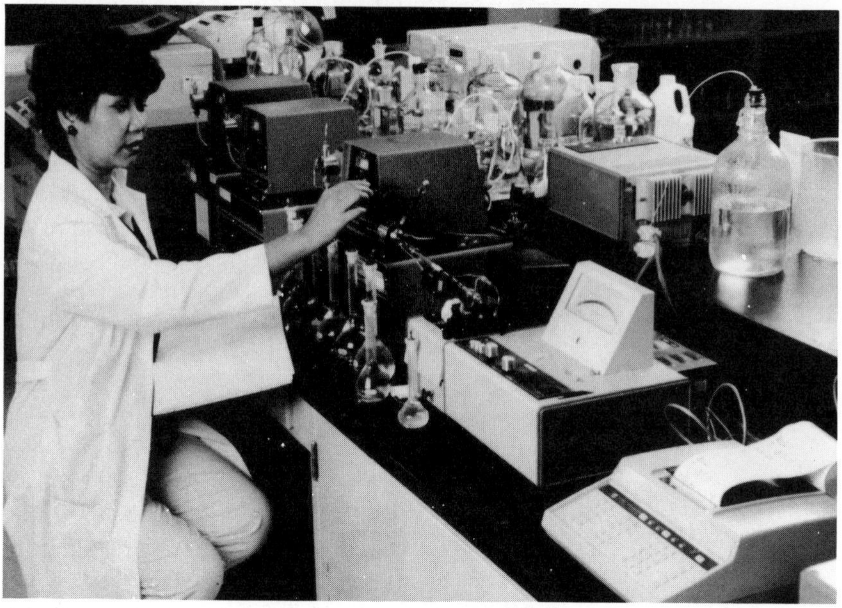

Research being done at Whiteworth Pharmaceutical Company in the United States.
Wide World Photos, Inc.

its ability to spread its R&D expenses over a global market rather than depending solely on domestic sales to recoup them. Also, the MNE has broader access to technical talent in many countries.

How to Utilize a Technology Advantage

Each firm is different from any other firm, if only because it employs different people with different skills. At the simplest level, **technology advantage** is any superior business knowledge held by people in one firm that is not held by people in another firm. As discussed in detail in Chapter 2, each firm should try to take maximum advantage of its technological edge over other firms. How can this be done? (The problem of *protecting* the firm's technology is discussed later.)

Consider Hoffmann-La Roche & Co.,[6] the Swiss-based multinational pharmaceutical firm. This firm innovated the two drugs chlordiazepoxide and diazepam (whose Hoffmann-La Roche brand names are Librium and Valium) in the early 1960s. Librium and Valium became two of the most successful tranquilizers in history. In order to protect the proprietary technology embodied in these drugs, Hoffmann-La Roche took out patents in each of the countries where it sold them. Patents gave the firm long-term legal protection against firms that might seek to copy the patented products. In most countries, patent protection lasts well over 10 years. (In the United States, for example, it lasts 17 years.) By registering Valium and Librium for patent protection around the world, Hoffmann-La Roche effectively gained a period of time in which it was the sole producer of the two drugs. Thus, the firm was able to sell enough Valium and Librium at a high enough price to repay the research costs of developing them and many less successful drugs, plus to pay for additional research to create new drugs for future sales. Because patent protection lasts for only a fixed period of time, additional R&D (and, hopefully, the creation of more successful products) must be part of the firm's strategy.

Hoffmann-La Roche sells Valium, Librium, and its other products through its own network of affiliates around the world. In a small number of cases, generally under government pressure, the firm has also licensed local companies to produce its proprietary drugs. Mostly, however, its sales take place through subsidiaries that it manages and owns. This is an example of internalized technology. (Also, the technology is *embodied* in products, which are then sold to customers.)

As a second example, consider Arthur Andersen & Co., the U.S.-based multinational accounting and management consulting firm. This firm's knowledge of accounting rules and practices and of business strategy is superior to that of many U.S. firms and many firms in other countries. Its proprietary technology is not in product or process technology, but rather in management knowledge.

Arthur Andersen is organized as a partnership, with individual accountants and consultants acting as both owners and managers. A legal entity called a "société coopérative" was formed in Switzerland, and it functions as a legal link among Arthur Andersen's widespread affiliates throughout the world and to the home office in Chicago. The main strategic links among Arthur Andersen affiliates are partners from affiliates in one country who are made partners in affiliates in other countries. By linking firms across countries through individual partners, Arthur Andersen is able to transfer its technology as embodied in its people. Thus, in its overseas activities, Arthur Andersen usually operates as a linked set of partners, although the legal entity is sometimes a corporation in which the parent firm owns some or all of the shares. In 1985, for example, Arthur Andersen acquired the Philippine firm SGV Group, with over 3,000 employees, via the Swiss Société Coopérative. The Philippine firm itself has affiliates in Thailand, Taiwan, Malaysia, and Indonesia.)

Arthur Andersen sells its knowledge as a service to other firms and to individuals. Its main businesses are auditing, tax accounting, and management consulting. Each service is sold to outside clients, a number of which are multinational firms, that can benefit from Arthur Andersen's knowledge of tax and other accounting rules in many countries.

These two examples show that there are numerous means for taking advantage of proprietary technology and that these means are very dependent on the kind of business involved. The possibilities include internalizing knowledge through a network of subsidiaries, working through partnerships (as discussed above), licensing local producers, and selling the use of the company name through a franchise. Let us examine these alternatives to see what company and product characteristics suit each of them best.

Internalizing First, there is the strategy of internalizing all technology. This translates into international business by requiring the firm to use local affiliates around the world to sell its products or services, or to use exports to some smaller or less important markets. **Internalization** tends to be best in these conditions:

1. The firm makes new *products* that cannot be copied easily by competitors.
2. Important economies of scale that the firm achieves on *products* would be lost if outside firms also used the technology and served part of the total market.
3. The *firm* depends greatly on the sale of the product or service that uses the technology.
4. The *firm* is so small that it does not have the personnel to both use the technology internally and sell it to outsiders; or the firm is so large that it can easily exploit the technology through its own affiliates.
5. The firm considers its *technology* to be more valuable than do potential buyers of the technology.
6. The *technology* is costly to transfer from one firm to another.

These conditions illustrate the kinds of situation-specific issues that a firm must take into account if it wants to properly utilize its technology advantage. They point out some of the company-specific, product-specific, and knowledge-specific considerations that (in these cases) would justify internalizing technology.

Recall the example of Polaroid Land cameras from Chapter 3. The key technology in that case was the knowledge necessary to produce high-quality, instant-developing film. Because no other firm was able to re-create equivalent technology, Polaroid gained a lasting competitive advantage in the photography market. There is no doubt that such firms as Eastman Kodak, Agfa-Gavaert, and Fuji have better distribution networks worldwide and perhaps other advantages over Polaroid. However, as long as Polaroid can keep the instant-developing segment of the photography market to itself, it will be able to compete successfully. By continuing to innovate and improve its film, Polaroid has been able to keep patent protection on its best technology through the years. The particular characteristics of this case, taken from our list above, are that (1) the product cannot be copied by competitors, (3) the firm is highly dependent on its technology for its success, and (4) the firm is large enough to exploit the technology through its own affiliates around the world. These conditions justify the internalization of instant-developing film technology in Polaroid Corporation and the sale of only the final product (i.e., *not* the knowledge by itself) to customers.

Externalizing As a second possible strategy for utilizing proprietary technology, the firm could contract with other firms under a licensing agreement, management contract, or other income-producing arrangement that involves the sale of the technology rather than the sale of a final product embodying the technology. This strategy (of **externalization**) would be appropriate in these conditions:

1. The firm's products are easily copied, but rival firms would still be willing to buy its product- or process-specific knowledge.
2. The firm's products are not central to its ability to survive in competition.
3. The firm has greater skill in creating the technology than in producing and marketing the final products.
4. The firm's financial and personnel capabilities make it desirable to let another firm incur the cost of producing the products.
5. The firm cannot protect its technology with a patent, and it could lose the benefits of that technology unless it contracted for the technology's use by rival firms.
6. The firm's technology is not costly to transfer between firms.

Each of these conditions tends to justify the sale of proprietary technology to other firms rather than (just) internalizing it in final products. Broadly, these product-, firm-, and technology-specific conditions relate to situations in which the technology is embodied in products that are not the lifeblood of the firm or to situations in which the technology itself, rather than the final product, is the most valuable factor.

The sale of "intermediate goods"—either components that embody proprietary technology or knowledge in the form of plans, blueprints, books, or other technical information formats—is common in many industries. The entire industry of management consulting is a form of externalizing business knowledge and skills. Similarly, public accounting and economic forecasting are businesses that sell knowledge for further use by firms producing final products or services. Arthur Andersen is an example of such businesses. Even in manufacturing, there are many consultants and capital equipment manufacturers that work independently from companies, selling their knowledge on onetime or repeated contractual terms to different firms.

Franchising Another interesting example of technology transfer through intermediate goods rather than final products is **franchising.** Many hotel chains, restaurants, and other service firms create a company or brand name that comes to connote good quality, rapid service, and so on. Once the name becomes established, its possessor can sell its use to other firms. This contractual arrangement is called franchising. McDonald's, Burger King, Hilton, Holiday Inns, Avis, and Hertz are just a few of the best-known franchisors.

The franchisor generally sells the franchisee the right to use its name plus some array of products and services. For example, franchisees contract with Burger King to buy plastic packaging, napkins, some food ingredients, and kitchen equipment used in cooking the hamburgers and other products sold in the restaurants that bear the Burger King name. Burger King maintains the right to control the quality of the franchise (e.g., through quality control of products and pricing strategy), so that franchisees cannot tarnish the company's image. In return for the use of Burger King's name and for these services, the franchisee must pay the company a fee based on the volume of sales. In this arrangement, the technology being transferred includes some production (of hamburgers) technology, some marketing skills, and some management policies.

The International Product Cycle

Another way to look at the use of technology as a competitive advantage comes from Vernon's product cycle analysis. By studying the stage of any product in the cycle in a given country, the firm can select a strategy that exploits its advantages. For example, when personal computers became extremely popular in the United States (about 1982), competition became fierce and these computers advanced quickly from the new product stage to the maturing product stage. At that time, the personal computer was still in the new product stage in Argentina. Thus, IBM or Apple Computer had opportunities to operate as new product producers in the Argentine market, selling with very little competition and facing a very price-inelastic demand. In the United States, on the other hand, these firms had to lower their prices and work on new software and hardware developments to maintain their market positions. The maturing product stage of the cycle required these actions, as well as increasing efforts to lower production costs. In fact, both IBM and Apple have turned to offshore, low-cost supply sources for such components as memory chips and peripheral equipment.

The international product cycle offers insights not only for high-tech industries but also for standardized products. Once production technology has become standardized, the firm must search for low-cost production sites and low-cost distribution channels. By taking a global perspective, a firm in an industry whose technology is fairly standardized, such as shirt or shoe manufacturing, can select production sites that offer cost advantages *and* markets in which particular shirts or shoes can compete.

A Continuous R&D Process

A general method of targeting research that avoids the dilemma of huge uncertainty in new product development, and one that many firms have selected, is to build incrementally on proven technology through a **continuous R&D** process. That is, the firms follow a strategy of developing modifications for the basic product or process, without undertaking major basic research in areas unrelated to the successful original innovation. Clearly, this is the strategy that IBM has followed in the development of its personal computer. Virtually all of the components used in making the first IBM PC were innovations that IBM or other companies had made in other applications. The PC itself is thus an amalgam of existing technologies, packaged in a valuable way and marketed very successfully. (IBM's competitive advantages in reliability and service, as well as its huge capital resources, enabled it to apply known technology to the product and to market the product with phenomenal success.)[7]

Dow Chemical Corporation is another MNE that follows the incremental approach to developing technology. Dow uses what are called **skunk works** (a term coined at Lockheed Aircraft Corporation in California), or small project teams that work on new applications of existing technologies or on the development of new technologies for specific uses. The skunk works are viewed as separate from the mainstream of the firm's production and sales activities, but the firm supports them in order to maintain an active presence in R&D. By remaining small, the skunk works allow the project teams to function more or less as entrepreneurs, though with potential substantial backing from the corporation in the event of a promising development. Because the skunk works generally focus on clearly defined new products or processes, they can be viewed as incremental builders on existing technology.

Control of Proprietary Technology

So far, we have examined the use of technology as a competitive advantage in international business. An important aspect of this advantage is its ability to be dissipated, that is, to be acquired by other firms and thus reduced in value to the original possessor. The next problem we will consider, therefore, is the *protection* of proprietary technology.

Whether the knowledge in question is production or management technology, there is a potential for rival firms to copy it. In some cases, the rival firm may assimilate the technology by simply looking at the innovation. In other cases, the technology may be complex or difficult to transfer, so the rival firm needs to spend substantial money to obtain it. In any case, the technology can be dissipated and the competitive advantage lost. A protection method is needed.

Methods for Protecting Technology

Once again, the appropriate strategy depends on the type of technology. If the knowledge possessed by the firm is a manufacturing process that produces a new product, that process and the product can be protected with a **patent** in most countries. If the knowledge is embodied in a book or manual that can be sold, then a **copyright** will protect the document against copying, though the knowledge itself will need patent protection as well. If the knowledge is embodied in the product, and it implies a high standard of quality or services, then often a **trademark** can be obtained for protection.

Three of the legal devices that protect proprietary technology are defined below.

Trademark "A technical trademark is a distinctive mark, word, design, or picture which is affixed to goods so that purchasers may identify their origin. In general, a trademark must be fanciful, arbitrary, unique, and nondescriptive."

Copyright "A copyright protects literary, musical, dramatic, pictorial, audio, and audiovisual works, but it is only the form of the work that is protected rather than ideas, concepts, or methods of operation. . . . The copyright holder is given exclusive right to reproduce, perform, or display the work, subject to what is known as 'fair use.'. . . The life of a copyright under [U.S. law] is 50 years beyond the death of the last surviving author."

Patent "Patent law represents a balancing of society's interest in promoting free competition against its interest in encouraging innovation by rewarding inventors with temporary monopoly rights. . . . A patent may be granted to any person on any new and useful invention of (1) a process, (2) a machine, (3) a product, (4) a composition of matter, (5) a new and useful improvement of a prior patented invention, (6) a growing plant, or (7) a design."[8] (Note the Hoffmann-La Roche example above.)

The trademark, copyright, and patent laws offer protection to innovating firms if their technology fits into one of the categories stated above. They do not protect all kinds of innovation, and in different countries the rules and enforcement vary widely even for technology of these three types.

Other methods for protecting technology include *hiding* it from competitors. This strategy works especially well when the key aspect of the technology is simple to understand but embodied in the product in a complex manner. Then, unless competitors can obtain the "formula" for using the technology, the proprietor can preserve its advantage. Another method is to require employees developing new products to sign an agreement prohibiting their use of the new technology outside the firm, so that they cannot leave the proprietor firm and use their knowledge of the new technology to compete against it.

Yet another method for protecting technology is simply to exploit it quickly, gain a large market share where it is used, and thereby discourage market entry by other firms. This strategy enables the firm to move quickly along the experience curve, lowering costs and creating a larger entry barrier as time passes.

Problems of Protecting Technology

Despite the methods of protection discussed above, there are still many situations in which adequate protection may not be available. For example, the Four Tigers of Asia (Hong Kong, South Korea, Singapore, and Taiwan) are notorious for producing imitations of branded, patented, copyrighted, and otherwise protected products.[9] From computers to videodiscs, from records to textbooks, a huge market exists in these countries for illegal imitations of such products. Similar problems exist in every country, particularly since interpretation of the law is required to judge whether an imitation is legal or not.

A problem that often thwarts the firm's efforts to protect its technology is **industrial espionage.** This method of obtaining technology from the possessor firm is also illegal, and it also occurs frequently. In a highly publicized case, IBM successfully sued Hitachi Corporation for stealing company documents containing proprietary information about a new mainframe computer introduced in 1981.[10] A scientist who had left his employment at IBM enabled Hitachi to obtain extensive documentation about the computer, thus placing Hitachi in a substantially better competitive position. While the espionage was detected and prosecuted in this case, much undetected espionage undoubtedly takes place.

A problem with which multinational firms in particular have to deal is the *difference in rules on technology use and technology transfer in different countries.* Less developed countries, often afford foreign MNEs less protection on their technology than is afforded by industrialized countries. The Andean Pact countries in Latin America, for example, do not allow patents for many proprietary products brought in by MNEs, and these countries do not allow local subsidiaries to pay royalties to parent companies for the use of technology.

A problem for firms involved with joint ventures or other contractual links with other firms is the *difficulty of constraining joint-venture partners* to apply shared knowledge only to the application under contract. In this type of situation, the firm supplying its technology to a joint project often finds that the partner is able to appropriate the technology for uses that the supplier cannot control or profit from. Thus, some of the value of the technology is lost to the supplier firm.

A final problem related to the protection of proprietary technology is the *mobility of employees.* Even if a firm successfully uses patents and copyrights on its technology, its competitive advantage may be lost if key employees (such as the scientists or managers who introduced the technology) leave the firm to work elsewhere. Since these people cannot leave their brains behind when they leave one company to join another, a tremendous amount of technology transfer takes place at relatively low cost through job mobility.

Country-Specific Concerns in Technology Use and Transfer

In Industrial Countries

The generation and use of technology in industrialized countries tends to be very market based, with the government playing the role of referee and rulemaker. Table 19-1 lists a few of the government rules related to technology in a selected group of developed nations. Note that patent life is fairly consistent among these countries (in the range of 15-20 years), as is the lack of limitations on intercountry transfer of technology. In fact, the main "limitation" is on the use of royalties to pay for technology transfer; these are limited to 6-10 percent of the firm's sales in a few countries. Perhaps a more important restriction is the immigration laws in most developed countries, which make it difficult to transfer skilled employees to different countries.

Despite the tendency of the governments in developed countries to allow market activity to determine technological advancement and diffusion, as shown in this table, another factor needs to be considered. The governments in each of the countries shown spend billions of dollars each year on military and other government-sponsored research. In fact, the U.S. government accounts for (i.e., finances) approximately 46 percent of R&D spending in the United States today (though industry carries out 74 percent of the actual R&D).[11] Viewed in this light, governments are clearly major players in the creation and diffusion of technology.

Companies doing business in industrial countries find that R&D is subsidized either through tax benefits or through direct government spending on

Table 19-1 **Industrial Country Rules Relating to Technology Use and Transfer**

Selected Countries	Limits on Royalties	Unpatentable Items	Patent Duration	Trademark Duration	Highest Tax Bracket on Royalties
Canada	None	Chemicals for food and medicine	17 years	15 years, renewable	25%
France	6% of sales	Nonindustrial items, animals, plants	20 years	10 years, renewable	33.3
Germany	10% of sales	Medical treatments	20 years	10 years, renewable	45
Italy	None	Theories	20 years	20 years, renewable	21
Japan	8% of sales	Nuclear transformations	15 years	10 years, renewable	20
United Kingdom	None	Scientific discoveries, artistic creations	20 years	7 years, renewable	30
United States	None	Noncommercial items	17 years	20 years, renewable	46

Source: Business International Corporation, *Investing, Licensing, and Trading Conditions* (New York: Business International Corporation, 1985).

company research. R&D is seldom restricted, except in cases where public health or safety is perceived to be at risk—for example, recombinant DNA research ("gene-splicing") or research on nuclear reactions.

When transferring technology between countries, a firm can usually choose among exporting, direct investment, and local licensing on the basis of market conditions, without concern for government intervention. In that case, the decision can be based on the factors discussed above, such as the technology's importance to the firm, its ease of transferability to other firms, and the size of the host country market.

Legal protection of proprietary technology is widely available in industrial countries, although industrial espionage and some illegal copying still take place in many industries. The countries of the European Community have standardized most of their rules on technology usage and transfer, and these rules differ fairly little from the rules in Japan and the United States. One major difference is in the amount and targeting of government spending on R&D in each country.

Another factor that firms operating in industrial countries need to consider is the level of competition and the length of product cycles. As modern telecommunications and transportation have virtually eliminated the distances between developed countries, innovations in any one country tend to be copied or transferred within MNEs very rapidly. Increasingly in the 1980s, firms introduce new products into several markets simultaneously, without waiting for the traditional international product cycle to follow its course. One can conclude that the dissipation process of proprietary technology is becoming more and more rapid and that innovating firms must be aware of the shortening life spans of their products.

In many cases, R&D by firms from industrial countries has become international. Large MNEs such as General Electric and IBM operate research facilities in several countries, benefiting from breakthroughs that take place in each country and spreading them to affiliates elsewhere. Several studies over the past few years have demonstrated the increasing internationalization of the R&D function within MNEs.[12]

Pfizer Corporation carries out basic research on new chemical entities in the United States, the United Kingdom, and Japan. It also has a large product development laboratory in France and numerous development facilities in other countries for the local product testing required by their governments. The Pfizer strategy is to maintain key research facilities in locations that have concentrations of research scientists and a relatively high likelihood of new product developments by many firms. Minor product adaptation is done when needed in Pfizer's plants around the world, but major research work is concentrated in the United States, the United Kingdom, and Japan.

In Less Developed Countries

The generation and transfer of technology are far more restricted in less developed countries than in industrial countries. Less R&D takes place in

LDCs, and more government policies constrain the use and transfer of proprietary technology. Table 19-2 shows some of the important government policies that influence technology use by multinational firms in LDCs. In comparison with industrial countries, LDCs offer less patent protection, place more limitations on international transfer of technology, and present greater demands for participation in the process of technology creation and diffusion. This should not be surprising, since these countries face a "technology gap" between their economies and the economies of industrial countries, and they see a need to catch up. Among the ways in which they attempt to catch up is to get MNEs to engage in greater local R&D activity and to transfer skills to local people—both of which are policies widely used in the third world today.

Multinational firms, for their part, generally find that local R&D in less developed countries is relatively inefficient (or not even viable) because there are far fewer skilled scientists, engineers, and managers in such countries than in industrial countries. Therefore, MNEs tend to concentrate their basic research in developed nations and to carry out a minimum of product development (often adaptation to local conditions) in the LDCs that require it. Moreover, as emphasized in Vernon's international product cycle, firms

Table 19-2 **Rules of Selected Less Developed Countries Relating to Technology Use and Transfer**

Country	Limits on Royalties	Unpatentable Items	Patent Duration	Trademark Duration	Highest Tax Bracket on Royalties
Argentina	None	Pharmaceuticals	5, 10, 15 years	10 years, renewable	n.a.
Brazil	1-5% of sales to unrelated firms only	Pharmaceuticals, foods, chemicals	15 years	10 years, renewable	25%
Egypt	None	Any substance; only production processes are patentable	15 years, renewable	10 years, renewable	40
India	8% of sales	Foods, drugs, chemicals	14 years	7 years, renewable	40
Korea	None	Food, drink, medicine, chemicals	15 years	10 years, renewable	25
Mexico	5%; many exceptions	Foods, drugs, agricultural chemicals	10 years	5 years, renewable	42
Nigeria	1% of sales	Plants, animals, biological processes	20 years	7 years, renewable	45
Singapore	None	?	Only UK patents are valid	UK registered only, 7 years	40

Source: Business International Corporation, *Investing, Licensing, and Trading Conditions* (New York: Business International Corporation, 1985).

prefer to do R&D in or near their large markets, so that they can respond to customer preferences and government policies. This is another reason for the small amount of MNE research done in LDCs.

The choice among exporting, direct investment, and licensing is often mandated by the less developed countries. Often they simply do not allow direct investment in a particular industry or they require the licensing of local firms. In other situations, they require local investment (i.e., FDI) and do not permit imports. Thus, the MNE manager's choice of the market entry method, and consequently of the technology transfer method, is often forced by the host government.

Even after the firm brings a new product or process into an LDC, the legal protection for proprietary knowledge is often either unavailable or less assured than in industrial countries. Many LDC host countries refuse to grant patent protection for some products, reasoning that the technology is not new, or that it should not be proprietary, or that the MNE has already earned a reasonable return on its patent in industrial countries. Any of these arguments leads to less protection for the technology than that available in industrial countries.

The competitive situation is far less pressing in many LDCs than in developed countries, so that in LDCs technology tends to diffuse more slowly and a technological advantage can be maintained for a longer period of time. Even when patents expire, local firms are often not quick to acquire the technology and compete with the originating firm. Because of a lack of competitive pressure, MNEs often continue to use production processes in LDCs even after they have been replaced by modernized processes in the MNEs' facilities elsewhere.

Finally, for the past two decades governments of LDCs have been pressuring the MNEs to use **appropriate technology.**[13] This is generally considered to mean less capital-intensive and more labor-intensive technology in LDCs with an overabundance of labor and a scarcity of capital. Long and heated debates have taken place between companies and governments, and the United Nations has even tried to create a Code of Conduct on Technology Transfer that would push MNEs into using technology that offers maximum benefits to LDC host countries. There has been no clear outcome as yet, but at least a better definition of "appropriate technology" has been developed. It is now defined as product, process, or managerial knowledge that is optimally adapted to local conditions.[14]

Conclusions

Technology is knowledge that has application in an industrial (business) setting. Such knowledge may be created through research and development or simply through experience in doing business, from which the firm develops managerial skills. It can also be purchased from innovating firms. Technology may be used through internal transfer and deployment within the firm or through sale to outside firms via licensing or some other contractual means. Ultimately, the competitive advantage obtained from technology may be dissipated, due to copying by other firms or to their creation of comparable knowledge.

Technology is at the heart of the multinational enterprise. Whether it be product, process, or managerial technology, the MNE usually depends on it for competitive advantage. This kind of firm benefits from technological advances made by an affiliate in one country that can be transferred within the firm to affiliates in many other countries. Production technology can be created through R&D in several countries, benefiting from the spillover effects of the activities of other firms there. The knowledge of market and supply conditions in many countries is itself a technological advantage possessed by MNEs.

Control over the use and diffusion of proprietary technology is a difficult task for the multinational manager. There are many protection measures, and these are sometimes effective in preserving the competitive advantage of proprietary technology. Eventually, however, all technology becomes diffused or outmoded, and the proprietor firm needs to develop or acquire new technology to create new competitive advantages.

Each country has established rules governing the use and transfer of technology by firms operating there. Developed countries tend to offer relatively few restrictions on the creation and dissemination of technology. LDCs generally limit the MNE's use of technology by imposing restrictions on licensing agreements, limiting patent protection, and otherwise trying to restrict the competitive advantage that the MNE derives from technology. The future will probably bring greater government attempts to control the use and transfer of technology, since the benefits of technology are important to countries as well as companies.

Questions

1. What is technology? How is it used by multinational enterprises in competition?
2. Explain the concept of a "public good." Why does this concept cause problems for innovating firms? How do governments view this issue? How does management?
3. By what methods can technology be transferred internationally? What are the key costs and benefits to an MNE for each transfer method?
4. How can an MNE create a technological advantage over other firms? Give several examples.
5. What is R&D? What is the optimal level of investment in R&D for a multinational firm?
6. Explain several methods that a firm can use to protect its proprietary technology.
7. What are the main kinds of problems that make it difficult for a firm to maintain its competitive advantage based on proprietary technology?

8. How do industrial countries and LDCs differ in their approaches to regulating technology use and transfer?
9. How can an MNE best deal with the regulatory structure facing technology in the less developed countries?
10. What would be a viable strategy for a firm such as Hoffmann-La Roche in international competition, given that its key proprietary pharmaceuticals have passed the period of patent protection?

References

Baranson, Jack. *Technology and the Multinationals.* Lexington, Mass.: D. C. Heath, 1978.

Behrman, Jack N., and W. A. Fischer. *Overseas R&D Activities of Transnational Companies.* Cambridge, Mass.: Oelgeschlager, Gunn, and Hain, 1980.

Caves, Richard. "Causes of Direct Investment." *Review of Economics and Statistics,* August 1974.

Caves, Richard. *Multinational Enterprise and Economic Analysis.* Cambridge: Cambridge University Press, 1982. Chapter 7.

Chudson, Walter. *The International Transfer of Commercial Technology to Developing Countries.* New York: UNITAR, 1971.

Contractor, Farok. *International Technology Licensing: Compensation Costs and Negotiation.* Lexington, Mass.: D. C. Heath, 1981.

Dahlman, Carl, and Francisco Sercovich. "Local Development and Exports of Technology." World Bank Staff Working Paper no. 667, September 1984.

Davidson, William, and Donald McFetridge. "Key Characteristics in the Choice of International Technology Transfer Mode." *Journal of International Business Studies,* Summer 1985.

Emmanuel, Arghiri. *Appropriate or Underdeveloped Technology?* New York: John Wiley & Sons, 1982.

Horst, Thomas. "Firm and Industry Determinants of the Decision to Invest Abroad: An Empirical Study." *Review of Economics and Statistics,* August 1972.

Magee, Steven. "Information and Multinational Corporations: An Appropriability Theory of Direct Foreign Investment." In *The New International Economic Order.* ed. J. Bhagwati. Cambridge, Mass.: MIT Press, 1977.

National Science Foundation. *National Patterns of Science and Technology Resources.* Washington, D.C.: National Science Foundation, 1984.

Organization for Economic Cooperation and Development. *Appropriate Technology.* Paris, OECD, 1976.

Teece, David. *The Multinational Corporation and the Resource Cost of International Technology Transfer.* Cambridge, Mass.: Ballinger Publishing, 1976.

Tinnin, David. "How IBM Stung Hitachi," *Fortune,* March 7, 1983.

Endnotes

1. Technology is "industrial science, the science or systematic knowledge of the industrial arts, especially of the more important manufactures" (*Webster's New International Dictionary,* 2nd ed). *Webster's* identifies two key points in this definition. First, technology relates to industry; that is, it is the application of science to business. Second, it relates to systematic knowledge of the various parts of industry such as production but also distribution, R&D, and even marketing and finance.
2. Jack Baranson, *Technology and the Multinationals* (Lexington, Mass.: D. C. Heath, 1978), defines three types of technology: product, process, and managerial. Walter Chudson *The International Transfer of Commercial Technology to Developing Countries* (New York: UNITAR, 1971), similarly defines technology as having three forms: product design, production techniques, and managerial functions.
3. See, for example, David Teece. *The Multinational Corporation and the Resource Cost of International Technology Transfer* (Cambridge, Mass.: Ballinger, 1976).
4. See, for example, Henry Grabowski and Dennis Mueller, "Industrial Research and Development, Intangible Capital Stocks, and Firm Profit Rates," *Bell Journal of Economics,* Autumn 1978; and E. L. Reynard, "A Method for Relating Research Spending to Net Profits," *Research Management,* July 1979.
5. Thomas Peters and Robert Waterman, *In Search of Excellence* (New York: Harper & Row, 1980), pp. 223-34.
6. Thomas Gladwin and Ingo Walter, *Survival of the MNE,* pp. 300-304; and the Harvard Business School case "Hoffmann-La Roche A.G."
7. "IBM: Colossus of Armonk," *Creative Computing,* November 1984, pp. 298-306.
8. Harold Lusk, Charles Hewitt, John Donnell, and James Barnes, *Business Law and the Regulatory Environment,* 5th ed. (Homewood, Ill.: Richard D. Irwin, 1982), pp. 984, 987, and 990.
9. See, for example, *Publishers Weekly,* 1982, p. 70.
10. David Tinnin. "How IBM Stung Hitachi," *Fortune,* March 7, 1983.
11. National Science Foundation, *National Patterns of Science and Technology Resources.* (Washington, D.C.: NSF, 1984), p. 3.
12. See, for example, Robert Ronstadt, *Research and Development Abroad by U.S. Multinationals* (New York: Praeger, 1977); and Jack N. Behrman and William Fischer, *Overseas R&D Activities of Transnational Companies* (Cambridge, Mass.: Oelgeschlager, Gunn, and Hain, 1980).
13. See, for example, Henry Norman and Patricia Blair, "The Coming Growth in Appropriate Technology," *Harvard Business Review,* November-December 1982.
14. Organization for Economic Cooperation and Development, *Appropriate Technology* (Paris, OECD, 1976), Chap. 1.

20

DEVELOPING A GLOBAL STRATEGY

This chapter moves to the highest level of decision making in the firm—the selection of a global business strategy. In fact, two levels of strategy must be established. First, top management must establish overall corporate objectives, such as the kinds of businesses to be in and the ultimate goals of the firm. Second, top management must establish broad strategies for the firm's strategic business units (SBUs)—strategies such as cost leadership, focus on specific market segments and so on. In addition to defining and clarifying the relationships between corporate goal setting and strategy determination, this chapter discusses the means of maintaining control over the firm's effort to pursue its chosen objectives. The main goals of the chapter are to:

1. Define overall corporate objectives.
2. Show how to create strategic business units and use them to pursue corporate goals.
3. Explain four generic SBU strategies that have shown excellent results for companies during the past few decades.
4. Examine the means by which the firm can control its activities to ensure that corporate goals are achieved.

Introduction

Throughout this book, our attention has returned repeatedly to the competitive advantages that enable firms to compete successfully in international business. In each context, from exporting and importing to technology transfer to financial management, selected key competitive advantages have been discussed and methods for utilizing them have been analyzed. This chapter moves one step beyond the previous types of decision making. Here we are concerned with overall corporate strategy for the firm.

The focus is on three aspects of overall corporate strategy. First, the firm must have a clear set of *overall objectives.* (For example, is the firm's goal to be in the transportation business, or in information services, or in chemical manufacturing?) These overall objectives then lead to such choices as diversifying into a new industry (e.g., going out of making trains and into making autos, or going into computers and telephones together) or serving a major new set of customers. Should a multinational steel producer enter a very different industry such as oil (as U.S. Steel did with its purchase of Marathon Oil in 1982)? Or should a diversified tobacco-producing MNE move heavily into processed foods (as R. J. Reynolds did with its purchase of Nabisco in 1965)? No simple answer can be given to such questions. The fundamental goals of the firm must be clearly established if it is to make decisions of this kind. Second, the firm must select optimal *generic strategies* for its major business units. That is, it must choose among basic overall competitive strategies, such as Porter's (1980, chap. 13) four strategies: broad-line competition, global focus, national focus, and protected niche. Each of these strategies has proven to be sustainable in competition for major firms, while mixing them has often led to serious difficulties for the firm choosing that approach. Third, the firm must *maintain control* over its widespread parts. Measurement and evaluation of financial decisions, production strategies, personnel relations, and other key operating activities are fundamental for a successful firm. Methods of achieving the necessary control and key areas that require clear control are discussed below.

Thus, global strategy encompasses overall objectives, specific operating strategies, and efforts to ensure acceptable performance of the firm's units. Figure 20-1 depicts the strategy cycle from the formulation of overall corporate goals, to the creation of operating strategies, to the measurement and evaluation of performance.[1]

We will look at these three levels of strategy sequentially in this chapter. But before examining each of the levels in detail, we wish to provide some additional clarification on them.

The formulation of overall corporate objectives requires some judgment as to the appropriate extent of the firm's activities. The question of optimal company size (in terms of sales volume, number of products, etc.) has not been resolved by either theoreticians or company managers.[2] Both diversification into new industries or countries and divestment of existing company

Nabisco products that now belong to the combined Company R. J. Reynolds-Nabisco.
Courtesy Nabisco Brands, Inc.

Figure 20-1 **Global Business Strategy in Perspective**

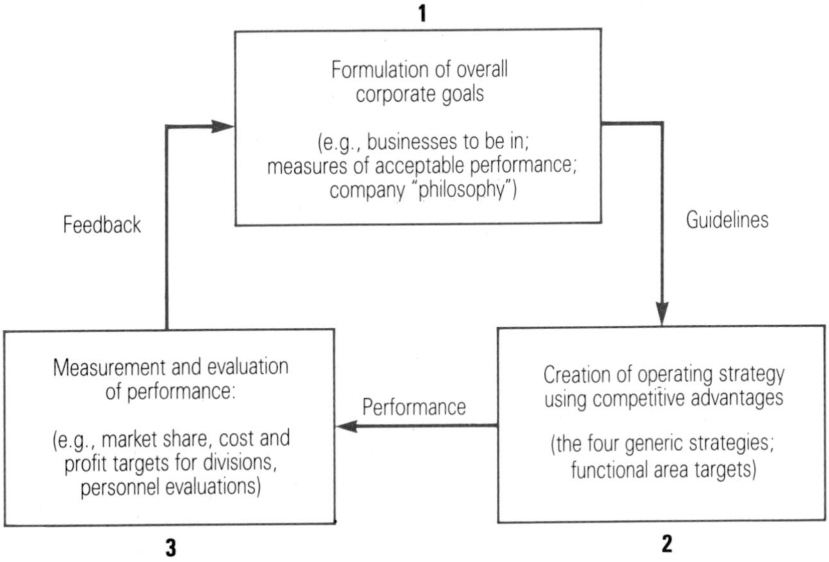

activities may yield helpful or harmful results to the firm. (Note that, in terminology that we have used before, this is the decision of whether or not to *internalize* a particular business activity.) Our approach is to point out major considerations that should be weighed in the expansion/contraction decision, rather than to attempt to answer the question conclusively. In this light, we also examine some of the major diversifications and divestments of the past few years.

Expansion/contraction decisions need to be made in the broad context of overall corporate policy-making. Although an almost infinite number of strategies have proven successful for firms over the years, in international business since World War II a handful of general or generic strategies have led to success in many industries and countries. These generic strategies, discussed in some detail by Porter (1980, 1985), enable firms to maximize the gains from their competitive advantages (such as possession of an international marketing network, proprietary technology, or government protection) and to build defensible positions to ward off rival firms. Each strategy is appropriate not necessarily for an entire widely diversified firm, but rather for each **strategic business unit** (SBU) in a firm. As a firm looks for new business opportunities or seeks to get out of existing businesses, it must carefully consider the fit of each activity into each SBU.

Strategic Business Unit

Strategic business units, which we have identified and discussed earlier (in Chapter 12), are groups of products, divisions, or other company activities that have sufficiently similar characteristics to justify their assignment to a single group for strategy development.* Each SBU is an operating unit with profit and loss responsibility for the activities within it. One criterion that may be used to create SBUs is to group product divisions that serve the same end users. Similarly, a second criterion could be products that utilize the same or similar technology, which then should be placed in the same SBU. In contrast, consumer products such as cosmetics should be assigned to a different SBU than bulk petrochemical products in a diversified chemical company. (The criterion is consumer versus industrial products in this case.)

Regardless of the number of industries or countries in which a firm does business, the fundamental strategic business units should be those that have sufficiently *dis*similar characteristics to justify the division of company activities into those units. For example, ITT unquestionably needs separate SBUs (and separate strategies) for its telecommunications division and its Sheraton Hotel division. The production methods of these divisions are very different; their customers are quite divergent groups; and their competition differs greatly. Similarly, no matter how many internal applications General Motors can find for its Electronic Data Systems subsidiary, this computer company needs a separate strategy if it is to continue serving customers outside GM.

A recent organization chart of General Electric Company, the firm that initiated SBUs in the early 1970s, appears as Figure 20-2. Notice that the 28 business units are divided broadly along global product lines, with a handful of matrix-type units such as the international

One method of dealing with rival auto firms is to work with them and learn from them, as in this Toyota-General Motors joint venture in Fremont, California.

Wide World Photos, Inc.

alternatives will help the firm avoid the hostage problem—the situation in which the firm is at the mercy of shifts in government policy in one country and has no options to ameliorate the impact of those shifts. These issues are discussed in Chapters 21-23.

Dealing with Rivals

Finally, dealing with rivals requires corporate-level control. Although the firm in question cannot determine or control the strategies of its competitors, it can assess those strategies. In addition, it can influence those strategies by its own actions. Monitoring the activities of competitors and attempting to estimate their reactions to the firm's own strategy can enable the firm to develop a better strategy.

At the international level, rivals include other multinational firms, local firms in each country of operation, and even firms in other countries that are potential competitors. While the complexity of analyzing international competition is much greater than that of analyzing domestic competition, the stakes are generally also greater. Much of the business strategy literature, and indeed this book, aims at developing sustainable strategies for firms involved in international competition.[8]

Conclusions

The development of a global strategy involves two levels of planning and the process of evaluation and control. First, the firm must establish overall corporate objectives—broad, long-term goals such as businesses to compete in and acceptable kinds of performance (e.g., in the risk/return framework). Second, the firm must develop for its strategic business units goals based on the four generic strategies: broad-line competition, global focus, national focus, and protected niche. Finally, the firm must establish clearly defined targets for performance, must monitor that performance, and must set up a feedback mechanism for realigning itself to meet targets better.

Overall corporate strategy must be to some extent ambiguous or open-ended, since the future business conditions under which the firm will operate cannot be known today and full contingency planning is impossible. However, the firm's top management can define broad corporate goals and acceptable means of pursuing them that will be able to survive changes in the environment. This level of planning needs to be fairly long term, since only over a period of years can the firm's performance and changes in the environment be observed adequately.

SBU strategy can be formulated and changed more frequently, since at this lower level more concrete, measurable goals can be established. Strategic business units can follow any one of the four generic strategies, from broad-line global competition to serving a protected niche, with the additional possibilities of focusing on a market segment worldwide or adapting to national market segments in different countries. Each SBU should be chosen to group activities of the firm that possess similar characteristics, such as technology, customers, location, and inputs.

Performance monitoring, evaluation according to some clear criteria, and reformulation of strategy are also necessary parts of strategy making. The MNE needs to develop methods for monitoring far-flung affiliates on financial conditions, personnel performance, government relations, and the activities of rival firms, as well as other key issues that may arise. More important than specific quantitative goals are targets that are designed to pursue the main strategic objectives of the firm.

Questions

1. What is a strategic business unit? How should SBUs be selected from among a firm's divisions?
2. Using your knowledge of ITT from the chapter and any other sources, what would be the appropriate SBUs for that firm today? Why?
3. How can you distinguish among corporate strategy, business unit strategy, and operating strategy for a firm? What are the key characteristics of each?
4. Explain the four generic strategies for business units. How does each of these strategies apply in international business?

5. On what grounds can a business unit choose between a global focus and a national focus?
6. Why is control an important aspect of corporate strategy? How can control be achieved in a multinational enterprise?
7. How can a firm decide whether or not to diversify into a new industry in a country where it has not operated before? What criteria can it use to make this decision?
8. What is different about corporate and business unit strategies at the international level as compared with the domestic level? That is, what is different about them for a multinational enterprise as compared with a domestic one?
9. Explain how a firm could establish a protected niche strategy for its business unit in the telecommunications industry. What forms of business activity would be possible, and how could the firm use this strategy in more than one country?
10. Discuss some major spillover benefits from other business activities that could aid the competitiveness of an MNE such as Dow Chemical in the pharmaceuticals industry. That is, what advantages does Dow possess due to its diversified business units (in industrial chemicals, agricultural chemicals, specialty chemicals, cosmetics, consumer products, etc.) that purely pharmaceuticals firms do not have?

References

Christensen, Roland; Kenneth Andrews; Joseph Bowers; Richard Hammermesh; and Michael Porter. *Business Policy*. 5th ed. Homewood, Ill.: Richard D. Irwin, 1980.

Davidson, William. *Global Strategic Management*. New York: John Wiley & Sons, 1982.

Donaldson, Gordon, and Jay Lorsch. *Decision Making at the Top*. New York: Basic Books, 1983.

Hall, W. K. "SBUs—Hot New Topic in the Management of Diversification." *Business Horizons*, February 1978.

Porter, Michael. *Competitive Strategy*. New York: Free Press, 1980.

_______. *Competitive Advantages*. New York: Free Press, 1985.

Endnotes

1. This scheme generally parallels that of Figure 12-1, with two exceptions. First, we do not cover the level of "implementing the operating plan" in the present chapter, which focuses instead on overall corporate strategy. Second, we do not consider organization structure in any detail in the present chapter.
2. See, for example, Edith Penrose's classic analysis of this issue in *The Theory of the Growth of the Firm* (Oxford: Oxford Univ. Press, 1951); also see

Anthony Sampson, *The Sovereign State of ITT* (New York: Viking Press, 1973), for the real-world case of ITT, a huge conglomerate in the 1960s and 70s and a drastically reduced telecommunications firm today.

3. Some people would argue that small firms are *more* likely to be flexible enough to leave unprofitable market segments, while large MNEs may be relatively inflexible and more likely to remain in weak market segments. This is an empirical question.
4. This uncertainty cannot be eliminated, but the problem can be managed somewhat by specifying a range of potential rivals' responses and examining the firm's expected performance in each case. Such analysis has been facilitated dramatically by microcomputers and sophisticated financial planning programs.
5. Gordon Donaldson and Jay Lorsch, *Decision Making at the Top* (New York: Basic Books, 1983), found in a survey of 12 large U.S.-based MNEs that their chief executive officers viewed *company survival,* rather than maximizing shareholders' wealth, as the primary objective of the firm. "They [the CEOs] are committed, first and foremost, to the enhancement of *corporate* wealth, which includes not only the firm's financial assets reflected on the balance sheet but also its important human assets and its competitive position in the various markets in which it competes" (p. 7).
6. Henry Ford, *My Life and Work* (Garden City, N.Y.: Doubleday, 1922), p. 72.
7. See, for example, Rita Rodriguez and Eugene Carter, *International Financial Management,* 3rd ed. (Englewood Cliffs, N.J.: Prentice-Hall, 1985), chap. 13.
8. See, for example, Roland Christensen et al., *Business Policy,* 5th ed. (Homewood, Ill.: Richard D. Irwin, 1980.)

PART 4

DOING BUSINESS IN . . .

21

INDUSTRIALIZED COUNTRIES

Chapters 21-23 examine issues related to doing business in each of three types of country: industrialized, less developed, and communist. This chapter begins the sequence with a discussion of some general characteristics of industrialized countries and of common problems and opportunities that occur when doing international business there. First, criteria are offered to distinguish industrialized countries from the rest of the world. Then specific aspects of the economies and government systems of industrialized countries are presented to give an idea of the kinds of international business that are most likely to be appropriate in these countries. Subsequent sections focus on government concerns and policies that relate to international firms and on company strategies that can be used to deal with the policy environment. Finally, entry and operating strategies are presented. The main goals of the chapter are to:

1. Demonstrate important characteristics of industrialized countries.
2. Show what kinds of international business are common and appropriate in such countries.
3. Examine the role of governments in industrialized countries and show how firms can deal with these governments.
4. Consider entry and operating strategies that international firms can use in industrialized countries.
5. Illustrate the general issues with the case of Japan.

Introduction

Definition of Industrialized Countries

The countries considered in this chapter are the developed nations of Western Europe and North America, plus Japan, Australia, and New Zealand. They are called **industrialized countries (ICs)** because their economies have become dominated by industrial production rather than agriculture. They all have relatively high standards of living, compared to the rest of the world, and they all use market-based economic systems (as opposed to communism). Table 21-1 lists the countries that are considered industrialized today and provides several measures of their economic performance, such as per capita incomes, unemployment, and real economic growth rates. Notice that Scandinavia, the United States, and Switzerland have the highest incomes but that Japan and Spain (both of which are countries that were substantially behind the others after World War II) have the greatest growth rates. The economic performance of the industrialized countries is significantly better than that of the communist countries. (In 1985 per capita GDP was $US 7,400 in the Soviet Union, $US 7,260 for Eastern Europe as a whole, and $US 340 in China.) It is tremendously better than that of the less developed countries (LDCs)—although such individual LDCs as Hong Kong, Korea, and Singapore have achieved very impressive economic records during the past decade or so, and several oil-exporting LDCs with small populations, such as Kuwait and the United Arab Emirates, have high per capita incomes. (In 1984, per capita GDP averaged $US 260 in low-income LDCs, $US 1,250 in middle-income LDCs, and $US 1,950 in upper middle-income LDCs.) More detailed comparisons can be made by looking at Table 21-1 along with its counterparts in the next two chapters, Tables 22-1 and 23-1.

In addition to the macroeconomic indicators shown in Table 22-1, many other measures of development distinguish the industrialized countries from the rest of the world. For example, all of the industrialized countries have well-developed securities markets in which private sector and government borrowers and lenders participate. While the markets in the United States and the United Kingdom are the largest and most influential in international financial dealings, even tiny Luxembourg has stock and bond markets and other financial markets. Broad financial systems of this kind are usually lacking in less developed countries and of course are legally prohibited in communist countries.

Industrialized countries generally possess an advanced system of *distribution*—roads, railroads, airports, and navigable waterways. These pathways for the transportation of products and people enable companies to get their products to customers and to move raw materials and intermediate goods to processing locations. Similarly, advanced *communications* networks allow rapid and efficient transmission of information through telephone, telex, television, radio, and print media. Also, the systems of *education* in industrialized countries generally offer high-level training in the skills needed to function in an industrial setting—particularly engineering, sciences, and business administration. Each of these types of infrastructure exists in less developed countries as well as industrialized ones. The key difference is their very wide availability and high quality in the developed countries as compared with the LDCs.

Table 21-1 **Selected Characteristics of Industrialized Countries**

	Measure					
Country	GDP per Capita, 1984 ($US)	Growth Rate of GDP per Capita*	Average Annual Inflation (%/year)†	Average Unemployment (%) 1983	Current Account BOP, 1984 ($ millions)	Manufacturing as Percent of Total GDP 1984
Canada	13,280	3.1	9.3	11	1,974	16
United States	15,390	2.2	7.3	7.25	−107,780	22
Australia	11,740	2.4	11.4	8.75	−8,302	20
Japan	10,630	6.1	6.9	2.5	35,148	30
New Zealand	7,730	1.5	13.1	7.25	−1,444	23
Austria	9,140	3.9	6.1	5.0	−633	27
Belgium	8,610	3.6	7.1	15.0	205	24
Denmark	11,170	2.5	9.9	10.0	−1,634	17
Finland	10,770	3.6	11.7	5.25	1	24
France	9,760	3.7	10.1	10.5	−820	25
Germany	11,130	3.1	4.9	7.75	6,130	36
Ireland	4,970	2.9	14.3	18.0	−916	14
Italy	6,420	3.4	16.0	10.25	−2,902	29
Netherlands	9,520	2.9	7.4	15.5	4,879	24
Norway	13,940	3.4	9.0	3.25	3,228	15
Spain	4,440	4.0	16.0	20.0	2,323	22
Sweden	11,860	2.4	9.9	3.0	356	22
Switzerland	16,330	1.9	4.8	0.5	4,019	n.a.
United Kingdom	8,570	2.0	14.2	11.25	1,417	22

* For the period 1960–1982.
† For the period 1970–1982.
Sources: World Bank, *World Development Report, 1984, 1986,* (Washington, D.C.: World Bank, 1984, 1986). For unemployment data. *OECD Economic Outlook,* July 1984, p. 43.

Main Forms of International Business in Industrialized Countries

Not surprisingly, the main forms of international business discussed throughout this book are the ones used among the industrialized countries. As noted earlier, about two thirds of world exports and imports take place among developed nations (which comprise one sixth of the world's population), and an even larger portion of total foreign direct investment occurs among them. International banking activity likewise involves mostly banks and clients in North America, Europe, and Japan—despite the emphasis of public debate on LDC debt during the economic crisis (especially in Latin America) of the 1980s. Table 21-2 shows some aggregate measures of the international business that occurs in the developed-country members of the OECD (Organization for Economic Cooperation and Development).[1] Note that by far the bulk of international business worldwide occurs among industrialized countries and that foreign direct investment is more concentrated among these countries than is international trade (or lending).

With this base of information, we can proceed to discuss major factors that company managers should consider when doing business in industrial countries. The next section describes a variety of attributes of industrial countries as they pertain to MNEs. The third section focuses specifically on the regulatory structure and government policies that affect international firms in these countries. The fourth section suggests entry and operating strategies for multinational firms. Some strategies for dealing with the host

Table 21-2 **International Business among Industrialized Countries**

From ICs	Exports ($US billions, 1986)	FDI Flow (1980)	Commercial Bank Loans (1985)†
To:			
ICs	1,083.8	27.5	1,945.8
Latin America	62.1	5.3	540.1
Africa	39.9	2.2	70.1
Asia	113.8	1.5	306.5
Oil-exporting LDCs*	62.8	n.a.	99.8
Communist Countries	28.8	n.a.	51.5

* These countries also are counted in the regional totals shown.
† Liabilities of borrowers in each group of countries owed to foreign commercial banks.

Sources: International Monetary Fund, *Direction of Trade Yearbook* (Washington, D.C.: IMF, 1986); and Bank for International Settlements, semiannual international lending report.

and home country governments are sketched in the fifth section. Then current international business activities and concerns in a particular industrialized country—Japan—are presented. The final section provides a summary and some conclusions.

Key Characteristics Relating to MNEs

The Concept and Function of the Marketplace

All industrialized nations use the free market as one acceptable means of organizing economic activity—subject to fewer or greater government constraints, depending on the country. This assertion is more or less a definition; the only countries that have high per capita incomes, well-developed economic infrastructures, and other characteristics similar to those of the industrialized nations are a few communist countries, such as the Soviet Union and the German Democratic Republic (East Germany). Those countries have rejected a **market-based economy** in favor of communism. In discussions of the three main groups of nations, the industrialized countries are often called the **first world,** the LDCs are called the **third world,** and the communist countries are called the **second world.** While these distinctions are intended primarily to distinguish countries on the basis of economic development, in fact the communist countries are quite varied between high-income and low-income countries, between industrial and agricultural countries, and so on. Nonetheless, we will retain the common classification of industrialized countries as those that use a market-based economy and have achieved relatively high levels of per capita income and other measures of development.

Even the market-based economies vary fairly widely in the degree of private sector and public sector (i.e., government) participation in business. France and Italy have placed ownership and control of a large number of companies and industries in the hands of government managers, in contrast with the United States and the Federal Republic of Germany (West Germany), where very few government-owned companies exist except for some public utilities.

The key point is that industrialized countries view the market as a legitimate means of organizing economic activity. By allowing markets to function, and firms to compete, these countries reap the gains from the efficient use of resources. This contrasts with the communist countries, in which the government largely allocates economic resources according to various nonmarket criteria and in which resource allocation has generally been relatively inefficient.

Recall that economic activity can be organized by markets, by governments, *and* by large firms that internalize business activities. As noted in

A customs checkpoint on the U.S.-Canada border in Montana.

Odyssey Productions/Robert Frerck

attract more direct investment (and consequent jobs and income) and allowed more foreign control of the economy.[6] Although not going to Canada's earlier extreme, all industrialized countries limit foreign ownership and other forms of participation in key industries such as national defense, telecommunications services, and postal service. Each of these limitations can be viewed as an attempt by the national government to preserve sovereignty over the national economy.

A second concern to keep in mind is **information disclosure.** Each country requires disclosure of some types of information by firms doing business there. MNEs are constantly being asked to provide information about foreign operations to national governments that want to assess taxes, to limit unfair practices, and even to protect consumers and investors. MNEs often argue that the information requested is overly expensive to collect and report and/or that it could be used by competitors if disclosed. A related concern is **information transfer** across national borders. National governments are seeking to judge the importance of transborder data flows, especially within MNEs. Such transfers place information that could be sensitive to national interests in the hands of company decision makers in other countries; the full implications of this concern remain to be seen.

Additional concerns such as pollution control, consumer protection, and labor protection sometimes present major hurdles for MNE managers, but they are usually not aimed specifically at MNEs; rather, they are directed at all firms operating in the given country.

Entry and Operating Strategies for MNEs

Entry Strategies

General entry strategies were presented in Chapter 2, and specific strategies for exporters in Chapter 18. This section raises a few additional points with respect to entry into industrialized countries. While conditions differ to some extent across industrialized countries, the main factor in determining **entry strategy** is usually *competition.* That is, the choice of a country, a product, and an entry mode (see Figure 18-1) depends on the kind of competition faced by the firm in each country.

In the television industry, for example, competition takes place among a half-dozen or so major manufacturers, whose plants are located in countries or regions with low-cost labor, plus many additional firms that buy televisions from the primary manufacturers and sell them through retail outlets, sometimes under their own brand names. Entry into the market of, say, Belgium, would most likely be through exports from a low-cost factory in another country. Whether the exports will be sold by the manufacturer itself or through a secondary firm and its retail network must still be determined. Sony, Panasonic, General Electric/RCA, and Siemens have entered through the establishment of sales offices and through direct sales to retailers, in both cases under their own brand names. Other firms sell televisions to retail stores, which place their own brands on the TVs and market them through their own channels. Virtually no manufacture of televisions takes place in Belgium.

There are no restrictions on foreign-owned television firms that want to enter the Belgian market. Such firms must follow the same rules as local firms and must compete with imports or local production. Since competition is very strong in this industry, a firm might consider setting up local production in exchange for government protection in some form. Such a strategy would probably be wasted, however, because the European Community countries would continue to have free access to the Belgian market and because any subsidy offered to one firm would be protested by other suppliers. Since the principle of free competition is clearly established in Belgium, a television maker would be concerned mainly with minimizing the delivered cost of getting the TVs to the market and with maintaining the quality of the product relative to the others that are available. Seeking government protection would most likely not be a viable strategy in this case.

The choice between entering with an owned **affiliate** and **contracting** with another firm to make the product or deliver the service raises another interesting problem. If we assume that the firm is from North America or Japan, then producing in, say, the French market constitutes an entry into the European Community (EC). If the firm does not specify the contract carefully enough, the French contractee may be able to use the product or service in other EC countries in ways detrimental to the supplier firm's overall strategy.

Volkswagenwerk entered the U.S. market first by exporting and later by setting up production in Pennsylvania.

Wide World Photos, Inc.

For example, if a small Japanese manufacturer of computer circuit boards chooses to produce and sell in France through a licensee, that licensee may want to serve the entire European Community. Unless the contract is written restrictively enough, the licensee may have the right to do so—even if the Japanese manufacturer wants to set up its own plant in Italy or elsewhere in the EC for a similar purpose. The initial manufacturer may find that France's participation in the EC requires an "EC strategy," rather than a strategy for the French market alone.

In fact, for the competitive reasons just discussed, the OECD countries can be divided usefully into North America, the European Community, and Japan (ignoring Australia and New Zealand). Within each of these areas, there are few legal barriers to trade and other transborder business activities (none in Japan)—and transportation costs are very low compared to the costs of interregional transport. In addition, there are few cultural barriers between the United States and Canada in North America; though there are often important cultural barriers between countries in Europe. Another barrier to interregional business that should be noted is the difference in time zones; North America crosses six of them, and the European Community crosses three. Japan, by contrast, is in only one, and that one has very little overlap of business hours with the other two regions. None of these points is an absolute barrier to interregional business, but they all tend to make firms view North America, Europe, and Japan as three markets.

Operating Strategies

Assuming that the entry strategy chosen is an owned affiliate, the firm must next consider the operating details. Given that government protection is not likely to be a viable option in many cases, the firm will need to compete on the basis of cost, product differentiation, or market segmentation. All three of these strategies have been discussed previously, and here examples are given to illustrate them.

Cost minimization strategies have been followed widely by domestic firms as well as MNEs. During the past half-century, many U.S. firms have moved production from the industrial Northeast to lower-cost locations in the South. During the late 1970s and the 1980s, dozens of European and Japanese firms set up manufacturing in South Carolina, Georgia, and other Southern states, because these states had a cost advantage over Michigan, Pennsylvania, and other Northern states, but they still offered access to the entire U.S. market.

For similar reasons, Monsanto, Dow, Ciba-Geigy, ICI, and several other multinational chemical companies have chosen to manufacture basic chemicals in Northern Ireland. This politically risky location has the advantages of low-cost labor (relative to the rest of the EC) and of a government incentive program that further reduces costs. In this case, where production costs are the key competitive variable, firms have been able to operate a European Community strategy with a supply of basic chemicals from their plants in Northern Ireland. Of course, such other costs as transportation and communication are also low, in comparison with what they would be at production sites outside the EC.

The strategy of **product differentiation** plays a very important role in the industrialized countries, where consumers have relatively large amounts of discretionary income to spend on both necessities and luxury items. Not only can McDonald's and Burger King succeed as fast-food outlets, but with different foods and pricing strategies, so can Wimpy's, Kentucky Fried Chicken, and Arby's. Entry into the U.S. market for this type of store still offers possibilities to additional participants, as long as they can sufficiently differentiate their menus and other characteristics to attract customers. The fast-food concept swept the United States first, but the other ICs have accepted it as well—so opportunities exist in Tokyo and Rome too.

Product differentiation by country or region is a strategy followed by such automobile manufacturers as General Motors and Ford. These two companies have introduced models in their European affiliates different from those they sell in the United States and Japan. Both Ford and GM have introduced "world cars" that they sell in both European countries and North America, but they also produce many models that they sell within only one or a few countries. In fact, they sell virtually all of their North American models only in the Western Hemisphere, and GM imports almost none of its Opel and Vauxhall models into this area.

Finally, **market segmentation** is a useful strategy in industrialized countries, whose markets are generally much larger than those in LDCs. Even when large competitors dominate markets for thousands of products, smaller firms or competitors not yet in the market can often find a niche for their sales.

Dealing with the Governments of Industrialized Countries

Much of the discussion in this chapter has focused on the central importance of competition in determining business opportunities and problems in the industrialized countries. It is also true, however, that the governments of industrialized countries do impose highly detailed rules on some industries (such as defense-related ones) and that they operate companies in others (such as utilities). Also, the government sector typically constitutes more than one fourth of the total economy, so the government is a huge consumer in each industrialized nation. This section looks at some of the central issues of government/business relations during the current decade.

Probably the most contentious issues in the mid-1980s in government/MNE relations have been:

- MNE financial policies that affect a country's BOP and taxes, such as transfer pricing and other funds transfer strategies.
- MNE decisions to locate production facilities, often made to minimize costs, that shift production and jobs away from high-cost countries.
- MNE allocations of markets to affiliates, which are then limited to serving only some markets and thus may not be responsive to national efforts to stimulate exports or to restrict dealings with specific countries.
- Overshadowing all of the above points, the multinationality of MNEs versus the uninationality of governments, which some governments argue creates unequal bargaining power in favor of MNEs.

Successful dealings with host and home governments require careful consideration of both sides of these issues. The MNE manager, while needing to pursue the goals of the firm, must be aware of the government's goals as well—and aware of the government's sovereign right to set rules that seek to achieve those goals.

On the issue of **financial transfers,** for example, the MNE manager typically wants to minimize the tax burden paid on transfers and to take advantage of the ability to move funds where they are needed in the firm. But when a country faces a balance of payments problem due to a trade deficit and/or capital outflows based on expectations that the currency will devalue, the MNE's funds transfers may add to the problem. There is no simple solution to this conflict, though the MNE can seek to improve government relations by exporting to other affiliates, importing less into the country, reducing funds outflows, and generally looking for ways to help the BOP of the country. Such a strategy might ward off government policies that would constrain the MNE much more significantly.

The MNE's decision to move production to low-cost locations has become a more and more crucial issue in the 1980s. U.S.-based firms have faced substantial criticism for **offshore production** in the electronics, clothing, automobile, and many other industries. Because MNEs can consider many national locations for production, while governments can regulate only one, there is an essential imbalance in positions between the two. A fundamental step for MNEs is to demonstrate clearly either (*a*) that employment is not lost through offshore manufacture but merely shifted into other tasks (e.g., the production of other products or more white-collar activities in the firm) or (*b*) that the employment would have been lost anyway, due to less costly foreign production by firms of other countries. Both of these contentions are difficult to prove, so the tension between government and MNE remains.

Market allocation by MNEs limits a government's ability to push companies into greater exporting or other domestic or overseas activities. Typically, the MNE will use a local subsidiary to supply the local market but not to supply its operations in other countries. If the Canadian government wants to stimulate exports, it would probably find it difficult to convince the affiliates of U.S. companies that they should ship products to the United States, whose needs the parent firm is already supplying. This problem becomes especially acute when the affiliate is a joint venture and the partner firm perceives itself as constrained from exports that would add to the joint venture's profitability. Again, the issue is not simple to manage. Perhaps the best alternative for the MNE is to consider ways in which the affiliate could export without too greatly affecting the firm's global strategy. Then government relations might be enhanced at a low cost to the firm.

Finally, the basic issue is **multinationality.** An MNE is bound to follow the rules in any country where it does business. However, it is not tied down by the laws and conditions in one country, because it also does business in other countries. When difficulties arise in one country, the MNE may be able to shift some or all of its business activities to another country. Since a government cannot pursue an MNE into another nation's jurisdiction, a situation of unequal power exists. However, as Vernon (1977) and others have noted, MNEs are not free to ignore governments; if an MNE wants to do business within a government's jurisdiction, it will have to follow the demands of that government. Sovereignty is not at bay. As additional questions about the transnational dealings of MNEs arise, MNE managers will need to develop responsive strategies to government demands, rather than utilizing multinationality as a tool to avoid them.

An Example—Competing in Japan

Overview

Since Japanese and American firms will continue to become more directly competitive in the years ahead and since both Japan and the United States are highly desirable target markets in terms of size and per capita incomes, managers from both countries will benefit from a better understanding of the functioning of each other's business system. This section lays a simple foundation for starting to understand the Japanese system; additional insights about human resource management in Japanese firms were offered in Chapters 16 and 17; and several excellent references to the issues are cited at the end of this chapter.

Since a detailed analysis of Japan's business system is not possible here, our approach is to discuss several key aspects of Japanese business that confront foreign firms seeking to operate in Japan. First, we discuss the largest and most important companies and industry groups; next, we note key aspects of Japan's indicative planning process (i.e., the government/business relationship); and finally, we consider some competitive strategies for foreign firms.

Major Local Competitors

The main local competitors for virtually any foreign firm operating in Japan are the nine largest trading companies, the **Sogo Shosha.** These few firms account for about one fourth of Japan's GNP and for about half of Japan's imports and exports. Table 21-4 lists the nine firms and some of their characteristics. These firms follow in the tradition of the pre-World War II **Zaibatsu,** Japanese holding companies that owned or otherwise controlled hundreds of affiliated firms in manufacturing, finance, and other business areas. The Zaibatsu dominated Japanese business at that time, but they were

Table 21-4 **The Nine Largest Sogo Shosha in Japan**

Name	1986 Sales (million yen)	Major Industries
Mitsubishi Shoji	16,331,782	Oil, industrial products, financial services, computers, communications
Mitsui Bussan	16,019,824	Chemicals, energy, steel, food products
C. Itoh	15,324,503	Banking, electronics, textiles, oil
Sumitomo Shoji	14,225,622	Steel, chemicals, precious metals, communications
Marubeni	13,916,508	Textiles, machinery, steel, food products
Nissho Iwai	8,821,216	Banking, steel, aircraft, machinery, ships, lumber, rolling stock
Toyo Menka	4,770,959	Cotton, food products, machinery, electronics
Nichimen	4,515,584	Banking, lumber, computers, machinery
Kanematsu-Gosha	4,246,748	Banking, textiles, machinery, electronics, oil

Source: Keizai Toyo, *Japan Company Handbook* (Tokyo, Japan: Keizo Toyo, 1986).

forcibly dissolved as a result of the war and the subsequent Allied occupation. While many of the Zaibatsu were effectively split up, a few retained business ties and in the 1950s redeveloped some of their ownership ties. This led to the reconstitution of the two largest groups around their original core firms, Mitsubishi and Mitsui.

Additional networks of firms formed around a number of large industrial corporations, such as C. Itoh and Marubeni in textiles and Nissho-Iwai in metals, as well as around banks, such as Fuyo (Fuji) and Sanwa. All of these groups once again established their **Keiretsu,** affiliating large numbers of suppliers, intermediaries, and other related firms into industrial power centers. A distinguishing characteristic of the postwar groups has been their extensive expansion into international business, through the creation of trading companies, the Sogo Shosha. Today, the dominant form of business entity in Japan is the industrial group, linked by ownership and business ties to a Sogo Shosha rather than to a family-related Zaibatsu. The Sogo Shosha function as marketing arms for the affiliated firms of the Keiretsu, seeking sales at home and abroad as opportunities are uncovered. Figure 21-2 sketches some of the relationships among members of the largest Keiretsu, the Mitsubishi group of companies. Note that the central components of the chain are the trading company, which provides markets and information for the group; the banks, which provide financing for the group; and a large number of manufacturing companies, which provide the main products sold by the group.

The Japanese trading companies and their associated Keiretsu pose a very real threat to potential foreign competitors, since they control a large portion of Japan's distribution channels and they operate cooperatively among many of the country's manufacturers, banks, and so on.

Government/Business Relations

Relations between the government and private sector firms have developed far more cooperatively in Japan than in the United States. While the private sector does own and operate most of Japan's business system, government policy is often used to support chosen industries and firms. Historically, government policy has been inward-looking as far as production is concerned and outward-looking as far as sources of supply are concerned. (Since Japan is not blessed with many fossil fuels or other minerals, oil, coal, iron, and so on must be imported—and export markets must generate funds to pay for these imports.)

The government agency responsible for implementing Japan's industrial policy is **MITI,** the Ministry of International Trade and Industry. After World War II, this agency was given responsibility for instituting a plan of economic development focusing on four major industries: electric power, steel, shipbuilding, and fertilizers. By setting up a system of incentives to prompt investment in these industries and to assist the successful firms in entering export markets—and also a strict system of protection against competitive

Figure 21-2 **The Mitsubishi Keiretsu**

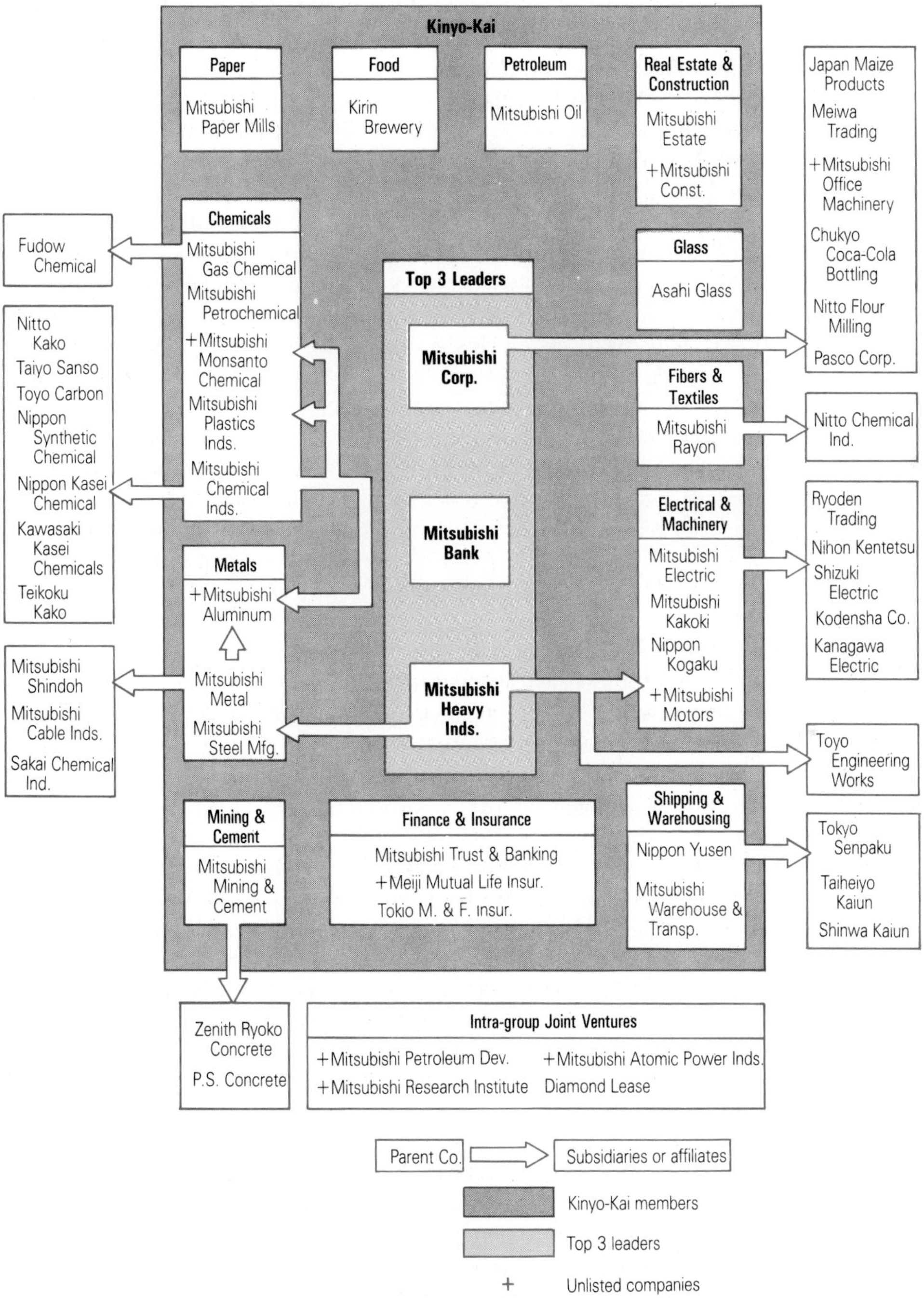

Source: Reprinted with permission from Dodwell Marketing Consultants, *Industrial Groupings in Japan*, 7th ed. (Tokyo, 1986) p. 48.

imports—MITI contributed substantially to Japan's "economic miracle" after the war. During the 1950s and 1960s, GNP grew about twice as fast in Japan as in the most dynamic of the other industrial countries.

In more recent years, MITI has maintained its role as a primary agent of indicative industrial policy, offering incentives to push business into desired activities, especially to stimulate investment in targeted industries, such as chemicals and computers. The policies of protectionism have been largely dismantled, so that Japan is now no more protectionist than other industrial nations.

MITI has historically dealt with business as a partner in development, rather than as an antagonist or opponent. (There is frequent movement of managers from private sector corporations into MITI and from MITI back to the private sector.) MITI tends to be highly supportive of the private sector rather than distrustful of it. This cooperative relationship has been noted widely as a reason for Japan's superior ability to put national economic resources into leading ("sunrise") industries and to avoid overcommitment to declining ("sunset") industries. MITI officials frequently meet with company managers in selected firms and industries to discuss business needs, government goals, and ways to cooperate. All in all, Japan's system of indicative planning has functioned very successfully during the past 40 years.

Successful Competitive Strategies

Foreign firms entering Japan in the 1980s have found that the legal restrictions are not overwhelming but that the cultural barriers are. The language is a major hurdle—Japanese is only remotely related to the Indo-European languages, such as English, French, and German—and the highly homogeneous society is quite inwardly biased. Japanese consumers tend to prefer to buy from domestic suppliers and to reject foreign goods in general. This presents a huge barrier to the foreign exporter or direct investor.

One extensively used strategy has been the **joint venture** with a Japanese partner. By linking up with a local firm that belongs to one of the key Keiretsu, a foreign firm can obtain distribution and promotion support that would be totally unavailable to the independent firm. By taking on a Japanese name, the foreign firm may avoid the negative customer reaction that prevails throughout the country. And finally, by truly working with a Japanese partner, the foreign firm may be able to absorb some of the managerial and technical expertise that has enabled many Japanese firms to succeed around the world in recent years.

Another strategy that has proven successful in Japan is the **licensing** of a Japanese firm to use the foreign firm's proprietary technology. After World War II, when the Japanese government restricted domestic industries to local participants, this was the only way (except for exporting) that the Japanese market could be entered. Foreign direct investment has been permitted more and more freely since the 1960s, but licensing continues to offer a low-cost alternative. The main advantage of licensing is that it allows immediate market entry without the start-up costs of setting up production, distribution and so on. The main disadvantages are that earnings are limited to the licensing fee, and that the proprietary technology must be given up to the licensee.

A **sequential entry strategy** might offer better results. In this strategy, the firm uses licensing to gain some knowledge about the Japanese market and subsequently sets up its own local manufacture or service facilities. (IBM initially entered the Japanese market through licensing agreements with various local firms in the 1950s. When the prohibition on FDI was lifted, IBM was able to enter with its own operations, and today it is one of the most successful foreign firms in Japan.)

In sum, all of the basic market entry strategies that have been discussed in this book are now generally possible in Japan. The difficulties that most foreign firms have encountered lie much more in the areas of product acceptability, distribution, promotion, and so on—fundamental business considerations—than in the area of government regulation. Japan's market, while very large and very affluent, presents major barriers of cultural and geographic distance from the experience of European and American firms.

Conclusions

Doing business in other industrialized countries is the main concern of most MNEs today. Problems in LDCs or communist countries may be more visible and more difficult, but most of the international business carried out today is between industrialized nations. These countries have market-based economies that permit many MNE activities. In fact, the main problem generally faced by firms in the industrialized countries is competition from other firms.

While government-owned companies do exist in every IC, the private sector plays a very large role in the economy. Government policies tend to be procompetition; they limit the activities of business mainly in order to assure that both local firms and MNEs deal fairly in employment, pricing, taxpaying, and so on. In industrialized countries, dealing with governments is largely the same for both local and foreign firms. A key concern in government relations is that MNEs are multinational, while governments are only uninational. This concern has led governments to share information about MNEs among themselves, to harmonize some of their policies that relate to MNEs, and to require that MNEs provide more information about their operations.

Strategies for doing business in ICs focus mainly on creating solid competitive positions. The basic strategies include cost minimization, product differentiation, and market segmentation.

Questions

1. Define "industrialized country." Does Norway fit into your definition? Does Spain? How about Kuwait? What would be an appropriate definition of industrialization?

2. Which countries are the most developed today? Which ones do you think will be the most developed by the year 2000? Why?
3. What are the general differences between the French and U.S. business systems, and what are the particular differences between these systems with respect to the treatment of MNEs?
4. How do IC governments participate directly in business? What implications does this situation have for the MNE manager?
5. Name four main concerns of IC governments in dealing with foreign multinational firms. What can the firms do to minimize tensions with the host government with regard to each of these concerns?
6. Name four main concerns of IC governments in dealing with MNEs based in their own countries. What can the firms do to minimize tensions with the home government with regard to each of these concerns?
7. What problems would arise for multinational firms if transborder transmission of information were restricted, as has been proposed in recent government discussions? How could MNEs cope with these problems?
8. Present three broad operating strategies for MNE affiliates in industrialized countries. Which of these strategies would have been appropriate for Monsanto Chemical Corporation when it was seeking to enter the European Community?
9. Explain the imbalance of power between MNEs and national governments due to the fact that the MNEs can operate in several countries, whereas the national governments are limited to their own jurisdictions.
10. Create a market entry strategy for a small German textile manufacturing company that wants to enter the U.S. market for synthetic fabrics. Make necessary (reasonable) assumptions so that your answer covers the organizational form of the venture, the channels of distribution, the structure of decision making in the firm, financial concerns, and any other issues that you feel are important.

References

Bergsten, C. Fred; Thomas Horst; and Theodore Moran. *American Multinationals and American Interests.* Washington, D.C.: Brookings Institution, 1978.

Boyer, Edward. "How Japan Manages Declining Industries," *Fortune,* January 10, 1983.

Gladwin, Thomas, and Ingo Walter. *Multinationals under Fire.* New York: John Wiley & Sons, 1980.

Grosse, Robert. *Foreign Investment Codes and the Location of Direct Investment.* New York: Praeger Publishers, 1980.

Hirschmeier, J., and T. Yui. *The Development of Japanese Business.* 2nd ed. London: Allen & Unwin, 1981.

Organization for Economic Cooperation and Development. *Declaration on International Investment and Multinational Enterprises.* Paris: OECD, 1976.

Safarian, A. E. *Governments and Multinationals: Policies in the Developed Countries.* Washington, D.C.: British-North American Committee, 1983.

United Nations. *National Legislation and Regulations Relating to Transnational Corporations.* New York: UN Center on Transnational Corporations, 1983.

Vernon, Raymond. *Storm over the Multinationals.* Cambridge, Mass.: Harvard University Press, 1977.

Yoshino, M. Y. *Japan's Multinational Enterprises.* Cambridge, Mass.: Harvard University Press, 1976.

Endnotes

1. The OECD is an organization that groups the industrialized countries of the world plus a few LDCs, such as Turkey, Yugoslavia, and Portugal. The organization provides a forum for the rich countries to cooperate on issues of concern—improving education and social services, harmonizing policies such as those on MNEs, and so on. The OECD was founded in the early 1950s and is headquartered in Paris.
2. Organization for Economic Cooperation and Development, *Declaration on International Investment and Multinational Enterprises* (Paris: OECD, 1976), sec. 2.
3. This, of course, is easier said than done. Language and other cultural differences hinder the creation of a true Community-wide labor market.
4. See "Beyond Unions," *Business Week,* July 8, 1985, pp. 72 ff.
5. See *Miami Herald,* May 26, 1985, p. 3F, for a listing of the taxes paid by 200 of the largest corporations in the United States in 1984.
6. See the "Investment Canada Act," *Investment Canada Regulations.* Ottawa: Government of Canada, 1986 [S.C., 1985, c. 20.].

22 LESS DEVELOPED COUNTRIES

This chapter examines business conditions and opportunities for international firms that seek to operate in less developed countries (LDCs). First, the characteristics of LDCs are presented; this is no simple task, since LDCs include countries ranging from relatively high-income Korea and Singapore all the way to very low-income Bangladesh and Ethiopia, with governments ranging from elected socialist and capitalist regimes to military dictatorships. In general, the aspects of these countries that are relevant to international firms are emphasized. Major emphasis is placed on the role of government in the economy, including both policies toward business and the widespread use of government-owned companies. Specific entry and operating strategies for international firms seeking to operate in LDCs are suggested and analyzed. The main goals of the chapter are to:

1. Demonstrate important characteristics of less developed countries for international firms.
2. Show what kinds of international business are common and appropriate in these countries.
3. Examine LDC concerns and government policies that relate to foreign MNEs.
4. Consider the entry and operating strategies that international firms can use in these countries.

Introduction

While no brief discussion of business conditions, policies, and opportunities in less developed countries (LDCs) can hope to offer detailed insights into particular countries, this chapter aims to raise the key issues facing foreign firms that want to do business in the nonindustrialized countries of Latin America, Africa, and Asia. Business conditions are far from uniform in these countries, which range from newly industrializing nations such as Singapore and Taiwan in Asia to the poorest, least developed African nations such as Ethiopia and Uganda, with most of Latin America somewhere in between. International firms in these countries engage in the full range of business activities, though a large part of their activities involve extractive industries and manufacturing assembly operations for exporting products to the industrialized countries.

This section provides a definition of less developed countries and a brief commentary on the main kinds of international business found in such countries. The next section discusses key aspects of LDC political and economic environments that particularly relate to MNE activities. The third section focuses on government policies and practices in dealing with foreign MNEs. Then, in the fourth and fifth sections, company strategies for entering and operating in LDCs are presented.

Definitions of Less Developed Countries

In principle, a **less developed country (LDC)** is one that is at a lower level of economic development than some other countries. This oversimplified definition just recognizes that some countries are poorer than others, and classifies them according to such measures as per capita income, average life expectancy, and average level of education. Since economic development continues to occur in all countries, the absolute measures of poverty, health, education, and so on continue to improve, though some countries must still be in the bottom part of the distribution and others in the top part. That is, the measures of economic development themselves change as standards of living rise worldwide—but some countries must still be below the average of all countries.

The World Bank uses a classification scheme that groups countries into six categories: low income, lower middle income, upper middle income, high-income oil exporters, industrial market economies, and East European nonmarket economies. Table 22-1 describes selected countries from all four third-world categories along several dimensions.

Another classification scheme is used by the United Nations, which groups countries into developed market economies, socialist economies, and developing countries. These categories group low- and middle-income countries together, with the exception of communist countries, which are listed as socialist nonmarket economies. The developed market economies here are

Table 22-1 **Selection of Countries Classified as LDCs by the World Bank**

Country	GDP per Capita, 1984 (US$)	Growth Rate of GDP per Capita*	Average Annual Inflation (%/year)†	Average Unemployment (%)†	Current Account BOP, 1984 ($ millions)	Manufacturing as Percent of Total GDP, 1984
	Measure					
Low income						
Ethiopia	110	0.4	4.4	n.a.	−201	11
Uganda	230	2.9	64.5	n.a.	−256	4
India	260	1.6	7.8	2.2	−2,429	15
China	310	4.5	1.8	n.a.	2,509	n.a.
Kenya	310	2.1	10.8	n.a.	−135	12
Haiti	320	1.0	7.9	n.a.	−110	n.a.
Lower middle income						
Bolivia	540	0.2	54.5	6.8	−178	20
Indonesia	540	4.9	17.4	15.9	−2,113	13
Egypt	720	4.3	13.1	3.8	−1,978	27
Nigeria	730	2.8	13.0	21.0	346	4
Nicaragua	860	−1.5	17.2	n.a.	−444	25
Upper middle income						
Brazil	1,720	4.6	71.4	3.0	53	27
Mexico	2,040	2.9	31.5	5.9	3,905	24
South Korea	2,110	6.6	17.6	4.2	−1,344	28
South Africa	2,340	1.4	13.2	n.a.	−1,098	23
Israel	5,060	2.7	84.4	4.1	−1,499	n.a.
High-income OPEC						
Libya	8,520	−1.1	10.8	n.a.	−1,803	4
Saudi Arabia	10,530	5.9	14.1	n.a.	−24,036	7
Kuwait	16,720	−0.1	9.2	n.a.	5,570	8
United Arab Emirates	21,920	−0.7	8.7	n.a.	7,137	9

* Average annual rates during the period 1965-84.
† Average annual inflation during the period 1973-84.
Source: World Bank, *World Development Report, 1986* (Washington, D.C.: World Bank, 1986); International Labour Office, *Yearbook of Labour Statistics* (Geneva: ILO, 1985); and United Nations, *Statistical Yearbook* (New York: UN, 1983-84).

equivalent to the industrial market economies in the World Bank grouping. This scheme simplifies the categories, but it also obscures the different situation of the key group of oil-exporting developing countries by placing them together with all other LDCs.

Finally, a new classification—**newly industrializing countries (NICs)**—has arisen to describe the LDCs that have moved farthest along the road to industrialization. Most of these are Southeast Asian countries that have succeeded in attracting large amounts of foreign investment in manufacturing. MNEs from Japan, Europe, and North America (as well as locally based MNEs) use facilities in these countries to assemble electronic equipment, clothing, machinery, and various other products. The attraction of these countries lies in their relatively high levels of education, low wages, and industrious work forces, all of which make local manufacturing profitable for domestic and foreign firms. Indeed, the phenomenal success of such ventures has led some people to contend that these countries, which they call the "Asian Challenge," will rival the United States and Japan for supremacy in manufacturing during the coming years.[1] Table 22-2 illuminates some key characteristics of the NICs.

Each of the classification schemes has useful aspects. Which scheme is best really depends on the type of presentation desired. For our purposes, it should be noted that important differences exist among oil-exporting LDCs, NICs, and other less developed countries, and that one should be aware of these differences when using World Bank, United Nations, or other sources of information.

Main Kinds of International Business in LDCs

The international business activities carried out in LDCs are at least as varied as those carried out in developed countries. These activities include exporting and importing, foreign direct investment, such contractual arrangements as licensing and franchising; and international banking. The most striking

Table 22-2 **Development Indicators for NICs** (newly industrializing countries)

	Indicator			
Country	GDP per Capita, 1984 (US$)	Annual Growth Rate of GDP per Capita, 1965–1984	Exports as Percent of GDP, 1984	FDI as Percent of GDP, 1984
Brazil	1,720	4.6	14.4	0.8
Hong Kong	6,330	6.2	92.4	19.9
Singapore	7,260	7.8	132.0	8.0
South Korea	2,110	6.6	35.1	0.1
Taiwan	n.a.	6.2	83.0	n.a.

Source: World Bank, *World Development Report, 1986* (Washington, D.C.: World Bank, 1986); and International Monetary Fund, *International Financial Statistics Yearbook* (Washington, D.C.: IMF, 1986).

characteristic of much of this business is that it is generally far more *regulated* in LDCs than in industrialized countries. The limitations placed on foreign business in LDCs far surpass those imposed by industrialized countries. This point will be discussed in some detail in the section "Government Policies."

Another striking characteristic of international business in less developed countries is its relatively small size—LDCs comprise more than 80 percent of the world's population but only about 25 percent of international business. Tables in Chapters 2 and 3 illuminate this issue to some degree, showing that LDC exports and imports each constitute slightly less than one third of the world total. (This measure can be divided between oil-exporting countries and other LDCs. In the mid-1980s, the former had a substantial trade surplus and the latter faced a substantial trade deficit.)

As far as foreign direct investment is concerned, Table 22-3 shows the distribution of FDI in the countries listed previously. Probably not surpris-

Table 22-3 **Flows of Foreign Direct Investment in Selected Less Developed Countries**

Country	1966–1971	1972–1977	1978–1983
Ethiopia	65	83	—
Uganda	24	−2	—
India	−42	−29	—
Haiti	0	33	48
China	226	—	—
Kenya	—	142	327
Bolivia	28	52	171
Indonesia	308	1,054	1,331
Egypt	—	130	2,922
Nigeria	683	1,822	1,021
Nicaragua	134	61	15
South Korea	136	419	−15
Brazil	922	6,155	11,181
Mexico	1,466	2,746	7,444
South Africa	1,240	448	−1,529
Israel	178	375	−366
Singapore	299	2,350	4,681
Libya	383	−1,631	−3,250
Saudi Arabia	−3	−1,730	17,207
Kuwait	—	—	−438

Source: International Monetary Fund, *Balance of Payments Statistics* (Washington D.C.: IMF Publications Unit, 1969, 1977, 1981, and 1986).

ingly, the largest amounts of FDI go to the largest economies, although the Southeast Asian NICs have attracted a disproportionate amount to their relatively small countries. Of total worldwide FDI, just under 20 percent is in LDCs, and about one half of that is in manufacturing. The service sector has become the second largest recipient of FDI in LDCs. It replaced mining after the wave of nationalizations of oil properties and other mining ventures of MNEs during the 1960s and early 1970s.

Although the use of **offshore assembly** to reduce production costs is becoming more and more popular, such manufacturing counts for only a small part of total FDI at present. Even if we assume that all U.S. FDI in Hong Kong, Singapore, South Korea, and Taiwan is for offshore assembly, it only constitutes about $US 2 billion of the total $US 18 billion in LDC manufacturing. The trend is dramatically upward, however, as shown by the fact that as recently as 1970 U.S. manufacturing FDI in those countries was less than $US 270 million out of an LDC total of $US 5.5 billion.[2]

International bank lending to LDCs has also grown dramatically during the past decade. Table 22-4 shows the change in commercial bank loans to developing countries from 1976 to 1985. Notice that the most internationally indebted countries are the large Latin American borrowers, followed by the newly industrializing countries. (This is somewhat misleading, because Hong Kong and Singapore are offshore banking centers, where large volumes of eurocurrency transactions take place separate from borrowing for domestic uses.) The countries that are least economically developed have attracted the least commercial bank financing (given their relatively low abilities to generate foreign exchange to repay such loans). Finally, note that the Arab OPEC countries incurred substantial foreign debt during 1982-1985. This was probably associated with the decline in the price of oil since 1981.

Key Characteristics of LDCs Relating to MNEs

Government Involvement in Business

As in the industrial countries, the government sector in LDCs constitutes a substantial percentage of the total economy. Figure 22-1 shows estimates of the size of the public sector in selected LDCs.
In fact, on average the government's activities account for a *smaller* portion of GDP than in the industrial countries (even when state-owned companies are included). This situation needs to be contrasted with the *regulatory* environment that confronts private-sector firms in DCs and LDCs.

While such industrialized countries as France and Sweden have a very great degree of government participation in business through government-owned companies and highly regulated industries, most industrialized countries allow firms substantial freedom to operate as the market dictates. Among LDCs, contrarily, the exceptions are the few Asian nations that allow broad competitive freedom to the market, while the rule is that LDC governments

Table 22-4 **Commercial Bank External Claims on Borrowers in LDCs, Selected Years** (in millions of U.S. dollars of loans outstanding)

Country	December 1976	June 1982	June 1985
Ethiopia	18	41	161
Uganda	7	57	46
India	571	1,577	4,892
Haiti	39	59	147
China	506	1,295	6,618
Kenya	102	830	729
Bolivia	448	1,053	644
Indonesia	4,010	8,155	14,142
Egypt	1,264	5,350	6,719
Nigeria	284	6,714	—
Nicaragua	634	796	523
South Korea	3,701	19,994	—
Brazil	18,461	55,300	66,662
Mexico	17,885	64,395	71,669
South Africa	7,624	14,125	17,003
Israel	2,033	6,126	5,558
Hong Kong	7,485	34,003	65,821
Singapore	9,168	33,690	62,671
Libya	148	830	926
Saudi Arabia	1,053	5,268	6,070
Kuwait	939	6,274	6,156
United Arab Emirates	1,172	4,449	4,383

Source: Bank for International Settlements, "Maturity Distribution of International Bank Lending" (Basle, Switzerland, June 1977 and December 1982).

place many limits on company activities and participate actively in the market through government-owned or -controlled companies. In most LDCs, a national airline dominates or monopolizes that industry (for example, Aeromexico in Mexico, Varig in Brazil, and Air India in India), a national oil company controls that industry (for example, YPF in Argentina, the National Iranian Oil Company in Iran, and Nigerian National Petroleum Corporation in Nigeria), and a national bank (in addition to the central bank) controls or greatly influences local financial markets (for example, Banco de la Nación in Peru; Arab Banking Corporation in Kuwait, Libya, and the United Arab Emirates; and the Bank of Korea and Korea Development Bank in Korea)—all in

Figure 22-1 **Government Participation in the Economy** (Central Government Expenditures as a Percentage of GDP, 1983)

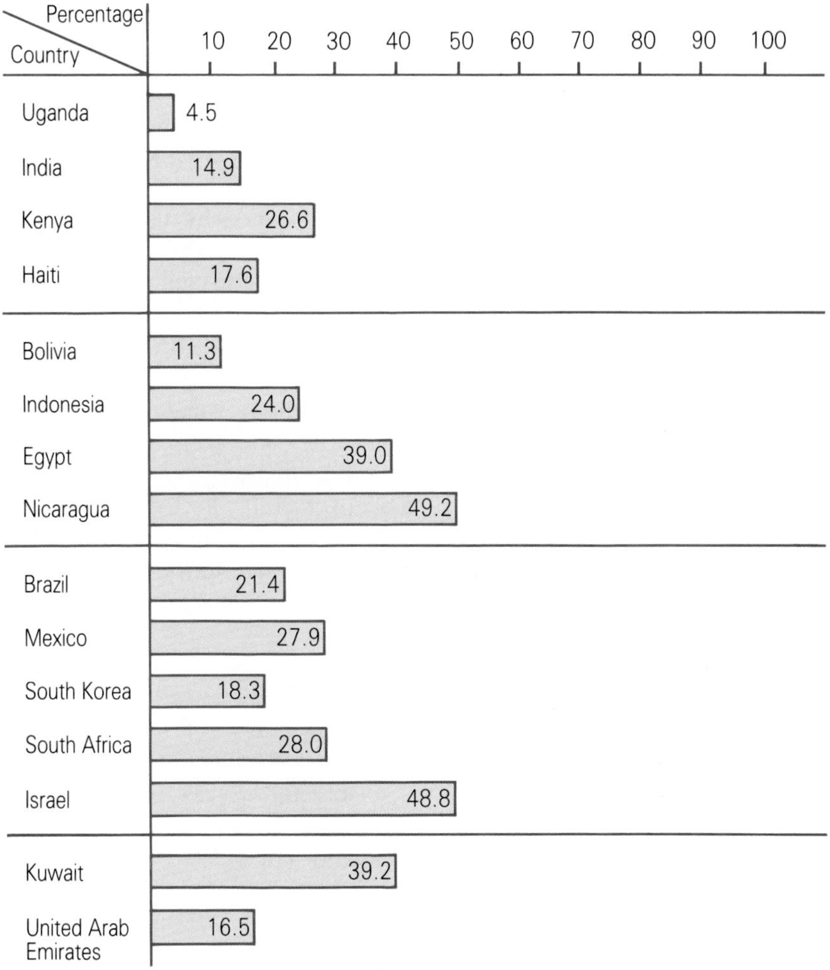

Source: World Bank, *World Development Report* 1986.

addition to government-controlled postal service and electric, telephone, and water utilities.

Even beyond these industries, the government in an LDC often operates through an owned or controlled company that competes with private firms in other industries. A national automobile company (for example, Hindustan Motors in India) may compete with General Motors, Toyota, Ford, and others in the local market. A national food processing company or cooperative (such as Food Corporation of India and the National Cereals and Produce Board of

Kenya) often competes with Borden, Kraft, United Brands, and others both domestically and in other countries. The list may extend to dozens of industries, depending on the country.

Finally, the government in an LDC may exercise considerable control over the private firms in an industry by setting rules that limit their power to import, transfer funds, hire and fire, and so on. In this manner, LDC governments attempt to guide business in directions deemed desirable—though of course they do not always succeed in forcing the expected results.

In all of the above ways, LDC governments participate actively in the business systems of their countries. To foreign MNEs seeking to enter such markets, these conditions present challenges different from those in the industrialized countries. In industries monopolized by the government, foreign firms can operate *only* through contracts with the government to provide needed products or services used by the national monopoly. In industries where a government company competes with private sector firms, the rules of competition are different from those in a wholly private market, and the managers of foreign companies need to understand the key differences. In other industries, managers of foreign companies need to deal with the regulatory structure in a way that satisfies the local government and still leads to acceptable profitability for the firm. The challenge is to maintain the acceptability of the foreign firm to the government while carrying out some business activity that has value to the firm as well.

Dual Economies

Much has been said in the literature on economic development about the existence of **dual economies** in LDCs.[3] That is, the economic environment in many LDCs contains two separate and distinct groups: people who belong to a traditional society and do not participate in international business or even in the national market economy and people who belong to the market economy, which includes manufacturing and other modern industry, with its links to foreign business.

In Latin America, the Indian populations of the Andean and Central American countries typify the traditional societies, with very low per capita incomes, often living in remote areas far from cities, and with few ties to the market economy, which predominates in a few cities of each country. In political science terms, these people represent the **periphery,** which fails to benefit substantially from the economic development of the **center,** that is, the cities. The populations of Latin American cities (of both European and Indian descent), while far from a wealthy class overall, include a wealthy elite group as well as middle-income and poor groups. The entire urban area generally has access to foreign products and to a functioning market economy; hence it is the center of economic development.

The multinational enterprise usually deals only with the **market sector** of a dual economy, that is, with the urban centers and more specifically with the middle and upper classes (which have sufficient purchasing power to buy foreign goods or sufficient education to work in the factories or offices of foreign firms). This presents quite a difficult social problem for the MNE to deal with, since the government officials who determine policy toward business generally come from the urban centers, while a large percentage of the population may exist on the periphery. The response of most MNEs has been to operate in the market sector and let the government worry about the **traditional sector.** This response has subjected MNEs to great criticism by LDC analysts and policymakers. Unfortunately, these firms are expert at producing and selling goods and services but not at redistributing income or choosing a country's economic development strategy. Because MNEs are a part of economic development, however, their managers must come to grips with such problems. Possible strategies are discussed below.

Political Risk

A third key characteristic of LDCs in general that tends to affect foreign firms is the high degree of political risk. Broadly speaking, less developed countries tend to present foreign companies with much more frequent and greater shifts in policy than do developed countries. While it is not every day that a shah is overthrown or a president deposed, the amount of political instability tends to be far higher in LDCs than in industrialized nations. Also, the frequent changes in political orientation—from leftist to conservative to centrist—tend to result in policy changes ranging from nationalizations to tax holiday incentives. The often unstable political environments lead MNE managers to perceive greater political risk in LDCs than in industrialized countries even if the instability does not have substantial effects on business activities.[4]

Government Policies

Important Government Concerns

As contrasted with governments in industrialized countries, LDC governments tend to focus their concerns on crucial development issues such as poverty, political instability, and social strife. Where European and North American countries seek to ensure a fair distribution of the benefits of MNE activities through taxation and antitrust rules, the Latin American, African, and Asian countries look for access to technology, capital, and managerial skills. In another view, the industrialized nations are largely concerned with sharing the benefits of MNEs fairly, whereas the LDCs are concerned with gaining more of those benefits and minimizing the costs of doing so. (It must be recognized, of course, that most of the world's multinational enterprises come from the industrialized countries and thus are "foreign" to the LDCs.)

The result of these concerns is a range of policies in LDCs that attempt to extract as much value as possible from MNE activities without driving away the firms that are providing the benefits. Table 22-5 lists a set of important

Table 22-5 **LDC Relations with MNEs**

Problems Different from Those of Industrialized Countries	Policy Reactions of LDCs
Sovereignty	Expropriation Require joint ventures "Unbundle" capital, technology, management, distribution, etc.
Lack of financial capital	Capital controls
Lack of technology	Technology controls Incentives for local R&D
Lack of infrastructure	Local content requirements
Lack of access to developed-country markets	Stimulate offshore assembly Encourage countertrade
Unemployment	Local labor requirements
All the concerns of the developed countries	

concerns of LDCs in dealing with foreign firms and notes some of the policies that LDCs are using currently. Each of the concerns is discussed separately below.

Sovereignty Since the 1960s, a fundamental concern of LDCs, especially those that are former colonies of European countries, has been the demonstration of **sovereignty**—that is, control over the national economy. Many of the most serious problems for foreign companies arose during the late 1960s and early 1970s, when LDC governments expropriated a number of oil, copper, and other raw materials investments and demanded that other investments be partially sold to local investors. Chile, for example, expropriated the copper mines of Anaconda, Kennecott, and Cerro de Pasco in 1969 and several other foreign (primarily U.S.) investments during the Allende regime, from 1970 to 1973. Even more striking were the oil company nationalizations during the mid-1970s, following the OPEC embargo and price hike in 1973. Most of the Middle East countries nationalized the properties of foreign oil companies during that period, as did Venezuela and Ecuador in Latin America.[5] (**Expropriation** implies forced loss of MNE property with inadequate or no compensation. **Nationalization** refers to forced sale of MNE property to local purchasers with compensation.)

Another policy that has become widely used to gain more local ownership of MNE activities is the requirement of a **fade-out** of foreign ownership over some time period. Instead of demanding that the MNE sell its local affiliate to nationals immediately, a number of LDCs have set rules requiring the sale of 51 percent or more of foreign-owned businesses over a period of 10 to 20 years. The Andean Pact countries currently utilize this policy. A somewhat similar policy, implemented by Mexico, India, and

One of the Bougainville Copper Company's mines in New Guinea, originally owned by the Rio Tinto Zinc Corporation of Great Britain.

Milton & Joan Mann/Cameramann International

Nigeria, requires new investments to take joint-venture partners with some prescribed minimum ownership (51 percent local ownership in Mexico; 60 percent in India; and 40 or 60 percent in Nigeria, depending on the industry). Each of these policies could be considered a partial nationalization, since the intent is to have local investors gain control over the affiliate.

Expropriation and nationalization have not been the only responses of LDCs to their concern about controlling the national economy. Many of the policies enacted by LDCs in the past two decades have aimed at **unbundling** the MNE into components that have value to the host country. For example, in order to force MNEs to transfer managerial skills to local people, LDCs have limited the use of expatriate managers in MNE affiliates and required local nationals to be employed. Similarly, to gain access to technology, LDCs have tried to force MNEs to sell their proprietary technology to local firms and have disallowed the payment of royalties to parent firms, so that the country will not pay (through transfer of funds abroad) for technology developed by the MNE elsewhere. Without totally disallowing the entry of MNEs, many LDCs have sought to obtain the valuable pieces of the firm separately.

Lack of Financial Capital Another concern of LDCs is a relative lack of financial capital for investment in productive activities. More specifically, this refers to a shortage of foreign currencies that could be used to buy foreign products necessary for supporting the local economy and to a lack of domes-

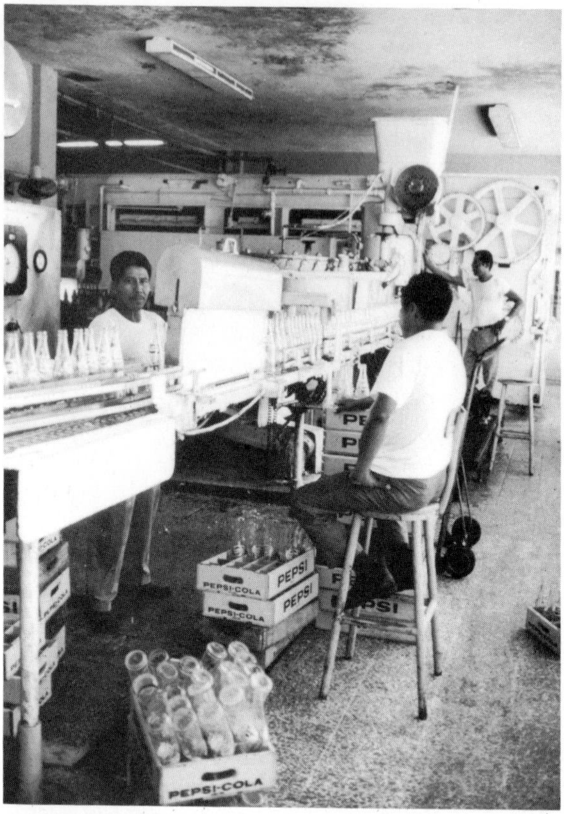

A joint-venture Pepsi-Cola bottling plant in Minatitlan, Mexico.

Odyssey Productions/Robert Frerck

tic long-term capital markets that could provide financing as well. While a government can print as much money as it wants, it cannot print the dollars or deutsche marks that are needed to buy machinery to run local factories. Nor can a government simply create long-term financial markets without substantial private sector participation and support, both of which are generally lacking in an LDC.

No simple solution exists to this problem. Many countries try to implement **capital controls** to limit transfers of funds abroad (which drain the country of foreign exchange). When capital controls are implemented, typically a black market arises for the purchase of foreign exchange and the problem continues.[6] Transfers of funds abroad are also taxed by host governments, thus reducing their profitability. This policy has some usefulness, though it does not stop the capital from moving. Many efforts have been undertaken to stimulate the development of capital markets in LDCs; thus far, the main successes have been offshore eurocurrency markets such as those in the Bahamas and the Cayman Islands, neither of which has provided any major amount of local access to the markets for local development.

The real basis of the problem is that investors, domestic and foreign, try to move their funds to safe and high-yielding investments. When an LDC demonstrates an unstable political climate, or a debt crisis that makes foreign exchange very scarce, these investors will try to place their funds abroad—and they occasionally cause such a massive **capital flight** that the crisis is exacerbated.[7] In addition to seeking funds from MNEs, less developed countries go to the private credit markets for international bank loans and bond issues and they attempt to raise their borrowing needs from international organizations such as the IMF and the World Bank.

Lack of Technology All countries have come to view technology as a critical factor of production. That is, no country is willing to follow simple comparative advantage and specialize solely in the production of raw materials, even if such specialization is dictated by cost conditions. Rather, every country seeks access to current technology in manufacturing, so that the economy can be diversified and not dependent on a narrow range of products (especially raw materials). Consequently, LDC governments want to obtain a continuing flow of current technology from suppliers such as MNEs at the lowest cost and to the greatest degree possible.

The policies used to achieve this goal range from refusal to recognize patents (which is intended to gain access to technology without paying for it) to incentives for local R&D. The Andean Pact countries do not allow payments to parent firms for technology transferred to local affiliates, although they still maintain patent protection. Most LDCs offer one form of subsidy or another to attract MNEs to do some local product development (the "D" of R&D), recognizing that basic research is usually centralized in one or two locations in the firm. In late 1984, Brazil required that all computers sold in the country be produced locally by local firms. This attempt to force the development of a domestic capability in such a key high-tech industry has led to great turmoil in the Brazilian computer industry, with IBM, Burroughs, and other MNEs still not certain of the full implications for their activities in Brazil.[8]

Lack of Infrastructure Not only do most LDCs lack major domestic companies in manufacturing industries; they also lack the necessary **infrastructure** to support such industries. That is, good roads, accessible electric power, good telephone service, up-to-date educational institutions, and other utilities and public services are often lacking in LDCs. These facilities tend to be extremely sensitive politically, and foreign firms are often not permitted to provide the services rendered by such facilities, though they may supply equipment and other inputs to construct the facilities.

The most common strategy used by LDCs to create the necessary infrastructure is to contract with MNEs to set up the telephone system, port, or power plant and then either to buy the project under a turnkey arrangement or to let the MNE remain as an adviser and perhaps licenser of the government-owned project.

Another tactic used by governments is to require MNEs and other firms that operate locally to obtain a substantial percentage of their inputs locally. In this manner, MNEs are compelled to carry out as much of the production process as necessary to reach the local content limit or to buy inputs from local suppliers. Thus, other local businesses are stimulated and a larger industrial sector is created. The supplier firms form part of the local infrastructure needed by MNEs to produce locally. The Venezuelan government, for example, requires that automobile firms obtain at least 40 percent of their sales value from local sources, either their own local production or purchases from local suppliers. General Motors, Toyota, and Jeep have expanded their local assembly operations to achieve the necessary level of local content under this rule.

Lack of Access to Developed-Country Markets Even when LDCs make products that can be competitive in world markets, they face another disadvantage relative to MNEs. LDC firms generally lack the knowledge of market conditions in the industrialized countries that they need to build distribution networks there. The enormous competitive advantage gained by an MNE that operates a distribution network in several countries and passes information among its affiliates cannot be overemphasized. Without such networks, the LDC raw material supplier or manufacturer faces little chance of success in competing with the MNEs.

In response to this problem, a number of policies have been tried. One interesting example, a result of the Latin American debt crisis, is Colombia's requirement that any firm importing specified products into the country must also find some product or service of equal value to export. This effort to balance trade and reduce the dollar outflow from Colombia is a form of barter or countertrade that attempts to gain the country better access to the markets of other countries.[9] Another example is the attempt made by many countries, especially in Southeast Asia, to attract offshore assembly by MNEs. By positioning itself as a location for assembly of manufactured goods, the LDC gains not only new production and employment but also access to the developed-country markets via the MNE that takes the assembled goods and sells them abroad.

Unemployment Unemployment is the last concern of LDCs that will be discussed here—though certainly not the last of the many difficulties faced by LDCs in seeking to improve their economic conditions. Rates of unemployment and underemployment in LDCs are estimated to be anywhere from a manageable 2-3 percent in such countries as Korea and Singapore all the way to 25 percent or more in such countries as Jamaica, and these rates are not even available from Ethiopia and Uganda. Thus, most LDCs experience far more unemployment than industrialized nations.[10] This issue represents a continuing critical problem for most LDCs, which look to MNEs as one source of additional jobs.

The main policy tool utilized by LDCs to push MNEs to hire as many locals as possible is the local labor requirement, under which limits are set on the use of expatriate staff. Typically, labor is required to be all local and management is required to be 90 to 95 percent local, depending on the country. Also typically, the MNEs have no trouble achieving these targets because they seldom transfer production workers overseas and because the high cost of using expatriates makes hiring local managers very desirable. The use of expatriate managers was a serious point of contention in the 1960s and 70s, when MNEs used far more of them, but most MNEs now have enough local managers in most countries to avoid conflict on this score.

A criticism of MNE employment practices in LDCs is that they are too capital intensive in countries where the abundant supply of labor calls for more labor-intensive production. This issue was discussed in Chapter 10 and will not be treated again here. In the present context, we are concerned with the fact that LDC governments are interested in stimulating MNEs to utilize more labor-intensive production and other activities. No specific policies to carry out this task are in wide use, probably because no one has been able to decide what **appropriate technology** really is. (For instance, more labor-intensive technology and production often leads to more costly products, which are not competitive in international markets.)

The Concerns of the Developed Countries The previous categories covered only problems peculiar to LDCs. In addition, the less developed countries, like the industrialized countries are concerned with their balances of payments, the distribution of the costs and benefits of MNE activities, and tax issues. Rather than repeat what has already appeared in Chapter 21, this section concludes with the reminder that the problems presented there also concern the LDCs.

Table 22-6 reviews the categories of problems specific to LDCs by presenting a selected listing of policies in 11 LDCs.

Broad Development Policies and Their Implications for MNEs

Solutions to the specific problems presented above are often offered in broad, macroeconomic treatments of the development process that follow Keynesian, Marxist, monetarist, or other models. The Keynesian view, for example, calls for government spending to stimulate production and national income and for government policies that encourage exports and reduce imports. The Marxist view, on the other hand, calls for government control over the entire economy and for participation by foreign firms only as suppliers of products or services that the country cannot obtain elsewhere. (The Marxist view underlies the policies presented in Chapter 23 concerning communist countries.) The monetarist view focuses on the use of monetary policy as the key tool in shaping economic development. This view is espoused by many University of Chicago economists, whose policies have been a key basis for the development of Chile since 1973.[11] Other broad development perspectives have also been followed.

But even such perspectives change with changes in a country's economic

Table 22-6 **Selected Policies in 11 LDCs**

Country	Ownership Rules	Financial Controls	Technology Controls	Local Content Requirement	FDI Incentives
	Policy				
Brazil	None, but government pressure for local majority	Foreign exchange controls; high tax on remittances	Technology contracts valid for five years	Encouraged; incentives	For FDI in specified regions
Chile	None	Foreign exchange controls	None	None	Few; for mining, oil
Egypt	No legal limits; few 100% foreign firms exist	Foreign exchange controls; remittance limits	Tight controls	None, but encouraged	None
India	40% for most firms	None	Close scrutiny; hard to obtain licenses	Maximum use encouraged	Numerous and varied
Indonesia	Foreign firms must fade out to 49% in 10 years	None	Very few	None	None
Israel	None	None	No approval necessary	None	Major incentives for FDI in selected sectors
Korea	Foreign ownership restricted but not prohibited	None	Liberal licensing rules; technological imports encouraged	Generally quite high	Wide range
Mexico	Limited to 49% foreign	Foreign exchange controls; remittance limits	Must be registered	Fairly high and enforced	For export-oriented ventures
Nigeria	40–60% foreign maximum, depending on industry	Foreign exchange controls; remittance limits	Approval required	Tax incentives	For pioneer industries and selected regions
South Africa	None	Foreign exchange controls	Licenses easily obtained	None	Area incentives
Venezuela	Fade-out to 49% foreign in 15 years	Foreign exchange controls; remittance limits	No royalties permitted	In autos, some other industries	Few

Source: Business International Corporation, *Investing, Licensing, and Trading Conditions* (New York: Business International Corporation, current edition).

situation. Chile, for example, shifted from fairly Keynesian policies in the 1960s, to Marxist policies under the Allende government, to monetarist policies under the subsequent military government.

In the international sectors of their economies, LDCs have pursued two broad policies in the post-World War II period: import-substituting growth and export-led growth. **Import substitution** calls for policies subsidizing the local production of goods that are being imported and for limiting the importation of products that have been successfully introduced into local production. In the extreme, import substitution could lead to complete self-sufficiency, though the cost of producing some products locally (for example, mainframe computers, airplanes, and nuclear power plants) would be so high that the country would be better off if it continued to import them. The intent of import substitution is to alter a country's comparative advantages by subsidizing the start-up of industries that could in time become cost effective—that is, less expensive than if their products were imported. Thus, available foreign exchange could be used to import products that could not be produced locally without great cost, and the country would be better off.

Export promotion calls for subsidizing the production and export of whatever products can be made locally and sold competitively in international markets. This development strategy has the same general goal as import substitution, namely the creation of economically viable local industries that add income and employment to the country. Export promotion is a more outward-looking strategy, however, because it focuses on the production of exportable goods whose foreign exchange earnings can be used for further imports.

Foreign MNEs should be aware of the policy orientation of the host government as regards these two views of international business. The import-substituting country will most likely use high tariffs and other import barriers as a part of its international business policy. On the other hand, the export-promoting country will typically subsidize production and sale of exports, without limiting (to the same degree) imports that the firm may want to bring in. Over at least the past few decades, export-promoting countries have allowed foreign firms more opportunities to participate in the local economy, whereas import-substituting countries have reserved much more of the economy to local firms and have placed much more stringent limits on the activities of foreign MNEs.

Entry and Operating Strategies for MNEs

Entry Strategies

The possible **entry strategies** for doing business in LDCs do not differ from those for entering industrialized countries, as they were presented previously. This section looks at some strategic considerations that may be important due to the relative political and economic instability of LDCs in comparison with industrialized countries. Because a change in government or any number of other factors can change the "rules of the game" rapidly and significantly, the MNE manager should consider measures to protect against risk at every stage of a project in an LDC. Government policies enacted to improve the balance of payments could cut off exports from some foreign affiliate of the MNE to its local LDC affiliate, which might affect the MNE drastically by eliminating its perhaps substantial imports. Foreign direct investment is, of course, subject to many more possibilities of adverse policy or other environmental changes, ranging from nationalization to a national depression caused by a worldwide decline in the prices of primary goods. Before entering into business in a less developed country, the MNE manager needs to plan for such potential problems.

The Obsolescing Bargain

Before deciding what protection plan for the business should be carried out in an LDC, the MNE manager should consider the firm's bargaining position relative to that of the host government. The firm is in a much different position *before* investing or setting up its other business activity in that country than afterward, when assets have been deployed and are committed to a particular use. For example, before setting up an oil refinery, an oil company possesses several desirable characteristics from the viewpoint of the host government. The company will bring in money, machinery, people who can train local workers and managers, access to foreign oil customers, and so on. With such a favorable set of components, the FDI project generally looks very desirable to a host government, and it can often be used to obtain very favorable tax treatment and other incentives for the MNE. Once the refinery is in place, however, the bargaining advantage shifts somewhat to the host government. Now the company has physical assets present in the country and links to its other operations elsewhere. The government can now raise taxes and impose other costs on the company, which is to some extent captive in the country. The MNE's bargaining power has faded away to some degree, or obsolesced. The **obsolescing bargain** is the "contract" between company and government that includes the rules under which the affiliate operates; very often those rules become much less favorable to the company once it has committed its assets and the government has gained a stronger position.

Operating Strategies

Once the firm has chosen an entry strategy and protected itself as well as it can against the problem of the obsolescing bargain, it must adopt an **operating strategy.** One consideration will continue to be the maintenance of a strong bargaining position relative to the host government. This can be accomplished through maximizing the use of the firm's competitive advantages, such as proprietary technology and its international information and distribution networks and other links to affiliates in other countries. The more ties the firm maintains to inputs and markets in other countries, the less the host country in question can constrain the MNE without facing a reduction in the benefits it obtains from the MNE's local operations. A clear example is that of offshore assembly. An MNE's local television assembly plant in Taiwan is probably fairly safe from the vagaries of government policy shifts, since any adverse regulation could cause the firm to shift its assembly to Singapore, South Korea, or Hong Kong, and in addition the main production inputs usually come from the home country and the market to be served is usually a developed country or countries. Each of these aspects of the business of offshore assembly gives the firm bargaining strength relative to that of the host government even after the plant has been established.

As in developed countries, the firm's operating strategies in LDCs may focus on cost minimization, product differentiation, or market segmentation. In the less developed countries, there is often a much greater possibility of market segmentation through government protection. That is, in LDCs, where governments play a much larger role in operation of the economy, firms may gain protected market positions by obtaining government contracts or by receiving government protection against competitors in exchange for setting up a local affiliate. Thus, although competition still plays a large role in LDC business, government policies can create profitable market niches for firms that plan carefully and negotiate skillfully for them.

In dealing with the particular risks inherent in LDC operations, the firm has many options. As with other risks, the firm may eliminate or reduce these risks by avoiding LDCs, by insuring the project with some public or private insurer, or by hedging the exposed assets with local liabilities. In addition, the firm can diversify its international activities into other countries so that a particular LDC does not affect too much of its total operations.

The hedging strategies for both political and exchange risks have been discussed previously. The governments of many industrialized countries offer commercial and political risk insurance to exporters and direct investors doing business with LDCs. In addition to the common financial hedges to offset exposed local-currency assets, such as local borrowing, MNEs have employed a variety of other strategies for dealing with this risk. When assets must be kept in the local currency, firms have generally tried to place investments in assets that tend to keep pace with local inflation, such as real estate, government-backed securities with values tied to inflation or the U.S. dollar, and the local operation itself.

Dealing with LDC Governments

The government is a much more important participant in the economies of most LDCs than in the economies of industrialized countries. For that reason alone, MNE managers in LDCs need to be extremely sensitive to the issue of government/business relations. In addition, because most MNEs are headquartered outside LDCs, they are viewed as "foreign" in the LDCs where they do business. Thus, relations with the government (and the public) generally play a much more important role in LDC business than in IC business. **Foreignness** may be the most important issue in dealing with LDC host governments.

Other central issues that create tensions in the relations between MNEs and LDC host governments include:

- MNE financial policies, especially remittances of earnings that contribute to capital outflow.
- MNE employment practices that result in fewer host country employees than the government would like and MNE use of technology that is more capital intensive than the government would like.
- The size of MNEs relative to the economic size of host countries, which gives MNEs substantial economic power.
- The multinationality of MNEs, which enables the home country parent to make decisions on activities in the host country and to transfer people, money, and other resources into and out of the host country, decisions that the government of the host country is unable to control.

To succeed in dealing with LDC governments, MNE managers need to understand both sides of these issues and to take steps that reduce the tensions they cause.

Company *financial policies* often focus on minimizing company assets in LDCs with rapidly devaluing currencies and unstable economic conditions. Host governments, of course, do not want to see funds outflows of this type, which exacerbate the capital flight problem, so they regularly look for ways to constrain firms from transferring their earnings abroad. The MNE manager needs to find ways either to reduce outflows or to generate funds inflows (for example, through exports) that will reduce BOP pressure on the host government. This is often a very difficult task for the affiliate manager, since the MNE home office would prefer to see as much of earnings as possible remitted from high-risk, rapid-devaluation countries. It might be argued that the MNE would be best off if it reinvested its earnings in the host country as wisely as possible and remitted some funds on a regular basis. Local asset values can often be maintained against devaluation, and by not contributing to capital flight, the MNE would create goodwill for its continuing activities in that country. This is by no means an ultimate solution for the MNE, but it may enable the firm to operate in an LDC on a continuing basis, with better government relations than it would have otherwise.

The *employment practices* of MNEs tend to be criticized mainly because of the high unemployment in LDCs and the high visibility of MNEs. In fact, several studies show that MNEs tend to offer better compensation and training to their LDC employees than do local firms.[12] The "appropriateness" of the technology used in the LDC operations of MNEs can always be debated, but if that technology enables the firm to operate efficiently and competitively, then it can be viewed as contributing to the country's ability to maximize use of its available resources. In many cases, MNEs perhaps need to make public the number of people they employ, so that host governments and pressure groups will be forced to recognize their contributions on this score.

The *economic power* possessed by MNEs can appear quite overwhelming to an outside observer. The annual sales of many firms are larger than the annual GDPs of many countries. The amounts that firms spend to construct facilities surpass the investment capabilities of many governments. What must be recalled is that each government has the power to set the rules of the game for business in its jurisdiction. So if any firm exercises economic power in some fashion unacceptable to the host government, that government can easily intervene to constrain the firm. Nonetheless, firms do possess bargaining strengths relative to host governments, and a government that wants to keep a firm operating locally cannot raise restrictions indefinitely. The result is a recurring set of negotiations and bargaining between the two sides over how the benefits and costs of the MNEs' activities should be distributed between them.

Multinationality is the final focal point of tensions between MNEs and LDC governments. A firm with access to funds, people, markets, inputs, and so on, outside the host government's jurisdiction, has a clear advantage over that government. This advantage cannot be completely negated, though international codes of MNE conduct creating a multinational government policy structure toward MNEs have been debated (and some have been enacted). At present, however, MNEs still occupy a position of strength on the basis of their multinationality, since the codes of conduct have not been able to limit their practices very much.[13]

Conclusions

Much more attention to government/business relations is required in LDCs than in industrialized nations. A wealth of government-owned companies, strict limitations on company activities, and frequent rule changes make the path of the MNE difficult in LDCs. Given the size of the government sector in most LDCs and the active roles that most LDC governments play in business, MNE managers need to pay close attention to these governments both as regulators and as customers.

At present, international business in LDCs accounts for less than a third of total international business. Since LDCs have most of the world's population and a large portion of its natural resources, they constitute valuable target markets and sources of production inputs. Thus, despite the difficulties of underdeveloped economic infrastructures and often changing regulations, LDCs present many opportunities to MNEs.

The MNE manager can gain important insights into the treatment that the MNE is likely to receive in a particular LDC by studying that country's process of economic development. An LDC that follows the path of import-substituting growth is likely to impose trade barriers and protect local industry against foreign competition. An LDC that uses an export-promotion strategy is likely to foster a much more open business environment. These two broad approaches to development give only a macro perspective on the LDC. The examination of other aspects of economic development theory and policy as they apply to the LDC may offer additional useful insights into the environment there.

MNE managers in LDCs will always face the problem of foreignness. No matter how responsive to host government rules and preferences the MNE may be, it still represents foreign owners and decision makers. The MNE manager must be aware of the tension that this foreignness may engender and must be prepared to minimize it when possible.

Regardless of the strategy that it adopts to do business in a less developed country, the MNE needs to consider methods of protection against political risk, exchange risk, and commercial risk. Those methods, which have been discussed in other chapters, should form a part of the total strategy for ongoing business in an LDC. Since the firm's ability to gain an advantage in dealing with the host government declines once it has committed real resources in the host country (and thus faces the problem of the obsolescing bargain), it requires both entry and operating strategies for risk protection.

Questions

1. Define "less developed country." Does Nigeria fit into your definition? Does Singapore? How about Portugal? Kuwait? What is an appropriate measure of economic development?
2. Describe the development strategies called export promotion and import substitution. Has either of these strategies demonstrated better results than the other in the past half-century? Explain.
3. Would it be possible to use the development strategy of Hong Kong in another country, such as Costa Rica? Why or why not?
4. Present a strategy that AT&T or L. M. Ericsson could use to compete in the Indian market for telecommunications. Use information from the chapter about rules on foreign business in India.
5. What risks does an MNE encounter if it agrees to accept a local partner and enter an LDC market with a joint-venture manufacturing plant? Assume that the company produces chemicals. How can the MNE deal with these risks?
6. Name four main concerns of LDC governments in their dealings with foreign multinational firms. What can the firms do to minimize tensions with the host government with regard to each of these concerns?
7. Explain how the "obsolescing bargain" operated in the case of any multinational oil company that was nationalized by a host government. What can a company do once nationalization has occurred?
8. Again considering the obsolescing bargain, what can a company do to

maintain its bargaining power even after it has committed resources to a plant or other facility in an LDC host country?

9. Create a market entry strategy for a small textile manufacturing company from a developed country that wants to enter the Indonesian or Taiwanese market for synthetic fabrics. Make necessary (reasonable) assumptions, so that your answer covers the organizational form of the venture, the channel of distribution, the structure of decision making in the firm, financial concerns, and any other issues that you consider important.
10. Explain how offshore assembly could be a viable strategy for a U.S.-based machinery manufacturer that wishes to enter the Jamaican market.

References

Cline, William. *International Debt and the Stability of the World Economy.* Washington, D.C.: Institute for International Economics, 1983.

Grosse, Robert. *The Multinational Enterprise in Latin America.* London: Croom Helm, 1988.

Hagen, Everett. *The Economics of Development.* 3rd ed. Homewood, Ill.: Richard D. Irwin, 1980.

Hofheinz, Roy, and Kent Calder. *The Eastasia Edge.* New York: Basic Books, 1984.

Kobrin, Steven. *Managing Political Risk Assessment.* Berkeley: University of California Press, 1982.

World Bank. *World Development Report, 1986.* Washington, D.C.: World Bank, 1986.

Endnotes

1. Roy Hofheinz and Kent Calder, *The Eastasia Edge.* (New York: Basic Books, 1984).
2. U.S. Department of Commerce, *Survey of Current Business,* August 1971 and August 1984.
3. See, for example, Everett Hagen, *The Economics of Development,* 3rd ed. (Homewood, Ill.: Richard D. Irwin, 1980), chap. 15; and I. M. D. Little, *Economic Development* (New York: Basic Books, 1982), chap. 6.
4. See Steven Kobrin, *Managing Political Risk Assessment* (Berkeley: University of California Press, 1982), concerning empirical measures of political instability leading to loss outcomes for firms.
5. See ibid. concerning expropriations in the international oil industry.
6. For example, see David Shirreff, "Arab Finance: Why the Black Market Thrives," *Euromoney,* May 1984; and Rudiger Dornbusch et al., "The Black Market for Dollars in Brazil," *Quarterly Journal of Economics,* February 1983.

7. Capital flight is considered to be a central cause of the continuing Latin American debt crisis. See, for example, William Cline, *International Debt and the Stability of the World Economy* (Washington, D.C.: Institute for International Economics, 1983).
8. Business International Corporation, *Investing, Licensing, and Trading Conditions* (New York: Business International Corporation, January 1985), Brazil section, p. 7.
9. Business International Corporation, *Investing, Licensing, and Trading Conditions* (New York: Business International Corporation, December 1984), Colombia section, p. 29. Only some specific products are subject to this countertrade requirement, although the list has been expanding since its initiation in 1984.
10. Unemployment rates are taken from International Labour Office, *Yearbook of Labor Statistics* (Geneva: ILO, 1983).
11. See, for example, Norman Gall, "How the Chicago Boys Fought 1000% Inflation," *Forbes,* March 31, 1980.
12. See, for example, Jerry Ingles and Loretta Fairchild, "Evaluating the Impact of Foreign Investment," *Latin American Research Review* (1978); and Robert Grosse, "The Economic Impact of Foreign Direct Investment: A Case Study of Venezuela," in Grosse (1988).
13. See Robert Grosse, "Codes of Conduct for Multinational Enterprises," *Journal of World Trade Law* (Sept/Oct 1982).

Case
Advanced Chemicals in Peru

One day in the summer of 1984, Robert London, general manager for Advanced Chemicals Corporation's Latin American Division, was debating his future at the company. The company had been growing rapidly and profitably in Latin America when he had accepted the offer to head the regional staff. Over the past three years, however, virtually every country in the region had suffered severe recessionary problems and a need to restrict the transfer of dollars overseas. This situation had made it impossible for London to demonstrate an aggressive, creative management style. His main function for most of the three years had been to serve as Advanced Chemicals' senior representative to each government in the region, pleading for the right to repatriate funds and to carry on his business without excessive new restrictions. Only in the past few months had any real hope appeared for an end to the prevailing crisis conditions.

Of the countries under London's control, Venezuela and Argentina were the largest markets, followed by Colombia and Peru. (Advanced Chemicals used a regional X product matrix for its international organization structure. Brazil and Mexico were each treated as a separate region, reporting directly to the home office.) At this time, the home office was negotiating a large joint-venture petrochemical plant with PDVSA in Venezuela, so London did not consider it opportune to pursue that market separately in his planning. The economic and political conditions in Argentina presented such a huge risk to major investment that he felt obliged not to spend time planning any large-scale venture there. In fact, London felt that of all the countries under his supervision, Peru probably offered the best combination of market potential and currently small Advanced Chemicals commitment, so that he could make a mark by creating a solid plan for business in that country.

Advanced Chemicals had at one time owned an agricultural chemicals plant in Lima and a paint plant in Trujillo. Neither of these investments had been very large, and both had been sold in the early 1970s, during the height of anti-American fervor in Peru and Chile. In 1963 Advanced Chemicals had established a pharmaceuticals formulating plant as a 50-50 joint venture with a Peruvian firm, and this operation had survived both the political problems of the early 70s and the debt crisis of the early 80s. According to the most recent internal records of Advanced Chemicals, the Peruvian venture had contributed $1.5 million to annual income and represented assets of about $4.2 million. For a $9 billion company, this operation was a drop in the bucket.

Advanced Chemicals periodically received requests from Peruvian companies to form joint ventures with them for producing products ranging from

This case was written by Professor Robert Grosse for use in class discussion, 1984.

cosmetics to polyethylene. In London's thinking, the goal of a country strategy should be to focus on a small number of products with good local market potential and a good fit in the company's global product plan. With this in mind, he began to put together a plan for Peru.

About the Company

In 1983, Advanced Chemicals was the third largest U.S. chemical company and the fifth largest chemical company in the world. Its annual sales were just over $9 billion, and its global assets were valued at about $15 billion. It owned 74 foreign subsidiaries in 26 countries, and it held a minority interest in 8 more foreign ventures. (Figures 1 and 2 present 1983 income statement and balance sheet data for Advanced Chemicals.) Latin American sales accounted for about 5 percent of the sales total, and assets in Latin America constituted about 3 percent of Advanced Chemicals' assets worldwide.

Advanced Chemicals' first Latin American business was a polyethylene plant built near Mexico City in 1951. This plant supplied a wide variety of plastic products to Mexico and other Latin American countries. The current value of the plant was over $100 million. In 1953, Advanced Chemicals undertook its first direct investment in Brazil, a plant to manufacture agricultural chemicals that it built near São Paulo. Within five years, it built two

Figure 1

ADVANCED CHEMICALS
Consolidated Income Statement, 1983
(in $ millions)

Net sales		$9,257		
Area sales:			Industry segment sales:	
United States	$4,528		Industrial chemicals	$4,387
Europe	3,016		Plastics	1,764
Canada	583		Specialty chemicals	1,351
Latin America	467		Agricultural chemicals	1,280
Brazil	214		Industrial equipment	475
All other	449			
Cost of goods sold		7,698		
Selling and administrative costs		911		
Operating income		648		
Interest income		108		
Exchange gains (losses)		36		
Net income before taxes		792		
Taxes due		264		
Net income after taxes		528		
Earnings per common share		1.72		

additional plants in Belo Horizonte, to produce plastic resins and specialty chemicals. After a period of slow growth in these subsidiaries, business boomed in the mid-1960s. Between 1962 and 1971, Advanced Chemicals established sales offices in 10 more Latin American countries and built new plants in Argentina, Venezuela, and Chile. Except for plastics and agricultural chemicals, the firm exported from the United States virtually all of the products that it sold in Latin America. At this time, it had the second largest sales volume of any multinational chemicals company in that region.

Advanced Chemicals was organized on the basis of five product divisions and six regional divisions, as shown in the organization chart in Figure 3. Each of the divisions was run as a profit center, with inconsistencies negotiated away at the home office in Chicago. Marketing responsibility for all products in the Latin American region was assigned to the division headquarters (as with other regions), whereas production of the five main product lines was determined primarily at each of the product division headquarters. While home office negotiations for corporate resources were highly competitive among divisions, the Latin American group had always been in a weak position because of its relative insignificance in the company's total business.

Figure 2

ADVANCED CHEMICALS
Consolidated Balance Sheet
December 31, 1983
(in $ millions)

Assets	
Cash	$ 215
Marketable securities	508
Accounts/notes receivable	3,080
Inventories	3,455
Plant and equipment	7,537
Deferred charges	288
Total assets	$15,083
Liabilities	
Notes payable	$ 957
Accounts payable	1,975
Taxes due	528
Long-term debt	3,909
Deferred taxes	895
Stockholders' equity	6,819
Total liabilities	$15,083

Figure 3 **Organization of Advanced Chemicals**

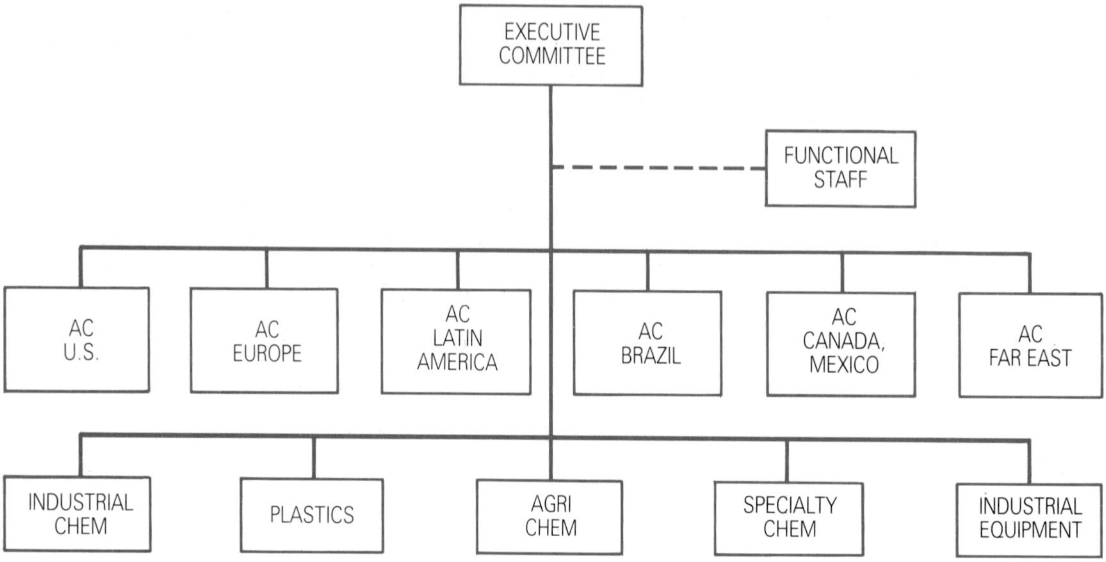

Nonetheless, success in that division had historically meant a step into the corporate executive committee for the person in charge.

The company had always maintained a large team of research and product development scientists, aiming primarily to generate new products for traditional industrial customers in the automotive, construction, agriculture, and health care industries. About 5.3 percent of its annual sales were devoted to the R&D budget worldwide. Products developed in the previous 10 years had generated over 80 percent of Advanced Chemicals' profits during its 60-year history. On the whole, the products that Advanced Chemicals sold in Latin America had already been sold successfully in the United States for several years and were fairly mature in the product life cycle.

Marketing in the Latin American region was budgeted at the regional office level, but advertising and other local marketing activities were initially established by each national subsidiary. In countries with no affiliates, marketing policy was set at the regional office. The marketing effort had traditionally emphasized product quality and availability, though price had become a critical factor in the past five years. Marketing managers at the regional office spent their time mainly in offering advice to affiliate managers and in monitoring the sales of affiliates and distributors in the region. Except for the products produced locally and agricultural chemicals, there was no coordinated effort to promote other company products in the region.

About Peru

The Peruvian market for agricultural chemicals was dominated by foreign competitors, selling mainly fertilizers and pesticides. These products were usually not recent innovations, but rather products that had been used successfully in other countries for several years. Market share was highest for the two foreign firms that produced locally, though each of the eight main competitors had at least a 20 percent market share for one or more products.

The Peruvian market for plastics was also dominated by foreign multinational firms, though Petroperu (the state-owned oil company) was seeking to integrate downstream into this business. Again, the technology used in the products of interest were not new, and the main barriers to entry were the need for assured supply of feedstock, a distribution network for output, and basic capital costs.

Market segments existed for sales of other Advanced Chemicals products, but none of these segments appeared to be large enough to justify the planning and investment required for entry.

The following Appendix, an article from *Business Latin America*, provides some current information about the Peruvian economy and business conditions in general.

Case Appendix 22–1
Business Outlook Peru[1]

Peru will be fighting its way out of a deep economic coma in 1984. Worse yet, it will try to mix a bitter dose of economy-stabilizing medicine with politicking for the presidential elections scheduled for 1985. Moreover, the global recovery will not boost Peruvian metals and minerals export prices until late in the year.

Also worrisome is the abrogation of a three-year Extended Fund Facility (EFF) with the IMF, which has stalled rescheduling negotiations with creditor banks for debt due in 1984 and frozen undisbursed monies from 1983 renegotiations. Even though the country will sign a one-year Fund standby agreement to replace the lost EFF, Peru will have a tough time arranging financing for a projected current-account deficit of close to $400 million.

Political situation. There is a 50/50 chance that the military will mount a preemptive coup if increased terrorism and broadened social upheaval further paralyze the government of Fernando Belaunde Terry. Heated campaign rhetoric pointing an accusing finger at the economic problems of the last few years could spark violent protest sufficient to goad the military into action.

Political and economic terrorism, emanating from the anarchic Sendero Luminoso, has spread into urban areas after being routed from the southern altiplano by a military sweep. Sendero will step up attacks on business operations, along with continued acts against utilities and military and police stations. MNC executives might be threatened by a rise in kidnapping. The undisciplined nature of recent military counterinsurgency efforts is a card in Sendero's favor; the armed forces risk spawning a broad-based rural guerrilla front should the present level of overkill in rural areas continue.

Barring a coup, politics will be heated and often bitter during the next year, as the contenders vie for power. The opposition center-left Alianza Popular Revolucionaria Americana (APRA) won a stunning victory in November's municipal elections, boosting the popularity of its leader, the youthful Alan Garcia, and giving the party a chance to win and take office for the first time in its history. While many think an APRA victory is assured, the most important question surrounds the party's choice of a coalition partner in Congress. The military would balk at a left-leaning bloc.

Belaunde's Accion Popular (AP) is reeling from its poor showing in last November's poll. In addition, internecine quarrels are debilitating the party and could leave it lifeless if the party does not find a unifying head for 1985.

The United Left (IU) placed Alfonso Barrantes as the Marxist mayor of Lima (where 42% of voters reside) and will run neck and neck with APRA through 1984. It is unlikely, though, that IU will figure into a coalition; the party will, however, be strong enough in Congress to influence policy. The other major party, the conservative Partido Popular Cristiano (PPC), will leave its partnership with AP in July to improve its chances for power.

Gross domestic product may show marginal growth but will be slow to recover from 1983's dramatic 13% decline. Growth will have to come from improved export prices, an upturn in the construction industry and agricultural production—socked by flood and drought last year. Some austerity in public spending will also cool recovery.

Industrial production will be flat—but a marked improvement on the 15% drop in output and market shakeout last year. Manufacturers will still cringe at the high cost of credit, but they will benefit from a rise in private consumption. Industry will finally get protection from cheap imports, which have hounded the sector since open competition began in 1981.

Textile manufacturers will increase production this year, benefiting from a countertrade deal with the USSR to cover arms imports. In addition, the sector will get a shot in the arm via higher levies on competing imports. However, a shortage of raw materials due to disease afflicting the cotton crop last year will mean higher imports; the resulting rise in costs could kill recovery.

The *chemical* industry will count on growth in agriculture to pull out of last year's doldrums. Those firms that can export will do well in 1984. *Pharmaceuticals* manufacturers will face more competition from generic imports as the government seeks to hold down costs of medicine subsidies. *Consumer goods* will benefit from a pickup in private consumption.

The *construction* industry, hammered last year by cutbacks in government contracts and foreign competition in ancillary industries, will rebuild thanks to protectionism and a rise in government-funded infrastructure and housing projects.

The *automotive* sector will no longer face unlimited competition from cheap imports. Local-content rules come on stream in 1984, and tariff hikes for finished imports will make locally produced cars more cost-competitive; nonetheless, sales will fall a further 20% unless purchasing power makes a dramatic comeback. Total 1983 sales were about 22,000 units (46% locally assembled), down 50% over end-1982.

Mineral production will remain steady—export volume rose an estimated 32% in 1983—but prices are the big question mark. Basic metals have not yet benefited from the global recovery. Shaky prices also mean a dearth of new investment and the shutdown of some government projects.

The 1984 government-spending program exonerates mining companies from a 5-10% export levy when prices fall below certain levels. Also, all export tax payments are credited against income tax.

Copper output will be up some 10% in 1984, after a 4% drop last year due to stagnant prices. Last year's output was 348,000 MT. *Silver*, on the other hand, could turn in a shining performance, with volume expected to increase 6% over last year, to 1.64 million fine kg, as prices rise steadily.

Iron ore output—3.5 million MT in 1983 (off some 7% from 1982)—will continue to drop this year owing to poor quality and lethargic markets. *Lead* production was up some 7% in 1983 and could rise by a similar amount this year—if prices go up. *Zinc* forecasts show a 5% price increase in 1984.

Petroleum output will be up some 4% this year. Flood-related disruptions knocked production down 11% to 174,000 bpd in 1983. Modest exports—around 30% of the total—are expected, maintained by a dampening local demand through dollar-pegged pump prices.

New investment prospects are getting tough competition from neighboring Ecuador, and Petroperu—the state oil company—will be pressing hard to discover new reserves. Proven reserve levels dropped to nearly 700 million bbl at end-1983, suggesting a need to import oil in the medium term.

Slightly over $200 million in new exploration investment is expected in 1984. Of that, Occidental Petroleum will invest around $100 million in jungle blocks; the firm will also upgrade existing wells and try to maintain current output at its old sites. Serpetro, Petroperu's technical subsidiary, may enter a $27 million joint venture with Hispanoil for seismic and drilling work. Belco plans to spend some $50 million on 32 new wildcats in 1984.

Agricultural production should rise 3% after last year's disastrous El Nino-induced weather wiped out most production for local consumption. The sector gets more emphasis and special credit facilities to upgrade existing enterprises in this year's budget. *Sugar* output will rise about 11% to around 500,000 MT, provided the weather holds, but an additional 16% will be imported to meet local demand. A high volume of other foodstuffs—rice, potatoes and consumable oils—will be imported.

The debt-laden *fishing* sector, once a major export earner, will be retooled away from fishmeal and into canning for local consumption as a result of severe 1983 losses. The disappearance of pilchard and anchovy resulting from the warm El Nino current wiped out the industry, and most fishing concerns will concentrate on meeting local consumption, with some exports of high-value shellfish products.

Investment. Public investment will be directed mainly at high-priority infrastructure rebuilding and new housing projects, with some upgrading of major hydroelectric and mining projects expected. Some S200 billion (S2,388:$1) in public bonds will be issued. Public investment equaled 7% of GDP last year, and it will be difficult for the government to prevent a widening of the budget deficit in an election year.

Private investment, normally heavily weighted to the petroleum sector, is another big question mark in 1984. Other private outlays will be in the form of reinvestment and will be contingent on perceived political risk and the cost of credit.

Labor costs will rise less than the rate of inflation, as high un- and underemployment—encompassing some 50% of the workforce—make job security a key concern. But the union movement will be highly politicized as workers flex their electoral power for the elections; union membership is expected to grow during the coming year. Labor will strike over the loss of purchasing power, as well as for political reasons. The APRA-affiliated CTP can be expected to do the party's bidding; rumors are rife that terrorists are infiltrating the communist labor confederation, CGTP. No changes are expected in the Labor Code or strike regulation law in this election year.

Prices will rise around 110% this year after a record 125% COL increase in 1983. Budget deficits in the range of 7-10% of GDP—mainly overruns in the bloated, inefficient state-company sector—were the main contributors, although the high cost of credit, currency devaluation, higher import costs, a strong dollar and gradual elimination of basic foodstuffs subsidies all fuel Peru's 70% structural inflation.

Credit availability will tighten and the effective cost of credit will increase—through up-front fees and daily interest charges. Dollar credit—now over 40% of the system's total—will remain expensive at about one to two percentage points above LIBOR. Dollar loans will get hit with an additional 0.25% levy on the total.

Imports and exports. Imports will drop another 6%—after a 23% fall in 1983—to around $2.5 billion, a response to higher costs and a move toward protectionism. Exports should rise more than 6% to $3.14 billion—after a 3.5% drop in 1983—as prices of metals and minerals begin to climb; full recovery in nontraditionals is still a ways off; oil exports remain stagnant. Peru's trade balance will be some $650 million in the black—on the heels of last year's $300 million surplus.

Exchange rate. The preannounced three-month exchange rate will be abandoned and minis reinstituted at or slightly above monthly inflation—with a possible maxidevaluation at the end of the first quarter. The sol fell nearly 130% last year, to S2,275:$1 at year-end, and is expected to drop to S4,800-5,000:$1 by end-1984.

Peru's *balance of payments* will continue to suffer from overborrowing by state companies and the high cost of credit. The country's loss of the IMF's EFF and its subsequent replacement with a one-year standby are making creditors edgy and reluctant to provide new loans. Foreign banks will lay out self-liquidating trade credit, but access to new monies needed for 1984—about $400 million—is jeopardized by uncertainty regarding the country's financial plans.

The current-account deficit could be as low as $400 million or as high as $1 billion in 1984, depending on whether new loans are forthcoming, undisbursed monies are released and the trade surplus increases by a healthy amount. It is highly likely, however, that a drawdown on reserves—$1 billion at end-1983—will be necessary in 1984.

Endnote

1. Business International Corporation, *Business Latin America* (New York: Business International Corporation, February 1984) pp. 44-46.

23

COMMUNIST COUNTRIES

This chapter examines business conditions and opportunities for international firms that seek to do business in or with communist countries. The communist countries include broadly those of the Soviet bloc plus China. The key aspects of these countries for international business managers are presented and discussed. Most important, the role of private business in such countries is considered. Since many forms of international business are restricted or disallowed in communist countries, emphasis is placed on those activities that are accessible to foreign firms. Methods for dealing with host country governments, which generally form the market as well as the regulatory environment, are presented. Finally, a view of East-West business from the perspective of the home country (Western) government is offered. The main goals of the chapter are to:

1. Explain the characteristics of communist countries that are important for international business managers.

2. Show what forms of international business are common and appropriate in such countries.

3. Consider entry and operating strategies for Western firms in this government-controlled environment.

4. Present the perspective of home country governments, so that the international firm's manager will see the range of economic and political issues raised by East-West business.

Introduction

This chapter discusses the issue of doing business with **communist countries,** or centrally planned economies. We use the term *communist countries,* rather than the term *centrally planned economies,* for two reasons. First, most countries today employ some degree of economic planning at the national level and many countries operate state-owned companies—so central planning is not confined to communist countries. Second, the serious ideological differences between communist and noncommunist countries should not be glossed over in discussions of international business. The informed international business person should be aware of the political and economic goals of both home and host countries in this arena. Very real national security risks are involved in doing business with countries that are potential enemies, and in East-West transactions these risks should be considered along with specific business goals.

This chapter is structured similarly to the chapters on industrialized and less developed countries. The first section defines the countries of interest and typical forms of international business that occur there. The second section notes key characteristics of communist countries that affect the MNE. The third section discusses government policies toward foreign MNEs. The fourth section sketches some entry and operating strategies for MNEs in communist nations. A special section covers the perspective of the MNE's home country, discussing such issues as national security and economic risk. Finally, some conclusions are offered.

Definition of Communist Countries

The nations of concern in this chapter are those constituting the **Eastern bloc** or the **second world**—that is, the USSR-dominated countries of the Council for Mutual Economic Assistance (CMEA, or Comecon) and the People's Republic of China.[1] These countries lie outside the realm of market economies, and thus they are often ignored by firms from the industrialized nations and the third world.[2] Because the "rules of the game" are very different in these communist countries, businesspeople from the rest of the world generally have great difficulty in doing business with them. Responsible managers should understand the issues involved in East-West business, whether or not they have any direct interest in selling to or buying from the Eastern bloc.

Selected countries of the second world are listed in Table 23-1, along with some broad characteristics of their economies. While China alone comprises more than two thirds of the population of the communist countries and indeed almost one fourth of total world population, notice that it accounts for only about 10 percent of the GNP of communist countries. Also notice that the economies of the East European members of this group (all of the countries listed except China) have macroeconomic characteristics sim-

Table 23-1 **Economic Characteristics of the Communist Countries**

	Measure					
Country	GNP, 1985 ($ billions)	GNP per Capita, 1985 ($)	Real Growth, 1985 (%)	Intra-CMEA Specialization	Inflation 1985 (%)	Exports, 1985 ($ billions)
Bulgaria	57.8	6,420	−0.8	Electronic peripherals, agricultural and food processing machinery	3.3	12.8
Czechoslovakia	135.6	8,750	1.7	Machine tools, vehicles, computers	2.2	17.8
German Democratic Republic	174.4	10,440	2.4	Ships, precision instruments, mining equipment, chemicals	0.0	24.0
Hungary	80.1	7,560	−0.9	Drugs, tractors, buses, measuring equipment	8.6	13.5
Poland	240.6	6,470	1.6	Ships, electronic equipment, metal products	16.2	17.8
Rumania	123.7	5,450	1.8	Petroleum processing, forestry	1.0	12.2
Soviet Union	2,062.6	7,400	1.2	Energy resources, chemicals	1.5	87.0
Yugoslavia	129.4	5,600	0.2	n.r.	72.4	10.7
People's Republic of China	354.3	340	12.0	n.r.	11.9	31.3

Sources: U.S. Central Intelligence Agency, *Handbook of Economic Statistics, 1986* (Washington, D.C.: CIA, September 1986).

ilar to those of the West European market economies—that is, they should also be considered industralized countries.

The communist countries are those that assign the ownership of property primarily to the government, (i.e., to communal ownership). They are led by totalitarian governments that allow only one political party to operate freely (i.e., the Communist Party). All of the communist countries except Albania, China, and Yugoslavia are considered part of the Soviet bloc, with varying degrees of political control from Moscow and varying degrees of economic relations with noncommunist countries. Free enterprise is substantially limited in the communist countries, though a small number of widely publicized experiments in private sector business have been allowed in most of them (and particularly in China since the late 1970s). Business operates through government-owned and -managed companies, with decisions on pricing and production levels largely determined by the central planning organs, rather than by consumer demand.[3] However, this broad picture of communist countries fails to give an idea of the real possibilities for noncommunist firms to carry out business with them. For that purpose, some evidence about the East-West international business that has occurred with these countries will be useful.

Main Forms of International Business

Very few examples exist of a communist country allowing foreign firms the opportunity to hold controlling ownership of business ventures within its borders. International business with such countries must be carried out through nonequity methods, such as exports and imports, licensing agreements, management contracts, and turnkey ventures, or through minority joint ventures.[4]

While data are very difficult to obtain about most business activities in communist countries, export and import information is relatively accessible. Table 23-2 presents some of the main characteristics of international trade flows involving communist countries. Most of the imports and exports are shipped between communist countries, but there is also a substantial amount of East-West trade. Much of the imports of communist countries from noncommunist countries consists of manufactured goods, especially high-tech electronics, instruments, chemicals, and the like. Grain shipments from the United States and Canada to Eastern-bloc nations also are an important part of such imports. Much of the exports from communist countries to noncommunist countries consists of raw materials, such as oil and natural gas (from the Soviet Union), and a variety of relatively low-tech, low-cost manufactures.

Table 23-2a **International Trade by Communist Countries, 1983** (in millions of U.S. dollars)

From \ To:	Czechoslovakia	GDR	Hungary	Poland	Rumania	USSR	China	Yugoslavia	United States	EEC
Czechoslovakia	—	n.a.	382	n.a.	331	n.a.	102	595	62	1,517
GDR	n.a.	—	518	n.a.	557	n.a.	170	412	58	1,137
Hungary	436	n.a.	—	342	112	2,758	45	275	177	1,354
Poland	n.a.	n.a.	337	—	383	n.a.	91	257	190	2,001
Rumania	341	508	141	367	—	1,892	362	108	503	1,469
USSR	n.a.	n.a.	2,217	n.a.	n.a.	—	401	2,738	341	15,023
China	90	59	28	164	292	319	—	14	1,713	2,460
Yugoslavia	689	391	281	246	124	3,769	49	—	385	2,877
United States	59	139	110	324	186	288	2,173	572	—	44,311
EEC	1,282	700	1,738	1,842	794	10,660	2,486	4,022	44,232	—

Source: International Monetary Fund, *Direction of Trade* (1984 yearbook).

Table 23-2b **International Trade of Communist Countries by Industry, 1984** (in millions of U.S. dollars)

	USSR	Czechoslovakia	GDR	Hungary	Poland	China
Exports						
Machinery and equipment	11,406	9,801	11,515	4,076	8,220	1,145
Fuels, minerals, metals	54,319	2,385	4,297	2,138	4,507	5,735
Agricultural and forest products	5,078	1,149	2,038	3,439	1,606	6,390
Manufactured consumer goods	1,283	2,698	3,707	2,111	2,090	5,735
Imports						
Machinery and equipment	29,417	6,003	5,701	3,506	4,946	7,620
Fuels, minerals, metals	9,077	7,096	9,121	3,998	6,435	215
Agricultural and forest products	19,090	2,065	3,881	2,070	2,349	4,840
Manufactured consumer goods	8,827	919	1,250	1,216	1,538	1,510

Source: Central Intelligence Agency, *Handbook of Economic Statistics, 1986* (Washington, D.C.: CIA, September 1986).

(In recent years, the exports of chemicals, food, textiles, and wood products from communist countries to Western Europe have become very significant.)

Other important categories of international business include **technology transfer agreements** in the form of licenses, turnkey ventures, and sales of process or product technologies. These are very common between East European countries and West European firms, but less so between U.S. firms and Eastern-bloc purchasers. Examples of these types of agreements are shown in Table 23-3. Generally, the agreements are between communist-bloc purchasers and large, well-established Western (or Japanese) firms. The communist firms or government agencies tend to prefer dealing with sellers whose long-established track records for sales and service inspire confidence that they will remain accessible to meet future needs.

Joint ventures in the Eastern-bloc countries are another category of international business that occurs between communist and noncommunist partners. While full or controlling ownership is generally not permitted to foreign firms in any communist country, partial ownership often is. Few such accords exist with Russian partners, but a wide range of industrial joint ventures exist in China, Hungary, Poland, Rumania, and Yugoslavia. A few examples of these ventures are presented in Table 23-4. Like the technology transfer agreements, these joint ventures tend to involve very large, experienced noncommunist firms. Most of the joint ventures are quite large, demonstrating that the communist governments are interested in attracting into their economies a fairly small number of foreign participants that can generate large amounts of production of known quality.

Table 23-3 **Technology Transfer Agreements between Western Companies and Communist Countries**

Company	Type of Agreement (date)	Country	Product
Aerospatiale (France)	License	Rumania	Assault helicopters
Akai (Japan)	License (1984)	Hungary	Video recorders
Bayer (Germany)	License (1978)	Hungary	Corn syrup and alcohol
Boeing (United States)	License	USSR	Passenger aircraft doors
Coca-Cola (United States)	License (1985)	USSR	Bottle and sell Coke
Combustion Engineering (United States)	License (1985)	Czechoslovakia	Process for upgrading ethylene feedstocks
Eastman Kodak (United States)	License	China	Color film and paper
L. M. Ericsson (Sweden)	License	Yugoslavia	Telephone switching equipment
Levi Strauss (United States)	License (1985)	Hungary	Blue jeans
Montedison (Italy)	License (1985)	GDR	Chemical plant
Occidental Petroleum (United States)	License	Poland	Metal-finishing process
Perkins Engine (United Kingdom)	License	Yugoslavia	Medium diesel engines
Philip Morris (United States)	License	USSR	Cigarettes
Royal-Dutch Shell (United Kingdom/Netherlands)	License	Poland	Insecticides
Shin Etsu (Japan)	License	Hungary	Polyvinyl chloride
Siemens (Germany)	License	Hungary	Recovery of pulverized paint
Singer (United States)	License	Poland	Sewing machines
Swindell Dressler (United States)	Turnkey (1972) venture	USSR	Kama River truck plant construction
Union Carbide (United States)	License (1985)	Yugoslavia	Compact disk record player

Sources: *The Wall Street Journal* (various dates); and Paul Surovell (ed.) *INTERFLO*. Maplewood, N.J. (1985-1986).

Table 23-4 **Joint Ventures between Western Companies and Communist Countries**

Company	Country	Name and Date of Joint Venture	Ownership (West/East)	Product
American Motors (United States)	China	Beijing Jeep	49/51	Production and marketing of Jeeps
Astra (Argentina)	Yugoslavia	Bosnalijek	25/75	Production and marketing of pharmaceuticals
BASF (Germany)	Hungary	1985		Production of polyurethane
Berlin Consult (Germany)	GDR	No name, 1985	n.a.	Incinerator in GDR to burn waste from West Germany
Bowmar Canada (Canada)	Hungary	Hirbow	49/51	Production and marketing of calculators
British Aerospace (United Kingdom)	Rumania			Production of Rombac aircraft and Rolls-Royce engines
Control Data (United States)	Rumania	Romcontrol Data	45/55	Production and marketing of computer peripherals
Daimler-Benz (Germany)	Yugoslavia	FAP-Famos	15/85	Production and marketing of trucks
Dow Chemical (United States)	Yugoslavia	DINA, 1978	49/51	Production and marketing of polyethylene products
Fiat (Italy)	Yugoslavia	Crevena Zastava	11/89	Production and marketing of motor vehicles
General Tire (United States)	Rumania	n.a.	Minority/Majority	Production and marketing of tires
Occidental Petroleum (United States)	China	No name	50/50	Development of coal mine and sale of coal
Société Générale (France)	Hungary	No name, 1985	49/51	Monetary information systems
Volkswagen (Germany)	China	No name	50/50	Production and marketing of cars

Sources: Josef Wilczynski, "Multinational Corporations and East-West Economic Cooperation," *Journal of World Trade Law*, 1975; John Ryans, Anant Negandhi, and James Baker, *China, the U.S.S.R., and Eastern Europe: A U.S. Trade Perspective* (Kent, Ohio: Kent State University Press, 1984), pp. 132-41; Paul Surovell (ed.) *INTERFLO* (1985-1986).

Key Characteristics Relating to MNEs

Concept and Function of the Marketplace

A fundamental commercial difference between the communist countries and the rest of the countries discussed in this book is that the communist countries do not allow prices and markets to function freely. Production and distribution decisions are made by managers who are guided by output targets that are established by government fiat rather than by consumer demand. Prices are set by decision makers who seek to serve social and political (as well as economic) goals rather than to maximize the firm's profits.[5]

The logistic problem of setting production targets for thousands of products and services is perhaps the greatest difficulty in the operation of a communist economy. (Another major difficulty is motivating the work force when competitive wages are not paid and when consumers face repeated shortages of the products they wish to purchase.) Consumer purchases lead to the depletion of the inventories of some products and thus to shortages. Sometimes the shortages are allowed to persist, and other times they lead to decisions to increase the output of the products in short supply. Insufficient consumer purchases of other products lead to excess inventories, which ultimately lead to a decision to reduce the output of these products. The flow of information about optimal production levels is generally much slower and less efficient in communist economies than in market economies.[6]

Long-range planning is one way in which communist countries attempt to reduce the inefficiency of nonmarket production and distribution decisions. Policymakers in each communist country construct five-year plans that delineate industries to develop and major capital budgeting commitments throughout the economy. Among the Soviet-bloc countries, an attempt is made to coordinate the plans, so that some production is assigned to one country for use in several or all of them. For example, East Germany has been assigned a wide range of chemical products, which it manufactures and ships throughout the CMEA. Similarly, Bulgaria and the Soviet Union produce almost all of the battery-powered vehicles sold in the CMEA and Rumania produces forestry products for sale in the entire Soviet bloc.[7] Although coordination is sought, the rate of success is far from perfect—as with planning in other country blocs, such as the Common Market and the Andean Pact. The key aspect of communist five-year plans for Western businesspeople is that the probable demands for Western products and technology can be ascertained by examining the five-year plans to see where each communist country is expecting to commit its resources during the period. Since the purchasing decisions of communist nations are not market based, the five-year plans offer a means of projecting demand conditions in these nations.

In practice, Eastern-bloc countries do not completely ignore market signals. Market activities exist in each of the communist countries. Especially in Yugoslavia and China, there are industrial firms partially or totally owned by individuals rather than by the state. In the 1980s, there have been numerous examples of Chinese experiments in capitalism through small, individually owned companies as well as efforts by state-owned enterprises to operate in Hong Kong, a British colony that will revert to Chinese control in 1997.[8] Throughout the Soviet bloc, farmers have been given the opportunity to produce some crops for their own account, in addition to their main jobs in communes or cooperative farms.[9] This small-scale capitalism has achieved widespread acceptance during the 1980s.

In order to buy from and sell to Western firms, the communist countries have no choice but to function in the market system. While production within Eastern-bloc countries remains primarily communal (i.e., owned and controlled by government agencies), export sales to the West and import purchases from the West are conducted along more or less capitalist lines. That is, exports must be sold through a marketing effort to find and contract with Western purchasers and imports must be contracted and paid through capitalist trade financing methods (although the specific financing methods include much more countertrade and forfaiting than are used in free-world trade). This means, essentially, that international business opportunities do exist for Western firms in the Eastern-bloc countries, whereas domestic business in these countries is limited to local, usually government-owned, firms or agencies.

Social and Cultural Differences

Social and cultural differences unquestionably play a major role in East-West business, just as they do in industrialized country/LDC business and in business between Western and Japanese firms. In East-West business, a wide range of countries are involved—from relatively less developed and racially distinct China to the industrialized European countries of the Soviet bloc. The main differences affecting business activities between East and West are simply the radically different ways of doing business. Decisions are made on different bases, the decision makers are motivated differently, and the legal rules differ greatly.

In addition to the differences in business practices, the problems of language, social practices, and ethnic preferences must be faced in East- West business. Overcoming the substantial hurdles involved in doing business in communist countries requires both an ability to deal with the radically different business systems and an ability to handle the cultural differences that exist between the Western firm's home country and the target Eastern-bloc country.

One recent study examined the factors that influenced success in business negotiations with the *Chinese.*[10] The study found that knowledge of Chinese business practices was very important to success but that knowledge of Chinese social customs and language was relatively unimportant. The Chinese were apparently more interested in the characteristics of the product or service than in the supplier's ability to communicate well in Chinese or to "fit in" socially. (This finding may be biased, however, because only Western firms were polled, and not Chinese partners.) The conclusion to draw here is that social and cultural differences probably do matter, and in particular that the issues related to differences in business practices are most important.

Government Involvement in Business

Government participation in business in communist countries dominates all activities. The vast majority of goods and services is produced by government-owned companies, financed by government-owned banks, and transported by government-owned carriers. As far as Western access to communist-bloc business is concerned, **foreign trade organizations (FTOs)**—that is, government trading companies—and government ministries form the first line of entry. Sales by Western firms are generally made to government agencies rather than to consumers, and the types of products sold generally include manufactured goods, especially those utilizing advanced technology. The perspective of the host government on East-West business is discussed in the next section.

Government Policies and Concerns Related to MNEs

Government = Market

The most notable aspect of East-West business for the Western firm is that all business must be done with or approved through the host country government. This implies that all such business is dependent on political relations between the firm's home country and the host nation. Any political disagreement between the two nations can completely disrupt business between them. This is an important risk factor that the firm needs to evaluate. It also means that the firm will need to create a strategy that focuses on the government itself as the market in a communist country. Whether the Western firm sells automobiles, machinery, or food, typically it will deal with an FTO and a ministry, such as the Ministry of Transportation, the Ministry of Industry, or the Ministry of Agriculture. For example, Swindell Dressler Company, when selling a truck plant to the Soviet Union, contracted with the Ministry of Foreign Trade and the State Committee for Science and Technology for its dealings. Similarly, Continental Grain Corporation has a continuing contract with Exportkhleb, the Soviet grain-trading FTO, and the Ministry of Foreign Trade for major annual wheat sales.[11]

While many of the business partners encountered by Western firms dealing in the Eastern bloc are companies, these companies are generally wholly government owned and controlled. Thus, even though negotiations may proceed on a fairly Western basis of discussing prices, quantities, delivery times, quality, and so on, a pervasive political factor affects the Eastern partner's decisions. Regardless of the technical and economic viability of such a business deal, the deal may be lost due to political concerns related to the Cold War or any binational dispute. For example, several billion dollars of contracts related to construction of an oil and gas pipeline to the Soviet Union were lost due to political conflict between the United States and the Soviet

Union in 1980, and in 1972 Ford's negotiations to construct the Kama River truck plant for approximately $1.4 billion were cut off by the U.S. Defense Department's objection to the project.[12]

The Soviet Gas Pipeline Controls

The difficulty of choosing and implementing U.S. economic policy with respect to the Soviet Union is well illustrated by the restrictions placed in 1981-82 on the participation by U.S. companies in construction of a natural gas pipeline from the USSR to Western Europe.

After the Soviet invasion of Afghanistan in 1979, Presidents Carter and Reagan imposed a variety of restrictions on the dealings of U.S. firms with the Soviet Union. Beginning with the highly visible and politicized boycott of the 1980 Olympic Games in Moscow, the Carter administration sought to cut back on U.S. business with the USSR. Actually, few limitations other than denying the American athletes permission to participate in the Games were imposed at that time—despite public rhetoric to the contrary. Grain shipments and the sale of nonmilitary goods continued through 1980.

When President Reagan took office in 1981, he quickly moved to cut back on U.S. trade with Moscow. At the end of 1981, he imposed an embargo on U.S. goods shipped for the construction of a pipeline connecting Russian oil and gas supplies with Western European markets. The embargo was lifted in November 1982. During the year of the embargo, such American firms as General Electric and Caterpillar lost contracts for shipment of industrial and construction equipment worth over $2 billion.

Initially, General Electric and other U.S. suppliers tried to switch the production of their equipment out of the United States into their European subsidiaries, to avoid the U.S. rules. By June 1982, the embargo was extended to cover the overseas affiliates of firms that operated in the United States. This policy led to a large number of lawsuits seeking to enjoin the U.S. government from extending its jurisdiction outside the country. Before the issue could be resolved in court, the sanctions were eliminated. By this time, however, GE and Caterpillar, among other U.S. firms, had lost very substantial business.

The political risk presented by conflict between the superpowers clearly places U.S. firms at a disadvantage relative to European and Asian suppliers to Eastern European customers. It appears that additional business was lost to U.S. firms as a result of the pipeline incident, since bids for future projects have gone increasingly to non-U.S. suppliers. This claim is difficult to document, but the evidence seems to support it. Komatsu (Caterpillar's main competitor worldwide) received an additional $800 million of Soviet contracts in 1982 and 1983, while Caterpillar's Soviet business dropped off dramatically. Similarly, some of GE's European competitors gained major new contracts for Soviet sales, while GE's Soviet business declined for several years.

Growth Policies

Probably the main reason for communist countries to seek business with capitalist firms is to promote economic growth. By purchasing products and technology from the West, Eastern-bloc nations can advance their economies without total dependence on internal supply. This strategy follows the simple concept of comparative advantage in international trade (though East-West business activities are **negotiated trade** rather than free trade). As Table 23-2b shows, the communist countries (especially the Soviet Union) are exporting, and thus presumably have an advantage in producing, petroleum-based products and some manufactured goods, while they demonstrate a relative disadvantage in producing electronic and other high-tech products and grains—all of which they import in large quantities from the United States, Western Europe, and Japan.

The specific growth policies pursued by Eastern-bloc countries are subject to change in each of the five-year plans that they adopt. As in LDC efforts at planning, in the planning efforts of communist countries there tend to be fairly substantial shifts in strategies to push some sectors actively while ignoring (or at least not favoring) others. This is especially true in the case of agriculture, which is allotted a high priority in some five-year plans and a low priority in others. Similarly, in the Soviet Union the approach to the production of automotive products has varied from tremendous support—in the case of the Kama River truck plant—to relative de-emphasis, measured by the failure of projects negotiated with Ford, Mack Truck, and other companies to come to fruition.

Countertrade and Other Efforts to Obtain Credit

Credit is a major concern of the communist governments. There is far more demand for Western products in Eastern-bloc countries than for Eastern-bloc products in Western countries. Because the communist currencies are inconvertible into dollars or other freely traded currencies, a large demand for Western currencies exists continually in the communist countries. One method that these countries use to avoid immediate payment in dollars or other hard currency is to finance imported purchases with bank credit or **supplier credit.** Another method is to force Western exporters to accept payment in products rather than money (i.e., **countertrade**). Both of these methods are widely used in East-West trade and other East-West business arrangements.

A major example of financing through countertrade is Fiat's contract in the Soviet Union. In 1966, Fiat Corporation, the large Italian automaker, agreed to construct an automobile plant worth about $1.5 billion in Togliattigrad. Payment for construction of the facility and for technical assistance has been made in the form of automobiles—that is, cars produced in the plant. Fiat then markets the cars in Western Europe in the same way that it markets cars manufactured elsewhere.[13] Other very large countertrade contracts have been undertaken by several different Western firms. A selection of recent countertrade deals is presented in Table 23-5.

Bank financing for importers in Eastern-bloc countries tended to be fairly widely available until the Soviet invasion of Afghanistan in 1979, due largely to these countries' histories of creditworthiness. Historically, Russia and its

Soviet workers on a Fiat assembly line in Togliattigrad, Russia.

Wide World Photos, Inc.

Table 23-5 **Selected Countertrade Deals between Eastern and Western Partners**

Company	Country	Date	Products Involved
Capsule Technology, Inc.	GDR	1985	Gelatin capsule manufacturing plant for future payment in capsules
General Electric	Rumania	1985	Steel plate for machinery
Hancock Prospecting, Inc.	Rumania (Australia)	1985	Rumanian mining equipment for Australian iron ore
Hoesch, A.G.	Czechoslovakia	1985	Gas pipeline for Czech goods
Montedison	Yugoslavia	1985	Ethylene and ethylene dichloride for naphtha feed stock
Occidental Petroleum	USSR	1985	Soviet ammonia for superphosphoric acid
UMC International Corporation	Rumania	1985	Thai rice, tapioca, rubber, and coffee for Rumanian fertilizer, chemicals, and machines

Source: Paul Surovell, *INTERFLO*. Maplewood, N.J. (various issues 1985-1986).

Gregory, Paul, and Robert Stuart. *Soviet Economic Structure and Performance.* New York: Harper & Row, 1974.

Marer, Paul, and Joseph Miller. "U.S. Participation in East-West Industrial Cooperation Agreements," *Journal of International Business Studies,* Fall-Winter 1977.

Organization for Economic Cooperation and Development. *East-West Trade: Recent Developments in Countertrade.* Paris: OECD, 1981.

Ryans, John; Anant Negandhi; and James Baker. *China, the U.S.S.R., and Eastern Europe: A U.S. Trade Perspective.* Kent, Ohio: Kent State University Press, 1974.

Surovell, Paul. *INTERFLO.* Maplewood, N.J. (monthly East-West Business Newsletter).

Szuprowicz, Bohdan, and Maria Szuprowicz. *Doing Business with the People's Republic of China.* New York: John Wiley & Sons, 1978.

Tung, Rosalie. "U.S.-China Trade Negotiations: Practices, Procedures, and Outcomes." *Journal of International Business Studies,* Fall 1982.

United Nations. "Manufacturing Enterprise Relationships in East-West Technology Transfer: Theoretical Models and Practical Experiences." New York: UN Economic and Social Council, 1975.

U.S. Central Intelligence Agency. *Handbook of Economic Statistics, 1986.* Washington, D.C.: CIA, September 1986.

U.S. Department of Commerce. "East-West Trade Update," *Overseas Business Reports,* January 1979.

U.S. Department of Commerce, *Doing Business with China.* Washington, D.C.: U.S. Government Printing Office, December 1983.

Wilczynski, Josef. "Multinational Corporations and East-West Economic Cooperation." *Journal of World Trade Law,* 1975.

Endnotes

1. We will not look at the less developed members of the communist bloc, which include Afghanistan, Cuba, Mongolia, North Korea, and Vietnam.
2. The East European countries are certainly not totally ignored by their neighbors in Western Europe. A substantial amount of trade takes place between East and West Germany—though far less than that between West Germany and other EEC countries.
3. See William Ebenstein and Edwin Fogelman, *Today's Isms,* 8th ed. (Englewood Cliffs, N.J.: Prentice-Hall, 1980) chap. 1, for a clear discussion of how communist economies function today.
4. Turnkey ventures usually involve continuing licensing agreements, so that the Western partner remains linked to the project even after the keys have been turned over to the Eastern-bloc purchaser.

5. Obviously, these statements overgeneralize the functioning of communist economies today. All of these countries allow some opportunities for markets to operate, from the Soviet Union's private small farms to Yugoslavia's numerous joint-venture companies.
6. See Paul Gregory and Robert Stuart, *Soviet Economic Structure and Performance* (New York: Harper & Row, 1974), especially part 2, for a discussion of how resources are allocated and prices set in the Russian economy in recent years.
7. See U.S. Department of Commerce, "East-West Trade Update," *Overseas Business Reports,* January 1979; and CMEA Secretariat, *The Council for Mutual Economic Assistance: 30 Years* (Moscow: CMEA, 1979), p. 55
8. See, for example, Julia Leung and Vigor Fung, "Entrepreneurs in China Are Quick to Seize Opportunity, despite Official Delays, Hostility," *The Wall Street Journal,* March 11, 1985, p. 32; and "Chinese Permit Private Firm to Sell Shares to Individuals," *The Wall Street Journal,* July 12, 1985, p. 26.
9. N. P. Condee, "The Farmers' Markets," *Institute of Current World Affairs,* 1985.
10. See Rosalie Tung, "U.S.-China Trade Negotiations," *Journal of International Business Studies,* Fall 1982.
11. These projects are discussed in Marshall Goldman, *Detente and Dollars: Doing Business with the Soviets* (New York: Basic Books, 1975), chapts. 7 and 9; and the Kama River project, specifically, is discussed in the United Nations, "Manufacturing Enterprise Relationships in East-West Technology Transfer: Theoretical Models and Practical Experiences" (New York: UN Economic and Social Council, 1975).
12. Ibid.
13. See, for example, Hartley Barclay, "The Soviet-Fiat Pact," *Automotive Industries,* August 1, 1966, pp. 27-29.
14. See Josef Wilczynski, "Multinational Corporations and East-West Economic Cooperation," *Journal of World Trade Law,* 1975; and Organization for Economic Cooperation and Development, *East-West Trade: Recent Developments in Countertrade* (Paris: OECD, 1981).
15. Fiat has faced some competition from its Russian licensee in Western Europe, and some other examples of such improper use of Western licenses do exist, but they are not common.
16. Ian Amariute, David Rutenberg, and Richard Staelin, "How American Executives Disagree about the Risks of Investing in Eastern Europe," *Academy of Management Journal,* March 1979.

PART 5

A LOOK TO THE FUTURE

24

INDUSTRY PROFILES

This chapter contains extensive case studies of four major industries—the petroleum, automobile, banking, and telecommunications industries—in which international competition is involved. Each section explores industry characteristics such as locations of production and consumption, recent history, and industry structure. In addition, individual firms and their competitive strategies are discussed. The main goals of the chapter are to:

1. Provide a clear picture of competition in the four industries in the late 1980s.
2. Illustrate the concepts developed throughout the book.
3. Show how both large and small firms participate in various activities within each industry.
4. Focus on the international aspects of each industry.
5. Offer a single framework of examination, so that all four industries can be compared and seen in a similar light.

Introduction

This chapter provides a view of four major industries that have figured prominently in international business in the 1980s: *petroleum, automobiles, banking,* and *telecommunications.* The purpose of the chapter is to explore the international aspects of these industries, from competition among multinational firms to international structure of production, looking at the various stages of production, from initial processing to consumer sales. More specifically, the purpose is to present basic information about the industries and then to examine the implications of current conditions and expected changes for international business managers.

The chapter offers an overview of the nature of competition in four extremely important international industries of the 1980s. While one cannot become an industry expert after reading these few pages, it is possible to gain from them a better understanding of the pressures facing firms in these industries and the relative positions of some of the larger firms. By selecting four distinctive types of industry (natural resource, high-tech, service, and smokestack), we are able to offer insights that have application to a wide variety of additional industries and firms.

Four Industries

The *petroleum* industry is arguably the single most important industry of the past 20 years. Oil is the most important energy source used in the 20th century, as well as being the base of the petrochemical industry. Oil is a relatively scarce natural resource, and supplies of oil are substantially located in less developed countries (especially the Middle Eastern countries). The cartel of less developed oil-producing countries has shifted the balance of economic power somewhat away from the industrial nations and toward the oil-producing nations during the past 15 years. And finally, in the present context, trade and direct investment in the oil business constitute a major portion of total international business. Beginning with the OPEC (Organization of Petroleum Exporting Countries) oil embargo and price hikes in 1973 and 1974, crude oil prices have gone from about $US 2 per barrel to almost $US 40 per barrel and then back to around $US 20 per barrel (by the mid-1980s). And after numerous nationalizations in LDCs during the mid-1970s, the petroleum industry has evolved from a fairly small number of vertically integrated MNEs (the "Seven Sisters" and a handful of others) to a multiplicity of firms and contractual arrangements. These changes have had an enormous impact on consumers, governments, and firms in other industries. Inflation in the industrialized countries rose from an average of around 6 percent per year in the early 1970s to well over 12 percent by 1980. (One reason for inflation was expansionary government monetary and fiscal policies in industrialized countries to mitigate the negative effects on employment and income caused by the huge transfers of financial wealth to the oil-exporting countries.) Worldwide recessions occurred in 1975-76 and 1980-83, after major hikes in oil prices. The ripples from these changes are still being felt today.

The *automotive* industry is a traditional "smokestack industry," that involves large-scale, capital-intensive production facilities with assembly lines, a heavily unionized work force, and fairly standardized (or at least mature) products and that places an emphasis on price competition in the final product market. Unlike the petroleum industry, this industry is not based on a single raw material but is a heavy user of a number of industrial inputs, among which are steel, glass, rubber, and oil. Competition in the production aspect of this industry remains the province of firms in industrial countries, with strong competitors in the United States, Europe, and Japan. However, the production of components, assemblies, and even full automobiles has been shifting more and more significantly to low-cost locations around the world. This is the youngest of our four industries, having first come into existence at the end of the 19th century.

Banking contrasts sharply with the petroleum and automotive industries. Banking is a service that requires few raw materials. The provision of domestic banking services is highly regulated in every country, though the eurocurrency market is relatively unrestricted in a few countries (primarily the industrialized nations). Banking has been closely tied to the oil industry, not only as a source of loans and deposits, but also as the major vehicle through which "recycling" of the money ("petrodollars") earned by OPEC countries in the 1970s took place. Both banking and the petroleum industry supply fairly standardized products. Competition in banking is often based on non-price factors, such as service or regulatory conditions. Banking is by far the oldest of our four industries.

The *telecommunications* industry differs greatly from the other three. This industry has existed since the advent of the telegraph in the 1840s, and it has continually faced dramatic competitive shifts as new technology has been developed. From telegraph to telephone to television, the industry has repeatedly led technological advancement in the modern world. In the 1980s, the advances have been related primarily to the integration of the computer industry with telecommunications. Building on the use of tiny transistors embodied in silicon chips, both computers and telecommunications switching equipment have become almost infinitely complex and at the same time relatively inexpensive and widely available to consumers during this decade. The competition among firms in the telecommunications industry has changed rapidly with each new generation of computer technology—from memory increases to communications advances and improvements in processing speeds. During the past decade or so, the telecommunications industry has become characterized by the use of offshore assembly in Southeast Asia for the production of telephones, televisions, computer chips, and many other products. In the 1980s, telecommunications has generally been regarded as the epitome of the high-tech industries.

International Aspects

Our intent in this chapter is to highlight the international aspects of each of the four industries it covers. The next four sections provide a look at the cross-country structures of each of these industries, at the history that has led to its current competitive environment, and at its major firms and some of their competitive strategies. Particular emphasis is place on the ownership arrangements that pervade each industry—for example, banking in most countries is fragmented geographically and primarily locally owned, whereas telecommunications equipment is produced globally by a small number of multinational firms. A wide variety of contractual agreements arose in the petroleum industry as governments nationalized oil production, but these governments still need the MNEs for technical assistance, access to foreign markets, and other services. Automobile manufacture remains the province of a small number of MNEs, but marketing, service, and parts production all involve thousands of smaller competitors in many countries. Although the examples presented below focus on MNEs, an attempt is also made to demonstrate the involvement of smaller firms in each industry.

Oil

Sources of Production and Consumption

Most of the world's proved oil reserves are located in the Middle East, as shown in Figure 24-1. Saudi Arabia alone has proved reserves totaling about 169 billion barrels, in comparison with the 27 billion barrels of the United States and the 63 billion barrels of the Soviet Union.[1] The numbers in Figure 24-1 portray a major shift in oil reserves since World War II. Before that time, the United States was the largest oil-producing nation, supplying over half of the world's demand. (Most of this U.S. production went to serve U.S. consumption, so the United States was not a major oil exporter even then.) Major discoveries in the Middle East during the late 1940s catapulted Saudi Arabia ahead of all other oil producers. The Ghawar oil field alone had proved reserves of 60 billion barrels.

On the demand side, as may be expected, the industrialized countries account for most of the world's oil use. The United States leads the consuming nations, with annual consumption of about 6 billion barrels of oil out of a total world consumption of about 22 billion barrels per year.

Recent History

The oil industry has been dominated by U.S.-based firms during most of its existence. Since the founding of Standard Oil of New Jersey in 1882, that firm (known today as Exxon) has been the industry leader. (In 1986, however, Royal Dutch Shell took over the position of industry leader, when the parent

Figure 24-1 **World Distribution of Proved Oil Reserves** (In billions of barrels as of January 1, 1984)

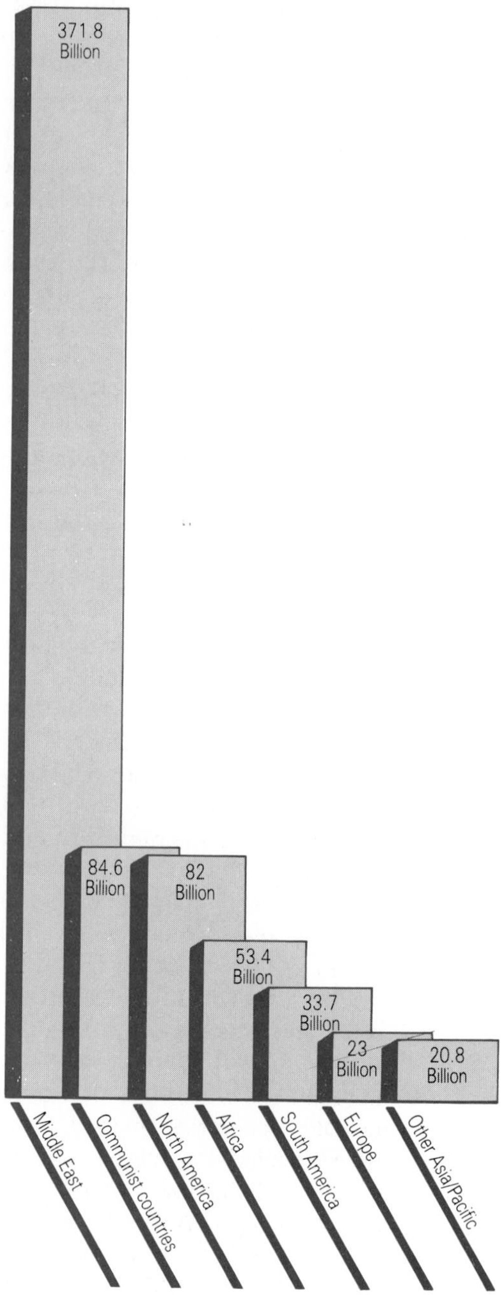

Source: Exxon Corporation, *Middle East Oil.* p. 2. © 1984 Exxon Corporation.

firm purchased the 49 percent of its U.S. subsidiary that was not already owned.) During the first half of the 20th century, a group of vertically integrated firms in the United States and Great Britain achieved substantial positions in all phases of the industry in the noncommunist world, from exploration to the operation of gasoline stations. These firms (Exxon, Mobil, Texaco, Socal, Shell, Gulf, and British Petroleum) were labeled the **Seven Sisters** because of the similarities in their size and strategies.[2] With the merger of Gulf into Socal (or Chevron) in 1985 and the increased importance of Amoco (Standard Oil of Indiana), plus the truly global nature of the oil business today, perhaps the leading oil industry firms should now be called the **"Major Multinationals."** (Table 24-1 below lists the largest oil multinationals and a few of their characteristics.)

Early Oil Producers The United States was the largest producer of oil during the first half of this century. As exploration in other countries grew during the 1940s, discoveries in the Middle East quickly led that region to surpass the United States as an oil producer. The companies involved in oil exploration and production in the Middle East were the Seven Sisters plus a few foreign competitors. Exploration in Algeria, Nigeria, Venezuela, Indonesia, and several other LDCs also led to expanded worldwide oil production, which reached about 18 million barrels per day in 1960.

Throughout this period, the multinational oil companies operated through **concessions** in oil-producing countries (i.e., agreements with governments to extract and sell oil in exchange for paying taxes, fees, and other charges) and controlled most of the oil being produced. The governments of the producing countries gained substantial revenues through fees and royalties on oil sales. Land was used by the oil companies under concession from host governments, and these governments were paid fixed per barrel royalties on the oil produced. It was not until the early 1950s that Middle Eastern countries began charging income tax (at a 50 percent rate) on sales of oil. Since the oil companies sold most of the oil to their own downstream affiliates for refining and subsequent processing, they were able to keep wellhead prices low, and thus to keep taxes to host governments low. In September 1960, five of the LDC host countries joined together to form **OPEC** (**Organization of Petroleum Exporting Countries**), specifically to protect their interests in obtaining stable and higher returns on oil production. Since then, OPEC has expanded to 13 members, which control about half of the noncommunist world's oil supply. During the course of the 1960s, the OPEC countries chipped away at the oil companies' control of the oil industry, mainly by raising royalties and taxes.

By 1970, the power balance in the oil industry had shifted dramatically in favor of host governments. "Whereas oil had accounted for about 10 percent of the total energy consumed in Western Europe in 1950, its share was more than 55 percent by 1970. In Japan over the same period, oil's share rose from 9 percent to 33 percent. Imports accounted for virtually all the oil consumed in both areas."[3] Even the United States began to import a substantial quantity

A Mobil Oil refinery in Beaumont, Texas.

Wide World Photos, Inc.

of oil from OPEC suppliers. Not only did global demand create a seller's market for petroleum, but supply conditions had shifted by 1970 to the point where OPEC provided about 60 percent of noncommunist output. And finally, through the education of increasing numbers of students from Saudi Arabia, Iraq, Venezuela, and other countries in the world's leading universities, a base of managerial skills was being developed to manage OPEC oil for the specific benefit of these countries rather than for the benefit of the oil companies. Each of these shifts pushed the obsolescing bargain farther in favor of the producing countries.

The Role of Arabian Gulf Oil Looking back at this period, two events appear to have set the stage for the incredible upheavals of the 1970s. First, the Arab-Israeli War in 1967 led to the closing of the Suez Canal, through which much of the Arabian Gulf oil was transported to Europe. This event highlighted the growing dependence of the industrialized countries on Arabian Gulf oil, and it also focused attention on U.S. support for Israel, which created very serious tensions between the United States and the Arab countries. Second, a construction accident in 1970 caused the temporary shutdown of the Trans-Arabian Pipeline, requiring all Arabian Gulf oil to be shipped much farther away—around the Cape of Good Hope in South Africa—to reach European buyers. This event led to increased oil prices and a successful demand for higher taxes by OPEC members, thus reinforcing the oil-producing nations' awareness of their bargaining strength.

In 1971, the Arabian Gulf countries and Libya successfully forced negotiations with the oil companies to set oil prices through agreements between the governments and the companies and to raise taxes on the oil sold. These agreements, signed in Tehran (Iran) and Tripoli (Libya), marked the first time that producing countries had achieved control over crude oil pricing. Following this success, the members of OPEC began pressing for ownership of the oil production facilities. By the end of 1972, Saudi Arabia, Abu Dhabi, and Qatar had negotiated to buy 51 percent of the oil-producing facilities within their borders over a 10-year period.

The **nationalization** of oil companies and the control of pricing by OPEC members jumped ahead again in September 1973, when another Arab-Israeli war broke out and the Arab countries unilaterally raised their oil prices and embargoed oil shipments to the United States and the Netherlands (because these two countries showed support for Israel in the war). Crude oil prices (at US$ 2.70 per barrel in early October) were raised 35 percent on October 16, 1973, and 131 percent on January 1, 1974. The OPEC governments raised taxes on the oil companies to 85 percent of income and royalties to 20 percent of the list price of crude oil. Greater government ownership of oil companies operating within the OPEC nations was also demanded, and by the end of 1974 most of the OPEC nations had achieved 60 percent ownership.

Since 1974, the nationalization of oil companies within the OPEC nations has proceeded to complete local ownership in most cases. Crude oil prices are now set by OPEC governments without negotiations with the companies. After a few years of price increases that approximately kept pace with inflation, the Iranian crisis of 1978, which led to the overthrow of the shah's government, disrupted the supply of oil from that country. OPEC raised prices accordingly throughout 1979. By year-end, consumers' fears of a new oil shortage and OPEC's reaction to panic buying had enabled OPEC to increase oil prices 95 percent, to $US 26 per barrel. This second oil price shock was followed by two years of steadily increasing OPEC prices, which peaked at $US 34 per barrel in October 1981.

Oil consumers reacted to the continuing upward spiral of oil prices by trying to conserve energy in their existing activities, by switching to alternative energy sources, and by simply cutting down on energy-intensive activities. The effects of these reactions were slow to be felt, but by 1982 the fuel efficiency of U.S. automobiles had been raised to over twice the 1972 level (mileage of over 30 miles per gallon was common for new cars, compared to about 15 miles per gallon in the early 1970s), coal and nuclear power were replacing oil in many electric utilities, and both residential and commercial electric power use (per customer) had dropped noticeably.

These reactions, as well as a worldwide recession and the emergence of major new oil supplies in the North Sea and North America, had created an oversupply of oil by the end of 1982.

By the mid-1980s, world oil sales had shifted away from the OPEC countries, which now sell only about 40 percent of the world total, to other suppliers such as the Netherlands, the United Kingdom, and Canada—countries that do not follow OPEC market-sharing practices. Also, sales of oil on the "spot" market, which, unlike OPEC sales, are not tied to long-term contracts, rose in the mid-1980s to almost one third of total crude oil sales. Some OPEC (and other) producers have placed substantial amounts of their production into this market, and many oil companies make their purchases increasingly without long-term contracts (i.e., on the spot market). Finally, the OPEC countries themselves have been discounting their prices substantially during the 1980s oil glut, so that the posted price published by OPEC countries is no longer a good measure of actual sales prices. In fact, in late 1985, OPEC abandoned attempts to control its members' oil-pricing policies. The cartel has failed to maintain its monopoly control over oil supply—though only after more than a decade of successful operations that led to huge transfers of wealth from industrial countries to OPEC members. (Renewed efforts to fix crude oil prices succeeded to some extent in 1987, when OPEC agreed to a price of $US 18 per barrel. This agreement was achieved despite the all-out war between Iran and Iraq and the widespread use of discounts and other efforts of OPEC members to sell more than their production allocations in the cartel.)

Industry Structure

The ownership of companies producing *crude oil* shifted from almost exclusively, the Seven Sisters and other private firms during the first half of this century to almost exclusive host government ownership (in the LDCs) by 1980. Figure G232 bears out this point. Both exploration for new oil and downstream processing of crude oil, however, are still dominated by the oil companies. One would expect the OPEC governments to be interested in downstream production, and indeed in 1984 refining capacity within OPEC was about 3.6 million barrels per day, compared to worldwide refining capacity of about 56.2 million barrels per day. Unfortunately for the OPEC refineries, oil demand dropped sharply during the early 1980s and refining has become an unprofitable or marginal venture in many cases. Several OPEC countries have begun to process farther downstream, into petrochemicals,[4] but petrochemical demand has stagnated in the past few years. While it appears that OPEC-based firms will supply substantial amounts of downstream products to world markets in the long run, their progress thus far has been curtailed by weak demand worldwide.

One can conclude that upstream oil production in LDCs has been very largely taken over by governments, in contrast with the production and

and a similar portion of consumption taking place in North America, Western Europe, and Japan. While substantial natural resources are used in the production of cars and trucks (and other motor vehicles), that production is still located primarily in the major industrial markets. Figure 24–4 shows the distribution of automobile production and consumption worldwide over the past half-century. Notice that although production in North America had fallen to about one fifth of the global total by 1982, consumption in that region still accounted for about one third of total world consumption. This implies, of course, that North America has been the major net importer of automobiles in the world during the 1980s. Among the reasons for North America's position as an importer of automobiles are lower production costs and greater precision in production in Japan (and Europe), the easy access of foreign producers to the North American market, a continuing bias of North American producers away from compact and subcompact cars despite consumer demand for such cars, and finally the huge size of the North American market relative to other markets around the world. These and other reasons for this situation are explored below.

Because automobiles are composed of fairly standardized components, there has been a tendency to place greater reliance on low-cost locations for the production of components and the assembly of automobiles. In the 1970s and 80s, Brazil, Mexico, and Korea in particular became important sources of supply of parts and assemblies to the auto industry. Brazil alone assembled almost a million autos (in addition to producing auto parts) in 1980, when about 27 million autos were produced worldwide. The increasing use of low-cost locations appears quite likely to continue into the 1990s.

The communist countries account for a small percentage of worldwide automobile production; they produced about 2 million automobiles in 1982. Virtually all of their automobile production is sold within the communist bloc, with little import competition and little effort made to export to the industrial countries or elsewhere.

Recent History

Historically, the automobile industry has been dominated by American firms, in particular by General Motors and Ford. This dominance began in the early 1900s, when Henry Ford's company brought standardized parts and mass production, plus the use of a continuous assembly line, into operation. Prior to 1900, for the first 20 years of the industry's existence, German and French manufacturers produced most of the automobiles in use. By 1923, Ford and General Motors (GM) together accounted for 91 percent of world auto production—and their combined share remained above two thirds of the world total until after World War II.[6]

Through strategies of foreign direct investment, Ford and GM obtained strong market positions in Europe and North America. During the 1930s, Ford set up manufacturing facilities in England, Germany, and France. GM chose acquisitions of existing European firms, buying Vauxhall in England

Figure 24-4a **Global Automobile Production**

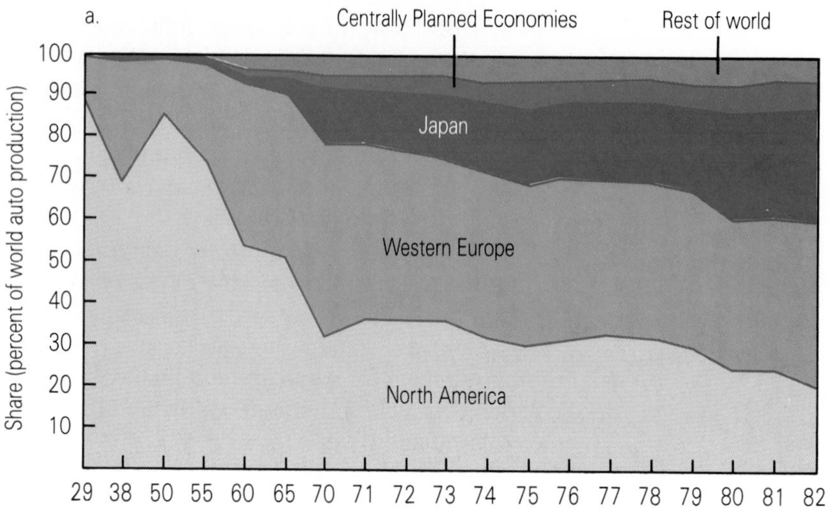

Share of world automobile production by region, 1929–82.
Source: Roos and Altshuler (1984), p. 20.

and Opel in Germany in the late 1920s. (Both firms were denied permission to establish manufacturing in Italy, where they would have competed with state-owned Fiat.) Both Ford and GM also operated manufacturing facilities in Canada.

After World War II, competition from non-U.S. firms began to heat up. High tariffs on imported autos, support for state-owned manufacturers, and rapidly growing European economies led to a boom in European production by such companies as Renault, Volkswagen, and Fiat. (The Ford and GM affiliates in England and Germany also grew rapidly in this environment.) When the European Common Market was established in 1958, European producers were able to take advantage of economies of scale that resulted from serving the six-country market instead of the relatively small national markets. By 1973, the European Community market was about the same size as the North American market, and European automakers were beginning to enter the U.S. small-car market very successfully.

At the beginning of the postwar period, auto production in Japan lagged far behind that in Europe and North America. Japanese auto production was less than 1 million vehicles per year until the late 1960s. By 1970, however, it had hit 3 million and Japanese auto exports to the United States had reached a market share of more than 4 percent. And by 1980, Japanese exports accounted for almost 23 percent of the U.S. auto market. Like the European autos, the Japanese autos were smaller than their U.S. counterparts and offered a low-cost alternative to U.S. buyers.

Figure 24-4b **Global Automobile Consumption**

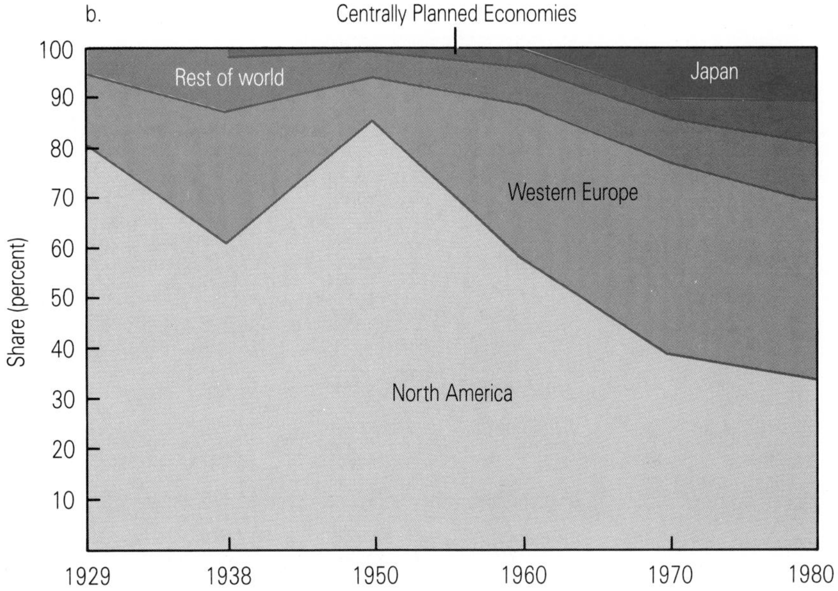

Share of world automobile market by region, 1929-80.
Source: Roos and Altshuler (1984), p. 23.

Industry Structure

In most countries, the automobile industry is dominated by models designed and produced elsewhere. That is, a small number of manufacturers in a handful of industrial countries make virtually all of the cars and trucks used in the world's almost 200 countries. (Six firms produce over two thirds of world auto output.) From a different perspective, the three major markets for autos are North America, the European Community, and Japan. All of the six largest auto firms manufacture vehicles in at least two of these areas in dozens of plants. In sum, the industry is highly concentrated among six firms: in descending order of size, General Motors, Ford, Toyota, Nissan, Renault, and Volkswagen. (Fiat and Peugeot-Citroen are not far behind Volkswagen in size, though they are far less multinational outside Europe than any of the six largest firms.) Table 24-2 depicts some features of the ten main competitors in the world auto industry.

As with the petroleum industry, the automobile industry includes thousands of additional firms that are involved in various stages of its operations, from the production of components to the final sale of cars and trucks to retail customers. What distinguishes the six (or eight) major multinational auto firms is their control of the *final assembly* stage of production. These

Table 24-2 **Major Competitors in the International Automobile Industry**

Firm	Home Country	Annual Sales, 1985 (in $ millions)	Competitive Advantages
General Motors	U.S.	$96,372	largest size and largest distribution network
Ford	U.S.	52,774	large size and diversification, innovative skills
Toyota	Japan	26,040	low-cost production, good labor relations, best financial situation
Chrysler	U.S.	21,256	relatively low costs and recent good image
Nissan	Japan	18,226	low-cost production, good labor relations
Volkswagen	Germany	17,831	government support
Daimler-Benz	Germany	17,800	reputation for very high quality
Fiat	Italy	14,193	government support
Mitsubishi	Japan	14,112	good labor relations
Renault	France	13,594	government support

Source: Fortune, *The International 500* (August 4, 1986).

final assemblers produce less than half of the total value added in the industry. The rest comes from suppliers, such as tire firms (e.g., Goodyear, Firestone, Michelin, Bridgestone) and drivetrain manufacturers (e.g., TRW, Borg-Warner, Dana); distributors, such as the thousands of independent new car dealers in the industrial countries; and financiers, such as the major commercial banks.

Among the six largest firms in the industry, General Motors and Ford are more vertically integrated than the others, while Toyota and Nissan are much less integrated than the others. Also, the Japanese firms have traditionally specialized in smaller, less expensive cars and have achieved a much better quality record than their foreign competitors. These positioning strategies have brought the Japanese firms greater success during the past two decades, when customer preferences have favored more differentiated and less expensive vehicles. In particular, the competitive edge of the Japanese firms has resulted from their ability to adapt models to changes in consumer tastes and to serve the low-cost end of the market with relatively high-quality products.

The Six Major Multinational Automotive Firms

The six largest multinational auto firms have somewhat different corporate strategies and structures. This section points out some characteristics of these firms that are relevant to global competition with their rivals. The firms are presented in declining order of size (i.e., annual sales).

General Motors has been the largest auto company in the world for most of the auto industry's history. In 1985, GM's annual sales were almost twice those of its nearest competitor. GM has traditionally made a wide variety of large autos that constitute over half of its total production, while filling out its product line with medium, compact, and subcompact vehicles. Among GM's main competitive advantages are its financial capacity to respond to problems and opportunities around the world with massive funds when needed, its highly diversified portfolio of production facilities in the industrial countries and in LDCs, and its base in the United States, the largest national market for motor vehicle sales. Recently, GM has also demonstrated a willingness to cooperate with foreign rivals in production and research, thus benefiting from those firms' skills as well as its own.

Ford Motor Company has been the second largest manufacturer in the auto industry for most of its existence. Ford's product line is similar to that of GM, though Ford has only half of GM's worldwide volume. Historically, Ford has been somewhat more vertically integrated than any of the other major auto firms, with its own very large steelmaking operation and its greater in-house production of other inputs. Ford's major competitive advantages include its long and successful experience operating in foreign markets, its base in the United States, and its innovative capacity, as shown (for example) by its introduction of the compact Mustang model in 1965 and its importing of the Fiesta model from Europe in the late 1970s.

Toyota is the larger of the giant Japanese auto producers, both of which have become multinational competitors only in the past two decades. Toyota's growth rate has far surpassed those of the American and European firms since 1970, and it has been one of the best examples of the "Japanese challenge" to world business in the 1980s. That is, with its advances during this period in competition with the other major firms in many national markets, Toyota has demonstrated most of the attributes of successful Japanese MNEs. Its competitive advantages include far lower production costs and greater production efficiency than those of any of the non-Japanese firms, harmonious labor/management relations, excellent quality control, vehicles with relatively low gasoline consumption, a successful focus on smaller cars, and great financial stability (with zero long-term debt).

Nissan, the manufacturer of Datsun cars and trucks, presents much the same success story as Toyota. The company became a major multinational competitor only during the 1970s and 80s, and its competitive advantages are much the same as Toyota's.

Renault, the French state-owned automaker, has fared far less well in international competition than its rivals in the top six. Operating from a protected base in the French national market, Renault has grown successfully at home. It has also established manufacturing operations in Spain and Mexico, and through acquisition of controlling ownership of American

Motors, it has moved into U.S. production too. Unfortunately for Renault, its American Motors venture did not gain a large market share in the United States, and it was sold to Chrysler in 1987. Renault's strengths lie in its protected position in France, its long European experience, and its production of a wide variety of smaller and relatively inexpensive cars.

Volkswagen is the most multinational of the European auto producers, with plants in the United States, Mexico, and Brazil. The Beetle, Volkswagen's initial entry into the American market (in the 1950s), was tremendously successful and led Volkswagen to dramatic growth through the 1960s. Since that time, the firm has not enjoyed such strides ahead of its rivals. Volkswagen became the first major foreign automaker to set up production in the United States, with its Westmoreland, Pennsylvania, plant, which it purchased in 1974. Although this venture has been only moderately successful, similar direct U.S. investments have been made by Volkswagen's major non-U.S. competitors. Volkswagen's major competitive advantages include its reputation for reliability (established by the Beetle), its protected base in West Germany, and its focus on the small-car market segment.

This overview of six of the largest automakers is offered as a sketch of the competitive conditions in the automobile industry rather than as a precise definition of the capabilities or difficulties of these firms. It is intended to give some insights into the current and future shape of the industry around the world.

Banking

Worldwide Distribution of Activities

The fundamental services rendered by banks are the lending of funds and the taking of deposits. The "raw materials" of the banking industry are deposits and other sources of funds, and the main "output" of the industry is credit in the form of loans and other instruments. In addition, banks offer many other financial services that generate income, such as issuing guarantees of performance on behalf of clients, serving as intermediaries for the purchase/sale of financial instruments other than deposits and loans, and making a market in such instruments as foreign exchange. Finally, banks provide nonfinancial services such as *information*—about market trends for various products, about economic and political conditions in various countries, about financial market conditions at home and abroad, and about other matters of interest to clients. In some countries, commercial banks participate directly in markets for stocks and bonds (i.e., in investment banking) and in markets for real estate, insurance, and other financial services. Our discussion will focus primarily on the two traditional banking functions: taking deposits and lending—and more specifically on these functions in the international context.

Every country has a domestic banking system that is regulated by a domestic monetary authority (typically a central bank) and involves participation by locally owned financial institutions. In this sense, banking activities are distributed across the globe—in capitalist and communist countries, in rich and poor countries. Many countries limit participation in domestic financial markets to locally owned institutions, with foreign banks allowed only to have representative offices or to operate only indirectly through relations with local banks. Such limitations exist throughout the communist world, and they are also fairly extensive in less developed countries. This means that much of international banking takes place through "correspondent banking relations," that is, through transactions in which a bank in one country deals at arm's length with its counterpart in another country. It also means that there are far fewer multinational banks than there are multinational industrial corporations.

In the industrialized countries and in a handful of LDCs (Panama, Hong Kong, Bahrain, the Bahamas, the Cayman Islands, and a few more), international banking transactions are relatively open to foreign-owned financial institutions and free of most limits (other than those intended to ensure prudent banking practices) on the lending and deposit-taking practices of participating banks. The eurocurrency markets flourish in this environment, as do dealings in foreign exchange and other internationally transferable financial instruments.

The international spread of bank affiliates outside their home countries is depicted in Table 24-3. Notice that the main centers of foreign bank activity are the main countries involved in eurocurrency transactions—the industrialized nations plus a handful of LDCs that offer legal incentives to attract foreign bank activity.

Recent History

In general, banking offices and services have followed industrial clients into new types of business and into new countries through the years. In the 18th and 19th centuries, this meant that British, French, Spanish, and Dutch banks established overseas networks of affiliates to support the business taking place within the colonial systems of their respective countries. Even today, the presence of British banks (e.g., Barclays and Lloyds) in former British colonies, of French banks (e.g. Crédit Lyonnais and Banque Nationale de Paris) in former French colonies, and so on, is greater than one might expect, considering the small markets of many of these nations and their distance from their former home countries.

In the first half of the 20th century, when Great Britain and the United States were the largest industrial powers, banks from these two countries extended their overseas activities as British and American multinational industrial firms spread their mines, factories, and sales offices throughout the world. By 1960, there were about 5,000 foreign branches and agencies of commercial banks headquartered in major industrialized countries (still dominated by the more than 4,000 affiliates of British banks in the British Commonwealth, mainly throughout Africa and Asia).[7] American banks in

Table 24-3 **International Spread of Banking Affiliates**

Country of Origin	Banks	Host Area: U.S.	UK	Fra.	Ger.	Switz.	Neth.	Other Eur.	Lat. A.	Jap.	Hong Kong	Other Far E.	Mideast	Africa	Carib.	Pan.	Sing./Mal.
United States	136	n.a.	56	21	22	8	7	60	85	32	31	69	30	16	188	19	26
United Kingdom	20	19	n.a.	21	8	8	6	66	102	8	87	357	142	148	78	5	59
France	24	11	13	n.a.	16	10	2	46	30	7	10	18	23	30	4	3	3
Germany	12	13	6	2	n.a.	0	0	1	1	5	4	5	0	0	2	5	3
Switzerland	12	8	8	0	0	n.a.	1	3	0	3	0	0	1	0	7	0	2
Netherlands	7	8	5	0	2	0	n.a.	8	28	3	2	5	10	2	9	1	3
Italy	6	11	4	0	0	0	0	6	6	1	0	0	5	1	0	0	1
Other Europe	32	18	158	79	7	1	1	20	22	0	3	0	6	1	1	0	0
Canada	7	28	15	2	6	0	2	5	26	0	2	3	7	1	138	2	6
Latin America	15	16	4	2	1	0	1	3	39	2	0	0	1	1	7	11	1
Japan	23	47	23	1	11	0	0	6	9	n.a.	7	16	0	0	1	0	10
Australia	9	7	17	0	0	0	0	0	0	0	0	528*	0	0	0	0	0
Other Far East	47	36	130	4	5	0	1	2	1	18	43	76	81	24	5	1	138
Mideast	21	17	20	6	8	0	0	3	0	0	0	4	106	10	3	0	0
Africa	15	0	8	4	0	0	0	0	0	0	0	0	13	15	0	0	0
Caribbean	1	0	0	0	0	0	0	0	13	0	0	0	0	0	0	0	0

*The Australia and New Zealand Bank moved its head office to Australia and is therefore counted as an Australian bank. Its branches, agencies, subbranches, and offices no longer appear as British owned. Branches, agencies, subbranches, and offices of the bank located outside Australia are included in the "Australia" row, "Other Far East" column.

Source: Page and Soss, "The International Spread of Banking Affiliates," Richmond Fed *International Banking*, p. 143.

particular faced a regulatory structure that encouraged overseas expansion, since domestically all banks were limited to expansion within one state only, and then often only on a restricted basis. The "money center" banks from New York extended their activities aggressively into Europe and elsewhere during this time.

During the 1970s, international banking was struck by the dramatic shift in wealth between industrialized nations and OPEC developing nations that resulted from the two oil crises; the banking industry responded by recycling the "petrodollars" generated by this shift. As was seen in the section on the oil industry, this recycling led to a very large increase in lending to nontraditional borrowers, such as governments in less developed countries. It also led to the establishment of new multinational banks in the oil-exporting countries and to the creation of a financial center in the Middle East (in Bahrain).

The structure of international financial dealings with LDCs changed remarkably during the decade of the 70s. In the two preceding decades, most of the lending to governments in less developed countries had come from official sources, such as foreign government departments (e.g., the U.S. Treasury) and international agencies (e.g., the International Monetary Fund and the World Bank). During those decades, approximately two thirds of the loan financing provided to LDC governments had come from official sources, and the remaining third from commercial banks. By the late 1970s, financing of this kind had grown dramatically and had shifted toward the private sector, so that commercial banks now provided about two thirds of such financing (particularly to large LDCs such as Brazil and Mexico), and official agencies the remainder.[8]

Among the industrialized countries, competition among banks has developed in line with changes in the competitiveness of manufacturing firms. That is, as U.S. (and British) firms have lost market share to competitors in Europe and Japan, so too have U.S. (and British) banks faced increasing competition from German, Swiss, and Japanese banks in many countries. Also, as national governments have permitted more participation by foreign banks in their economies, the competition among banks has become much more international.

Industry Structure

The banking industry is structured somewhat differently in each country. In the United States, there are over 14,000 commercial banks. Federal law substantially limits an individual bank's activities in more than one state. Nonetheless, about 20 of the largest banks, with assets of over $US 20 billion apiece, carry out almost half of the value of U.S. banking transactions. In Great Britain, where nationwide banking is permitted, a group of six very large banks (Barclays, National Westminster, Midland, Lloyds, Royal Bank of Scotland, and Bank of Scotland) dominate the domestic market and own most of the 14,000 bank branches throughout the country. Over 400 foreign banks participate in the international segments of the market. In Venezuela, seven local banks hold 60 percent of the banking deposits, and they control most of the international segment as well. Foreign banks are limited to ownership of 20 percent of the equity in a Venezuelan bank.[9] All in all, domestic banking activities are much less concentrated in the United States than in other countries, but international banking activities are fairly concentrated everywhere.

The *eurocurrency* market, the largest financial market in the world, is located mainly in the financial centers of the industrialized countries,[10] plus a handful of offshore sites such as Hong Kong, Panama, and Bahrain. The banks participating in this market at any location generally belong to the group of multinational banks noted in Table 24-4. (The eurocurrency market is discussed in some detail in Chapter 6.)

Participation by government-owned institutions is especially important in banking, since governments establish the rules of the game in each country and since they can pursue goals other than profit as part of their banking strategies. Typically, the largest and most important commercial banks in less developed countries are state owned, and this situation also exists in a few industrialized countries, such as Sweden and France. The major French banks, which are all government owned, provide an excellent example of such institutions, dominating the domestic market and competing actively in the euromarkets. The services offered by state-owned banks do not differ from those offered by their private sector competitors; in international banking the only noticeable difference between state-owned and private sector banks is that the state-owned banks serve some captive clients (namely, government agencies and companies).

Major Banking Competitors

The 50 most important commercial banks in the world are listed in Table 24-4 according to their rankings by assets. Notice that the dominance of U.S.-based banks has disappeared over the past decade and that there is a fairly even distribution of leading banks among the United States, Japan, Canada, Germany, France, Great Britain, and a few other European countries.

The particular competitive advantages possessed by the multinational banks listed in Table 24-4 are somewhat difficult to assess. If we use the number of foreign affiliates as a measure of experience in international business, then the British banks have a large advantage. If we consider the diversity of financial services offered, then the Japanese banks with ties to large trading companies are probably the most active outside the realms of deposit taking and lending. To some extent, the banks that can minimize their costs of providing financial services show the greatest profitability, since the cost of obtaining funds is fairly similar for all of the banks in question. In this case, it is the diverse group of banks that show the greatest returns on assets that possess a cost advantage. (Clearly, the multinational banks that have access to funds in a number of countries have a probable cost-of-funds advantage over local banks in any one market that offers limited borrowing sources.) The advantage of a well-known brand name is possessed by all of

Table 24-4 **The World's Largest Commercial Banking Corporations, 1985**

Bank	Assets ($ billions)*	Pretax Profit on Assets	Pretax Profit on Capital
1. Citicorp	142.7	1.15%	25.32%
2. Dai-Ichi Kangyo Bank	119.0	0.48	18.66
3. Fuji	115.1	0.55	18.96
4. BankAmerica	113.7	0.40	8.84
5. Mitsubishi	110.7	0.53	18.54
6. Sumitomo	107.6	0.61	26.62
7. Banque Nationale de Paris	98.9	0.35	22.84
8. Sanwa	96.4	0.51	18.78
9. Crédit Agricole	92.4	—	—
10. Crédit Lyonnais	90.4	0.37	31.37
11. Société Générale	87.1	0.25	18.09
12. Barclays	85.1	0.95	23.56
13. Norinchukin	83.0	—	—
14. National Westminster	82.7	1.02	24.35
15. Industrial Bank of Japan	81.7	0.57	23.63
16. Chase Manhattan	81.6	0.80	16.54
17. Tokai	76.0	0.45	17.54
18. Deutsche	73.3	0.87	26.47
19. Manufacturers Hanover	73.0	0.84	18.96
20. Midland	71.1	0.24	7.53
21. Mitsui	71.0	0.39	16.27
22. Bank of Tokyo	66.1	0.56	23.64
23. Long-Term Credit Bank of Japan	65.4	0.37	17.33
24. Royal Bank of Canada	64.4	1.02	24.01
25. Mitsubishi	61.6	0.26	11.77
26. J. P. Morgan	61.2	1.20	19.93
27. Taiyo Kobe	59.7	0.39	21.19
28. Hongkong and Shanghai	59.7	—	—
29. Mitsui Trust	58.4	—	—
30. Sumitomo Trust	58.0	0.31	12.74
31. Compagnie Financiero de Paribas	56.2	0.66	16.77
32. Dresdner	55.5	0.53	19.85
33. Bank of Montreal	55.4	0.55	13.74
34. Daiwa Bank	51.9	0.32	14.98
35. Lloyds Bank	50.9	1.14	22.05

Table 24-4 *(concluded)*

36. Union Bank of Switzerland	50.6	0.73	14.26
37. Chemical Bank of New York	49.8	0.79	15.96
38. Canadian Imperial	49.4	0.61	14.89
39. Banco do Brasil	47.4	3.41	45.01
40. Yasuda	46.2	0.21	10.60
41. Swiss Bank	46.0	1.10	22.07
42. Banca Nazionale del Lavoro	45.8	0.38	14.41
43. Westdeutsche Landesbank	44.8	0.12	4.05
44. Security Pacific	44.8	1.09	24.38
45. First Interstate	44.0	0.80	15.87
46. Bank of Nova Scotia	43.5	0.64	17.09
47. Bankers Trust	42.6	0.99	20.24
48. Algemene Bank Nederland	41.4	0.45	16.78
49. Nippon Credit	40.7	0.37	17.09
50. Standard Chartered	39.85	0.92	22.40

*Assets do not include contra accounts.
Source: "The Euromoney 500," *Euromoney* (June 1986).

the banks listed; indeed, any bank with over $US 40 billion in assets is generally considered trustworthy! A final competitive advantage worth noting is an existing customer base in one country that can be extended overseas as clients establish operations in other countries. Banks based in the United States, home of the largest number of multinational enterprises, should have an advantage in this regard, with their access to more clients in the domestic market.

An interesting aspect of competitive advantage in banking is the positioning of large multinational banks in competition with smaller local banks in national markets. Since such competition usually occurs for domestic banking activities, it will not be discussed here. However, a number of useful analyses of the subject are available in the literature.[11]

Telecommunications

Telephone Service and Production Worldwide

In every country, telephone *service* is provided by a local company (typically owned by the government), regardless of the skills needed to operate the system or the source of the equipment used. The *production* of telephone equipment, on the other hand, is dominated by half a dozen firms worldwide. Because the provision of telephone service is viewed as a strategic issue in the national economy, this industry is influenced by political as well as economic factors. While historically companies such as ITT (International Telephone & Telegraph) have operated telephone systems in some less developed countries, by 1985 the ownership of national telephone systems virtually everywhere except the United States had become the province of national governments or their chosen domestic companies.

Producing the high-tech equipment that is used to transmit and receive telephone and other telecommunication signals requires huge capital and technological resources. Therefore, the production side of telecommunications still remains in the hands of corporations—though often with strict contractual arrangements between these corporations and governments to disallow corporate activities perceived to be against the national interest.

The production of telecommunications equipment ranges from sophisticated manufacture of incredibly tiny integrated circuits to assembly of the telephone units used in homes and offices. While most of the really technology-intensive work is done in a few industrialized countries by very large MNEs, assembly of telephones and some components, such as silicon chips, is now done in a wide variety of countries, especially in the low-cost LDCs of Southeast Asia (namely Taiwan, Singapore, Hong Kong, and South Korea). Because of the pervasive nationalism in the provision of telephone service, equipment standards have never become standardized and a wide variety of standards still exists among countries.[12]

Recent History

The recent history of the provision of telephone service largely follows the pattern of raw materials production around the world. That is, less developed countries have declared the telephone service industry to be a "national resource," and in the 1960s and 70s such countries nationalized their telephone systems.

On the other hand, telephone equipment production has followed the spread of new technology, with competition among a few large firms supported by their national governments and with fewer than 10 major competitors dominating production worldwide since World War II. The most important technological changes during the past 40 years have been the development of satellite transmission, the use of optical fibers in telephone cables, and the introduction of silicon chips of increasingly tiny dimensions to replace vacuum tubes and then transistors for information storage and switching. As these changes occurred, the competitors in the industry remained mostly the same, but their competitive positions shifted, depending on the extent to which they took advantage of the new technological opportunities.

The most important recent events that have altered competition in the telecommunications industry have been the nationalizations of telephone companies in most less developed countries and, in industrialized countries, the opening to competition of telephone equipment production and the

A technician checking electronic telephone switching equipment at AT&T.

Milton & Joan Mann/Cameramann International

provision of some telephone service, rather than continued monopoly by the existing telephone service provider. These events are discussed in more detail below.

Industry Structure

This discussion focuses on the production side of the telecommunications industry and on international telecommunication service. Domestic telecommunication service, which is either government owned or greatly government controlled in all countries, will not be discussed here.

The telecommunications industry is now in a state of rapid transition. Due to the "information revolution," microelectronics has become the focal point of the communications business. Tiny silicon chips that can store more than 256,000 bits of information per chip are being widely produced, and 1 mega-bit chips are coming into large-scale production. Such chips are used in typewriters, telephones, computers, and even in the equipment that switches telephone calls from one location to another (that is, telephone exchanges). Manufacturers of telephones and other telecommunications equipment must act quickly to master the new technology and create prod-

choose to buy its integrated office equipment (LME hopes to develop a market niche in this way) but that it risks serious difficulties if customers choose another supplier's system or do not buy integrated office systems at all.

Nippon Electric Corporation has a far smaller overseas marketing network than the other four companies. Therefore, one aspect of its strategy is to expand the international part of its business, focusing especially on the United States. NEC relies on its image as a supplier of high-quality electronic products, though its after-sale service is viewed as poor by many critics. Much like AT&T, until recently NEC sold much of its equipment directly to the Japanese telephone company, a related firm. Since NEC began to look for outside customers, its approach has been weak in the marketing area. Its strengths lie in its ability to produce very reliable equipment and in its low costs due to the use of low-cost Japanese and Asian labor. Its present strategy is to merge its activities in the computer and communications areas toward the emerging industry of information technology. NEC expects to lead this industry in technology development.

Siemens is the second most diversified of the five companies. Its products range from light bulbs to nuclear power plants, with about a third of its sales in telecommunications. Except for its telecommunications division, Siemens is quite similar to the U.S.-based General Electric Company. As the largest private sector company in Germany, Siemens plays a very important role in that country's economy. Its competitive advantages appear to lie in a reputation for reliable, well-designed products and for after-sale service. A major criticism of the company is that it moves very bureaucratically, reacting to competitors' advances rather than leading the market. In the telecommunications market, the ability to introduce products that use the latest technology has become more and more important during the past decade. Thus, Siemens will probably have to become more innovative to compete effectively in this market in the future. Through licensing and joint ventures with two California firms, it has entered the market for computer chips. This strategy is expected to help Siemens design state-of-the-art telecommunications products.

No one can know the future. It is not possible to forecast exactly which of the five companies will produce the best results through the 1980s and into the 1990s. Nonetheless, based on the competitive advantages and the current strategies of the companies, it is possible to gain some useful insights into the likely direction of future competition.

Conclusions

Each of the four industries that have been examined in this chapter has been important internationally during the 1980s. All four are linked through financial transactions and information networks, though no individual firms own businesses in all four. Each of these industries also involves competitors ranging from the largest multinational enterprises all the way down to the smallest local bank, gas station, or telephone vendor. While the discussion has focused on large firms that participate in several segments of the market, the activities of thousands of smaller firms play an important role in the total picture—especially when the large MNEs are excluded from market segments that are protected for local, typically smaller, competitors.

Despite the great importance of government regulation and participation in these industries, the dominant firms in the international parts of the industries are mostly private sector corporations. Thus far in the current century, government-owned enterprises have not gained the level of international diversification that their private counterparts have achieved. This fact does not deny the growing activities of such firms as Petrobras (based in Brazil), Crédit Lyonnais (based in France), or Nippon Telephone & Telegraph (based in Japan) in other countries. In the future, a much greater share of global business may very well be held by public sector corporations, depending on how firms, both public and private, respond to future competitive challenges.

While only the telecommunications industry is necessarily based in the rapidly changing electronics field, the banking industry has clearly become more and more dependent on international communications and data processing, and the petroleum industry utilizes sophisticated electronic equipment for information processing, production machinery controls, and even exploration. Companies in the automobile industry are moving to "factories of the future," which feature extensive use of industrial robots. The nature of competition in each of these four industries is changing as such technological shifts occur and as government policies toward foreign private sector enterprises change.

Questions

1. Explain the importance of *technology* in the petroleum, automobile, banking, and telecommunications industries.
2. What firms are major competitors in the oil refining business in the United States, Europe, and the Middle East? What firms are major competitors in the gasoline sales business? Why is there a substantial difference between the two?
3. What are the key factors that determine the competitiveness of banks in domestic markets in (*a*) the United States and (*b*) Latin America?
4. What are the key factors that determine the competitiveness of banks in international financial markets in the United States and Europe?
5. Describe the competitive positions of AT&T, LME, and NEC in the production of global telecommunication equipment production. Which strategy do you think will work best in the next five years? Why?
6. The oil industry is based on a natural resource that governments have increasingly chosen to nationalize in the past two decades. Why does the telecommunications industry, which uses almost no natural resources, face similar government restrictions?

7. Do you expect to see more or fewer international banks in the next 10 years? Why?
8. Which countries are the main producers of crude petroleum? Which countries are the main consumers of oil-based products? What can multinational oil companies do to benefit from this situation?
9. How would you expect IBM's entry into the telecommunications industry to affect competition in that industry? What will be the probable impact of IBM's entry on the other firms mentioned in the text?
10. Describe a set of market segments in the petroleum, automobile, and telecommunications industries that would be appropriate ones for small firms to enter. Explain why each of these segments would be potentially viable for a small firm.

References

Aliber, Robert. "International Banking: A Survey," *Journal of Money, Credit, and Banking,* November 1984, part 2.

Altshuler, Alan, Martin Anderson, et al., *The Future of the Automobile.* Cambridge, Mass.: MIT Press, 1984.

American Petroleum Institute. *Oil & Gas Journal.* Various issues.

Anderson, Robert. *Fundamentals of the Petroleum Industry.* Norman: University of Oklahoma Press, 1984.

Crane, Dwight, and Samuel Hayes. "The Evolution of International Banking Competition and its Implications for Regulation," *Journal of Bank Research,* Spring 1983.

Exxon Corporation. *Middle East Oil.* New York: Exxon, 1984.

Federal Reserve Bank of Richmond. *International Banking.* Richmond, Va.: Federal Reserve Bank, 1981.

Fortune, "The International 500," (August 4, 1986).

Odell, Peter, *Oil and World Power.* 8th ed. Middlesex, England: Penguin Books, 1986.

Roncaglia, Alessandro. *The International Oil Market.* Armonk, N.Y.: M. E. Sharpe, 1985.

Sampson, Anthony. *The Seven Sisters.* New York: Basic Books, 1979.

________. *The Money Lenders.* New York: Penguin Books, 1983.

World Motor Vehicle Data. Detroit: World Motor Vehicle Association, various editions.

Endnotes

1. Exxon Corporation, *Middle East Oil* (New York: Exxon, 1984), p. 4.
2. Gulf is now part of Socal (Chevron).

3. Exxon, *Middle East Oil,* p. 24.
4. Ibid, pp. 38-9.
5. Anthony Sampson, *The Seven Sisters* (New York: Basic Books, 1979); Robert O. Anderson, *Fundamentals of the Petroleum Industry* (Norman: University of Oklahoma Press, 1984); and Peter Odell, *Oil and World Power.*
6. *World Motor Vehicle Data.*
7. Dwight Crane and Samuel Hayes, "The Evolution of International Banking Competition and Its Implications for Regulation," *Journal of Bank Research,* Spring 1983, p. 41.
8. Data calculated from World Bank, *World Debt Tables* (various issues), and Bank for International Settlements, *Lending by Group of 10 Banks to Nonresident Borrowers* (various issues).
9. Data on United States, Great Britain, and Venezuela are from Business International Corporation, *Investing, Licensing, and Trading Conditions* (New York: Business International Corporation, 1985 country issue for each country).
10. Bank for International Settlements semiannual data on nonresident deposits in group of 10 commercial banks, June 1985.
11. See, for example, R. Alton Gilbert, "Bank Market Structure and Competition," *Journal of Money, Credit, and Banking,* November 1984, pp. 617-45; also see Gerald Hanweck and Stephen Rhoades, "Dominant Firms, 'Deep Pockets,' and Local Market Competition in Banking," *Journal of Economics and Business,* 1984, pp. 391-402.
12. See, for example, *Business Week,* March 31, 1986, pp. 68-70.

25

MULTINATIONAL ENTERPRISES AND THE WORLD ORDER: A LOOK TO THE FUTURE

This chapter attempts to project the key concerns of international business managers into the 1990s. It looks at government policies, internal company activities, the economic environment, and the political environment. It suggests changes that will take place in the kinds of business carried out by multinational enterprises. In general, it extrapolates into the future and interprets with respect to international firms some of the key technological, regulatory, and social trends that are already under way. The main goals of the chapter are to:

1. Demonstrate the importance of technological change in determining business patterns.
2. Discuss possible shifts in government policy toward MNEs.
3. Consider the likelihood of the MNE's survival.
4. Project likely shifts in competitive conditions in international industries.
5. Project likely shifts in relationships between managers and workers, between managers and company owners, and among managers within the MNE.

Introduction

This chapter looks to the future. What will be the key concerns of MNE managers in the 1990s? How will MNEs deal with home and host governments and societies as the number of MNEs grows and as national priorities shift? And what will be the major characteristics of international business a decade from now? The answers to these questions cannot be known for certain, but some of the broad outline of future conditions can be read from today's circumstances. Without speculating too extensively, we will give an outlook on some of the important issues that are likely to face managers in international business during the next 10 years.

The next section discusses a range of issues that will present major challenges to managers in international firms in the future. Then comments are made on the sometimes rocky, sometimes smooth, but always important relations between international firms and governments. It is argued that as a reaction to external pressures, such as government demands on firms, companies will increasingly become **international contractors,** using contractual relationships rather than ownership in many international business situations. The fourth section examines key aspects of the structure and conduct of competition in global markets. This is followed by a look at important developments in internal company relations among workers, managers, and owners and, finally, some conclusions.

Major Managerial Considerations for International Firms

Technology

Technology is arguably the most important input in the production of goods and services, since it determines the manner in which capital, workers, and other factors are utilized. Since it is not possible to know what inventions will be made in the future, it is likewise impossible to know what key innovations will transform the workplace.

In the industrialized countries, we have seen a continuing trend toward the production of such services as recreation, government, and computer programming during the past half-century. *Employment* in agriculture, fishing, and other sources of food products has been declining, while the *production* of food products has continued to grow (due to laborsaving advances in production technology). Similarly, employment in manufacturing has ceased to grow substantially, and has even been declining in some countries—again while output has continued to rise due to greater efficiency and more use of other production factors. The trend toward greater employment in the provision of services will probably continue in the industrialized countries, though not to the complete exclusion of manufacturing and the production of raw materials.

One important reason for continuing to manufacture in industrialized countries, despite the lower production costs that often exist in LDCs, is the importance of **spillover benefits** from manufacturing. When a firm produces automobiles in Detroit, that production leads to related production of tires, steel, glass, and so on to supply the automakers, which in turn leads to the development of new products and processes through the experiences of the various manufacturers. Such spillover benefits help maintain the technological advantages of the innovating countries—which would be lost if manufacturing were fully transferred to other countries.

There are other important reasons for continuing to manufacture. For one, some products can be produced only where technical knowledge is available; these products include high-tech electronics, specialty chemicals, and aerospace vehicles. Another reason is that firms do not want to subject all of their manufacturing to "country risk" problems (which are particularly prevalent in LDCs), so they typically diversify production into both DCs and LDCs. Finally, some products are simply cheaper to produce and distribute in industrialized countries, which are the main markets. All of this implies that manufacturing will continue to be a very significant base of the economies of industrialized countries.[1]

An important aspect of technological development is its impact on the workplace. The clearest tendency in technological change is that such change generally leads to a reduced need for production inputs, or to changes in the amounts of certain inputs needed, or to greater satisfaction of consumer demands—in each instance raising the economic welfare of society. Based on this reasoning, we can expect future technological change in industrialized countries to reduce the amount of time required for work and to increase the amount of leisure time. Though the tendency is the same in less developed countries, high levels of unemployment and highly skewed income distributions will continue to limit the benefits of technological change in such countries as compared with industrialized countries.

A specific change in workplace activity that has occurred recently and promises to continue into the future is office computerization. Microcomputers have revolutionized the performance of many business tasks—from typing to copying, to mailing, to financial forecasting—and this has led to greater decentralization of work. More people carry out office activities at home, with less frequent trips and more telecommunication to the office. Since more and more people are employed in office-type activities, in manufacturing firms as well as service providers, and in government as well as the private sector, computer-related changes in the office environment are radically altering how people do their jobs. From the perspective of the MNE manager, those firms that carry out this transition most effectively will gain a competitive advantage over rivals.

Government/Business Relations

If we ignore the possibility of a third world war between capitalist and communist countries, which would dramatically alter government/business relations, then changes in government policies are likely to be incremental during the next decade. That is, national governments recognize the benefits and costs of allowing MNEs to operate. Therefore, these governments will continue to impose policies that constrain MNEs from undertaking what they view as undesirable activities (e.g., massive destabilizing currency transfers, production switching to avoid labor disputes, pollution-causing production, electronic transfer of "sensitive" information across national borders), and they will continue to try to attract MNE activities that they view as desirable (e.g., local R&D, manufacturing, transfer of knowledge).

At the transnational level, intergovernmental agreements on policy toward MNEs remain very elusive. The attempts of several organizations to formulate codes of conduct and other transnational policies have been relatively unsuccessful. Aside from further agreements to share information about company activities and some standards on corporate behavior, such as nonintervention in government affairs, major transnational policies that would affect the investment or major operating decisions of MNEs appear unlikely.

The United Nations began an effort to create a **Code of Conduct on Transnational Corporations** soon after the call in 1972 for a **New International Economic Order** that would redistribute wealth to give the less developed countries a greater share. The aim of this code is to prescribe guidelines or rules whose observance will ensure that multinational firms more fully serve national goals in the countries where they operate. Issues such as technology transfer, international financial transfers, labor relations, and information flows, constitute the core of the proposed code. Although the United Nations members have been negotiating for more than 15 years, several major disagreements still block the final passage of the code. However, the United Nations members are fairly well agreed on the main provisions of the code, most of which are noted in the accompanying box.

The United Nations Code of Conduct on Transnational Corporations*

In early 1987, final agreement on this code still faced a number of hurdles. However, the overriding structure of the code was in place and was broadly accepted. Major sections of the code cover the following subjects:

Policy toward MNEs

1. *Observance of Domestic Laws in Host Countries.* Local subsidiaries, branches, and other affiliates of MNEs are to be subject to the national laws of the country in which they operate.
2. *Settlement of Disputes between MNEs and Countries.* The host government has the right to choose the court or other legal arbiter of disputes involving firms within its jurisdiction.

3. *Noninterference in Domestic Political Affairs.* MNEs should not engage in activities that undermine the host country's political, social, and constitutional systems.
4. *Respect for National Sovereignty.* MNEs must respect the national sovereignty of host countries and the right of host countries to exercise sovereignty over their natural resources and wealth.

Policy toward Governments

5. *Fair and Equitable Treatment.* MNEs should receive fair and equitable treatment from host governments.
6. *National Treatment.* Subject to needs for national security and other government policy goals, MNEs should receive treatment similar to that received by domestic enterprises in similar circumstances.
7. *Nationalization and Compensation.* States have the right to nationalize assets of MNEs, and compensation is to be paid according to applicable legal rules.
8. *Funds Transfers by MNEs.* MNEs are entitled to transfer all payments legally due. Transfers are subject to relevant legislation of the host country such as foreign exchange laws.

The bilateral assignment of responsibilities to companies and governments follows the structure of the OECD Code (1976) and is intended to create a stable business environment conducive to foreign direct investment and other company activities that stimulate economic development.

* See, for example, United Nations Center on Transnational Corporations, *CTC Reporter*, January 1986, which discusses the code effort from several perspectives.

The policies of individual countries toward MNEs have been becoming more and more selective about permitted activities. Although industrialized countries continue to use the free market as the fundamental base of their economies, they have been requiring increasing compliance with "fair" labor practices (see the account of the Badger case in the accompanying box), greater responsibility to consumers, and stricter standards on reporting to government agencies.

The Badger Case

One interesting example of labor relations policy that has been applied to a multinational enterprise is the case of Badger Corporation and the government of Belgium. In this instance, a U.S.-based MNE (Badger, Inc., a subsidiary of Raytheon Corporation) was sued for failure to provide financial backing to its Belgian subsidiary, which declared bankruptcy and then failed to offer its 237 laid-off employees sufficient funds to cover Belgium's required termination payments. A group of Belgian labor unions brought the case to the Belgian government, arguing that the MNE had failed to live up to an international agreement among OECD countries (including Belgium and the United States) that required MNEs to follow national labor relations rules. The Belgian government argued that Badger, Inc., should bear financial responsibility for the termination of its affiliate's labor contracts in Belgium. Ultimately, Badger, Inc., settled directly with the Belgian government and agreed to pay the termination costs of its Belgian subsidiary beyond those paid by the bankrupt subsidiary. This example demonstrates that although industrialized countries are quite willing to permit MNEs to operate locally, they are scrutinizing the activities of such firms more closely and discouraging undesirable practices.

Source: For a complete history of the situation, see R. Blanpain, *The Badger Case* (Deventer, the Netherlands: Kluwer, 1977).

Less developed countries, on the other hand, have shifted toward more favorable regulation of MNEs in the 1980s compared with the previous two decades. They have moved from the strategy of inward-looking development, characterized by heavy emphasis on import substitution, to a more outward-looking view, in which greater participation of foreign firms is permitted. As LDC government managers become more expert in dealing with MNEs, however, they are tending to follow the industrial countries in demanding more from these firms. (Since 1985, for example, the Brazilian government has demanded that all computers sold in the country be locally manufactured.)[2] Very important exceptions to the basic trend are firms in raw materials industries and public services whose ownership LDC governments took or kept in the 1960s and 70s. These governments show every sign that they will continue to operate and control such state-owned firms without private sector participation. As a result, opportunities are growing for MNEs to supply services to state-owned resource firms through licensing and management contracting.

Company/Society Relations

Despite popular movements that favor smaller firms (promoted, for example, in E. G. Schumacher's *Small is Beautiful*) and a less-bureaucratic society, large MNEs, whose competitive advantages include technology, scale economies, and information transfer capabilities, play an increasing role in business worldwide. This is not to say that all business is becoming more concentrated, but rather that more firms are becoming multinational. In the United States, the rate of growth of small firms is far greater than that of large MNEs—but so also is the rate of failure of the small firms.[3] On balance, one may conclude that small local firms and large MNEs will continue to coexist, without any trend toward either smaller or larger average firm size.

An interesting phenomenon related to **corporate social responsibility** and portending future conditions has been occurring in MNEs during the past decade or so. Multinational firms often go to great lengths to establish legal ties among their affiliates around the world. These firms choose legal structures to minimize taxes, to ensure control, to conform to host country requirements, and so on. Nonetheless, when some liability arises in a foreign affiliate (regardless of how that affiliate is legally structured), the parent company very often steps in to support the affiliate. For example, when Union Carbide's joint-venture plant in Bhopal, India, leaked deadly gas that killed over 2,000 people in 1985, the parent company took responsibility for compensating the victims.[4] The joint venture itself, a limited-liability company, had far too few assets to settle those claims. The Badger case, discussed above, is another example of such parent company support.

Industry Structure

The mid-1980s have witnessed a dramatic rise in very large corporate mergers in the industrialized countries. From Socal's (Chevron) purchase of Gulf Oil, to CGF's purchase of ITT's telecommunications operations in Europe, to Hoechst's purchase of Celanese Corporation, these "megamergers" have become almost commonplace. At the other end of the size spectrum, thousands of tiny firms have become multinational in the same industries in which the megamergers have occurred. And even the largest firms have either chosen or been forced to contract out some of their activities, rather than internalizing, again adding to the number of competitors. Industry structure is perhaps becoming more changeable, though not any more or any less concentrated on average.

One result of the mergers and acquisitions that have been taking place is that newly formed competitors often shake up previous industry structures. When a chemical company buys an oil company, the vertical linkages involved affect competitive conditions in both the oil and the chemical industry. The chemical company (e.g., Du Pont) obtains a guaranteed source of supply of raw material at a relatively low price, and the oil company (e.g., Conoco) gains a customer for a substantial part of its output. This kind of competitive positioning is sure to continue, resulting in major realignments of firms in each industry. (Note that such realignments are due to the acquisition strategies of firms, rather than to technological changes, which are another factor tending to remake industry structures.)

Company Internal Relations

One of the most intractable problems of industrial society has always been the **alienation** of workers from their jobs.[5] When jobs consist of carrying out a few functions within a large, impersonal assembly line or a complicated production process, such alienation is commonplace. Over time, industrial psychologists and other investigators have developed ways to reduce the severity of this problem. One way is to move workers into different kinds of work during the day, to maintain mental alertness. Another is to involve workers in company decision making, whether through worker representation on plant councils or boards of corporate supervision (as in Germany's codetermination), or through quality circles, or through the Japanese "ringi" system of consultative decision making. The goal of all these techniques is to create a more productive, more satisfied work force. As the problem of alienation has become more widely recognized, solutions are being more extensively implemented.

The problem is far from solved, as demonstrated by the occurrence of strikes and demonstrations from time to time in all of the noncommunist industrialized countries. However, as manufacturing and raw materials production become more mechanized and as more workers function in office environments rather than in factories or fields, the severity of the problem is reduced to some degree. The future human relations problems of companies will tend to relate to fair treatment and participation in decision making. As noted above, many methods of increasing participation have been tried, and more are being developed all the time. One key source of future competitive advantages will be the skill to manage human relations within the firm so that employees are motivated and productive and the human capital investment they embody is challenged and tapped.

Relations among First, Second, and Third Worlds

The political environment plays a part in the MNE's future, not only through dealings with individual host and home countries but also through broader political relations among major blocs of countries. If communist and capitalist countries avoid war but enter a period of greater confrontation and opposition to each other, then surely international business between countries in different blocs will decline, perhaps drastically. If less developed countries become more integrated into the international capitalist economic system, then substantially greater MNE activity will develop in those countries.

Because the LDCs each face different levels of economic development, different resources, different political goals, and so on, no grouping of such countries appears likely to confront the MNEs in the future. Barring the emergence of successful interest groups, such as OPEC in the 1970s, the LDCs will probably continue to cooperate with industrialized countries, seeking financial aid and other assistance and not opposing the basic market economy that is used. This does not mean to say that relations between the two groups of countries will proceed smoothly in the future, but rather that the disputes between them will probably not lead to fragmentation of the international economic system.

Survival of the MNE?

Concerns and Bargaining Strengths

Previous chapters have discussed the relative bargaining positions of MNEs and governments in industrialized, less developed, and communist nations. Drawing from those discussions, a list of significant factors that should determine bargaining positions in the future is shown in Table 25-1. As long as a country can supply raw materials used in production or offer a market significant enough to attract MNE business, that country will possess a bargaining capability vis-à-vis MNEs that enables it to channel their activities in

Table 25-1 **Bargaining Chips of MNEs and Governments**

Governments	Companies
Control over raw materials	Control over technology
Control over market access	Control over international transmission of information
Setting the rules of the game (e.g., the role of private enterprise, the operation of state-owned firms)	Production-switching capability
Setting specific rules on MNEs—taxes, permissions, etc.	Flexibility to change strategy and activities limited only by preferences of owners
The obsolescing bargain	Economies of scale and scope

return for allowing them access to the materials or market. On the other side of the coin, as long as an MNE has some proprietary capability that governments see as desirable, such as product technology or distribution channels into foreign markets, plus the ability to move to another country if a government is not sufficiently cooperative, that MNE will possess a bargaining capability relative to the governments. (MNEs are limited in their choice of strategies by their owners' preferences for management of the firm, while governments are limited by their constituents' preferences, as expressed through either a voting process or some more authoritarian method of control.)

The relationships between MNEs and governments will continue to operate as bargaining situations—favoring one or the other as political, technological, competitive, and other conditions change. The obsolescing bargain will continue to characterize business/government negotiations, requiring company managers to plan their entry and operating strategies to recognize the "hostage" effect of placing fixed assets in any government's jurisdiction (including that of the home country). While governments are discovering new methods of obtaining benefits from MNE activities all the time, there is no tendency to eliminate MNEs as actors in international business, since many of their bargaining advantages remain proprietary and highly "appropriable" (i.e., capable of being protected by the firms).

The New MNE—The International Contractor

From the bargaining situations described above, and due to increased competition from other firms, MNEs are experiencing more and more pressure to externalize their activities. Whether it be the demand of a host government to take on a local partner or the enticement of a joint research project with a rival firm to reduce R&D costs, pressures are mounting toward increased contractual arrangements between firms. Simultaneously, the previous reliance on wholly owned affiliates, especially preferred by U.S.-based firms, has shifted toward a greater willingness to utilize nontraditional methods such as joint ventures, licensing or service contracting, turnkey ventures, and combinations of these, as managers realize the relative profitability and strategic viability of such arrangements.

As additional small firms become multinational (by establishing affiliates in three or more countries), the tendency is again to externalize some activities, especially when the firm's resources or skills do not permit it to go beyond its core activities. What we are seeing, in essence, is that even small firms are looking at multiple countries as their markets—rather than being constrained by national borders in their strategy making. Then, as corporate expansion occurs, and given low costs of international transportation and easy communication, they seek new markets or products in different countries. Just as small domestic firms often contract out for parts of their business, so too do the new small multinationals, which face similar constraints on their activities.

In sum, large MNEs are utilizing more externalized contracting due to regulatory constraints and small firms are using externalized contracting due to their internal economic and managerial constraints. Both of these trends foreshadow the rise of a new class of multinational firm, the **international contractor (INC).** The INC is defined as a firm that carries out business activities in at least two countries, but without necessarily owning affiliates in both. The INC operates from a home office that controls the use of its key competitive advantages, such as proprietary production technology and its international information network. The home office also decides when to utilize the INC's competitive advantages through internalized operations such as local and foreign subsidiaries and when to sell knowledge or some other intermediate goods to potential customers. The INC is still a multinational firm, in the sense that it possesses multinational operations; its difference from the MNE lies solely in its lack of dependence on ownership of affiliates as the main vehicle for using its competitive advantages in different national environments. (The MNE, in fact, is a subset of the INC.)

The international contractor, like the MNE, may be a small or a large firm. The INC is in principle more open to nontraditional means of doing business around the world. For example, when Citibank discovered that its data processing skills were in demand by clients and competitors around the world, it chose to sell more than just its banking services. Now Citibank sells dozens of services to outside clients—access to a global computerized information network, technical support to clients that want to use the system, the software for record-keeping in such banking activities as customer deposit and loan accounts, technical support for use of that software, and so on. Rather than internalizing these services completely, Citibank has chosen to contract out for their use and expand its sales into markets that the bank itself cannot enter and into services that it previously limited to internal use.

Many other examples of international contractors exist. General Electric Company, the U.S.-based diversified electrical products manufacturer, has added a trading company to its portfolio of businesses. The trading company

Glossary

absolute advantage The production cost advantage that one country may have over another when one (or both) of two products is cheaper to produce in the first country.

accidental exports Those that are not really planned by the firm. Agents buy from the firm and export without the firm being aware that the sales to the agents are for export.

accounting system A numerically based method for keeping track of assets, how assets are funded, sales, expenses, and so on.

accounts receivable management The strategy used by some MNEs to adjust their A/R to reduce exchange risk and to optimally time funds transfers.

achievement motivation The desire of individuals or groups of individuals to accomplish objectives.

affiliate A partially or wholly owned unit of an MNE. Affiliates include wholly owned subsidiaries and branches, joint ventures, and any other legal form that implies control over the entity.

airway bill A document analogous to the bill of lading but used for air transport.

alienation The problem in industrial societies that some workers become dissatisfied with their jobs due to boredom, lack of stimulation, and impersonality.

American basis A method of quoting exchange rates, in U.S. dollars per unit of foreign exchange. That is, $US 0.147/FF1 is an American quote.

Andean Pact A regional integration group formed in 1967 that today includes Bolivia, Colombia, Ecuador, Peru, and Venezuela.

appropriability The nature of a technology that enables the innovator to protect it from use by competitors and to obtain economic rents from it.

appropriate technology Technology that is suitable for the distribution of factors of production in the country where it is used. In countries where labor is relatively abundant, for example, appropriate technology would be relatively labor-intensive.

Association of Southeast Asian Nations (ASEAN) A regional integration group formed in 1967 that includes Indonesia, Malaysia, the Philippines, Singapore, and Thailand.

automatic adjustment mechanism The economic response that occurs when a BOP imbalance arises. When a trade deficit exists under flexible exchange rates, a currency devaluation usually occurs to stimulate exports and reduce imports. Under fixed exchange rates, domestic inflation is expected to be lower than foreign inflation, leading to relatively lower domestic prices and again increased exports and reduced imports.

back-to-back letter of credit A form of pretrade financing in which the exporter uses the importer's letter of credit as a basis for seeking credit from a bank, which in turn backs its letter of credit to the exporter with the demonstrated likelihood of ability to repay that the importer's L/C represents.

balance A portfolio concept acknowledging that there may be a randomness to the factors causing success or failure at geographically dispersed operations, or that the correlation coefficient relating operations in one area with those in another is other than +1.00. The concept pertains to risk diversification by having a portfolio with co-variances equal to other than +1.00.

balance of payments (BOP) The financial record of all transactions between residents of one country and the rest of the world for some given time period.

balance of payments accounting A double-entry bookkeeping system that is used to record transactions that appear in the balance of payments.

balance of payments adjustment The automatic response of an economy to an imbalance in a country's international transactions. If a trade deficit occurs, it usually leads to a currency devaluation and/or reduction of domestic prices relative to prices in other countries.

(balance of) trade deficit The situation that occurs when a country's imports (in value terms) exceed that country's exports for some time period.

balance sheet hedging The MNE strategy of using financial hedges (such as forward contracts) to avoid translation risk that would potentially adversely affect the firm's balance sheet.

bank draft The means of payment for an export/import transaction. The draft may be a *sight draft*, i.e., payable when received, or a *time draft*, payable at the time specified on the document itself.

bankers acceptance A form of posttrade credit for the exporter, in which the exporter sells the account receivable to a bank at a discount in exchange for immediate payment.

bargaining unit All employees in a group that are covered by the same labor contract.

basic balance A balance of payments that measures all of the current account items plus the country's net exports of long-term capital during some time period.

bill of lading A shipping document that is used as evidence of a contract for shipping merchandise and as a claim of ownership of the goods.

board of supervision A group of employee-elected and shareholder-elected representatives that has major control over management decisions and that appoints the top managers. Usually found in Germany, Benelux and Northern Europe.

bona fide resident One who legally resides in a foreign country and meets the foreign residency requirements of his or her home country.

branch An office or extension of the parent company in a foreign country that is not incorporated in the foreign country.

brand or trade name A name, often protected by a trademark, used by a firm for its product(s). The name may, over time, come to connote high quality, good service, or some other favorable attribute that attracts purchasers away from similar products made by other firms.

broadline global competition The competitive strategy that implies production of a wide range of products in one or more industries with sales in many countries.

brokers' market The market for exchange of financial instruments between any two parties using an intermediary (broker) similar to an auctioneer to unite buyers and sellers. The foreign exchange brokers' market in the United States makes up a large part of the trades that involve two banks as buyer and seller.

business unionism A union philosophy stressing maximizing economic returns to union members rather than social or societal reforms to advantage working classes.

buy American policy A U.S. Government policy of buying supplies from U.S. firms unless foreign suppliers offer substantially better terms. Some purchases are completely restricted to U.S. suppliers; for example, defense-related materials.

buy-back agreement A form of countertrade in which the initial export sale is for a capital good that is used to produce products which are subsequently used as payment by the importer.

call option An option contract that entitles the purchaser to *buy* a fixed amount of foreign exchange at a fixed price in the future.

capital controls Limits on access to foreign exchange. These controls limit not only capital outflows but also imports, which cannot be paid for if capital controls disallow the payments.

capital flight The export of financial resources by residents of a country, typically in response to a situation of economic or political crisis.

Caribbean Basin Initiative (CBI) A U.S. government policy begun in 1983 that attempts to stimulate private-sector business in the Caribbean and Central America through tariff reductions and other incentives.

Caribbean Common Market (Caricom) A regional integration group formed in 1973 that includes former British colonies in the Eastern Caribbean.

cartel A group of producers of a product that attempts to monopolize the product and fix prices and quantities to maximize their gains. OPEC is the most successful cartel of countries in history.

centralized cash management The strategy used by some MNEs to place the responsibility for managing corporate cash balances from all affiliates in the hands of a single, central office (usually in London or New York).

certificate of origin A shipping document that states the country of origin of the merchandise.

Code of Conduct on Transnational Corporations An intergovernmental agreement sponsored by the United Nations that is intended to spell out rules of good corporate behavior for MNEs in host and home countries. The Code still was not approved within the United Nations by the end of 1987.

combined transport document A document analogous to the bill of lading but used for shipping when there is more than one form of transport involved.

commercial invoice The exporter's bill of sale that describes precisely the merchandise and terms of sale.

common market A customs union which additionally allows freedom of movement of capital and labor (i.e., factors of production) between member countries.

comparative advantage The advantage gained by both countries that agree to trade, when each produces the product that is *relatively* cheaper to make there (and imports the other product).

comparative cost theory The cost-based theory of international trade developed initially by Ricardo and now extended in the Heckscher-Ohlin theory. This theory shows how production cost differences between countries account for trade flows.

competitive advantage Any characteristic possessed by a firm that enables it to achieve lower costs, higher revenues, or lower risk than its competitors.

concession A legal agreement between a host country and a firm in which the country gives the firm the right to explore for, extract, and sell, oil in exchange for specified taxes, fees, and other charges.

consolidated report *See* Consolidated statement.

consolidated statement An accounting statement showing the combined operations of parent and subsidiaries.

consolidation The process of preparing a consolidated statement whereby line-by-line summations of parent and subsidiary accounts are ultimately presented.

Continental basis A method of quoting exchange rates in foreign currency per U.S. dollar. That is, FF6.8/$U.S.1 is a continental quote.

contingent liability A contractual commitment that requires the issuer to deliver whatever instrument is specified, (for example, foreign exchange) if the buyer chooses to exercise it.

continuous R&D A strategy under which the firm develops new technology incrementally, based on extensions of its existing technology. This can be contrasted with R&D in new areas where the firm is not already active.

control Monitoring operations, taking decisions to conform to plans and, when necessary, taking decisions to change plans or behaviors to eliminate variations from plans in any organization.

controlled foreign corporation A foreign corporation 50 percent or more owned by U.S. shareholders, that is, U.S. citizens or corporations holding at least 10 percent of the common stock each.

conversion loss Receipt of lower revenues than expected because the exchange rate has changed and the foreign-currency receivable was originally worth more of the home-country currency than was ultimately received. Conversion losses may also arise from an increase in foreign currency payables and are realized losses.

copyright A legal contract under which a government agrees to protect the originator of a literary, musical, dramatic, or other work, from unauthorized use by outsiders.

corporate culture The totality of behavior patterns, values, institutions, and so on, that are distinctive to corporations.

corporate social responsibility The principle that firms should adopt behavior that serves social needs in host countries.

cost method A method used in preparing a parent company's non-consolidated accounting reports that treats income at the affiliate's level as being received by the parent only when the affiliate's dividends are actually received by the parent.

cost minimization An operating strategy under which the firm or SBU attempts to compete based on low prices and low costs.

Council for Mutual Economic Assistance (CMEA or Comecon) The regional integration group led by the Soviet Union and comprised primarily of Eastern European countries, though also including Vietnam, Cuba, and Mongolia. This group is also called the Soviet Bloc.

counterpurchase A form of countertrade in which the initial export sale is paid for by later shipments of goods by the importer.

countertrade A means of posttrade financing that involves payment in goods rather than money for an export sale. Barter of one product for another is the simplest form of countertrade.

cross rates Exchange rates constructed by combining rate quotations of each currency involved in terms of a third currency. For example, a DM/FF cross rate can be determined by obtaining quotes for DM/US$ and FF/US$ exchanges.

cross-hauling Trade in similar products in both directions between two countries. For example, there is cross-hauling of autos between the United States and Canada, since auto parts and finished cars are exported in both directions.

cultural risk The risk inherent in operating cross culturally. The potential for loss because of a firm's inaccurate reading of a foreign culture or the manner in which the corporate culture and the foreign culture interface.

culture The socially transmitted behavior patterns, values, institutions, and so on, that are distinctive to a country, region, community, or population.

culture-based products Products whose configuration, function, and so on, are essentially responding to consumer tastes that are culturally determined; for example, chop suey or Panamanian molas.

currency diversification The strategy of reducing the impact of unexpected currency fluctuations by undertaking activities in a variety (portfolio) of different currencies.

currency inconvertibility The situation that arises when a firm is unable to gain access to foreign exchange in the normal market(s) of a country. This is generally the case in communist countries and often occurs in LDCs when economic crises arise.

current account balance A balance of payments that measures a country's exports of goods and services, minus its imports of goods and services, plus its net receipts of unilateral transfers during some time period.

customs union A regional economic integration group that uses both unrestricted trade between member countries *and* a common policy toward trade with outside countries.

de facto protectionism Non-tariff forms of protection used by countries to restrict imports. The United States uses "voluntary" quotas on Japanese autos and has tried to "jawbone" other countries to reduce their exports to the United States and to increase their imports of U.S. goods.

debt/equity ratio The capital structure of a firm. The average debt/equity ratio differs from country to country.

delivered cost The cost of producing and shipping a product to the target market. This includes total production cost, cost of insurance and freight, tariff cost, and any other cost involved in getting the product to the market.

demand patterns Measures of the characteristics of goods and services purchased by consumers in different countries. Demand patterns tend to be similar in countries at the same stage of economic development.

diffusion The spread of new technology throughout the market.

direct quote A method of quoting exchange rates that uses units of foreign currency per unit of foreign exchange as the basis. That is, in Germany, DM1/0.40 British pounds is a direct quote.

disinvestment Divestiture. Disinvestment occurs when a firm sells or otherwise disposes of a foreign direct investment.

diversification Entry into a different business activity outside of the firm's traditional business. This may be a different product, stage of the production process, or country.

documentary collection A means of paying for an export/import transaction that uses only a draft and other informational documents, but *not* a letter of credit.

documentary draft A sight or time draft that is accompanied by instructions and other documents but no L/C.

Domestic International Sales Corporation (DISC) A separate subsidiary through which exports could be directed at substantial (U.S.) tax savings. The DISC was replaced in U.S. legislation by the Foreign Sales Corporation.

dumping Selling at an unfairly low price in an import market. The U.S. Government has defined dumping as selling below the cost of production or selling below the price in the firm's domestic market.

eclectic view Dunning's theory of international business that explains MNE activities based on their ownership advantages, their use of internalization, and on locational factors.

economic integration Expansion of commercial and financial ties among nations. It is expected that greater economic integration of the world will lead to more efficient production and greater output, thus potentially making all countries better off.

economic risk The foreign exchange risk that future cash flows of the firm will be unexpectedly affected by future changes in exchange rates.

economic union A type of economic integration group that uses all of the policies of a common market, plus it calls for harmonized monetary and fiscal policies among member countries.

embargo A quota with maximum imports of zero units. That is, a total disallowance of imports of the product being embargoed (or on all imports from the country being embargoed).

enterprise union A union comprised of employees at a single company. Typical to Japan.

entry strategy A method used by an MNE for entering a foreign market. These include exports, direct investment, licensing, franchising, turn-key ventures, and other contractual forms.

equity method A method used in preparing a parent company's nonconsolidated accounting reports that treats income at the foreign entity's level as being received by the parent (for reporting purposes) when it is earned by the foreign entity.

ethnocentrism A style of decision making in the multinational enterprise that is dominated by the parent company. Its values, knowledge, and interests are reflected in decisions at the subsidiaries.

eurobond A bond denominated in any currency other than that of the country where it is issued.

eurobond market The market for bonds denominated in any currency other than the local one in any country. Most eurobonds are dollar-denominated bonds issued outside of the United States.

eurocurrency market (or eurodollar market) The market for short-term foreign-currency-denominated instruments such as bank deposits in any country. The bulk of the eurocurrency market involves dollar-denominated bank deposits outside of the United States.

eurodollar A U.S. dollar-denominated bank deposit located outside of the United States. Most eurodollars are time deposits or certificates of deposit.

euromarkets Markets for short- or long-term financial instruments in any country in which the instruments are denominated in currencies other than the local one.

European Community (EC, or Common Market) The association of Western European countries formed in 1957 that has eliminated most tariffs among members, established a common external tariff, harmonized some fiscal and monetary policies, and broadly attempts to increase economic integration among the member countries.

European Currency Unit (ECU) A composite currency similar to the SDR, whose value is based on a weighted average of the currencies of the European Community. Although it is only an accounting convention (i.e., an ECU bill does not exist), the ECU is being used increasingly to denominate international bond issues and other large international financial transactions.

European Monetary System (EMS) A mini-IMF organized by the members of the European Community. The EMS observes exchange rate fluctuations between member-country currencies and makes loans to member governments, primarily to serve the goal of balance of payments stability.

exchange controls Government-imposed limits on use of foreign exchange, generally used to restrict outflows of funds from a country. They include limited access to foreign currency at the Central Bank, and multiple exchange rates for different users, among other methods.

exchange rate The price of one currency in terms of another.

exchange risk The possibility that a firm will not be able to adjust its prices and costs to exactly offset exchange rate changes. Not only must exchange rates be able to vary, but the variations must not be fully anticipated.

exchange risk adaptation The strategy of adjusting the firm's activities to reduce the potential impact of unexpected exchange rate changes. This may be done through financial hedging or other adjustments in the foreign currency activities of the firm.

exchange risk avoidance The strategy of avoiding dealings in currencies that are viewed as having high exchange risk, and/or charging higher prices when exchange risk appears to be higher.

exchange risk transfer The strategy of eliminating or reducing exchange risk by contracting with insurance providers to cover possible exchange rate-induced losses.

exercise price The price at which an option may be used to buy/sell foreign exchange.

Eximbank The Export-Import Bank of the United States, the main U.S. Government agency responsible for assisting U.S. exporters via loans and loan guarantees.

expatriates Employees, typically in managerial and/or technical positions, who are not nationals in the countries where assigned; for example, an American working for a U.S. multinational enterprise on assignment at a Canadian subsidiary, or a Canadian in the same company on assignment at the U.S. headquarters.

experience curve effects The effect of repetition and experience on the cost of doing something. The more often something is done, the more efficient or cost-effective are the labor and management resources involved in its production and delivery.

export commission agent One who buys products and exports them on behalf of a foreign client.

export department The organizational unit within the firm that is responsible for exports.

Export Management Company A company that specializes in promoting and handling another company's exports.

export merchant One who buys products for its own account and then sells them to foreign buyers.

export promotion A strategy for economic development that focuses on increasing a country's exports to generate foreign exchange and stimulate domestic production. This is an outward-looking development model.

Export Trading Company A company owned by several small and medium sized companies to facilitate exports from all its owners while being exempt from U.S. antitrust law.

export/import transaction The basic activity of international trade.

expropriation The forced takeover of a company's assets by the host government without compensation (or with inadequate compensation).

externalization The opposite of internalization. A market or production process is externalized when the firm stops carrying out the activity itself and contracts with an outside firm or agent to do it.

extractive FDI Direct investment used by the MNE to obtain raw materials such as oil, copper, or other metals, agricultural products, etc.

factoring Selling an account receivable at a discount to an intermediary company called a factor. The exporter receives immediate (discounted) payment, and the factor receives eventual payment from the importer.

fade-out A government policy toward FDI that calls for progressive sale of ownership of foreign firms to local investors, ending with either complete local ownership or with some maximum foreign percentage ownership.

fair value The portion of a firm's activities that can be determined to be carried out in a given jurisdiction. The fair value is crucial to efforts by governments to tax MNE activities.

financial accounting disclosure The presentation of the consolidated statements, showing both income and balance sheet accounts.

financial transfers Methods used by MNEs to move funds internationally, such as profit remittances, fee payments, payments for intracompany shipments, and loans.

first world The industrialized countries. These are primarily members of the Organization for Economic Cooperation and Development (OECD).

flexibility The ability to adapt to changes in customer demands or other aspects of the marketplace as those conditions change.

flexible multi-item factory A factory that is usually labor intensive and thus capable of producing several different products without large capital costs.

follow-on market The market where a product is introduced following its introduction in a *lead* market.

follow-the-leader strategy The strategy of oligopolistic reaction. It implies that the follower waits to see how an industry leader operates (e.g., in introducing new technology), and then pursues a copycat strategy in areas that appear profitable.

foreign-base company A *controlled foreign corporation* that derives a substantial portion of its income from investments, sales, services or shipping.

Foreign Corrupt Practices Act A U.S. law that prohibits certain kinds of bribes and questionable payments, requires internal accounting control procedures regarding such payments, and the imprisonment of company officials guilty of evading these requirements.

foreign currency option An option contract that gives the holder the right but not the obligation to exercise it to purchase a given amount of foreign currency at a fixed price during a fixed time period. Contract specifications are similar to those of futures contracts, except that the option requires a premium payment to purchase (and it does not have to be exercised).

foreign direct investment The extension of controlling ownership by a firm from one country over a firm in another country through new investment or acquisition.

foreign exchange A financial instrument that carries out payment from one currency to another. Common instruments of foreign exchange include bank drafts, wire transfers, telephone transfers, forward and futures contracts, and cash.

foreign exchange arbitrage Use of simultaneous contracts to buy and sell foreign exchange at different prices or at different times, such that a profit is made and no exchange risk is undertaken.

foreign exchange hedging Protecting against the possible impact of exchange rate changes on the firm's business by balancing foreign currency assets with foreign currency liabilities.

foreign exchange market The market(s) in which financial instruments denominated in one currency are traded for instruments denominated in other currencies. Typically, a country's main foreign exchange market is carried out through the commercial banking system.

foreign investment controls Government-imposed limits on the ability of firms to undertake foreign direct investment. These typically restrict FDI *inflows*, though they have been used to try to limit the outflow of FDI as well.

Foreign Sales Corporation A legal entity through which a firm can channel exports and derive special income tax benefits.

Foreign Sales Corporation (FSC) Act A U.S. Government law that replaces the Domestic International Sales Corporation (DISC) legislation. The FSC is a foreign company that exports for a U.S. firm, which may show its export profits in the FSC and avoid U.S. taxation on a percentage of the earnings until they are remitted to the parent U.S. firm.

foreign sourcing Producing or purchasing products or production inputs from a foreign location, typically to lower costs. Many electronics firms source their memory chips in their own plants or through contracts with local firms in Taiwan or Singapore to lower the costs.

foreign subsidiary An operating unit within the firm that is incorporated in a foreign country. It may be wholly or partially owned by the parent company.

foreign trade organization (FTO) A government trading company operated by a communist country.

forfaiting A means of posttrade financing analogous to factoring. Forfaiting is used primarily for large capital goods exports to Eastern European countries.

forward foreign exchange market (forward market) The contractual form used by commercial banks to offer their clients the opportunity to fix an exchange rate for future delivery of one currency for another.

four Ps Product, Place, Price, and Promotion—the traditional decision making areas which determine consumer responses on whether or not to buy a product.

franc area The group of former French colonies that continue to use the French franc as an acceptable currency and/or tie their currency values to the franc.

franchising A contractual arrangement under which one firm (the franchisor) agrees to allow another (the franchisee) to use its good name and often some product and process technology in return for direct compensation. This is a non-ownership form of business in which an intermediate product (viz. the franchisor's name) is sold.

free-trade area A regional economic integration group that implements policy for unrestricted trade between member countries, but leaves each country free to set its own policy with outside countries.

functional currency The "home country" currency of the parent or the subsidiary which is used in preparing and presenting accounting reports at the operations level.

functional structure Organizational units within the firm defined on the basis of what they do; for example, marketing, finance, production, and so forth.

futures foreign exchange contract (futures contract) A legal contract similar to a forward contract, except that it is traded on a securities exchange and has fixed specifications such as maturity date, contract size, and trading limitations during the contract's life.

gain-sharing agreement An agreement between management and labor (typically in the United Kingdom) to share economic gains, usually because of new equipment being installed.

GATT The General Agreement on Tariffs and Trade, the world's main intergovernmental organization that seeks to reduce barriers to international trade. GATT currently has 90-member governments.

geocentric organization One in which different operating units within the multinational enterprise come together on decision making to optimize results for the global enterprise, rather than for the individual units.

global focus The competitive strategy that implies concentration on one industry segment or a narrow product line with sales in many countries.

global international An organization of trade unions from countries around the world.

global logistic network The pattern of intra-company product and component flows as production at one location is transferred to another location for further work or for sale.

goodwill The ability of a firm or product to earn a rate of return above that which is typically competitively experienced, based on its image of good quality or service. In this sense, "goodwill" is similar to a market "franchise," economic rent or monopoly income.

government protection Direct or indirect assistance to a firm by which the government enables that firm to compete. Two main types of protection are restrictions placed on other firms, and government contracts that enable the firm to sell to the government, (e.g., trade, tariffs, quotas, etc.).

the managerial skills that enable a firm to compete by using its resources efficiently.

manufacturer's export agent An agent that promotes the exports of a manufacturer's products (for a commission, usually).

market absorption curve A graph depicting the percentage of the market that has purchased a product (on the ordinate) since the product was first introduced in the market (on the abscissa).

market allocation The strategy used by MNEs to restrict activities of each affiliate to specified markets, to avoid competition among these units.

market sector That part of a dual economy that is marked-based and is connected to international business with the industrial countries.

market segmentation An operating strategy under which the firm or SBU attempts to compete based on defining and pursuing a niche or segment of the total market, such as the highest quality segment, or the smallest size segment, and so on.

market-based economy A national economy in which the free market is used to determine prices, output quantities, investment patterns, and so forth. No country uses *only* a market-based economy, but the noncommunist countries are considered to have substantially market-based systems.

marketing mix The manner in which product, place, price and promotion are determined by the firm to come together on the purchase of that firm's products.

market-serving FDI Direct investment used by the MNE to produce and sell its products or services in the host country.

master strategy A definition of the basic methods to be used in achieving a strategic objective; for example, locating a plant in France to be close to the market.

matrix structure Some organizational units within the firm have defined reporting relationships with two or more other units; for example, marketing in Europe may report to both a functional manager (marketing) and a geographical manager (Europe) in terms of hierarchical relationships.

mature MNE The firm with geographically distributed product markets and resource markets. Having evolved from a purely domestic firm, the mature MNE takes a global perspective on operations, seeking to serve customers wherever they are and to produce at lowest cost, wherever low cost resources may be.

maturing product A product which is produced by several firms, whose technology is no longer monopolized by the innovating firm, and which faces increasing price elasticity of demand.

microrisk The political risk that exists for a particular firm or industry in a given country.

mission statement The definition of the fundamental purpose of the enterprise, usually including profit orientation, consumer needs addressed (e.g., transportation), recognition of community responsibilities, and so forth.

MITI The Japanese government agency; the Ministry of Trade and Industry.

monopoly power The economic strength that MNEs possess relative to other firms and relative to governments because of their size, their availability of information, and their multinationality.

most-favored-nation A principle in international trade regulation that is used by members of GATT. If a trade barrier is reduced between any two members of GATT, that same benefit is automatically extended to all other GATT members under the most-favored-nation principle.

multilateral netting The strategy used by some MNEs to reduce international funds flows between affiliates by canceling redundant cash flows and transferring only the net amounts necessary.

multinational enterprise (MNE) A firm that operates owned subsidiaries, branches, or other controlled affiliates in at least three countries.

multinational marketing Selling the product in several different country markets.

multinational sourcing A capability that exists for MNEs to find or set up production sources in more than one nation, thus enabling the firm to lower its costs relative to firms that produce or buy in only one country.

multinationality The essence of the MNE. By operating simultaneously in several countries, the MNE is able to transfer information about prices and demand conditions, move funds and products to safer or otherwise preferable locations, and generally escape the limitations imposed by the environment in a single country.

national focus The competitive strategy that implies adaptation of products to each national market in which the firm operates.

nationalization The forced takeover of a company's assets by the host government *with* compensation. Sometimes this is achieved by requiring sale of controlling ownership to local investors, still leaving the MNE with some partial ownership.

negotiated trade Exports and imports arranged by government agreement rather than by the free market.

New International Economic Order An idea created in the United Nations in the early 1970s that intended to develop mechanisms for redistribution of income between rich and poor countries. The effort was essentially dropped after the oil crisis of 1973–74, though the concept remains in discussion.

new product An invention that is successfully introduced into the marketplace. The new product constitutes the first stage of the international product cycle. It is characterized by price inelastic demand and reliance on technology as a competitive advantage.

newly industrializing country (NIC) Among the LDCs, one of the rapidly-growing countries that have proceeded farthest along the road to industrialization. NICs include South Korea, Hong Kong, Taiwan, Singapore, and Brazil.

next best alternative The project that would be undertaken using the available resources if the one under consideration were foregone. The cost of foregoing this alternative is the opportunity cost of the project.

nontariff barriers (NTBs) Government-imposed restrictions on imports other than tariffs which also limit imports. They include licensing requirements, prior deposits, bureaucratic delays, and many more restrictions.

obsolescing bargain The situation that exists *after* an MNE commits its capital and human resources to an investment project in a host country. The MNE's bargaining position relative to the host government diminishes (obsolesces), since it has important resources at risk in the host country. Over time, the government typically gains even greater ability to force the firm to follow its desired goals as the firm becomes more integrated into the local economy.

official settlements balance The "bottom line" balance of payments when all private sector transactions have been accounted for and all that remain are official exchanges between central banks (and the IMF). This balance measures the country's net inflows of official holdings of foreign exchange, SDRs, gold, and the country's borrowing position at the IMF.

offshore assembly The overseas production of goods whose inputs are fabricated in one country, typically done to reduce labor costs. That is, basic materials are made in one country, they are shipped abroad for assembly or processing, and then the final products are shipped to the target market for sale.

offshore production Either offshore sourcing or offshore assembly.

operating plan A detailed program on how organizational units will function together in achieving strategic objectives.

operating strategy The day-to-day method of doing business that an MNE must tailor to conditions in each host country. Operating strategy is dependent on the degree and kind of government regulation, competitive conditions, and other factors.

opportunity cost The potential gain foregone in any business activity that is given up by hedging against the risk of loss on that activity. The opportunity cost of a forward contract is the lost foreign exchange earnings that would have occurred if the contract were not used and the exchange rate had changed favorably to the firm. For a country the opportunity cost of using resources in one activity is the cost of foregoing the next best alternative use of those resources.

orderly marketing agreement An intergovernmental agreement to limit imports of a product(s). These agreements are usually made when imports are visibly hurting the domestic industry and the importing country cannot demonstrate that the importing firms are dumping or otherwise operating illegally.

Organization for Economic Cooperation and Development An intergovernmental organization that has as members the industrialized countries (the first world). The OEC is concerned with economic and social issues.

Organization of Petroleum Exporting Countries (OPEC) The multinational cartel of oil producing countries that successfully raised the price of oil by over 400 percent in 1973-74 and again by over 200 percent in 1979.

patent A legal contract under which a government agrees to protect a possessor of proprietary technology from use of the technology by unauthorized outside users.

pattern bargaining An industry-wide bargaining strategy characterized by a contract settlement with one company that establishes a basis for other firms in the industry to follow.

periphery That segment of a country's population that is least advantaged economically. Also, the periphery countries of the world are the LDCs.

personal selling A form of promotion that involves personnel who meet potential buyers and seek to directly influence their purchase decisions.

place The location where the product is marketed.

political risk The possible increase or decrease in a firm's value that may occur because of unexpected changes in the external political environment.

political union A type of economic integration that calls for full political integration between countries, that is, creation of a single political jurisdiction (country).

polycentric organization One in which decision making in the multinational enterprise is distributed among several geographically distributed units, each of which makes decisions affecting its own operations which reflect its own values, knowledge and beliefs.

portfolio investment The purchase of financial instruments such as stocks, bonds, bank deposits, and so forth, by an investor; in our context the investor would be from one country and the investment in another country.

posttrade financing Credit extended to the exporter or importer after shipment but before this firm receives its payment for the goods.

pretrade financing Credit extended to an exporter to enable that firm to produce the goods that will be exported. This is a form of working capital financing.

price controls The setting of prices or price ceilings by a government.

price escalation when exporting Increasingly higher prices for export products because some expenses and tariffs are percentage add-ons to the export price; that is, the monetary value of the add-ons escalates since they are percentages applied to percentages.

pricing strategy The use of product price as a means for achieving higher corporate objectives, for example, profit maximization, market share growth, and so on.

process technology The knowledge used in production to organize the inputs and operate the machinery. Process technology relates to the process by which a given product or service is produced.

product That which the firm offers to sell in the marketplace.

product differentiation An operating strategy under which the firm or SBU attempts to compete based on non-price factors such as quality, service, and other product characteristics.

product modification Adapting a product to meet local conditions without changing the core concept of the product; for example, marketing smaller cars in Europe because roads may be narrower and fuel more expensive than in the United States (where larger cars have historically been popular).

product structure Organizational units within the firm defined on the basis of what they produce; for example, automobiles, trucks, and so forth, or televisions, VCRs, and the like.

product technology The knowledge used to produce any product, that is, the information that specifies the product's characteristics and uses.

production allocation Assigning production that is needed globally to various subsidiaries.

production smoothing Allocating production to various subsidiaries with the intention of maintaining relatively steady output levels at all locations.

promotion Encouraging people to buy a product.

proprietary asset A skill or other company-specific characteristic (competitive advantage) that one firm possesses and which enables the firm to achieve lower costs, higher revenues, or lower risk than its competitors.

proprietary technology Knowledge about how to make a product (or service), how to operate a production process, or how to run a business, that one firm possesses and that other firms do not. The innovating firm is able to protect this technology for itself, either through legal means (e.g., patent or trademark) or by secrecy.

protected niche The competitive strategy that implies obtaining government protection for the firm's activities in the countries where it operates.

Protestant work ethic Hard, physical work is a valued personal and social behavior. The concept finds its origin in the middle ages when Protestantism sought to distinguish itself from other forms of Christianity with its belief that "work is prayer."

public good A product that can be used repeatedly without being used up. Technology is a public good, because using it does not deplete it.

purchasing power parity The condition that an inflation differential between any two countries is eliminated by an offsetting change in the exchange rate between their currencies.

put option An option contract that entitles the purchaser to *sell* a fixed amount of foreign exchange at a fixed price in the future.

quota A quantity restriction on imports. The number of Japanese cars imported into the United States has been limited by a "voluntary" quota during much of the 1980s.

regional economic integration Expansion of commercial and financial ties among countries in a regional group, leaving the rest of the world outside of the group. Five forms of regional economic integration have been identified during the post-World War II period, ranging from free trade areas to full economic and political unions.

regional international An organization of trade unions from a specific region of the world, for example, Western Europe.

relative productivities The output produced by production factors in one country compared to the output produced by the same amount of production factors in another country. Due to differences in production abilities, output will be different in each country.

repatriation The return of an *expatriate* to a home country assignment; or the return of foreign subsidiary profits to the parent company.

reporting currency The parent company's currency used in preparing and presenting accounting reports at the parent level.

rugged individualist One who relies mainly on himself or herself as the source of sustenance or success; for example, the pioneers.

scale economies in advertising The condition where the incremental costs of each unit of advertising expenditure are declining, for example, where fixed costs of advertising copy preparation can be allocated to an increasingly large total market as additional ads are placed in different markets.

scale economies in distribution Cost reductions achieved by shipping large quantities of products, thus lowering the unit shipping costs relative to competitors that ship lower quantities.

scale economies in financing Cost reductions gained by borrowing large quantities of funds at lower interest and other cost than charged to borrowers of smaller quantities.

scale economies in production Cost reductions achieved by a large size production facility. When large-scale output is achieved, low unit costs result (relative to competitors operating smaller-scale facilities).

scale economies in purchasing Cost reductions gained by buying large quantities of inputs at lower unit costs than those paid by buyers of smaller quantities.

second world The communist countries, primarily members of the Soviet bloc (Comecon).

seasonal factory A factory that can handle large variations in employment and capacity usage over the year, for example, at Christmas time.

sequential entry strategy An MNE strategy that implies market entry through a relatively inexpensive step such as exports or licensing, and a buildup of commitment into joint venture ownership and/or full subsidiary ownership.

Seven Sisters (or the Major Multinationals) The world's largest oil companies. In the late 1980s they include: Royal Dutch Shell, EXXON, Mobil, British Petroleum, Texaco, Chevron (Socal), and Amoco.

short-term national financial markets Money markets in different countries; that is, markets for short-term financial instruments such as bank deposits and Treasury bills in different countries.

Shunto The "spring wage offensive" in Japan characterized by coordinated collective bargaining by *enterprise unions* seeking wage increases that mainly pertain to cost-of-living and industry productivity concerns.

skunk works A think-tank environment used by some MNEs to encourage researchers to pursue new projects in small teams without excessive bureaucracy from the mainstream business of the firm.

social benefit/cost ratio The sum of all social benefits generated by a potential project divided by the sum of all social costs generated by the project. If the ratio is greater than one, the project should be undertaken, from the host country's perspective.

social Darwinism "Survival of the fittest," in a societal context.

societal culture The totality of behavior patterns, values, institutions, and so forth, that are distinctive to a country, region or community.

Sogo Shosha The Japanese trading companies, such as Mitsubishi Shoji and Mitsui Bussan.

sourcing FDI Direct investment used by the MNE to produce its products or inputs overseas for eventual sale back in the home country (or in other countries).

sovereignty Control over the national economy.

Special Drawing Right (SDR) The official currency of the IMF. The SDR is a composite currency based on the weighted values of the dollar, yen, mark, French franc, and the British pound. New SDRs are issued infrequently by the IMF, and this currency is used as the unit of account for transactions with the IMF.

specialized international A component of an intergovernmental agency which represents workers' interests and views within that agency.

spillover benefits Positive externalities. To a country, spillover benefits accrue when a business activity is undertaken and it has positive impact beyond the success of the venture itself (such as additional employment, improved balance of payments, etc.) To a company, spillover benefits accrue when an activity is undertaken that has a positive impact on the rest of the firm's business in addition to the activity's own success.

standardized product A product that is produced by many firms, whose technology is well known, and which faces very price-sensitive demand. Commodities are generally standardized products.

sterling area The group of former members of the British Commonwealth that continue to use the British pound as an acceptable currency and/or tie their currency values to the pound.

Stewards' Council An elected group of worker representatives, not a union, to negotiate with management on labor agreements and the solving of workers' problems. The Stewards' Council more commonly found in the United Kingdom.

strategy A plan of action based on an analysis of the variables affecting success, the method which the firm wants to use in achieving success, the allocation of resources necessary to achieving success and the monitoring and adjusting, as required, of this plan of action as it is being implemented.

strategic business unit (SBU) A group of products, divisions, or other company activities that have sufficiently similar characteristics to justify their assignment to a single group for strategy development.

strategic management Managing at the Corporate and business unit levels regarding issues that are crucial to the long run success of the firm; for example, markets to serve, products to produce, location of plants, etc.

strategic objectives Goals which are important to the long run success of the firm.

strike A group of employees' refusal to work.

structure The horizontal and vertical set of reporting relationships among the organizational units within the firm, and the allocation of responsibilities among those units.

Subpart F income Income received from a *foreign-base* company.

subsidiary A foreign corporation whose stock is more than 50 percent owned by the parent company and is therefore controlled by the parent company.

subsidy As refers to international trade, a subsidy is some cost-reducing privilege offered by the government to domestic firms to stimulate their competitiveness so that they may be more successful against imports.

SWOT analysis The evaluation by the firm of internal strengths and weaknesses and environmental opportunities and threats. SWOT analysis is part of the strategic management process.

synergy A situation where one operation benefits from the other; for example, where the design of a high-speed, high-quality zipper production machine is usable at the parent level, perhaps in Japan, and at the subsidiary level, perhaps in France and/or the United States. The competitive result is that zippers produced in France and the United States by such machinery don't have to bear the (direct) cost of the design expenditures. In the (incremental) cost sense, they do not have to pay for the design costs already paid for in Japan.

tariff A tax placed on imports that thereby raises the price and restricts the quantity of imports.

Tax Reform Act of 1986 A major overhaul of the U.S. income tax system which, effective January 1 of 1987, allows a U.S. citizen to exempt the first $70,000 of foreign income from U.S. income taxes provided certain requirements are met—for example, regarding the time spent in actually working and living outside the United States.

technology advantage A competitive advantage gained from creation or obtaining of proprietary technology.

technology intensity The amount of technology used relative to capital and labor in production of a product or service.

The 10/70 Rule This rule pertains to the deferral of income at the controlled-foreign-corporation (CFC) level. If less than 10 percent of the income at the CFC level is *Subpart F* income, full deferral applies; if the percent at the parent level is more than 70 percent, there is no deferral. If the subpart F proportion is between 10 and 70 percent, income is allocated to Subpart F on this same ratio.

third world The less-developed countries, primarily in Latin America, Africa, and Asia. These countries have relatively low per capita incomes and relatively high importance of primary products in their economies.

three-way (or triangular) arbitrage Exchange arbitrage among three currencies which involves beginning in one currency, passing through each of the other two, and ending in the initial currency.

time orientation Behavior that is sensitive to the clock; for example, punctuality.

trade adjustment assistance (TAA) A U.S. government policy that offers aid to workers laid off because of competition from imported goods. This mechanism attempts to alleviate the burden on people who are hurt by the operation of comparative advantage in international trade, which leads to contraction of some domestic industries and expansion of others.

trade balance A balance of payments that measures a country's exports of merchandise minus its imports of merchandise for some time period.

trade creation Generation of new exports between members of an economic integration group, due to lowering of trade barriers between them.

trade diversion Reduction of imports from outside countries into members of an economic integration group, and replacement of those imports by intra-group trade, due to continued restrictions on imports from outside.

trade financing Credit extended to an importer by the exporter, or a commercial bank or some other intermediary, that enables the importer to pay for the merchandise, presumably until it is sold and the importer receives funds to pay with.

trademark A legal contract under which a government agrees to protect the originator of the distinctive mark, word, design, or picture, from unauthorized use by outsiders.

Trading-with-the-Enemy Act A U.S. government law that forbids U.S. firms from doing business with countries that are from time to time listed as enemies; for example, North Korea, Cuba, and Vietnam.

traditional sector The poorer part of a dual economy that is based on traditional agriculture, hunting, or fishing, and is weakly connected to the market sector.

transaction efficiencies The gains of economic welfare generated by operation of MNEs because they are (sometimes) more efficient than smaller, uninational firms.

transaction risk The possibility that a foreign currency-denominated transaction will be worth less (or more) than expected in local currency when the transaction is completed in the future.

transfer price The price for products, components, and so forth, traded among units within the same multinational enterprise.

translation loss An accounting loss reflected in adjustments to accounting statements at the end of an accounting period to record changes in home-country currency values caused by changes in foreign currency based receivables, payables, or other assets or liabilities.

translation risk The possibility that a firm's balance sheet entries will be changed in domestic currency due to changes in exchange rates that affect foreign-currency accounts.

tricultural setting The total cultural environment affecting the multinational company, consisting of the home country culture, the host country culture and the company's own distinctive culture.

trigger price mechanism A system used by the United States during 1978–82 to limit imports of steel products. The trigger price was the estimated cost of producing each steel product in Japan, the world's low-cost producer of most steel products. Firms attempting to import at prices below the trigger prices faced penalties for dumping in the U.S. market.

INDEX

F

Q–R

S

X–Z

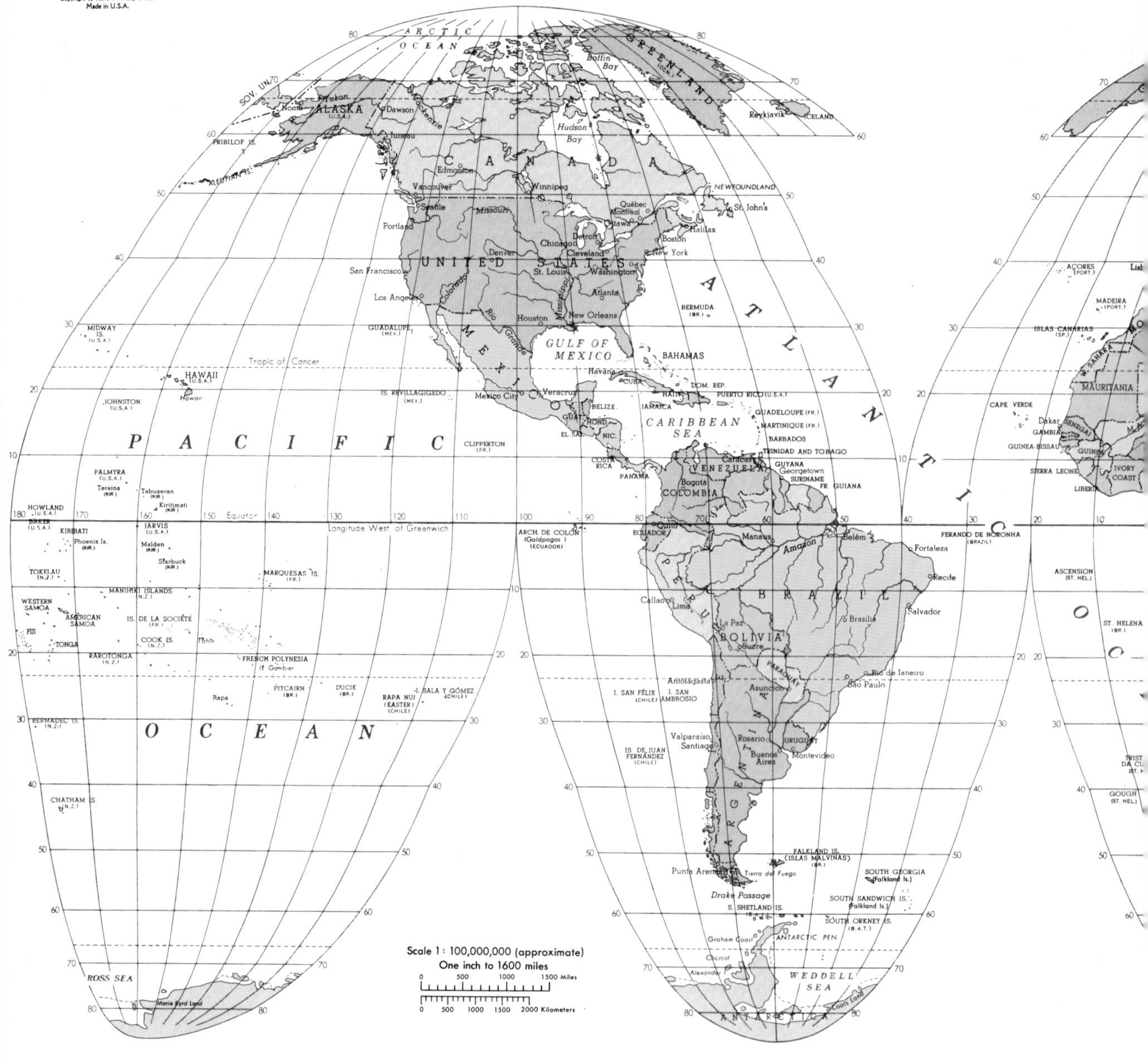
ARCTIC OCEAN
GREENLAND (DEN.)
Baffin Bay
ICELAND
Reykjavík
ALASKA (U.S.A.)
Nome
Yukon
Dawson
Juneau
PRIBILOF IS.
ALEUTIAN IS.
SOV. UN.
Hudson Bay
C A N A D A
Edmonton
Vancouver
Winnipeg
NEWFOUNDLAND
St. John's
Halifax
Québec
Montréal
Ottawa
Seattle
Portland
Missouri
Chicago
Detroit
Boston
New York
Cleveland
Denver
UNITED STATES
San Francisco
St. Louis
Washington
Los Angeles
Atlanta
Colorado
Mississippi
Houston
New Orleans
Rio Grande
BERMUDA (BR.)
GUADALUPE (MEX.)
MEXICO
GULF OF MEXICO
BAHAMAS
Havana
CUBA
DOM. REP.
HAITI
PUERTO RICO (U.S.A.)
JAMAICA
Mexico City
Veracruz
IS. REVILLAGIGEDO (MEX.)
BELIZE
GUAT.
HOND.
EL SAL.
NIC.
COSTA RICA
PANAMA
CARIBBEAN SEA
GUADELOUPE (FR.)
MARTINIQUE (FR.)
BARBADOS
TRINIDAD AND TOBAGO
Caracas
VENEZUELA
GUYANA
Georgetown
SURINAME
FR. GUIANA
Bogotá
COLOMBIA
Quito
ECUADOR
ARCH. DE COLÓN (Galápagos I.) (ECUADOR)
CLIPPERTON (FR.)
Manaus
Amazon
Belém
Fortaleza
Recife
BRAZIL
PERU
Callao
Lima
La Paz
BOLIVIA
Sucre
Brasília
Salvador
PARAGUAY
Antofagasta
Asunción
Rio de Janeiro
São Paulo
I. SAN FÉLIX (CHILE)
I. SAN AMBROSIO
Valparaíso
Santiago
IS. DE JUAN FERNÁNDEZ (CHILE)
Rosario
URUGUAY
Buenos Aires
Montevideo
ARGENTINA
CHILE
FALKLAND IS. (ISLAS MALVINAS) (BR.)
Punta Arenas
Tierra del Fuego
SOUTH GEORGIA (Falkland Is.)
Drake Passage
SOUTH SANDWICH IS. (Falkland Is.)
S. SHETLAND IS.
SOUTH ORKNEY IS. (B.A.T.)
Graham Coast
ANTARCTIC PEN.
Charcot
Alexander
WEDDELL SEA
Coats Land
ANTARCTICA
ROSS SEA
Marie Byrd Land
MIDWAY IS. (U.S.A.)
HAWAII (U.S.A.)
Hawaii
Tropic of Cancer
JOHNSTON (U.S.A.)
P A C I F I C
PALMYRA (U.S.A.)
Teraina (KIR.)
Tabuaeran (KIR.)
Kiritimati (KIR.)
HOWLAND (U.S.A.)
BAKER (U.S.A.)
KIRIBATI
Phoenix Is. (KIR.)
JARVIS (U.S.A.)
Malden (KIR.)
Starbuck (KIR.)
Equator
Longitude West of Greenwich
TOKELAU (N.Z.)
MARQUESAS IS. (FR.)
MANIHIKI ISLANDS (N.Z.)
WESTERN SAMOA
AMERICAN SAMOA
IS. DE LA SOCIÉTÉ (FR.)
FIJI
TONGA
COOK IS. (N.Z.)
Tahiti
RAROTONGA (N.Z.)
FRENCH POLYNESIA
Îl. Gambier
PITCAIRN (BR.)
DUCIE (BR.)
RAPA NUI (EASTER) (CHILE)
I. SALA Y GÓMEZ (CHILE)
Rapa
KERMADEC IS. (N.Z.)
O C E A N
CHATHAM IS. (N.Z.)
A T L A N T I C O C E A N
AÇORES (PORT.)
MADEIRA (PORT.)
ISLAS CANARIAS (SP.)
W. SAHARA
MAURITANIA
CAPE VERDE
Dakar
SENEGAL
GAMBIA
GUINEA-BISSAU
GUINEA
SIERRA LEONE
LIBERIA
IVORY COAST
FERANDO DE NORONHA (BRAZIL)
ASCENSION (ST. HEL.)
ST. HELENA (BR.)
GOUGH (ST. HEL.)
Scale 1: 100,000,000 (approximate)
One inch to 1600 miles
0 500 1000 1500 Miles
0 500 1000 1500 2000 Kilometers